McColl

The Man
with America's Money

Ross Yockey

LONGSTREET
Atlanta, Georgia

Published by
LONGSTREET, INC.
A subsidiary of Cox Newspapers
A subsidiary of Cox Enterprises, Inc.
2140 Newmarket Parkway
Suite 122
Marietta, GA 30067

Printed in the United States of America

1st printing 1999

Library of Congress Catalog Card Number: 99-61753

ISBN: 1-56352-539-9

Jacket and book design by Burtch Hunter

Visit Longstreet on the World Wide Web
www.lspress.com

For JoAnn and Jane

McColl

McColl

PROLOGUE

David, nearly naked, impatience-chafed, stretched across the soft cotton sheet in the valley of Goliath's shadow.

No word from the enemy camp on when the battle would be pitched or where, so it was no good planning thrusts and parries and the fit of the rock in your sling. Better simply to lie still, breathe deep and set the mind somewhere else for a while. Forget about the handshake that could put half the nation's money in your grip.

The ceiling of the hotel room—an expensive room, no doubt, though he'd taken little notice of it—was the same dimpled white of all the hotel rooms he'd slept in in a hundred cities. Other than its fancy light fixture and elaborate fire sprinkler, there was nothing about this ceiling to tell him how much BankAmerica might have paid to put him up in this suite at the Ritz-Carlton. Hugh McColl closed his eyes to the ceiling and stared instead up into the crisp blue sky of Bentonville, North Carolina.

He'd been here before in his imagination, contemplating the miracle of Duncan Donald McColl's survival and his own eventual conception seventy years later. Sounds of war and dying encased him like the red March mud.

Bentonville was one of the places he came to await the battles of his personal war, imagining the near-death experience of the McColl family hero. For this moment he could forget that he was only Duncan Donald McColl's great-grandson, Hugh, staring at the ceiling of a San Francisco hotel room, trying not to anticipate the handshake that would transform a slow-talking South Carolina farmboy who never learned to drive a tractor straight into the most powerful banker in the known universe.

The only noises on Hugh McColl's San Francisco battlefield would be words. Body language, not body count, would tell which way the fight was going. This was March of 1995, not 1865, but at bottom it was the same old war winding down: power in the balance, power measured by the ignorant in money but power all the same. (And the axis of power had shifted so that the North might call itself "West" and pitch its tents in San Francisco, but it was still the North and it still looked on Hugh McColl as the threatening, ignorant South.) When the last rounds of words were fired, the deal would be settled in a handshake, just the way Lee and Grant had settled things in Wilmer McLean's parlor, only one state away from that tent where Duncan Donald McColl lay clutching at life. This time it would be the South's turn, a McColl's turn, to win.

McColl in San Francisco turned his thoughts to Goliath, to the North-slash-West. He had drawn the room's blackout curtains to keep BankAmerica executives from invading his solitude; their office windows were hardly more than a paper airplane's throw away from the hotel. What he could not figure out was why Dick Rosenberg had taken so damn long to set up this meeting. When was it—sometime before last Thanksgiving—that Jim Hance had come to him to say he was "getting signals" that BankAmerica wanted to talk merger? Hance, NationsBank's chief financial officer, was approached by a go-between, someone high up at Merrill Lynch. Somebody playing power broker. There were vast sums to be gained or lost in a merger between the banks that were, at this snapshot of time, America's largest and fourth largest. Hance had brought the Merrill Lynch people in for a meeting in Charlotte. They had a book all prepared showing the holdings of the two banks, the two territories all complement and no overlap. It was beautiful. It was the largest bank in America, the first coast-to-coast bank. No wonder Rosenberg wanted to talk.

Then again, if Rosenberg really wanted this meeting, why were the Merrill Lynch people taking so long to bring him to the table? Why were the two CEOs having such a hard time getting together? For

McColl's part, once he let himself imagine the possibilities, the deal was in his blood and he could concentrate on little else. He told Hance he would drop anything to meet with Rosenberg. "Hell," he said, "I'll go anywhere anytime to get this deal done. I'll leave my new grandbaby in the delivery room if I get the call from you there."

"Anywhere" should not have been San Francisco. This sort of deal was usually discussed on neutral territory. Denver, say, or St. Louis. Still, just as he had promised, when Dick Rosenberg called, McColl accepted the invitation to meet. In all the history of banking no one before had ever dreamed a deal this big. But at the hotel desk there had been no message waiting from Rosenberg. McColl's agitation swung from excitement to annoyance and back again. He decided that if Rosenberg called he should not be in the room. Instead he would scout the enemy camp.

In the elevator, he thought about a new name for Rosenberg's bank. Depending on where it showed up in print, the bank might be called either "BankAmerica"—the official name of its holding corporation—or "Bank of America," BofA for short, which was what A. P. Giannini had called it after starting it out in life as "Bank of Italy." The trend seemed to be toward the steamlined "BankAmerica." Maybe NationsBank West would have a better ring.

He crossed the street from the hotel, stepped onto the BofA plaza, not nearly as welcoming as his own plaza back in Charlotte, street din softened by cascading water. Here was a twelve-foot-high black marble glob of a sculpture, and he'd heard what the people here called it: the banker's heart. Cold, hard, black. Maybe he'd get rid of that sculpture when all this became his. Inside, the lobby was nondescript. A plaque on the wall contained some nice sentiments about the bank's founder, A. P. Giannini, dead nearly fifty years but still treasured in San Francisco's memory. There was a bronze bust of Giannini, too, and he actually saw a man touch the shoulder as he walked past to the elevator, like a Catholic dipping holy water as he entered the sanctuary. McColl stayed there for a few minutes, watching the people. Generic bankers to the eye, yet each a real person, a man or a woman with feelings, history, family. Busy-busy employees of the United States' largest banking institution.

They're bigger, McColl thought, *but we're smarter. And that makes us stronger.* He watched the plates of the escalator slip naturally into place. The tectonic plates of world banking were sliding just as naturally. *Power is shifting,* Hugh McColl told himself. *California needs North Carolina more than North Carolina needs California.* Southern banks were still the poor, pitiable cousins in 1974, when interest rates on NCNB (not yet "NationsBank") short-term borrowing climbed off the chart, to 25 percent. Investors were afraid for their cash. His own quick thinking got the bank through the near-crippling Fourth of July holiday, but a week later London's Israel-British Bank, Ltd., went under and took NCNB's $3 million short-term investment with it. He and then-CEO Tom Storrs had bet the farm on commercial paper, only to find out that no commercial investor would touch it. BankAmerica Chairman Chauncey Medberry came to the rescue, helping their stumbling little bank to its feet. Medberry doubled NCNB's line of credit to $20 million. Dick Rosenberg's predecessor had reached out a paternalistic hand in 1974 to Hugh McColl's predecessor, and had put some money in the hat. This time it would be McColl putting money in Rosenberg's hat, but the money didn't matter. Only the handshake mattered.

BofA's building with its businesslike lobby was nothing approaching the "Taj McColl," as the satirists dubbed it, on the Square in Charlotte. It had nothing like the monumental Ben Long frescoes McColl had personally commissioned. Probably nothing like the view, clear to the mountains, from the NationsBank tower, tallest building in the Southeast. This San Francisco building was fifty-two stories and his was sixty. Back home no one would have passed Hugh McColl in his lobby without a wave, a hello, a handshake. Here nobody knew who he was. Just a tanned, rugged little Brooks Brothers man, dressed like a banker but shorter than bankers were supposed to be and an inch taller because of his hand-stitched cowboy boots. How many of these busy-busy people would be working for him in a few months' time?

Back in his suite, McColl stripped to his shorts and lay down on the bed to clear his mind with a chapter of the book he wanted to write someday: tales of the modern business hero laced with flashbacks to the time of his personal hero, Duncan Donald.

McColl was determined not to anticipate the meeting with Rosenberg, not to go over every what-if and then-what. That was how Tom Storrs had done it, approaching each encounter with options neatly labeled and prioritized. Storrs, a soft-spoken, cautious man, nonetheless boldly set the cycle of growth and acquisition in motion. Storrs had gotten McColl to the table, staked him to the game. Then McColl changed the game. Storrs had been a master of bridge, all planning and innuendo; McColl was a genius at poker. You can't play a hand of poker until the cards fall and you look your opponent in the eye.

Eyes closed, breathing deeply, McColl made a significant observation: North and South played on the same team in bridge. When he'd started out in banking's minor leagues, alliances were customary—though North naturally insisted on relegating its little banking buddies down South to the role of dummy. A lot had changed in thirty years. Banking 1990s-style was army against army, no allies, no prisoners. It was the War Between the States, still being waged in 1995, North against South, East against West, every major player egged on by the Seouls, the Tokyos, the Londons. Yet, down at the pit of every stomach (just as Abe Lincoln had insisted) every one of us was simply an American. Even the Koreans, Japanese and English, now, all Americans at the bottom line.

Bentonville, North Carolina, was the Confederacy's last mad stand after four years of madness. Duncan Donald McColl, volunteer in Company A of the First Heavy Artillery Battalion of North Carolina, was part of the ragtag army held together by General Joseph Johnston, Lee's last hope of stopping Sherman's army before it could join up with Grant's. Duncan Donald, Unionist before the war, was just another filthy, loose-hung Johnny Reb uniform to the Union infantryman who put the bullet in his chest. Johnston's retreating army left McColl's body in the mud and sent word to his parents that he was dead.

"*But Duncan Donald lived on,*" Hugh McColl's grandmother had said so many times, laying on the nineteenth-century-style patina she'd perfected in her own Southern childhood, "*to be a hero once more on the battlefield of commerce. Yes, child, a hero on the battlefield of commerce.*" Duncan Donald was household god to the McColls of Bennettsville, South Carolina.

"They say if a man was great alive," Grandmother McColl would recite, "he'll be tenfold greater dead." And Hugh McColl's mother had inherited, or usurped, the role of storyteller for the children. The two women together fed their family hominy grits at breakfast, heroes at bedtime. The shelves in Bennettsville were filled with *Ivanhoe, The*

Three Musketeers, Beowulf and Homer. No child, male or female, passed through the matriarchal sphere of influence without shouldering the staff or the millstone of these heroes.

Shortly after 5 P.M. the phone rang. McColl awoke with a start from a nap he wasn't certain he'd taken. Rosenberg's secretary. Could he meet Mr. Rosenberg at the front desk at five-thirty? McColl rose, showered, dressed, opened the blackout curtains and looked out the window. Rosenberg's building was craggy, with bay windows projecting at irregular intervals, rather like a mountain, dark and forbidding on a cloudy evening. He smiled, thinking of his own acrophobia. He'd conquered the Alps, trekked Kilimanjaro, daring his own terror to stop him, winning every time. He loved being at the summit. He remembered standing at windows in other cities, Tampa, Dallas, Atlanta, feeling the thrill of conquest, telling himself, *You have just become the largest financial player in this metropolis.* The feeling of power was undeniable. And would he wake up in this room tomorrow morning with that same feeling, the new proprietor of the City by the Bay?

Dick Rosenberg was waiting near the bell captain's desk when McColl stepped off the elevator. A medium-sized man, Rosenberg stood only a bit taller than McColl's five-seven, but he was considerably thicker around the shoulders and waist. His dark complexion seemed not born of Marine Corps training and Texas hunting, as was McColl's own tan, but came rather from some deep Middle Eastern roots.

"Hugh, it's good to see you. How was the flight?" Rosenberg's natural northeastern brogue had been replaced by homogenous California clip.

"Well, it was longer'n a country sermon, but it's good to be hyeah." That mixed-Carolinas accent was McColl's badge and his stigmata, salt to rub in the ears of a wounded foe. He could stretch it and thicken it like a vaudevillian milking laughs. McColl never permitted himself to lose his drawl.

He wished he knew his adversary better. They had clashed only once, in the late 1980s when Rosenberg was head of Wells Fargo Bank. McColl and NCNB had embarrassed Wells Fargo then, with their paradigm-shifting takeover of First Republic of Texas. They had met at conferences over the years, but McColl attended far fewer of those than Rosenberg did. Each had been quoted by the financial press as paying compliments to the other, unusual in the banking business. Rosenberg's greatest strength, McColl understood, was his marketing savvy.

McColl's handpicked successor had been Buddy Kemp, head of NationsBank's Texas operations. When Kemp lay in a Dallas hospital dying of brain cancer five years earlier, he had recommended Rosenberg as one of only two men in the country who should be considered to replace him. But by that time Rosenberg was already CEO of BankAmerica.

At BofA, Dick Rosenberg had turned around a bank in trouble. After writing off huge loans to Brazil and other less-developed nations in the eighties, BankAmerica saw the air go out of its stock, taking a billion-dollar loss and nearly falling to a hostile takeover bid by First Interstate of Los Angeles in 1986. In the last few years Rosenberg had been forced to sell nearly half his foreign operations. But when he pulled off the acquisition of Security Pacific Bank for $4 billion, BankAmerica Corporation became the largest bank in the country, with $190 billion in assets, twenty-four hundred branches in ten states. Yet McColl sensed that BofA under Rosenberg was in a retrenching mode, with infighting at high levels and dissension in the ranks making the rumor rounds, something like the bank McColl had gone to work for back in 1959. Rosenberg put an arm around McColl's shoulder, leading the way. McColl felt himself edging closer to the handshake that would crown his career. He thought he detected just a whiff of apprehension rising from the wool-blend suit beside him.

Instead of going to a private dining room, Rosenberg ushered McColl into the hotel's main restaurant, an oddly public place for a conversation like this, but the maitre d' seemed to know Rosenberg, showing him to a solitary corner table. Because it was early, they had the place almost to themselves. McColl ordered his favorite single-malt scotch, Lagavulin. Rosenberg began with pleasantries and questions about the health of old acquaintances. McColl worried his responses to small talk might reveal too much of substance. After months of waiting he'd flown six hours and spent three more in a hotel room. His engine was racing and he wanted Rosenberg to wave the green flag.

The dinner was nothing memorable, but with it came another round of drinks. *Always safe in a hotel,* McColl thought, *where they pour so little whiskey in the glass. I won't lose any edge . . . but, then, neither will he.*

They did not talk about money because money was not the issue. At this level, they were beyond money. Their discussion was about control, about whose hands would hold the reins of the merged megabank. At first, Rosenberg seemed to be yielding it all to McColl.

"You run the show," he said. "We'll work out all the details later, but you'll be in charge. Imagine, Hugh, running the largest damn bank in the world."

There it was, the capitulation. Grant handing his saber to Lee. *The showstopper of my career,* McColl thought, *the performance nobody can top.* It was to McColl an excursion to the outer limits of his dreams. He permitted himself a smile, sipped on his scotch.

"Then, just to make our board of directors happy," Rosenberg went on, "when you retire in five years one of our people will take over. Of course that won't be until the year 2000. What do you say?"

McColl concentrated on body language. *Say nothing.*

If there ever could be, in the mists and confounds of Big Business, such a thing as a "merger of equals," this certainly did not sound like it. Rosenberg's deal sounded rather like a thinly disguised acquisition of NationsBank. Hugh McColl, the man who had rewritten America's banking rule book, would have five years to bask in the glory and wonder of it all, a right short reign for David over the Philistines. Meanwhile, the bank he and Tom Storrs and Addison Reese and so many others had built would quickly crumble around him, coming to an end, like a family tree ended in a fruitless generation. *The deal he wants me to do is to sell out my company and my team.*

Hugh McColl would be a lame duck. People in the organization would immediately line up behind the successor, the BofA man, the CEO-elect. In effect he would be delivering to BankAmerica Corporation his company, sacrificing all his lieutenants who had helped him get to this point. Five years was nothing. He'd retire remembered as the man who sold out the South.

In the convenience-store commentary of newspapers and magazines, Hugh McColl was a man of few dimensions, good copy, easy headlines. Media descriptions made him "straightforward," an "ex-marine" who "pulls no punches," a "no-nonsense tough guy" who "always lets you know where he stands, even if he's standing on your toe."

That March evening in San Francisco he felt more like Uncle Remus's tar baby. He smiled, nodded, hmmed, swirled the melting ice in his glass, said nothing. *The press should see me now.* Viscerally, he felt insult and deep disappointment, but he fought against letting it show, refused to let his body language give him away. To McColl, Dick Rosenberg's offer said: "This guy can be bought." Rosenberg might have argued that anyone should be flattered by his offer, that it was more than generous, a huge concession on the part of BankAmerica. But McColl had nothing for sale and Rosenberg thought he could buy him cheap. A shiny crown for Hugh McColl and maybe a fancy new castle, but he would have to surrender his entire army. Having his successor named was simply a nonstarter. *Purely and simply a nonstarter.* The deal could never work.

"Look, Dick," he said at last, "we both want this deal to happen. This deal makes sense for everybody. But you didn't invite me to this dance and I didn't invite you. You don't want to sell your company and I don't want to sell mine. We're being pinhooked."

Rosenberg squirmed, looked puzzled.

McColl said, "That's an expression exclusive to eleven or twelve counties in South Carolina. It comes from the tobacco leaf that has a 'pin' or curve to it. When I was a kid, when the tobacco wagons rolled by you could steal a lot of leaves by hooking those pins. Then you'd take your ill-gotten goods to market and make a profit on a crop you never had to plant or tend or harvest. So a pinhooker became a low-life. That migrated into the real-estate world and came to mean a promoter who promises to put one person in touch with another before he gets either one of them to agree. It's somebody selling something he doesn't have any right to offer for sale. I'm not sure there's anything for sale here. You and I have been pinhooked by our friends at Merrill Lynch."

He pushed back his chair and rose. Rosenberg had signed the check already.

The two men shook hands, but it was not The Handshake they both had come expecting. Hugh McColl walked away from the merger that would have made him, for a while, the undisputed monarch of American banking.

"I still think about it," he told a friend back in Charlotte two years later. "The deal's still floating around out there. Somewhere."

CHAPTER 1

"You know anything about bookkeeping, boy?"

Hugh McColl stood stiff, heels planted together on the hardwood floor, eyes straight ahead, staring through a cloud of cigar smoke over the head of his new boss. His hair, four months past the last brush-cut, might be growing out, but the corps varnish had been laid on thick. A marine stood at attention before his CO.

The boss's name was Bedford Boyce and he couldn't have been more than twenty-two, if that, which was exactly two years younger than Hugh McColl Jr. What made one the "boss" and the other the "boy" was that Boyce had started at the bank right out of high school, whereas McColl had graduated first from the University of North Carolina and then from the United States Marine Corps. All that study-ing, kowtowing and drilling, just to wind up in his first real job nervous and hoping like hell he could figure out a way to impress this lanky kid.

Boyce was at home here, like a squirrel in a hollow tree, tucked behind random stacks of papers; dusty, thick ledgers and teeth-pocked pencils. His desk had a pull-out shelf where a typewriter was meant to go, but Boyce used the shelf as a footstool, stretching his long legs and tilting back in his chair.

"Yes, suh," McColl answered him quickly. "I kept the books at my daddy's gin."

Soon as the words were out of his mouth, McColl wished he hadn't said them. He felt like he must have hay sticking out from behind his big country ears. He had no idea what he was doing here and cursed his father for making him come. *You're not smart enough to be a farmer, boy. You'd better be a banker.*

"Drinkin' gin or cotton gin?"

"Cotton."

"Where you from?"

"Bennettsville, South Carolina."

Boyce masticated his cigar. He seemed to be trying to place the name of the town. "Marlboro County, right?"

"Yes, sir."

"You got a lot of sheep down in Marlboro County?"

"Mules, mostly. They call it the mule capital of the world."

"Mules." Boyce smiled around his cigar, sucked in and blew smoke. "Then you probably don't know how a sheep feels to be dipped."

"Dipped?" McColl began to feel stupid standing at attention, so he eased into parade rest, hoping Boyce wouldn't notice.

"Shearing time, they dip the sheep. One dip kills the lice, next dip gets the cooties off. You know, soak 'em in this tub, then that tub, then another tub. That's what they're doing to you. You just enrolled in the American Commercial Bank Sheep-Dip Program."

"Mr. Kirby told me this was the PQ Program. Promotion Qualification."

"Ol' Bob calls it PQ, everybody else calls it sheep dip. This is your first tub, the bookkeeping department."

"What will I be doing?"

"*Doing?* You won't be doing anything, McColl. You'll be watching. Just watch what we do around here. Ask questions—but not so many questions you bother anybody—write down everything you see and make your report back to Kirby. Then you go on to your next dip. Thirty months of this and then you'll be ready to *do* something."

"Thirty months? That's nearly three years."

"Used to be forty-two months. That's nearly four."

Hugh McColl hated banking, starting September 1, 1959, his first day on the job.

He found out they hadn't even expected him at American Commercial Bank in Charlotte. Bob Kirby recruited the people he wanted from Chapel Hill, from Duke, Wake Forest, Davidson, the

University of South Carolina. Nobody had recruited Hugh McColl. And Kirby already had his contingent of five trainees signed up before he ever interviewed Hugh. It was "don't call us, we'll call you." Only a call from his father to the president had got him a place in the training program. The others had started in June, right out of school. McColl came in late, off the bench. He was the sixth man on a five-man team. And this definitely was not the varsity squad.

He found out Day One that sheep-dip boys at American Commercial were lowlier than pledge recruits at a fraternity house. Boyce shared all the great lines with him. "P. J. Cooper, over in Credit, you know what he says? He says he never saw a college boy who could pour piss out of a boot that had the directions written on the heel. Har-har. Johnny Kabus, guy I work for, says keep you out of his way. Dead weight, he says."

That was not what Bob Kirby, assistant vice president of personnel, had led him to believe. According to Kirby, American Commercial was the Bank of Destiny, the Bank of the 1960s, the bank that was going to challenge North Carolina powerhouse Wachovia Bank & Trust. "How'd you like to be a pioneer, Hugh?" Kirby asked him when he finally found out McColl had been told to report to work. "How'd you like to go places nobody's ever taken a bank before? Well, here's your chance. Here's your chance to board this big, fast train that's leaving the station right now. You've got your ticket, McColl. Don't miss your ride."

It was Kirby's standard locker-room speech, and McColl found out soon enough that he made the same pitch to all the trainees. Moreover, the other recruits seemed to lap it up. They met together regularly, just so Kirby could pump them up and make it seem like they were doing something of importance. More often than not, his pep talk would include something about their responsibility to the bank and to its president, Addison Reese. According to Kirby, Reese saw their recruits as "leaders of the future."

"Look around you as you go through this program," Kirby told his trainees. "Look at the bank's senior officers. You'll see a lot of good people, a lot of them close to retirement. They've all been through the Depression. They've got ideas about what a bank's supposed to be and they aren't going to let go of those ideas. They want to play it safe. Well, Mr. Reese isn't interested in playing it safe. Mr. Reese wants us to beat The Wachovia. Now, nobody in his right mind would say this little bank could ever beat the biggest bank in the state, but Mr. Reese thinks we can. And you know what keeps me getting up and coming to work every morning, gentlemen? Chasing The Wachovia."

From what McColl could make out, there was not much chance of American Commercial ever catching the giant bank from Winston-Salem. Every morning when he got off the bus or, splurging, pulled his beat-up Chevy into a parking lot, the big sign painted on the building across Fourth Street would hit him with a strong dose of reality: *Wachovia Bank & Trust, the largest bank between Philadelphia and Dallas.* Kirby made it sound like a game. But, if it was a game, this contest was between his old Bennettsville high school team and the Chapel Hill varsity. If McColl's father really had wanted him to succeed in banking, maybe he should have gotten him a job at The Wachovia.

He wondered how much his father really knew about banking. Hugh Senior had owned a bank at one time, the Bank of Marlboro. Kept it going through the Depression only to shut it down. Hugh's uncle, D. K. McColl, had controlling interest in another Bennettsville bank, Marlboro Trust Company, but he'd never even given Hugh a summer job there. Now here he was in Charlotte, the biggest city in the two Carolinas, carrying a ring binder and a pocket full of pencils, making notes about bookkeeping, listening to people like Bedford Boyce and Mike Gheesling and John Kabus who seemed determined to overwhelm and intimidate him.

McColl learned the first week that his degree in banking and finance from Chapel Hill had thrown him without a life jacket into the cold sea of banking reality. This was simply drudgery. Worker bees posting checks and deposits by hand in alphabetized ledger books, pulling down the slot-machine arm of a Burroughs posting machine, cross-checking totals. As he watched, listened and scribbled frantic notes about the bookkeeping department, twenty-four-year-old Hugh McColl became aware of a strange feeling, one he'd never known in all his years of growing up, of quarterbacking football teams and taking the point in basketball, of playing poker and shooting pool, of daydreaming through college and suffering through boot camp. This new feeling was fear. For the first time, he doubted his ability to see a task through. He was afraid he didn't have whatever it took to be a banker. He was afraid of disappointing his mother and father. He was afraid of failing Jane Spratt, the girl he'd be marrying October 3.

As much as he despised the training at American Commercial Bank, his fear forced him to work at it. He wrote down words he'd never encountered, like "float," then found someone he could quiz on his lunch break. "Float," he learned, referred to the time it took the bank to collect the money on a check. *I should have been able to figure that out on my own,* he told himself. Settling for easy, average grades at Chapel Hill might not have been such a smart strategy after all. Not only did he feel seriously unwanted at American Commercial, peering over the hunched forms of fifty-year-old clerks who perhaps were earning even less than he was, he felt stupid as well. McColl had no way of knowing he was, in a very small way, part of Addison Reese's master plan.

In fact, McColl knew almost nothing about where his new company was headed, although he did have some idea of its history. When his father made the call that got him the job interview, he said he was telephoning "American Trust," despite the fact that there had been no bank by that name in Charlotte for more than two years. American Trust had merged with the bank next door, Commercial National, forming American Commercial in 1957.

But to Hugh McColl Sr. it would always be American Trust Company, the bank that had helped him survive the Depression. It was American Trust, the "banker's bank," lending money to smaller banks around the Carolinas, helping them to make loans to their customers in amounts greater than the little-town banks could handle. This "correspondent banking" had been the principal line of business for American Trust Company all along.

Hugh remembered dinner-table conversations about American Trust from his childhood, in the days when his father was still running the Bank of Marlboro in Bennettsville. He could recite the story of how South Carolina bankers had let Charlotte, North Carolina, "steal" a branch of the Federal Reserve in 1927, a branch that by all rights should have been set up in Columbia, South Carolina. He knew it was the chairman of American Trust, Word Wood, who sold Washington on Charlotte. He understood, too, that having a Fed branch in town gave Charlotte banks quick access to the Fed's "discount window" when they needed to borrow money. More importantly, as a "reserve city" bank, American Trust could act as a correspondent bank, or clearinghouse, for checks drawn on banks elsewhere, and then deposited in small-town banks and rural banks throughout the Carolinas. That was an advantage. And in a regulated industry, his daddy always said, any advantage was a *big* advantage.

McColl decided that his family's history with the bank could be a slight advantage for him in his competition with the other trainees just to get noticed. Not that Bob Kirby or Bedford Boyce gave a hoot about Hugh McColl's grandfather or great-grandfather, but McColl thought he might understand things about the bank other recruits didn't know. He knew something of his company and his industry's *history*. It might be to his advantage to learn even more about that history. He wasn't sure yet even whether this company was Hugh McColl Jr.'s friend or his enemy, so he started asking questions, getting the lay of the land. There was a lot more history to be learned.

When Hugh McColl started work in September 1959, American Commercial Bank was in a state of turmoil. To begin with, it wasn't so much one bank as two. American Trust, the bankers' bank, had recently merged with the bank next door, Commercial National, which did business primarily with individual consumers and with corporations. Over the past two years, the two Charlotte banks had combined their boards, their executives and their funds. On the surface, the changes were hardly noticeable.

To the average downtown (or "uptown," as McColl was learning to say) customer, the merger did very little to alter the status quo. People in Charlotte still walked into the twelve-story, skinny-as-a-rail Commercial National Building on the corner of South Tryon and Fourth Streets to deposit their paychecks. Correspondent bankers still did most of their business by mail or telephone with their trusty American Trust account managers. When small-town bankers came to Charlotte, they still pulled up to a parking meter on South Tryon Street and entered the squat, three-story vault they knew as American Trust Company, with its six Doric Order columns framing tall, tinted windows, its steel grates and brass doors defying distrust.

Nor did the financial world take much notice of the change. This first bank merger in Charlotte was a merger of little economic consequence. When "American Commercial Bank," with its combined resources of $234 million, was born in 1957, the most visible change was a hole in the wall of each building, enabling employees—and the occasional confused customer—to pass from one side of the operation to the other.

Then, in mid-1958, plans were unveiled for the two buildings to be replaced by an eighteen-story edifice at the same location. It would be three stories taller than the building Wachovia Bank was planning for West Trade Street two blocks away. That meant all of American Commercial's operations had to be transferred to nearby temporary office space, while the old structures were torn down and replaced with the new.

In Charlotte, razing tradition was something of a tradition in itself. The city had grown from an Indian-path campsite to a wagon-trail town to the crossroads of Carolina boosterism, mainly by tearing down whatever stood in the way of the next thing somebody wanted to build. In April 1959, as Hugh McColl was winding up his stint in the Marine Corps, Addison Hardcastle Reese, CEO of American Commercial Bank, was winding up like a baseball pitcher. In his hand was a brick knocked off one of his old buildings. Reese sent the brick crashing through one of those majestic front window panels of the American Trust Company Building, to the clicking of cameras from the *Observer* and the *News* and the cheering of dignitaries and bank workers. Addison Reese and his brickbat were progress.

Reese's flair for the dramatic came naturally. As a child, he had been entertained by performers who worked his grandfather's theater in Baltimore. Dorothy and Lillian Gish are said to have gushed over little Ad. His great-grandfather was the Ford of Ford's Theater in Washington, where Abraham Lincoln was assassinated. When Reese threw his brick, he was standing almost on the very spot where Jefferson Davis, president of the Confederacy, had been standing when he learned of Lincoln's death, a cosmic connection Reese certainly appreciated, since there was a curbside marker to identify the site.

A tall man with striking good looks and piercing eyes, Addison Reese worked his way through the Depression as a bank examiner with the Reconstruction Finance Corporation. In 1936, at twenty-nine, Reese became the youngest senior examiner in the United States. In 1951 he was back home in Baltimore, chairman of the County Trust Company of Maryland, when Word Wood's successor, Torrence Hemby, invited him to North Carolina. A touch antiestablishment, with no roots in the good-old-boy clay of the Carolinas, Reese was nonetheless sophisticated, urbane, polished, patrician, a Southerner of the Jeffersonian line. He made a smooth impression on directors and important customers when he arrived in Charlotte.

Reese was a man who liked a challenge, and he was intrigued by the possibilities of North Carolina's liberal banking laws. Unlike most states, North Carolina did not prohibit banks from operating in more than one county. Yet, for a century and a half, the only bank that had taken advantage of that open door was Winston-Salem's Wachovia Bank & Trust Company. With branches stretching from the Blue Ridge mountains to the Atlantic beaches, Wachovia controlled one dollar out of every five in North Carolina banks. Wachovia was also the state government's bank, and its wish was the virtual command of the state banking commission, which issued charters for new banks and approved new branch locations. Wachovia held North Carolina business and government in thrall, and outside the state it was recognized as perhaps the most important bank in the Southeast. Yet Reese was convinced that "The Wachovia," as it was called by its venerating minions and meek competitors, was vulnerable.

Before American Commercial could slay the giant, Reese's bank had to get a little bigger. That meant buying smaller banks, which would take less time than starting up new branches, in outlying counties. Reese's first and most formidable obstacle in going after smaller banks was his boss. Torrence Hemby did not want to frighten off his largest customer base—smaller banks—by seeming overly acquisitive. Before Reese took command Hemby actually had turned down a merger proposition from First National Bank & Trust Company of Asheville, a customer with three-quarters of a million dollars on deposit at American Trust.

"We're not in the merger business," Hemby declared. Even when Reese became president of the bank in 1954 he had Hemby as board chairman, watching over his shoulder. It was not until November 1957 that Reese consummated the merger with next-door-neighbor Commercial National. Ironically, that sent Hemby's rejected suitor, First National Bank of Asheville, flying into the arms of Union National Bank, headquartered just across South Tryon Street from the Mutt-and-Jeff buildings of American Trust and Commercial National. The marriage of the Union National in Charlotte and First National of Asheville created First Union National Bank. Now there were two banks in Charlotte bent on overtaking Winston-Salem's Wachovia to be the dominant bank in North Carolina.

In addition to external growth, there was a second element to Reese's strategy. He was determined to surround himself with people who would follow his leadership. He wanted bankers who were neither mired in the old ways of doing business in the Carolinas nor so beaten down by the Depression that they couldn't tell a good risk from a bad one. Bankers like that were not easy to find, so he opted for developing his own new breed. When he hired Bob Kirby in 1956 to scout the college campuses for management candidates, Reese's instructions were both explicit and, in the context of the period, extraordinary.

"Don't get all Baptists," Reese told Kirby. "Don't even get all Southerners. Eventually I'm going to want you to look for Blacks, for women, for people of different backgrounds." Kirby, who like Reese had grown up in the South, was astonished and somewhat alarmed.

"Now, I'm not telling you to go do that now, but I want you to start thinking about it. Because what I want is *variety*. I want this, Kirby. I don't want us to be vanilla, I don't want us to be chocolate. I want us to be something else, maybe Neapolitan. And that's going to be good in terms of doing business. It's going to be good for the state. It's going to be good because we're going to catch those guys at The Wachovia and we're going to pass them. And the kind of climate and culture we want to create is going to attract good people."

That culture grew slowly. When he arrived in 1959, McColl had no way of knowing that the progress of the sheep-dip program was closely monitored by the higher-ups at American Commercial. Except for the pep talks by Bob Kirby, McColl's early contacts with management were at a level that did little to convert his fear of failure to the sort of "team spirit" Addison Reese had in mind. The thing that made him interested in his new career was that, for the first time in his life, he was going to be responsible for the welfare of someone other than himself.

One month and two days after he started working at American Commercial, Hugh McColl married Jane Spratt, daughter of a prominent lawyer and principal stockholder in the Bank of York, South Carolina. They had met at the railroad station in Charlotte, on the first leg of a "Grand Tour" of Europe, and it was only after he fell for her that Hugh discovered Jane's family had money. They were both children of small-town South Carolina, both extroverts, both risk-takers. He found her "cute." She thought he was "goofy." They fell in love to mandolin music under the stars on the Grand Canal of Venice. They had their picture taken, holding hands on the *Fontana di Trevi*, for a postcard that Jane sent to her parents. On the postcard she wrote: "This guy wants to marry me!" Her mother was mortified that Jane would casually write this sort of thing on a postcard where the mailman could read it and gossip the story all over town, but Jane rarely bothered about what other people thought.

Hugh was at least discreet enough to seal the news inside an envelope, in a letter written to his mother August 4 from Hotel Rosenkranz, in the Norwegian seaport of Bergen:

> *Jane and I have been dating every night and of course are together quite a bit during the day. There is no reason for you to worry about us doing something rash, because she is very level headed. We think we are in love and of course have talked of marriage. . . . Jane is a rising senior at USC. She is not an excellent student, more like I was, but she is intelligent. She is not beautiful, but very attractive. She is more fun than anyone I have ever known. Everyone loves her to death. She is by far the most popular girl on the tour. The best thing is that she appreciates me and whatever I might do for her. Unusual among women. I never have to be anything but myself around her. . . . All of this means very little until I get home and we see how this works out. I only wanted you both to know that we are serious and could conceivably get married. However, we need not worry about this for quite a while yet, she may change her mind. Who knows?*

Two months after he wrote that letter, Hugh McColl was a husband. Jane moved into the upstairs room Hugh was renting at Mrs. S. L. Bagby's on Berkeley Avenue. This was just behind Covenant Presbyterian, one of the most prestigious houses of worship in a city that seemed to have a church on every corner. Hugh proudly moved Jane's clothes into the walk-in closet—the likes of which he'd never seen—and was astonished at how quickly a woman's wardrobe could eat up space. He showed her the fancy new shower stall in their bathroom. Not only did it have a nozzle to pour water down on your head, it had a second nozzle down near the floor for your feet and a third, right in the middle. (Mrs. Bagby had not explained what the middle nozzle was used for.) He was surprised that Jane wished they had a bathtub instead of that fancy shower stall.

Barely had they settled into married life when they had to contemplate the pending demands of parenthood. Hugh confessed to Jane that he hated his job, but, for her sake and for the sake of the baby that was on the way, he would succeed at it.

After what seemed like an endless string of weeks in the Bookkeeping Department, Hugh McColl handed in his notes to Kirby and was told to report to Mr. Shaw in the Proof Transit Department. Once again, McColl found himself standing at awkward attention before a man to whom he felt innately superior. That feeling was mutual. Benny Shaw evidently thought even less of the college recruiting program than Bedford Boyce did.

"Let's get one thing straight, Mister McColl." The *mister* was dragged through all the sarcasm Shaw could manage with his sawtoothed drawl. "I didn't ask for you. I don't want you. I don't like college boys. I don't like you. So don't get in my way. Don't cause me no problems."

It wasn't Benny Shaw that angered McColl so much as the stupid training program that forced two men into conflict. Whatever Mr. Reese had in mind by bringing in college graduates, he had failed to convince people like Benny Shaw, people who had worked their way up through the ranks, that it was the right thing to do. Benny Shaw and Hugh McColl should have been playing on the same team.

McColl knew Shaw from the minute he opened his mouth. Benny Shaw was a Dead-End Kid, like the boys who played the toughest football in Bennettsville, played so hard that the Lord Fauntleroy teams from the other side of town would holler and run home to mama. Kids like Benny had always made little Hugh McColl glad his family's land wound up on the "wrong side" of the railroad tracks his great-grandfather had laid through town.

Benny Shaw had gone from high school into the army and fought in that big war Hugh had listened to on the radio and followed on his daddy's wall maps. Somehow after the war, Shaw had talked himself into a job at the bank instead of doffing spinning frames at some lung-clogging cotton factory. He'd even put himself through two years of college night school. Now, at age thirty-five, Shaw had worked his way up in eleven years to manager of the American Commercial Proof Transit Department.

"This is the heart of the bank," Shaw told McColl, showing him around. "This is where we prove all the deposits, separate all the checks. We create all the totals for the Bookkeeping Department. We send out cash letters to the Federal Reserve and other banks for pay-ing checks. We post the controls and the general ledger and the statement of condition of the bank."

McColl heard an edge of pride in Shaw's explanation. He decided to stop taking notes and simply listen as his new supervisor led him around a corner. "Now this here's the Analysis Department, where we analyze the bank accounts and the corporate checking accounts for profitability, you understand? And we also handle all the collections for the bank. So they call it proof transit, but it's a whole lot more than just proof transit. Right here's just about all the important operations of this bank."

No matter how much Mr. Reese's training program was set up to make them enemies, Hugh McColl decided Benny Shaw would become his friend. He knew it wouldn't be easy because, this time around, it was the Dead-End Kid who owned the ball and, quite reasonably, expected to play quarterback. Hugh McColl decided to make Benny Shaw respect him.

McColl saw that bookkeeping operations at a bank were more complex than what he had done at the cotton gin in Bennettsville. The Transit Department was where checks were batched according to Federal Reserve District, added up and balanced. It was a labor-intensive process that had to be done mostly after-hours. It was no fun and there was no room for error. As soon as McColl saw what went on in the Transit Department, he understood it. It was the kind of work that had to be done no matter how dull and boring it might be, the kind of work you learned to do in the marines. Sometimes you had to stay late to get it all done.

He made friends with one of the women who did the "checking off," Margaret Brown, and she agreed to let him help her. They started with a stack of checks that had a batch header—a blue sheet of paper attached to a list of figures. The batch header informed them that the checks in the stack added up to $1,182,003.27. Miss Brown showed him how to use the ten-key number pad of the mechanical sorting machine to key in the amount of each check, then put it in the appropriate "pocket" of the sorter—one pocket for the Richmond Federal Reserve, one pocket for the Atlanta office—twenty-seven pockets in all. At the end of the process, the machine would provide a total, which was supposed to match the figure on the batch header. More often than not, the two totals would be different. To reconcile the totals, each separate item had to be "checked off" the pre-sort list and the sorted list. If there was a discrepancy in the numbers, they would locate the specific bank check and identify the error. There were nights when the lights in the Transit Department stayed burning until 2 and 3 A.M. Every night, trainee Hugh McColl stayed on the job until it was finished. If the checkers wanted food or coffee, he'd be the one to go for it.

It didn't take long for Benny Shaw to figure out that Hugh McColl was not Bob Kirby's typical trainee. The kid was okay, a member of the team. Maybe his family owned a bank, but he wasn't ashamed to get his hands dirty. There was something different about Hugh McColl, something Benny Shaw liked. He decided to take on the young man from Bennettsville and teach him what *really* went on in the bank, who made the big calls, who you needed to steer clear of, who you wanted to impress. Benny Shaw worked with numbers, but his specialty was people.

Shaw learned that McColl's bride was John Spratt's daughter, and that led to a lesson in correspondent banking. Before the merger, Shaw explained, nearly half of American Trust's deposits were from other banks. "Banks like that one your daddy used to own," Shaw explained. "Banks like John Spratt's down in York County, Bank of Fort Mill. Nonpar banks."

"Nonpar?" Another term that had somehow escaped the curriculum at Chapel Hill. Shaw told him how nonpar banks deducted a fee for each deposited check drawn on another bank.

"Now, just about half your banks are nonpar banks, and that means the Federal Reserve won't accept their checks at all. Plus there are other banks who aren't members of the Federal Reserve, so they can't send their checks to the Fed. So we've got to clear the checks for all those other banks. It's a big thing. It's a heck of a job. 'Course, in our department, we don't have to deal with the customers a whole lot. Mostly that falls to Louis Henderson over in Correspondent Banking."

"Henderson?"

Shaw smiled. "You were in the marines. You ever have one of them really mean-ass old drill sergeants that would sooner kick you than ask you to move out of the way?"

"Oh, yeah."

"That's Louie. You're gonna have to rotate into his clutches sooner or later."

With Hugh putting in such late hours in the Transit Department, Jane had little to do besides read and listen to the radio in Mrs.

Bagby's parlor. One night Hugh came home to learn his wife had found herself a job, working the telephone and sales counter for a fire alarm company on Hawthorne Lane. Jane was proud of her enterprise, but Hugh was not pleased. His mother and grandmother were the Great Ladies of Bennettsville; McColl women never worked. He was disappointed to learn that Jane had used her married name on the job application. He told her to quit, but she refused, insisting they needed the money. They would soon have to find a bigger apartment, because Mrs. Bagby's room was already too crowded, and, after all, there was a baby on the way.

Nights Hugh was home, he stayed awake late, adding up anticipated expenses, subtracting them from the meager salary that netted them only about eighty dollars each week. With every dime a matter of some importance, he was shocked to come across their bank statement in the wastebasket. Jane explained that this was the way she always handled it: she just looked at the last line to see how much was left in their account. No one had ever taught her how to balance a checkbook. Her father would receive a telephone call from someone at the Bank of York, warning it was time to "put some more money in little Jane's checking account," and it would be done. John Spratt loved to spoil his daughter.

Hugh decided he'd better find a way to "spoil" her too. Jane deserved something better than a room in some other woman's house. At the bank he was told that Charlotte had few "quality" apartments. Although new housing developments had mushroomed everywhere to accommodate returning GIs and their growing families, there were not many places suitable for a fledgling officer of American Commercial Bank. He was handed an application form for the Selwyn Village Apartments, off Park Road. It would mean a longer bus ride, but it was a respectable location. In fact, the Selwyn was owned by one of Charlotte's leading families, the Spanglers.

On a Saturday they went for an interview with the apartment manager. McColl carried his completed application form along with a letter of recommendation signed by a top bank executive. Apparently, the McColls passed the Selwyn Apartments test. All they had to do now was figure out how to squeeze seventy-two dollars rent out of Hugh's before-tax salary of $375 each month.

Hugh knew there would be no raise forthcoming for the near future. He could not turn to his father for help because, as Daddy was sickeningly fond of saying, a man should never spend a dollar he didn't have in his pocket. Rather than buying furniture for their new apartment, they accepted hand-me-downs from their mothers and from a cousin. The only piece Hugh could contribute was a hi-fi he'd won in a Marine Corps poker game. His collection of Ella Fitzgerald, Louis Armstrong and rhythm-and-blues, along with Jane's classical records, provided most of their entertainment. Jane loved her new apartment, but Hugh resisted spending the money on curtains for the windows.

"No sense putting down roots here," he told her. "We probably won't be here very long." His dissatisfaction with the job and with Charlotte was unsettling to Jane. She wanted to make this her home and her baby's home. But Hugh kept telling her he wouldn't be working for the bank any longer than he could help it.

As Jane got further along in her pregnancy, she gave up the alarm company job and the paycheck that went with it. Hugh's only financial recourse was to throw himself into his work at the bank, the work he hated, hoping somebody would take notice and reward him accordingly.

He began to see the bank as a battlefield, the theater of a war he detested but had to win. Maybe, as Bob Kirby maintained, the big enemy was Wachovia Bank of Winston-Salem, but inside the bank there were countless private skirmishes to be fought, and, if you were going to work your way up the chain of command, every skirmish had to be won. McColl began to look on the other young men in his "pledge class"—his fellow dippees—as competition. The five men Kirby had handpicked for officer training were Jim McDavid, Bob Wright, Bob Mauldin, Ken Harris and Fred Price. Hugh McColl was shorter than any of those men, the runt of the litter. He was a walk-on, an afterthought who arrived, along with Mauldin, three months after the first training shot was fired. While McColl was chasing Jane Spratt across Europe, four competitors were already scoring points with the brass.

McColl felt out of place in their company. His Bennettsville suit wasn't quite right for a banker. He only owned four dress shirts. His hair was still being discharged from the Marine Corps and his sideburns weren't quite down to where he wanted them yet.

Looking at the up cards, Hugh McColl figured to fold and walk away from the table. But McColl wasn't one to show what he had in the hole. His aces, he decided, were brains and balls. He could outthink the others and he would take chances they'd never dream of taking. Like his strategy of actually *working*, putting in long, uncompensated hours, while the others just drifted through the PQ program. While they were dutifully observing, department by department, writing their notes and chumming it with the people in Personnel, McColl was forming friendships, allegiances, relationships with the people who did the actual work.

Benny Shaw, a man who understood personalities, told him not to worry about Personnel, not to worry about competition from the other trainees. Instead, Shaw pointed out which people at the bank McColl truly needed to impress, which ones didn't matter very much and which ones should be avoided at all cost. Even after he rotated into the Note Department, McColl paid frequent visits to Benny Shaw and his other friends in Bookkeeping.

The Note Department was definitely a step up. Whereas keeping books had been a cloistered, humdrum assignment, now McColl actually got to interact with customers, when they came in to make payments on outstanding loans. Again, rather than simply observing, he talked himself into a job, this time as a note teller. Again there were accounts to be balanced late into the night. Again the practice he'd had keeping books at the McColl Cotton Gin in Bennettsville gave him a degree of proficiency that impressed his fellow workers.

This was the way to get through basic training. Make friends, let people know you understand the importance of their work. In the entire American Commercial Bank there were only about 230 employees, so getting to know people was not a daunting task, not for a man who had been voted "most likely to succeed" in high school. But on the morning of April 9, 1960, as Jane was nearing the end of her pregnancy, McColl read the news on the front page of the *Observer* that would change his life almost as dramatically as fatherhood was about to.

The story, written by Business Reporter Rolfe Neill, said that Charlotte's American Commercial Bank would join forces with Security National Bank of Greensboro, North Carolina, creating the state's second largest bank. Only Wachovia's $658 million in resources would top the new bank's combined resources of about $500 million. Neill called it a merger and speculated that the new entity would be named "American National Bank of North Carolina."

From what McColl could pick up around the water cooler, it seemed as though Addison Reese had won the first big battle in his declared war for supremacy against The Wachovia. McColl wondered how he could get out of boot camp and move up to the front lines.

> *"All of us were trying to climb the corporate ladder. In the '60s, we were* The Man in the Gray Flannel Suit. *We were the company."*

CHAPTER 2

Working at a bank in Charlotte was about the last thing Hugh McColl would have dreamed of in the spring of 1959. He wasn't dreaming about much then, except maybe that trip to Europe his poker buddy Dave Michaux had signed him up on.

"Come on, Hugh, we won all this money. Let's go spend it. Let's have one last fling." Leave it to his father, somber and solitary man, to bring him down to earth.

"Son, what you planning do when you get out of the Marine Corps?"

They were in the kitchen of the house in Bennettsville, Hugh, his mother and father, all around the chipped enameled-iron-topped table with the square legs. It was a Sunday evening and they were eating bacon, lettuce and tomato sandwiches. Hugh was just back from the Caribbean, tanned and lean, a month away from his discharge, a month away from his twenty-fourth birthday.

"I don't know, Daddy. I thought I'd come home and help you."

His father took a bite of his sandwich, chewed slowly, as though contemplating the flavor and consistency of it all, then said, "Well, I'll tell you, we're getting along fine without you."

He was not needed, not even wanted. It was the first time Hugh perceived that he would not succeed his father by right of primogenitor, that he would not ascend the family throne and run the family businesses. He knew he wasn't cut out to be a farmer, but he could leave that to his brothers, Kenneth and Jimmy. On the other hand, there was the cotton merchant business, the gin; with his flair for deal-making, couldn't he handle that? Apparently, his father simply had no more use for him.

"Mmm-hmm. Getting along *fine* without you. You better go up there to American Trust Company and get you a job."

Hugh McColl fancied himself a fighter, a competitor, but at the end of the day he always obeyed his father's command.

"Let's drive up to Chapel Hill and get you in college."

"Yes, Daddy."

"And what are you thinking you'd like to major in, Hugh?"

"Uh . . ."

"Dean, you can go ahead and sign the boy up for banking and finance."

"Yes, sir."

To Hugh McColl Jr. there simply was no greater authority than Hugh McColl Sr..

Next day he drove up to Charlotte in his beat-up Chevy for the appointment Daddy had set up on the telephone through his loan officer. The guard at the front door pointed the way to the personnel office. He was to ask for Mr. Kirby.

The first time he laid eyes on Hugh McColl, Bob Kirby saw a cocky and self-important young man, starched and polished in his blue marine uniform, wondrous in a world of dark-suited men and white-gloved secretaries. McColl stood at attention, a ludicrous posture in a bank office, until Kirby told him to take a seat. Kirby had work to do and broached this unscheduled interruption only because his boss had insisted. He asked the requisite questions, completed the necessary forms, then said: "Well, Mr. McColl, I'm sorry to tell you that we're just full-up. They won't let me hire any more trainees this year."

To Kirby's surprise, the young man brightened. "Well, that's just fine," he replied. "I'm nearly done with the Marine Corps and I'll be heading to Europe for a month or two. How about I check with you when I get back in the States?"

"That'll be just fine," Kirby said, standing and extending his hand. "Why don't you do that?" He watched the boy lieutenant execute a neat about-face and march out the office. *There's one I'll never see again,* he thought. *Mr. Reese would never go for him, anyway. Likes his bankers tall.*

Kirby had not been apprised of the fact that the young marine's great-uncle, D. K. McColl, owned 5 percent of the stock in American Trust Company before the merger, nor that Torrence Hemby was on the board of D. K. McColl's Marlboro Trust Company. The relationship between American Commercial and the McColls of Bennettsville ran far deeper than Kirby appreciated.

"How'd the interview go, son?" Hugh McColl Sr. inquired next morning.

"Well, Daddy, they don't want to hire me."

Hugh watched his father pick up the telephone, calm as ever, going through operators and secretaries until he got his high-placed friend on the line. "I understand that y'all are not interested in hiring my son."

There was a pause, an assent from his father, a hand placed over the receiver. "Son, when can you go to work in Charlotte?"

Hugh stuttered, "I . . . I . . . Daddy, I'm going to Europe and. . . ."

The father shook his head in resignation, eyes narrowing.

Hugh stood his ground. "I'm not sure when I'll be back."

"September first," his father said into the telephone. "Unfortunately, the boy has an engagement he can't break, but he'll be out of the Marine Corps and finished with his other commitments by then. You can expect him the first of September."

By the end of his first year of employment, Hugh Leon McColl Jr., now the proud father of Hugh Leon McColl III, found himself in the thick of a company in flux. The merger between American Commercial Bank and Security National of Greensboro produced an entity to be known henceforth as North Carolina National Bank. The "National" came from the Greensboro bank's charter, which placed it under the jurisdiction of the United States of America. The new bank would operate under that charter, rather than under the state charter that had licensed American Commercial.

By asking questions, McColl learned that this business of the charter had important ramifications for Addison Reese, chief executive officer of North Carolina National Bank. For one thing, Reese's moves would no longer be subject to approval of the Wachovia-pleasing North Carolina Banking Commission. Instead, NCNB—as people tended to call the new bank—would operate under the auspices of the Comptroller of the Currency, who was eager to have a strong national bank in the state. In fact, with its half-billion dollars in assets, nearly one thousand employees, and forty offices in twenty cities, NCNB instantly became the largest nationally chartered bank in the entire Southeast.

More subtly, the national charter caused the Comptroller to direct that Charlotte, the Federal Reserve city, should be identified as the primary mailing address of the new bank. This gave Reese the upper hand in his battle for control with the Greensboro bank's former CEO, Neil Vanstory, who was named NCNB chairman under the merger agreement. While the new bank would have dual "headquarters" in both cities, the bank's operations would be run out of Charlotte. The insiders told McColl that this arrangement was less than satisfactory to Vanstory and his former Security National management. Clearly there was more going on than what he read in the papers.

Not that Hugh McColl could *do* anything with this information. He was putting in even longer hours since his rotation from the Note Department to the Trust Department, which seemed to be in a state of disarray. McColl learned that one of the Trust Department's key officers had simply walked off the job the previous week. This individual had been responsible for insuring all the properties held by the bank in trust. Instead of doing his job he had spent his time looking for work outside the bank. Records had been poorly maintained and the bank could not be certain what was insured and what was not.

McColl was pulled out of the training program and put to work on special assignment, sorting through the trust documents and verifying insurance coverage. McColl had never seen an insurance policy in his life, but he was a quick study. For eight weeks he labored at setting things straight, out of his element and maybe out of sight as far as promotion was concerned. But as weeks went by he began to sense a change in the attitude around him. In the Trust Department he had responsibility for an important job and he was getting that job done. Hugh McColl was developing an identity of his own—not just the son of a big customer or that short kid from the sheep-dip program. He felt his stock rising.

In the summer of 1960, the world was contemplating the widening rift between Communist China and the Soviet Union. Vice President Richard Nixon was fighting off a challenge for the presidency from

Senator John F. Kennedy of Massachusetts. Across the South, the Civil Rights movement was gaining momentum.

In Charlotte, a group of students from the all-black Johnson C. Smith University sat down for lunch at the all-white Kress five-and-dime lunch counter, around the corner from North Carolina National Bank. This prompted Mayor James Smith to form what he called a "Friendly Relations" Committee, which ultimately recommended that all the city's lunch counters be integrated.

With so much change in the air, Addison Reese decided it was time to begin the internal course correction NCNB would have to make if it was ever going to supplant Wachovia as the number-one bank in North Carolina. Reese's management challenges started at the top. To begin with, both his chairman, Torrence Hemby, and his board of directors were far too intimately involved in daily management decisions. Even more unsettling was the constant tug of war for control between Charlotte and Greensboro—still "us" vs. "them." Finally there was the matter of succession; Reese needed someone in the copilot seat who could take over controls at the appropriate time.

Reese decided to look outside the bank for someone shrewd and decisive, an Androcles he could throw into Neil Vanstory's lion's den in Greensboro. To the old management team from Security National, someone from outside the company might seem untainted by any long relationship with Charlotte. If Reese could identify a man to help him tame Vanstory and his unassimilated people, such a man might have the leadership qualities needed to run the statewide bank he envisioned.

Reese found his candidate just a few blocks down South Tryon Street. He was the recently appointed manager of Charlotte's Federal Reserve branch, Thomas Irwin Storrs. Brought in from the main Federal Reserve Bank in Richmond less than a year earlier, "Buddy" Storrs had earned a doctorate in economics from Harvard, then had grazed the relatively peaceful pastures of government banking for about as long as he could stand it. He was ready to try his hand at something more competitive, something with growth potential. At just over five-and-a-half feet tall, Buddy Storrs was not the physical image Reese sought to project, but Reese could overlook that flaw if Storrs would agree to be his man in Greensboro.

Storrs agreed to move with his wife Kitty and their children to Greensboro, with great hopes but no contract. At the appropriate time, if he did what needed to be done, he expected he would be summoned back to Charlotte. Considering the eventual position Reese had in mind, he suggested Storrs drop the nickname "Buddy." In October, as Kennedy was making his stretch run against Nixon, "Tom" Storrs took over the operations of NCNB in Greensboro.

In Charlotte, Hugh McColl was pulled out of the training program seventeen months early. His hard work had won him a real job, in Correspondent Banking under the dreaded L. W. "Louie" Henderson. He was on the fast track to management, but he hated the assignment.

"I want to be a loan officer some day. Those are the people that have all the prestige in the company," he complained to Jane. "This is a wrong turn in my career. I want to go to work for a guy like Jack Tate in commercial banking. Tate's been to Harvard Business School. You can't believe how articulate the guy is. Charming. Instead they want me to be one of Louie Henderson's traveling salesmen. He's the guy Benny warned me about, the toughest, meanest son of a bitch in the company. Blows you all over the place for no reason. The man's obtuse, belligerent and belittling. Never spent a day in college."

The word that caught Jane's attention was "traveling." In her opinion, Hugh already spent far too much time away from her and the baby. Now this sounded like things were going to get worse before they got better. She suggested they take a weekend drive to Bennettsville in the new Ford Falcon her father had given her for Christmas, so Hugh could get some advice from his daddy.

Sitting again at the old enameled kitchen table, Hugh McColl Sr. listened to his oldest son complain.

"I'm being derailed, Daddy. I've been putting in all these long hours, doing jobs nobody even asked me to do, and they put me over on this sidetrack. I'm thinking, maybe I ought to quit."

His father's advice was exactly what Hugh should have known it would be: "Son, you go back up there and do what they ask you to do. You know that they know what's best for you and for American Trust, or whatever they call it now. A good job is something you cherish, something you honor."

Monday morning at eight Hugh reported to Louie Henderson.

Henderson was already on his third Camel of the day. It was drooping down from the side of his mouth, with a long ash about to fall and burn another hole in his white shirt. McColl stood at attention, watching the smoking ash. Henderson looked up at him, but did not speak. He was unwrapping something, a sort of bar, swathed in brown paper. Slowly, deliberately, he peeled the paper away, letting it dangle down to the floor beside his desk chair. At last he got the wrapper off and held up a three-surfaced bar, studying it like it might be some oracle. McColl recognized the shape of a newly minted, official North Carolina National Bank desk nameplate. Henderson turned it so McColl could read the inscription and he began to speak. The cigarette wobbled and the ash tumbled onto his shirtfront, glowing red.

"C'n you read that, boy?"

McColl read aloud: "Louis W. Henderson, Senior Vice President."

Absentmindedly, a brown-stained finger flicked away the cinder, along with a few blackened threads of Henderson's shirt. "*Senior Vice President*. Boy, you do what I tell you and you'll git one of these one day."

Welcome to Correspondent Banking, McColl thought.

When it came to leading his group, Louie Henderson proved to be a minimalist. Underlings were rarely let in on the reason for a job or precisely what Henderson's expectations of that job might be. He only told them what the job was.

"I need you to get me some information, McColl," he said.

"Yes, sir."

"I need to know the average size of the cash letters we're sending to the First National Bank of Cincinnati."

That seemed like a simple enough assignment to McColl. He hopped in the elevator and went down to see his friend Benny Shaw in the Transit Department. After some discussion as to the apparent mindlessness of the mission, McColl and Shaw decided to go to the Cincinnati bank's records for the previous month, select five days at random and run an average. McColl wrote down his number and brought it back to Henderson.

"How big was your sample on this?"

McColl confessed it had been only five daily cash letters. Henderson crumpled the sheet of paper and tossed it in the wastebasket.

"Well, *that's* not a damn average, boy."

McColl went back to Shaw and together they pulled an entire month of checks for First National of Cincinnati. Still, Henderson was not satisfied.

"Well, look, that's just February. What about the rest of the year?"

Seething, McColl picked up an adding machine and went to the warehouse where North Carolina National Bank stored its boxes and boxes of records. Still short on wardrobe, he carefully draped his jacket, shirt and tie over a hand truck and sorted through the dusty shelves in his suit pants and undershirt. For hours he opened boxes and pulled out files until, on several sheets of legal paper, he had recorded to the penny the amount of every cash letter that had been sent to the Cincinnati bank in the course of 1959. Sitting there in the warehouse with a manual adding machine, he summed the figures, then divided by the number of entries. On the bottom of the last sheet he wrote the average in large print and circled it.

Back in uniform at the bank, he presented his work to Henderson. His boss looked at the figures, turned the pages and took in the total. He grunted, then tore the sheets of paper in half and, methodically, tore them again. Then he threw the scraps into the wastebasket.

Louie Henderson sent McColl into South Carolina under the tutelage of one of his best people. Jack Ruth was a graduate of Davidson College, the Presbyterian school situated just outside Charlotte in the northern part of Mecklenburg County. While Davidson had a reputation for turning out topflight businessmen, it also provided a firm education in the humanities. Jack Ruth's human qualities proved to be even more valuable to McColl than his banking savvy. He took McColl under his wing, treating him as not only a business associate, but a friend. He and his wife, Betty Kate, had the McColls over to dinner, then invited them to attend church with them at Covenant Presbyterian, near their first apartment. Soon Hugh and Jane joined the church.

On the road with Jack Ruth, McColl learned how much he still had to learn about his business. They took to the highway, heading south, every Monday morning. They'd travel U.S. 521 to Lancaster, Kershaw and Camden; U.S. 601 to Pageland, Hartsville and Darlington; South Carolina 49 to Union. They would hit every little bank in every little town and talk to bankers on subjects that, McColl admitted to Ruth, "I don't know a damn thing about."

The most important thing for him to understand, Ruth explained, was that they personified their company to the customer. They were big-city bankers, calling on isolated small-town bankers and businessmen. Their customers naturally assumed Jack Ruth and Hugh McColl were in on the big secrets—what was going to happen to the interest rates, the bond market, commodity trading. In fact, the only thing McColl or, for that matter, Jack Ruth, knew very much about was collecting checks. They knew a world about collecting checks.

To better educate himself, McColl developed the habit of making the rounds of all the different NCNB departments, as soon as he got back to town at the end of the week. He pretended he was still in training, learning from the people who did the work. This time around, because he was a junior officer rather than a trainee, his wandering met with more respect.

Out in the field, Jack Ruth taught him to be a good "customer man," responsive, quick to do whatever a customer needed done. McColl learned the importance of always having an opinion. Put forth aggressively, most of his opinions seemed to receive more value than they deserved. Even when he wasn't sure, he was sure. Correspondent bankers wanted to be *confident* in their upstream men.

McColl saw that the correspondent banking system had evolved over the years, first out of the devastation of the Civil War, then out of the rubble of the Depression. State-chartered banks could make no individual loan that was greater than 15 percent of the bank's total capital. Consequently, if a merchant in Conway, South Carolina, wanted to build a new store, the local Conway bank would lend as much as it could, then invite its upstream bank in to write the balance of the loan. If the Conway bank happened to enjoy a good relationship with Wachovia, then Wachovia would very likely get the business. Looming over all the major Southern banks was the threat that, if the total amount requested was too high or the proffered service less than perfect, the Conway banker might pick up the telephone and call New York. That was the "money center," where the real dollars resided. Most Southern bankers persisted in the belief that it was undercapitalization, not General Robert E. Lee or his soldiers, that had lost the War. Hugh McColl perceived that, when it came to capital, the South still felt inferior.

He also perceived the misery of the traveling salesman's life. To save money against the standard per-diem, they put up in little hotels and motor inns. Four dollars a night, some of them, plus 3 percent sales tax. They drove out of their way to save money.

At least Jack Ruth seemed to empathize with Hugh's situation, one child and another on the way, no help coming from his steel-willed father. Jack Ruth was the nicest person Hugh McColl had met at the bank. Ruth's only flaw, as far as McColl could see, was that his gentle nature made it too easy for a customer to tell him no, or else to cut NCNB a smaller piece of the pie than they might merit. McColl wished he could see Ruth push just a little harder, charge a little faster. To some degree, they might be working a seller's market, but McColl smelled competition out there. Keeping the business would be no less a challenge than getting the business in the first place. He needed to be on the lookout for loan officers from Wachovia Bank and Charlotte's First Union, from Atlanta banks like Trust Company of Georgia and Citizens & Southern Corporation, from in-state banks like State Bank & Trust Company.

A few months under Jack Ruth's tutelage and McColl was on his own. Nights on the road he spent studying maps and reading history books. He formed the opinion that no American state was ever fought after the way South Carolina had been. When Sir Henry Clinton captured Charleston in 1779, it nearly spelled the end of the American Revolution. Only a victory by the Over-Mountain men and the South Fork Boys at King's Mountain, just west of Charlotte, thwarted Lord Cornwallis's plan to turn Americans against Americans. The Civil War began, April 12, 1861, when South Carolina troops fired on Fort Sumter. Nearly four years later, just before the fire that nearly destroyed Columbia, General Sherman said his entire army was "burning with an insatiable desire to wreak vengeance upon South Carolina."

McColl's home state was still a battlefield. Only now the invading armies were bankers and money investors, and, hell, he was one of them. He drew himself a map, with South Carolina a down-pointing triangle. He sketched in the fall line, formed by rivers flowing toward the sea from the North Carolina border, merging northeast of Spartanburg. His fall line forked near Columbia, in the center of the state. One fork split off to the south, heading toward Augusta, Georgia, and the other ended at the ocean, above Charleston. Thus the state triangle was divided into three four-sided figures, each of more-or-less equal area. His home part of the state, where Bennettsville was located, was in the upper right section, the Pee Dee. The Pee Dee River was its dominant feature. To the left of the Pee Dee section, toward the Blue Ridge Mountains, was the Upcountry. At the down-pointing apex of the triangle was the Low Country. Cartographers could take issue with his precision, but the map was what Lieutenant McColl required for a plan of battle.

Whatever industrial strength the state could claim was located in the Upcountry, around Greenville and Spartanburg. Consequently, this part of the state had the greatest appeal for the Northern banks, as well as for those coming out of Atlanta. The Low Country harbored what remained of the region's Old South plantation mentality—what McColl termed "attitude." The Low Country was fertile ground for the State Bank & Trust, headquartered now in Columbia, the state capital. The majority of NCNB's correspondent accounts were in the Pee Dee section, where McColl had grown up. Most of the money in the Pee Dee came from farming, with cotton and tobacco the cash crops. The Pee Dee was his to defend, McColl decided, while he raided the Upcountry and Low Country to extend North Carolina National Bank's sphere of influence.

One of his strongest allies in infiltrating enemy territory was, in fact, one of the competitors. W. W. Johnson, known to all as "Hootie," was heir apparent to the chair of Columbia's State Bank & Trust, which had grown out of the Bank of Greenwood, founded by Johnson's father in 1943. While State Bank & Trust had branches in many parts of the state, it also did its own correspondent business with smaller banks in rural areas. Often these little banks needed help with cash flow when they had to cash "foreign" checks, those drawn on an out-of-town bank. State Bank & Trust would become the little bank's "upstream" bank, accepting the foreign check, crediting the account of the smaller bank, then collecting the money from the bank on which the check had been drawn.

Quite often State Bank & Trust needed an upstream bank of its own to provide that same service, a bank it could turn to whenever a larger source of funding was called for. Hootie Johnson's father had looked to American Trust in Charlotte as one of his upstream banks. After the mergers created NCNB, that relationship continued, as Hootie Johnson prepared to take over State Bank & Trust and Hugh McColl prepared to take over the South Carolina territory for NCNB.

Johnson, four years older than McColl, was not fond of McColl's aggressive approach to business, but if his own bank was to continue growing it required a dependable relationship, if not with NCNB, then perhaps with Wachovia. But Johnson would give McColl the benefit of the doubt, for the time being at least. The two men met regularly, sometimes in Columbia, sometimes at crossroads luncheonettes, where a farmer might be looking for $300,000 to build a grain elevator or a cotton gin. The local bank's limit was $50,000. Could NCNB put up the $250,000? That way the local bank could keep the farmer's business and State Bank & Trust could keep the local bank's business.

"Let's take a look at the property," McColl would say.

Federal regulations were few in those days before truth-in-lending laws. In the pockets of his suit coat, which usually was slung over his shoulder, McColl carried bank notes. Perched on the back of a tractor, surveying the property, he'd ask the farmer where he planned to build and how much he'd need to get the job done. After passing a few pleasantries under the broiling sun, he would feel sure that, yes, he probably could talk the bank into approving that loan. The farmer would be concerned about how long that approval might take. McColl would flash his wide grin and whip out a bank note from his pocket.

"How's today suit you?" he'd ask.

This was not the way Jack Ruth had instructed him to handle loans. He was supposed to fill out paperwork, formally present the request to the bank in Charlotte, obtain approval, *then* write the note. But approval was not strictly required until the amount of a single note exceeded $99,999. McColl figured that just about any loan could be structured in increments smaller than $100,000.

An unwritten law of the correspondent banking trade was that no upstream bank would attempt to do direct business with customers within the downstream bank's territory. That kept the relationships fairly clean, at least as far as NCNB was concerned. But the rules were rewritten in 1962 when Addison Reese set up a new, aggressive division in the bank. It was to be called the National Division of NCNB and correspondent banking was to be one of its primary functions.

The mission of the National Division was to bring in business from wherever in the United States business could be found. Not only business from banks, but from corporations, manufacturers, builders and consumers. While McColl still reported to Jack Ruth, Louie Henderson's function was taken over by Yates Faison. The entire South Atlantic Region of the National Division became the responsibility of young John Robison, a protégé of Reese's chief advisor, Julian Clark. At the top of the National Division, reporting directly to Clark, was Patrick Calhoun, who had come from the Greensboro side of the merger.

Among the many personnel shifts arising from the birth of the National Division was that of Benny Shaw's promotion to "call officer" in South Carolina. Shaw, whose experience of McColl had been restricted to conversations in the Proof Transit Department, saw a different side of his friend when he accompanied McColl to meet with Ernest Patton, president of People's National Bank in Greenville, South Carolina.

Shaw assumed the meeting was a washout from the get-go, when the two men walked into Patton's office and he immediately looked at his watch. "All right," Patton said. "I'm going to give you about five minutes and that's it."

God almighty, thought Shaw, *I'm ready to get out of here fast. 'Cause this guy is cold. Lord, he's cold.* But McColl started talking and wouldn't let up. By the time Patton looked at his watch again, thirty minutes had gone by and he was still lapping it up. McColl walked out with a new customer. As they left the bank, Shaw shook his head and smiled, "Hugh, my opinion of you just shot up a long ways."

"I'm a closer," McColl said. "I can make the sale, actually make it happen, and not take no for an answer. Part of it is realizing that if you are driving another man to a decision, if he makes it, you'd better be ready to perform. You won't be able to say, 'Well, gosh, I'll just take that back.' You see?"

McColl was learning that he could get along fine in the business world if he approached it as a game. As long as he could play at work the way he played at sports, he might even come to enjoy it. On weekends he honed his competitive edge by joining a YMCA basketball league and by playing Sunday football on the Selwyn Village quadrangle. It was touch football, played by young banking, law and business professionals, with their wives cheering and fussing from the sidelines. McColl usually talked the other guys into letting him play quarterback, his position in high school. He got "touched" to the ground regularly, but he loved it. Monday morning aches helped him keep the edge as he settled in behind his steering wheel for the long drive south.

His gas pedal never spent much time in the raised position. Everything was a contest. Could he pass that fertilizer truck before the two-lane road curved? How many calls could he get in that day? More often than not, lunch would be a pack of Lance crackers, an apple and a carton of milk, downed as he drove thirty miles to the next town, the next county, the next bank or business office. Unless he could pick up a baseball game on the radio, he'd be planning his next move as he drove, how he'd sweet-talk that next banker into starting or deepening a relationship with NCNB.

Sometimes, though, he found himself dreaming about freedom, about never having to work at all, about never having to report to anyone on how many calls he made or how much money he loaned. He dreamed about just traveling with Jane, his mind drifting back to that summer, 1959, before he became a banker, when he'd finally met a girl who saw him for the romantic rebel he was, and loved him for that alone.

He'd found her sitting on the railroad station bench in Charlotte, waiting for the train that would take them to New York, where they would board a steamship for England. Brown hair cut short, flashing smile, full skirt, bobby sox, incessant laugh. Someone called her Jane. He pulled a slip of paper from his pocket. There were always slips of paper in his pockets, filled with important information, notes to himself.

"Jane Spratt from York?"`

She stopped chattering, looked up at him, curious, slightly annoyed at the curt interruption.

"Sister Padgett said I should look you up." Bonita Padgett, a Converse College student who lived in Bennettsville. Jane Spratt had spent two years at Converse before transferring to the University of South Carolina. Her dorm room had been next to Sister Padgett's. McColl always took notes, always made connections. This was how he met people, how he kept score. Jane Spratt's attitude told McColl she was not interested. She found him pushy, no doubt far too sure of himself. He and his buddy David Michaux were older than any of the other young people on the tour, and she'd been told to watch out for older men. McColl noticed she favored one of the college boys. That made it a contest, with him as the underdog. His favorite sport.

There was no headway on the ship: Jane dancing with her college boy, playing shuffleboard with the group. It wasn't until London that he got his opportunity. The group guide and self-appointed chaperone, Miss Louise Thomas of Thomas Tours, announced that she could buy tickets for *My Fair Lady*, starring Rex Harrison and Julie Andrews, for those who had the money. McColl had more than enough. That fifteen-hundred-dollar tour ticket had barely dented the big poker purse he'd carried away from the marines. He bought tickets for himself, Michaux and Jane and paid for a taxi to take them to the theater. After the play, riding back to the hotel, he told her he was crazy about her. She said, no, he was just crazy. But he could tell she was thinking about it.

In Brussels he looked out of the window of his hotel room and saw a flower cart, filled with roses. He told Michaux he was going to buy every one of those roses and send them to Jane. That got her attention: a train of French-snickering bellboys with arms full of flowers. Even the bidet got called into service as a vase. Next morning on the train, Jane was all smiles until she saw another girl giving Hugh a peck on the cheek and thanking him for the bouquet he'd bought for her—just in case Jane didn't respond.

That was the last bet he hedged. In Rome he put all his time and spent all his money on Jane. He rented a Fiat, no bigger than a sofa, and drove on the wrong side of the winding roads to the beach. In Venice they eluded the ever-vigilant Miss Thomas for a night of romance: the gondola, the wine, the mandolins, the stars. In Florence, over a dinner of steak and Chianti near the *Ponte Vecchio*, Hugh pulled out a scrap of paper and began scribbling figures, adding up what he had left of his poker winnings, the imagined cost of airline tickets, diamonds, apartment rentals. He announced his plan to fly the very next day to Amsterdam, to meet Jane at the train station when she arrived. He would have an engagement ring and all the plans for their wedding. She laughed and told him no, that he was *definitely* crazy. But from the Hotel Milano he wrote to his mother that this was the girl he would marry.

And now there was little Hugh, with a second child on the way. The poker winnings were long gone. Rent at Selwyn Village had soared to $82.50 a month. His highway dreams of freedom always ended at a nose-in parking spot on the main street of some South Carolina cotton market town, pulling his jacket from the back seat of his car, walking through the big doors of a little bank. If he hurried, maybe he'd make a big city, like Greenville, by evening, find the Y and shoot a few hoops before he turned in and got back to whatever book he was reading.

It was the Friday before Christmas and McColl had the afternoon off in Charlotte. He decided to put in an hour of basketball at the YMCA, but had barely worked up a sweat when the attendant opened the gym door and called him to the telephone. He was astonished to hear the voice of his "big boss," division director Pat Calhoun. His first thought was that he must have done something wrong, but Calhoun had a problem with a customer and wanted McColl to solve it. McColl listened, answered, "Yes, sir," and raced to the showers.

A few minutes later he was heading down Highway 21 to Columbia. It was nearly a hundred miles, two hours under the best conditions. McColl made the trip in ninety minutes. He pulled up to the headquarters of State Bank & Trust Bank—recently renamed Bankers Trust—and headed for Hootie Johnson's office. Johnson met him at the elevator and took him aside.

Although he appreciated NCNB's quick response, Johnson wasn't sure anything could be done to save the situation. It involved a large regional automobile dealer, a man who had multiple dealerships and was highly visible in Columbia. The dealer had expanded, using money borrowed from Bankers Trust, from First National Bank of South Carolina and from elsewhere. Now the bankers had caught the dealer using a ploy called "selling out of trust," turning over cars on his lot without reporting the sales to his creditors. Johnson felt that the other banks were ready to demand payment in full on their loans, which would have sent the dealer into bankruptcy. Since Bankers Trust was already into the dealer for the maximum credit limit of 15 percent of its deposits, there was nothing Johnson could do to replace the other banks' investments. At the same time, Johnson's bank had the most to lose if the dealer became insolvent. Hootie Johnson let McColl know he had called Pat Calhoun rather than his counterpart at Wachovia Bank because he felt NCNB might be quicker to respond. At the mention of Wachovia, McColl felt the competitive fires in his gut.

"Wachovia! They're always ready to lend you an umbrella when the sun's shining, then take it away soon as it starts to rain." He practiced lines like that between pitches during ball games on the radio. "Hootie, you know we don't cut and run when the cards don't fall. We might could do something to help you out here."

Johnson escorted McColl into his boardroom, where the president of First National Bank of South Carolina and several other of the top bankers in Columbia were gathered, along with the guilty auto mogul and his lawyers. McColl sensed that a deal was his to make. He was a first-level bank officer, little more than an assistant cashier, sitting down with the high rollers. But he realized that, from their vantage points, he represented Big Money. As Jack Ruth had taught him, whether or not these men knew Hugh McColl from Adam's house cat, they respected the power of his company.

He began to talk, putting the Columbia bankers at ease, parroting back what he'd learned from his briefing by Hootie Johnson. He let them understand that he understood their various and difficult positions. The others corrected a point here, a point there, but by and large McColl had his facts straight. He spent a few minutes going over the dealer's balance sheets and he spotted several assets that were not yet pledged as security. At the end he put it succinctly: "Seems like you fellows find yourselves in a game ain't nobody can win. So what we need to do," he said, looking first at the president of First National, "is take you all out of it. We'll buy your loans, providing Mr. Johnson keeps his money in."

Hootie Johnson let out his breath and nodded agreement.

"Okay," McColl said, turning his attention to the car dealer. "Here's what we'll do. We'll take all of your real estate and we'll work with you to get you out of debt. You've got enough other assets to cover what we call the collateral shortfall. That gives us some comfort if we can get through to the other side, and if we can't, we sell the assets and make good on the loan, you understand? Because the thing we don't need to do is put you into bankruptcy, 'cause for sure every damn one of us'll be taking losses then."

Go down there and see if you can save the situation, Pat Calhoun had told him. That was all the authority McColl needed, no matter what the rule books said. He was confident, decisive. He felt a thrill as he shook the hands of the bank presidents and the car dealer and the lawyers. They all were in his debt. Hootie Johnson would be his friend, from now till the cows came home.

*"They judge you on force and leadership and aggressiveness. . . .
I ought to get a pretty good aptitude mark."*

Hugh McColl
Letter from boot camp, 1957

CHAPTER 3

For Hugh McColl or anybody else in 1961, if you wanted to keep your mind on business you needed to avoid the evening news or the morning headlines. No news was good. Even McColl's marines falling on their face in the Bay of Pigs invasion, Fidel Castro grinning through his Communist beard. The Soviets' cosmonaut thumbing his nose from space at the U.S. Russia's fifty-megaton hydrogen bomb, bigger than anything the U.S. had. That Berlin Wall.

But the news back home at North Carolina National Bank: business was getting better and better. Addison Reese struck north of Charlotte, acquiring first the Statesville Bank, then moving into Wachovia territory, buying the First National Bank of Winston-Salem. NCNB now had forty offices, covering almost the entire state. McColl and his buddies at the bank knew those Wachovians were looking in their rearview mirrors now, a tad nervous.

The bankers of the forty branches of NCNB had their enmity toward Wachovia in common, but they were bound by little else. Reese was building not so much a union, as a confederation of separate institutions. His bipartisan board of directors—one foot in Greensboro, the other in Charlotte—remained far more involved in banking operations than he would have wished. NCNB was running hard, but as yet it had no policies, no guidelines, nothing that could be called a corporate culture.

Finally, however, it did have a new building. The eighteen-story NCNB Building opened to great fanfare early in 1961, the first new structure built in Charlotte since 1925 that was tall enough to require an aircraft warning beacon on top.

Hugh McColl was impressed. By now he'd been inside so many banks he thought he must have seen them all, all of them depressingly alike. This NCNB Building, on the southwest corner of South Tryon and Fourth Streets, was different. It reminded McColl of a big movie theater, so much more than a century removed from that tiny brick storefront Bank of Marlboro, the one his great-grandfather had started on Bennettsville's Main Street in 1886. Instead of the dark, crypt-like traditional bank, this new building had a wide and friendly lobby, with a two-story ceiling and a mezzanine-level balcony. Behind the line of tellers loomed huge sculptures, like figures from the pages of books his mother used to read aloud: Industry, Transportation, Agriculture, Medicine, Education, Science. Fifteen feet tall and five hundred pounds apiece. It was a place where heroes could transact business and feel right at home.

To reach Valhalla, one ascended the wide, carpeted stairs to the mezzanine. Addison Hardcastle Reese's office was there, to the left, with one window that made it possible for him to look out over the floor of customers and tellers, another window overlooking Fourth Street—and the inescapable Wachovia billboard. The mezzanine plateau held desks for assistants and secretaries, behind them the Loan Administration Department. And to the right of the stairway, in a position of evident expectation, the new NCNB National Division.

Part of Reese's charge to his National Division was "no more Mr. Nice Guy," no more polite avoidance of stealing business away from correspondent banks. From this point on, any bank's loan customer was a potential NCNB loan customer. As a result, officers of the National Division, with their offices located so near the seat of power, began to see themselves as a sort of elite corps. They could write their rule book as they went along. Reese was their commander-in-chief, and he had declared war on Wachovia. Every bank or business that did or might do business with Wachovia was a hill to be taken. With his Marine Corps training still fresh enough to motivate him, McColl picked up his loan forms and marched.

From what he learned over morning coffee and evening beer,

McColl perceived that others in the bank were not so eager to get in line behind Reese. Charlotte officers returned from excursions to Greensboro full of gossip about the old Security National organization and its lingering loyalty to conservative chairman Neil Vanstory. The injury to Greensboro's pride, after little more than a year, was far from healed.

"They're all 'us' up there," an Accounting Department clerk reported, "and we're 'them.'"

There were lots of laughs in Charlotte over Vanstory's refusal to leave even the most routine Greensboro operations to Reese's new man from Harvard and the Fed, "Dr. Tom" Storrs. Among old-line Security National managers, an order was not an order unless it came from "Mr. Vanstory." Storrs even had to contend with the chairman's son, Neil Vanstory III, who was in charge of the Greensboro branch operations. On a January afternoon, the Charlotte mezzanine tittered over a new joke from upstate. That morning Storrs had taken an angry call from a customer who slipped on icy snow in front of one of the branch offices. McColl was filling out his weekly report when the loan executive arrived with the story. People gathered around the secretary's desk outside Julian Clark's office to hear him tell it.

"Storrs drew up the damn snow removal plan himself," said the messenger. "The man practically told them how long the shovel handles had to be and how much their bags of salt had to weigh. Storrs wants every detail perfect. He can't believe the first day it snows this old lady falls on her can. So he calls down to the garage for a driver and a car. He tells them to put snow chains on it. This guy's from the north, right? Snow chains in Carolina? So he heads out in this freezing weather to make the rounds of the branches. Guess what? About half the banks still have snow and ice everywhere. So he calls in and tells his secretary he wants Neil Vanstory—'Little Neil'—in his office when he gets back. And I'm standing there when Storrs comes in. He's got ice on his shoes. You wouldn't believe the language. I mean, he kicked Neil Vanstory's ass till his nose bled."

"Probably wishing it could be the old man instead of Junior," chipped in a fellow from the retail side.

Everybody laughed. But Hugh McColl recognized this was serious stuff. "It's a contest of wills," he told Benny Shaw. "If we can see it from down here, imagine what it must look like from where Mr. Reese sits."

Over soup in the new company cafeteria on South Tryon Street, Chairman Vanstory became known as "the thorn in Mr. Reese's side," the butt of jokes and a perceived obstacle to NCNB victory over Wachovia. Orders that came directly from Vanstory were viewed as "imperious dictates" by much of the National Division cadre. Although it did little for the cause of corporate unity, this anti-Vanstory sentiment served to build the fighting spirit of the men who served under Addison Reese and his popular second-in-command, Julian Clark. No matter what went on in Greensboro, Hugh McColl and his compatriots believed themselves to be the heart of NCNB. The National Division was McColl's team, his family, a place where he fell into ranks securely and naturally behind John Robison, Yates Faison, Pat Calhoun and even Julian Clark.

While Calhoun was designated as the executive vice president responsible for the new National Division, Clark, as the bank's chief credit officer, exercised his prerogative of going over McColl's loan write-ups personally. Clark's practiced eye never failed to spot omissions that would provide clues to the questions McColl forgot to ask, in the fever of writing new business. Clark always began with a pleasantry, putting his foot soldier at ease. Then came the question to which McColl had no good answer. It would be, "Has this fellow already shopped Wachovia or First Union?" or "Does he have any property in another county that we could use as collateral?" Whatever the question, Hugh McColl's answer could only be, "I don't know, sir," or "I forgot to ask."

McColl shook his head to John Robison in disbelief. "That Mr. Clark's got to be the smartest man in the world. The first question he asks me, every damned time, is the one I didn't know the answer to. I'd know the answer to any other question that he could possibly ask. How come he always figures out the one thing that I don't know?"

Clark always found a thrust that drew blood, even when McColl was complimenting the work of someone else at the bank. "Mr. Clark, this guy's really a great analyst."

"How do you know?" Clark shot back.

"Well, I've seen his work. It's obvious he knows what he's talking about."

"You don't know whether the guy is a great analyst or not, Mr. McColl. Not until five years go by and you find out whether the things he thinks are going to happen actually have happened. Come back in five years and tell me he's a great analyst."

McColl got the point. *Thinking skills. He's trying to teach me how to think, like putting one foot in front of the other.* He began to enjoy the game. It was like the Marine Corps. You had to hump the load and slog the mud, but you were part of the team. No need to prove that. You could show the brass your individual strengths and talents, but just wearing the uniform made you part of the team. You could only prove you didn't deserve to wear it, by not following the rules.

In 1962 Addison Reese wrote a new set of rules. Suddenly North Carolina National Bank had a corporate organizational plan. Job descriptions materialized along with definitions of each officer's previously vague duties. Julian Clark introduced formal loan guidelines, which the bank's younger loan officers had never encountered. At first, these formalities went against the grain of a free-wheeling lender like Hugh McColl, but McColl was used to setting rules, making game plans and following guidelines. He came to view the guidelines as actually playing to his strengths. Since both the loan guidelines and the corporate policy placed a premium on human relations, McColl detected a conscious decision on Reese's part to focus less on dollars in and dollars out, more on managing people and developing client relationships. The more he studied the plan, the more McColl recognized his own ideas. He was on the team less than three years and he'd already played a role in mapping the bank's future.

To lay out his new corporate philosophy, Reese brought in a New York consulting firm, Cresap, McCormick and Padgett. From Bob Kirby and others, McColl learned the consultants were talking about building something called a "corporate culture." Rather than a company divided like the city of Berlin, run by remnants of two distrustful armies, Reese wanted to build something new, something he could control. He wanted every foot soldier in lockstep to his beat-Wachovia beat.

The consultants recommended structural modifications in both Greensboro and Charlotte, but reported to Reese that they were "running into one human resistance problem after another" in implementing their changes. What Reese was running, argued the consultants, was actually sixteen small banks, most of whose employees had at one time been competitors with one another. Now he was attempting radical change, forcing them all into his single-minded mold. They urged Reese to bring in reinforcements in the form of an industrial psychologist, Dr. James Farr, who could work with the people Reese had in mind as his future leaders.

In mid-1962, Farr began traveling to NCNB's city offices all over the state. His instructions from Reese were to use his psychological knowledge and resources "in any way that supports the bank's purposes and intentions." Farr took his orders directly and solely from Addison Reese. In Greensboro he had two assignments, both very hush-hush. First, minimize the Vanstory influence, and, second, groom Tom Storrs to follow Reese as president.

"Tom may be lacking in people skills," Reese coached his new shrink, "but he's exceptionally bright, a realist. He's highly motivated and he's organized. I see this guy becoming the chief executive, and I'd like you to spend a lot of the next five years coaching him." At the same time, Farr was instructed to develop a second tier of leaders in the bank. He should look not at longtime employees, whose habits were too ingrained, whose leadership potential had been stunted by exposure to fallout from the Depression, but at younger, more aggressive, hungrier types. He should look at employees like Hugh McColl in the National Division.

On his days back at the office, McColl usually found himself scheduled for a session with Dr. Farr. Growing up Baptist, he'd never been to confession, but he figured this was something like what Catholics must feel, letting it all out regularly, accepting penance, receiving absolution. It was a cleansing feeling. Even on days when he wasn't scheduled for a session with the Doc, McColl would hunt him up for a spoonful of free advice. McColl knew Dr. Farr was one sure channel to Mr. Reese's heart. As Farr listened to McColl discuss his work and his vision of NCNB's future, he picked up on a tantalizing phobia deep within the psyche of this smallish young man with the ewer-handle ears and the wide grin. Was it paranoia or simply a fear grounded in parental rejection? Farr continued to listen. McColl was bright, ambitious, determined. Yet he seemed to question his own ability to rise to the top of the company, due to forces beyond his control. And now those forces were personified in the form of a tangible competitor, a newcomer named Luther Hodges Jr.

McColl picked up the scuttlebutt on Luther Hodges. Word was Reese had recruited him personally from his teaching position at the University of North Carolina's college of business. McColl actually remembered Hodges from Chapel Hill. They'd attended a couple of naval ROTC classes together. One year McColl's junior, Hodges came away with a Phi Beta Kappa key while Hugh McColl earned mostly Cs. After college, while McColl was off learning to shoot a rifle in the marines, then suffering through Reese's training program, Lucky Luther was at Harvard getting his M.B.A..

McColl saw in Hodges a perfect Reese protégé. He was six-feet-two and handsome, just like Reese. Thin lips and wide forehead, under a prematurely receding hairline, put him over as a junior deity, a smooth understudy for leading man. Hodges came equipped with an air of authority, seemed somehow more mature than country-boy McColl, who was still an awkward fit in banking's vested pinstripes. McColl's full features, long sideburns and quick-drawl repartee gave the impression of a salesman at home on the South Carolina backroads, but not a full-blooded member of the mezzanine executive officers' club. Hodges seemed to have left his Southern accent in concrete work boots at the bottom of the Charles River. To make matters worse, Hodges's father, Luther H. Hodges Sr., of Rockingham County, had just completed two highly acclaimed terms as governor of North Carolina.

Hugh McColl knew a coup when he saw one, and he saw Reese's motives plain as day in young Luther Hodges. One of Governor Hodges's closest personal friends was none other than Wachovia Bank's chief executive, Robert Hanes. Now the governor's son was in bed with Hanes's worst enemy. That had to hit Hanes where it hurt. Even better for Reese, Hodges Junior had to know a lot about Wachovia, just from growing up in the company of Hanes—how Wachovia thought, how they could be expected to react to events. McColl pictured Mr. Reese spending a hundred happy hours playing "what if. . . ?" with Little Luther while Hugh toiled lost and forgotten in the red clay fields of South Carolina.

Though he never said so, psychologist Farr realized McColl was not suffering from delusions. Hugh McColl had every reason to be concerned about the potential negative effect of Luther Hodges on his career at NCNB.

For his part, Luther Hodges was glad to run into McColl again. He saw in McColl a man he understood, a man who had changed very little in six years. Hodges felt McColl was "totally consistent with what he was at age eighteen." There was "no guile about him, no surprises."

Hodges would learn he was wrong, at least about the element of surprise. Hugh McColl's open arms and broad smile were sincere, but they masked an intensity that bristled at the approach of competition. He succeeded best in life when he could turn a challenge into a contest. He demanded, of himself and anyone who played on his team, victory in any encounter. Only the best was good enough. His grandmother had taught him that, back in third grade.

"How'd you do on the test, Hughlie?"

"Great, Grandma, I got the second highest grade in the class."

"Well, that's all right, honey. I know you'll do better next time."

By this time McColl thought he had a good idea of all the players on the Charlotte team of NCNB, if not the ones in Greensboro. He knew their positions and how well they played the game. When he looked at them as competition for advancement, as other people who wanted to be captain or quarterback, there were not many challengers. Before Luther Hodges, only John Robison had loomed as a contender for leadership of the next generation in the bank. Robison might be smarter than McColl, and he had made considerable progress in a relatively short career with the bank. But, to McColl, Robison seemed to lack aggressiveness; and McColl suspected it would take a reservoir of aggression to scale Addison Reese's corporate ladder. On the other hand, when he looked at Luther Hodges, McColl saw a man who was both smart and aggressive. Since he and Hodges would be wearing the same uniform, McColl decided he wanted Hodges to think of him as his friend, not his enemy.

Dr. Farr's advice was even simpler. McColl should quit worrying about how he stacked up against other people and look at what he himself needed to accomplish in order to get ahead. McColl liked that advice. He decided that what he needed to get ahead was a team-within-the-team, a group of players who saw him as their natural leader, who would support Hugh McColl's efforts and help him achieve his ends in the company. Leadership, in the Farr lexicon, was the ability to identify the goals of other people and then—with a minimum of coercion or manipulation—to convince them that in order to achieve their own goals, they must work toward your vision.

Without even telling Hodges there was a game on, McColl started choosing up sides. He was looking for a team of people he called "tigers," who could stalk and charge along with him. Among the earliest players he signed were Benny Shaw, his friend from the Transit Department, and Bob Kirby, who had indoctrinated McColl into the company. Since a team had to spend time together off the job as well as on it, McColl and his growing family moved from the Selwyn apartment complex to a neighborhood at what was then the southern outskirts of Charlotte, Beverly Woods. Benny Shaw and Bob Kirby lived just down the street. They hung around together, played golf and tennis on weekends, cards in the evening. McColl made sure to include Luther Hodges in as many group activities as possible, though Luther lived in a more expensive part of town.

Beverly Woods was a modest neighborhood with homes averaging about twenty-five thousand dollars, which was more than the McColls could afford. Hugh sold some of Jane's stocks and borrowed cash from her father in order to make the six-thousand-dollar down payment. Their second child was soon to arrive and McColl was not too proud to let his father-in-law know they were "always struggling" for money.

McColl opened up with John Spratt far more than he did with his own father. He could tell his father-in-law how things were, complain that he still didn't like his job very much, despite his advancement. Spratt would listen and commiserate. Hugh McColl Sr., on the other hand, would simply dismiss him, driving Hugh to frustration. Jane liked the fact that her father listened without giving her husband too much advice.

"Just let him get it off his chest, Daddy. He'll be all right."

Jane found the two men alike, certainly in their dedication to work. Consequently, she was not surprised that Hugh seemed to take more interest in his job than he seemed to take in her. She only wished that work didn't keep him so much away from home, especially after the birth of their second child, John Spratt McColl, in January 1963.

With two children, Hugh knew he was going to need a second car. To save money, he had sold his old Chevy and driven the Falcon that actually belonged to Jane. He hated to think of taking on a car note, but he stayed up late one night and came up with a plan. Driving a certain number of miles each week, taking the company's standard ten-cent mileage allowance, then deducting the actual cost-per-mile of the car—2.7 cents—buying a little Volkswagen Beetle could actually return a profit of 7.3 cents a mile for him. A Beetle was good business.

Instead of going to the local dealer, McColl went to the nearby town of Gastonia, where dealers claimed to offer lower prices. He paid fifteen hundred dollars for a white VW, the sole amenity of which was a radio.

During Hugh's long weeks on the road, Jane found herself leaning more and more on her parents, on Hugh's parents, and on the other women in the neighborhood. Suffering from what she thought to be recurring influenza and colds, Jane wrote her mother- and father-in-law—"Dear Fran and Big Hugh"—long letters that showed her determination, as well as her husband's commitment to his job. On St. Patrick's Day 1963, Jane wrote:

"The two Hughs have gone to Sunday school so I have a chance to write you. This is Hugh's Sunday to keep the nursery. . . . But I'm telling you, all this sickness and Hugh's being out of town so much has just about done me in. Hugh says my disposition is rotten! We always get sick on Monday as he rides off and by Friday, when he gets home, the worst is over and he can't understand why I'm so tired. I told him he was lucky to be getting a good night's sleep in that motel."

Jane made friends with other young women in the neighborhood who were "in the same small boat" that she was in. Women without jobs sat in the unfenced back yards in lawn chairs, "complaining, griping, raising our children, cooking supper together, pooling our food. And the children just ran in the yards. We all hung our clothes out together." When her father made her a present of a clothes dryer, Hugh worried about the added expense. "He thought we couldn't afford it, that it would run the electricity bill up."

If Hugh was on his way to winning at the bank, it was Jane who paid the table stakes. That was what McColl men expected of McColl women. Jane was only bearing the burden his own mother, Frances, had, playing "the perfect mother" not only to her children but to her husband as well. "I'm just trying to make a living and get ahead for the family," he told her. "This is how it is and how it has to be. I can't do anything about that."

Jane was beginning to understand the man she married. What Hugh McColl wanted was to succeed, and from what he told her, he did not see himself as much of a success so far. That meant he had to push harder, run faster, work longer hours, no matter the loss of time with his family that might never be recovered. Jane's father worried. "He's too much away from you," he told her. "But when he's with the children I see that gleam in his eye, and I know it's going to be all right." That gleam was there any time Hugh McColl felt himself feeding his sons' imaginations, the way his own imagination had been nurtured by his mother, Frances, back in Bennettsville.

Little Hugh had climbed down from his mother's lap to sit on the rug at her feet, listening all the while to her readings of great dreams and romances. Little pigs boiling bad wolves grew into knights beheading dragons. By the early 1960s it would be a matter of some embarrassment for a banker to confess finding inspiration in legends of pirates and princes, but McColl could not get them out of his soul. They belonged there. He knew damned well he would not have joined the Marine Corps but for *Beau Geste*. And Patricia Smith.

Tricia, as he called her, was four years younger than Hugh, but had been his sweetheart since he was a senior at Bennettsville High School and she was in eighth grade. College-man McColl stayed stuck on her, searching the daily mail for a sign of Tricia's poodle stationery and her news of the goings-on at home or at Myrtle Beach. But by the time he'd been at Chapel Hill two and a half years, Patricia tired of correspondence dating and set her eye on a boy her own age.

Hugh wrote home brokenhearted: "I want her, Mother. No one else will ever do. I will never give up while I am still alive. I have not missed a single day of asking God to give her back to me. Maybe someday he will."

Still awaiting God's intervention toward the end of his junior year, McColl learned he must decide whether to finish up his ROTC training in the navy or switch to the marines for his senior year. Maybe all the World War II movies had something to do with it, but far more likely it was *Beau Geste*.

Hugh had John Geste fixed in his soul's heaven like a polestar. The hero believes one of his brothers has stolen a valuable jewel. In order to shift blame to himself and protect his brother's honor, John runs away to join that "romantic-sounding, adventurous corps of soldiers of fortune, called the French Foreign Legion." The author, Percival Christopher Wren, daubed the walls of Hugh McColl's imagination with lusty prose: "hot life and brave death . . . battle and bivouac." Hugh McColl, like John Geste, would "win his way to soldierly renown under a *nom de guerre*." Like John, he would return from military service, "bronzed and decorated, successful and established, a distinguished Soldier of Fortune," to claim the hand of his true love.

With no Foreign Legion recruiter on campus, Hugh wrote home:

"I want to be a marine, and since I doubt if I will be married, foreign service will be appealing." His mother fretted, but Hugh sent words to soothe her heart: "Don't worry about my being in the marines. . . . If God decides we must die, we will, no matter what we are doing. I am convinced of that." Bo Geste, at least.

In boot camp they shaved away his hair and all the advantages of his birth. No longer a McColl of the Bennettsville McColls, no longer president of Beta Theta Pi, Hugh's silver spoon was melted down to a brass buckle, demanding a constant devotion of polish. Now surviving the marines became his single purpose. He survived. In March 1958, boot camp behind him, McColl traveled down the eastern seaboard to Camp LeJeune, North Carolina, where he was commissioned as a second lieutenant, USMCR, Second Artillery Battalion, Tenth Marine Regiment.

His two best marine buddies were John Cain, a University of Mississippi graduate who loved poker almost as much as McColl did, and David Michaux, a friend from UNC. Neither man had ever seen a card player like Hugh McColl, whose mastery of poker, gin and other essential skills came in eighth grade, under the tutelage of young Tommy Hamer, left in a wheelchair by polio and cards his only pleasure.

At the BOQ—bachelor officers' quarters—Cain studied McColl. He learned to ignore Hugh's incessant, rapid-fire chatter, saw that nobody was better than McColl at distracting opponents. Instead Cain watched McColl's hands. When the fingers started to quiver, it was time for a smart player to fold. Others around the table took it as a sign of nervousness, thought Hugh might be holding a weak hand, bluffing. In fact, Cain knew Hugh was shaking with sheer anticipation, sure he held the winning cards and worried the others might not raise his bet. Gambling was strictly against base regulations, but McColl learned from older marines how to get away with it.

In July, McColl, Cain, Michaux and thousands of others at Camp LeJeune were ordered to sharpen their bayonets and make out their last wills and testaments. They mounted out aboard a truck convoy for the port of Morehead City, whence they would sail for Lebanon. But before the USS *Hermitage* was halfway across the Atlantic, new orders were issued. President Eisenhower determined that his first wave of fifteen hundred marines would be sufficient to quell the Communist threat in Lebanon. The Second Artillery Battalion, Tenth Marine Regiment was diverted to the Caribbean to await further orders. For two weeks, aboard an air-conditioned troop transport known as *LSD 34*, off the tiny island of Viequez, near Puerto Rico, Hugh McColl's status as a poker player went from formidable to legendary.

The game was organized by McColl's CO, Captain Jack "Killer" Kane. Each marine had been issued three months' pay in advance. For first lieutenants McColl, Cain and Michaux, the pay was $250 a month, or a total of $750. There were tens of thousands of dollars on board and very little to spend them on. At first they played table stakes, with a relatively conservative limit, but as days drifted by the game grew more serious. It floated from one jammed, sweaty, eye-burning cabin to another.

By the time they steamed into Morehead City, McColl had more than forty thousand dollars stuffed in a lockbox. He would travel to Europe on that money, but he blew a lot of it first on good times with his buddies Michaux and Cain.

Back at LeJeune, poker made way for basketball. One afternoon McColl went for a steal and felt his knee buckle. It was the same damn knee he'd cracked up in '51, during his sophomore year in high school. On his way to a card game then, he'd lost control of his daddy's car on rain-slick Main Street and turned it over in Emmett Matthews's front yard. That knee had kept him off the football varsity and he'd lived with pains and sprains ever since. This time the base medical staff put him into surgery, then confined him to bed. For the next three weeks, Cain and Michaux led nightly raids on the hospital. One man distracted the nurse on duty while the others picked up McColl and smuggled him out a rear emergency entrance. Good thing he didn't weigh much, because the BOQ poker game couldn't go on without Hugh.

On holidays like Christmas, whenever they had extended leave, McColl would drive down to South Carolina to spend time with the family and his friends back home. Usually he'd invite John Cain to go with him. Cain had no family of his own nearby, so generally he was glad to accept. They would load their gear in the trunk of McColl's '57 Chevrolet and head south along U.S. 17 to Wilmington, west on U.S. 74, then pick up U.S. 401-15 south to Bennettsville, passing through the town of McColl, named after Hugh's great-grandfather Duncan Donald. Every trip down, Cain had to hear some Civil War story.

Cain had grown up a navy brat, uprooted every time his father got transferred. He was touched by the closeness of the McColl clan in

Bennettsville. But even with that closeness, he could see the tooth-and-nail competition between Hugh and his two younger brothers. He and Hugh took on Kenneth and Jimmy in basketball and you'd think Hugh was going after a straw man in bayonet drill. Skinned knees and elbowed eyes under the goal, hugs and backslaps around the dinner table. And every trip Hugh had to visit Tommy Hamer for a game of penny-ante poker. There was no trace of pity in the way Hugh propped his feet on the wheel of Tommy's chair, no pretending to lose, either. Polio or not, the only way to beat McColl was to beat him.

Hugh McColl didn't learn life in the Marine Corps, but the marines confirmed the one value he could distill out of all his childhood experiences—wheeling Tommy Hamer to the pool hall, completing spiral passes to swivel-hipped mill kids, sharing a Coke with the children of the "colored help," watching his father treat every sharecropper as his equal. He knew at the core of him that every human being was every bit as good as Hugh McColl was. No black skin or withered legs or hardscrabble labor could make him less a human being. His one value was that everyone was valuable.

At Camp LeJeune and aboard *LSD 34*, McColl sat down with juvenile delinquents, hayseeds and ghetto rats. They were all marines, no better or worse than any other marine. As an officer he was called on to judge their actions, but not their accents or the color of their skin. What mattered was how much weight they could hump and how fast they could walk. Could they deploy a howitzer and get it firing quickly? Could they lay a gun out and hit the target? Could they fix a broken truck? What mattered were results. Things like that were the subjects of long conversations on the rides back from Bennettsville to LeJeune.

"You know, there's no such thing as an ex-marine," Cain told him, trying to convince McColl to stay in the service. Cain figured to make it a career, like his father in the navy.

McColl thought about it seriously. "You know, John, I might take you up on that except for one thing: the time. It's just gonna take too goddamn many years for us to get where we can lord it over somebody else the way those bastards lord it over us now."

"You're a marine, Hugh," Cain said. "Whether you're a marine on active duty, or a marine who's not on active duty, you've got that USMC stamped on your rear end for the rest of your life. You're part of the *team*."

McColl liked that part. "You're never attacking alone. You always have people with you when you attack, because you have invested the energy, the time and the effort, and the concern in them. You've built a team. And they reciprocate. They invest their time and energy and talent in going where you want to go."

Where Hugh McColl wanted to go, notwithstanding *Beau Geste*, was somewhere other than the Marine Corps. If his father would not let him run the cotton gin, if his uncle would not let him run the Marlboro Trust Company, then McColl would find something he could run. He didn't yet know what it would be, but he knew he had to start by building a team, tigers who would invest their time and energy and talent in Hugh McColl's leadership.

Benny Shaw watched McColl build his team and he wondered where it would all end. There was something about him that made him stand out from the old-fashioned bankers, men who gave orders with no regard for the degree of intelligence an order might display. Shaw saw McColl consciously projecting a new image, an identity, in order to inspire his team.

In fact, this image was nothing new. It was an outgrowth of the persona McColl had worn as a child and refined in the marines. He still felt alone in a world of equally valuable individuals, but now he could mask his sense of isolation with a rapier grin and disarming conversation. Now he buried his fear of failure under a single-minded commitment to boldness. He made himself known as a player who would always push the stakes, always raise the limit. He would be Hugh McColl, Risk Taker.

On the road in South Carolina, while his rivals from Wachovia, First Union and C&S asked questions, urged prudence and sought approvals, Hugh McColl wrote the loans. He sought out the "owner-class family"—like the McColl family—in every little town, the "people who make it happen," and he found out what they needed money for. A haberdasher in Pageland, a construction company in Sumter. Inevitably, getting to know the people told him where to lend the money. He showed them that the road to their goals led through his vision. In Florence, the "capital city" of the Pee Dee region, he made so many loans that he could walk into the country club as though he held a membership.

One of the leading lights of the Pee Dee was Craig Wall Sr., an entrepreneur from Conway who took a liking to McColl. He had stopped doing business with American Trust Company about the time Hugh was born, but he had kept right on making money. "Your bank screwed me good back in the thirties," Wall said, his arm around the young man's shoulder. But he was drawn to McColl and decided he would do some business with him. McColl spent more and more time playing golf with Craig Wall and getting to know his friends.

"Meet my buddy Hugh McColl. Boy's got money to lend. Drives one of them little bitty Volkswagens, so you know he's not gonna mess with you."

All over South Carolina, thanks to Hugh McColl, NCNB was investing in the sort of projects Southern banks had never been interested in—golf courses, shopping malls, office parks. McColl found out where the people were, where the population was likely to grow, which people could be trusted. He drew his maps and made his lists.

Even in the rural areas—Dillon and Marion Counties—he would seek out the big tobacco brokers as their crop was coming in, talk with them in language they understood, and hand out on-the-spot loans, so they could buy up more of the new leaf crop, then resell it to the tobacco companies. He developed a one-page agreement in simple language that said the bank owned the tobacco until the warehouseman paid off the loan. Both he and the broker knew the contract was worthless, since the tobacco would be moving faster than any banker in Charlotte could get his hands on it.

McColl moved faster than the tobacco. Most bankers, constrained by experience and banking laws of the Depression, sat on their bank's money. "You don't want to wait on Wachovia," he'd say. "Hell, over there everybody and their dog's got to sign off on something. Ain't nobody taking any risks." McColl, the risk taker, made his loans without getting anyone to sign off on anything. He was a banker. His role was to deliver to his customer the entire bank, or whatever part of it that customer needed. When he got back to the mezzanine in Charlotte, he treated his superiors like the customers, selling his idea of why NCNB should do the loan. He knew all this enhanced his reputation.

As it happened, Addison Reese was working along similar lines to enhance NCNB's reputation as the bold, risk-taking banking force in North Carolina. In March 1963, the bank installed a new $1.5 million computer system. Among other advantages, the computer-speeded processes gave the bank a new attraction for downstream banks, stealing check-clearing customers away from the Federal Reserve.

At the same time, the bank agreed to lend millions to Duke Power Company, the principal supplier of electricity in North Carolina's Piedmont Region. Duke needed the loan for the purpose of preparing homesites along the shores of a lake, which as yet did not exist, about twenty miles north of Charlotte's center.

Duke's chief engineer, William S. Lee Jr., completed work on Cowan's Ford Dam, a power generating plant, and the company began flooding a 32,500-acre reservoir along a stretch of the Catawba River. "Lake Norman" would take the next two years to fill, and other banks seemed to doubt there would be much interest among home builders in developing what would be 520 miles of shoreline—more than North Carolina's Outer Banks. NCNB took the risk and Hugh McColl was proud.

In September that same year, NCNB merged with the Bank of Chapel Hill, giving it a branch in Research Triangle Park. The bank's growth was keeping up with the growth of North Carolina. Over the previous decade the state's population had increased by 10 percent, with a 50 percent rise in per capita income. Technology industries were beginning to move in, not only in the Research Triangle, but in Charlotte as well. Targeting small- to medium-sized businesses, the bank had written more than $300 million in North Carolina loans. By the close of 1963, with the nation still reeling from the assassination of President Kennedy, NCNB resources were listed at $654 million, making it roughly three times the size of the bank Hugh McColl went to work for in 1959, just four years earlier.

It was all "interesting enough" to McColl, but he hardly felt part of it. He was a big man in some little South Carolina communities, but he still felt isolated. Despite his team-building posture, he sometimes resented his father for condemning him to this life. But maybe that was simply resentment at being told by his father—or anyone—what to do. What McColl thought he wanted was *freedom*, just like all those Civil Rights marchers he saw on the late news in the motel rooms: *What do we want? Freedom! When do we want it? Now!* Now. He was sick of life on the road. He felt like the only thing he'd really learned in four years was how to be a great driver in a small car. He joked about being able to drive a Volkswagen "better than anybody else in the world."

"You're just frustrated," Jane told him. She knew he was very intelligent, perhaps more intelligent than most of the people he worked with. Even worse, he had a lot more energy than he needed. She could tell he was bored, and he was not a patient man. He wanted to jump over the waiting and just take charge of everything.

In the worn, hot bucket seat of his little car he built what he called sky-castles, wondering where he really stood in the bank, wondering whether he really had a chance for advancement, with guys like Luther Hodges Jr. in the group. More than once McColl told himself, "You're not learning a damned thing. You really need to quit and find yourself another job." But what would his father say to that? He'd say, "Just do your job, son." And maybe he'd be right. Maybe if he just went after it, the way he'd gone after that poker money in the marines, he would get ahead.

McColl looked around and saw few decisive people above him in the bank. Only a handful had that "deal closer" quality he prized so highly in himself. One of those would be Mr. Reese himself. He did not really know the president, but he pictured Reese alone, isolated, like McColl was isolated, only at a higher level than other men. Reese seemed to radiate strength and power, intelligence and class. He was coolly detached, always passing judgment, never threatened. On the rare occasions when McColl had faced the president he felt Reese looking at the back of his brain, knowing all his secrets.

Addison Reese had no children. McColl wondered whether he looked to the young crusaders of the bank as his "pride and joy." It might be. If one of those young surrogate sons set his mind on emulating Addison Reese, perhaps he truly could get ahead at NCNB. Perhaps Hugh McColl would not need to find another job.

In his car, in motel rooms on South Carolina highways, he went on building his sky-castles, sometimes jotting numbers on one of the scraps of paper he always carried in his pockets. In three years Vanstory would be forced to retire and Reese would be chairman. In ten years Reese himself would be sixty-five. Who would take his place? Julian Clark? Unlikely, since Clark seemed about the same age as Reese. In ten years Hugh McColl would be thirty-eight. That seemed frighteningly old, but not old enough to be handed a whole bank. McColl might conceivably find himself in the right place, but it wasn't likely to be the right time. So who would step up? McColl told himself Reese must be asking himself that same question.

Betty Wright had been Addison Reese's secretary since 1954. She always had his mail ready and sorted when he arrived promptly at

8:30 A.M. every morning. Late in December, Reese called her in even before he opened his mail, and that was most unusual. There was a memorandum in Reese's head, ready to be dictated. He instructed Wright to assemble all the bank's top officers, city executives from around the state, headquarters executives and chief lieutenants. She could tell this was going to be an important meeting.

When the senior executives were all seated in the auditorium, Reese shocked them with new tactics in his campaign to beat Wachovia. He had developed these tactics on the advice of his consultants, Cresap, McCormick and Padgett, and of Dr. Farr, the house psychologist. From now on, NCNB's number-one priority would be something that would never show up on the balance sheet. He had their attention.

With the growth Reese foresaw in the coming years—the growth that would be necessary to overtake Wachovia—the key commodity would not be cash on hand or loans outstanding; it would be *people*. They must step up the pace of developing young managerial talent. For every key position in each division and city of North Carolina National Bank, Reese told his senior executives that they must identify not one but *two* replacements. Each man in the room realized he must develop two understudies who could do his job just as well as he could. Maybe better.

Reese told them NCNB's executives of the future would have to be flexible. They must be experienced in more than one area of the bank, more than one geographical territory. They must not be hidebound by tradition. Instead, their hallmark must be *adaptability*.

"We are not looking for brilliant credit analysts or keen-eyed bookkeepers," Reese said. "We want *people skills*. We want talent for community relations." Adaptability and growth, Reese proclaimed, would be the defining characteristics of the bank he envisioned. For the first time some of the executives were forced to confront the term "corporate culture." At the end of the meeting, Reese left the group speechless with a final warning. In the uncharted waters ahead, he said, some of the executives in the room, regardless of their seniority, were going to be left behind.

Once again, it was as though Addison Reese had been looking at the back of Hugh McColl's brain.

CHAPTER 4

Looking out his window at South Tryon and Fourth, Addison Reese, a Southerner from Baltimore, saw Jim Crow dying. It was 1964, and across the Southeast voter registration drives were lighting hope-fires that couldn't be doused by state legislatures, whose bucket brigades seemed forever tripping over Robert Kennedy's Justice Department. Politicians and seersuckered executives in "Deep South" states like Louisiana, Alabama and Mississippi wrapped their resolve in the old Confederate battle flag. They could claim, with a degree of legitimacy, that the pressure for change was strictly from the outside, exerted by "Northern liberals," which everyone understood to be a polite term for "Communists."

That no longer worked in North Carolina, home to the South's first sit-in, right in Neil Vanstory's Greensboro. Four years earlier, even before the quiet protest in Charlotte, students from the all-black North Carolina Agricultural and Technical College challenged segregation by demanding a meal at the all-white lunch counter at Woolworth's downtown Greensboro store.

Now President Lyndon Johnson was pushing ahead with President Kennedy's civil rights legislation, banning discrimination in public places and denying federal funding to discriminatory state programs. The Twenty-Fourth Amendment to the United States Constitution, outlawing the old Southern ruse of poll taxes, had been passed by Congress and was awaiting inevitable ratification by the states.

North Carolina had its share of diehard states' rights advocates. Anti-Vietnam War demonstrations at Chapel Hill prompted the General Assembly to pass the Visiting Speakers Act, banning "known Communists," along with those who refused to answer questions about their loyalty, from speaking on the state's college campuses. Nevertheless, in 1964 Governor Terry Sanford was completing a four-year term that was widely recognized as the state's turning point, away from the segregationist policies of Dixie toward a peaceful abolition of intolerance. Sanford had defeated segregationist-intellectual I. Beverly Lake, in a campaign described by then-Governor Luther Hodges as one of the most important in the state's history.

Charlotte's political leaders continued to roll with the punches of progress. Students from Johnson C. Smith University marched down Trade Street. Martin Luther King Jr. arrived to speak at six black high schools and had high praise for the city's leaders, who were sitting at uptown lunch counters in biracial groups. Addison Reese was ready for his bank to be counted among the champions of progress.

Bob Kirby got the go-ahead to include college women and blacks in his recruiting efforts for management training. Kirby brought in Hernon Floyd, one of the first African Americans to graduate from the University of South Carolina, and put him into the training program. Floyd, however, got no further than the Credit Department before being diagnosed with sickle-cell anemia; he opted to find a less stressful job and resigned from NCNB. He was followed by William Clement Jr., whose father was president of one of the nation's largest black-owned companies, North Carolina Mutual Life Insurance in Durham. The first woman in the training program was Lucy Otis, who would later marry one of the bank's lending officers, David Anderson. Although many of NCNB's old-line bankers found it difficult to welcome black and female trainees into their departments, for Hugh McColl, the changes were welcome.

"The ladies don't stand the ghost of a chance of getting fair play," Hugh's great-grandfather had written to his bride-to-be. Now McColl was watching his own sister, Frances, going through a personal crisis that hardly seemed fair. Had Frances given herself the option of a professional career, he believed, her life might be turning out very differently.

Instead she had forced herself into the expected wife-homemaker-mother role and now she was paying the price.

As a child, Frances was a natural leader. Nobody could climb a tree higher than Frances. Nobody could slip a verbal stiletto between a wise guy's ribs faster than his big sister. Frances was not just a girl; she was the person he looked up to, the person who showed him what leadership was all about. She was Supergirl: athlete, actress, composer, writer. She called him Hughlie and he called her Pal. After nailing her master's degree in journalism at Chapel Hill, she got a job writing the Charlotte Chamber's newsletter. But that was all just treading water, waiting for Mr. Right, who had to earn not just Frances's approval, but the family's as well. That turned out to be Roy Covington, business writer for the *Charlotte Observer*. Homemaker-motherhood proved to be a difficult transition for a free spirit. Her mother had made it work, but this seemed to be a wrong turn for Pal. Even though he expected Jane to stay home and mind the children, McColl was coming to see that some women needed careers, the same as some men did. He believed Mr. Reese was doing the right thing.

As for African Americans, McColl was well aware that it was past time for times to change. Back in Bennettsville, emancipation had succeeded only in transforming slave into servant. His parents had their maids and cooks—professedly proud to be "better-class coloreds," working in the homes of "better-class whites." The farmers of Marlboro County had their field hands. Grandmother had Sherman, the yard man, to help tend the prize irises in her garden. Hugh, his sister and his brothers all had "nurses," black women who looked after their every need. Anna was Hugh's nurse and he never learned her last name.

He hated himself for taking Anna for granted, like nearly every white in South Carolina took nearly every black for granted. He remembered that the first female breasts he'd ever laid eyes on were black, breasts of women nursing their babies on the curb on Main Street, on hot Saturday afternoons when the cotton came to town so his daddy could buy it off the wagons for his gin. Breasts, such a taboo in his culture, yet, every market day, in plain sight. Just colored women.

He should have known better, even then. Living on the "wrong" side of Bennettsville's tracks, Hugh played enough basketball with the children of the help to know they were every bit as good as the Eastside kids his grandmother wanted him to court. Junior—the biggest kid, black or white, he'd ever seen, strong enough to lift Daddy's tractor out of a ditch at fourteen—never got past fourth grade, and nobody thought that was unusual. Junior was just a colored boy.

Back then, none of this had bothered Hugh in the least. As long as Joe DiMaggio and Ted Williams and Lou Boudreau kept hitting, as long as there were girls for chasing and music for shagging, nothing else seemed to matter, back in the forties and fifties.

Hugh was at Chapel Hill when the first black student was admitted. One of his fraternity brothers wanted to organize a cross-burning in front of South Building, where the black student lived. That never came to pass, but the same fraternity brother came back with another invitation. *"Hey, I heard about this big Ku Klux Klan meeting on Saturday, down in Society Hill. Let's go."*

Society Hill, South Carolina, on the Pee Dee River in Darlington County, hours from Chapel Hill. But Hugh McColl let himself be led along, one of a group of young sheep penned into a little Lark automobile, only to be scared shitless at the sight of three crosses ablaze and hundreds of white sheets milling around a parking lot. They turned that Lark around and headed right back to Chapel Hill.

It wasn't until Hugh McColl hit basic training that he couldn't hide the facts from himself any longer. He came from a typical white family in a small Southern town. He had either to accept their racist standards or to build some standards of his own.

He got his chance to start building when he took Jane back to Bennettsville to meet his old school friends. That was the first time he recognized the ugly side. It was *the goddam niggers* this, and *that bastard Bobby Kennedy* that. After a few beers, McColl had enough. He reminded his old gang that, even as they spoke, young black men were in the jungles of Vietnam fighting right alongside young white men. *"So, they're good enough to lie in a ditch and get killed with your little brothers, but they're not good enough for you to piss in a public toilet next to them. Is that what you believe?"*

That was a guaranteed conversation-stopper in 1964 Bennettsville. Yet, talk was still easier than action. Back in Charlotte, when Jane asked for help with the housework and the two boys, she had no trouble finding a woman who would work Wednesdays and Fridays for a few dollars a day and bus fare. Like Anna, his nurse, like big Junior back in Bennettsville, the woman was black and had too little education to get a better-paying job.

At the bank, blacks and nonclerical women were certainly novelties, but not the youth movement. One management trainee, James Thompson, was so shocked at the sight of so many young men that he nearly turned down a job at NCNB. With so many people his age, Thompson wondered, could there be anyone to learn from? Could there be any chance of advancement? Then Thompson talked to Hugh McColl, who convinced him that "the opportunity is here for individuals who can get down and make things happen, individuals who can make a difference."

Unbeknownst to Hugh McColl, Addison Reese was pleading the same case to his house psychologist, Dr. James Farr. With the help of Farr and Tom Storrs, Reese selected two dozen young officers who could "get down and make things happen" for his bank, an elite corps of young executives who, it was understood, all believed they deserved to have Addison Reese's job some day. Officially, the chosen two dozen were known as the Information and Advisory Panel. Soon they came to be called "the Young Turks."

Reese told Farr to work with the select twenty-four, just as he had worked with Storrs. Reese had picked his own successor in Storrs, now he wanted to make sure he had the upper hand in choosing and molding the man who one day would follow Storrs. With Farr's help, Reese believed he could "psycho-engineer" leadership.

In the fear-crippled, regulation-bound banking industry of post-Depression America, role models for leadership were scarce. At North Carolina National Bank the list of universally recognized role models began and ended with Addison Reese. Thus, one of Farr's regular monthly boardroom exercises was for the Young Turks to consider the question, "What makes Mr. Reese such an effective leader?" The query had all the earmarks of a self-fulfilling prophecy, yet McColl found it intriguing. It gave him something new to ponder as he crawled the arteries of the Upcountry and the Pee Dee in his Beetle. One element of leadership certainly had to do with demanding leadership of those who followed. It stood to reason that, even though McColl was pretty well restricted to followership at the moment, he would have to demonstrate the capacity for leadership before he'd be given the chance to lead.

When he heard Hugh McColl express thoughts like that, it became clear to Jim Farr that McColl was one of two dominant Young Turks. The other was Luther Hodges. While all the two dozen were animated and opinionated, none were more eager to solve any problem than Hodges and McColl. Farr noted that whichever of these two entered the boardroom after the other, he would invariably take a seat on the opposite side of the table. Whatever the subject, Hodges and McColl approached it from opposing points of view. Farr found Hodges the more loftily idealed of the two, weighing and doubting and considering. McColl was like a ferret, darting from cause to effect, effect to cause, single-minded, relentless, challenging the others to keep up with him. Hodges the humanist, McColl the *magister ludi*, the gamemaster.

Dr. Farr found it all fascinating. Here was a laboratory where the rats loved him for studying them. His one-on-one sessions with McColl were particularly energizing. Farr loved to play-argue with McColl because he saw the learning process build as the arguments intensified. McColl's positions, at first simple and predictable, would become deeper and more complex each time Farr challenged his assumptions. Farr reported back to Reese that this one was "very bright, very motivated and very smart." Furthermore, despite what Farr saw as a strong, assertive nature, McColl was "fundamentally very respectful of people—*his* people."

On the debit side of McColl's ledger, Farr reported, was a tendency to "fight harder than he really needs to at some points. Sometimes he gets too assertive, too aggressive, too competitive." That was especially true whenever McColl found himself in a debate with Luther Hodges. The intensity of their rivalry, unmatched by any others among the Young Turks, gave Farr the feeling that one of these two men would be in charge of NCNB one day. McColl and Hodges saw it that way, too. On weekends they would get together and talk about "how it's going to be when we run the bank."

One of the things they saw eye-to-eye on was the need to throw out the almost obsequious deference displayed by their fellow Southern bankers at the mere mention of The Money Center—New York. The same NCNB stalwarts who bared their fangs at big, bad Wachovia sat up and begged whenever some junior officer from a New York bank arrived on a missionary trip. An assistant vice president from J. P. Morgan or Chemical would merit a full-dress reception by everyone in Charlotte, up to and including the chairman himself.

"One day," McColl said, "we'll have those guys bowin' and scrapin' when they come down here looking for our business."

Hodges smiled and nodded.

In the Young Turks' boardroom laboratory, the two self-proclaimed candidates for NCNB stardom could agree to disagree, but McColl had no intention of alienating Luther Hodges. In his heart of hearts, McColl believed that one day he would be working for Hodges. He saw Hodges as more intellectual, more politically astute, more adept at charming wives and board members. In short, Luther Hodges was more like Mr. Reese.

But Hugh McColl was far from conceding the game to Luther Hodges. In sports, McColl had always compensated for his lack of size with agility and speed. He began to look for ways to apply that strategy at the bank. He needed to demonstrate his willingness and capacity for leadership, and he found it on the South Carolina highways.

South Carolina was still by and large an agricultural state, yet even such staid institutions as Columbia's South Carolina National Bank were beginning to mention "leisure" and "travel" in their descriptions of the Palmetto State's economy. The state was pinning its hopes for tourism on its oceanfront resort towns, especially Myrtle Beach, where nearly half the upper-crust families of Charlotte spent their summer vacations, where Hugh McColl and the other kids from Bennettsville had learned to shag and still look cool and to open a beer bottle with their bare hands, many years before the "twist-off cap." Myrtle and its county, Horry, had long-stagnant economies, but from what he picked up in his golf-course conversations with people like Craig Wall, McColl believed there was more money to be made along the Palmetto coastline than NCNB was getting. If he could help South Carolina banks clear their checks faster, they could make more money, and some of that would trickle up to Charlotte.

Even though NCNB had its big General Electric computer now, clearing checks remained a time-consuming, labor-intensive process. Whether the smaller bank sent its checks to NCNB, Wachovia, First Union or the Federal Reserve, they usually traveled by mail. Depending on the correspondent bank's location, the checks could spend a night, or even two nights, in a post office sack before they reached their destination. McColl saw a way to do it better.

His first thought was to switch check delivery from mail to bus. However, Benny Shaw reported that bus schedules between the South Carolina beaches and Charlotte were even less suited to their needs than were the mails. McColl drew up a plan for an overnight courier service that would carry checks from Myrtle Beach to Charlotte, where they would be processed after-hours and posted to the correspondent bank's account before nine the next morning. However, this Night Transit

System, as McColl named it, would be cost-effective only if he could sign up other banks along the way from Myrtle Beach to Charlotte. That way the evening courier could pick up checks at multiple stops.

With Benny Shaw in tow, McColl hit the highway. In one day they visited eight banks—in Pageland, Jefferson, Hartsville, Florence, Marion, Mullins, Myrtle Beach. By the end of that day, they had cash letters, the equivalent of deposits, from every one of the banks and the Night Transit Department of NCNB was in business. Twenty years later, overnight mail and package delivery would be standard operating procedure for American businesses, but in the mid-sixties, it was an innovation that gave McColl's company another edge. Shaw enjoyed telling a good story, so he made sure to spread the Night Transit tale around headquarters. "Eight in one day!" Benny made it sound like *The Brave Little Tailor*.

McColl spoke his mind, let the world know he wanted his company to go somewhere and by God he was ready to help it get there. After-work beers at Leo's went down along with Hugh McColl's view of the impact of international monetary policy on NCNB's commercial overseas prospects. If some of the National Division team was winding up lunch hour with a few games at Rex's Pool Hall on Tryon Street, McColl would bound up the alley stairway next to Tanner's orange juice shop to the second-floor hangout, shoot a round and leave, talking up a hurricane the whole while.

"When I'm in charge, no more of this chicken-shit retail, small business banking. We're gonna concentrate on the real business. You hear what I'm saying? Six-ball in the side pocket."

His company really ought to become a merchant bank, in the style of Morgan-Stanley or Rothschild or Barings, McColl declared. They should concentrate on underwriting securities, syndicating bonds, taking equity positions in big investment opportunities. Since his pool game, like his poker game, had been honed to a fine edge back in his misspent Bennettsville youth, McColl generally emptied the pockets of his banking buddies as his bank shots filled the pockets of Rex's tables.

After Hugh was gone, there'd be a round of laughs and head-shaking. Imagine some two-bit Southern hustler daring to dream Hugh McColl's big dreams! They all understood that only the money center banks could play on such a grand scale. For most of NCNB's new-breed bankers, the goal was simply to fulfill Addison Reese's "beat Wachovia" mission of becoming the largest bank in

North Carolina. That in itself seemed near enough to impossible.

McColl knew he needed more than big talk and bigger dreams. He had to clearly demonstrate his team's contribution to the company's profitability. In the 1960s this was not such an easy task. While each department was required to account for its expenses, down to the last penny, the revenues of that department were simply lumped in with all other income rather than being tracked systematically. McColl only learned about this when he went to the comptroller's office and asked to see a breakout of the National Division's South Atlantic Region books, so he could figure out which accounts were bringing in the most money. He was told this could not be done.

Once again, McColl put one of his most highly regarded team members on the case—Benny Shaw—and told him to start a new ledger. Methodically, Shaw traced each customer account for which Hugh McColl was ultimately responsible. Quickly, it became clear that the South Atlantic Region of the National Division was doing very well, thanks in large part to McColl's accounts. Although the term had not yet been popularized, McColl had established a "profit center," the first at the company.

In September, as he ended his fifth year of employment, twenty-nine-year-old Hugh McColl knew he was, as Benny Shaw put it, "climbing the pyramid." However, events in his personal life were making it difficult to savor his business success. Frances— Pal—was in and out of the hospital. Mother was worried sick about her, Daddy almost as worried about keeping up with the medical bills. Hugh and Jane were worried, too, over the welfare of Frances's four children, ages one to six.

Then, in November 1964, the McColls of Bennettsville suffered another blow. Hugh's grandmother, Gabrielle Drake McColl, suffered a stroke that put her in the hospital. On the thirteenth of December she left the hospital, and Hugh was looking forward to seeing her at Christmas. But on December 17 she was stricken again and died at the age of eighty-two. She left without acquiescing to the minister who lived across the street and had made one last-ditch effort to bring the old woman into the fold. She was as resistant to religion as her husband Hugh had been.

"Don't you want to go to heaven?" the preacher asked her.

"I'd rather be in hell with Hugh than in heaven with everybody else," Gabrielle answered.

When McColl talked about the people who influenced his childhood, his grandmother generally headed the list. She had survived her husband by thirty-three years, holding the McColl clan together by her personal strength and determination. She was "by any measure the greatest lady of Bennettsville," Hugh believed. He spoke of a fragile woman, "a China doll," and yet "an iron magnolia," a lady who had convinced her grandson that respect was in no way dependent on physical stature. More than anyone else, she had infused him with the conviction that he was a child of significance, a child of destiny.

Most of her life Gabrielle Palmer Drake McColl was the queen frog in a small, self-sufficient pond. She was head of the most prestigious family in Bennettsville, South Carolina. She had married the son of one of the three "merchant princes," second-generation Scottish immigrants, who had built what the state of South Carolina officially recognized as its "first Great Town." The lines of the other two princes—H. A. Matheson and C. S. McCall (from a branch of the same Clan McColl in Scotland)—had splintered and worn away with time, but her husband's succession thrived and maintained its preeminence. Gabrielle saw personally to that.

To Gabrielle Drake McColl, family history was something of a religion. She wasted few opportunities to gather her children, grandchildren, nephews and nieces around her in the parlor on Jennings Street for another telling of "How the McColls Came to Bennettsville." Sometimes the story began back in Scotland, with the brave defeat of the Highlanders at the Battle of Cullodon in 1746. Sometimes it began with Solomon McColl of Appin, Scotland, arriving at Wilmington, North Carolina, about 1785. Sometimes the stream surfaced in Scotland County, North Carolina, in the old Stuartsville Cemetery where the headstones all read "McColl." Sometimes it began with Peter McColl, traveling down the Great Pee Dee River to Marlboro County, South Carolina, to join a colony of Welsh farmers. Wherever she began, Gabrielle's listeners always sat up when she reached the time of Duncan Donald McColl.

Reading from a manuscript biography of Duncan Donald by his son, D. D. McColl Jr., Gabrielle would tell how the great Duncan Donald was born in 1842 and raised on a farm a few miles from the "backward and isolated" village of Shoe Heel, now called Maxton, North Carolina.

"What we would now consider poverty and hardship, what to us would be the dearth of opportunity, were in those days the common portion of all, merely reflecting the hard and primitive conditions of a new land," Gabrielle read aloud. *"Too much importance cannot be attached to the heritage of a good name, high principles and strong virtues which Mr. McColl received from his Scotch ancestors."* The story went on to tell how Duncan Donald was brought to Bennettsville by his childless Great Uncle Peter, a bachelor son of Solomon McColl, at the age of sixteen. Duncan divided his time between school and assisting his Uncle Peter at the Marlboro County Courthouse, where Peter served as full-time clerk of court, responsible for daily operation of the crenelated brick courthouse, with its high, thin windows and brace of towers, the central feature of the town of Bennettsville. Bachelor Peter McColl was a "stern, austere" man of "rugged, sterling qualities."

In the middle of the nineteenth century, Bennettsville, South Carolina, was virtually isolated from the outside world. The nearest railroad depots were fourteen miles away, the nearest freight terminal six miles away at Gardners Bluff on the Pee Dee River. Such seemingly insignificant distances were imposing in those days of washed-out roads and muleback travel. Slave-labor plantations, near the river and larger creeks, raised most of Marlboro County's food and nearly all its cotton. When Duncan Donald McColl arrived in 1858, the plantations were producing more than thirteen thousand four-hundred-pound bales of cotton each year. Just over half the people in the county were slaves. That entire economy and way of life were only three years from extinction.

South Carolina was the first state to secede from the union, following Abraham Lincoln's defeat of Stephen A. Douglas. Three Marlboro men, including William D. Johnson of Bennettsville, were among those to sign the Ordinance of Secession in Charleston, five days before Christmas in 1860. Peter McColl had argued passionately against secession, but at his Marlboro County Courthouse, the Stars and Stripes was replaced by the Palmetto flag.

In April 1861, in Charleston harbor, the inevitable war began. At the age of nineteen, Duncan Donald McColl returned to North Carolina to join his older brother, Hugh, in the state's First Heavy Artillery Battalion. The battalion served at Wilmington, then Fort Caswell, then was sent to reinforce Fort Fisher in the port of Wilmington, North Carolina, the South's most impassable coastal stronghold and the Confederacy's last remaining port of entry for blockade-running supply ships. On January 15, 1865, Union sailors, marines and infantrymen stormed Fort Fisher and overran the First Heavy Artillery's cannon placements. Duncan Donald McColl and the rest of the battalion that made it out were attached to the brigade of South Carolina's General Joseph E. Johnston, consisting mainly of Tennessee volunteers. General Robert E. Lee was working on a plan to slip out of besieged Richmond to join Johnston in North Carolina. Meanwhile, General William Tecumseh Sherman had an army of ninety thousand men, sweeping up from Atlanta, bent on joining General Ulysses S. Grant in Richmond to bring a swift end to the war.

On March 4, 1865, President Abraham Lincoln delivered his Second Inaugural Address at the Capitol in Washington. "With malice toward none; with charity for all; with firmness in the right, as God gives us to see the right . . ." As Lincoln was writing his speech, Sherman tore through Marlboro County on his way to North Carolina. On March 6, Sherman occupied Bennettsville, declaring Peter McColl's courthouse local headquarters of the Union Army.

Young Nellie Thomas had been sent out of harm's way by her father, pastor of the town's little wood-frame Baptist church. As she returned home, Nellie—who would become Hugh McColl's great-grandmother—recorded the aftermath of "Sherman's horrific march." Blackened chimneys stood "like lone sentinels over the ruins of homes." A trail of "ruin and deprivation" testified to "the progress of fire and sword as the war-god rendered his way through the prostrate State. As we approached our home, I missed many familiar buildings . . . . Homes had been pillaged; meat houses robbed; horses carried away."

March 19, Sherman's army reached Bentonville, North Carolina, about a hundred miles northeast of Bennettsville. General Joe Johnston's army was waiting there to stop him in what would prove to be the Confederacy's last stand. About 250 members of the First Heavy Artillery Battalion fought at Bentonville and close to 150 of those men fell in the three days of attack and counterattack. One of the casualties was Duncan Donald McColl. When his retreating companions saw the blood and gore spilling from the left side of his tattered jacket, they left him on the battlefield. Word was sent to his parents that he was dead.

A few days later, the president of the Confederacy, Jefferson Davis, slipped out of his burning capital of Richmond and moved his cabinet to Charlotte, North Carolina. On Palm Sunday, April 9, 1865, General Lee surrendered.

Carried from the battlefield and nursed back to health from his supposedly fatal wounds, Duncan Donald McColl returned to Bennettsville, to "confusion and demoralization," as his son would tell the tale. Fewer than half the men of fighting age came back to Bennettsville alive, and many of those survivors were cripples. Duncan found a "chaotic condition of public affairs and the total absence of any common community purpose. The old institutions had been overturned by the hand of revolution and no substitutes had yet been erected in their stead." There was a vacuum of leadership and Duncan Donald McColl stepped into that vacuum.

He began by helping his Uncle Peter rebuild the county's legal system. In the process, he taught himself the law and, in only a year, got himself admitted to the bar. By November 1866, Duncan Donald was a Solicitor in Equity, then a Magistrate, who saw his job as being "to promote law and order and to discourage unnecessary litigation . . . and to promote the peace and harmony of the community," in a time of "turmoil, confusion and internal strife." His misgivings about secession having been upheld, Peter McColl and, by close association, his grandnephew, became respected central figures in the county's efforts to rebuild. Because they had supported South Carolina and the Confederacy in spite of their misgivings, the McColls were also trusted. When Peter McColl died in 1871, the full benefit of the community's respect, along with the full responsibility of its trust, fell to Duncan Donald.

These were the years of radical reconstruction in the South, when freed black men were thrust into public office alongside whites. Public schools were instituted, even though there was no money to pay teachers. The plantation economy of Marlboro County gave way to a sharecropper system, in which the majority of families, both white and black, raised crops on land owned by the slightly less poor white minority. The landowners received a portion of the sharecroppers' output as rent. The only reliable cash crop was still cotton. More than two decades after the Civil War began, the region had become the ghost of its Old South past. But change was in the wind, and Duncan Donald McColl was in the right place to feel the first breeze.

"There is a New South," Henry Grady proclaimed to the New England Society in 1886, "not through protests against the old, but because of new conditions, new adjustments and, if you please, new ideas and aspirations." Grady was the Prophet of the New South and his newspaper, the *Atlanta Constitution*, was his pulpit. In Charlotte, one of Grady's most devoted disciples was the publisher of the *Charlotte Observer*, Daniel Augustus Tompkins.

In the closing decade of the nineteenth century, these two newspapers and others like them preached that the South could pull itself up by its own bootstraps. It could build mills to process the cotton that grew so abundantly in its rich soil, thereby diversifying from a monolithic agrarian economy to a balance between farm and factory. To deliver manufactured goods to market, the South would have to build a better transportation system—roads and railroads. Eventually, the region would need a strong banking system as well, to finance steady growth, even though it would take substantial investment from the North to get this New South economy up and running.

In 1884 Duncan Donald McColl put together a group of Bennettsville citizens to capitalize the grandly named South Carolina & Pacific Railway Company. A year later the first train from Bennettsville arrived at the North State Improvement Company's line at Fayetteville, fifty-seven miles north of the town. Now Bennettsville cotton could reach the port of Wilmington by rail and then travel by ship around South America, all the way to the Pacific Ocean. It was an ostentatious title for a fifty-seven-mile spur, but the South Carolina & Pacific did indeed put Bennettsville in touch with the great wide world. One of the depots on the new line, just below the North Carolina border, was named in McColl's honor and, almost immediately, the farming community of McColl, South Carolina, became an actual town. Donald Duncan McColl was elected president of the railroad company. Six years later he succeeded in extending the Charleston, Sumter and Northern Railroad from Darlington to Bennettsville, enabling for the first time the convenient passage of goods and people across the Pee Dee to Charleston.

Larger merchants in the Pee Dee region had funds on deposit with factors or bankers in Charleston or Wilmington, so that they could purchase goods as they were delivered. There was, at this time, not a single bank in the county of Marlboro. Indeed, there were only a handful of banks in the entire Palmetto State, other than those in the port city of Charleston and the capital city of Columbia. With ready money hard to come by in Bennettsville, in 1886 Duncan Donald McColl decided he had better build himself a bank.

The tiny Bank of Marlboro, of which he was the president, chairman, chief executive officer and chief operating officer, immediately occupied all of Duncan Donald McColl's time and energy. He was forced to abandon his law practice. In his son's words, he managed the bank as though it were his child, "watched it zealously, guarded it constantly and devoted his entire energy and splendid financial judgment to the upbuilding of this enterprise which meant, especially in its early years, so much for the prosperity and continued progress of the community." McColl came to be recognized as one of South Carolina's leading bankers and, in 1910, was elected president of the state bankers' association.

Deposits in the Bank of Marlboro gave Duncan Donald McColl the resources he needed to pursue the New South grail. After only two years as a banker, he brought together some of the county's most prosperous citizens and used his solicitor's powers of persuasion to convince them that it was time to stop merely growing cotton and begin to manufacture cotton yarns and fabrics. Instead of using his railroad to ship raw cotton elsewhere, why not spin that cotton into yarn right in Marlboro County and then ship it out? Manufactured cotton brought a much higher price per pound than raw cotton. Furthermore, the mills meant employment and paychecks and economic growth. That would stimulate sales at Marlboro County stores and, not incidentally, put more money into his bank.

The county's first postwar cotton mill, with 3,260 spindles, was built in McColl with thirty-five thousand dollars cash capital. It was called McColl Manufacturing Company and Duncan Donald McColl served on the board of directors. The first years were difficult, and more than once Duncan Donald had to dip into his personal account to rescue the mill. When McColl Manufacturing found itself of the verge of bankruptcy, Duncan Donald McColl recommended that the company issue bonds to be sold in the money markets up north. He and several other directors made a pilgrimage to the Bank of Boston and to other shrines in New York, but their supplications went unanswered. In desperation McColl went to his own bank and personally guaranteed a loan that would be enough to pay the company's most pressing debts and see it through another season of production. The spindles whirred on and the worst was over.

By 1897 McColl Manufacturing was such a success that Duncan McColl and his shareholders invested in two additional factories—named the Marie Mill and the Iceman Mill—making McColl the most industrial town in Marlboro County. Duncan Donald was afraid his beloved Bennettsville was in danger of being left behind. At the bank, he called his shareholders together for a meeting and warned them that their prosperous Bank of Marlboro was growing too big for its community. The bank had more accumulated surplus of capital than they could possibly invest within the corporate limits of Bennettsville. Consequently, the bank would pay shareholders a one-time cash dividend of 100 percent—effectively doubling their investment.

Then he asked the shareholders what they planned to do with their windfall of cash. He was ready with a suggestion: they all would invest in a new company, the Bennettsville Cotton Mill. Some took their money and socked it elsewhere, but McColl convinced a significant group of local investors to buy into the mill, provided McColl sign on as its president. Less than two years later, Duncan put together a merger of the four Bennettsville and McColl mills into a new corporation, the Marlboro Cotton Mills, with a capital stock of $1 million.

That story, like so much of what is known about Duncan Donald McColl, comes from the fifteen-page manuscript written in 1916 by his son, Duncan Donald Junior, and copied sometime thereafter by another son, D. K. McColl. The manuscript treats the rescue of McColl Manufacturing and the undergirding of Bennettsville's economy as examples of Duncan Donald McColl's character, which one day would be burned into the clan memory of Hugh McColl Jr., establishing a sort of Platonic ideal, up to which the leadership principles of Addison Reese and James Farr would have to measure. Toward the end of the essay, the son attempts to limn this character of his father, always referred to as "Mr. McColl."

Mr. McColl disregarded the ordinary rules of business and, acting only upon his keen knowledge of human nature, loaned money without security .... Mr. McColl was willing to encourage a man he considered worthy and deserving by advancing money (that) was not only repaid but proved to be the foundation of a successful business career. Two of the largest business houses now in

*Bennettsville owe their foundation to financial assistance ren-
dered to their owners when they had no security to offer, save what
appeared to the keen discerning eye of Mr. McColl as industry,
character and a determination to succeed.*

An addendum to the manuscript is an accompanying letter, written by
Duncan Donald's son, D. K., to "each of my father's living grandchildren and each great grandchild." D. K. writes that he has made seventy
copies of the original. "I am sure if you will read this carefully, you will
greatly appreciate it and hand it on down to your children and admon-
ish them to take care of it and see that their children's children have an
opportunity to read it. . . . I think it will do you good to get it out of the
place you keep it and read it occasionally just like you would read your
Bible. I am sure it will do you a great deal of good in many ways."

Duncan Donald McColl, not a religious man himself, fell in love with
the daughter of Bennettsville's struggling Baptist minister. This was
the same Nellie Thomas who set down in her girl's diary the "horrific
effects" of the Yankees upon Marlboro County. After her graduation
from Converse College, Nellie returned to Bennettsville, married
Duncan Donald, and gave him three sons. The first was honored with
the name of Duncan Donald's older, childless brother, Hugh Leon. It
was Duncan Donald and Nellie's son Hugh Leon McColl who would
marry Gabrielle Palmer Drake, from a land-rich rural Marlboro
County family. And it was Gabrielle who would give Bennettsville, in
addition to three McColl girls, its third-generation merchant crown
prince, Hugh Leon McColl Jr., in 1905. (This Hugh would become
"the Hugh" upon the death of his father, thereby granting his son the
privilege of becoming "Hugh Junior," though not until it had been
cleared by the passing of Gabrielle, Mrs. Hugh Senior.)

Like her mother-in-law Nellie, Gabrielle Drake had the distinction of
attending Converse College. Her 1898 graduation photograph shows
a slight, attractive young woman. Dark hair is pulled back above a
long neck with a severity that emphasizes the softness of her facial
features. High collar and puffed sleeves support an imperiously tilted
head, suggesting that she has disdained the portrait photographer's
suggested pose for one of her own. In another picture, taken perhaps
shortly after her marriage, Gabrielle's high-piled hair reveals ears that

are just a bit large and protruding, a trait that would be handed down to successive generations of McColl men.

From the first, Gabrielle McColl seems to have fashioned for herself a sort of "power behind the throne" role. A Christmas letter written in 1909 to her father-in-law, Duncan Donald, might have come from the still-unspotted hand of young Lady MacBeth:

> *Dear Mr. McColl,*
>
> *You have told me many times "to take care of Hugh." And I want to say that to look after him is indeed my first object in life. I have his entire confidence and we work together for his welfare and the children's. I realize that he holds a position of great responsibility and I would suffer anything rather than see him err from the lines of strictest rectitude and necessary caution. It is on my mind day and night that I must be to him a tower of strength and a pillar of comfort, that I must keep him well and make him happy.*
>
> *If it shall come to pass that men speak of him as they do of his father, so that to call his name is to imply honesty, up-rightness, utter integrity and true charity, then will my dearest ambition be satisfied. Hugh and the little Hugh after him are the links between us and that they shall be an honor to the name you have given them is my first prayer.*

The "little Hugh after him," her son and male heir—the crown prince of Clan McColl—elevated Gabrielle to a position of greatness. Gabrielle understood her role. She was active in the Daughters of the American Revolution as well as the Daughters of the Confederacy. She studied the stock market, learned to invest and developed a lifelong interest in the performance of stocks and bonds. She rose late to take breakfast in a dressing gown. She made an annual shopping excursion by train to Philadelphia. She was, as her grandson James would recall, "an awfully fine lady."

Besides her family and its furtherance, Gabrielle's passion was gardening. However, hers could not be simply a garden. It had to be a showplace for all Bennettsville. It had to be officially recognized by the South Carolina legislature as a "state garden." Like Duncan Donald's bank and railroads and mills, Gabrielle McColl's Greengate Gardens brought prominence and pride to Bennettsville with its grand display of day lilies and bearded irises, azaleas and camellias.

When Confederate veteran Duncan Donald McColl died in 1911, his three sons divided up his business interests. Duncan Donald Junior was a lawyer, embroiled in state politics. David Kenneth—D. K.—took over the mills. Hugh Leon McColl—Gabrielle's husband—became president of the Bank of Marlboro. The bank was doing remarkably well, with deposits nearing an all-time high of $600,000. An advertisement in the 1913 Marlboro County Fair program would boast of "Capital, Surplus and Profits" of $250,000. The bank's slogan was "The Old Reliable."

Hugh McColl Sr. (our subject's grandfather) was a man of varied interests with a gentle, yet insistent way of channeling the conversation into those pools of interest. "Genial waggery" was how his nephew, David, described his style. He was a man of "homespun philosophy" and "inimitable mannerisms." Those who knew him well knew him as honest, conservative, steeped in family tradition.

His greatest pride was his namesake, Hugh Leon McColl Jr.. A hand-tinted photograph from around 1915 shows this Hugh (our subject's father) as a boy of ten or so, dressed in a suit and bow tie, standing stiffly beside a cast-iron park bench. His high-top shoes are laced up and his long stockings disappear under the elastic bottoms of his knickers. The photo provides no hint of his growing reputation as a rascal, hellion and firebrand. The boy's nickname is "Peck," as in the novel, *Peck's Bad Boy.*

It may have been his penchant for unruliness that got Hugh Junior packed off to Bailey Military Institute in Greenwood, South Carolina, where an inscription in the yearbook suggests that he made no secret of the nickname, but told no one where he got it. Peck played football and baseball at Bailey and informed his friends he would be matriculating at good old prestigious Furman University. According to his senior yearbook in 1923, Peck "shines in his pronunciation of French" and was "the shark" at trigonometry. He was "one of the fellows who keeps the third floor from becoming too dull." The yearbook editor sends him off to Furman with "So long, 'Peck.' We know you will keep close company with Lady Luck."

Notwithstanding Peck McColl's aspirations, his father and mother sent him to the University of North Carolina. While only a few of his letters from Chapel Hill were preserved, one written during his senior year indicates that the wild hair was rooted still. He tells his mother that "there has been quite a stir" over the student council's judgment against fourteen men for playing poker. "The council used coercive measures to convict them and the students are pretty mad about the whole affair."

Peck was not known for his achievements in class. For all his alleged proficiency in high school languages, Hugh Junior is said to have sat in a Spanish class for half a semester before realizing it wasn't French. Friends joked about him "dancing his way through college." He was sent home at least once for infractions, but somehow he persevered. Just before the final examinations, in the spring of 1927, Dean D. D. Carroll wrote his father, "H. L. McColl, Esq.," recommending that Hugh Junior be permitted to follow his graduation with a trip to Europe.

"I have developed a great fondness and respect for Hugh," the dean writes, "and feel confident that he is going to make a business man of high quality . . . as he proceeds through the last lap of what, to him, has been a long and tedious journey."

When he returned from abroad in the fall of '27, despite his growing reputation as a gay blade, Hugh Junior went to work for his father in the "old reliable" Bank of Marlboro. These were hard times in the Cotton Kingdom. The devastating boll weevil infestation had spread from the lower states up into South Carolina and, inevitably, into Marlboro County. Farmers in the county were looking to less vulnerable crops, others to raising beef or pork or to dairy farming. Meanwhile, the cost of transportation was rising while the prices farmers could get for their yield were falling. Instead of trying to market such crops as Irish potatoes and melons, Marlboro farmers found it more economical to simply feed them to the hogs. Already Bennettsville had lost two of the banks that had grown up to compete with Duncan Donald McColl's Bank of Marlboro. Hugh McColl Sr. kept a wary eye on the economy and spent long days at his bank. At home, he and his wife shared a growing concern as to whether their miscreant son would have the ability to carry on the business successfully and to solidify the McColl dynasty's hold on Bennettsville.

Perhaps it was his father, but more likely it was Gabrielle who decided that the best way to settle down "Peck's Bad Boy" was to get him married to the right woman, someone of strong character, someone who would curb young Hugh's tendency to stray from the straight and narrow. With their son's apparent blessing, they settled on a young lady who was expected to return home from college in a few months, Frances Pratt Carroll.

The youngest and most precocious of five sisters, Frances Carroll was only nine when her mother died in an accident that shook Bennettsville in 1915. Mrs. Carroll had been raking leaves in her front yard, helping her husband. Mr. Carroll started burning the leaves, and all of a sudden his wife turned and her long black taffeta skirt swung into the flame. The fire almost instantly swallowed up the taffeta and Frances's mother was gone. Raised by her father, Frances became something of a local legend. Everybody in Marlboro County knew the girl was brilliant and talented. She was also a tomboy, a free-spirit daredevil who would dive off bridges and climb over slippery creek-bed rocks. In 1923, at the age of seventeen, Frances went off to Winthrop Female College in Rock Hill, South Carolina. That was the year her father died.

At Winthrop her leadership skills, her wit and her intelligence made her a favorite of teachers and students alike. She became a skilled painter and sculptress and set her heart on a career in art, a tall-order dream since her family had no money and Frances had no means of supporting an artist's life. Her friends and advisors urged her to return to Bennettsville and teach. In 1928, during her senior year, she received a proposal of marriage by mail, from a boy she had known as a friend back home, Hugh "Peck" McColl. Suddenly, Peck seemed to love her. Frances wrote back that the friend with whom Hugh was "in love" was not really the woman Frances Carroll. This woman was someone new, someone Hugh could not really know deeply enough to love. Besides, she had no intention of returning to Bennettsville; Frances the artist had her heart set on New York.

As she neared the end of her senior year, destined to be valedictorian of her class, Frances was walking across a campus playing field with a group of her friends when an airplane buzzed them. The pilot flew low enough that the young ladies could see his face. He waved and they waved back. And then he set the single-engine plane down, right in the field, and taxied up to where the girls were standing.

"Who wants to take a ride?"

Frances simply could not resist the opportunity. Just a year earlier Lucky Lindy had captured the world's imagination by flying alone across the Atlantic. Lindbergh made flying seem as reckless and exciting as bridge-diving or art, and she had never even been in an airplane. Her friends warned her not to go. It was against the rules for any of the students to set foot off campus.

"Well, I'm not setting foot off campus, am I?" There was a general titter and a shriek under the roar of the lifting biplane.

The ride was wonderful. Frances enjoyed it so much that she would always remember it with delight, though it cost her dearly. The college stripped her of her honors for violating the rules. She was allowed to graduate, but at the bottom of her class. No scofflaw could be permitted to deliver the valedictory at Winthrop Female College.

True to her promise, Frances Carroll went to New York in 1928. There she found a job with an insurance company, shared an apartment in Greenwich Village with five other girls and pursued her art studies. Back home, Hugh McColl Sr. and Gabrielle determined to bring her back. Apparently, Hugh Junior was not opposed to the idea. He continued to court Frances through the mail, though she let him know she was dating other men.

The following spring, 1929, Hugh Senior sent his son to New York. The outward purpose of the trip was for Hugh Junior to call on the "upstream" banks upon which the Bank of Marlboro depended. The young man scheduled as many appointments as he could, as far apart as he could, so that he could spend as many evenings as possible with Frances.

The circumstances of 1929 joined the McColl family conspiracy against Frances's art career. As the economy grew worse and worse, Frances worried about her ability to make a living, even as a secretary in an insurance office. In October, the stock market crashed. Frances left New York for Bennettsville. She agreed to set her wedding date with Hugh on November 14, the anniversary of Hugh Senior and Gabrielle's marriage.

Frances would not only share Gabrielle's wedding date, she would share her home. The young couple moved into the two-story Victorian house on Jennings Street where Hugh Junior had spent his entire life, other than his dormitory years. It was the house Hugh Senior had built for Gabrielle. Now Gabrielle and her Hugh would sleep downstairs, Frances and her Hugh upstairs. It was an odd situation for an independent young woman who had always placed herself out of the mainstream, avant-garde and rebellious. It also seemed an odd fit for a young man who never had been one to walk the straight-and-narrow line chalked by his parents. Yet the young couple's furnishings, china and silver were Gabrielle's, as were the servants, the meals, the whole atmosphere of the place. Just as Hugh Junior assisted his father at the bank, Frances must assist her mother-in-law in making a home. This was not the life she had sketched out for herself.

If Hugh Junior had any plans for his own life, surely they could not have included his current condition, working for a father whom everyone revered, but who put no stock in his son's ability to take over the business. Hugh Junior learned, to his shock, that his father was even thinking of selling the family bank.

Letters written in the spring and summer of 1930 show Hugh McColl Sr. in failing health, doubting he could rely on any member of the family to maintain the bank's profitability. When his oldest brother, who had become State Senator Duncan Donald McColl, died on April 11, Hugh's interest in holding on to the bank flagged.

Hugh Senior met in Florence with Robert S. Small, the Charleston banker who created South Carolina National Bank. "There is no bank in South Carolina which we would rather see affiliated with us than the Bank of Marlboro," Small told McColl. With the current state of the economy, Small thought he could get McColl's bank at a bargain price, probably less than $25,000, for a bank whose net worth had been advertised as $250,000 seventeen years earlier.

In early May, McColl began contacting his major shareholders to feel them out on Small's embarrassingly small offer. His sister Pearl Bunyan, wife of a Presbyterian minister in Ontario, wrote Hugh that she would rather liquidate the bank than sell it. Pearl, who owned the building in which the bank was housed, pleaded with her brother not to continue operating the company "under the present difficult and burdensome conditions."

Hugh's brother, D. K. McColl, was in favor of selling, but not at the paltry sum offered by the South Carolina National Bank. D. K., who had been elected mayor of Bennettsville, instructed Hugh to demand at least $30,000. Small wrote that while "Mr. D. K . . . . may be correct in his thought that someone will pay $30,000 for it, I am frank to tell you that we cannot. We do not believe that any bank which does pay such a price can possibly succeed."

By August Hugh McColl's medical condition had worsened. He wrote Small that he had suffered "three hard attacks in twelve hours" and had been ordered to bed for two weeks. He begged Small to consider a counteroffer he had made in Florence, because other interests were forcing him to look elsewhere for a buyer. He assured Small that other bankers—not "any of our South Carolina banking friends," but out-of-state interests—had said they would like to move into Bennettsville and that, should he choose to liquidate, they would pay at least $30,000 for the fixtures. Why, the bank vault doors alone were worth $10,000. Small reminded him that the vault doors were attached to a building that the bank did not own.

The out-of-state interest turned out to be none other than Word Wood and Torrence Hemby of Charlotte's American Trust Company. But, in a letter of September 17, 1930, Hemby dashed McColl's hopes. "Our people have always preferred not to go into the branch business," he wrote. Furthermore, American Trust did not have the resources to administer "out-of-town banks that we would become interested in." Therefore, "our people have decided that we will not undertake to operate a bank in Bennettsville."

Immediately following Small's refusal to up the ante and Hemby's decision to maintain a local profile, both the health of Hugh McColl Sr. and the economy of Bennettsville took a turn for the better. In a letter dated October 15, 1930, Aunt Pearl wrote, "I hear from all sides that you look better and are better than you have been for years. . . . I think you did the wise thing to postpone the business about the bank."

The bank seemed on the mend as well. As 1931 began, McColl received congratulations from both Word Wood at American Trust and Hillary Locke at City Bank of New York on his year-end financial statement. "You have the strongest bank in the world," wrote Wood, somewhat tongue-in-cheek, "with far more cash on hand and in banks than you have debts. The Bank of England and the Federal Reserve cannot match you in strength." Locke sent praise for "the high degree of liquidity which you are continuing to maintain. It is indeed encouraging at a time when there have been so many bank failures to see the strong condition of some of our friends around the country."

Healthy again, McColl Senior threw himself back into the business of banking, writing letters to state legislators and other officials in opposition to a bill that would allow out-of-state banks to do business in South Carolina. If they weren't interested in buying his bank, McColl did not want them competing for his business. He received word from State Bank Examiner Albert S. Fant that the administration was pulling out all the stops to defeat the bill, since "enactment of this bill into law would be a serious handicap to state banks as far as competition with national banks is concerned."

In March 1931, Frances and Hugh Junior celebrated the birth of their first child, Frances Carroll McColl. Quite obviously, Gabrielle and Hugh Senior had been hoping their first grandchild would be a male, for Frances wrote to one of her husband's aunts, thanking her for "such a darling, encouraging letter." Frances expressed relief that at last she had heard "a McColl say that a girl is welcome in the family."

On April 11, 1931, one year to the day after his brother's death, Hugh Leon McColl Sr. died at his desk in the Bank of Marlboro at the age of fifty-six, collapsing into the arms of his son, Peck. Immediate cause of death was an acute heart attack. Bennettsville's businesses shut down so everyone could attend the funeral. The *Pee Dee Advocate* eulogized him as a man absorbed in business and finance, "a man of sound judgment, guiding his large business interest . . . in a careful, conscientious and successful manner. He clung to the 'way of his fathers,' and in this he was wise.

"The Bank of Marlboro has long been recognized as a bulwark of strength, a Gibraltar in the world of finance. Through the recent panicky years this institution remained solid, and it is today recognized as truly one of the outstanding banks of the state and as for that matter, the entire nation."

Now it was Peck McColl's turn to run the bank. He wrote his Aunt Pearl in Ontario that "I have been elected to fill Daddy's place here in the bank. I don't mean fill it, because no one could ever do as well as he has done. However, I realize just what a grave responsibility I have assumed and I will certainly do my very best." Immediately he felt the pressures of an unstable economy. "We are going slow on local loans," he wrote to South Carolina National's J. W. Norwood, "as the price of cotton is far from encouraging." In another letter, he agrees with Norwood that "one of the sure cures for this depression will be when people get down to hard pan and live within their income instead of spending more than they earn, with never a thought of trying to save part of the year's salary. Personally, I try to lay by a little each year so in the future I will not be dependent upon others or the times."

He paid himself $125 a month to run the bank. His tax return for 1931 shows a total income of $1,551. For $10 Frances could sew herself ten dresses. Peck McColl, the bad boy of Bennettsville, the gay blade of Chapel Hill, had become Hugh McColl, the fretful, insecure, pinch-penny banker.

Hugh McColl Jr. (his mother remained "Mrs. Hugh L. McColl Sr.") began corresponding regularly with banks outside the state, opening a savings account at National City Bank of New York with money received from his father's estate. When asked for advice about setting up a trust account, he always recommended City Bank or Guaranty Trust in New York. "I would not consider any company in the South or nearer home," he warned. "You should choose two large companies in New York City." Neither his own money nor others' was secure in this backslid New South his grandfather had helped create.

Of course, the South held no franchise on economic problems. When President Franklin D. Roosevelt took office on March 4, 1933, his first action was to proclaim a four-day "bank holiday." During that hiatus he signed the Emergency Banking Act, which described the conditions under which banks could reopen. The Bank of Marlboro could fulfill those conditions, but some of the Carolinas' largest institutions could not and were forced to remain closed. It was not until August 21 that South Carolina National Bank, or SCNB, Bennettsville's rejected suitor, was allowed to reopen.

In the newspapers and on radio, at the barber shop and in the drugstore, people were blaming banks for the Depression. The men who ran banks were dubbed "banksters." In 1934 banks were paying the lowest savings interest rates in history. Roosevelt's New Deal provided no instant cure. In Bennettsville, where the seed planted by Duncan Donald McColl had grown an economy once strong enough to support ten banks, now only two banks were gasping along. Besides the Bank of Marlboro there was only Marlboro Trust Company, in which Hugh's Uncle D. K. was a principal stockholder.

Not even the birth of his first son, Hugh Leon McColl III (our subject), on June 18, 1935, seemed to make life easier for Hugh Junior. He felt weighed down by the responsibility of keeping the bank solvent, particularly since so many of the people who owned stock in the company were his relatives. Old maid aunts, his severe and unforgiving inebriate Uncle D. K., his own mother—people who seemed to consider him some sort of black sheep—found themselves with their future in his hands. Whatever decision he might make at the bank, there was always someone looking over his shoulder, second-guessing him.

At home, Mother Gabrielle was omnipresent. Hugh and Frances

might be better off with a house of their own, but what could he do? It was the Depression. If they moved now, Gabrielle would be left alone in the big house on Jennings Street. And the house certainly was big enough for all of them, even when child number three, David Kenneth, arrived on July 28, 1937. It seemed roomy still when baby James Carroll came along on April 9, 1939. The house on Jennings Street was where Peck had grown up; now his four children would grow up there, secure, tended like the irises in his mother's garden.

By 1939, Hugh McColl Jr., grandson of the New South pioneer Duncan Donald McColl, had endured all he could endure of banking and business. He liquidated the Bank of Marlboro. "Mr. D. K.," Hugh's uncle, at first pleaded, then ranted. His father, Hugh's grandfather, had started that bank, and, by God, no McColl was going to shut it down. It was solvent, even healthy. Hugh shut it down anyway.

Despite that insult, somehow, Hugh McColl prevailed upon his Uncle D. K. to take him on as bookkeeper at McColl Mills. He was still a "shark" at numbers, whatever his other skills might or might not be. When he wasn't needed at the mills, he would work the land, become a "yeoman farmer," uphold the Jeffersonian ideal. He developed a gentlemanly farmer attitude and smiled at folks who put too much stock in deskwork and money-lending and machines. It takes brains to be a farmer, Hugh McColl told people; any damn fool can be a banker or a businessman.

A quarter-century later, Gabrielle Palmer Drake McColl was gone. She had lived in that house on Jennings Street, lived with her furniture and her silver and her china, lived with her irises and her daylilies and her servants, right up until the day she died. Not yet thirty, Hugh McColl III—our Hugh—wasn't quite sure what had been lost when his grandmother went away, but he felt it was something important.

With Gabrielle's death, there would be no more official, state-sanctioned Greengate Gardens. The McColl family compound in the center of Bennettsville would be parceled away. South Carolina's "First Great Town" would begin to slip out of the McColl family hold. Hugh and his sister Frances were making homes for themselves up in Charlotte. Brother Kenneth was getting on with First National Bank of South Carolina in Columbia. Jimmy had gone to work for Citizens and Southern Bank down in Charleston. If Gabrielle's life work had been to establish an unbroken line of succession to the "throne" of

Bennettsville, she had failed.

When they came of age, each of her son Hugh's boys had been pushed out of the nest and driven to Chapel Hill. Following their compulsory two years of service, each one had been told by their father, "You're not smart enough to be a farmer, so you'd better be a banker." And the banks of Bennettsville were not what Gabrielle's son Hugh—or perhaps her daughter-in-law Frances—had in mind for their three boys. They were dispatched beyond the sphere of Gabrielle's influence.

Frances had her own dreams for her children, dreams that would send them far from the confines of the little Bennettsville pond. Just weeks before Hugh was born, Frances clipped a page from the Sunday *New York Times* and folded it into the box that held her letters and important keepsakes. She hoped her son-to-be, the next Hugh, would read it some day. Maybe he would take inspiration from it.

The page was filled with stories about the brave and episodic life of Colonel Thomas E. Lawrence, Lawrence of Arabia, killed May 20, "hurled from his motorcycle on which he was traveling at breakneck speed through the peaceful Dorset countryside, swerving to avoid a boy cyclist."

Lawrence was "the most strikingly individual leader and the most puzzling enigma" to emerge from World War I. "Seldom in the course of history a hero emerges, and legends grow up about him until they reach the dimensions of a Homeric epic. Such a hero was Thomas Edward Lawrence, who having created kingdoms, scorned honors and riches, died after his brief hour in dramatic self imposed simplicity. His was a story of dazzling intrigue and adventure with the vast tapestry of the World War its background and romantically mysterious Arabia its setting."

Frances believed that heroes like Lawrence could arise out of places as humdrum as Jennings Street. Perhaps one of her children would be such a hero. She would read to them, night after night, tales of adventure and courage and sacrifice and camaraderie. If her mother-in-law wanted to include Duncan Donald McColl in their pantheon of heroes, that would be all right, but she, Frances, would paint their dreams.

> *"Some day, Luther . . . we'll be the power."*

Hugh McColl
To Luther Hodges, December 24, 1964

CHAPTER 5

On the afternoon of Christmas Eve, 1964, McColl stood with Luther Hodges at the top of the mezzanine staircase, watching Charlotte's lords of business and industry perform their annual court ritual. Textile kingpins William Barnhardt and Harold Lineberger, George Snyder of Coca-Cola, real estate mogul James Harris and the other members of the NCNB board trooped up the staircase, waving to friends spotted in the bustling throng below. On the mezzanine, they paid their jovial respects to the managers of their feudal depository. Each visiting board member would drop in unannounced, yet expected, on Addison Reese, then on Julian Clark, Pat Calhoun and Herbert Wayne. After season's greetings and invitations were exchanged, the directors would descend the staircase and stride purposefully to the tellers' windows, where they would withdraw several hundred dollars from their personal checking accounts, usually in ten-dollar bills. The cash envelopes would be stuffed into suit pockets and they would exit the bank, stocked with this year's Christmas largesse for the men and women who drove their cars, shined their shoes, delivered their mail, mopped their floors.

"That's the power," McColl said to his friend. "Those guys own this town. That's the power. And some day, Luther, we'll be doing that, and we'll be the power."

Hodges smiled and nodded. He believed, as his good friend Hugh McColl believed, that a day would come when Luther Hodges would be chief executive officer, Hugh McColl president of the largest bank in North Carolina. The Harrises and Barnhardts would call on them on a Christmas Eve and they would all be jovial. Hodges's office would be the first stop, because of the two he was the most like Addison Reese in style and looks and eloquence. McColl? Well, he had a style all his own.

Perhaps the bank's most serious challenger to Hodges and McColl was John Robison, the man who along with Jack Ruth had introduced McColl to the South Carolina sales routes. Robison was smart, sophisticated and savvy when it came to loans and intrabank politics. Moreover, although he was only a few years their senior, he had started at NCNB's parent, American Trust, when he graduated from the University of North Carolina in 1952, one year after Addison Reese arrived and more than seven years ahead of McColl. Robison worked at the bank for just six weeks before he was drafted into the Korean War, but the American Trust job was waiting for him when he returned from his tour of duty in 1955. He was there for the mergers that created NCNB and the start of the campaign to over-take Wachovia as North Carolina's biggest bank.

After introducing McColl to the correspondent bankers of South Carolina, Robison had helped recruit Hodges into the bank and then helped him find a place to live, in Robison's neighborhood. Like Hodges', Robison's family was well connected in the social circles of both Carolinas. In fact, his father-in-law happened to be the Bennettsville doctor who delivered Hugh McColl. Hodges and McColl wondered if the combination of seniority and connections would give Robison an edge over either of them.

If Robison wanted to run the bank, as Hodges and McColl did, he tended to keep his ambitions to himself. McColl only remembered his letting it slip once, on a July evening in the Greenwood, South Carolina, VFW Club. He and Robison were cooling off with vodka and orange juice after a day of calling on slow-talking South Carolina bankers. Both men were in their cups, mulling over the question of how one could work his way to the top of this upstart company. Robison grabbed a handful of peanuts from the bar and leaned closer.

"McColl," he said. "I can work with you, but not for you."

Recounting that story to Hodges, McColl said he had gone "stone-cold sober" when he heard the line. Not only did it hint at Robison's own ambition, but if Robison could contemplate the possibility of one day having their positions reversed—Robison working for McColl—then it must *be* a possibility.

"He wants the power, but he realizes we could beat him, Luther. He wants it, but he knows we could beat him."

The waiting, though, was beginning to chafe at McColl. He wanted badly to *run* something, to be in control. For all intents and purposes, he still was NCNB's drummer, traveling the backroads of South Carolina. This second-largest bank in North Carolina was too much like the United States Marine Corps to suit him. If he wanted to advance through the ranks, he just had to stay around, stay alive, get promoted.

McColl was ready to be in charge of something, *anything*, as long as it made him some money. He began plotting with Jane's brother, John Spratt Jr., to build what the two young men believed could become a "banking empire" in South Carolina. If he played his cards right, Hugh McColl might one day soon control all the banks in York County. And if his own daddy wouldn't help him do that, he believed Jane's daddy just might.

"*What we'll do, Mr. Spratt, is we'll put your Bank of Fort Mill and the Bank of York together. We'll merge those two. Then we'll form our own little holding company and buy the Bank of Clover. Then we might be big enough to buy Rock Hill National. Our family could own the whole darn county. We'd have the power, the control.*"

John Spratt considered, then he shot down the Big Plan. He simply would not, could not buy the Bank of Clover. Why? On account of one of the big shareholders in that bank being a widow, whose husband's estate had been handled by none other than Attorney Spratt. And now what would people say? People would say John Spratt stole that bank from that that poor widow lady. No, sir, he wouldn't have it. His reputation was at stake, and that was something no amount of money in any number of banks could buy. McColl knew he would have to bide his time, but he began to feel that, somewhere out there, some bank must be waiting for him to take it over.

In fantasizing about their possible turn at the NCNB helm, the concerns of Hugh McColl and Luther Hodges were an entire generation removed from the more pressing problems confronting Addison Reese. The two young men were still learning about the complex relationships that directed the flow of power and authority in the company, relationships that shaped decisions at the top. Facing mandatory retirement in 1974, when he would reach the age of sixty-five, Reese had but ten years to train and acclimate his successor. This hardly seemed like a long time in the torpid environment of banking. While Reese already had made up his mind to promote Tom Storrs, he was very much aware of resistant pressures from the board, applied from at least four different directions.

When Reese and Torrence Hemby created NCNB out of Charlotte's American Commercial and Greensboro's Security National, each of those banks was still bleeding from its own previous merger operation. American Trust Company and Commercial National in Charlotte had combined two twenty-five-member boards into one twenty-five-member board. In Greensboro, the city's two most prominent banks, Security National and Guilford, had only just announced a merger when they, in turn, were merged into the Charlotte operation. In Greensboro then, two twenty-five-member boards wound up being distilled into just twelve members of the "unified" NCNB board.

Since, ultimately, only a total of twenty-five people were selected for the new board, that left out seventy-five "advisory directors," who felt slighted. Reese recognized that the mergers had more splintered than unified his bank. Both actual and advisory director groups contained people who felt lukewarm, if not downright hostile toward Tom Storrs, Reese's man in Greensboro. At least among the deposed advisory directors, there were several who felt no love whatsoever for Addison Reese. There had developed a tendency to form camps and take sides, a divisiveness that worked its way through every level of the company. The arguments over who should have power and how power should be directed served to diffuse the real power—Addison Reese's power to energize the bank through a single vision.

North Carolina National Bank had a chairman, Neil Vanstory, who came from Security National Bank. Its president and CEO, Addison Reese, had started just nine years earlier at American Trust Company. Julian J. Clark, generally thought to be Reese's right-hand man, actually was the "first among equals" in a triumvirate of executive vice presidents.

In addition to Clark, once the popular choice to attain Reese's seat of power, the other EVPs were Patrick N. Calhoun, whom Reese had spirited away from Greensboro's Guilford National Bank (against

Neil Vanstory's wishes), and Herbert M. Wayne, who was the highest-ranking survivor from Commercial National Bank after its buyout by American Trust. Thus in Vanstory, Reese, Clark, Calhoun and Wayne, all four premerger corporate cultures were represented.

Clark was in charge of finance, credit and investment. Calhoun's duties included oversight of all correspondent and corporate banking in the National Division. Wayne headed up "back office" operations, the headquarters office in Charlotte, and had responsibility for so-called "city officers" in the bank's branch locations throughout North Carolina. Thus Wayne was responsible for "in-town" activities—that is, within the jurisdiction of any branch town's management—Calhoun for "out-of-town" activities, in all locations that did not have a branch of NCNB.

The three-man combination might have been volatile, but for one stabilizing influence: all of the EVPs were from the same generation. Neither Calhoun, Clark nor Wayne would be young enough to follow Reese to the chief executive's dais in 1967, when Reese was scheduled for elevation to chairman. As a triumvirate of nominally equal stature, the three very dissimilar executive vice presidents provided Reese with a nonthreatening support group that could keep the wolves of the board at bay while he trained his somewhat impersonal economist, Thomas "Buddy" Storrs, in the soft art of personality management.

Just as Hemby had brought Reese in from the outside, Reese imported Storrs from the Federal Reserve system. But instead of following Hemby's lead and throwing Storrs to the wolves, Reese eased his protégé's entry by assigning him to a position that would not attract quite so much attention. Storrs was posted outside of Charlotte, and he received the less imposing title of senior vice president, or SVP, one step down the ladder from that of the three EVPs. This was despite the fact that Storrs's responsibility, as director of the Greensboro Region, was essentially identical to that of Wayne, who ran the Charlotte Region, but whose health was failing rapidly.

In early 1965, the stiff, moralistic Methodist, Herbert Wayne, died of the cancer that had been consuming his body for years. With his triumvirate broken, it was time for Addison Reese to make his next move. He left Pat Calhoun as executive vice president in charge of the National Division. Julian Clark remained executive vice president of finance. Reese moved Tom Storrs up one rung, to executive vice president for administration. But he gave Storrs both the Charlotte and the Greensboro regional operations. This effectively shifted the weight of power within the EVP group to the younger Tom Storrs's office in Greensboro.

To those in the bank who had a personal interest in the matter of succession, Reese was sending a clear signal. This move meant that of all the people closest to the throne, Storrs and Storrs alone had the potential for ascendancy. Reese seemed oblivious to the fact that few if any executives in the Charlotte office knew a great deal about Storrs and his abilities. The tendency of Reese's officers—at coffee shops, Rex's Pool Hall, after-church lemonades and other small-talk gatherings—was to poke fun at "Doctor Buddy" Storrs.

Hugh McColl got the joke, though he didn't much care for it. He realized that his fellow Charlotte bankers considered Storrs "a glorified branch manager." He was "saddled with a doctor of economics degree," and to those who had studied banking in college, economics was regarded as "the dismal science." McColl saw Storrs as "generally not well liked. He came in as an executive vice president, in a world that was very small and had very few big titles. And here was somebody from the *outside* using up one of those big titles. He had the dubious honor of being disliked by both of the camps in the company." In Greensboro, Storrs was considered Ad Reese's man, "one of *them.*" In Charlotte, everybody assumed Storrs was Vanstory's toady, "one of *them.*"

From the little he knew of Tom Storrs, McColl found him, if a bit too weak in personality skills to be called "likable," at least a very reasonable man. There was a lot to appreciate about Tom Storrs. For one thing, he was every bit as short as Hugh McColl, and that put a large number in his plus column. Even better, McColl had a feeling Storrs thought highly of him.

Three years earlier, in 1961, only a few months after accepting Reese's offer to change careers, Storrs had been trying to sort out who did what in the curious in-town-versus-out-of-town management structure of NCNB. A loan officer approached him with a problem concerning a local commercial customer in Greensboro who had an affiliate in rural South Carolina. The affiliate needed a loan to expand operations, but the bewildered loan officer wasn't sure how NCNB could help. Feeling like a man to whom the buck had just been passed, Storrs called the Charlotte office. After being shuttled from one secretary to another, he got someone named Hugh McColl on the phone. He explained the problem, giving McColl only the name and telephone number of the affiliate in South Carolina.

"Mr. Storrs, I'll get right on it," McColl said.

Storrs hung up and told the customer they would get back to him "very shortly." But he was feeling uneasy about holding on to that customer. You never knew which side of the team you were depending on, whether they might open up a path for you or get in your way. In the Greensboro office, Storrs found relations between Guilford people and Security people to be "very, very cold. I always speculated that the chairman of one of them may have gotten his officers out in the lobby every morning and made them raise their hands and swear they'd hate the other one all day long, more than they had hated them the day before."

To his everlasting astonishment, Storrs's secretary buzzed him that same afternoon to let him know that Mr. McColl from the National Division was on the phone.

"It's all taken care of, Mr. Storrs."

"Taken care of?"

"We got them the loan and they'll be able to move ahead with their plan."

Storrs looked at the clock on his desk and read 2:33 P.M. His mind—constantly keeping records, making notes, adding things up—told him that a mere three hours and seven minutes had gone by since the voice on the Charlotte telephone promised action. This was unique in his NCNB experience. It was the sort of response he had grown to expect at the Fed, but he doubted it could happen in the business world. Now, here was this man McColl, seeming to take actual responsibility for his company and its relationships with customers. Tom Storrs filed the name away.

McColl did his level best to keep to his place in the curious chain of command. This was not always easy. EVP Julian Clark could not resist poking his knowledgeable fingers into the operations of the National Division, even though McColl's nominal "big boss" was Pat Calhoun. Under Calhoun was Yates Faison, followed by John Robison, followed by Hugh McColl. It was McColl's duty to jump at any command from any one of his superiors, and he believed his performance would be judged on how quick and how high he could jump. In the bank, people got a real charge out of watching him do that.

Near the head of the mezzanine stairway were the desks of two secretaries, Mary Covington, reporting to Pat Calhoun, and Martha Hendrix, reporting to Julian Clark. Mary Covington always knew when Mr. Clark had business with any of "her boys" in the National Division, and nobody responded to a call from Mr. Clark as expeditiously as Hugh McColl did.

"Mr. Clark would ask Martha to call Mr. McColl, just to give him a message," Covington recalled. "Well, she would dial his number and he was sitting over in the corner where we could see. And I would hear Martha say, 'Hugh?' And she would hang up the phone. And he would come out that door and we would watch him, pulling on his coat and running around there to Mr. Clark's office. And she'd say, 'You didn't have to come around here, I just wanted to give you a message.'

"And the next time she'd do the same thing, and she'd say, 'Now Mary, watch this.' And we'd go through the same routine. He'd come out that office just flying around her. I mean, if Mr. Clark wanted him over there, he was going to be there *instantly*. And he didn't give her an opportunity to tell him what he wanted, he just showed up."

McColl saluted the uniform, not the man, just as the corps had drilled him. He was used to saluting Mr. Clark and Mr. Calhoun. Now, if Mr. Reese, the commander-in-chief, wanted him to salute Mr. Tom Storrs and Tom Storrs was wearing the brass eagle, he had no problem with that. McColl would show Mr. Storrs the same respect he showed the others. He would respond with the same alacrity, no matter what others in the bank might be saying about Storrs behind his back, or about Hugh McColl behind his.

It might even be that a Storrs promotion might have some bearing on McColl's own career. If indeed Addison Reese was planning to set up Storrs as the next CEO, that would require some rethinking on McColl's part. Up till now he had always assumed preference would go to Luther Hodges first, Hugh McColl second in the pecking order as decreed by Addison Reese. On the other hand, while Hodges was clearly the adopted offspring of the patrician, crowd-pleasing Reese, there was no special relationship—none that McColl knew of— between Hodges and Tom Storrs. In fact if you stood the four men together in a room, you'd be likely to pair off Storrs and McColl as readily as you'd pair Reese and Hodges.

McColl had one of those flashes of recognition, like the moment with Robison in the Greenville VFW bar. Should the day ever arrive when Tom Storrs took over North Carolina National Bank, well then, Hugh McColl's star could be hanging high and shining bright.

In early 1966, John Robison was reassigned from the National Division to run the headquarters office in Charlotte, reporting to J. A. "Jack" Tate Jr., who reported to the newly minted EVP, Tom Storrs. Some in the bank considered Tate a product of one of Addison Reese's "blind spots." This was a perceived tendency on the part of the CEO to kowtow to "Old South Aristocracy." Critics of the Reese style believed he wanted desperately to "belong" in the social circles that ran Charlotte and the Carolinas. In order to be accepted, some said, he would attach more weight to social status than to productivity and talent in assessing an executive's value to the bank.

Social standing had been part of Reese's personal, all-out recruitment of Governor Luther Hodges's son. Reese clearly resented the fact that North Carolina's capital-S Society was in the thrall of Wachovia Bank. To beat The Wachovia, NCNB had to succeed on the social front as well as on the deposits front, and that might require a very different style of warfare. To lead that sort of battle, Reese wanted people like executive vice president Pat Calhoun, a big, handsome Clemson man, a member of one prominent South Carolina family married into another. To Reese's critics, this was an example of "more-form-than-substance" executives brought in simply so that Addison Reese could "cozy up to the social set."

"Society" in Charlotte could trace its roots no further back than two generations. As an example, the three Belk brothers—Tom, John and Irwin—were on the board of three different banks. John had Wachovia, Tom NCNB and "Ike" First Union. The Belk family was as prominent as any in Charlotte, but they were hardly aristocratic. They ran a string of *department stores*. Their father had started out with a dry goods emporium advertised as "the cheapest store on earth." He probably never stocked hoop skirts and his wife certainly never wore them.

Ironically enough—although few at the bank recognized it—their most likely candidate for inclusion in the "Founding Fathers of Charlotte Club," had there been a club like that, would have been none other than backwater Hugh McColl. His wife was a Spratt, a linear descendant of one of the two original settlers at the intersection of two Indian trading paths that became Charlotte. Jane Spratt McColl of York was about as Old Charlotte as they came.

Instead, Jack Tate was the bank's aristocratic touchstone, and Tate picked John Robison for his team, creating a vacancy in the National Division. Robison learned that his old Southeast Region was about to be placed in the hands of an executive who, in John Robison's opinion, would be ineffectual as a leader. Robison decided to take matters into his own hands, going outside the chain of command, confronting Addison Reese. He told Reese that there was "no one in the bank for this job except Hugh McColl." Robison's recommendation, perhaps along with input from Farr and Storrs, brought an executive decision that would have far-reaching consequences.

In what came as a complete surprise to him, McColl found himself named a "deputy director" of the National Division. He was only thirty years old and in his sixth year with the company. "It was a new title that they made up, which really allowed me to have a lot of say in what went on. And the reason, I think, was that I was decisive, and I had been working for people who struggled to make decisions." McColl found himself filling a "vacuum of leadership," not so different from the one Hugh's great-grandfather, Duncan Donald McColl, had filled when he returned to Bennettsville after the war in 1865.

If there ever was a time for decisiveness, for leadership in the company, the mid-'60s was that time. Hugh McColl, in his new position of deputy director of the National Division, was attending meetings at which frustration ran right to the edge of desperation. Suddenly, every NCNB loan was being scrutinized. Unless something was done soon, NCNB and other Southern banks were going to find themselves in much the same position as those 1880s' would-be industrialists of the nascent New South, wondering what it would take to bring in some Union money.

It wasn't from any lack of business in Hugh McColl's area of the bank. On the contrary, Southern business and industry was in an expansive mood, fueled by inflationary policies in Washington. Everybody wanted to build, consume, borrow. The economy was so bountiful, in fact, the only question was how best to distribute its fruits. President Lyndon Johnson was building his "Great Society" on borrowed money, persuading Congress to accept an $11.5 billion tax cut at the same time he poured more money into his domestic social programs and into an escalating war in Vietnam. Washington's expenses were rapidly outpacing its revenues.

The expansive government budget deficit resulted in monstrous increases in the prices of goods and services. Instead of cutting back on purchases, people demanded more money to pay for those goods and services. Companies needed money to grow, so they could meet the growing demands of customers. Everyone wanted to borrow money from their bankers. The problem was, the banks had no money to lend them. Deposits were being drained out of the banks by opportunities to invest in Washington. The United States government, in order to help pay its bills, was selling savings bonds at higher interest rates than banks were allowed to offer savers. Regulation Q of the Federal Reserve banking laws prohibited banks from raising their interest rates to match those of the bonds.

Led by New York's First National City Bank, the money-center banks found a way around "Reg-Q." They issued certificates of deposit, or CDs, which were negotiable instruments that could pay interest rates. Because they wrote these certificates with a penalty for "premature withdrawal," banks were not prohibited by Reg-Q from paying interest, as they were on deposits in checking accounts. Sold in bulk, in denominations of $1 million, money center CDs were sweet music to the ears of Big Business CFOs. Corporations and wealthy individuals began to move their short-term cash reserves from non-interest-bearing checking accounts into what, from their perspective, looked very much like *interest-bearing* checking accounts. For the money center banks, the CDs began to generate impressive amounts of cash. First National City chairman Walter Wriston excitedly proclaimed that overnight CDs had changed the world of banking.

In North Carolina, Wachovia introduced negotiable CDs in one-thousand-dollar denominations, which had some appeal for smaller corporations and individuals. NCNB applied the same tourniquet, but the bleeding continued. The higher the money centers dared to go with the unregulated rates on their million-dollar CDs, the more large corporations responded by shifting their money supplies North.

At NCNB, time and savings deposits, which had climbed to over $280 million, now began to shrink. More dollars were leaving the bank, in the form of loans and withdrawals, than were coming in through deposits. To old-timers, this was a nerve-jittering reminder of the

Depression. This time, though, it was not the "banksters," but regulators who were causing the money well to dry up.

Anticipating even greater demand for loans on a bank that was trying to grow while running out of cash, Addison Reese convinced the board to let him sell the Tryon Street headquarters building. In what was at that time the largest real estate transaction ever recorded in Mecklenburg County, Reese sold the NCNB Building, which had been the source of much company pride, for just under $9 million. The new owners then leased it back to the bank. For a while at least, that would stanch the wound.

Reese was still looking for money as McColl, Hodges and his other "Young Turks" kept on bringing in the loan customers. January 1966, was the end of the line for Cornelius M. "Neil" Vanstory and his five-and-a-half-year contract as chairman of NCNB. The contract had been written to expire on the day Vanstory reached the age of sixty-five, thus establishing a "tradition" of mandatory retirement by the chairman at sixty-five. However, the board did not act immediately to crown Reese as chairman.

Vanstory's hold on the bank remained strong. Despite all headquarters operations and all decision-making coming out of the Tryon Street building, board meetings still alternated between Charlotte and Greensboro. Perhaps the single common denominator between Vanstory and Reese in their half-decade-long marriage of inconvenience had been the driving passion to "Beat Wachovia." Vanstory left with that goal unattained, yet tantalizingly within reach. With total resources at $949 million, NCNB was less than $350 million behind Wachovia's $1.29 billion. Yet, as runaway inflation continued to push the money demand further ahead of the money supply, Reese and his advisors were running out of ideas.

The smaller banks, NCNB's correspondents, were scratching just as frantically for cash. For them, one option was to write "over-lines," loans that exceeded the bank's limit, but which could be sold to their upstream partner, NCNB, for cash. That cash could be turned over in the bond market, generating more cash to write more loans at the smaller bank. If the borrower renewed his loan, the small bank could resell the loan to NCNB, generating more cash and more bond market interest. One of the most successful over-line players was a bank in Dillon, South Carolina, a customer of Benny Shaw. The bank was turning over its loans with such regularity and gusto that McColl decided to pay a visit himself to Dillon. McColl hit it off with the president of the bank, a gregarious West Point graduate, and got his permission to spend a little time in his back office.

"I started going through their note department and looking at their loans. And then I tried to find some particular record. That got me into the accounting side of it, trying to find some information about the payments and renewals. And I found discrepancies." McColl's sheep-dip training made him suspicious. Something was not right about these Dillon loans. He found entries in subsidiary ledgers that were not included in the general ledger, in spite of the fact that all the books balanced out. Without raising any hackles, "I thanked them and left."

Back on South Tryon Street, he conferred with Faison, Calhoun and Storrs. McColl told them he smelled a rat, though he couldn't be certain how large or how fraudulent that rat might be. He recommended that NCNB no longer renew the Dillon bank's loans, but should demand payment as each loan came due. The others agreed. Under new pressures, the Dillon banker resorted to even more desperate measures, which brought him to the attention of the Federal Reserve. Soon his loan books were being examined not by McColl but by agents of the FBI.

The federal men discovered that, in many cases, the original borrowers had long ago paid off their loans, never applying for renewals. The signatures on the bank's renewal request forms turned out to be clever forgeries, rubber-stamp impressions inked in by hand. When the case went to federal court, there turned out to be a great deal of money involved, but none had been lost by NCNB. Tom Storrs recognized that things might have turned out quite differently were it not for the decisiveness of Hugh McColl.

As 1967 approached, McColl's "nose" for good loans and bad loans was becoming almost legendary in the bank. Up close, Storrs could see that this young man who had impressed him at first encounter, possessed unusual skills, both in organizing his work and in leading other people. Nevertheless, he considered McColl "a very brash young man. He could say things very quickly that other people found damaging.

"Looking at Hugh McColl in the 1960s, you'd never say 'there is a warm fuzzy bear that I'd want to nuzzle up against.' But on the other hand, he was a person that I wanted to be associated with, because I had a high regard for his ability. And my only concern was whether, over the long haul, the edges or the brashness would get rubbed off, to the point that Hugh could take full advantage of the strengths that he had."

McColl never hesitated to speak his mind. Impatient as ever, he wanted Storrs to accelerate his rise in the company. He was convinced that his own wagon would roll faster hitched to Storrs's star. The sooner Storrs moved into the chief executive spot, the sooner he could prove that theory. He was disconcerted by the fact that Storrs continued to make his home in Greensboro, commuting to Charlotte, spending three or four nights a week in a hotel apartment. At a cocktail party one evening, fortified by several scotch-and-waters, he was introduced to Mrs. Storrs. As soon as he could barrel through the small talk, he blurted out: "You know, if your husband wants to run this bank, he's going to have to move to Charlotte." Kitty Storrs, who couldn't bear the thought of leaving her home in Greensboro, now understood her husband's descriptions of Hugh McColl.

Brashness notwithstanding, McColl's track record of good loans made him exempt from the tight-fisted scrutiny most other NCNB officers had to undergo before they could write a loan of any sizable amount. The only other member of the Young Turks who seemed to share this executive privilege was Luther Hodges. For both of them, the bank's top management seemed to have a wealth of confidence.

McColl felt it was a matter of results. "Luther and I were both willing to take more risks than anybody in the company." What was it the story said about his great-grandfather? *He lost practically no money, yet he often took chances. He disregarded the ordinary rules of business. He acted upon his keen knowledge of human nature.* Trust and risk. Duncan Donald had risked his life for the sake of his fellow Southerners, and they later entrusted him with their future. His mother had risked her college degree by jumping into some stranger's airplane. Now he and Hodges were aggressively lending money in the face of an ever-rising economic environment. In the 1960s, McColl considered himself "smart as hell."

As their reputations grew inside and outside the bank, McColl and Hodges developed an attitude of invincibility. They looked into the future, beyond Addison Reese, even beyond Tom Storrs, and they saw NCNB growing too big to be hemmed in by the boundaries of North Carolina. They would be regional bankers, perhaps even national bankers.

"We would sit around my kitchen table every evening after work," Luther Hodges reminisced. "We'd have a drink and talk about what we could do. We talked about some big acquisition, like buying the Bank of America or Citibank or Chase. We could see that it would eventually be a regional bank that would be able to get that big. It wouldn't be the Atlanta banks, because they couldn't expand into the rest of Georgia. Even the New York banks couldn't get out of New York City. None of them could diversify the way we could in North Carolina."

But for the moment the laws of other states prevented a "foreign" bank like NCNB from setting up branches on their turf. Until he and McColl had the influence to change those laws, Hodges would concentrate on expanding their base in North Carolina. Meanwhile McColl made South Carolina bankers, industrialists and businessmen ever more beholden to him—and, of course, to NCNB. Whatever it took, he'd get it done.

"We actually helped some banks get started, like the Spartanburg Bank & Trust Company. We started one in Hendersonville called Home Bank & Trust Company. And we helped Phil Stevenson start a bank down in Florence, South Carolina. I would bring a team, and we would help them actually begin a bank. You know, create one. Sales of stock and all. We would cradle-to-grave it. We were creating our own customers, in effect. And we would be engaged with them for weeks at a time. We would do their processing. There were times we even did item processing for other companies, their customers, bookkeeping for other companies. I mean, we did everything.

"I was a very aggressive person. Luther and I made a reputation of being willing to lend money and take a risk. Of course, our critics called us 'gun fighters' and 'hip shooters.' But I think that part of being a good lender is having a good judgment about people, about whether a person will pay you back or not, and understanding whether an idea is good or not, the *value* of it. And so my team—not just me, my team—proved their capabilities over an extended period of time. But nevertheless, I had a reputation as somebody who would take risks. And that's not a bad reputation to have for your customers. We were the people. If you needed money, this is where you came."

In both McColl's estimation and Hodges's, and in John Robison's as well, the two people who drove that reputation were Hugh McColl and Luther Hodges.

Boldly going where no Carolina bankers had gone before, NCNB was developing the image Addison Reese wanted: aggressive, competitive, up-to-date. It was the very antithesis of stodgy Wachovia. NCNB's advertising boasted of fifty-one offices in ten cities, stretching from Wilmington on the ocean to Tryon in the southwestern mountains, covering "principal money centers in the state."

Eager to project this image to the public, NCNB's marketing and public relations people came up with a spanking new logo. An eight-pointed starburst against an oval black hole, with a moon-like orb peeking over its left shoulder, the logo proclaimed "North Carolina National" to be the "dominant new star in Carolina." The PR people believed they could borrow excitement from the public's fascination with America's blossoming space program. After all, you could hardly pick up a newspaper without being confronted by a new set of photos of the moon's surface. So far all those photos had been snapped by robot cameras, but the National Aeronautics and Space Administration promised they'd have real people up there before long.

North Carolina National—which they considered a far more descriptive and catchy name than any obscure set of initials—was the bank that could take you and your company to the stars. The logo seemed like such a great idea that the marketing department had it minted in bronze and set in the sidewalk in front of the main entrance on South Tryon Street. "Cast in stone," as it were, all this hubris may have been premature.

On January 27, 1967, three Apollo astronauts—Col. Virgil I. Grissom, Col. Edward White II and Lt. Commander Roger B. Chaffee—were killed in a fire that swept through the cabin of their spaceship during a simulated launch. The disaster threw a pall over NASA's space program and many wondered whether Congress would ever finance a manned voyage to the moon. Reaching for the stars suddenly seemed like overreaching for brash mortals.

That very month, the aspirations of Hugh McColl and Luther Hodges were called into question by the arrival of a new player. His name was Bill Dougherty, his title was management services executive, and all of a sudden here was a third Young Turk who might be in line for the leadership prize. Dougherty was tough, decisive and savvy, at least when it came to numbers. Moreover, he seemingly had fewer of those "rough edges" so irritating to people who came too close to Hugh McColl. He was, in the minds of some, another Tom Storrs, although without Storrs's academic veneer.

When he arrived in January 1967 William H. Dougherty Jr. was thirty-six, five years older than McColl and Hodges. He was an accountant who had risen to prominence in Pittsburgh's Western Pennsylvania National Bank and Trust Company by moving its financial system onto a computer platform. Since NCNB was converting to its third generation of computers, it seemed on the surface that this was the immediate cause of his hiring. Very quickly however, the other executives realized that Dougherty's franchise reached into nearly every fief of the company.

In his first weeks at NCNB, Dougherty swept a new broom through the Charlotte accounting office. He found an entire room filled with checks waiting to be cleared, kicked out of the computer and left to molder for months on end. Here was a font of cash that could be put to good use by a cash-thirsty bank. Since no one had bothered to enter the checks manually into the books, the cash accounts had been out of balance for more than a year. Dougherty's astonishment, conveyed to the mezzanine executives, resulted in drastic action, a sudden shift from building people to reinventing processes.

Reese directed Dougherty to develop an entirely new set of accounting tools, all based on the computer. Dougherty established a system of compiling and assessing data unlike anything the bank had in place. Profit planning, long a staple of American corporate management, had been ignored by bankers; suddenly it was required at NCNB. Performance measurement and profit centers—concepts advocated earlier by McColl—forced NCNB executives into a new world of accountability. Some of the executives did not thrive in the atmosphere of that world. Bill Dougherty, a steelworker's son, took neither guff nor prisoners. The first syllable of his last name wasn't pronounced like "dough," but rhymed with "rock." He had no patience with the accounting traditionalists.

Jim Farr liked Dougherty, considering him to be "a good, moral, ethical, well-meaning guy." However, Farr expressed to Reese his concern that Dougherty might not be "highly skilled in the *people* stuff."

This sounded very much like Addison Reese's complaint about Tom Storrs and Storrs's complaint about McColl.

Dougherty's "cutting edge profit-planning and financial system" was not well received in certain areas of the bank, Storrs observed. "There were a lot of people who thought it was much more important to go do business than to write a lot of stuff on how you'd done it and things like that." One of those who resented Dougherty's fixing things that were not visibly broken was Hugh McColl. His people had no time to fill out Dougherty's endless forms. They were too busy servicing customers. Storrs watched the less- than-friendly relationship between the two men and suspected that if and when Hugh McColl learned how he could use the tools that Dougherty offered, and if he could convey that value to the people who worked for him, that would be a milestone in Hugh McColl's development from platoon leader to general.

Dougherty's irritating innovations put a new surge in the power grid of NCNB. For a bank to grow the way Reese and his followers wanted to grow, they would have to learn to take advantage of something called technology, the new wave of data processing and number crunching. If they did not, their company of high-flying lenders would be consumed by the "back office beast." For those who failed to understand the urgency, Dougherty's intrusions simply added to the concern that Reese, through Storrs, was taking the bank in a direction it should not go.

On St. Valentine's Day 1967, having left the NCNB chair unfilled for thirteen months after Vanstory's retirement, the board at last elevated the president and CEO, Addison Reese. Now Reese's title was chairman and chief executive officer. At the same time, it accepted Reese's recommendation to elect Thomas Storrs vice chairman. Julian Clark was named president of NCNB. Since up until this point there had been no such thing as "vice chairman," there was some confusion as to what this all implied.

To the vocal faction that held Tom Storrs in about the same esteem as they held The Wachovia, the announcement was a sign that Storrs had been rejected by the board of directors. Why else would he be thrown this "vice chairmanship" bone?

Addison Reese had been president and now the universally admired Julian Clark would be president. Maybe, after all, the board intended to give Clark a turn at being chief executive, while someone younger—say, Jack Tate or John Robison—was being groomed for the CEO spot. Given this interpretation, the board's action seemed to indicate dissatisfaction with Storrs. As a result, the anti-Storrs venom was released to flow freely through the bank offices and in all the places where bankers gathered. There was, as McColl saw it, "a great hue and cry over who would be the next CEO."

Luther Hodges was "sitting on that mezzanine the day Julian Clark was named president of the bank and Storrs vice chairman, and it was a signal . . . that their man had won. And one of the guys . . . came wandering down the mezzanine and said, 'Well all you *Buddy lovers* have lost now.'" Tom Storrs's boyhood nickname had become a pejorative.

Almost immediately Hodges was taken off the front lines, promoted to city executive in Chapel Hill, the place Addison Reese had found him. His wife, Dorothy Duncan Hodges, had given birth to their first child there in Chapel Hill. The state capital, where his father had cracked the whip of government, was just up the road.

It all started him wondering whether he, Luther Hodges Jr., was really cut out to be the new "banker of the future." Hodges was beginning to think he might make a bigger mark on the world somewhere other than this little bank that his friend Hugh wanted so badly to run. People told him he was a natural for politics, that he could rise even higher than his old man. Maybe so. At NCNB, it seemed to Hodges that if Tom Storrs ever really seized the power, then Hugh McColl was much more likely than he was to be next in line. Hodges had difficulty communicating with Storrs. He suspected Storrs didn't find him "analytical" enough.

Had McColl and the rest of the Young Turks known about Hodges's self-doubts, they would have told him he was way off base. The others saw the Chapel Hill city executive appointment as a big step up for the man they considered Reese's odds-on favorite. In their minds, Hodges clearly had the inside track to the top. But they did not have a chance to tell him so, because Hodges kept his own counsel.

Hugh McColl began wondering whether he ought to rethink *his* career. "In March of '67 I had been with the bank seven and a half years. I was making $14,500 a year. I remember that distinctly. I had gone to work for $4,500. And after seven years I was making $14,500. And that was a lot less than my contemporaries were making, who had gone into other fields, like medicine or law or industry. And I was really just a traveling salesman and I was getting tired of it. Didn't feel like I was going anywhere and didn't feel like the company was going anywhere in particular."

It was a pleasant surprise when his friend Hootie Johnson asked him to drive down to Columbia for a meeting. He wanted McColl to come to work for him at Banker's Trust of South Carolina. Recognizing that, "particularly in our credit area, we needed a higher degree of sophistication that was hard to develop from within," Hootie Johnson "talked with Hugh about coming. I offered him what I thought was a very bright future, and I think he seriously considered it."

McColl considered it seriously all right, but he turned it down. Johnson sweetened the pot, but McColl wasn't ready to walk away from Charlotte and NCNB. "Finally Hootie offered me $30,000, with a guaranteed 15 percent bonus, another $4,500. That came to $34,500 and I was making $14,500. I still said no."

Johnson dropped the subject of money and turned to power. That got Hugh McColl's attention. "He said he was going to make me president of his company. And I was only a vice president at the time. He would make me president. And finally he said he would put me on the board of directors. That triggered something in me. I thought, *Boy!*" He told Johnson he'd have to sleep on that one.

From Columbia, McColl drove to Bennettsville, where he found his father sitting at the kitchen table. Over a glass of sweet iced tea, he told the man who had watched his own father die at a bank president's desk, the man who had guided a bank through the Depression only to shut it down when times got better, about Hootie Johnson's amazing offer. He thought he was going to knock his daddy's socks off. He had just been offered a twenty-thousand-dollar raise, more than doubling his income. He was going to be president of a bank and a member of the board of directors.

"I told Daddy this story and he said, 'Son, you and Jane getting along all right?' I said, 'Yes, sir.' He said, 'You need anything?' I said, 'No sir, not really.' He said, 'Well then, the money is not important, is it?'"

"Yes, Daddy, I know," Hugh sighed. It was as though his old man hadn't heard a blessed word. "But they're going to make me *president.* They'll put me on the board of directors, and I don't know that I'll ever be on the board of the company I work for now." Hugh McColl surprised himself with that statement. This was the first time he had ever admitted to anyone else that there could be any doubt of his making it to the very top.

At the age of sixty-two, Hugh McColl Sr. had lost the nervousness that had soured his own banking career. He had heard his son the first time, understood his dilemma. He sipped on his iced tea and blew his nose before he answered.

"Well," he said at last, "it's been my experience you can always go from a big bank to a little one. But you *never* go from a little one to a big one." He took another swallow of tea. "And if I were you I'd go back up there to Charlotte. You got a good job. I'd go up there and do my job and it'll work out."

And that, Hugh understood, would be all the advice he would get from his father. Before giving Hootie Johnson his answer, though, McColl decided to consult a less caustic oracle, his father-in-law. Once again, he laid out what still seemed like an irresistible offer.

"Hugh, how many people working for Addison Reese's bank now?" was John Spratt's response.

"Mr. Spratt, there are about six hundred people working for North Carolina National Bank now."

Spratt looked up from his figuring. "Six hundred people! My God."

"So, what do you think? Should I go on down there to Columbia?"

"Son, you are in the big leagues. Don't come back to the bush leagues."

Hugh McColl telephoned Hootie Johnson and turned him down.

Not long afterward, McColl received an invitation to dinner from Tom Storrs, who was spending more and more of his nights in Charlotte, away from his wife and children. The dinner would be at Quail Hollow Country Club, where Addison Reese was a member and therefore was required to pay for a number of meals each month. Storrs enjoyed dining on Reese's tab, using the country club dinners as a means of getting to know the people who worked for him, and letting them see there was more to him than numbers and columns and bottom lines.

The two men left uptown Charlotte in Storrs's car and drove south along Park Road, passing near the Selwyn Apartments, where Hugh and Jane had lived during his first years with the bank. They continued past the neighborhood of Beverly Woods, where they lived now, passing the public golf course, where Hugh and Benny Shaw paid greens fees for the privilege of teeing off at dawn, and turned into the posh Quail Hollow course, pulling up to the modern club-house. If Addison Reese had been "Old Charlotte," they would have taken an entirely different route, ending up at Charlotte Country Club, rather than these upstart suburban digs.

Storrs turned the dinner conversation to "the opportunities we had in taking business that Wachovia wasn't in a position to handle and things like that. And also we talked about the need for building manpower, because we really didn't have any people." Storrs spoke of his goals for the company and he made it clear that McColl had a bright future with the bank. He said he was sure he could "count on" McColl to help him realize that future.

Hearing that, the thought flashed through McColl's mind that Storrs had gotten wind of the Hootie Johnson offer. He must know that other banks out there were becoming aware of his lieutenant's extraordinary talent. Maybe this was the right moment to let Storrs know he was going to have to pay handsomely for that talent if he wanted to keep it.

"Absolutely, Mr. Storrs," he answered. "You can count on me. Just as long as I'm here." *That ought to do it. For a shark like Hugh McColl there are lots of oceans to swim in.*

Storrs nodded, let the remark pass, and continued the conversation. As they drove into the parking lot uptown, they were speaking once again of the future, of Hugh McColl's chances of leading the National Division into its next stage of growth. As they got out of the car, Storrs to walk to his apartment, McColl to go to his own car, Storrs concluded with his main concern: building leadership through the ranks.

"We've got to do a better job of team-building," he said. "We need everybody at the top of this organization to concentrate on making this a solid team, with players we can count on."

"Well, Mr. Storrs," McColl said, shutting his door and leaning over the roof of the sedan. "You can count on me. As long as I'm here, you can do that. You can be sure to count on me."

Storrs stiffened. "You know, Hugh, that is the second time that you've said that to me tonight. If you continually raise the question of whether or not you are going to be here, people will start to plan around you."

It would be the last time Hugh McColl would ever hint at leaving NCNB.

"I never said it again, ever, in my whole life. Never after that night in '67, did I ever threaten to leave, act like I was going to leave or anything else. I made up my mind, then and there, that it was counterproductive. I understood that if you were going to leave, then leave. . . . I learned a lot from Mr. Storrs. I think Mr. Storrs taught me a lot just by osmosis, just by my observing him, but he taught me a direct lesson that night. He taught me that I couldn't be cocky with him and give him conditional commitment. Conditional commitment wouldn't work."

Perhaps Hugh McColl learned another important lesson that night: if he stuck with Tom Storrs, he had his best chance of attaining the level of power he desired. If Tom Storrs one day became the chairman of NCNB, then one other day Hugh McColl could become chairman. All he needed to do was play his cards right and not make any more dumb mistakes. He would even start getting on his people about those reports for Dougherty. He would follow General Storrs and never break rank.

McColl's resolve was tested almost immediately.

Addison Reese had hoped to sidestep all the factionalism by bringing in a "clean" outsider like Tom Storrs to run the bank. He had nursed Storrs and trained him patiently until Vanstory was out of the way. But the factionalism wouldn't retire. Instead, Reese seemed to have given members of the various factions a cause against which some of them could unite. Whether you came from American Trust or Commercial National stock, whether your bloodline was Security or Guilford, you could coalesce in resentment against whatever it was you imagined that Tom Storrs stood for.

Exactly what it was that Storrs represented to his adversaries is difficult to pin down. It had something to do with his single-minded approach to running a business with tight controls. From Storrs's point of view, if you couldn't keep records and balance accounts, if you couldn't stick to procedures, if you couldn't look at a loan prospect with a hard eye that didn't cloud over from friendship or other considerations, then you by-god had no business working for a bank.

From the other side, Tom Storrs was too much business and too little warmth. You resented the fact that Storrs had no truck with handshake deals and good-old-boy understandings. You hated that Tom Storrs had no respect for the "Southern Way," for the concept that one must be a gentleman first and a businessman second. With Buddy Storrs, there were no secret understandings—such as what your grandfather might have done for his grandfather, or the fact that your families had helped found the same church. If you couldn't put a fact down on paper, preferably reduced to a mathematical term, then it wasn't a fact for Tom Storrs, or, for that matter, for the new guy, Dougherty. The two of them were basically telling a lot of old-line bankers they didn't know what they were doing.

Tom Storrs admitted to having "a few rough edges of my own"; otherwise, he might have found a way to ease the hurt feelings of people in the company who came at banking from a different perspective than his. By March 1967, it was too late for peacemaking.

Reese and Storrs were so intent on building their team, they wanted to hold onto every individual who showed a spark of leadership and self-direction, even if some of them did not exactly adhere to Reese's vision. Now several of the brightest young leaders—including Jack Tate and John Robison—did what they had been trained to do: they took decisive action. Bypassing Addison Reese, they went to a member of the board they believed they could trust to see things their way.

Watching from the safe distance of Chapel Hill, Luther Hodges dimly saw the coup unfold. It took him by surprise, particularly in the number of high-minded individuals who took part in it. Hodges believed the anti-Storrs faction was acting in good faith, for what they felt was the good of the bank, but that they "made the classic mistake" of talking to a director of the company, who immediately reported the insurrection to Reese.

McColl was more directly involved than Hodges. The rebels sent a junior-level envoy to recruit McColl into the cause, expecting him to take their side. Assuming he was aware of what was going on, the envoy demanded to know, "Are you with us or against us?"

"I don't know what the hell you are talking about," McColl answered.

He replied, "You know, we're going to get Tom Storrs."

McColl shot the young man a quizzical look, remembering the promise of commitment he had made to himself only a few days earlier. "Actually," he responded, "I work for Mr. Storrs. So I guess I'm not with you. No, you can't count on me."

For the first time, McColl saw his job in terms of a military operation. He was a marine lieutenant informed of a cabal against his general. McColl put on his jacket and knocked on the door of Tom Storrs's office.

"Mr. Storrs, you need to understand what's going on," he began.

Storrs quietly listened, thanked McColl and told him the matter would be looked into.

"Within hours there was a mass execution." McColl was awed by the display of vengeful power. "Everybody that was in the cabal was slaughtered, in a corporate sense, within hours. All of 'em—*splat!* Gone. Clean-out-your-desk gone.

"I learned that if you allowed any one of your people to be challenged, then you yourself could be challenged. If they could kill the crown prince, they could kill the king too. So the king killed everybody else. And it went on and on and on. . . . And I had done nothing but report to my boss that he was being attacked, which I would do again, no matter what."

McColl assumed he bore sole responsibility for bringing the wrath of Reese down on the heads of people he'd worked with and shot pool with, people who had shown him the ropes, people whose families had shared meals with him and Jane and their boys. Tom Storrs, still short on people skills, never thought to correct this impression. In fact, Storrs already knew what was going on. Reese had warned him only moments before McColl knocked on his door.

The anti-Storrs group would always look on the moment with bitterness, believing that their way was the better way, that right was on their side. Some of them went to work for other banks in the Carolinas, some of them changed careers. John Robison left Charlotte to join Hootie Johnson's Bankers Trust in Columbia. J. R. "Jack" Tate announced he would leave NCNB to run for mayor of Charlotte. He lost by forty-four votes to incumbent Stanford Brookshire, whose administration was noted for its cooperation with the city's business interests.

The goings-on at NCNB made for fascinating conversation in "New South" Charlotte, at clubs, restaurants, golf courses and churches. Many of the losing faction had influences that ran deep within the veins of Charlotte and the Carolinas. Resentment against the "massacre" stretched far beyond South Tryon Street. Kitty Storrs, Jane McColl and other wives of the survivors found themselves ignored at social functions and shunned at supermarkets. Since Robison's wife came from Bennettsville, even Hugh's mother heard the noise down in Marlboro County. It was, to Hugh McColl, "a really snotty period. It went on for several years."

But it was also "a watershed moment for the company." Suddenly, McColl saw the corporate culture of North Carolina National Bank shift into focus. "It changed, moving from what I would call a highly politicized environment to a hard professional environment. Whether anybody understood it had happened, it had happened. It had happened in spades."

It happened because at that moment Tom Storrs became the legitimized heir to the crown of NCNB. Julian Clark, who just might have been able to stifle the insurrection had he known about it, once again came through for Addison Reese. He helped to unite the troops as he had done when Torrence Hemby anointed Reese. Clark helped others in the bank to see that his elevation to the presidency had been a gesture of appreciation by Reese for his long and distinguished contribution to the company. As for Storrs's position, everyone left in the upper management team understood that, at least until further notice, *vice* chairman meant *next* chairman. Any word from Tom Storrs was understood to be The Law.

"And Mr. Storrs really then brought to the management of the company a steel-trap logical mind," McColl believed. "He relied not one iota on intuition or feelings, but only on facts. Many of us who were right-brained, and people who went on their gut emotions a lot, had to learn to communicate differently, to communicate totally with facts and with logic, especially in dealing with Mr. Storrs. It took me some while to learn that, but I learned. And he made us a different company. And he was my real mentor. He taught me how to run a big company. He really had the vision. And he was able to articulate that vision for those of us who were younger, so that we grasped it and came with him."

Commitment to Tom Storrs clearly had been McColl's best move. Just a short time later, he was promoted to senior vice president. The title came with a raise of two thousand dollars a year, "which was a big raise by the bank's standards. A huge raise. Again if you look at percentages it seemed a large raise at the time." Yet it made him think again about the opportunity he had turned down. At Banker's Trust he would be earning $34,500. That was more than double his new salary at NCNB. Somehow, though, he believed he was happier where he was, closer to a goal that was beginning to define itself.

"More than money, I always wanted freedom, nobody telling me what to do, an absence of power over me." McColl believed that "the most sensible thing I did was realize that I needed to work and earn money to live before I could have anything. Then, the harder I worked, the more power I accumulated. My mistake was to assume that with the power would come freedom."

Now McColl found himself higher in the chain of command, with only EVP Pat Calhoun ahead of him in the National Division, which was mutating dramatically in the fallout of the coup. For the moment, the matter of rank could be ignored; Hugh McColl, for all practical purposes, began reporting directly to Tom Storrs.

McColl could only hope that Storrs thought as highly of his leadership potential as McColl himself did. He couldn't be sure, because Tom Storrs was a close-lipped man who didn't throw around his big ideas the way Hugh McColl did. You never heard Tom Storrs talking about whipping Wachovia as he banked a six-ball at Rex's. In 1967, only a few people had an idea where Storrs stood as far as taking hold of the reins and then handing them to someone else. But if you had a lot of money invested in NCNB, things like that seemed important. So, occasionally, the matter of who followed Storrs would come up in conversation among board members. As director Tom Belk saw it, "Addison Reese was sort of pushing Luther Hodges. And then there was Bill Dougherty, and then there was Hugh McColl. And, when Tom Storrs got the job, you might say, Hugh McColl was Tom Storrs's man."

Hugh McColl didn't speak much with directors, so he could only *hope* it was that way. Tom Storrs didn't give it a thought. He had McColl, he had Hodges, he had Dougherty. He had three good men, and if they stayed committed, maybe one of them would follow in his footsteps. That would come much later. For the moment, Storrs had business to conduct. Now, more than ever, the bank needed good people, loyal people.

Luther Hodges was called back from Chapel Hill to assume what had been Robison's responsibility, that of Charlotte city executive. Together, he and McColl went on a mission to recruit new talent into the bank. Having witnessed a team breakdown firsthand, McColl took the assignment very seriously.

As *de facto* director of the National Division, now McColl could build a team for the bank's future. He brought in men like Jim Sommers, Bill Covington, Alec Wilkins and Francis "Buddy" Kemp. Bill Vandiver was another who came into the bank at that time. He had battle scars from two years in Vietnam, an M.B.A. from the University of South Carolina, a wife who taught school in Columbia and "no earthly idea of what I wanted to do." A friend suggested that he "talk to this little bank in North Carolina, called North Carolina National Bank. I said, 'Why would I want to work for a bank?' He said, 'Well, I don't know.'"

"My image of banking was all men, old, gray hair, black suits. And I didn't think that was very exciting. I wanted to go work for Exxon or some big multinational company." But Vandiver needed a job, so he called and set up a campus interview with NCNB's Personnel Department. They invited him to Charlotte, to meet with executives of the bank. "And one of those people was a young thirty-one-year-old senior vice president of the bank named Hugh McColl. He told me he was from Bennettsville and used to be a marine. He and I kind of related to each other, because I had just come out of Vietnam, and I'm from South Carolina."

McColl decided he wanted Vandiver on his team. He and Hodges were after as many M.B.A. graduates as they could get, not only because of their education, but also because they tended to be a bit more mature and self-directed than were undergraduates. Wasting no time, he called Vandiver at home that evening and told him, "I want to send two of my top lieutenants down and talk to you. We want you to come to work for us." The next day, Richards Roddy and Bill Covington flew to Columbia, took Vandiver to lunch and offered him a job at eighty-two hundred dollars a year. With all his misgivings about old men in black suits, Vandiver went to work as a management trainee for the North Carolina National Bank's National Division. Among his fellow trainees in 1967 was Francis "Buddy" Kemp, who became a close personal friend of Vandiver's and was never instructed to drop his nickname as Tom Storrs had been.

The bank needed good people and it needed them in a hurry. Reese was determined to pull women into the executive ranks, so he wrote an article in the company magazine, *NCNB News*, headlined "The Best Man for the Job May Be a Woman." He cautioned that women would have to understand it was going to take some time before they would gain "acceptance by our customers," but that ultimately, "women can hold down any job in the bank." Mildred Gwinn became the bank's first female vice president. An accomplished racquetball player, Gwinn forced the Charlotte YMCA—McColl's basketball bastion—to accept women as members.

Whenever the personnel office saw a particularly impressive candidate, they would make sure to run them by McColl or Hodges. If the candidate was too good to lose, they would ask both senior vice presidents to work him over. Hodges and McColl worked out routines in which they would anticipate every possible objection—such as the "old men in black suits" cliché—and have a counterargument ready to fire off. From candidates who knew something about NCNB, and about the two power players who were courting them, a frequent objection would be: "Why would I want to work at NCNB, where I'd have to compete with you two guys?" To that, McColl would move right into a sports analogy. "Well, wouldn't you rather play with the New York Yankees rather than play with some bush-league team?" And Hodges would add: "With us you'll be on a team with nine great starters and a sensational bench. Why would you want to go somewhere where you'd be the only star on your team?"

In most cases, arguments like that won the day. One notable exception was the time they worked over a young graduate of Wharton Business School, who was looking at Wachovia and several other banks in addition to NCNB. When they lost the young man to First Union National Bank, Hodges called to find out why he'd rejected them. "Well," said Edward Crutchfield, "you two guys really convinced me. I decided I'd really rather be the one big star instead of being on a team full of stars." Two blocks south on Tryon Street, Ed Crutchfield started right into hanging the moon at First Union and McColl knew the opposition's gain would be NCNB's loss.

Recruit Bill Vandiver reported to the personnel office of NCNB at 8:30 on September 11, 1967. He had his picture taken and was sent to a small office to fill out forms and answer questions on Jim Farr's aptitude tests. After an hour, the personnel secretary summoned him to the telephone. It was Hugh McColl.

"What are you doing?" McColl asked sharply.

"I'm up here filling these forms out," Vandiver replied.

"Quit filling the damn forms out and come on down here to my office. It's time for you to go to work."

Bill Vandiver said, "Yes, sir." He was about to become a "kit man" for NCNB's new weapon in the war against Wachovia, the credit card.

For nearly a year, Addison Reese and Tom Storrs had been studying the advantages of buying the North Carolina franchise for BankAmericard, the credit card that had started a modern-day gold rush for San Francisco's Bank of America. Since BankAmericard's rollout in 1958, local banks across the country had tried to imitate its success, with less than spectacular results. A consortium of Chicago banks was losing millions on its investment in a local credit card. In Charlotte, First Union had been trying for nearly a decade to penetrate the state with its poorly received "Piedmont Card." NCNB's board of directors looked on the whole credit card scheme with suspicion and distaste.

Reese and Storrs saw something different about BankAmericard. Its anticipated national marketing effort would help convince North Carolinians of its value as a means of managing their money and for making purchases in this spendthrift era of inflation. More importantly, this would be the first bank card that could be used out of state, in effect taking NCNB across state lines. Charlotte cardholders could make credit purchases at Myrtle Beach. Raleigh legislators could use it on trips to Washington. Businessmen from Wilmington and Greensboro could use it to entertain customers in New York. No matter where the card was used, NCNB would earn a fee on every transaction. BankAmericard might just prove to be the leverage NCNB needed to pry some customers away from The Wachovia, which continued to embarrass Reese in its dominance of North Carolina's consumer deposits.

Deciding not to wait for board approval, Reese and Storrs sent their twenty-five-thousand-dollar deposit check by special delivery to Bank of America. It reached San Francisco one day ahead of Wachovia's bid, and NCNB was awarded the only statewide BankAmericard franchise east of the Mississippi River.

What they may have failed to appreciate, in weighing the virtues and risks of BankAmericard, was its value as an internal motivator. The blue, white and gold gift from California became a standard around which the men and women of NCNB could come together. It had nothing to do with Greensboro or Charlotte, nothing to do with

Tom Storrs or Julian Clark. It was a product, pure and simple, something that NCNB owned and nobody else had, something they alone could sell. For the very first time since the creation of NCNB, Reese called all his officers together for a meeting, a pep rally, to explain this exciting new venture. Both he and Storrs wondered why on earth they had never thought to gather the troops like this before.

John Pipken was one of the five hundred officers bussed to a furniture exposition hall in High Point, just down the road from Greensboro. He listened to the hoopla, learned about all the wonders BankAmericard would perform, then waited for the other shoe to drop. "Ultimately," Pipken figured, "what we had to do was get the cards distributed to our depositors. But the cards were no good unless the depositors had some place they could use it." Pipken became a member of the 125-person task force assigned to attack the retail establishments of North Carolina and sign them up as places where BankAmericard was welcome.

Like McColl, Pipken was a marine, so he accepted the challenge, even though it wasn't "his" job. *Every man a rifleman,* the corps had taught him. "If push comes to shove, cooks, mechanics, generals, everybody has enough competence and ability that they can pick up that rifle and use it. So we put everybody to work as a rifleman to saturate North Carolina and call on merchants and sell BankAmericard."

Pipken identified this as "the defining moment in the formation of the North Carolina National Bank, because it pulled all these diverse groups together and gave them a common goal, a common purpose, a common vision and then we went out and accomplished it, and we got to share a common accomplishment. And from that point on, we were then the North Carolina National Bank and there was no more of this 'us' and 'them' kind of mentality."

To Hugh McColl, the BankAmericard franchise was rich in opportunity. In addition to the merchants, if he could sign up correspondent banks in the Carolinas, NCNB would effectively control the franchise in the major cities of both states. By handling the bookkeeping and billing in Charlotte, splitting the transaction fees, he could offer the correspondent banks, in effect, "something for nothing." McColl tapped Jim Sommers, from the Credit Department, as the leader of his task force. Trainee Bill Vandiver was assigned as a kit man.

"Jim Sommers told me, 'You are going to go with me to Asheville, North Carolina, tomorrow. And you'll probably be there for four weeks. You are going to help sell the Bank of Asheville on BankAmericard. And then you are going to be the point person there, to install it, and get all the merchants.'"

Vandiver was taken by surprise. "I don't know anything about BankAmericard."

"Don't worry about it," Sommers answered. "I'll tell you everything you need to know in the car on the way to Asheville."

On the way home to his little apartment, Bill Vandiver stopped at Kmart and bought himself a briefcase for $3.65, "so I'd look the part of a banker. I didn't have a briefcase." The next morning he kissed his wife goodbye and headed for the mountains. It was his third day working for Hugh McColl and NCNB, and he was about to become the company's ambassador to the one big city in North Carolina that did not have a branch of NCNB.

"I walked into a board meeting at the Bank of Asheville with Jim Sommers. And Sommers introduced me as though I was a veteran of BankAmericard, a guy that had been forever at NCNB. And he told them I was going to be on the point. And that I was the guy to really help them. And this was a very major relationship for us, as I understood it. And so I bluffed my way through for six weeks. I was guru for BankAmericard. And they never knew the difference." Vandiver realized he was in on something important and he wasn't going to let Hugh McColl down. McColl trusted him with something big. "It was a rallying point in the history of our company. We had kind of a fire in our belly to make it happen."

It was also Jim Sommers's first time working under McColl. "He just told us, 'Go do it.' And we did it."

"BankAmericard, that was a great time," reflected Luther Hodges, an audible smile in his voice. "That was where some of the girls come in, the BankAmericard Girls. I don't know whose idea that was, but they were a very *positive* force in the marketing of the bank."

The BankAmericard Girls were hardly the female executives Reese had been looking for, but they did achieve a certain "acceptance by our customers." They were thirty miniskirted stormtroopers in eye-catching, if skimpy, battle garb of gold, blue and white. They traveled in gold station wagons with the kit men, to every store and restaurant and service station that agreed to sign up for the new credit card. Just like the models on television's *The Price Is Right*, NCNB's BankAmericard Girls struck fetching poses for photos with the store owners—giving readers of the small-town press something to gossip about. They set up point-of-purchase displays, applied decals to front doors, and demonstrated just how easy it was to use the BankAmericard imprinting machine.

A far cry from Bill Vandiver's image of old men in black suits, the BankAmericard Girls were more like go-go dancers, those carefor-saking denizens of discotheques that symbolized the stop-at-nothing spirit of the late sixties. If you had money, or credit, you could afford to dance. The evening news reports of war between the Arabs and Israelis, of China exploding a hydrogen bomb, of race riots in Detroit, were just a barely audible pedal-point to the real music. Anybody could hear it: computer tapes whirring, credit card imprint-ers swiping, cash registers *ka-chinging*, construction crews hammer-ing. Business everywhere, especially in the Southeast, especially in North Carolina, was damned good. The BankAmericard Girls were NCNB's chorus line, kicking into the era that would always be known as *go-go banking*.

In September of 1967, a huge roar went up from the mezzanine at South Tryon and Fourth Streets. The cheer cascaded through NCNB headquarters, traveled over telephone wires to Greensboro and to the bank's offices in all parts of North Carolina: NCNB had at last accu-mulated assets in excess of a *billion* dollars. One billion. The "B word." The number would have been inconceivable to Word Wood and Torrence Hemby in 1951 when they first got the notion to expand through mergers and go after The Wachovia. Sixteen years later, NCNB might be still looking at Wachovia's tailpipe, but it was close enough to count the flakes of rust.

September 30, there was cause for celebration at the house in Beverly Woods. The McColls' third child, a daughter, was born. Following the Southern tradition to which both families adhered, she was named after her mother, Jane. Her parents figured it was time to start look-ing for a bigger house, maybe in a more prestigious neighborhood. After all, the family was growing, the company was growing and Hugh's prospects were fair.

"My talents are limited to business and finance, but in those areas I have no modesty and feel that I am competent."

Hugh McColl
Letter to his Aunt Marjorie, January 24, 1972

CHAPTER 6

Yearning for the Carolinas' embrace, Addison Reese embraced Carolina's art. He brought in a full-time art coordinator, Sarah Toy, who organized a series of regional art competitions in NCNB branch cities. At the South Tryon Street headquarters in Charlotte, Toy tattooed the walls with works by Carolina artists. Her *pièce de résistance* was the lofted main lobby, where brobdingnagian figures of business and industry, surmounted by a wingspread eagle, had loomed over tellers and customers since 1961. Those solid, stolid representations were yesterday's perception of banking. To replace them, the bank commissioned Richard Lippold's *Homage to North Carolina*, a "modern" sculpture of gold and silver wires, suggesting that tomorrow's banking would be an art in its own right, a light, complex, airy construction of many strings and many angles. Its design would be glittery and formless, defined in the eye of the beholder. The NCNB publicity department crowed so long and loud over the bank's commitment to beauty that *Esquire* magazine could not resist selecting NCNB to receive its Business in the Arts award. But then, banks all around the country were changing and the world was taking notice.

In July 1968, First National Citibank of New York, bellwether of the industry, at last played the card it had been contemplating for more than a year. Citibank would now operate as the subsidiary of a holding company, Citicorp. By the end of the year more than fifty banks would follow Citi's lead, selling themselves to their own holding companies. This allowed the country's most aggressive bankers to pursue nonbank activities, such as real estate investment and insurance, activities that could bring unprecedented amounts of cash into the banks. The holding company (managed by the same people who ran the bank) could control the operations and revenue streams of finance companies, insurance agencies and investment firms, directing all the positive cash flow into that other company, the bank.

This new-order financial octopus became known as a one-bank holding company, because it controlled many entities, only one of which was an actual bank. The structure effectively negated the laws that agencies of the federal government had been writing since the Depression aimed at keeping bankers *out* of nonbank activities.

An *American Banker* article declared that the one-bank holding company would allow "virtually unlimited" expansion by banks into other businesses, including even manufacturing. *Business Week* suggested the holding company would change the image of commercial banks from "the Step'n Fetchits of the business world" into that of a "strangely exciting . . . free-wheeling conglomerate." The *New Yorker* declared there were many who believed the day of the Citibank announcement would go down as "the most important day in American banking history."

The New York media missed the fact that Citibank's place in history should be shared with a bank located in the hinterlands of the Southeast. On July 5, 1968, almost simultaneously with the creation of Citicorp, a new North Carolina company, NCNB Corporation, filed articles with the Secretary of State in Raleigh. Addison Reese was listed as chairman of the board of this new company and, in a reversal of their roles with the bank, Julian Clark was named vice chairman, Tom Storrs president. Encouraged by the bank's Executive Committee, Storrs had been studying the holding company option ever since the credit crunch hit in August 1966, making it painfully apparent that a small regional bank's access to customers and money was too restricted, and that Regulation Q was effectively keeping regional banks from competing with the money center banks for national business.

A holding company was not a bank, so it should not be constrained by the laws of banking. For one thing, a holding company could begin to build a base of customers outside the borders of North

Carolina. It could engage in any number of pursuits designed to bring in money—insurance, aggressively marketed mortgage lending, high-risk consumer lending. As long as it sold those services outside the bank, it could sell them almost anywhere.

Just as importantly, the holding company could have a board of directors quite distinct from the board that ran the bank. For NCNB Corp., Reese structured a board that would be less restrictive to his vision and less hostile to his chosen successor, Tom Storrs. With such a board in place, he could turn over operations of the holding company to Storrs, make it his baby. Word at the bank had it that Reese used the new entity to convince Storrs it was time to move to the headquarters city.

"You move to Charlotte and I'll name you president," Reese said.

Storrs shot back, "You name me president and I'll move to Charlotte."

That was how the story went. In any event, the swap was made and Tom Storrs headed down the highway to head up a one-bank holding company with as yet but one holding, North Carolina National Bank.

As with its BankAmericard franchise, NCNB was out in front of a trend. Despite whatever dissension might remain among his directors, Addison Reese was developing a reputation for pushing through the ideas that he felt were important. Director Tom Belk saw this as a critical moment in the development of the company. "Addison pretty well mapped out a program. If there hadn't been somebody like Addison Reese heading that bank, it's no telling what would have happened."

Citibank's highly publicized entry into the holding company game generated a nationwide debate over what a bank was permitted to be. Bankers and legislators worried that banks would use their subsidiary companies as bait to attract customers, who then would be given preferential treatment when funds were tight. Media analysts warned that bankers would become indistinguishable from stockbrokers and insurance salesmen, spinning the nation's economy into a no-holds-barred era like that of the twenties, perhaps crashing America into another Great Depression.

Quickly, the big money center banks became the target of Washington. House Banking Committee Chairman Wright Patman roared that a holding company was simply a ruse to benefit big eastern bankers, just one step away from what he called "a cartel-ized economy." Patman failed in his efforts at legislation to prohibit one-bank holding companies, but by the end of 1969 Congress declared that bank holding companies and their subsidiaries could engage only in those activities that the Federal Reserve Board determined to be "so closely related to banking . . . as to be a proper incident thereto." In other words, a bank's holding company could only buy and sell products and services approved by the Fed. For the moment, at least, that meant bankers would be allowed to plead their cause on a case-by-case basis.

Away from the bright lights and big cities, Charlotte's upstart bankers moved to expand their holdings. Reese assured the bank's shareholders that, while "much remains to be decided by the Board and the courts before we will know the precise limits," he believed the holding company law would be given "reasonable interpretation." Unrestricted by directors whose ideas differed from his own, unrestricted by federal and state banking laws, Reese was a lion freed into the sunlight after long years of viewing it through the bars of a cage.

In his annual report, Reese wrote, "We are convinced that the decision in 1968 to form a one-bank holding company was sound. We adopted this organizational structure for two principal reasons— to meet the changing needs of the marketplace, where individual and corporate customers increasingly seek one-stop financial services and to create a better-balanced corporation which would minimize the effects of cyclical fluctuations characteristic of the banking business."

The Corporation started by buying a Charlotte insurance company, American Commercial Agency, which had been born years earlier as a subsidiary of American Commercial Bank. Next the Corporation formed NCNB Properties, a real estate management firm, which purchased much of the property owned by the bank, thus taking liabilities off the bank's books and injecting $12 million cash into the bank's coffers. The Corporation then created NCNB Mortgage Corp., which bought the bank's entire portfolio of mortgage loans, and acquired a high-risk lender headquartered in Rocky Mount, North Carolina, Continental Acceptance Corporation.

More innovative was the Corporation's move into the still-calm waters of real estate investment trusts, or REITs. NCNB Corp. joined with First & Merchants Corporation of Richmond and First National Holding Corporation of Atlanta to sponsor the formation of Tri-South Mortgage Investors. Shares of the trust amounting to $275 million were sold on November 20, 1969, and by year's end the Tri-South REIT was a going operation. Exempt from federal corporation taxes, the REIT could invest its shareholders' money in income-producing property such as shopping centers and apartment buildings, from Virginia down through Georgia and into Florida.

The bank had a number of clients in the textile and apparel industries, the largest manufacturing group in the Carolinas. However, Wachovia Bank's conservative presence dominated textiles and NCNB-the-bank could only chip away at this important customer base. But NCNB-the-holding-company could get in by a different door, buying a successful factoring company, Factors, Inc., of High Point, with assets of more than $6 million and an annual volume of about $50 million.

Factoring is a common method, albeit a rather expensive one, of doing business in undercapitalized industries like garment and textile manufacturing, where the manufacturer has to buy materials and pay his workers as soon as he takes an order, but cannot collect from his buyers until the finished goods are delivered. To tide themselves over from order placement to goods delivery, many manufacturers sell their accounts receivable to a factor for cash. The factor accepts all risk, delay and collection responsibilities—for which the manufacturers pay dearly. The factor usually manages a large portfolio of receivables for each of its clients, so the factor must be able to judge the creditworthiness of the ultimate buyers as well as the capabilities and stability of the manufacturer.

From the manufacturer's perspective, the factor's depth and breadth of financial resources become critical elements in production planning. Consequently, having one's operations underwritten by the state's second-largest bank might seem like an excellent idea. To make sure everyone knew who stood behind whom, Storrs changed the name of the High Point factoring company to NCNB Financial Services.

To finance these business purchases and start-ups NCNB Corporation sold $40 million worth of NCNB Corporation debentures on the New York market. These were unsecured promises to pay, backed only by the general credit of the issuer, which was not the bank, but the holding company. The debentures would be payable in 1995, with a coupon rate of 8.40 percent. It was another bold step. NCNB became the first one-bank holding company in the United States to issue debentures as a means of financing its affiliate activities.

In early 1970 McColl and Hodges were not invited, though Bill Dougherty was, to travel with Reese and Storrs to New York, San Francisco and six other cities to present the case for their holding company and NCNB stock to securities analysts. Flying on a borrowed DC-3 they barnstormed the big markets, telling them about North Carolina, Charlotte, and the Southeast's fastest-growing bank. Reese regaled the analysts with "a story of the future, not a story of the past." He told them about a bank driven by youthful management, where "brains, education and training" were more important than experience. He told them that among executive and senior vice presidents, the average age was forty-seven. "Profit center managers" averaged just forty-three. Reese showed them how the bank used Dougherty's computer-based tools to measure, predict and analyze, allowing his bank to make decisions "based on hard and timely facts." The analysts were impressed. Before the DC-3 made it back to Charlotte, NCNB stock had jumped six points.

Dougherty had responsibility for all the nonbank subsidiaries as well as the operations of the "back side" of the bank. Hodges and McColl controlled the "front end" of the bank, anything having to do with customers, sales and marketing. Growing the holding company and its variegated affiliates was not really McColl's job, but when Storrs looked at potential targets for high-risk consumer lending, the company with the most appeal turned out to be one of McColl's clients, Stephenson Finance in Florence, South Carolina. Storrs assigned McColl to the case.

McColl's efforts at convincing Phil Stephenson to sell his profitable company turned into an awkward moment, due to an unrelated sequence of events in New York, Detroit and Washington. These events were a signal that the era of the Great Society was over; Richard Nixon was in the White House and Americans were learning to be suspicious.

One of the first dominos to fall was Penn Central Railroad. It went bankrupt, leaving investors holding $83 million in unsecured commercial paper. The next domino in line was the Chrysler Corporation, which needed to roll over its commercial paper in order to stay in business. If Penn Central-spooked investors insisted on cashing in their notes, Chrysler would go the way of the railroad. Frantically, the Federal Reserve began calling every bank in the country that held any Chrysler paper, arranging a deal to roll over the notes in exchange for the Fed's easing up its interest-rate restrictions on certificates of deposit. One of those banks was NCNB. Meanwhile bank stocks, including NCNB's, began sliding as investors lost confidence in anything that smelled like risk.

From Florence, McColl called Charlotte to report progress on the Stephenson negotiations. Phil Stephenson was about ready to sign an agreement to swap shares of his company for those of the bank. "Our stock is dropping out of bed," McColl heard the voice on the phone say. "You'll never get him to go through with it."

McColl hung up the phone and went back into Stephenson's office, where he launched into nonstop monologue. He had to keep the man occupied, keep him a prisoner in his own office until he signed. If he left the room, he might contact someone to see how financial stocks were trading. The tactic worked. McColl bought Stephenson, then stepped back as Storrs folded in Continental Acceptance and created a company called TranSouth Financial Corporation, a consumer lender with nearly nine hundred branches in the Carolinas, Georgia and Tennessee.

The holding company strategy allowed sales and office staffing of affiliate companies to be conducted in many far-flung locations, while all matters of policy remained under tight control of the bank in its Charlotte office. This provided a significant advantage for Luther Hodges. As Charlotte city executive, Hodges took the opportunity to strengthen the bank's local social and political connections, along with his own. That was an ace only Hodges could play in the three-man contest for Top Turk.

For his part, McColl made absolutely no effort to form social and political ties in Charlotte; his only focus was on growing the bank, on taking over the number-one spot from Wachovia. He even made it a policy among his team that such extracurricular activities as charity drives and community involvement were to be discouraged. He considered them diversions.

At Jane's continuing insistence, Hugh agreed to move to a house large enough to accommodate their three children. They found a place on Colville Road, less than two blocks from the homes of Addison Reese and Tom Storrs. This was the socially prominent neighborhood of Eastover, where homes cost a great deal more than they did in Beverly Woods. Even as senior vice president of the National Division, McColl could not come up with the eighteen thousand dollars they needed for a down payment. His annual salary was only twenty thousand dollars. Once again, McColl knew he could not get help from his father, a man who drove a car without a radio because a radio was not necessary to transport him from point A to point B. Hugh Senior expected his sons to live in houses they could afford.

Jane's father was more generous. Hugh deposited John Spratt's check for eighteen thousand dollars in his personal NCNB account on a Monday morning in June. Over his lunch hour he shook hands with the real estate agent and handed over the largest check he had ever written on that account. As a banker schooled in the vagaries of check floating, McColl should have anticipated that the Spratt deposit would not yet have cleared. Since his account contained only $942.35, Hugh McColl's check bounced.

Even more embarrassing was the memo he received two weeks later from NCNB's Checking Account Services. In accordance with Reese's Administrative Bulletin No. 100-5-63, employees' checks were not permitted to bounce. "The below listed employees," began the memo, had checks presented against their accounts "which were returned for reason: Insufficient Funds. . . . We should appreciate your counseling with them and explaining to them the seriousness of this act." Employee Hugh L. McColl Jr., the only name listed, was admonished.

But nobody told McColl to stop writing checks to buy banks. Small-town banks, big-town banks, they were for sale from the ocean to the mountains, and NCNB was ready to move into any North Carolina neighborhood it could find.

All around the state, bankers who had been thirty-something executives during the Depression were getting ready to leave the institutions they had jealously guarded for the past three decades. They had one final opportunity to make money for themselves, their heirs apparent and their stockholders, and that opportunity was to sell out to one of the bigger banks—Wachovia, NCNB or First Union. Most of these small-town bankers were conservative old men who were owners, managers and members of their own board. Sometimes they were CEOs, other times dominant shareholders. Either way, the "exit strategy" was theirs to formulate, since in most cases theirs was the only opinion that really counted in their bank.

This new world of banking was not their world. They were uncomfortable with CDs and credit cards, nervous about the dilution of Regulation Q, worried about money flowing to the highest rate and therefore straight out of their towns and their vaults. They didn't trust the economy, so they couldn't be sure which loans would be good and which would turn sour. They couldn't stop their customers from watching television, beamed in from the larger cities, where commercials for Wachovia, NCNB and First Union hit them every night right along with the weather and the baseball scores.

Many of these aging bankers knew and respected young Hugh McColl from their relationships as NCNB correspondents. Now they found themselves invited to NCNB parties, entertained at NCNB convention suites, called on by McColl, Luther Hodges and other high-level executives at NCNB. They enjoyed being courted. Over a period of weeks and months, they would come to an understanding that the old small-town banker, washed in the blood of experience, was in the process of moving on to a better place, the Elysian Fields of finance, with halo, harp, wings and bonus supplied by his good friend, Hugh McColl.

Hugh learned he could not bluff his way through a deal like this. He had to demonstrate a respect for the experience he was buying, for the roots that went deep into local soil. He had to see his father in every banker he dealt with, had to appreciate that no matter how tight the old white knuckles might squeeze, there was a great deal more at stake than money.

Sometimes alone, sometimes with Luther Hodges, sometimes with Louis Henderson or Corporate Planning Officer Joe Holzinger, McColl worked North Carolina the way he'd worked South Carolina in years past. Only this time instead of looking for customers, he was looking for prey. He hunted down banks in small communities like Farmville and Woodland. In the textile town of Henderson, he and Luther Hodges convinced Marshall Cooper, the head of the family that owned the town as well as the bank, that a merger with NCNB would be as good for the people of Henderson as it would be for Cooper himself. McColl bought the $4 million Marion Bank & Trust Company and the $15 million Industrial Bank of Fayetteville. On their way to the northeastern part of the state, to deal for the Bank of Washington, McColl and Hodges considered the strategy they were developing for buying banks.

"I guess, what you learn is like any other sale," shouted McColl. They could barely hear one another in the cabin of NCNB's single corporate airplane, a Cessna 421. "I mean, its simplest form is that you 'catch more flies with honey than you do with vinegar.'"

Hodges agreed. "You have to be accommodating in your conver-sations. You have to keep your body language nonthreatening."

"Yeah. Low-key."

"And you've got to recognize the pride that other people have in their institutions."

"That's hard for me to do," McColl admitted. "I know it's true, I know all of that, but I don't always act it out."

"If you can't do that, you can't make the sale," said Hodges.

When the target bank was big game, Storrs and even Reese might join the hunt. For the $20 million State Bank & Trust Company of Greenville, Tom Storrs led the safari, the first time he and McColl had hunted together. To seal the deal with the bank's board, Storrs agreed to leave the old bank's name on its buildings, adding a second line of fine print reading, "Office of North Carolina National Bank." McColl chafed at the concession, but Storrs overruled him.

Most times, Storrs would tell McColl where the game had been spotted and send him out to bag it. More often than not, the key to a purchase was a single, highly visible individual. In the furniture man-ufacturing triad of Greensboro-High Point-Thomasville, one of the most prominent businessmen was George Hundley. As a long-time member of the state highway commission, Hundley had amassed great quantities of power and capital. He was also the majority stock-holder of High Point's State Commercial Bank. Storrs called McColl into his office with Julian Clark, and the two instructed him to see if State Commercial could be bought.

"Watch out for this fellow Hundley," Clark warned. "He's very smart, very shrewd and very aggressive."

"Right," said Storrs. "But see if you can get something going with him."

As Storrs had learned in their first encounter, he could count on McColl to be a good soldier. Give McColl an order and it was as good as done. Immediately, McColl had Hundley on the telephone, mak-ing an appointment for the following day.

In one meeting McColl negotiated the deal. The men put it in writing, shook hands, and McColl drove back to Charlotte to report the good news to Storrs, feeling on top of the world. No matter how shrewd, aggressive or smart they might be, they couldn't resist the persuasive powers of Hugh McColl. He'd bought another bank.

The air hissed out of the balloon the next morning when he was summoned into Addison Reese's office, a thing that almost never happened. McColl knew "there was a big problem. You don't get sent for by Mr. Reese. This was like the Pope sending for you, only stronger, more important."

McColl's body stiffened as he felt the tension in the room. The chairs in front of the chairman's desk were occupied by an uncharacteristically stern Julian Clark and a somewhat puzzled Tom Storrs. McColl took a seat on a small sofa to one side. Reese looked over his glasses as his senior vice president shrank into the upholstery.

"What's this I understand about the State Commercial Bank?"

McColl sat up straight and proud. Reese knew about his big deal. They had gathered to praise him, not to bury him. "We've got an agreement to merge them, sir. I got it yesterday."

Reese's voice lowered. "On whose authority?"

The question plunged McColl into the darkest confusion. His mind recognized instantly what had happened. Clark and Storrs dreamed up the Hundley approach without consulting Reese, who must have been negotiating a deal with one of Hundley's competitors in Davidson County. Now what should he do? Rat on Mr. Storrs and Mr. Clark? Weasel out? Play the scapegoat? In the few seconds he could take to answer, none of his metaphoric solutions seemed right. Blessedly Storrs and Clark raised their voices like an angelic chorus: "Addison, we sent Hugh to Thomasville."

Reese looked across his desk. "Well you don't have that authority," he said.

Not waiting for a response, he turned to McColl. "You can just go back up there and undo what you've done. That's it."

"Yes, sir." And Hugh McColl was out of there.

Reese indeed had been stalking with another Davidson County prey, the Lexington State Bank. He'd simply neglected to tell anybody about it, which was the boss's prerogative. Now the problem was McColl's to solve.

On the drive up to Thomasville, McColl came up with a plan. He would suggest that the Federal Trade Commission was snooping around NCNB, questioning its runaway expansion activities. The FTC had nothing to say about bank mergers, but maybe George Hundley would miss that point.

After an hour of nonstop arm-twisting, McColl convinced Hundley that the risk of "confronting the FTC" simply wasn't worth it. Hundley might announce the merger only to see it fall apart. McColl didn't want Hundley to lose face, lose the respect of his board, lose customers. "Hell, Mr. Hundley, you could wind up losing a lot of *money*." Finally, the deal was off.

After two days, McColl had heard nothing more about the banks in Davidson County. Suddenly, Reese's secretary, Pat Hinson, summoned him to the inner sanctum again. This time only Reese was there, so McColl remained standing at attention.

"We are ready to move forward with the merger," said Reese.

"Sir? The merger in . . . ?"

"Thomasville."

"Mr. Reese, I did what you told me to. We terminated our contract."

Reese nodded. "Well, go reinstate it."

"Yes, sir."

Back in Thomasville, McColl delivered the good news that, after all, the FTC had decided not to meddle in NCNB's Davidson County expansion plans. Smelling opportunity, Hundley tried to raise the price. McColl stood his ground. His bank was not interested in paying any more than had been negotiated. He got the bank for the second time at the price he had agreed to pay the first time.

Luther Hodges knew George Hundley's reputation as a horse trader and he was impressed. McColl had pulled off another coup. To celebrate, Hodges and a few of their buddies took Hugh out to dinner that night at the City Club.

In 1970 Charlotte's entry into the American mainstream was still impeded by blue laws, invented by the Puritans of New England to keep their moral spine stiff. Charlotte stores did not open on Sundays and Charlotte restaurants could not serve alcoholic drinks. Consequently, the town was liberally spiked with "private clubs" of widely varying repute. The City Club, located in an uptown office building, was one of the more sober spots, its membership roll a testimony to the good taste of Charlotte's business elite. The City Club was a quiet, discreet place, done in rich woods, antiques and leather. It also had an excellent selection of single-malt scotch whiskeys, and therein lay its principal attraction to Hugh McColl.

The night McColl celebrated his double victory of the merger deal in Thomasville, Chuck Cooley, NCNB's newly hired number-two man in personnel, was at a corner table in the City Club. It was his farewell dinner with Bob Butts, his boss at the Celanese Corporation until recently. Cooley was delighted at the unfettered camaraderie displayed by his new teammates. They were loud, playing by their own rules. He was going to enjoy working with them. It would be fun. Noticing his friend Butts stop in mid-sip of his French onion soup as McColl let out a steel-edged laugh, Cooley gestured in McColl's direction. "There's the man who is going to really take this company somewhere," he said.

Butts emptied his soup spoon. Cooley had worked for him for more than ten years and they had spent long hours hashing over the qualities of leadership. What was Chuck thinking of? "He just sounds like any other smart-ass to me."

"He may sound that way," Cooley insisted. "But this guy is special."

"Yeah? You'd never know it to listen to him."

A few weeks later, McColl received a visitor from Thomasville, not the wily Hundley but his wife. Mrs. Hundley was accompanied by her attorney, who expressed his outrage at the way McColl had "taken advantage" of her poor, unsuspecting husband. Gentle, parochial George had been bamboozled by the sharp, slick-talking banker from the big city. McColl leaned back in his chair. At first he wanted to throw them out, but then he saw the humor in the situation. Hundley's deal-making savvy was legendary in North Carolina.

"Ma'am, I'll tell you what," he said. "If you'll put on the front page of the *Charlotte Observer* and the *Greensboro Daily News* that Hugh McColl has taken advantage of George Hundley, we'll be glad to pay you more money. I'll see to it you get it. You just come back with those newspaper headlines and we'll do business."

That was the last he heard from Mrs. Hundley.

While McColl was barnstorming the state for acquisitions, Bill Dougherty was tightening the screws on the bank's back-office operations. Dougherty's commitment was to "run this ship lean and mean," to turn it into "a very accountable place." His new system was supposed to make it possible for the executives in Charlotte to know just what was going on in the ever-multiplying branch offices across the state. For the first time control would be centralized and, in theory, the top executives would know almost instantly when and where trouble might be brewing. Using Dougherty's tools, a manager should be able to plan, for a quarter or even a year, and evaluate how well his people were performing against that plan. Thanks to Dougherty, Hugh McColl's "profit center" notion was implemented throughout the company. McColl was unimpressed. Dougherty's efforts seemed merely to confirm what he already knew: he and his people were making money.

McColl was unsettled by Bill Dougherty's meteoric rise in the company. While he respected what a CPA could do, McColl found Dougherty to be "only an accountant." He appeared unappreciative of the sweet intricacies of banking, like a man who could be happy filling in only the words that came easy on a crossword puzzle. Dougherty wasn't turned on by the almost sensual pleasures of deal-making. Worse, McColl never felt like he got a straight answer out of Dougherty. It was as though the Pittsburgh transplant might have something to hide, some kind of black magic on those big reels of computer tape. McColl knew that to the old-time bankers, the ones with green eyeshades and automatic pencils and fountain pens, the new high-tech accounting department was a sanctum sanctorum, Dougherty its dreaded high priest, demanding tribute from all, then auditing his own books and theirs in shrouded, whirring mystery.

To accommodate Dougherty's computers, accountants and data collections, Reese proposed and his board approved a $4 million commitment to a new Corporate Services Center building, three blocks southwest of the Charlotte headquarters, at the corner of College and Second Streets. Reese directed one of the city's top architectural firms, A. G. Odell Associates, to give him a computer building that would have "a good visual image, not extravagant, but one of permanence, character and conservatism, that would appeal to the average businessman."

Leadership in the growth-happy environment was clearly a concern. By the middle of 1969, it was apparent that Julian Clark's health was failing and that he would soon be out of the picture. In the fall Clark and his wife Mackey joined the first group of tenants at Sharon Towers, a new assisted living complex. A lifelong smoker, Clark was dying of lung cancer and would not be returning to the bank he'd helped to build.

Julian Clark was more than an executive at NCNB. He was, in Hugh McColl's eyes, "the glue that held us together." Clark simply knew everything there was to be known about credit policy, the check-and-balance system of the bank. In addition, he was in charge of investments—what would come to be called liability manage-ment—balance sheet and bond portfolio. McColl was one of many who "looked to Mr. Clark for guidance on what to do about a credit opportunity." Whenever a big credit decision had to be made, Julian Clark made it.

In an upper echelon that included the unapproachable Addison Reese and the unappreciated Tom Storrs, Julian Clark was easily "the most loved person in the company." When he left, McColl felt that "some of the heart and soul of the company changed. He was a link with the past. And he was a great teacher. He taught a lot of the people like me, and John Robison and others. Mr. Clark taught a lot of us how to be bankers."

Nobody felt the need for leadership as pressingly as Tom Storrs did. Storrs recognized that there was "a generation gap" at NCNB Corporation, the company he was poised to take over in just a few years. Instead of sixty-five-year-old retirees being replaced by men and women in their early fifties, relatively inexperienced young men in their thirties were being pushed into positions of greater and greater importance, to run a company that was growing, perhaps faster than even he appreciated.

To support its own expansion, the bank and the holding company needed growth on the revenue side, wherever it might come from. Storrs was being urged by Addison Reese and the board to trim back expenses wherever possible. Even the recruiting and training program, Reese's own creation, could be sacrificed to the bottom line. Storrs was deeply concerned that the company was about to "eat our seed corn." Recruiting and training were investments in the future, "not track maintenance on a railroad that could be varied from year to year."

Working with personnel director Joe O'Shields, Storrs came up with an alternative plan. Instead of cutting out the recruiting program, he proposed to turn his new recruits into personal profit centers. They would dump the time-honored "sheep-dip" training program and replace it with something entirely new.

"Look," Storrs said, "we are going to stop this thing of people sitting around and looking over other people's shoulders trying to learn the banking business. Instead we are going to take these people out of college, and we are going to put them to work and we are going to get production out of them the first day they are here. And what we'll do then is oversee their job assignment to make sure they're under supervision of people who are really going to teach them something while they are working. And we are going to use classroom instruction to supplement that."

For Storrs, the system was a jewel of logic, "a very critical decision." He hated the inefficient, time-wasteful, sheep-dip days. "We were paying college graduate salaries to get clerical work done. And so we said, we'll let clerks do that. And we'll use these young people right off the bat to do analytical work, rather than doing clerical work."

Critical to the plan's chances of acceptance was Storrs's final carrot: for each new recruit hired into a specific department, an existing employee in that department would be terminated. "We'll simply bring them in and they will displace the least productive people we have at the bank," he explained.

Reese immediately recognized the simple beauty of the Storrs-O'Shields plan. "So we'll be getting rid of an expense item and we'll also be getting people into production. That suits me fine."

It became personnel director O'Shields's duty to approach each manager and say, "We've got three people we are going to put in your organization. They'll be here in June." When the manager protested that his department had no vacancies, O'Shields would inform him that he would need to "identify the three people you can do without. And we'll let them go and we'll put these people in place of them."

The new second-line executive in the Personnel Department, Chuck Cooley, worried that Joe O'Shields was taking far too much pleasure in the new ritual of replacement. O'Shields had "a personality flaw that caused him a lot of problems in his relationship with people. Mr. Reese was using him as a hatchet man . . . and his personality flaw was that he appeared to like it."

For Cooley, the critical piece of the new program was the classroom training. To help set up the curriculum, Cooley consulted the man he saw as the company's most energetic driving force, Hugh McColl, a man who agreed with Storrs on abolishing the sheep-dip method.

Active for some time in the recruiting side, McColl now expanded his interests into the training of those new hires. He took every opportunity to beard them in their classroom—a captive audience that would be influenced enormously by his energetic style. Cooley watched him mold his new players "in terms of values and the culture and things that are important. He spent more time there than he spent with the other VPs."

The unofficial "sheep dip" designation disappeared, although the training process retained its official name, the Promotion Qualification Program. Trainees were officially "PQs," but more commonly referred to as "moles," since their credit analysis training area was in the windowless bowels of the NCNB building. One of the first moles was a graduate of Shaw University in Raleigh, Ed Dolby. After two years in the Peace Corps and a brief stint at Prudential Insurance, Dolby thought he might find his niche in a company where they talked about succeeding on the basis of merit, where a person could learn the rules of the game and compete to get ahead. Dolby found himself in a basement, spreading and analyzing the financial statements of companies applying for NCNB loans. His reviewer was Ken Lewis, but there was another fellow, a shorter man, who was always looking over the moles' shoulders.

"Hugh McColl," he introduced himself, sticking out a hand. "You're Ed Dolby, right?"

"Right."

"See that spread you're working, can I?"

Dolby pushed aside his goldenrod legal pad and pencil and moved his calculator aside to give McColl a better look. "Just a little company I'm working on." He pronounced it "own," confirming McColl's suspicion that Dolby had grown up around Raleigh.

"Never heard of it. Damn, it's a little bitty ol' company, ain't it?"

Dolby laughed. "Pretty small."

"But you know what, Ed, you start looking *into* these numbers instead of just *at* that and you'll start connectin' some dots. Could be this little company might get big."

Dolby listened rapt as a mathematician contemplating Bach for the first time. McColl talked to him about what he called the "character" of a balance sheet, told him what to look for, what the *practical* applications of the numbers would be. He pointed to the line item labeled inventory and explained that this had to be thought of as something tangible, something real, a collection of goods or products that would turn over and appreciate and depreciate. Take a look at that line over a stretch of time, McColl instructed, and watch how it shrinks and grows and see what effect it has on other lines. Understand how that inventory is *managed*, how that management might be improved.

Ed Dolby looked at the spreadsheet and saw it for the first time. It was a kind of history book, a story of someone's dream. And the dream was one that he could influence by what he said to the loan officer who would have to sell the dream to a loan committee. He would never again be able to say simply, *here are the numbers, this is the acceptable risk.* Hugh McColl had made the numbers real. Moreover, he showed Dolby how to look for clues as to what kind of people were in charge of the little company.

"Ain't the company gonna pay us back the money, Ed. It's the people. Remembuh that. Tell Ken Lewis I said he should kick the tires on this one after you write it up, okay? See you latuh."

Dolby came to value the moments he spent in the company of Hugh McColl. During their conversations he could almost be unconscious of the fact that Ed Dolby was black and Hugh McColl was white.

A few weeks into the PQ program, McColl drew Dolby aside at a cocktail party, a quarterly event hosted for new recruits and their spouses in the bank's twelfth-floor auditorium. He told Dolby he and others had been "kind of assessing" him, and he wanted to assure him that "everybody thinks you are doing okay." The one thing McColl wanted him to understand was that at NCNB "we realize talent comes from everywhere. You may have gone to a small school, compared to a North Carolina or a Duke. But talent is talent and we think you have that. And as long as you are prepared and you stay prepared, then it really doesn't matter what color your skin is. And you just ought to know that."

Instantly, Ed Dolby felt more relaxed in his new company.

As the cocktail party drew to a close, McColl surprised the trainees by telling them to leave the auditorium, to wait in an anteroom while he had a word with their wives and the few husbands who were there. Driving home, Dolby's wife Dee told him what had gone on. She said McColl was "the most energetic man I have ever met." He was candid, frank. Dee could tell McColl really liked what he was doing, that he loved his company.

His reason for talking to the spouses was to make them feel like members of the NCNB team as well. He knew how much he depended on Jane to succeed. These other men and women were going to demand the same kind of support from their wives and husbands. There would be some late hours, he warned them, even a few drinks after work to celebrate victories. There may be times when couples would be separated, because NCNB's business wasn't all in North Carolina anymore.

Dee Dolby gripped her husband's hand across the front seat of the car. "I think we're going to be happy with this company," she said, "as soon as you graduate from mole school."

McColl's effectiveness with the trainees was not lost on Chuck Cooley. He recognized that McColl was using his influence and persuasiveness at every level of the bank to establish the kind of training the new recruits would receive, who would train them and how their success would be measured. From this point forward, Cooley believed, it would be very difficult for anyone to come into this company and succeed without following the Hugh McColl Way. Even the curriculum was designed by McColl, drawn from McColl's experiences and limited by McColl's biases.

Cooley saw that McColl wanted to develop a new breed, young bankers who would appreciate the value of getting to know the customer, who would be ready to "talk with the people, about opportunities they might have to restructure their balance sheet. Or to understand why they aren't more profitable, offer financial solutions to that. He wanted us to teach people to do 'gap analysis'—where is the gap between what we provide and what this person already has?"

McColl and his designated tutors might not be able to do anything about a new employee's instincts or personality traits, and only experience would make them effective bankers, but intelligent young people could learn the value of preparation. "Don't go before a customer until you really do understand their business and our business." That was a lesson repeated over and over in the PQ classroom.

"The difference between the world you have just entered and the world of business school case studies," McColl told the new recruits, "is that here *the case fights back.*"

Based on his own classroom career, McColl's assumption that he could teach anything was high chutzpah. He had sputtered through college unconcerned about impressing his teachers, permitting himself to believe that only those who could not practice a profession would spend their lives trying to teach it. He'd been a sheep all right, not just in the bank's training program, but from the first day he set foot on the campus of the University of North Carolina, following wherever his father led.

"Dean, you can go ahead and sign the boy up for banking and finance."

"Very good, Mr. McColl. You know, we only have about five other freshmen who want to be bankers, so I know some professors who'll be mighty glad to see you, Hugh. Now, where do you think you'd like to live on campus?"

"He wants to live in Ruffin Dorm, same place I did. You know, maybe he can get my old room, 307."

He never said a damn thing, just got in the car and drove home. A month later he was living in Ruffin Dorm and majoring in banking and finance. Later his father would lead Hugh's brothers down the very same path. Kenneth and Jimmy, both banking and finance majors, both residents of Ruffin their first year, until each one pledged their big brother's fraternity, Beta Theta Pi, and moved into the fraternity house. Hugh had tried to get into a dozen fraternities, most of which had blackballed him. During his last two years, Hugh shared his room at the Beta house with Ken. And when Hugh graduated, Jimmy took Hugh's place in the same room.

Even in college I had no ambition. My father worried I would not amount to much. I assumed I would finish college then go home and run the family business. I was mostly just a gym rat. I lettered in lacrosse. I played a lot of poker and gin rummy. What the hell was I doing still going to school?

Hugh's letters home, scribbled and misspelled, on loose-leaf, postcards and stiff fraternity stationery, told part of the story.

Dear Mother,

I am really snowed under with work. I study three hours every night and a lot during the day . . .

P.S. I made a C+ on my first English paper. Pretty good for me. I have blisters all over my feet from playing basketball.

Dear Mother,

School is really hard. I am studying very hard and still can't make above a C in English and Spanish. I know I can pass, but it is going to be a grind. I am going to have the cleaners send the bill to Daddy if it is all right with you.

Dear Daddy,

I noticed where cotton prices on futures had dropped some last week. I hope that doesn't affect us to much. Maybe you will be able to make a cotton man out of me someday. The experience of keeping the farm books sure helped a lot in accounting and I am sure that the accounting course has helped me to be able to keep them better next time you need me.

Love,
Hugh

Hugh Leon McColl Jr. received his B.S. in business administration on June 3, 1957. He finished with five As, in physical education, math and accounting; six Ds, in Spanish, government, public finance and business cycles; six Bs and thirty-three Cs. He considered it a significant achievement that he made it through four years without failing a single course.

Outside the classroom, however, McColl's college years had convinced him that you could win at any game—poker, lacrosse or business—if you understood the people you were playing against and if you picked the right people to play with. In his newfound teaching role at the bank, if there was an ulterior motive, it was that the more he controlled the training process, the better he could identify the players he wanted on his personal team.

Benny Shaw watched his onetime assistant doing "a heck of a job in selecting people that surrounded him." No sooner did a class complete its training, Shaw observed, than McColl and his department heads would put in their assignment requests. "And Hugh would fight like the dickens to get people. Where Hugh would see somebody that impressed him—and he'd look at all of them—he would talk to those people about what he expected to do. And he would sell them on his department, and tell them to ask for his department. And you know, he could be quite persuasive. He got some good people."

One of those people, Bill Vandiver, recognized in McColl a man who could have a radical impact on his own career. During his service in Vietnam, Vandiver "saw good leaders and I saw bad leaders. And there were people you would follow into hell. You'd follow them into the furnace. You'd say, 'Why would I do it?' You come down to one thing—it's trust in that person."

When he joined the company, Chuck Cooley decided immediately that NCNB took its direction and energy from McColl. Addison Reese was chairman, Tom Storrs president, but "Hugh was the spiritual leader of the company, the one people rallied around."

Chuck Cooley was six months older than Hugh McColl, born in the little mining town of Nitro, West Virginia. He had spent his career to that point assessing people in terms of their competencies and skills, forecasting their ability to succeed. His passion was understanding people, figuring out what made them tick. If he had not found his way into personnel, he might have become a psychologist. What stood out more than anything else about Hugh McColl was that, like Cooley, he truly cared about people. And it was that trait that caused Cooley to take his troubles not to Tom Storrs but to Hugh McColl on the day he was ready to walk away from his new company.

The caring environment nurtured by McColl had led Cooley to deal with people rather than with "problems." This brought Cooley into conflict with personnel director Joe O'Shields, who saw his understudy as "getting out in front." O'Shields accused Cooley of what he called "unethical behavior" by going around him to deal with people directly. Tall, broad-shouldered and athletic, Cooley enjoyed a reputation as a reserved, comforting man. But with his honor challenged, he sprang to his feet and screamed at O'Shields, ordering him out of his office. Business on the mezzanine came to a halt and all eyes turned to the personnel area as O'Shields moved back to his office. Cooley grabbed his coat from its hook behind the door and prepared himself to confront Tom Storrs. *It's either him or me*, he would say. *This bank's not big enough for both of us.*

On second thought, he headed to Hugh McColl's office. McColl listened to his story, let Cooley vent his spleen, then asked him to be patient. He had Cooley marked for a tiger and didn't want to lose him. He called Luther Hodges in and asked Cooley to go over it all again. The more he aired the grievance, the less volatile it would be. McColl and Hodges had been instrumental in recruiting Cooley away from Celanese Corporation. They were intensely interested in the future of the Personnel Department because they recognized its potential for building a base of internal support.

"Chuck, just give us a little time," McColl said. "Let the hand play out, because things are going to change."

"I can be patient with it," Cooley decided, "if that's your game plan, to do something."

"Don't worry," McColl said, "it won't be long before we're all playing on the same team."

The assumption was that when Reese stepped down, McColl and Hodges—and perhaps Bill Dougherty—would rise up to the dais level vacated by Tom Storrs. Then McColl and Hodges could decide who ran the Personnel Department. They were about to learn that no bet was a sure one.

Despite his success in managing the board of his new holding company, Reese could not kill off the persistent dissension of the Greensboro contingent on the NCNB board. If a big wheel squeaked loudly enough, Reese had no choice but to grease it. When the board learned of Julian Clark's failing health, one of the most persistent anti-Storrs directors, Huger S. King, demanded the bank bring in someone near the top who was older and more experienced in credit than any of the next level of executives.

King was a prominent lawyer in Greensboro and had served two terms as the city's mayor. He was heir to the Richardson-Merrill Corporation and its fortune, founded on the famous liniment, Vicks' VapoRub. King's voice on the board was a persistent vote of no confidence in Tom Storrs. He felt, as another board member observed, "that Mr. Storrs just would not come to heel." Feeling compelled to give the board another option, Reese directed Joe O'Shields to conduct a high-level executive search for someone "more experienced" than Storrs. At the dawn of the 1970s there was no professional migration to the metropolis whose principal claim to fame was being "the largest city between Richmond and Atlanta." O'Shields found the man he and Huger King were looking for in Elliott "Pete" Taylor. Formerly the CEO of TransAmerica Financial Corporation in San Francisco, Taylor was unlike any executive the NCNB group had ever encountered.

West Coast Pete Taylor came to Charlotte with a style all his own. In his Gucci shoes and double-breasted Italian suits, Taylor breezed into the office that most everyone felt still belonged to Julian Clark, right next to Addison Reese on the mezzanine. He immediately boxed up Clark's belongings and outfitted the office to look like the California desert at sunset, with lavenders and earth tones and indirect lighting. "It looks like a *fornicatorium*," said Reese the first time he walked in.

Taylor joined the company just about as close as anyone could get to the top. His titles at the bank were executive vice president and vice chairman of the board. In addition, Reese gave him responsibility for all nonbank subsidiaries, which had been part of Storrs's domain.

Taylor's style of doing business was as flashy as his outfit. No decision could be made without going through a series of committee meetings, often over lunch. His contract called for a personal driver, the first and only one in the company. He brought with him a wife who seemed to have a doctorate in entertainment. Among the first guests at the Taylors' posh new home were Mr. and Mrs. Hugh McColl and Mr. and Mrs. Luther Hodges. Like Storrs and McColl, Taylor wanted to know which members of this NCNB team he could count on.

The conversation was light, the dinner heavy, accompanied by several expensive bottles of wine. The evening would be the subject of many subsequent tellings by Hugh McColl.

"At some point, the men—as men used to do—went our separate way from the wives, and Taylor took us for a walk in the garden. He said something like, 'If you boys play ball with me, you've got a great future.'

"Well, Luther and I probably had had a reasonable amount to drink, as we were wont to do, and I remember leaning across Taylor and saying to Luther, 'Is this son of a bitch talking to us?' Because you know, we thought we ran things. We were not people who thought we needed any help with anything.

"From then on, we were estranged. I didn't get along with him at all. I didn't think he knew anything. And it didn't take me long to figure that out. I think Mr. Storrs, truthfully, didn't like him much at all, although he never would have shown that to any of us."

Storrs's displeasure with Taylor, though unspoken, ran as deep as McColl's. He blamed himself, along with Reese, for bringing Taylor into the company "without doing adequate background research." Storrs came to view Taylor as "a man who did not have substantive knowledge of the job we were putting him in." Storrs did not really feel threatened as far as succession was concerned. His chief concern was that the company might suffer from entrusting any substantial part of its operations to the outsider.

"Taylor may have felt that he was coming in as Reese's successor. The director who sponsored him may have thought that there was a chance that he would. And it may be that some of the people in the organization thought there was a chance he would succeed. But I did not have the feeling that he had the ability to run this company."

McColl, on the other hand, could only look at Pete Taylor as an enemy, a spy from some other army in the NCNB camp. Otherwise his own code of behavior would have forced him to salute Taylor just as he saluted Reese, Storrs, Calhoun and Faison. Since he wore his corporate emotions like chevrons, McColl made no effort to hide his distrust and dislike of Taylor, not even in front of Addison Reese.

McColl and Reese had few moments alone, so they never would become close. The first time they made a customer call together was to Fort Mill, South Carolina, where they met with Bill Close, the CEO of Springs Mills. After a productive meeting, Reese—who, unlike Taylor, had no chauffeur—drove McColl back to Charlotte.

Reese seized the opportunity to heal the rift he saw developing in his company. After all his efforts to merge the banks of Charlotte and Greensboro, along with the dozens of other banks he'd brought into the fold, the old animosity was rising up to bite him again. He was determined to play out the Pete Taylor hand his divided board had dealt him. NCNB was too close to overtaking Wachovia to let any internal squabbles get in his way. He looked over at his passenger, the young man Jim Farr saw as the front-running successor to Tom Storrs. Even his own favorite, Luther Hodges, seemed to think a great deal of McColl. "Hugh," Reese said, "you don't get along very well with Pete, do you?"

McColl bit his tongue and answered simply, "No, sir."

"You know what I think, Hugh? I think you and Luther could learn a lot from Pete Taylor."

The acid frothed up in McColl's mouth before he could swallow it. "Yeah? And what would that be?"

No sooner had he uttered the words than McColl knew he had made a mistake. Honesty was one thing, disrespect another. He'd never sassed Addison Reese before. He found himself wanting to crawl under the seat. He wished Reese would stop the car and tell him to go cut a switch from a privet hedge the way his mother used to do when he swore, even take off his belt like his daddy did when he was really bad and double it up so it would make a loud pop when it slapped against a boy's bare legs. But Reese was not his father. Reese was a cool hard man who was frightening on his best days. He only narrowed his eyes and looked over the long black hood at the highway.

"To start with," he said, "Pete could teach you something about organizing."

The ride back to Charlotte was chilly and quiet. McColl was left to weigh Reese's perception of him as disorganized, at least as compared to the meticulous Pete Taylor. *Organization about nothing,* he thought. *Ask him if he's got a minute and the man pulls out an appointment book.*

It may be that Reese told Storrs of the drive back from Fort Mill, because McColl's stock seemed to rise even higher in Tom Storrs's appraisal. In the National Division, Storrs let it be known that Hugh McColl was the man in charge. McColl had no doubt that he "ran everything. Everybody looked to me for decisions. Everybody. Probably including my boss, Pat Calhoun."

Storrs, who never felt befriended by the people who worked for him, knew he could trust McColl, no matter how unlike their methods might be. It was, in fact, McColl's pugnacious, damn-the-torpedoes attitude that Storrs needed to "get the ball and move the ball forward down the field." As the fruits of the holding company acquisitions began to mature, the National Division loan portfolio doubled in just two years under McColl's direction to $580 million.

It was a period of intense education for McColl. He realized his loan-savvy reputation was based not only on his intuitions about people, but on the careful study of their businesses and their positions within that business. Nevertheless, he steadfastly refused to remove his blinders about any part of NCNB Corporation that did not have a direct bearing on his own bottom line. McColl considered himself to be "a driven, single-minded person, building up the earning power of the National Division. And I paid little or no heed to anything else. I had a great disdain for the Marketing Division and the consumer bank."

But because the bank held the purse strings of the nonbank companies, McColl was expected to serve as a resource for the factoring company, the real estate trust, the mortgage company. As the holdings expanded, his advice and acceptance were sought on transactions in areas about which he knew nothing—everything from sweater knitting to steel making. He had to gather a great deal of information in a hurry, studying as he'd never studied in college.

"I learned a terrific amount about the businesses we were lending to. I knew nothing except the basic farming business, the cotton business that I had grown up in. Now I had to learn about textiles, about hot metal. I learned about dozens and dozens of businesses that we didn't know anything about." He also learned the intricacies of the law, about perfection of collateral, how to take mortgages, how to get chattels and liens, and what the enforceability of those might be.

All this made him better at running his part of the company. The

National Division, rooted in correspondent banking, was recognized by every knowledgeable executive as the corporation's most reliable enterprise, the division with the longest history of steady growth. McColl felt that Storrs and Reese were looking to him and his team to supply the information and intuition when it came to buying other banks. "We were the bankers and my team were the caretakers of the relationships we had with these banks. We were the depository of information about them, including financial information. And so we got brought into some of the discussions about acquiring other kinds of companies."

The goal was still "Beat Wachovia," which they would achieve primarily through acquisitions within the state and through internal growth. And now there was a growing sense of urgency about reaching that goal. Addison Reese was due to retire at the end of 1973, and NCNB simply *had* to be the largest bank in North Carolina before Reese left. No memorandum was issued to that effect, but everyone got the message. Whatever the nonbank affiliates might be doing in other states, it was only the activity they generated in Bill Dougherty's Charlotte computers that counted. NCNB-the-bank had to have more dollars on deposit than any other bank in North Carolina. It was that simple for McColl. "Our horizons were limited to our state. And our goal was to beat Wachovia."

Reese's plans for expanding the bank, except for the correspondent business, always had stopped at the borders of North Carolina. Even though many of the bank's customers were involved in exporting textiles, tobacco and other Carolina-manufactured goods, Reese was not interested in stretching his bank's already thin management line any thinner by starting up an overseas operation. He was too close to overtaking Wachovia for such distractions.

Yet, to some degree, it was Wachovia's success in the international arena that kept it just a step ahead of Reese. Wachovia handled most of the business of R. J. Reynolds Tobacco. Most leaf tobacco growers in the eastern United States were longtime Wachovia customers. Because the overseas tobacco market was big and getting bigger, Wachovia had moved its international division from its central Winston-Salem headquarters to the port city of Wilmington, where it was doing a respectable business.

Bob Barker—whose work for Julian Clark on foreign exchange and letters of credit in the sixties made him the closest thing NCNB had to an international banking expert—believed it would be a mistake for them to copy Wachovia and try to build an international business out of a domestic port. The vast majority of overseas transactions happened either in New York or somewhere outside the United States, notably in the London financial market. Barker repeatedly urged Julian Clark to open up a branch overseas in order to provide additional financing services for some of their textile and tobacco customers. But he found that Clark "didn't think very much of lending to foreigners," so the idea went nowhere. Then in 1969, with Clark out of the picture and Barker reporting to McColl, one of the bank's major textile customers gave the international dream new life by throwing a scare into the National Division.

Pharr Yarns of McAdenville, just across the Catawba River from Charlotte, was beginning to realize unexpected profits from a factory it had set up in the Netherlands. That profit could grow substantially if Pharr could expand its Dutch mill's manufacturing capacity. To make that happen Pharr needed a loan. The company's executive vice president, J. M. "Bip" Carstarphen, was not pleased to learn that his North Carolina bank, NCNB, could not make that loan without charging the Netherlands subsidiary a substantially higher rate of interest than the rate it charged the parent company in McAdenville. McColl and his teammates realized they had to come up with a solution fast if they didn't want to lose Pharr's business to a New York bank or, even worse, to Wachovia.

The Pharr Yarns problem was rooted back at the end of World War II, when the Soviet Union began hoarding U.S. dollars at its own bank in Paris, then loaned those dollars to European traders at substantial interest rates. The Soviet strategy was not lost on other European bankers. During the 1950s European traders could bring their American dollars to the United States and exchange them for American gold at a guaranteed rate of thirty-five dollars an ounce. This led to a national fear that foreigners would spirit away America's wealth. To discourage the lending of dollars abroad—thereby protecting the United States' gold stockpile—President Kennedy imposed a so-called "interest equalization tax" in 1963, a tax on loans by American banks to foreigners.

Unwittingly, Kennedy created the "Eurodollar market," a trade in American dollars conducted outside the borders and outside the laws of the United States. Anyone who could accumulate U.S. currency overseas could lend out that money in Europe, where firms were eager to get their hands on dollars. Since the transaction was done outside the U.S., the interest rate could be higher than the going interest rate in the United States, yet still lower than the net after-tax rate a domestic U.S. lender would have to charge.

The expansion-happy sixties led thousands of American companies like Pharr to establish plants and offices abroad, uncorking a sudden spew of currency from the United States into Europe—the very opposite of what Kennedy had intended. The dollars were overseas to be bought and sold at a premium—provided you had an overseas office to handle the transactions. By 1969, this Eurodollar market had topped $15 billion which, as they say, was a lot of money in those days.

To keep Pharr Yarns' business, NCNB was forced to take a letter of credit to Big Brother Citibank which, like all the big money center banks, had an office in London. This got Bip Carstarphen the money he needed in the Netherlands, but no sooner had the transaction been posted than the Citibank national sales staff had its "first team" in the quaint company town of McAdenville to see if there was any more textile business to be taken away from NCNB. Barker reported to Hugh McColl that Citibank was trying to sell Pharr "every other service they had." NCNB couldn't "just sit back and give the business to New York." It was time, Bob Barker pleaded, to open up an overseas branch.

McColl was fascinated by the idea of turning his "National Division" into the "International Division." He knew that his domestic opportunities were drying up. Small North Carolina banks were getting harder to find, what with Wachovia, First Union and NCNB all frantically beating the Tarheel bushes. The correspondent banking business had about reached its peak; in South Carolina, McColl's old territory, ninety-nine out of the state's one hundred banks already did business with NCNB.

McColl saw in Barker "a smart man and a good man in terms of watching risks." Ultimately, McColl let himself be convinced that there was substantial money to be made in financing the movement of textile machinery and agricultural machinery to Latin America and Europe. These were things Wachovia could not do from Wilmington. McColl only worried about the expense of creating an office and a staff in London. At Reese's insistence, and with Dougherty's growing influence, Storrs was squeezing the budget for every nickel.

What Barker told McColl opened his eyes. They did not actually need an expensive office in London. They could dip their toes in the international waters much closer to home, in the Bahamas. And they didn't actually need an office or a staff down there. All they really needed was a Nassau telephone number, which could ring a telephone in Charlotte. McColl agreed to take the recommendation to Storrs.

Storrs gave the go-ahead, Barker did the research and McColl cut the deal. Essentially, it came down to paying a Bahamian attorney twenty-five thousand dollars to fill out a business charter form and take it down a hall to a magistrate, who seemed to be one of the lawyer's relatives. McColl learned from that experience the importance of having "the right lawyer." The first headquarters of NCNB International Division was a one-room booking office in an unimposing Nassau office building, opened in September 1969, a few weeks after the death of Julian Clark. The trading room, with its bank of telephones and money traders, was in uptown Charlotte. Hugh McColl was off on a new phase of his career.

On a dreary winter night, Jane McColl wrote to "Fran and Big Hugh" in Bennettsville, with a glimpse of her life as the wife of a big-time international banker:

> *Can't beat a Saturday night alone while your husband is sailing around Nassau. . . . Naturally while Hugh was gone the plumber had to come and tear a hole in the ceiling downstairs to see about a leak in the shower. They are going to have to tear out tile and rebuild the old drain, etc. etc., all amounting to $400. . . . Tough luck if Hugh doesn't approve.*
>
> *He won't be back until late Monday night. It has been a long rainy weekend. Do hope he is getting sunshine. What could be worse than being on a sailboat in the rain?*

But at NCNB Corporation they liked what Hugh was doing. His part of the company was profitable, so he came in for a big raise. McColl started 1970 with a new salary of thirty-four thousand dollars. Jane could pay the plumber.

"I believe I have really found my calling. As you know, I've always loved big business and I believe that the international banking scene provides me with an outlet for my imagination and ambition."

Hugh McColl
Letter to his parents, November 1971

CHAPTER 7

Sitting in on executive-level meetings, McColl basked in the beam of Addison Reese. He believed everything Mr. Reese said about the North Carolina market being a money-lender's paradise. He grinned ear-to-ear when Mr. Reese said a man would have to work mighty hard in this day and age to fail at the business of banking in the Tarheel State. Hell, the REIT was working on its second $50 million in loans, the mortgage company just hitting stride. Mr. Reese had the Midas touch. So when he heard about the big new building going up in Mr. Reese's mind, it was about all he could do to keep from shouting.

Shouting wasn't what you did in one of Addison Reese's executive meetings, though. You listened. So McColl listened to Reese talk through his idea. Talk about the "Odell Plan" for uptown Charlotte. Talk about the history of Independence Square with the two Indian trading paths. Talk about generating jobs and tax revenues. But that wasn't the talk McColl wanted to hear. It was the other part, the part about dominating, the part about the biggest goddamn structure in the city, the tallest, the best, the most. Thirty stories, maybe more. Fifty million dollars, maybe more. Maybe put in a hotel, shops, a skating rink even. Call it NCNB *Tower*.

Reese said it all so calmly, and then: "You know, you boys really have to want to do this, because I'll be gone, and you all will have to pay for it."

More confident at that moment than he'd felt after any raise or new title, McColl wanted to go on record.

"Of course we want to do it, sir. Damn the torpedoes, full speed ahead."

Tear down the eyesore that was uptown Charlotte. Who would lament the passing of a Kress dime store? A little history would bite the dust, like the old *Charlotte News* building, the Buford and Central Hotels, Tanner's lunch counter, the barbershop of Thaddeus Tate, a black man who took in business tips from white bankers and amassed a fortune of his own. But Reese said and McColl believed that none of those buildings could help a city grow and prosper in the 1970s the way a real skyscraper could. The one loss, as far as McColl was concerned, would be Rex's Pool Hall. Of course Rex's was fairly ratty and he was getting too busy to stretch his lunch breaks into pool games anyway.

McColl got behind the new building 100 percent, not because of all the talk about making uptown Charlotte a better place—that was just Chamber of Commerce puffery to his way of thinking—but because it was something bigger and better for his company, a taller pole for flying the NCNB flag. He and his team were going after the state championship of banking and this new tower on the square would be their trophy.

Jim Martin, a local candidate for Congress, heard McColl talk about NCNB's plans at a public meeting. Somebody asked whether there was an environmental impact study being conducted on this proposed new edifice. "I'll give you an environmental impact statement," McColl blurted. "It's gonna blot out the sun!"

Candidate Martin found the quip good for any number of laughs, but his brother and campaign strategist Joe Martin was appalled that a banker of all people could make an insensitive remark like that. This McColl was "too arrogant, too combative, too insensitive." Joe Martin knew instinctively that he and Hugh McColl "would not like each other or that either of us would want to hear much of what the other one had to say."

It was no longer simply managing a profit center that mattered to Executive Vice President Hugh McColl. As part of what he called the "senior team-elect, the people who were going to run things," McColl began taking a broader view of his company. Thus he gleefully participated in the decision to erect a second new building for NCNB, not in Charlotte but in the center of North Carolina. This would be an $11 million, fourteen-story office building, the bank's largest facility outside its headquarters city, in downtown Winston-Salem. NCNB would become a permanent eyesore to the executives and directors of The Wachovia, right in their hometown. They would be one up on Wachovia for that billboard NCNB executives had been forced to endure for so long in Charlotte.

Even more exhilarating to McColl was the realization that Wachovia was about to lose its bragging rights to being the "largest bank between Philadelphia and Dallas." It was beginning to seem inevitable that NCNB would overtake Wachovia before Reese retired at the end of 1973. "Turn up the faucets," McColl told his team. "Drive up the volume."

Despite McColl's tendency to jump into his mouth with both feet, Reese and Storrs liked the results he achieved. Between McColl's commercial banking success and Luther Hodges's growth of the consumer side, NCNB-the-bank was making its shareholders *very* happy. By 1971 NCNB was on the list of the top fifty banks in the United States, based on earnings growth over the past year and the previous five.

NCNB was the most progressive, most aggressive bank in a state that was no longer flying below the radar of the federal government agencies and the money center banks. During the decade of the '60s, commercial bank deposit growth in North Carolina had nearly doubled the national pace. Total loans by banks within the state increased 182 percent from 1960 to 1969, about thirty percentage points higher than the national increase. Reese told his shareholders that this growth reflected NCNB's development as a "statewide branching system." By forcing Wachovia into competition, NCNB and First Union had kept within the state working capital that formerly had been "siphoned off to other financial centers." Reese believed this competition had been one of the essential ingredients in the state's economic growth. Not incidentally, his use of the word "other" was an intentional gauntlet thrown at the feet of New York City.

To better manage the bank's growth, Reese and Storrs came up with a new operations chart with new titles and new leaders. Retail banking would be known henceforth as Banking Group I. Commercial business, both foreign and domestic, would be conducted by Banking Group II.

On May 1, 1970, the new designations became official. Bill Dougherty was named executive vice president in charge of operations and nonbank subsidiaries. Luther Hodges was named executive vice president in charge of Banking Group I. Hugh McColl was named executive vice president of Banking Group II at a salary of forty-one thousand dollars. All three men would have seats on the bank's board of directors. Still six weeks from his thirty-fifth birthday, McColl was a director of the bank that hadn't wanted to give him a job.

Under Tom Storrs's growing influence, Reese became mildly interested in the formerly uncompelling subject of international banking. McColl found himself free to beef up his staff, so he quickly rounded up some of the best people, the "tigers," from other parts of the operation. He partitioned the globe into four "NCNB International Regions," so there could be sales competition among the team players. Within each region the group chased down short-term, security-pledged "call loans" to brokerage houses. Export financing increased dramatically, and NCNB became a sought-after lender to U.S. corporations' overseas operations, to foreign banks and even to foreign governments.

As he studied international banking McColl came to believe that the only way he could become a big-time player in Eurodollars and overseas financing was to put a branch in London. That was the place the big players went to put together big deals, and that was where he needed to be in order to get in on those big deals. He wasn't going to hear about the deals, let alone make them, out of a telephone closet in the Caribbean. Having an office in Nassau was interesting but McColl wanted more.

By June 1971 McColl and Bob Barker put together a convincing argument for spending whatever it might take to open up a branch in London. Storrs agreed to help McColl sell the board on the idea that in London they would not be "subject to controls on the free movement of capital." They would have a foothold in "a nation soon to join the European Economic Community." Reese was dubious about the company's ability to make money so far away from their home base, but in the end he let Storrs and McColl have their way. His only reason for not formally opposing it was that it would not be his bank much longer. Like the new building, it would be up to Storrs, McColl and the others to pay for what he was convinced would be their mistake, after he retired.

McColl could speak more bluntly to his team than to the board. They had been forced to join the international game in Nassau or they would have started losing some of their own existing customers. "From now on," he told his troops, "we go after other banks' customers."

McColl and Storrs flew to London together. There were a number of formalities involved, and Storrs wasn't certain how McColl's Southern-marine-cardshark style would go over in the seat of British propriety. Storrs himself was impressed by the stiffness of the Bank of England officer who assisted them with their application. He thought the fellow might have just stepped out of a Gilbert and Sullivan guardsman's uniform.

"Now where do you plan to have your offices?" the Bank of England gentleman asked.

Storrs answered that any convenient office building would do.

"Ground floor, of course?"

"Well, sir," said McColl, "it's not likely we'll be doing much walk-in business. Don't imagine there's any need to pay street-level rent."

The British executive looked up from his stack of forms, over his bifocals at Storrs. His tone was matter-of-fact with just the right touch of severity. "I never heard of a proper-run banking business *not* on a ground floor."

Storrs directed McColl to find them a proper street-level location.

When the preliminary negotiations were finished, lawyers retained and formalities dispensed with, Storrs returned to Charlotte and Bob Barker joined McColl in London. On a Sunday afternoon they walked around the city looking at locations and found a building McColl really liked, a perfect location.

The following day their attorney confirmed that the building was indeed available, and he called in a real estate agent. Negotiations went forward as to price and date of closing, and McColl began taking care of other details. Then, in the course of a routine meeting, McColl mentioned that he just couldn't wait to get his bank operating in that wonderful location.

"Excuse me," the lawyer interrupted. "Did you say you want to put a *bank* in that building?"

"Of course," McColl told him, "we're bankers."

"I'm sorry, but you cannot do that," the lawyer said dryly.

"Why the hell not?"

"It simply isn't done. This is not a proper bank building."

McColl was astonished to learn that London zoning laws were unflinchingly rigid. "A pub is a pub," the lawyer told him. "It may change hands, but it always will be a pub. A clothing store is a clothing store. There are buildings proper for banking and others which are not proper for banking."

McColl felt he had been hoodwinked. "Why in the hell would you let us walk down this path?" he demanded.

"Well, you didn't ask, did you?" the lawyer calmly responded. "You asked if you could buy this building and the answer to that particular question was 'yes.' You didn't say, 'May I use it for banking?' did you?"

McColl had his first taste of doing business abroad. Unlike Americans, the British would not volunteer information. He decided he had better ask the question he wanted the answer to. He suspected that every nation was like a commercial loan customer: you needed to learn a lot about their business before you could be sure about doing business with them.

Another curious London banking regulation was that any newly established foreign bank office must hire a foreign exchange officer who was British. McColl asked around and came up with Bernie Furlonger, who was BankAmerica's chief dollar trader in London. Furlonger liked McColl's offer and asked if he might bring a couple more BankAmerica people with him to the new office. McColl gave the approval and resignations were duly submitted at BankAmerica London. Immediately, McColl got a somewhat anxious telephone call from Storrs asking what was going on. When McColl explained, Storrs told him that Tom Clausen, chairman and CEO of BofA, had called to tell him he had made his last "contribution" to NCNB's international gambit. "He said we had better not hire any more of his people."

McColl was fine with that. What he needed now was someone from his own team to head up the operation, "a man in London we could trust, a man who understood our language, when we said something to each other across thirty-five hundred miles of cable or Telstar." He selected George Campbell, a Harvard Business School graduate whom McColl had stolen out of Luther Hodges's Marketing Department and put to work with his correspondent banks in North Carolina. Campbell would be NCNB's London office chief, just as soon as the red tape could be slashed and the office finally opened. Meanwhile, Hugh McColl started bringing in customers.

Frankfurt, Germany
1 November, 1971

Dear Mother and Daddy,

Tonight I flew over the English channel in a small twin engine plane, similar to that owned by NCNB. It was quite an experience to fly from London to Frankfurt much as we might fly from Charlotte to Washington, D.C. My host for the flight was Korf Industries. Which owns the Steel Mill at Georgetown, S.C. Tomorrow I meet with Mr. Korf and his bankers to discuss a $6 million loan we propose to grant them.

Last Wednesday I arrived in London at 8:30 A.M. and at 11:30 participated in a $30 million loan, closing with Sonotracht, an Algerian oil company. I believe I have really found my calling. As you know I've always loved big business and I believe that the international banking scene provides me with an outlet for my imagination and ambition. . . .

We are in final negotiations on the establishment of an office in London. The project is one of my brainchilds and I am of course, very excited and pleased to be nearly in business in London.

My job certainly has its penalties. Jane is always mad with me because I am out of town so much and I miss my children and I have obviously been remiss in seeing you. Perhaps I can make it all right with everyone soon. I love you both very much and regret that I have not seen you lately. I promise to come home before Christmas.

Love,
Hugh

December 9, 1971, McColl cleared the last barrier to becoming a full-fledged international banker when the Federal Reserve Board in Washington approved NCNB's application for a banking office in London. On January 1, 1972, NCNB International Banking Corporation would officially open its doors on the ground floor of a building known as Prince's House at 93 Gresham Street, corner of Basinghall Road, less than two proper blocks from the Bank of England, in the old Roman sector, the City of London. NCNB became the only bank from the Southeastern United States to have a branch on the far side of the Atlantic.

From London, George Campbell and the other members of NCNB International corralled more and more Eurodollars to secure more and more loans. When he looked at this new set of foreign customers, McColl realized it was something new and different and vaguely worrisome. In the Carolinas he had customers who were deeply committed to NCNB because NCNB was so deeply enmeshed in those customers' businesses and cultures. Now, as he scooped up foreign deposits to fuel overseas loan growth, he had a net filled with customers who were indifferent to NCNB. They had "no natural reason for doing business with us other than rate," McColl realized. Customers like that could vanish as quickly as they materialized. On the other hand, every one of those new customers brought NCNB a step closer to fulfilling its destiny: *Beat Wachovia.*

As the first quarter of 1972 ended, the senior management team got some very good numbers from Bill Dougherty. Their bank was worth just under $3 billion. A few weeks later, the *Observer* published first-quarter earnings reports, and there it was in black and white: NCNB $2.9 billion, Wachovia $2.7 billion. This was the news Reese had been waiting to hear since he arrived in Charlotte in 1951. This, he told his stockholders, was the moment of destiny, the "one basic reason" for which NCNB had been created. "There was one bank which dominated the state and a large part of the Southeast. We saw a need for increased competition." Now NCNB was the largest bank not only in North Carolina but in the entire Southeastern United States.

Of course, in business a finish line is nothing more than the starting line of the next lap. Reese might be retiring, but Storrs and his executives would be working to hold onto first place long after December 1973. For McColl now, work meant traveling, even more than in his Beetle days down South Carolina farm roads. Jane's letters continued to lament her husband's long absences from his wife and children. Even on those rare occasions when Hugh was in Charlotte, he would let business overshadow their personal life.

"We are having all the men and their wives that work for Hugh for a light Sunday supper." Jane wrote to her in-laws. "The number comes to 75. Hopefully some will be out of town. But no one has called to say they can't come. When this is over I hope the summer will be mine and the children's."

But McColl's time belonged to the bank. Letters from England, Europe, Asia and South America were his principal means of communication with his family, letting them know that Hugh McColl was making a substantial impression on the important figures of foreign countries. Likewise, those countries were making an impression on him.

1 March, 1972
Dear Mother and Daddy,

Arrived in Managua, Nicaragua, on night of 29 Feb. . . . On Monday I had an audience with the president of Guatemala, General [Carlos] Araña. And tonight I am giving a party in honor of the president of the Republic of Nicaragua, General Anastasio Somoza. This is one part of the world where bankers are popular. On one of my side trips in Guatemala I flew over a live volcano in a light plane. . . . The poverty is shocking, but everyone looks well fed. Certainly we should learn to appreciate what we have in the U.S., there is nothing like it.

Love,
Hugh

United States bankers were indeed welcome in Latin America. Yet from West Germany and Japan, where economies were at last regaining the vigor that the World War had sapped from them, U.S. economic supremacy was beginning to feel pressure. America's balance of payments deficit was over $10 billion and climbing. The U.S. inflation rate was also headed up, already at 4 percent. As the United States imported more oil, automobiles and electronics, the nation's trade surplus became a deficit for the first time in nearly a hundred years. With Regulation Q continuing to shackle America's lenders, dollars kept on pouring out of the country to seek higher yields on the Eurodollar market. For NCNB it made sense to get as much of that Eurodollar trade as it could, and the best man to get it was Hugh McColl.

McColl found England exciting. He fell in love with London. "I liked the big city, liked the streets packed with people, and the hustle and bustle. I liked it a lot better than New York." London helped change his outlook on a lot of things. The stories he read in the *Times* gave him insights he never got from reading the *Charlotte Observer*.

He realized his view of life, of history, of business had been a provincial view. In London he felt like a citizen of the world.

He walked the vibrant streets—streets with marvelous names like Austin Friars and Moorefield Highwalk—and wondered why Charlotte couldn't have streets like this. In the evening he found his way to friendly pubs and quiet little restaurants, all in peaceful coexistence with some of the planet's most frenetic commerce.

As soon as he could manage it, he got Jane to make a London trip with him. They went to the hotel on Russell Square where they'd stayed with Miss Thomas's York County tour group. "Not quite as uptown as I remembered it," Jane smiled. They rode a hansom cab along the Thames, and near the Savoy he brushed her brown hair back and touched the nape of her neck with his lips, just the way a pitcher-eared kid had gotten fresh fourteen years ago, and she remembered the words she'd iced him down with that night: "You know, young men shouldn't kiss young women on the neck."

When he pondered what it could be that made London so magical, McColl settled on something very mundane, very simple. It was the Londoners' refusal to stray from their own history. It was why he could only put his bank in a place that was proper for a bank to be. He realized what "Draconian zoning" could accomplish, "making things happen in a way that you wanted them to happen." He learned that if a man saw what should be in a city, and if he could lead others to share his vision, then anything might be possible. Perhaps even in a place like Charlotte, North Carolina. London began to change McColl's feelings about Charlotte.

Back in his office on the mezzanine, McColl returned a call from the dean of students at the city's new outpost of his alma mater, the University of North Carolina at Charlotte. The dean was Dennis Rash, who had left one of the city's most prestigious law firms for a career in academia. Rash was just back from a European tour and a stop in London, where he'd spent some time with his old college roommate, none other than George Campbell, the man McColl had picked to run his London office.

Rash was a student of literature and history, whose Anglophilia played a sweet harmony to McColl's growing London infatuation. The two men began a series of lunchtime meetings in which they talked about cities. Rash found McColl's perception of London's allure refreshingly simple. He heard this banker describe a place whose greatness "had relatively little to do with Buckingham palaces, wonderful rivers or gigantic parks, and much more to do with the kind of twenty-four-hour-a-day operating of the city, where people lived over their shops and strolled down the street to the greengrocer or the butcher or the baker every day. It was that kind of urban live-liness that attracted McColl. And he wished that for Charlotte, under the kind of simple credo that you can't have a great bank without a great city. Ergo, we should do everything we could do to make Charlotte a great city."

McColl was an inspiration. Rash recognized that what he wanted was to build a great university, just as McColl wanted to build a great bank. Both their dreams could be more readily realized if they could somehow make Charlotte into a great city—which it clearly was not in the early 1970s. Similarly, Rash inspired McColl to spend a little more time looking into what might be done. After all, he might some day have one of the two controlling voices in the city's largest bank. Maybe that would translate into power. McColl never really had con-templated *power* on this scale before.

Someone in Charlotte who seemed to understand the use of power was a close friend of Addison Reese, architect A. G. "Gouldie" Odell. Until now, McColl had dismissed Odell as "sort of a country-club type." In fact, the architect was Charlotte's most progressive visionary and a dominant influence in the city's current course. He had drawn up a plan for revitalizing uptown in 1966 and now that plan was tak-ing shape, with urban renewal in the Second Ward and NCNB's new office tower going up on the Square. It was Odell, not Mayor Belk, who'd convinced Reese to build the tower. McColl started spending time with Odell, listening to his ideas, becoming "extremely fond of him." Soon the architect was drawing blueprints in the mind of McColl, becoming "in a lot of ways, my spiritual advisor or muse. . . . He had a great effect on me."

In his travels, McColl rekindled the passion for reading sparked in his mother's lap in Bennettsville. Now, instead of manly adventures and wilderness tales he read history, government, books of social change and civic discourse. Most of his waking hours were devoted to business and to his unbroken habits of note-taking and after-hours calculating. But now he made himself make time to think about change. For the moment, there was little he could do to make a bet-ter place of his city, let alone of the world, but one day the chance might come to him, if the power came.

For now, the dreams of others would have to suffice, the dreams of people who needed money to finance those dreams. McColl and his team barnstormed the globe in search of customers long on plans and short on cash. Meanwhile, Tom Storrs began to wonder what recourse he would have if one of these exotic offshore borrowers went belly-up. In the age of go-go banking, the practice was to sign up the loan customer first, and find the money to lend him later.

In fact, NCNB had become a highly leveraged company, with barely more than a quarter of its portfolio funded by direct deposits. While there was no regulation stating what the ratio of capital-to-liabilities should be, investors grew suspicious if a bank's ratio fell below 8 percent. Around the country, many major banks were extending themselves well beyond that limit, and, in fact, Citibank's capitalization would drop to 4.1 percent within the next eighteen months. Citibank CEO Walter Wriston, whom Storrs admired, assured his investors that only small banks needed to worry about large capitalization, since small banks were less diversified and less well-managed than his big bank. Storrs felt the same way, since NCNB certainly would qualify as at least an almost-large bank.

Nevertheless, Storrs thought it prudent to establish a "Country Limits Committee," which met monthly to discuss what was going on in each of the countries where NCNB was doing business. The committee's purpose was to determine how much money should be loaned in any foreign country at a given time. National politics and international relations seemed, for the first time, at least as important as the ruminations of the North Carolina legislature and the price of cotton in Columbia. In Europe, where NCNB was now a player, Great Britain, Ireland and Denmark were about to join the Common Market. In Washington, a scandal called Watergate was shaking President Richard Nixon's administration to its roots. In Charlotte, North Carolina's largest bank was feeling invincible.

Reese and Hodges staged a big party on the Square in July for the "topping out" of the forty-story NCNB Tower at Trade and Tryon. The last steel beam sent up five hundred feet on the construction crane bore the signatures of dignitaries and ordinary citizens who packed the streets below. The National Drum and Bugle Corps flew in to play "The Star-Spangled Banner." "Up, Up and Away," the Fifth Dimension's anthem of the '70s, was thunked out by a steel drum band. Reese and

Storrs unveiled a crisp new logo, bright letters that seemed to be carved out of solid red plastic, timeless in a modern sort of way: no more sputniks and stars, just *NCNB*. Simple, solid, trustworthy, hip.

Addison Reese was going out in style. His $3 billion bank had twenty-four-hour cash dispensing machines operating in ten cities with more on the way. His NCNB Corporation had picked up another big mortgage company, C. Douglas Wilson and Company out of South Carolina, doing $250 million in mortgage loans. And, when he arrived back in Charlotte from a summer vacation in Nantucket, Reese discovered his bank now owned a little one-office operation in the Central Florida orange-juice town of Orlando. How that ever happened should have told Reese something about how much his once closely held power structure had changed; it might also have given him a peek into NCNB's future.

Hugh McColl was in the middle of a discussion in Luther Hodges's office when Bill Dougherty came in and told them about the Orlando opportunity. Dougherty had just got off the telephone with a former associate who was now CEO of Pittsburgh National Bank. He told them, "This guy wants to know if we're interested in buying a little trust company down in Florida."

"How much money is it losing?" McColl wanted to know.

"No, no, it's not that," Dougherty protested "It seems he forgot to ask his board if he could buy it and now they want him to get rid of it. He says he'll sell it to us at cost. And Mr. Storrs is out of town."

McColl and Hodges looked at each other.

"Why not?" asked McColl.

"Sure," Hodges agreed. "Go ahead and buy it."

So Dougherty bought it. The Trust Company of Florida had only $35 million in assets, pocket change to a bank like theirs, but it might get larger someday, especially with Walt Disney building that new tourist attraction down there.

In NCNB investors saw a company on the move and they kept buying. At the end of 1972 NCNB stock was selling at twenty-six times its earnings, unheard of in the banking business. That was the best price/earnings ratio in the country. The bank had more than twice the number of stockholders it had just three years earlier. Hugh McColl had "a feeling of accomplishment" about that P/E, though he admitted being but "superficially interested" in the stock side of things. Still only thirty-eight years old, McColl let himself remain "essentially naïve" about many aspects of the bank and the holding company that were outside his purview. "I had been told to make loans, make money, don't worry about the capital, we'll worry about that. And when people tell me not to worry about something, I don't. I mean, I went on and did my thing."

Still, a P/E of twenty-six was something to crow about, and few bankers could crow like Hugh McColl. He made sure his team took every opportunity to get under the competition's skin. They spread the word like a price-earnings rash at every bankers' gathering they could attend. "We thought we walked on water. We were arrogant—but 'arrogant' just barely covers how we felt about ourselves." McColl even took a perverse pride in being "universally disliked, thought to be completely out of line," by the men who ran the other banks.

Now, thanks to their nonbank subsidiaries, they were disliked not only among bankers, but in several other industries as well. McColl's South Carolina plum, Stephenson Finance Company, was doing a big business as TranSouth Corporation. TranSouth was writing second-home mortgages for Southeastern executives, whose prospects were going up faster than they could dig into debt. Beachfront or mountainside, if you had a yen for seasonal migration, TranSouth had your money.

On the other end of the employment ladder, if you were a shift worker in the booming textile industry, you might want to consider a fancy new mobile home. Those double-wides were being pieced together like blue jeans in Carolina factories. Before the credit crunch of 1969, mobile homes in the Southeast had been financed mostly by banks and finance companies in the Midwest and Northeast. When money got tight, these institutions pulled in their tentacles, at the very moment NCNB-the-holding-company was reaching out of the cradle. The way Addison Reese put it to his shareholders, NCNB's TranSouth "took the opportunity to start working with mobile home dealers throughout the Carolinas." TranSouth could get you in a "home of your own" for little or no money down. It was just as easy as financing a car: Sign here. Mobile home sales became the holding company's favorite cash crop, high volume and low maintenance.

In the past, many families had been reluctant to buy mobile homes because of the lack of land to sit them on. But in 1972 the FHA's decision to guarantee loans for mobile home parks opened up yet another opportunity, this time for the holding corporation's NCNB Mortgage Company. By 1973 NCNB Mortgage was a much larger contributor to the bank's revenues than even Tom Storrs had projected six years earlier when he led the drive to create a one-bank holding company. By absorbing two other mortgage lenders—C. Douglas Wilson and Blanchard & Calhoun—NCNB Mortgage now operated throughout both Carolinas and Georgia. It also had footholds in the Florida markets of Jacksonville and Orlando, which, with the completion of Walt Disney World, was growing into one of the healthiest economies in the United States. In fact, the entire Southeast was booming. In North Carolina, for example, fully 97 percent of the workforce was gainfully employed, and new homes were going up everywhere.

The business of NCNB Mortgage Corp. included much more than new home financing. Office buildings and shopping centers, condominiums and resort developments, manufacturing plants and industrial parks, golf courses, even a Myrtle Beach amusement park called "Pirate Land"—whatever you wanted to build, NCNB Mortgage would come up with the money. The mortgage company financed construction, then shopped the financing to its list of thirty big-name investment houses for long-term money.

"From volume, credit and handling standpoints, our experience with this financing has been excellent," reported Reese to his shareholders. "In all cases, we review the developers' plans for compliance with state and federal financial, construction and conservation requirements." As the construction fever rose, so rose NCNB Mortgage Corporation commitments, on loans of nearly $700 million. All these figures found their way into Bill Dougherty's computers, making the bank look better and better.

One of the few missteps in these go-go days was the attempt by Storrs and McColl to cross the state line into South Carolina. In the process they would resurrect the name American Trust Company, one of NCNB's grandparent institutions. Storrs believed that a trust company located near Columbia could bring in business from all over South Carolina. The NCNB Trust Department had studied estate executions in the state and determined that the South Carolina banks were inadequately serving the market. But when South Carolina bankers learned of the plan, they issued a formal protest and the Federal Reserve opened full-scale hearings in Charlotte. Storrs "took a pretty hard line on it," insisting that South Carolina's bankers were "not meeting the public need. We'd like to go down and meet the public need." But Hugh McColl's own grandfather had lobbied against out-of-state banking in South Carolina back in 1931, warning the bank examiner that this would be "a serious handicap to state banks." Forty years later, that creed had a fair number of adherents.

In the end, the Federal Reserve held up the American Trust application long enough so that the South Carolina legislature had time to pass a new law to prevent the deal. Tom Storrs got the message that his bank was not wanted in the Palmetto State, not by its bankers at any rate. No doubt this had something to do with the fact that so much South Carolina money was already being siphoned north to Charlotte, thanks to NCNB TranSouth, NCNB Mortgage and NCNB's correspondent banking raiders led by Hugh McColl. An even more important lesson was the resolve of the state legislature. McColl had not appreciated how quickly a group of politicians could respond to an external threat.

McColl's success—or notoriety—in South Carolina stemmed from his remarkable ability to grow relationships. As he put ever more emphasis into foreign lending, McColl sensed that this old-fashioned way of doing business was passing out of favor in the go-go age. He read what was happening at industry-leading Citibank, where Walter Wriston was determined to change the corporate culture of his company to something that operated more like Wall Street: swift, efficient, impersonal. As Wriston biographer Phillip Zweig puts it, Citi's new culture would be one in which "officers were branded either as Transactors or as Administrator-Managers." McColl's relationship banking "was going the way of the drug store soda fountain."

Wriston had concluded that centralized authority and slow-building revenue streams were "turn-offs" to the young and highly talented people he wanted to attract. One-time transactions were entrepreneurial, long-term relationships dull and stodgy. Hugh McColl was trying to attract the same people as Wriston was, but he remained committed both to the hierarchical leadership structure he'd learned in the Marine Corps and to the person-to-person banking style developed in his correspondent days. McColl felt he could train his new-breed bankers to build relationships that would last, accounts that might expand and deepen over time.

This philosophy was nothing more than an extension of the

relationship-building he was doing within the company. As the leader he must be one with his troops and, as much as possible, they should be one with their customers. McColl refused to believe a leader and his team—much less a banker and his customers—could not or should not be friends.

For ten years McColl had been building that kind of relationship with a Spartanburg businessman named Jerry Richardson and his partner Charlie Bradshaw, a couple of former college all-American football heroes. Richardson had gone on to help the Baltimore Colts win the National Football League championship in 1959. Richardson was the rookie receiver who caught the winning touchdown pass from Johnny Unitas to beat the New York Giants. Two years later, he quit when Colts management refused to give him a $250 raise to bring his salary up to $12,000. Richardson took the $10,000 he'd managed to save up to that point, borrowed another $10,000 and went into partnership with Bradshaw to open a Hardee's fast-food franchise in Spartanburg.

When Richardson wanted to expand into the mushrooming Charlotte market, he talked to Hugh McColl about a loan. McColl did his homework and learned about the fast-food business. He pegged Richardson and Bradshaw as "hard-working, very determined men who could turn out a pretty good hamburger." He loaned them $25,000 and they opened up a Hardee's at the Charlottetown Mall on King's Drive. Business boomed and they added several other locations in Charlotte. They borrowed another $25,000 and another, and they made all their monthly payments to NCNB. McColl was asked to sit on their board of directors, where he learned even more about fast food. He loaned Richardson more money as the company expanded through the Carolinas and Georgia, going public in the process. Also in the process, McColl and Richardson became close friends.

In the summer of 1973 Jerry Richardson proposed a raft trip down the Colorado River through the Grand Canyon for the Richardsons and McColls. Jane, who had been waiting months for a little rest and relaxation, thought this fell a little short of her idea of a great time. "Daggone, Jerry Richardson, I could kill you," was her greeting to the big man at a basketball game. "I'm going on the damn Colorado River for my vacation." But in the end, as Richardson had anticipated, Jane was a good sport about it. She left six-year-old Little Jane with her grandparents and packed up the rest of her family for an outdoor adventure that actually helped atone for all those weeks Hugh had been away from his family in pursuit of international business.

Four McColls and five Richardsons, ten days on a raft, camping every night, 290 miles of white water and canyon walls, all the way through the canyon—Glen Falls Dam to Lake Meade. Richardson hired a guide who was a geologist well versed in the eons of erosion on either side, but who could not swim if the raft happened to encounter an unfriendly rock in the middle of the river. They all spent some time in the water, buoyed by orange life-vests and cama- raderie. They lit campfires and cooked the trout they caught. They slept in tents and swatted horseflies. It was dangerous and sweaty and fun. McColl returned to Charlotte with two weeks' growth of beard and a closer relationship with his sons, thanks to the banking rela- tionship he had built with Jerry Richardson.

Another McColl relationship that figured prominently in the bank's activities of 1972 was the one he'd formed with C. D. Spangler Jr., whose family owned the Selwyn Village apartments. Dick and Meredith Spangler and Hugh and Jane McColl were neighbors and friends at the 234-unit apartment complex. Spangler recalled the "pretty fierce" games of touch football he and McColl played on Sunday afternoons, when "each team had twelve quarterbacks."

Now Spangler considered his friend at least the second-string quarterback of the town's biggest bank, and Dick Spangler needed to learn some banking plays in a hurry. Spangler's father was one of North Carolina's construction giants. In fact, C. D. Spangler Sr. had built Camp LeJeune, where McColl spent part of his Marine Corps days. While working on the military base in eastern North Carolina in the late forties, Spangler Senior became frustrated with the service he received from banks in the area and decided he would just build his own bank. With nine partners he started up the Bank of North Carolina in Jacksonville.

In 1972 Spangler Junior found himself on the board of a bank headquartered in Raleigh. It had seventy branches and big-time problems; in fact, he believed it was about to fail. When McColl brought Spangler and his problem to Tom Storrs and Luther Hodges, the four decided that the best course of action would be for Spangler to force out the rest of his board and most of his management team. NCNB would lend him the money—and even the management expertise—he needed to get over the hump. It would have to be, as

Spangler learned, "an adversarial process." He was going into the banking business "basically uninvited," and it would not be easy.

"Hugh and Tom traveled with me to the Federal Reserve Bank in Richmond and also to the Comptroller of the Currency's Office in Washington," as Spangler tells the story. "And we laid out a plan to save the Bank of North Carolina. Then they lent me several executives to help, and I recruited some others. And then of course, we did restore the Bank of North Carolina to substantial profit, because they had lent me money to do that." The money was slightly more than $10 million, which Spangler considered "a pretty gutsy transaction."

This relationship banking was critical not merely to NCNB's style, but to the substance of its success. That was how John Pipkin saw it from his NCNB lending office in Greensboro. The philosophically inclined Pipkin realized that it was much easier to produce more business out of an existing account than it was to develop new business. "The more you get somebody entangled with you, and enmeshed through involvement with ancillary activities, then the more difficult it is for them to ever make the decision to break away and go somewhere else. It's like being caught in a spider's web," mused Pipken. "Regardless of your size, like Gulliver and the Lilliputians, you can't get up and move away."

The other side of that coin is the banking proverb that if you lend a man a dollar, you own him; if you lend him a million dollars, he owns you. In other words, there comes a point at which a relationship may go *too* deep. A borrower in trouble can deceive his lender, and perhaps himself as well, about his ability to repay a loan. If the size of the debt is great enough, the bank may have more to lose than does the customer.

NCNB had positioned itself as the most likely bank in North Carolina to succeed in the flashdance age of *banking a go-go*. But in mid-1973, if you got close enough, the whole idea was beginning to take on the feel of a fad past its prime, like scuff-toed disco boots. Around the United States, newspaper business sections were beginning to report local companies filing petitions in bankruptcy court. In the beginning Reese, Storrs, McColl and the others thought it was probably nothing but a few sour notes in an otherwise sweet song.

Their first big problem loan was one made by the factoring company to W. B. Lea Tobacco Company, a dealer in Carolina tobacco leaves. Sent to eastern North Carolina on a rescue mission by Storrs,

McColl saw that Lea was "up against the wall" and about to go broke, so he extricated the bank from the relationship. That one was easy enough, requiring only a few meetings and phone calls and smooth talk. Then, not long after the Colorado River adventure, Reese himself called McColl in to discuss a company called Chadburn Gotham. This was a textile knitting company that had come into the bank through the Charlotte office, now Luther Hodges's domain, yet Reese thought McColl might be the best person to handle it. Chadburn, he explained, was on the verge of bankruptcy.

"How much are we in for?" McColl asked.

Reese looked him in the eye without blinking. "It could be as much as $30 million," he said. "If they go down, we might go down with them."

The word "bankrupt" derives from the Italian, *banca rotta*, which suggests a money-lender fractured. Indeed, when the borrower needs fixing, it is his banker who may go broke. A bank has two basic options in dealing with a customer on the verge of bankruptcy. The first and worst option is to foreclose the loan (usually *loans*, plural) and liquidate the customer. Since the customer invariably has more liabilities than he has assets, the bank will never collect more than a portion of the amount due and generally, during the course of the operation, the patient dies. The bank loses both the money and the customer.

The second option is called a "workout agreement." Under this option, the banker may help the customer to reorganize the business, restructure the indebtedness and over time repay all or at least most of the money he owes the bank. While that sounds like the obviously better course of action, workouts can be difficult and time consuming. They may even be risky, since the banker may have to become a venture capitalist, pouring more money into the business in order to get money out.

To salvage Chadburn, Hugh McColl saw that he was going to need help from some of the best minds he could assemble. They would come together in the crisis as NCNB's first "workout team." To assure the team's success the first member McColl had to recruit was the man who headed up the failing textile company, Tom Roboz.

Roboz was a colorful character, a native of Hungary whose father fought with the Russians against Hitler. Tom Roboz fled Europe with his mother, then nearly died attempting to reach the United States when his ship was torpedoed by a Nazi U-boat. At the age of sixteen he lied himself into the U.S. Army and returned to Europe to fight. After the war he got a job selling ladies' hosiery for the Gotham Gold Sock company in New York, working full-time and attending New York University Law School full-time as well. In the late fifties, Gotham was bought out by a Charlotte hosiery company called Chadburn, which was a client of American Commercial Bank, later NCNB. By 1968, Tom Roboz found himself president and chief operating officer of a multinational up to its waist in the lucrative manufacture of panty hose. In 1970 he became chairman, CEO and treasurer of a highly leveraged company, trying unsuccessfully to compete with Hanes Hosiery, which was filling its basket with the supermarket sales of L'Eggs, the panty hose packaged in a plastic egg. Roboz's banking relationship with NCNB had been nurtured first by Julian Clark and then by Luther Hodges, whom Roboz found to be "a charming man, extremely affable." In 1973 he met, for the first time, Hugh McColl.

Roboz walked into McColl's mezzanine office. Their handshake was still warm when "Hugh started bawling me out like a barracks sergeant major. Having been a first sergeant, I knew the type. I listened to him, then I finally said, 'Hugh, you know I didn't cause this problem. I know you didn't cause this problem. Now we've got two choices. We can sit here and scream at each other, or we can get down to it and try to solve the problem. Either one is perfectly satisfactory to me.'

"There was a desperately long silence—or one that seemed at the time to be desperately long. Hugh looked at me and he said, 'You and I are going to get along just fine.' And we did. We did."

The Chadburn workout would demand toughness beyond anything McColl and his team had faced in the course of normal operations. Workouts required the bank to take the point at the head of a band of uncooperative creditors. They had to turn these potential enemies into allies that would see Chadburn as a damsel to be rescued rather than a dragon to be slain.

Chadburn's indebtedness involved several other banks, notably the First National Bank of Boston, which had provided payroll and raw-materials funding to Chadburn since before NCNB had found its way into the factoring business. Like most old-line factoring institutions, the Bank of Boston tended to view its manufacturing customers as producers of collateral goods that would provide a decent return for the lender in the event that the borrower went broke. As long as there was some sort of collateral that could be loaded onto a truck and driven to market, the factor had little concern over the balance sheet.

The Bank of Boston now served notice it would not cover Chadburn's payroll for the coming weeks. McColl saw that as the thread that might unravel not only Chadburn, but the largest bank in North Carolina as well. If NCNB's multilayered relationship with Chadburn went under, McColl told his workout team, NCNB might well go under too. Their first battle would be for the minds of the Bank of Boston.

In addition to Tom Roboz, McColl's assault on Boston would involve one other non-NCNB player. This was Harry Grim, a lawyer with Lassiter, Moore and Van Allen who had been doing contract work for NCNB since 1961. Grim's loan contracts for John Robison, John Pipkin, Louie Henderson and others had made him almost a member of the family. One reason Hugh McColl liked him was that Grim had flown helicopters for the Marine Corps in the late fifties. That seemed a daredevil occupation for a lawyer.

As his second-in-command, McColl selected the man he had his eye on to become the bank's chief loan executive some day. This was Jim Berry, another aggressive player whom McColl had stolen right out from under Luther Hodges. Five years older than McColl, Berry was a native of Tulsa. Like McColl, he was the son of a banker. Also like McColl, Berry was a high school basketball player with a torn-up knee. Except for the injury, Berry would have fought with the army in the Korean War. He had worked two years for the Comptroller of the Currency as a bank examiner, then in 1969 became the senior credit officer for NCNB in Greensboro. In McColl's estimation Berry was "an Okie, 25 percent Cherokee and sort of rough around the edges," a man with "really good business instincts" who would be tough in a fight. Jim Berry, McColl believed, would have "the kind of native charm, and also the balls, to muscle through the Chadburn deal, a company that should have failed sixteen times."

Tom Roboz agreed—at least with the part about Berry. He seemed to be "an extremely good banker because he plays the country boy bit from Oklahoma to a fare-thee-well," the type that could "look you right in the eye and say, 'Look, I'm just a country boy from Oklahoma.'"

The other member of the workout team was Roboz's loan officer, Jerry Thompson.. Together, the team sized up the Chadburn situation as potentially explosive. In Jim Berry's estimation, the knitting company had "three levels of debt, and we had the unfortunate position of being in all three." NCNB could force its way out of any one of those situations, Berry concluded, but only by bringing the other two down. It was "like pointing a gun at somebody, except if you pulled the trigger, you blew your own head off."

From what they saw in the ledger books, the group decided that Chadburn could work its way out of its predicament within a reasonable number of years by divesting itself of the panty hose operations. Roboz convinced the others that he had "a pretty damn strong apparel operation. We had knits and wovens, t-shirts and sweat shirts. And all these good things were hot. Western wear was hot, and we made most of Levi's Western jackets for them." In those operations McColl gave Roboz a fair chance at making money.

Roboz had quickly come to trust McColl and he believed the trust was mutual. There could be "no monkey shines, none of the usual baloney of fake invoices to the factors or anything like that. . . . Hugh knew that I would run a clean operation or I would leave. Life is too short."

The team set up the meeting in Boston, where they would be joined by representatives of three other banks from New York, Atlanta and Germany. Because these banks had lesser stakes in Chadburn's indebtedness, it would be up to NCNB to lead the charge and convince the others to follow.

McColl, Grim, Berry, Thompson and Roboz boarded an Eastern Airlines flight for Logan Airport. On the way, they formulated a strategy. McColl would play the good cop, Berry the bad cop. Grim and Thompson would listen hard for loopholes, escape valves and mistakes by the other sides. Roboz would wait in another room until such time as his presence might be required. They talked through their game plan once, but McColl wouldn't let them do any rehearsing or role-playing. He had to go through that exercise with Tom Storrs every time they attended an important meeting together. He considered it worse than useless. Rehearsing was all right for the stage, but in business you never really knew what the other players might extemporize. It was better to be ready for anything.

The game around the Boston conference table started out friendly enough, McColl entertaining the group with somewhat fanciful tales of Roboz's heroics in the war. At the far end of the table, Berry could hardly believe his ears. "You would have thought that Tom Roboz was

General George Patton. Hugh made him out as being this big hero . . . and they were chewing it all up and swallowing it."

However good a soldier Roboz might be, the Boston bankers were determined he would lose this war. It was obvious from the start that they wanted out. They were ready to walk away from Chadburn no matter the consequences to NCNB and the other banks. The workout team from Charlotte hunkered down for a long session, the most "rough-and-tumble" negotiation Harry Grim had ever attended. Late in the afternoon, realizing he had failed to push the Boston platoon back from their position, McColl tried a new approach, based on Grim's suggestion that Boston had been playing fast and loose with banking regulations, paying Chadburn checks that were drawn on their own bank, returning checks drawn on other banks.

"You know," McColl said almost innocently, "it looks like you've been sending our checks back and paying yours." When the senior member of Boston's factoring group vehemently denied the charge, the Charlotte team knew they had found a chink in the wall. Berry jumped into his role. "Dammit, you've been pissing in our ear and calling it rainwater too long," he shouted.

"Ease off, Jim," good cop McColl soothed. "It's probably not up to us to decide. Maybe we ought to just let Tom file for bankruptcy. Put the whole thing in the courts."

Bad cop Berry slammed his hand on the table and lifted up from his chair. "Fine," he said. "Let's kill off the sonofabitch and get out of here."

It was the third-level member of the Boston bank team who caved. "What about this . . . ?" he began. Finally, negotiations were under way. By five-thirty they had a deal worked out—tenuous, fragile, but a deal. They brought Roboz in to get his approval, only to have him start asking questions and raising objections that threatened to sink the ship. Thompson held Roboz's hand and helped get him through the painful realization that being rescued is not altogether easy. A secretary put the agreement on paper, everyone signed and the Charlotte team left the building.

Tom Roboz was happy to promise that he would "repay every penny to NCNB . . . every penny of interest due." It would take the better part of the next two years, but all his inherited company's debt would be paid, he assured them. He would sell off whatever remained of the hosiery company. He would get rid of the stigmatum of the name "Chadburn" and come up with something entirely different—

like "Stanwood." He would make it all work for Hugh McColl.

By the time their taxi made it across the bay tunnel to Logan International Airport the workout team had missed the last flight to Charlotte. They boarded a shuttle for LaGuardia and spent that night in New York, celebrating over a steak dinner. Roboz continued to wax delirious over McColl's salvation of his company. McColl allowed himself a share of the delirium, because he had saved his own company in the process. He hoped it would be the last time the bank came that close to disaster. They told themselves that night in New York that this was an isolated incident. NCNB would continue as before, damning torpedoes and throttling the engine full.

Someone reminded McColl of the memo Addison Reese had written soon after the bank had passed Wachovia in total deposits. After congratulating the troops he had added, "I'm not going to let you crow about it until you catch them in domestic deposits. We've caught them, but you can't brag about it until you catch them in domestic deposits." McColl raised his glass of single-malt scotch in a toast. "Pedal to the metal, boys. Let's move this machine forward."

The lesson of Chadburn was not lost on the bank's board of directors. At the next monthly meeting in Greensboro the contentious Huger King took Bill Dougherty's latest earnings report with a grain of salt. "Dougherty," he said, "what are you going to do if your commercial paper won't sell one day?"

Realizing his bank was so highly leveraged that any loss of confidence by investors could tip it over, King wanted some sort of safety net. How about old-fashioned lines of credit, assurances from other banks that they would provide short-term money for NCNB in the event of an emergency? Not necessary, Tom Storrs answered King, just as Walter Wriston had assured his board. The security brokers at Shearson Lehman "told us not to worry about backup lines." In the unlikely event that assistance was needed, the bigger banks in New York and San Francisco could be counted on to underwrite NCNB's commitments to borrowers.

Storrs never much cared for backup lines, reciprocal "what-if?" agreements that involved no balances or fees. Still, King's question gnawed at him. What *would* they do in the unlikely event their IOUs went begging? He decided to get to work setting up bank lines of credit, covering at least a reasonable amount of NCNB's current liabilities. "Directors can be very important," he decided, "not in running a business, but in raising questions on issues which to them seem important."

One issue on the minds of directors and executives alike was that of international expansion. NCNB International Banking Corporation was now a holding company subsidiary in its own right, generating breathtaking revenues for a start-up venture. In the first year operating out of the London office, McColl's international income had more than quadrupled, to $61 million. He had a cadre of experienced lending officers working a sophisticated "call program," selling short-term loans to brokers who used the money to finance underwriting and to secure advances to customers with margin accounts. Selling to brokers in Latin America, Asia-Pacific, North America, Europe, the Middle East and Africa, the call program produced an almost instant 130 percent increase in average loans.

In the summer of 1973, with Congress debating an end to United States air support of the Cambodian government, the NCNB international policy committee decided the twelve-year war in Southeast Asia was about over. The bank should take steps toward becoming a major player in the economies of China, Japan, Korea, Thailand and the other nations of Asia and the Pacific. Immediately, McColl made a trip to Hong Kong, where he met with Chinese-British bankers to discuss the possible purchase of an existing Hong Kong bank. When that deal fell through, McColl settled for opening up a branch office of NCNB International to be known as Inter-Asia Finance, Limited.

In Hong Kong, McColl looked up his uncle, David Carroll, the most mysterious member of his family. Rumor had it Uncle David was with the CIA, although nobody ever proved it. Carroll was pleased to see his favorite nephew, whom he remembered as a lad with great potential and impressive skills, one whose "counter always was up pretty high, even as a little boy." Carroll gave Hugh a taste of Hong Kong nightlife. At the Mandarin, he was introduced to Lena Horne and Janet Auchincloss. Brandishing his license for a Hong Kong branch like a newly forged saber, McColl told his uncle, "Hell, this opens up the Orient for us. We can come over here and plant cotton if we want to." Then he was off for New York, where NCNB had more business to conduct. For the first time, a bank from North Carolina would open a branch in "the money center."

As Addison Reese gradually handed over more and more responsibility to Tom Storrs, their bank was evolving into something never before seen in the New South. Reese might have been content to go out wassailing from Wachovia's grail, but Storrs already was onto the next quest: *interstate banking*. Storrs wanted to be a banker not merely of North Carolina, but of an entire region. He believed that eventually the provincial protective laws that kept bankers from grazing in one another's fields would be struck down so the nation might compete more effectively in a world-based economy. To McColl those laws were as outmoded and stifling as Charlotte's blue laws, which would have to be amputated before his city would be able to compete nationally.

Up until now NCNB's interstate business, outside of correspondent banking and credit cards, was being conducted by nonbank subsidiaries of the holding company. Storrs wanted somehow to create a banklike presence in the nation's only real money center, New York, to which McColl and Storrs alike were weary of paying homage.

The bank's legal advisors found a chink in New York's wall in a 1919 amendment to the Federal Reserve Act. Under the amendment, known as the Edge Act, any state- or nationally chartered bank could form a separate "banking corporation" to finance international commerce. This "Edge corporation" was allowed to sell notes, drafts and bills of exchange in order to complement the international banking activities of its parent bank. Unlike the parent bank, however, the Edge Act bank was permitted to operate interstate branches.

In 1919 the only beneficiaries of this amendment could have been the banks in New York, Philadelphia and a few other big cities, giving them yet another "edge" in taking import-export business away from smaller banks in smaller cities. But in August 1973, North Carolina National Bank opened an Edge Act bank in Manhattan, yet another brag in state banking circles and in the annual report. In addition to being the first and only Southeastern bank with an office in London, shareholders could be proud of "NCNB's establishment of an office in another of the world's great financial centers—New York."

For all its achievements, McColl's bank was something of a pariah in North Carolina banking circles. For generations the state Bankers Association had been controlled by the patriarchal heads of small banks who professed disdain and distaste for the upstarts from those too-big-for-their-britches banks down in Charlotte. McColl went to

Storrs with a plan for McColl to run for president of the association. Storrs laughed. McColl understood just as well as he did that "running for president" was an oxymoron when it came to the NCBA. The nominating committee already knew whose turn it was, John Forlines from Granite Falls.

"We can beat him," McColl said.

"Go for it then," replied Storrs.

McColl was determined that the rest of the state's bankers understand that they had to reckon with NCNB. "They couldn't adopt lobbying postures that ignored our views." Even if he didn't win, he would send the association a message: "You cannot have your little clique and run your association the way you want to. You will have to deal with us." With Storrs's blessing, McColl assigned Buddy Kemp to "manage the campaign." Kemp pointed out to him that the office had never been contested, not in living memory at any rate. McColl wasn't fazed, because he had gone over the association's bylaws with a fine-tooth comb. "It says you're entitled to one vote for every branch you have, provided the manager of that branch is present to cast his vote."

"You mean we have to get . . . ."

"Right. I want every damn branch manager in Pinehurst for that vote."

"Hugh, that's about a hundred people. You have any idea how much that's going to cost us?"

"Just get 'em there, Buddy, just for one day. Let 'em vote, send 'em home. No hotel. Rent a couple of buses. Meanwhile, let's see if we can't round up some other banks' votes."

McColl went on the road and asked for support from banks NCNB had helped out in the credit squeeze. He got votes from First National Bank of Eastern North Carolina, First Citizens Bank and a handful of others. He was not surprised to hear that Wachovia was organizing its managers against him, but he was surprised at the anti-McColl sentiment coming from a few blocks down South Tryon Street. He would have thought First Union could see their bread was buttered on the same side as NCNB's. Disregarding the First Union and Wachovia interference, Buddy Kemp bused in managers from around the state. Their one-day registrations paid, he trooped them off the buses, got their votes registered and loaded them up again for the ride back to their branches. Hugh McColl won the first contested election in the annals of North Carolina Bankers Association history.

The other members knew they were in for a long year, and McColl's reputation as a ruthless gunslinger was assured.

After setting up the Edge Bank office, McColl's next trip to New York was in October, on his first investment outing on behalf of NCNB. He, Hodges and Dougherty accompanied Reese and Storrs to Wall Street for the wooing of investment bankers. McColl found himself impressed at how thorough Storrs and Dougherty had been in setting up the negotiations and laying out the figures for potential investors. But when the talks bogged down in consideration of whether shares should be priced at thirty-five and five-eighths or thirty-five and seven-eighths, McColl became impatient. Never one to let details get in the way of "getting it done," he told the group they were in New York for only one reason, to raise capital. "Where I come from," he said, "when you're talking about any number that begins with 35 million, the number to concentrate on is the 35 million, not the pennies that go after it. In other words, let's sell it."

That was just the sort of utterance that made McColl a polarizing influence in his company. While a Chuck Cooley might find McCollisms amusing, even motivational, another newcomer to NCNB, like Joe Martin, might take offense. Either you liked Hugh McColl or you didn't. From the outset, Chuck Cooley liked him and Joe Martin didn't, though Cooley and Martin found each other kindred spirits. After helping his brother get elected to Congress, Martin had accepted Cooley's invitation to apply for a position at NCNB. Martin, the son of a South Carolina Presbyterian minister, had a doctorate in English literature from Duke University and a penchant for the hot 1970s field of corporate social responsibility. Cooley set up an interview for Joe Martin with Luther Hodges.

Martin found Hodges "exciting," with "a real commitment to social justice, to civil rights—and a personal interest in a political career that made me think he would be serious about building a good record." His curiosity piqued by Cooley, his social passions aroused by Hodges, Martin's intellect was stimulated in an interview with Tom Storrs.

Dazzling Martin with his grasp of statistics, Storrs explained that NCNB had maximized its penetration of the traditional North Carolina banking market. Martin was astonished to hear Storrs say, "But fully one-third of the people in the NCNB market are precluded from mainstream economic activity simply because they are black. Anything we can do to move them into the mainstream will give us a bigger banking market, and we'll get more than our share of that growth." Then Storrs added something even more radical: "And one-half of our people are precluded from full participation because they are female."

A white male corporation acknowledging its responsibility to minorities and women? Joe Martin was impressed. He decided that NCNB must have "its brain engaged in the commitment, as well as its heart, that it had a corporate stake in community development, and that it would not turn back under profit pressures."

Joe Martin turned down a marketing offer from Ed Crutchfield at First Union when Luther Hodges offered him a job as NCNB's "director of public policy," a newly created position. Initially Martin was expected to coordinate the charitable contribution budgets of city offices across the state. This put him in regular contact with the executive group in meetings that, for the most part, seemed perfunctory, but which gave him "a crash course" in the bank's vocabulary and in its executive dynamics. "There was only one person in the group as intimidating as Mr. Reese and Mr. Storrs," Martin concluded. "Hugh McColl was the most aggressively hostile person I had ever run into."

McColl used meetings like these to perfect the managerial techniques he had learned from Julian Clark and others. Martin suffered through "detailed questions about the most inconsequential contributions in obscure city offices" only to lose McColl's interest "unless I did not have an answer." Just like Julian Clark, McColl could do rapid-math calculations in his head and invite Martin to challenge his conclusions. "If Luther attempted to rescue me, the attack would intensify. I learned to be prepared, and I learned never to attempt to bluff Hugh McColl."

After a few of these meetings, Hodges suggested that Martin propose a new initiative to further NCNB's commitment to "corporate social responsibility." Martin came up with a pilot program to determine whether the bank should provide day-care for children of low-income employees. Martin prepared for the presentation as meticulously as he had prepared for his Ph.D. exams. "I pre-calculated every possible combination of numbers. I anticipated every detail McColl could ask about the operation of a pilot program."

But just as Julian Clark had done to him, McColl honed in on the one number that Martin never thought to look up: exactly how many children would be eligible for his day-care program, should this pilot prove workable? Martin had no idea; he wanted only to set the agenda. McColl scoffed at Martin's lack of preparation, then blistered Hodges for "wasting executive time on such nonessential issues" in the face of serious matters the group had to deal with.

To Martin's relief, Reese adjourned the meeting without a vote on corporate day-care. But no sooner had he got back to his desk than he received a call from Pat Hinson summoning him to the CEO's office. When Martin walked in, Reese kept his seat and did not offer one to his junior executive. "You're doing a good job," the chairman said. "Don't let McColl get you down; he's a good man." That was the end of the conversation and the only private meeting Joe Martin would ever have with Addison Reese. He left the office determined to act under the assumption that Reese was correct in his assessment. He must be wrong. He would begin "looking for the good" in Hugh McColl. But he knew it wouldn't be easy to find.

What Martin could not appreciate—perhaps not even Reese or Storrs could—was the intensity of the rivalry between Hugh McColl and Luther Hodges. As much as Reese wanted to beat Wachovia in deposits, McColl and Hodges wanted to beat each other in profitability. McColl was not hostile to the idea of a day-care center; he was hostile to the notion of any more gold stars going on Luther Hodges's report card.

As an NCNB executive you were always being graded, examined and compared; that was part of Reese's management style. His final and perhaps most elaborate scheme for stacking his players in a pyramid of merit was the Leadership Climate Study of 1973. Under this microscope, each of twenty-six chosen executives was questioned by house shrink James Farr. The questions had to do with each person's view of the other twenty-five. Farr methodically recorded the answers to the same list of questions by every team member about each of his or her teammates.

"They all filled out things on each other. So that we had everybody's scores on everybody. Who's the most bright, who's not, who's cooperative, who's not." For each executive, Farr then compiled a score sheet, which would allow every individual to know how his peers rated him. In an extraordinarily candid session, Reese called all the executives together and let a somewhat trepid Farr read aloud all twenty-six score sheets. The psychologist found the process "fascinating. We were all face-to-face, together. I don't know if I'd have nerve enough to do that again that way. But it was fascinating."

Farr felt embarrassed for the one executive who "came out just clobbered in that study." It was Elliott "Pete" Taylor, the man recruited under orders from the board as Reese's possible successor. About the only contribution Taylor had made, as most of the other executives saw it, was his successful campaign to trade in the company's little Cessna for a used but respectable twin-engine King Air 90.

Reese by this time was painfully aware of Taylor's ill fit in the company. His shortcomings went deeper than his personality and his unbankerly taste in furnishings. During 1973 there were hints that all was not right in some of the nonbanking areas, annoying problems in factoring and mortgaging that Tom Storrs felt should have been nipped in the bud. Taylor had been given responsibility for all non-bank holding company subsidiaries and he had been found wanting. Now Storrs forced Reese's hand, letting him know there was no room in the company for both Pete Taylor and Tom Storrs.

The next Monday morning when Reese conducted his weekly conference-call meeting Taylor was not in attendance. Using a pull-down microphone over his Charlotte conference table, Reese spoke to the key management people in Greensboro and other cities, allowing them to comment and ask questions over telephone lines. On this Monday the meeting covered a number of topics, none out of the ordinary, until Reese rose to his feet and said:

"For your information, Pete Taylor resigned Friday. Those functions that reported to him now report to me. And since there are no questions the meeting is ended." Reese hit the master telephone receiver button and the only sound in Charlotte as well as in conference rooms around the state was the hum of a line gone dead. Reese left the room.

Neither McColl nor Hodges had given Taylor a prayer of beating out Tom Storrs. In their private thoughts as well as their weekend conversations Storrs was the man who would lead them on the next stage of their journey. McColl felt that this provided him with a new opportunity to run down Hodges. From their first encounter, McColl had proven himself loyal and useful to Storrs, and Storrs—unlike Reese—had made himself accessible to McColl. He and Hodges both had qualities that Storrs lacked as a leader. Luther had grand public appeal as opposed to McColl's barracks rapport. But as yet McColl had no clue as to which one of them Storrs might consider most essential to the company's success and to his own as CEO.

What McColl knew all too well was that Luther Hodges was a formidable opponent. In 1973 Hodges's Banking Group I came up with two programs that both Reese and Storrs praised to shareholders as indicative of NCNB's "willingness to break from the orthodox" that separated them from banks like Wachovia, from banks that allowed themselves to be bound by "regulation or inertia." Hodges's bold initiatives made headlines around the state and got him dozens of speaking engagements. Together, the one-two marketing punches delivered thousands of new customers to the bank, helping to realize Reese's dream sequel of beating Wachovia not only in deposits but in *domestic* deposits.

Punch number one was a retail lending gut-buster. Traditionally, banks made loans only to people with good credit ratings and a number of years on the job. Traditionally, women had a hard time getting loans unless their husbands cosigned. Yet North Carolina's manufacturing economy was strong in young working people and in unmarried working women. Hodges and his marketing group came up with a plan to suck in this new borrowing market and a slogan to soften it—although the slogan may have come first and the plan second. Breaking with all that tradition, NCNB advertised loans to anyone who had a steady job and enough salary to pay it back. The ads trumpeted: "Your Name is Your Collateral."

With high-impact advertising, the bank began raking in loans for televisions and appliances, furniture and automobiles. Shareholders were pleased to read that "no longer is the mere lack of a credit record (as opposed to a poor credit record) grounds for denying a loan or requiring collateral or cosigners. This unorthodox commitment struck a responsive note in thousands of people and contributed substantially to a 29.3 percent increase in consumer credit outstanding in 1973."

Even more unorthodox, dramatic and well-received was Hodges's number-two punch, the announcement in September that NCNB would make conventional home mortgage loans at *8 percent interest*. It was an extraordinary move in extraordinary times, but Hodges convinced the executive management team that it was the right move at the right time.

By summer's end in '73, conventional mortgage loans were the hens' teeth of North Carolina's economy. Interest rates had been rising so rapidly that to "protect the little guy" the state legislature passed a usury law making it illegal to charge more than 8 percent interest on a first home mortgage of fifty thousand or less. When the prime rate oozed over the 8 percent limit, banks were forced to stop lending money on moderate-income mortgages. Consequently, most "little guys" had no way of purchasing a home. By September 1973 the prime hit 10.5 percent. And that, said Luther Hodges to the executive committee, would be just about as high as it would go.

Hodges proposed a "limited-time offer" of NCNB Mortgage Corp. loans at 8 percent interest. Storrs felt that Hodges "made a very reasonable case," convincing the rest of the executives that rates would soon drop to 7 or even 6 percent. At that point NCNB could sell off the 8-percent loans at a nice profit. If the bank moved now, Hodges argued, hundreds of middle-income home buyers in North Carolina would come in for financing on thirty-year mortgage loans up to forty-five thousand dollars. NCNB would be the good guys in the white hats. The positive publicity sure to be generated would be like pouring acid directly into the Wachovia esophagus. "In the long run," said Hodges, "we're going to get new customers and new friends for the bank."

In the short run, Hodges looked like a genius. Almost the very day his Eight Percent Plan hit the media ("NCNB proudly announces, both as a service to its customers and as an aid to the entire NC economy...") the interest rates dropped a quarter point, down to 10.25. The morning after the media blitz, applicants were standing in long lines at NCNB Mortgage offices. Loan officers virtually drowned in applications. First Union executives snarled at each other for missing the idea. Wachovia officers watched stunned as home buyers literally walked out of their banks to chase down a loan from NCNB.

By the end of the first week, the mortgage company had processed more than $6 million in loan applications, by the end of six weeks more than $33 million. Meanwhile, the prime rate—the amount NCNB was paying for the mortgage money it was lending—kept inching lower, causing an equal and opposite reaction in the case of Luther Hodges's prestige. Hodges just couldn't wait for the prime to get back down where it belonged so his Eight Percent Plan would start paying off in real dollars.

Yet, in the fall of 1973, who could be sure where anything was headed? Vice President Spiro Agnew resigned. President Nixon—accepting responsibility but not blame—hired a special prosecutor to investigate the break-in at the Democrats' Watergate headquarters, only to fire him. The United States quit Southeast Asia without winning anything. For a month Israel battled Egypt and Syria in the Yom Kippur War, the deadliest ever in the Middle East, only to sign a peace treaty with Egypt that brought the wrath of the other Arab nations down on the head of the United States. The oil embargo by the Organization of Petroleum Exporting Countries (OPEC) told Americans for the first time that their lives were largely in the hands of strangers. It was hard to figure out just what was going to happen, hard to be sure of anything.

One thing was certain: the year about to end, 1973, was the last year Addison Reese of Maryland would serve as the czar of North Carolina National Bank and its universal holdings. It was time for Reese to retire and turn the bank over to Thomas Storrs of Virginia. As of January 1, 1974, Storrs would become chairman of the holding company, chairman of the executive committee of the bank, and CEO of both entities.

The Executive Committee of the board proposed, and the full board approved, that Luther Hodges would become chairman of the board of the bank and would continue to be responsible for all retail banking operations. William Dougherty would be president of the corporation, supervising all operations and all nonbank subsidiaries. Hugh McColl, continuing to manage the corporate and international banking business, would become president of North Carolina National Bank.

Just fourteen years earlier McColl was a trainee on a salary of forty-five hundred dollars. As president his salary would be one hundred thousand dollars, come January. One day, he had promised his father, he would run this bank. Now, at least in title, it was his to run. He was the president.

Yet Reese and Storrs had set up this troika that made it impossible to "run" anywhere fast. The bank was like a sled with three lead dogs—four if you counted the man holding the whip, Tom Storrs. In his heart, McColl still believed Luther Hodges was the one both Reese and Storrs intended to be the next generation's chief executive. McColl had knowingly allowed himself to be set up, chasing the carrot of leadership they dangled so that he would work twice as hard to be number two. McColl could deal with that because he respected Hodges and his way with other people, especially his way with the troops. Luther could emulate both Reese the patrician and Storrs the intellectual. If that was what they wanted, Hodges was their man. McColl had to be in the trenches and on the point.

The odd-man-out was Bill Dougherty. McColl had to ask himself, "Is Dougherty really a competitor?" His first answer was, "No, not really." Then he had second thoughts. "Yes and no" would be the more accurate answer. When it came to competing for the attention of Storrs, Dougherty was very much in the hunt. But if the question was "Can Dougherty run this company?" the answer from both the other men would have to be a resounding "No."

McColl knew Hodges considered himself to be "the best marketing officer, with the best conceptual ideas about what to do." McColl saw himself as "the best customer man, the best salesman . . . the person who knew how to make money the best." As to Dougherty, "Bill thought of himself as the financial guru of the company and that he knew best what should be done based on returns on equities, or whatever returns or models he built. He wanted to run the company off models." McColl had no patience with Dougherty's methods, considering him evasive, uncooperative and unwilling to share essential information.

As soon as Storrs told him he was going to be president of the bank, McColl wanted to see what was going on in all the bank's profit centers. This information was kept by Dougherty in the "orange book." But the comptroller said he was forbidden by Dougherty to turn over a copy of the orange book to McColl. In a rage, McColl stormed into Storrs office and demanded to know, "What the hell is going on here? I'm the president of the bank, so why don't I get this information?"

From the outset, his relationship with Dougherty had been "tense, combative. . . . I don't think we were ever very fond of each other." McColl continued to admire the precision of Dougherty's accounting system, but argued that the system was intended more to keep control in Dougherty's hands than to assist bankers in servicing customers. McColl decided he would find a way to get rid of both Dougherty and his system when he finally got the power. McColl envisioned an accounting system that could produce, in addition to financial control data, information for and about customers that could be used in marketing. Accounting should enable rather than restrict his company, but that kind of thinking ran contrary to Dougherty's approach.

Most of those who followed the contest from the sidelines were putting their money on either Hodges or McColl. Bob Kirby, the personnel manager who once had turned McColl down for a trainee position, felt that Hodges's strengths lay outside the bank, McColl's inside. For Hodges, the son of a politician, "politics was his first love." Kirby saw that "as he rose in the company Luther spent more of his time outside than inside the company in terms of developing, and he did it for business . . . . But I always thought that he had a personal political agenda as part of all that.

"And all the while Luther was becoming quite prominent, quite well known, Hugh was quietly doing his thing, building account relationships, building business relationships and building networks and making money for the bank. I always thought that Luther never quite had the profit motive. I know he didn't, not nearly to the extent that Hugh did. But they were contemporaries and they were colleagues, they were pals and they were buddies."

Outside the bank the two men could be the best of friends. They had gone into business with each other and Craig Wall to buy land in South Carolina; they had chipped in with Wall on a cottage at Myrtle Beach. But when it came to Banking Group I versus Banking Group II, retail business versus commercial business, they were rivals to the death. They were like two high school chums who found themselves captaining the North Carolina and Duke basketball teams in the Atlantic Coast Conference championship game. McColl was dedicated to winning, so if he could block one of Hodges's shots, he would block it. He stole Hodges's people like he might steal the ball off Hodges's dribble. Sometimes the rivalry worked to the good of the bank. Other times, as in the case of Joe Martin's day-care proposal, it worked to the ill.

The rivalry between McColl and Hodges, the tension between Dougherty and the other two were acceptable losses to Tom Storrs. He believed his company to be "very thin on executive leadership" and he was not about to signal any one of his top lieutenants that either of the others was his choice as successor.

"Each one brought something very important to the company," and Storrs did not feel required in 1973 "to make a decision as to which of them was going to be the number-two person." Storrs's goal was "to keep them as evenly balanced as I could, and hold on to all three of them."

That effort ran contrary to the ambitions of Hodges, McColl and Dougherty. "I think Luther would have liked very much for me to have made a decision at that point. And he would have liked to have been the president. But they each ended up with a meaningful title. No one of them reported to one of the others. And we worked together there, I would say, on a reasonably good basis for several years. . . . I bought some time. And that's what I wanted to do. And since I didn't have to make a decision, I didn't make one. In other words, if you say, 'What would I have done if I'd had to make a decision?' I'd tell you, 'I don't know,' because I never made that decision."

The title of president helped McColl more outside the bank than inside, where he had worked for a number of people who now worked for him. Some of those relationships refused to turn upside-down simply because Reese and Storrs painted a new title on Hugh McColl's office door. It was Louis Henderson—"Mister Henderson" to McColl in his first days at the bank—who cleared up any misunderstandings on that score. It began with a simple phone call.

"Hugh, I'd appreciate if I could come see you."

President McColl was busy, but said, "Fine. I can see you at five o'clock." He had decided to make most of his appointments with associates after five.

"Well, that won't do," said Henderson. "I go home at four thirty."

"Well, when would you like to come?" The tone was submissive, almost contrite.

The appointment was set for ten o'clock the next morning, at which time Louis Henderson stated his purpose: "Hugh, I've been working for this bank for forty-seven years, since I was in high school. And I think I've earned the right to retire without having to go to sixty-five. And I want to do that."

Without hesitating, McColl said, "Yes, sir. We'll do that."

The new rule became known as the Henderson Relief Act. It stated that anyone with at least forty years of service was eligible for full retirement benefits at the age of sixty. McColl found it remarkable that he could be president and still be told what to do by Louis Henderson, but to him the bank was like a family. He might have greater power than his father or his uncles, but if they wanted to direct him, that was their prerogative.

As the Reese era ended and the Storrs era began, both men were in daily meetings with marketing and public relations executives over just what face to put on the annual report to their shareholders. To be sure, there was a wealth of good news. Earnings were through the roof. The forty-story NCNB Tower was almost ready, with nearly all its leasable space taken. International activity was better than anyone could have hoped for.

Yet, there was gnawing evidence of trouble. That Chadburn near-disaster, those problems in the nonbank companies. The Fed was clamping down, making it impossible to sell insurance the way they wanted to, so they would have to sell off the American Commercial Agency. These could be signs that go-go banking was going, going. . . .

In the last days in his office on the mezzanine, Addison Reese could afford to write the story his way. In a personal message entitled "A Banker Retires," Reese sounded like a proud father marrying his daughter to the suitor of his own dreams. The most important part of his job, he wrote, had been finding the right people. There might have been "a few strikeouts," but "my batting average has been pretty good."

He called on this team he'd assembled to maintain and strengthen the image he had built, an image of "progressiveness backed by solid management and good judgment." While they must "continue to grow in size and profits," even more important would be to provide good customer service, maintain quality assets and increase the bank's social awareness. Reese concluded his remarks with what could have been taken as either a boast or a cautionary tale:

"Above the portals of the National Department of History and Archives in Washington, these words are carved in stone: 'What is past is prologue.' A tourist riding by in a taxi read the words and asked the cab driver, 'What in the world does that mean?' The driver replied, 'Lady, that means you ain't seen nothing yet!'"

Across the mezzanine, Tom Storrs was writing it his way: studied, calculated, suggesting much but promising nothing. It was his first solo report to the shareholders and he wanted to get it right:

> *The past year was one of uncertainty for the nation's banking industry as inflation, national money market mechanisms and politics became closely entwined. As a result, for much of the year the prime lending rate was held at arbitrarily low levels in relation to other market rates and rapidly rising money costs. Rates*

on loans to smaller business borrowers were changed only frac-
tionally during the year, and for many borrowers were well below
the banks' out-of-pocket expense.

The Federal Reserve Board placed higher reserve require-
ments on demand deposits and negotiable certificates of deposit
and relaxed Regulation Q to allow banks to pay higher rates on
consumer savings deposits. The competitive response immediate-
ly raised the cost of these funds.

These events all held the potential for dampening the earn-
ings of NCNB. They sharply narrowed the spread between funds
costs and lending rates even as operating costs were feeling the
impact of inflationary forces.

The bank however increased its level of earning assets con-
siderably and showed substantial gains in fee income as well as
in income from international operations. . . .

The high money costs adversely affected the earnings of cer-
tain of our bank-related subsidiaries which borrow interest-sen-
sitive short-term funds and lend at relatively fixed rates. This
factor plus several large loan losses contributed to a 7.7%
decrease in 1973 earnings for these subsidiaries. . . .

The year ended with a host of uncertainties, and 1974
promises more of the same.

Like that woman in the taxicab, Tom Storrs, Hugh McColl and the
NCNB shareholders hadn't seen nothin' yet.

"Bankers are like sharks. When there is blood in the water they swirl and swarm around and they know. There are no secrets. . . . You can feel people seeking money in the marketplace."

Hugh McColl
May 18, 1998

CHAPTER 8

In the breeze of 1974's first quarter, Hugh McColl could feel what Storrs meant by "a host of uncertainties." It started with one of Charlotte's most prominent home builders, the Erwin Company. Erwin had grown so fast that it attracted a deep-pocketed purchaser, American Cyanamid Corporation. That made Erwin appear "bullet-proof" from the effects of the national recession. Word at the City Club was that American Cyanamid would never let its subsidiary fail. McColl knew the bank had a lot of loan money outstanding to Erwin, but it seemed secure enough.

When the notes came due, however, McColl discovered that assumption was "180 degrees out from the truth. American Cyanamid was so big that they could let the Erwin division go under and never miss it. So they did." And American Cyanamid's name was not on the loan paper. "We lost right much money on it. Great lesson in that. We learned that nobody stands behind something they don't have to." McColl and his team had not made the loans; the loans had come through NCNB Mortgage. But the lost money came out of his bank. In 1974 there were, as he put it, "a hell of a lot of lessons" about to be learned.

The next yardstick to the knuckles came from the South Carolina affiliate McColl had purchased for the Mortgage

Corporation, C. Douglas Wilson & Company. On loan from the bank to ease Wilson's transition, Bill Covington uncovered several bad loans that should have surfaced earlier. To make sure NCNB Mortgage Corporation was adequately covered, its loan loss reserve was pumped up by 50 percent. McColl heard the hiss of oxygen leaving his bank's tires.

With the prime down to 9.5 percent, NCNB Mortgage had more than two thousand happy customers delighted with or ready to move into their new homes. Thanks to Luther Hodges and NCNB, their monthly mortgage payments were fixed at only 8 percent for thirty years. The good publicity long milked out, Storrs directed Hodges to close the door on this 8 percent mortgage money. By this time, NCNB had over $50 million invested, and the prime still needed to drop another two points before the loss began turning into profit.

Instead of moving down, the prime started back up. Mid-February it was flirting with 10 percent again. Most of NCNB's assets had fixed rates while most of its liabilities had floating rates, floating in the wrong direction. The water was up to Storrs's and McColl's waists already, and neither was a tall man.

Yet in the eye of the beholding public, NCNB was standing tall indeed, all grown up into the nation's twenty-sixth-largest bank. It had more than $3.6 billion in assets. The nonbanking subsidiaries of NCNB Corporation had 250 offices in six states and two foreign countries. Overall earnings were up 13 percent, and the company was about to take command of the most impressive building ever erected in Charlotte. The only fly buzzing around this ointment was the bothersome fact that everything was financed by borrowed money.

McColl had heard Storrs assure director Huger King that was really no problem at all. Yet, in his very first quarter as chairman and CEO, Tom Storrs was wondering just what he'd walked into.

Deciding he didn't have all the information he needed, Storrs set up a group of analytic magi at the bank who would be referred to as the Balance Sheet Management Department. Their job would be to monitor the economic heavens for any signs of "interest rate risk," as Storrs put it. This department's daily report, "drawing on yesterday's numbers as to what kind of exposure we would have" would be one of the most important auguries NCNB's Finance Committee would consult each morning before the day's work began.

There were almost too many numbers to think about at one time, because of the bank's increasing international exposure. With the end of the convertibility of the U.S. dollar into gold in 1971, the relative value of each country's currency was determined by factors such as the country's account balance, the general strength of its economy, its rate of inflation and interest as compared to those of other nations. This was known as the floating exchange rate, and it was almost a floating craps game. Dollars, deutchmarks, francs, yen and cruzeiros were rolled like dice, blown on by recession and inflation.

Thanks to the United States' official and public sympathy for Israel, the Arab nations were enjoying their discovery of crude oil-as-weapon. Oil prices were up more than 400 percent, America was sitting in lines at gas stations and the world economic order was changed forever. By turning down the flow of oil, OPEC turned up the flow of cash into its bank accounts, guzzling at an annual rate of over $100 billion. Thanks largely to higher energy prices, the United States and the rest of the industrialized world was now in the grip of the worst recession since the 1930s, and domestic loan demand was rapidly evaporating. If a bank's management made the wrong throw or tried to cheat the game, snake-eyes was a distinct possibility.

The NCNB Finance Committee decided something like that might be going on at the nation's twentieth-largest bank, Franklin National. A $3.7 billion go-go challenger to the money center giants of Manhattan, Long Island's Franklin was one of the banks with which NCNB had entered into a reciprocal "interbank deposit" agreement. This was different from Huger King's "backup lines," which basically allowed one bank to support loans called against another bank. With interbank lines, each bank essentially maintained an open account in the other bank, like a well it could go to whenever its own bucket needed a quick refill. In the first quarter of 1974, Franklin National was making too many trips to the NCNB well, and Hugh McColl decided it might be time to end the agreement. He sent Jim Sommers to call on the president of Franklin.

Meeting with all the senior executives from the bank, Sommers found himself being called on the carpet. Didn't he realize he worked for an upstart country bank in—where was it, Charleston, South Carolina? His boss, McColl, surely did not understand what he was doing. "You probably don't understand this," condescended one of the Franklin execs, "but our loans are going to Mexico. The proven petroleum reserves in Mexico alone, at forty dollars a barrel, will pay every bit of the Mexicans' external debt. So what are you worried about?"

Sommers thought for a moment, then answered, "Well sir, you are right. I didn't know that. So I guess that oil is forty dollars now, and the Mexican oil's in the ground now. And that may or may not be the price later, when they get the oil out of the ground."

A few minutes later the chairman of Franklin National was on the phone with McColl, demanding that he fly up personally and take control of the situation. McColl agreed since, after all, this was a major bank, a New York bank, even though it was on Long Island. But after sitting down with the Franklin executives, McColl agreed with Sommers that there was no future in this relationship. By the end of the meeting the interbank line to Franklin National was closed. Payment of the outstanding debt would be expected upon the due date.

April 18 the rest of the banking world found out what McColl and Sommers suspected. The bottom had dropped out of Franklin National. Its first-quarter earnings were down to two cents a share, from sixty-six cents in the first quarter of 1973. Within a few weeks the Federal Reserve declared Franklin failed. The industry had never imagined that a bank worth nearly $4 billion *could* fail. In Charlotte the message was painfully clear: NCNB was almost exactly the same size, with the same self-determinate attitude as the late, lamented Franklin National Bank.

Determined to keep his bank from sharing Franklin's fate, McColl paid attention when Tom Storrs told his senior team that times were about to get "really tough on the availability of funds." If America's economy was going to the bears, McColl agreed it would become even more difficult to find money in the United States. So, before the end of April, McColl proposed that NCNB should go on the offensive and buy up all the Eurodollars it could lay its hands on. Again, Storrs liked McColl's ability to move quickly and decisively.

"Hugh went and picked up the telephone and called the man in London and said, 'Go get all the money you can on extended securities.' And he did." McColl borrowed millions in six- and nine-month notes from European bank offices. That would help NCNB stay liquid and out of trouble for the time being. But it was a little pill for a major pain. If investors in New York and on the West Coast found out the true state of NCNB's dependency on Eurodollars, they would lose confidence in NCNB stock and NCNB Corporation commercial paper. McColl knew the worst was yet to come, fast and hard. He was not looking forward to the merry month of May.

The first Sunday of the month, May 5, the *New York Times* business section featured a photograph of NCNB's tower and an article applauding the bank's fast track to success. That was faint praise compared to the damning truth hidden within the gray matter of the story. The *Times* pointed out that Southern banks had been hit hardest by the first-quarter economy. So was the NCNB hayride about to end?

McColl read the irony in that. Ever since he could remember, ever since he'd half-listened to his grandmother's dinner-table complaints about the ignorant Yankees, Southern bankers and businessmen had been trying to catch the attention of "the money center." Finally, the Northern establishment was starting to notice what was going on in Charlotte, just in time to watch it crumble from the edges. *Wait until the* New York Times *and the* Wall Street Journal *get a look at our first-quarter earnings report. Here come the I-told-you-so's.*

About two weeks later, late on the afternoon of Thursday, May 23, the NCNB executive team took their places at the front of a New York hotel room filled with securities analysts. McColl hoped the stock-and-bond people had availed themselves of the complimentary drinks, what with Wall Street closed for the day. They would be hearing nothing but bad news from Storrs and company. By this time, it should come as no shock to anyone that the U.S. economy was in a jam. But NCNB was about to become the first bank to pillory itself before the nation, publicly admitting that Federal Reserve Chairman Arthur Burns was right: America in general and the Southeast in particular had fallen on hard times.

Before Storrs could finish explaining the reasons behind NCNB's first decline in earnings after forty-one straight quarters of success, McColl saw the trickle of traders heading for the exits. They still had time to place sell orders with their West Coast offices. *Forty-one good quarters,* McColl thought, *and the marble just rolls off the table.*

In Charlotte, every day at NCNB became an emergency. Storrs advised McColl—the man he knew he could count on in emergencies—that each morning would start with a Finance Committee meeting. They brought in Rufus Land, who managed the balance sheet; Bob Barker, who was familiar with marketing concerns and the international side; Jim Thompson, who handled bonds and funds management, and others as needed. McColl liked Thompson not simply because he was a graduate of the University of North Carolina, but because he had a way of looking at the bigger picture, rather than focusing on running a single profit center as McColl himself tended to do. McColl had promoted Thompson to manage the bank's investment portfolio and begin laying plans for invasion of the brokerage houses' turf.

The Finance Committee held its early-morning sessions in the new tower, even though it was not quite ready for occupancy. A seventh-floor trading room had multiple phone lines installed, and there was no chance a director would walk in on them there. The floor was bare concrete, the walls unpaneled Sheetrock, the tables the kind with fold-up legs and pressed-wood tops that could take a lot of coffee rings. They called it the war room.

"The reason it sounds dramatic is that it was." Hugh McColl understood the meetings were critical "to fund the bank. And every day we would go down and meet and discuss it with our key lieutenants. About what was happening. And they would bring us up to date, and we would stay there until we knew we had it funded for the day. You know, it was really sort of hairy."

In the Marine Corps, McColl had practiced for war, but had never gone into battle. This seemed a lot like what he'd practiced, like what he'd learned about war as a child. When the Big War started, Hugh was six years old. He remembered it like it was six days ago.

The whole town was watching the air show that chilly Sunday afternoon, out at the Bennettsville airport, where the Army Air Corps had set up a training base, just in case. Engines roaring, planes cartwheeling around the sky, then a surprise: the big loudspeakers said the show was over and everybody should go home and listen for the president's announcement.

"Turn on the radio, Hugh."

The console stood taller by a foot than Hugh was. He could reach the knob, though. He turned it *click*, heard the hum, climbed into Daddy's lap. Mr. Roosevelt's voice came on and said it was a day that would live in infamy. He saw his mother and father looking into each other's eyes, quiet, so he looked at his sister's eyes, but Fran didn't understand any more than he did.

It got exciting then, the living room papered in battle maps from the *New York Times* and *Life* and *Colliers*. Daddy would draw the lines with colored pencils as the war moved around Europe and the Pacific.

"This is France, Hugh, what they call Normandy."

"Now right here are the Philippine Islands."

He and Fran and friends pulled red wagons around town collecting flattened tin cans. Those would be turned into ammunition for the GIs who were getting shot at. A confirmed patriot, Hugh gave up his bottlecap collection and every one of his lead soldiers too. The GIs needed bullets.

In the summer the family went to the beach, down to Conway, and it was spooky at night because you couldn't turn on any lights. Black curtains on every window, dinner by candlelight, early bedtimes, all the cars with their headlights' top half painted black like sleepy eyelids.

On the beach at sunset, the kids could watch the convoys of supply ships headed for England. Through binoculars they could make out the navy destroyers riding shotgun. *Those German subs wouldn't dare to come this close to America, would they? Reckon not. Be durned crazy. Like to see them try.* Then one evening, BOOM! Right before his eyes, an oil tanker shot flames up a hundred feet, lighting up the east like that was where the sun went down. *Like the fires of hell,* Daddy said. A U-boat got it with a torpedo. Gunfire from the destroyers, airplanes overhead, circling. *Imagine anybody made it off that ship alive?*

Some of their relatives would not be returning from the war. One cousin died in the Pacific. Another cousin, Duncan McColl, wrote about how a torpedo almost got him. They said thank God he was on the swimming team at Chapel Hill. Duncan pushed himself to the surface, water on fire all around him. Fifteen hundred men killed that day.

The soldiers fought on and on and Hugh lived his childhood with the war. Strange gifts came from overseas: a Nazi helmet, two Japanese battle flags, one of them covered with blood, a Japanese bayonet picked up off a dead soldier at Iwo Jima. He was just a boy and the war was far away, but it would be part of him forever.

Now, in the war room, chalk walls covered with scribbled numbers of instantly lost import, Hugh McColl found himself wistful over last spring's go-go days, long-ago as that boy and his wagon.

"Scrap metal for the war, sir?"

"Money to lend, sir."

No more playing soldier. This was real war and it was hell.

McColl simply could not recall his division ever losing any money for the bank, though he might have lost some sleep over a few loans that got on the edge. So where had they gone wrong?

Nights now were seeming long, the hours of sleep few. The new house on Colville Road maybe needed blackout curtains. Jane looked at her husband's hair and thought she saw the gray coming in. She wanted Hugh to stop for a while, stop trying to prove something to himself. Or more likely, to his father. His sister Fran told her, *"You know, Daddy thinks Hugh's absolutely worthless."* He'd been riding that one on his back too long.

Drinking helped Hugh McColl get through the evenings, but he knew he had to watch that. Heavy drinking was part of the McColl curse. His Uncle D. K. had it, always angry at life and at lives that bumped up against his. Old-timers at the bank told him Uncle D. K. had tried like the devil to take over the board, first at the old American Trust, then American Commercial, but they wouldn't have him, even though for a while he was the largest stockholder. Too much drinking and bad temper. Hugh's mother talked about inbreeding—McColl marrying McColl over generations of isolation in America, clannish to a fault, she said. He knew all that was behind his Daddy's deal with him and his brothers in college. *"Stay away from the bottle and I'll give you a ten-thousand-dollar savings bond when you get out."* That had worked. He went through four years of college, including fraternity life, without even so much as a beer.

Poor Fran had it now, the McColl depression. In and out of hospitals, Hugh picking up the bills so his Daddy would worry less. It was Fran's children that worried Hugh. And right now he didn't need another damn thing to worry about. He couldn't give in to the bottle and he couldn't give in to his moods. Funny, he thought, how depression could kill him the way a depression could kill his bank.

In sleepless nights on Colville Road and morning meetings at the bank he analyzed and dissected the situation. McColl couldn't absolve himself completely. It was his own can't-fail, brass-assed recklessness that infected the company. He had gone and got himself elected president of the state Bankers' Association, even though they didn't want him, then forced them to spend their dues on lobbying for higher credit card interest rates instead of smiling at each other's wives at a bunch of dull parties. It was nobody but Hugh McColl who'd bulled the bank into London's china shop, nobody but McColl who'd stoked the raging corporate ego by working the bank out of a few problems. Now he had to face the fact that things were "moving very quickly on us. And we had no way out of it because of our heavy dependence on the short-term CDs and short-term Euro-market."

NCNB had become more susceptible than most American banks to the pain of high interest rates. He saw a bank "so highly dependent on purchase money out of the Euro-markets and out of the national CD market that our rates started ratcheting up immediately on the buy side, the liability side." That's what brought profits to a crashing halt. "We had also made the error of making placement with a lot of foreign banks, that is buying money short and lending it long, buying it on three months and lending it six months. And as the rates ratcheted up, the second three months we were having negative spreads on placements. And in addition to that, we had credit risks, performance risks."

Finally, as interest rates rose NCNB had to charge higher rates to its existing customers, "and whatever profit margins the customers had began to shrink." Which made those customers shrink from doing any more business with NCNB. Some of McColl's long, deep relationships were beginning to go dysfunctional.

And it all had seemed like such a good deal until the interest rates headed to the moon.

As Storrs bore into his executive team for any veins of promise, he began to use phrases like "retrenching" and "closing branches," putting Luther Hodges on the defensive. Hodges argued at planning sessions that "you've got to stay with it and you've got to build, even in difficult times." Storrs may have been simply searching for anything that might help, but Hodges took him in dead earnest.

From Luther Hodges's vantage point, "Tom Storrs panicked a little because he had just gotten the reins and all of a sudden it was going sour. He panicked about some loans that he wanted called, even though we had made commitments." One of these, according to Hodges, was the commitment the bank had made to C. D. "Dick" Spangler, now chairman of the Bank of North Carolina. Spangler's bank was still "in trouble and needed help," Hodges insisted. "And then he wanted to get out of the retail business. . . . And he wanted me to sell the Trust Company of Florida. And I said, 'You can't do these things.' He was in retreat and I thought that was wrong."

Hodges recognized that "McColl's side of the business, the wholesale side of the business, was doing better than anything else. The real estate side of the business, which was one of the things that Dougherty ran, was doing terribly. That was the real problem. Storrs was trying to find liquidity to deal with Dougherty's problems. And one way to get more liquid was to retreat in North Carolina, because it wasn't making money."

Hodges felt that with McColl's international business bringing in the desperately needed capital and Dougherty's subsidiaries constantly in the spotlight, his North Carolina branches—the same branches that had enabled the bank to overtake Wachovia—were now becoming "stepchildren." In fact, Hodges was beginning to feel something of a stepchild himself. He saw in meeting after meeting that Storrs was "more comfortable with Hugh McColl" than he was with Luther Hodges. Storrs and McColl and Dougherty refused to listen to Hodges, pruning limbs from the trees without stepping back and looking at the forest. He urged them to "take a longer view of things," to be visionaries in the fashion of Addison Reese, but he knew the others considered him "not as quantitative and not as tough vis-à-vis the current month's earnings."

Hodges considered taking the opportunity to leave the bank and let his pal McColl have it all. If he got out now, he could run for governor. A lot of his friends were urging him to do that, telling him he'd make an even better governor than his father had, telling him the Republicans had blown their opportunity, thanks to Nixon's White House. But he also heard people saying that his bank was a flash in the pan, that NCNB's ride was over. Hodges didn't like that. He knew the bank, like the economy, was simply in a down cycle, a cycle that could be ridden out. He willed himself to stay with the bank, to "win that particular game and show that we were the quality bank we had said we were."

It was the quality of information that disturbed Storrs and McColl. They could not be sure that Hodges was getting an accurate picture from the people he had out there pushing loans. Had McColl's cornering of the "tiger" market left Hodges with a flock of sheep masquerading as carnivores? At the same time, McColl began to doubt the information Dougherty was feeding them about his nonbanking subsidiaries. As overall head of back-office operations, all the numbers were Dougherty's to present, and he could put them in whatever light he wanted to shine. McColl wondered whether it was fair for the bank that one team's captain should also be the scorekeeper of the game. He felt certain that his own people were honest. "We weren't out there fooling ourselves, hoping things would get better."

At last ready to move into his new office on the twenty-third floor of the tallest building in Charlotte, Tom Storrs boxed up a few personally important items. One was a framed picture Mr. Reese had presented to him a few months back. It was autographed: *To Tom Storrs, Captain of the best team in the business, Addison Reese.*

There were five people in the black-and-white photo. One was Addison Reese, looking the way he always looked, dark-rimmed eyeglasses like a steelworker's goggles in reverse, protecting the outside world from the sparks and the splinters of metal those eyes could hit you with. Storrs noticed Reese's hair was almost gone now. Looking at his own hair in the picture, he saw it was going too. Dougherty and Hodges had receding hairlines as well. Not McColl. His hair was too long, sideburns like some disco singer framing his wolfish ears. He had unbankerly bushy eyebrows, full lips. Put a chaw of tobacco in his cheek and McColl could pass for a second baseman dressed for church. Dougherty seemed plump, pigeony, gray-faced, next to McColl. Hodges looked like a politician passing through the bank to shake a few hands and collect a few campaign contributions.

Best team in the business? There were things about each one of those men Storrs would change if he could. McColl's quick mouth, for example. He knew all too well there were a lot of things McColl and Dougherty would change about each other. No way to do that, no more than Rex Harrison in *My Fair Lady* could make a woman be more like a man. This was his team, personalities fully formed long before he got hold of them, not like the raw midshipmen he'd trained at gunnery school. You had to take these men the way they were, use them for what they could give you. Put tape over McColl's mouth and you'd lose the man's greatest value, his candor. McColl would always tell you what he thought. Three different personalities, though, made for a volatile combination. His job, his gift from Mr. Reese, was to keep the three of them functioning as a team for as long as he could. He wouldn't hang the picture on the wall. That would be immodest. Better to keep it in a closet and take it out now and then, to remind himself of the challenge.

Addison Reese's most precious office possessions were his antique clocks. On moving day he asked his secretary, Mrs. Hinson, to help him carry the clocks across South Tryon Street and up to the new office where he would settle as an interested bystander in the daily operations of the company he'd built.

Pat Hinson waited with her boss for the light to change, then started across. "In the middle of the street he turned around and looked at the old building, with really a nostalgic look on his face, and he said, 'Mrs. Hinson, I never thought we'd leave that building.'" Hinson fought back tears.

There was no "mezzanine" in this new tower fashioned from Reese's imagination. Nor was there a spot for Reese among the suite of executive offices on the twenty-third floor. That suite was designed for Storrs and the other three men he had anointed to run the company. From now on Reese would concentrate on his two favorite projects, the University of North Carolina at Charlotte and Mercy Hospital.

The new NCNB Tower was completed at a cost of $60 million. Its forty stories of glass dwarfed anything else on the Charlotte skyline. It had parking decks for 450 cars, a 50,000-square-foot shopping arcade and soon would add a 371-room hotel, uptown Charlotte's first new hotel in half a century. NCNB Corporation was committed to occupying 370,000 square feet of office space at $6.50 per square foot, a rent bill of $2.4 million a year. McColl figured they could have gotten offices elsewhere uptown for just over half that figure, $3.50 a square foot. "You boys will have to pay for it," Reese had said. And pay and pay. In McColl's eyes, red from late-night figuring of NCNB's liability flood and asset drought, it appeared that bodacious tower of Addison Reese's was going to drain at least a million dollars a year out of Hugh McColl's bank for the next thirty-five years. That was assuming the bank and the tower and McColl stayed together that long.

In a way, McColl supposed, the pendulum was swinging back to 1968 and 1969, when the money left Southeastern banks for better CD rates at the big banks in New York. Only this time the pendulum looked like an ax blade. Money center banks were simply better credit risks than upstarts like NCNB and other regionals. "The money is moving to quality," Mr. Storrs kept saying, and McColl did not like the sound of that.

Most years summers could be counted on: sluggish, business like a stalled engine you tried to crank while the people you depended on waved towels from a beach somewhere. Not the summer of '74. NCNB had more business than it could handle, and it was bad business.

It started Monday, the first day of July, with word from New York and their new investment banking partner, Salomon Brothers. Just a few months back, Salomon had been so proud to sign on NCNB as its first bank client. Now the representative regretted to inform NCNB that it simply could find no market out there for the bank's commercial paper. Any short-term money available to the bank would be priced at the unheard-of interest rate of 25 percent. Instead of rolling over its existing commercial paper obligations, the bank would have to pay back the holders of the paper, with interest, when they became due.

They became due in four days. A frightening number of obligations would hit them on Friday, July 5. The finance committee ordered a reckoning from Bill Dougherty's computers. By Tuesday, July 2, the committee had all the numbers they needed to realize the bank was going to be caught short, by about $40 million. Unless they could come up with an instant infusion of cash, the company was going to flatline.

The calendar gave them more cause for alarm. Banks around the United States would be closed for the Independence Day holiday on Thursday, the fourth, and Friday, the fifth. That meant any possible source of money in the United States would also be closed come Thursday. Around the table, the leaders of North Carolina's largest bank looked into each other's eyes and saw nothing but desperation. NCNB was about to fail.

It was McColl who came up with a plan.

His office in London would be open Thursday and Friday while America picnicked. He picked up the phone and called Bernie Furlonger across the Atlantic, where the Tuesday business day was winding down.

"Bernie," he said, "I need you to raise $40 million and I need it by Friday."

And then they waited, because there was nothing else they could do. Everything would depend on the competency of people halfway around the world, many of whom were complete strangers to most of the top executives in Charlotte. Only Hugh McColl knew all of them. He had invested them with trust and now he would find out whether they really accepted their responsibility. The telex and phone lines heated up as McColl's international team went to bat.

Meanwhile, McColl had another critical patient, one that might not survive the weekend without surgery. This was a long-time NCNB customer, Blythe Brothers Construction, one of the region's best-known paving contractors. In the late '60s Blythe heard the siren song of leisure and recreational development. Now they found themselves holding unfinished and unwanted resort property in the Myrtle Beach area, not to mention an entire golf course in the fried-seafood capital of Calabash, North Carolina. Getting into all this debt had required a great deal of help from NCNB Tri-South and NCNB Mortgage Corporation as well as from NCNB-the-bank, where one family member, Jack Blythe, sat on the board of directors.

It was Buddy Kemp who brought McColl the chart showing Blythe Brothers' condition, and Kemp's reading of the prognosis was not good. He thought they needed at least $4 million to keep from going bankrupt, which was another way of saying "break the bank." McColl and Kemp pored over the Blythe books and came up with a solution. The company owned some rental property that was generating a cash flow of just over thirty-thousand dollars a month. If they had someone who could buy that property, Blythe just might survive a while longer. McColl picked up the telephone and called his friend Dick Spangler, who wasn't sure he ought to get involved. Spangler said he'd like to sleep on it. McColl told him to wake up early with the right answer.

In fact, Spangler had trouble sleeping. His Bank of North Carolina was still in trouble, and he did not feel comfortable in the world of banking and high finance. He went out in his backyard at Hempstead Place and looked up into the sky. It was full of stars, a propitious sign. He found the constellation Leo unusually bright that night, and remembered that Hugh McColl's middle name was Leon, a derivative of Leo, the lion. He decided he'd be bold, lionlike.

The next morning, at McColl's office, Spangler agreed to help, provided the bank would advance him the money. To minimize his personal risk, he would create a new corporation.

"What do we call it?" asked Buddy Kemp.

"Leo Corporation," answered Spangler.

"Okay," said McColl to Kemp. "we'll create a sale for Blythe using our own money." Kemp pointed out that the bank didn't actually *have* any money, but McColl was certain his London people were going to come through. And if they didn't, another $4 million wouldn't make much difference.

When he took Spangler down to meet with loan officer Neal

Trogden, Kemp was appalled to discover Spangler's net worth listed at only $1 million. Trogden said he would have to turn down the $4 million loan. McColl took a quick look at Spangler's financial statement and saw that Selwyn Village was being carried at a value of only thirty-thousand dollars. "That property's worth at least $5 million," he said. On McColl's authority, Trogden made the loan. Spangler signed a note for $4.1 million, dated July 3, 1974, and Blythe Brothers survived to build another day.

McColl joined the family at the beach house they shared with the Hodgeses and the Craig Walls for an abbreviated Independence Day holiday, some hot dogs and firecrackers. Walking the sand with Jane that night he drifted back to the Palmetto Billiard Parlor in downtown Bennettsville, circa 1947. That was where he'd first encountered a telex machine.

He could always hear it ticking, like the clock in the crocodile in Peter Pan, even back at the third table where he'd be shooting five and nine, the two money balls. A quarter on the five and a quarter on the nine. If he made them both and there were four players, he could make a dollar and a half in five minutes. Under the clacking of billiard balls, the boasts of boys and the muttering of old men, the tape wire against the wall ticked out baseball scores every summer day. Inning by inning the scores would come in, the bell would ding and the games would pause for a report. There were quarters riding on the telex, too.

"It's St. Louis 3, the Cubs nothing after six."

"Breechen still got his no-hitter working?"

"Yes indeed."

"Anything on the Yankees yet?"

McColl's team was the New York Yankees. Imagine. Every evening he'd bring the Yankee stats to Tommy Hamer, crippled with polio. Tommy loved the Yankees too. They talked about how one day the South would get a major league team, maybe in New Orleans or Nashville. But if McColl had no hometown team to root for, he'd always go with the winner. Starting in 1947, Casey Stengel's Yankees would win the World Series seven out of the next eight years. The only other team to win in that span was the Cleveland Indians, Harry Easterling's favorite team.

"Check the telex, Harry. See about the Yankees."

With so much more than quarters at stake, the tickertape back in the office would be clacking now, laying down the stats on a team of bankers he'd put together that might be even more impressive than Casey Stengel's pinstripers. Bob Barker, Jim Thompson, economist Al Smith—they all had instructions to call him at the beach with any word, any time. He was splashing in the waves with little Jane. And talking with his buddy from college, Paxson Glenn.

"Seem a little uptight, Hugh."

"Ha. Just waiting for a call from England."

"Something serious?"

"Huge, Pax. We don't get it, we're down the tubes."

"Phone, Hugh." Jane shouted and he could hear the tension in her voice. He ran for the house, telling Glenn to keep an eye on the kids.

The loans came in. Four million. Twelve. Thank God the British didn't celebrate the Fourth of July. Up to thirty-two. *Forty . . . Fifty-five . . .* Okay, the four-mill to Spangler was covered. God bless Bernie Furlonger. He could swim naked in the Thames and McColl wouldn't care. As long as Hugh McColl had a say in the matter, Bernie Furlonger had a job. He went back to the beach and Pax Glenn could tell by the big grin that McColl still had his job.

Before the bank opened for business after the holiday, their paper was secured. But escaping the frying pan did not actually extinguish the fire.

The very next Thursday, July 11, the war room committee got hit with still more bad news. NCNB was holding a $3 million short-term note from London's Israel-British Bank, Ltd. The note was due to be repaid on July 12, tomorrow, freeing up that money for pressing needs. The London office regretted to inform Charlotte that this payment would not be forthcoming; Israel-British had just failed.

Jim Sommers was devastated. This wasn't like a loan to a real estate developer; this was a bank deposit and it was not supposed to carry any risk. Everybody worked on the assumption that the Bank of England would stand behind its authorized subsidiary banks. Now it seemed the United Kingdom was giving notice that it would not provide an open purse to every foreign banker. It was the American Cyanamid-Erwin Construction story all over.

The NCNB committee realized that the big New York banks had seen the failure coming and pulled their money out. "All the 'major friends of Israel' pulled out and left the people who didn't have any suasion in. And we kind of got tagged real hard." Maybe, Sommers suggested, regional banks shouldn't be playing in this global game.

McColl disagreed. He looked at the options and decided that there was a chance to save some of the Israel-British investment, if they had the courage to take it. Instead of simply losing his shirt, McColl did the unheard-of. He bought the shredded shirts of other bankers. Anticipating a 100-percent loss, bankers agreed to sell NCNB their notes at ten cents on the dollar, thereby losing only ninety cents. But when the immediate crisis passed, the Israel-British Bank resuscitated itself. McColl wound up recovering half of NCNB's original investment.

From now on, McColl and Storrs decided to become even more selective about which banks they would put their money in. Despite NCNB's own reputation as a Jack in Giant-land, NCNB's deposits, Storrs assured his shareholders, would from this point on be only "with the largest banks in the world" and "at very short maturities."

Trouble was coming from too many quarters now, and Tom Storrs knew he had no choice but to seek help. Storrs had been the one to resist when his boardroom nemesis Huger King demanded lines of credit with other banks. Now Storrs was about to find out whether King's security blanket was real. He and McColl divided up the banks that had signed reciprocal backup credit agreements with NCNB and they got on the phone.

Most of the bank executives responded gallantly. BankAmerica chairman Chauncey Medberry said he would double the $10 million line of credit NCNB had established. Chemical Bank, on the other hand, retreated from its commitment, unless NCNB would agree to go public with its problems—a condition tantamount to rejection.

After all the promises were called in, McColl wished they had protected themselves completely, because this line-of-credit blanket still left them uncovered by about $25 million. Storrs packed up Dougherty in the King Air for a hasty trip to New York and a call on Walter Wriston. After first telling Storrs he would have to go back on his word to Citibank's board, Wriston finally agreed to make the loan. Storrs telephoned McColl and let him know they would be able to hold things together a while longer.

More bad news from the economic crystal ball-gazers.

Now the prime interest rate was up to 12 percent and looked to be going higher. Storrs was angry with himself for not seeing this coming. Why couldn't Luther Hodges have been content with giving away dishes the way other banks did? Those 8 percent mortgages and "Your Name is Your Collateral" loans were killing him. The bank was paying dearly in short-term notes for the $55 million NCNB Mortgage Corporation had loaned out. Instead of turning a profit, Hodges's 8-percent mortgage scheme was like an open gash, draining cash-blood out of the bank while McColl and Storrs did everything they could to pump more cash in. Now even those "signature loans" were starting to go bad, and this bank had never before lost money on consumer lending.

Luther Hodges was beginning to feel like a tall target among short, angry men. He recognized that Storrs was "standing there...holding the ship together." And yet, "when the situation got worse, and those loans not only just didn't make money, they started losing money, that was another 'liberal foolish Hodges scheme.'" Hodges felt that the entire leadership team should share responsibility. "Everybody participated in the decisions, I mean nothing was done unilaterally, it was all four people. But when it went bad, you said, 'well that was Hodges.'"

Some of the worst problems, in fact, were in Bill Dougherty's subsidiary companies. Most notable was the mobile home program, representing one-fifth of TranSouth's entire loan portfolio. Mobile home sales were tied directly to Carolinas manufacturing, but the Arab oil embargo and the plummeting economy were playing havoc with orders for furniture and fabrics. As textile mills and furniture plants cut back production from three shifts to two to one—sometimes none—many workers lost paychecks, others lost jobs. In just twelve months fifty thousand North Carolina factory hands were laid off. The state's unemployment doubled, leaving 10 percent of the labor pool out of work.

In mobile home parks across the Carolinas, out-of-work couples threw their essential belongings into pickup trucks, left their double-wides and their monthly payments, and went home to mama. Storrs felt that perhaps "we had gotten a little exuberant" in the mobile home business. "We thought of the mobile homes as being like real estate, and were somewhat surprised to find that when people lost their jobs, they just up and left the mobile homes . . . and our collateral of the mobile home was always less than the notes outstanding. But also the market for mobile homes dropped out of bed. Even if we took them and refurbished them, there weren't a lot of people standing in line waiting to buy them. So we were stuck with substantial losses."

McColl saw the mobile home program as one instance of lenders in the field misrepresenting information they did not have in their possession. "We were financing the mobile home dealers themselves. They'd make a sale and we'd buy their paper. So we really didn't know the borrower. And whatever credit checking they were doing was certainly inadequate. I believe that we had a view at the time that mobile homes were just like any other homes, and that people were not going to give up their homes very easily. That turned out to be a flawed theory."

Only after repossessing the collateral did the slapdash lenders discover that "mobile homes weren't mobile. They really were premanufactured housing sitting on cinder blocks. And if you tried to move them you tore them up. So if you had a premanufactured home in the wrong place, it had very little value. So we lost a lot of money. A lot of what we did in '73, very aggressive lending, came home to haunt us in '74, '75."

NCNB found itself in possession of an armada of mobile homes for which it had no use. In fact, the bank had to pay a small fortune to have the lumbering structures dismantled and towed to small country airstrips for long-term storage. Many of them would have to be substantially refurbished before they could be resold, provided buyers could be found at any price. TranSouth's cash cow was NCNB's white elephant.

For the moment, Storrs believed he had seen the worst of it, that "we had a very good chance that our loan losses would sort of be stuck over this mobile home thing. But it wasn't very long before the real estate market was in trouble. And these were not mortgage loans to somebody buying a house, but loans to developers to buy land and make plans for development and things like that."

Except for a dwindling handful of oldtimers, the worst lending crisis anyone in his bank had experienced was the credit crunch of 1966, and Tom Storrs knew that was "really a wholesale sort of crunch, not loans going bad and things like that. For bankers who had not seen all this happen in their experience, it really was frightening, because we did not know where the bottom was. And this led us then to go into a defensive posture."

The four executives of this foundering ship decided their first action should be making sure they would not wake up one morning to find themselves with a fleet of used cars in drydock next to the used mobile homes. They put a stop to the practice of buying receivables from automobile dealers, which, like the mobile home paper, was an "arm's-length" business. Hodges directed one of his lieutenants, Connie Owens, to make the rounds of consumer credit offices and instruct managers to stop buying paper from dealers. This reduced the bank's exposure, but it also reduced the flow of new loans. Storrs immediately perceived another, more regrettable side effect: "It created a mindset that made people very reluctant to take risks."

David's knees were knocking. The culture built on boldness was cringing, afraid of the long shadow it was casting in the land of the giants. Chuck Cooley heard the whimpering in the next meeting of the Information and Advisory Panel, where McColl and Hodges had developed their rivalry. Cooley had given the current crop of "Young Turks" the assignment of designing the kind of bank they thought NCNB ought to be. What they designed, to Cooley's dismay, was "a company so safe we couldn't make any money."

The group Reese had formed to challenge his meek, Depression-sensitized Old Guard had become so terrified of risk that it would rather close down the bank than chance losing any more money. Instead, Storrs told Cooley it was time to close down the Information and Advisory Panel. That would be the last meeting of the Young Turks.

Hugh McColl's trainees were not the only ones worried. Nor were 1974's problems restricted to the southeastern United States. The international money trading world, so important to McColl and NCNB's future, suffered a serious shock on Wednesday, June 26, when the West German government failed the prestigious Bankhaus I. D. Herstatt. Until that moment, Herstatt Bank had appeared upright and responsible in the eyes of the world's banking community. However, like Franklin National, Herstatt had taken insupportable risks in foreign exchange trading, betting that the dollar would rise against the mark and losing $190 million on the gamble.

The failure came at the end of the business day in Cologne, which was still morning in New York and Charlotte. Some banks refused to pay notes that were supported by Herstatt, and CHIPS—the Clearing House Interbank Payments System computer in New York—was unable to settle accounts around the world. For McColl and other bankers, the week dragged into a nervous weekend. Now, as a banker who traded dollars overseas, McColl had to consider the "Herstatt Risk." Payments he was counting on might not be made, simply because the customer who owed the money might be open while he was closed, closed while he was open.

Foreign exchange markets were so spooked by the Herstatt failure that trading activity dropped to half what it had been in mid-June. The world banking system that had come of age with the Eurodollar market now seemed on the brink of collapse. McColl read in the business press daily reports of "financial time bombs" and an "economic doomsday." Even as Richard Nixon's administration sank into its own quicksand, the president's counselor, Kenneth Rush, went on national television to accuse the "greedy" banks of making "risky loans."

Bankers like Hugh McColl saw things differently. Nixon's monetary and fiscal policy had doomed the nation to rampaging inflation. In four years, public debt had grown by more than $100 billion. Nevertheless, Fed Chairman Arthur Burns continued to insist that wage and price controls and "going slow" would get the nation out of the mess it was in. The events of that summer reinforced both Burns's concerns and his convictions. The failure of Franklin National and Herstatt, he said, "transformed incipient unease into serious apprehension." Burns and his worries were inherited by Vice President Gerald Ford, sworn in to succeed Nixon in August. There seemed to be little Ford could do but follow the advice of his chairman.

Tom Storrs and the other members of the American Bankers Association found out what Burns's advice to the president would be in October, when they traveled to Honolulu for their annual meeting and lecture from the chairman. Burns put down his ever-present pipe and put on his sternest face. It was not federal economic policy that had failed, it was the bankers of America. The bankers had allowed equity capital to decline. The bankers had become overly dependent on volatile funds, foreign exchange dealings and overseas operations. It was the bankers who had made excessive loan commitments and eroded the quality of assets. "Innovative" banking had seen its day, Burns proclaimed. The Fed, which had the right to declare which new activities were appropriate for any bank, was hereby imposing a "breathing spell" on bank holding company expansion. Go-go banking was officially gone.

Third quarter reports showed Wachovia back in front of NCNB. What else could go wrong? Christmas was coming and Hugh McColl knew he'd find nothing but coals in his stocking. He was making more money than he'd ever dreamed he would, one hundred thousand dollars a year plus bonuses. But this year would bring no bonuses and he had no time to enjoy the fruits of his labor. Instead, he found himself contemplating what success and failure were all about. Sometimes he thought about Tom Storrs and what must be going on in his mind, although Storrs was not inclined to share that mind with anyone.

He saw now that "Mr. Storrs took on a very difficult assignment when he came into that job, certainly with limited backing and with limited followership. He was more like an admiral who had been assigned a new command, who had not previously been with the ship. He had not been the gunnery officer or the navigator, had not been promoted from a second position on the ship but rather came in on the bridge, with all inherent nervousness and concern on the part of the people who were operating the ship."

Tom Storrs had spent five and a half years in the navy, during the war that filled McColl's childhood imagination. While little Hugh was collecting tin cans and giving away his lead soldiers, Storrs had been torpedoed, bombed, shot at. He had survived. Part of that time he'd instructed younger men in the fine art of operating big guns. Most of the time he spent engaged in activities that would ensure his waking up alive the next day. He had hands-on experience in survival.

Watching Storrs operate now, McColl grew ever more aware of the fact that this commanding officer did not enjoy the enthusiastic support of his crew. They would respect him, probably never mutiny the way some former officers had, but he doubted many of the crew would ever *enjoy* working under this admiral.

Storrs was a navy man and McColl knew the navy did not like its officers getting too close to the seamen. He'd been on board navy ships and the mess-with-the-troops mentality of the Marine Corps was never much in evidence. It was an important point of disagreement between McColl's view of leadership and that of Tom Storrs.

"The navy believes that familiarity breeds contempt, that you should be aloof from the troops. Otherwise you can't order them into combat, because if you feel so close to them, how can you ask them to go and die?" McColl realized that this I-and-you distinction was by and large the attitude among the heads of large corporations, with their executive washrooms and executive lunchrooms and executive privileges. If that was what it took to be a successful business leader, he guessed he would never be good at it.

The books McColl read were more about military history than about business. He was curious about his great-grandfather and the Civil War, starting to collect books about that period. One of his favorite figures was Stonewall Jackson, who refused to wear an officer's uniform, "no plumed hat or anything. Just an old short-brimmed campaign hat."

What McColl learned from Jackson was that the information a commanding officer needed most could come only from the troops. A large part of McColl's own success could be traced to the fact that he knew so many of the four thousand-plus people in the company, knew what they did and how they did it. As long as the company didn't grow too large, he figured he would always be able to do that. He'd learned that tactic his first months out of college, from Captain Proudfoot, the Blackfoot Indian who was his commanding officer in basic training. Captain Proudfoot, USMC, taught him to "go ask the snuffies what's going on, go ask the grunts."

He also learned that an officer, be he second lieutenant or bird colonel, would never ask his team to go anywhere he wouldn't lead them. He would be at the head of the column, he would carry the same weight, he would make sure they changed their socks and kept their feet dry. In the process, they would learn to trust him with their professional lives and with the truth. Also in the process, he would be responsible for them. At NCNB, the troops in the column could not help noticing that they were marching behind Hugh McColl, no matter where the direct orders might be coming from. Nevertheless, while many of the troops seemed wary of Tom Storrs, McColl considered Storrs a fair and fearless leader. It was a surprise, then, to hear a frightened thought escape from the customarily guarded mind of the CEO.

It came late one afternoon, after another day of fighting off the wolves and scrabbling for dollars. The two men were alone in Storrs's office, looking down on the pyramided roof of the stark white civic center. Storrs, hands behind his back, lost in thought, let the words slip out: "I never thought it would come like this."

McColl swallowed the thought, but it haunted him: *Mr. Storrs believes it might be over.* Later he would repeat the words and Storrs would deny them, almost angrily. Never had he thought their company could be going under. McColl must have heard him talking about the credit market, not the bank.

"Yes, sir," he answered, but Hugh McColl knew what he heard that evening, regardless of what Mr. Storrs might have intended to say.

It wasn't just Storrs and McColl. Americans everywhere were wallowing in what author Robert Pirsig, in his 1974 book *Zen and the Art of Motorcycle Maintenance*, called a "gumption sump." With the Arabs in charge of our destiny, how could we *do* anything? With inflation just climbing higher and higher, how could the Fed *help* but push the interest rates up? And what could we *expect* from that but worsening recession? Bankers everywhere wiped their brows, waiting for the feverish malaise of 1974 to break.

McColl could not stand around and wait. Just before the holidays, he and Storrs traveled to London and Europe, to clear up any "misunderstandings" the overseas bankers might be having about NCNB International. McColl wrote his mother from Brown's Hotel shortly after his arrival in England.

Dear Mother:

Mr. Storrs and I just arrived in London after all night flight from Washington, D.C. Will sleep today (Sunday.) Have business here Mon. and Tues. Fly to Zurich Tues. nite, Wed. in Zurich, fly to Frankfurt, Ger. on Wed. nite, Thurs. in Frankfurt, fly to Brussels on Thurs. nite. Friday in Brussels and fly home Saturday. We hope to determine the true state of economic and political affairs in these countries and in Europe in general. Weather is mild so far. Tell Daddy that so far have taken care of all of Fran's bills OK. Have written her today and will at every stop. This has been a difficult year for us all but I have a feeling that we have turned the corner and 1975 will be better on every score.

> *I love you both,*
> *Hugh*

The North Carolinians went on the offensive, posing as bulls in a bear market, seeking advice on just how much larger their presence should be in Europe. However, instead of the hear-hears and back slaps they were hoping for, they found themselves on the receiving end of lectures on the proper way to run a bank. Clearly bankers in the southeastern United States knew little enough about it. McColl was frustrated, looking for loans, not advice. "We were just trying to keep our international bank lines in place so that we would survive. It was a brutal trip. I'll never forget it. Worn to a frazzle."

There was no time to rest when he got back. McColl hit the airports again, shopping American banks that were not yet suffering the way NCNB was suffering. He was trolling for heftier lines of credit.

The biggest fish he caught were in California and Texas, where local economies were holding their own, in spite of the energy crisis. In fact, just like those emirs across the ocean, Texas bankers were living high on the crude oil hog. The Lone Star economy was booming. McColl found himself feted by the twenty biggest guns at Dallas' Republic National Bank. They all spoke Southern and ate barbecue, pretty much as he did, and they were pleased as they could be to set up a line of credit for their little brothers up in North Carolina. McColl thought he could probably get along great with Texans. He just wished he had their money.

Despite his success in the face of blistering adversity, Hugh McColl found his portrait left out of the NCNB Annual Report of 1975. In fact, the report's only photo was a black-and-white of Tom Storrs looking stern. This annual report was quite a contrast to the four-color separation booklet of past years, stuffed with expensive location photos and screened graphics. This stark, thin duochromatic printing spoke voluminously of hard times. Tom Storrs, after his initial year as CEO, had the distinction of presenting NCNB's first-ever negative report. The company's earnings had dropped from $26 million the year before to $17.6 million at the end of 1974.

Tom Storrs began his report by telling shareholders that it had been "a year of testing for a number of executives who found themselves in new roles, confronted by a rapidly changing environment that made unexpectedly severe demands on them." Storrs was proud, however, to report that his executive team and the nearly forty-five hundred other associates "responded well" under pressure.

Unrecovered losses on Luther Hodges's consumer side were at $6,300,000 and counting; on McColl's commercial side the net loss—ultimately due to subsidiary company loans—was $2,761,000.

Business in North Carolina was experiencing "its first full-scale recession since 1958." On the international front, banks in six countries had failed during the year just ended. NCNB responded to these catastrophic events by instituting "policies designed to ensure liquidity and asset quality."

With all the bad news, it would seem unlikely that shareholders took any comfort in the fact that the McColl-Hodges-Dougherty impulse-buy, the little Trust Company of Florida, had turned a pre-tax profit of fifty thousand dollars for the company, a pretty turnaround from the previous year's thirty-thousand-dollar loss. Another bit of drama played out in Florida, very much behind the scenes, was the state legislature's enactment of legislation to prevent other out-of-state banks from sneaking in the way NCNB had. With the help of Orlando attorney Sid Ward, who owned a piece of NCNB's Florida Trust, the NCNB legal department made certain the bank was "grandfathered in" to the legislation. Since NCNB had established its foothold in Florida before the law was written, it would be allowed to stay.

While McColl continued to keep the bank on its feet, his job was made tougher due to the stumbling of the nonbank subsidiaries in Bill Dougherty's court. By the start of 1975 NCNB Mortgage Corporation had more than $37 million in nonperforming assets, the bulk of those bad loans in condos, apartment buildings and resort complexes, now the ghost towns and ghettos of the construction industry. Without ever intending to be caricatured as a Jolly Roger-waving band of marauders, the bankers at NCNB now found themselves the owners of "Pirate Land," whose half-built roller coasters and rides baked like the bones of dinosaurs in the Myrtle Beach sunshine. Just down the shore, on the island of Hilton Head, there were plush condos the company could not unload at the bargain price of forty thousand dollars. NCNB Mortgage owned ski resorts in the mountains and land nobody else wanted just outside Cincinnati. All these development and property deals had been entered into with the purpose of drawing in big revenues for the bank. Instead, each one became a new hole in the vault where money could only leak out.

McColl toyed with the notion of leaking out himself. Through the offices of a prominent corporate headhunter, he found himself being courted by a bank in San Francisco that was looking for a new CEO. The headhunter liked what he heard about Hugh McColl.

"Here we were in the middle of these horrible problems and I was tempted to go out to California." To McColl the notion "seemed romantic," but when he went out for an interview he found the West Coast bankers "more interested in membership in the yacht club than they were in making money. I was the wrong person for the job. My wife, bless her heart, said she would go there if that was what I wanted to do. But she didn't want to go. We had our families here, and all we had in the world was between York and Bennettsville." McColl decided against running away from his troubles.

Despite the problems of Bankhaus Herstatt, Israel-British and a few others, McColl believed the bank's best hope was to continue playing an aggressive game on the international chessboard. But the finance committee was uneasy about the tactic being employed by some of the larger American banks, pouring money into third-world nations. McColl cautioned his international team to play it safe in nations where not only the language and customs were unfamiliar, but where it was often difficult to figure out which numbers were in which columns in the ledgers.

To McColl, getting the numbers straight was the first step to doing business. During Hugh's childhood, his father and grandmother had passed earnings and profit numbers around the dinner table along with the mashed potatoes and field peas. "There were stacks of annual reports everywhere around the house. Dividend checks would arrive each week in the mail. There was a lot more talking about that sort of thing than about the Bible. Daddy insisted we know about things like that."

Before he could get to the neighborhood ball games on Saturday, Hugh had to go with his father, walking the family property lines. "I knew where every iron stake was buried. Then we'd go riding around the county, looking at every piece of land. He made me memorize who owned it, how much cotton it would grow, how much the land was worth and how much you could borrow against it." At fourteen Hugh McColl was tutored by his father in the arcane principles of double-entry bookkeeping. As soon as he got the basics down, the son began keeping the books at the cotton brokerage, every entry scrutinized by the father. There was no room for error on either side of the decimal point.

When it came to NCNB International, McColl wanted to be just as meticulous about the numbers his people were feeding into Dougherty's computers. Until they could be more certain about the future of the world economy, they would leave the bulk of the third-world business to the banks in New York, Chicago, California and Texas. He came up with what was called the "Commonwealth Strategy." NCNB would restrict its primary activities to members of the British Commonwealth, countries bound by a common set of laws, a common language, and the very same accounting principles McColl had used back at the family cotton gin.

NCNB's moves would be made on the friendliest playing fields McColl could find. "So we opened an office in Johannesburg. We opened an office in Sydney. And we already had the ones in Hong Kong and in London. Canada was handled out of here." McColl suspected that "frankly, that broad-based strategy would keep us out of a hell of a lot of trouble."

One problem nibbling at McColl's ankles was a growing difficulty in hiring good people, experienced in the banking tradition of a specific foreign country, to go to work in NCNB's foreign offices. He wanted to believe that at least overseas his bank's reputation was untarnished, but, as Jim Sommers kept reminding him, they were very small frogs in some large and unfamiliar ponds.

"Who's going to come to work for the North Carolina National Bank in London? I mean get a grip. Who *good* is going to come to work for North Carolina National Bank?" Jim Sommers wanted to know. Those who applied for the jobs McColl had to offer were, in Sommers estimation, the misfits, "incredibly bright, tough people, who were excluded from the system because they didn't wear the right school tie or they hadn't belonged to the right club or whatever."

One young man, who traveled all the way from London to Charlotte for a job interview was a Cambridge Ph.D. named Peter James who was employed as an economist in Paris. James showed Sommers a report he had written on the inevitability of American banks reducing in number through consolidation. One day, James was sure, there would be only a handful of very large banks dominating the United States economy. Curious, McColl agreed to join Sommers and James at the City Club. He smiled when the young economist informed him that the United States eventually would end up with no more than ten major banks, one of which would be North Carolina National Bank. NCNB had the right combination of location, outlook and aggression to make it to the top.

"That's why I decided I would come to work for you," he said.

"Wait a goddamn minute," McColl snapped. "We decide who works here, not you."

"Quite right, sir. Quite right." Peter James's accent was clipped and faintly annoying to McColl. "But I would like to work here."

"Well, Pete, you're an economist. You don't know anything about banking."

"Well, sir. That's correct. That certainly is correct, Mr. McColl, but I've read eight to ten books on it. It's not so complicated."

"Just a minute."

McColl pulled Sommers to one side and whispered, "Hire the sonofabitch. Put him in the credit department and break his ass."

Instead of breaking, James proved himself and eventually went back overseas as manager of the NCNB London office, reporting to Jim Sommers, head of international operations.

McColl's caveat to Sommers was that, while NCNB's foreign operations were essential to growth, NCNB International itself still had a lot of growing to do. "Remember four basic truths," McColl said. "One, we are not as big as 99 percent of the people you are competing with. Two, you won't have the capital or the long-term lending capacity they have. Three, you've got to figure out ways to get around those issues. And four, the biggest disadvantage we have is that we are operating out of Charlotte. We don't *know* people. That means you don't have information you need. To some degree, it is an old boy's club and you've gotta find a way to get around that."

Sommers took opportunity where he found it, even in non-English speaking countries, as long as the risks were manageable. In Guatemala he set up a joint-venture consumer finance agency, which became, in effect, the only option for small businesses and individuals for financing the purchase of a car or a truck. NCNB also loaned money to Guatemalan coffee growers, cattle ranchers and farmers, much as the bank had always done in the Carolinas.

Guatemala was a volatile nation, its political history steeped in violence, terrorism and demagoguery from the right and from the left. In 1974 the military government found itself with a new president, General Kjell Laugerud, into whose gene pool flowed such diverse cultural streams as Norwegian and Mayan. Recognizing the growing

importance of American banks in general and NCNB in particular—
to his own future as well as to Guatemala's—Laugerud invited the
president of NCNB to pay him a visit.

McColl accepted. At the Guatemala City airport he was met by a
motorcade of the nation's top banking officials. They drove him in a
limousine flanked by armed military guardsmen to the city's most
elegant hotel, where the entire top floor was reserved for him. "It was
almost a head-of-state visit," marveled Jim Sommers. Others in the
entourage, along with Sommers, were NCNB's head of international
credit, Bill Baker, and their senior man in Latin America, Mario
Delamico. That evening, to Sommers, "was like a movie. This huge
colonial dining room in the presidential palace, and the servants with
cutaways and white gloves, tall distinguished Spanish-looking fellows.
And there were three big harlequin Great Danes stalking around the
room while we were eating dinner."

After dinner the president asked the NCNB contingent to visit with
him in his study. Wrapped in a soft leather chair, McColl sipped
cognac. Laugerud asked his visitor whether he knew anything of the
history of Belize, the place the Yankees persisted in calling "British
Honduras." In fact, McColl had read about the region on the flight to
Guatemala City, astonishing Sommers with the depth of his "instant
information." He was only just beginning to realize "how incredibly
well read Hugh McColl is, and how many things he knows. I wouldn't
put any banker up in the world against him on geography or history
or political science."

McColl also seemed to impress *El Presidente* with his knowledge of
the seventeenth-century British logging industry's deforestation of
ancient Mayan territory. He knew that Spain had failed in its efforts
to dislodge the British and he knew the Guatemalans still refused to
admit the British claim to Belize. He also knew there might be oil
deposits in British Honduran waters and that there were British gun-
boats stationed permanently in the harbor at Belize, just in case
Guatemala should become enflamed by its own rhetoric.

As Sommers and the other Americans glanced at each other ner-
vously, President Laugerud asked McColl whether he did not think it
was a logical thing for Guatemala to try and "reclaim their territory."
McColl admitted there was a good deal of logic, assuming one admitted the claim in the first place.

Well, then, said *El Presidente*, should he take his troops across the border? And if that should turn into more than just crossing the border, what reaction might that cause with Señor McColl's bank? And what of other *norteamericano* banks?

McColl had contemplated the use of power, but until this moment he had never imagined being consulted on the question of war or peace between two nations. He reached out and scratched the ear of one of the Great Danes that had settled at his feet. "Mr. President," he began, "I suspect that, like me, you are a student of history, so you will know of the Monroe Doctrine, which has guided the United States for more than a hundred years." While he could not quote the 1823 doctrine, McColl remembered the gist of it: the independence of every nation in the Western hemisphere was considered important to the "peace and safety" of the United States.

Laugerud reminded him that the Monroe Doctrine was originally intended to keep European powers, including the English, *out* of the hemisphere.

True enough, countered McColl, yet there were places like British Honduras and Bermuda, where the British were "grandfathered in," just as his bank was grandfathered into Florida. McColl believed that this created a special relationship between Great Britain and the United States in the hemisphere, one that the president would be wise to consider. Another important consideration would be the likelihood that banks would stop lending money to nations at war.

The president passed around Havana cigars and wrapped up the conversation. He thanked McColl, assuring him that views quite similar to his had been expressed by the minister of finance and the head of his central bank. Nevertheless, Laugerud wanted to discover for himself how a commercial bank might respond to a "hypothetical effort to liberate Belize" from the colonial British.

Jim Sommers could not be certain, but he thought his boss might have had a hand in preventing a war.

Despite his problems, McColl was enjoying these experiments with power, much as Benjamin Franklin must have enjoyed his dicey kite-flying experiments with electricity. He was in a receptive, energetic mood when he received a telephone call from his visionary lunch companion, Dennis Rash. He decided to take his mind off banking for half an hour and find out what the university dean had on his mind.

Rash had spoken first to Joe Martin, who recommended he take his case to Luther Hodges, not to the unpredictable Hugh McColl, who was dealing with too many problems at the moment. Martin knew that more than a few of those problems involved well-intended real estate deals. And that was the sort of deal Dennis Rash was talking about—turning one of the city's most run-down areas of flop-houses, warehouses and brothels into a first-class residential neighborhood. Martin suggested that Rash's subject would find a more receptive ear in Hodges, who was active on the Urban Affairs Committee of the American Bankers Association. When Rash said he would rather talk about his plan with Hugh McColl, Martin said he considered that, well, a rash idea.

To Martin's surprise, McColl went for it. He agreed to commit thirty thousand dollars in seed money. That would help Rash get his "Fourth Ward Project" started with the renovation of the old Berryhill house, to show the city what could be done. McColl also committed the assistance of Joe Martin, the bank's hired social conscience, to work with Rash. McColl was glad for an opportunity to pull Martin into his camp, away from Hodges. No matter what Martin might think of him, McColl believed Martin might be one of the tigers he wanted on his team. Martin questioned McColl's motive in getting involved with the Fourth Ward renovation. He considered it "a power issue for Hugh."

In a sense, Joe Martin was correct. McColl was learning how to harness power and put it to his own use. Traveling ever more frequently to other cities, he had begun to see Charlotte as a city of potential, the key to its future being mixed-use development. That was what Dennis Rash was proposing for Fourth Ward, one of the original wards of the city, laid out more than a century earlier, long before anyone thought of suburbs. But while McColl might have enjoyed spending more time pumping up his influence in Charlotte, he was too preoccupied with plugging holes in his bank.

More money was leaking now from Atlanta, where the NCNB real estate investment trust Tri-South was headquartered. The NCNB REIT was a product of the 1960s fairy tale that real estate would always, always, always go up in value. It turned out that more than half of its portfolio was going downhill fast.

REITs represented the worst lending disaster to bare itself to the American public since the Depression, a Frankenstein's monster of government social engineering infused with bad credit judgment.

Before they began whirling under the disco ball, banks had been confined by their old-line credit men, like NCNB's Julian Clark, to finance only the construction phases of real estate development. As soon as the developer had his long-term financing in place, the bank would pull out its money and look for another safe place to lend it. But when banks spun off into REIT subsidiaries, they began risking their short-term money on long-term projects. They financed everything from the purchase of raw land, often at exorbitant prices, to management of the finished building—or whatever the end result turned out to be. By the first quarter of 1975, McColl was ready to engrave the pavement at Trade and Tryon Streets with the warning that developers will fill the world with empty buildings as long as lenders can be found with empty heads.

With the go-go music segued into the slow dance of recession, real estate was the wallflower. Like interest rates, construction costs were heading for the ceiling. NCNB Tri-South had a ton of paper maturing and no one even remotely interested in buying it. Since more than half of what Tri-South owned was earning zero or less, the European banks that had put up the corporation's $15 million grubstake were ready to call in their notes. It was all McColl could do to keep them from foreclosing.

Since he had a man like McColl, "particularly skilled" at this sort of deal-making, Tom Storrs devoted most of his own time to external relations, such as those he could nurture within the Association of Reserve City Bankers. Storrs felt it was "clearly an advantage" for the bank to have contacts and friends within the banking community, so for the first quarter of his tenure he had tried "to get out and represent the company in a favorable light in some nonbusiness situations that indirectly helped us in the business." These contacts at least helped the company to get a clear and early view of the oncoming high-beams of the next truck highballing right at it.

Storrs's visibility led to an appointment to the small group of bankers that served as advisors to the Federal Reserve Board. In May he traveled to Washington, to the marble castle guarded by the glowering huge eagle, in which the seven governors and chairman of the Fed held sway. There Storrs and the Federal Advisory Council met with Chairman Arthur Burns. Since his appointment in 1969, Burns had been warning that the amount of money in circulation was dangerously out of control, not only for the dollar but for the rest of the world's currency as well. Now Burns prophesied to his select group of bankers that the world was flirting with another depression. Clearly frustrated at the refusal of American banks to shut down the flow of credit, Burns told his advisors that the economy was overheated and OPEC's rise of oil prices was about to rupture the vat. "What do we have to do," he pleaded, "to make you fellows stop lending money?"

Tom Storrs returned to Charlotte convinced that Burns was not just crying wolf to set the villagers trembling, and McColl listened to his account of the meeting with a deepening sense of gloom. Hodges and Dougherty and all NCNB's high-priced consultants had bet the bank on the price of money going down. Now Arthur Burns insisted—and Tom Storrs believed him—that the ceiling on interest rates was still nowhere in sight. Moreover, the Fed was serious about cutting off loans. McColl might soon be unable to buy, at any price, money to lend. Investors would spurn NCNB stock. NCNB Corporation's commercial paper would be suspect as well, making it impossible to roll over and keep those ever-present and very real wolves from the door.

None of this news was good.

"Mr. Storrs," said McColl, "if you believe what the Fed is saying, then we need to get moving to cover our losses. Because we *will* have losses." It was past time to stop the bleeding, he insisted. The bank should move in quickly enough on the faltering clients of its non-banking subsidiary companies to salvage the outstanding loans before they self-destructed. If there was any day left to be saved, Hugh McColl and his workout rangers would have to save it.

The case-by-case workout process began with the recognition by Storrs, McColl, Hodges and Dougherty that a loan officer had gotten into a relationship over his head, through inexperience, inattention, underestimating risk or simply "falling in love with the customer." Storrs considered it critical that the executives establish "a willingness to take the responsibility away from the loan officers when we concluded that it was not productive to leave it with them."

When McColl looked at the number of questionable loans and the extensive job ahead of him, he knew he couldn't handle everything that needed to be done by himself. He could head one workout team, but he'd need two other teams that could go out and do the preliminary bush-beating, bringing him in for the kill when they thought he was needed. For one team leader he picked Jim Berry, the slow-talking, fast-thinking Oklahoman. To head the third team he picked the man he'd had his eye on for a long time, Francis "Buddy" Kemp.

McColl had seen a winner in Kemp from his first days at the bank. Eventually, he stole him out of the Credit Department and put him in charge of Mergers and Acquisitions. It didn't matter that there were no more North Carolina banks to be merged or acquired, McColl just wanted Kemp on his team. He had everybody believing that was the "preferred place to work. The most exciting, sort of the paratroopers of the bank." Kemp was about ten years younger than McColl, just as McColl was about ten years younger than Tom Storrs. McColl found him a perfect understudy, "very, very smart. Very tough. We had a friendship that was a good one, forged out of adversity." It wasn't hard to steal people like Kemp from Luther Hodges because Hodges wasn't focused on his people.

"Luther would do things that were expedient. He wanted to move forward in the bank himself, so he would put somebody in charge of something who wasn't quite qualified, or who wasn't the best, simply to get it filled and move on." Hodges found people for his jobs, McColl found jobs for his people. When he needed to pull people he could trust for the most difficult workouts, he knew where to find them, people like Bill Vandiver, Ed Spears and Ron Savas.

One of the most critical workouts on the table was that of Blythe Brothers Construction. Notwithstanding the $4.1 million bailout from C. D. Spangler and his Leo Corporation, Blythe Brothers found themselves on the rocks and foundering. If the construction company went under, they would take more than $35 million of NCNB's money to the bottom—and in all likelihood they would take NCNB down too. When senior credit officer Jim Berry realized the extent of the problem, he asked McColl to join him in Tom Storrs's office.

"I need to give you some information," he said, "but maybe y'all better sit down first."

Berry described a destroyer of Old Testament proportions. The size of the loan, the prominence of the family, the member of the board—if the lost money didn't sink them the bad publicity would. Storrs asked Addison Reese to join the discussion. He would bring Buddy Kemp in as well. They would meet on a Saturday, with the key members of the Blythe family and an outside attorney.

The critical factor for Reese, Storrs and McColl to recognize was that the Blythe family was not overly concerned about declaring bankruptcy. They were sufficiently well-off to be ambivalent about the company's future. It was NCNB director Jack Blythe, playing double agent, who convinced his sister and brother to let the bank move in and take control.

The story, as Hugh McColl read it, was complicated. The only possible happy ending seemed for the bank to put more money into a subsidiary called Blythe Brothers of Puerto Rico. That company was doing well, and if it could be recapitalized to the tune of ten million additional dollars, Blythe Puerto Rico would be able to handle the work on the parent company's books while those books were straightened out. McColl believed the plan might work, but there was a third party to be convinced. Almost as exposed as the bank was Blythe Brothers' bonding company, Reliance Insurance. If Blythe sank without finishing all the jobs currently under contract, Reliance could lose $20 million or more. NCNB and Reliance, McColl could see, were "in the same boat although paddling in different directions."

With the preliminary work completed, Buddy Kemp and Hugh McColl summoned the key players at Reliance Insurance into a Saturday meeting at the NCNB Tower. The group occupied a loan committee room, with no interruptions, no distractions and no way the Reliance representatives could call for help. McColl had discovered that he and Kemp could read each other's body language, gestures and eyes without exchanging words, almost as though each knew the thoughts of the other, rather like the members of a small jazz ensemble, improvising as one. With that in mind, McColl took one end of the conference table, Kemp the other.

Their goal that Saturday was to convince Reliance to go fifty-fifty on the $10 million loan to Blythe Brothers Puerto Rico. By lunchtime there was no agreement and Kemp went out for sandwiches. Hours went by and the haggling continued. The sun was going down and McColl was about out of angles. It was his role to be emotional while Kemp, balding and a bit round, sat at his end of the table like Buddha. McColl nearly always let himself "show a lot of emotion when I'm negotiating. And part of it's acting and part of it's real." McColl shot a look into Kemp's eyes and met recognition. He tried to color his voice with disgust, with lightly threatening overtones.

"Okay," he said, "fine. We have been talking to you for five or six hours now. That's enough. We're just going to let them go into bankruptcy. We're bigger than you, we've got more money than Reliance, so what difference does it make to us, anyway? Hell, let's go home."

The Reliance team asked for a break so they could huddle. McColl and Kemp stepped into a nearby office and stretched. Neither man was sure what the outcome would be. They were skating on excruciatingly thin ice. The Reliance executives huddled for nearly thirty minutes before calling the others back into the loan committee room.

"Look, we just can't do what you want," said the head insurance man, "but we'll do something else. We will guarantee your loan with Blythe."

It was all Hugh McColl could do to keep himself from jumping up and clicking his heels. This was a thousand times better than what they had asked for. Why would NCNB need $5 million of Reliance's cash if it could have $35 million worth of its credit? Just as he was about to shake hands and pass out cigars, McColl noticed Kemp at the far end of the table, unswerving, stoic.

"What about our *interest?*" Kemp demanded. McColl was flabbergasted. Kemp "never showed any pleasure." Here was Reliance Insurance "guaranteeing our damn loan, and he wanted to know about our *interest.*" In McColl's estimation, Kemp had just reinvented balls.

There was no more fight in the insurance group. Emotionally, they had caved in. Sure, why not guarantee NCNB the interest it was due on all those bad loans? Wasn't it the same as guaranteeing some developer that a construction company would finish a job? McColl was not about to let the Reliance people walk away and calmly contemplate what they had just done, not without signing a piece of paper. They signed a handwritten agreement to do the deal.

After showing their guests to the elevator, McColl took Kemp to Tom Storrs's private wine cabinet. Kemp protested. He was terrified of upsetting "Mr. Storrs." Anyone with a Ph.D. from Harvard, in M.B.A. Buddy Kemp's estimation, must know everything there was to know about everything. McColl didn't think twice. "It was a liquor cabinet. It had a lock, and we just broke it open."

The celebrants concluded that the Reliance team must have acted the only way they could. The only deal permitted was one that would not show up immediately on their balance sheet. "They probably had plenty of broke clients and they were desperate as well," reasoned McColl. "And we figured that was a cheap way out for them. But I think we were euphoric. I remember we were on a high, and we were superpleased with ourselves and we knocked off that bottle of wine posthaste."

That would not be the last bottle for McColl, Kemp, Berry and the others. "We did a lot of drinking that year. Nineteen seventy-four was a tough year. We were under so much stress. We would go from one problem to the next. Kemp and I—that's when we became really tight with each other. We were dealing with the fate of the company. I don't want to sound dramatic, but we were. And it was a very important period of our lives."

McColl's workout team members were assigned responsibility for submitting to top management a monthly "Storrs Report," named after its chief designer. Tom Storrs, Luther Hodges and senior credit officer Jim Berry would review each workout, assess the team's results and recommend further action. McColl, the one in charge of taking the action, found himself running the triage section of the NCNB emergency room.

The steel manufacturing company McColl had helped get started in Georgetown, South Carolina, three years earlier, was in a down cycle, unable to pay back nearly $20 million of NCNB's money. Steelmaker Willy Korf, undaunted by debt, had expanded with a second mill near Beaumont, Texas, and the sinking construction industry was not exactly living up to Korf's expectations.

Jim Berry and his wife were supposed to be going to look for a house when McColl called and told him he needed to leave for Bern to meet with the Union Bank of Switzerland. McColl understood "they were managing a great deal of money for the Kuwaiti government. See if you can get some of it for Georgetown Steel." Berry was too embarrassed to tell the boss his passport was expired, so he got on the phone with his congressman, Jim Martin, and someone set up a renewal for him en route, at Kennedy Airport. He talked the Swiss bank into the Georgetown credit deal for $25 million.

After that he met with bankers in Texas—"where they still didn't know what a problem loan was"—in Rhode Island, Ohio and Virginia. He met with lawyers in Amsterdam and government officials in Kuwait, holding together a $150 million consortium of lenders on behalf of a struggling steelmaker in South Carolina. Invariably, Berry's argument came down to, "Okay, we close them down. When do you want your share of the steel beams delivered to your lobby?"

Berry "couldn't let anybody get out. Once you let one out, you have a mess." With attorney Harry Grim, Bill Vandiver and Neal Trogden, Berry spent an entire Saturday at the bank, "calling Hugh at his hotel in Paris, and he's calling us back." It wasn't until Sunday evening that they got all the banks to agree. It was just mid-seventies business as usual to Berry, "just one crisis after another."

Ultimately, NCNB would get back all but about $2 million of the $20 million it had at risk in Georgetown Steel, another successful workout, cutting the losses to something the bank could withstand. Willy Korf, German-born nouveau-Texan, was so grateful that he bought a giant pair of mounted longhorns and had them shipped to McColl in Charlotte. Jane would have them nowhere in her house except for the basement, but Hugh liked the sentiment.

Any time he called in McColl's workout teams, Tom Storrs knew "we had taken our gloves off and our real concern was getting the money. We might not get all the money, but we were going to get as much of it as we could. We were going to do whatever was necessary to get it." However, there were times when Hugh McColl took off the gloves and immediately lost control of his emotions. This was the area of least compatibility between the two executives. McColl knew this was "a tremendous problem" for Storrs. "I had a mouth. I mean I was a hundred and eighty degrees out from him." While McColl could be nothing but direct, Storrs was "the kind of guy that doesn't tell you anything if he doesn't *want* to tell you. In other words, if he didn't say it precisely to you, he didn't say it. He only meant what he said to you, not one word more. And here I was, a 'Type A.' He's a left-brain type. I'm a guy who feels everything, goes on intuition, how I think people feel about things. And we were working with each other and it took me a long time to understand the differences."

During 1975, Tom Storrs's tendency to pick his words carefully had board members uncertain of the direction he was leading them. One director in particular, Bruce Cameron, demanded to know why Storrs and his team failed to anticipate loan problems before they occurred. Under the surface lay the concern that their chairman might not be telling them everything he knew. As he looked at the men and women on his board, Storrs saw a range of support, "from understanding to being concerned whether we were being completely candid. And I don't know how you convince somebody you are telling them everything if he's disposed not to believe that you are."

By the end of 1975, the board was convinced. Even though Tri-South and NCNB Mortgage continued to lose at the rate of nearly $5 million a year, constituting a drag on the corporation, Storrs could report that, "as far as the bank was concerned we had worked out of it." In his annual report, considerably less dour and more encouraging than that of the previous year, Storrs wrote: "The bank's earnings rose despite the unusual severity of the economic decline in North Carolina. International banking made a strong comeback from the problems of 1974, and there was continuing growth in earnings from national account business, the bond trading account, leasing and BankAmericard."

Meanwhile, down in Orlando, the little Trust Company of Florida chugged along, reporting a pre-tax profit of fifty-eight thousand dollars, up eight thousand dollars from the previous year. Like an annuity fund plodding through its course of interest, it drew little attention.

The bank's most telling loss of 1976 had nothing to do with money. Doctors at Mercy Hospital, which Addison Reese had helped to build, found that Reese's body was losing a battle with cancer. He would not recover. Reese continued reporting to the office each morning, until at last he was forced to check into the hospital. Even there, Pat Hinson sat by his bed, taking dictation and bringing letters for him to sign.

His mentor's flame flickering, Luther Hodges began to doubt his chances of fulfilling the destiny that both he and McColl had assumed was his—to lead North Carolina National Bank. Hodges felt he had done his career a disservice by not walking out of the bank two years ago and committing himself to public office. Watching the North Carolina gubernatorial race blow through the hot summer, he told himself the Democratic nominee about to win the state's biggest office should be Luther Hodges, not glad-handing Jim Hunt. This race might have been his best chance to travel the path his father had blazed.

Hodges could have gotten out before the bank started to slip in public opinion. Instead, he had done his duty, had looked at the rough weather ahead and decided to remain at his post on the ship. The thanks he got was Tom Storrs's blame for every leak and every rusted cable. If he'd put his own future ahead of the bank's, Hodges felt he might now be headed for the governor's mansion in Raleigh, with a chance to really make a difference.

One of the few people at the bank Hodges consulted about his political aspirations was Joe Martin, who had helped his brother Jim get elected to Congress. Hodges used Martin as a speechwriter, along with John Jamison, one of the bank's top public relations people. He knew the two men kidded him about his tendency to appear aloof and his less-than-colloquial speaking style, but he felt sure they and nearly everyone else at NCNB would get behind him if he decided to make a run for the United States Senate the following year. It was agreed that the Senate would be an excellent stepping-stone to the governor's mansion.

Indeed, in his years of traveling around North Carolina for the bank Hodges had made a lot of friends and Martin believed there was a "brain trust of people around the state who were ready to sign on with his campaign when the time came." At a meeting in Raleigh, one of Hodges's advisors suggested that if Luther was serious about running for office then he should concentrate less on influencing business leaders and spend more time with factory workers. Only half-kidding, Jamison responded, "Well, we could schedule a squash match with them. They probably don't play polo." Martin, a Republican, couldn't help wondering how his "patrician" banker would play in the tobacco fields plowed by North Carolina's less genteel Democrats.

Hodges's not-quite-secret aspirations were given a considerable boost by the national elections in November. The Republicans were thrown out of the White House by a moralizing Southern Democrat named Jimmy Carter. North Carolinians surely were as fed up with the disastrous economy and the scandal of Watergate as was the rest of the country. Surely they would be ready to elect a Democrat to the Senate. Luther Hodges decided his moment had arrived.

At the bank, McColl's moment seemed to be at hand. He knew—and he knew that everyone else knew—that he and his team had saved their company. McColl was convinced that "all the problems were in Luther's part of the bank, and that Storrs, by main force, was holding this company together with me and my team. My team saved the bank. Storrs saved the bank, too. He muscled it through and he had the brains and the skills to keep us alive. Storrs had to talk to other bankers and keep the line of credit coming to us."

After two and a half years of fence-straddling on the subject of his own succession, Storrs was prepared to make at least a partial commitment. If he was not yet sure which of his three executive vice presidents would follow him as CEO, he knew which one it would not be. Storrs recommended to the executive committee of the board that they award raises of twenty-five thousand dollars to McColl and Dougherty. He recommended no raise for Luther Hodges.

These raises would not take effect until January and, under normal conditions, Hodges should not have learned about the preferred status of McColl and Dougherty until publication of the proxy statement the following spring. But instead of waiting, Storrs forced Hodges's hand by telling him what was going on. Immediately, Hodges went to see Reese in the hospital. Reese responded by summoning McColl.

McColl found Reese clearly wounded by Storrs's display of favoritism. "Do you realize what Tom has done?" he asked. "Luther is going to leave the bank."

McColl felt guilty but he had no answer except, "Yes, sir."

"This is not what I wanted to happen," Reese said.

"I didn't ask for it, sir," McColl answered. "I didn't need to have that raise."

Reese said, "You need to call Tom Storrs and tell him that."

"Yes, sir."

McColl tracked down the CEO in San Francisco and told him about the conversation. "Mr. Reese said it was a mistake to pay me more than Luther." He told Storrs he was prepared to continue working at his present salary.

There was nothing but breathing coming from the telephone receiver. McColl felt the silence as sharp as a pop of his father's belt. Finally Storrs's eternally calm voice returned to the line. "Do you understand what you are asking me to do?"

"Sir?"

"Hugh, you're asking me to go back to my executive committee and tell them I made a mistake, that I didn't know what I was doing when I gave them this recommendation. That's what you are asking me to do."

"No, sir. I hadn't thought of that."

Storrs resolutely concluded the conversation. "If I were you, I'd go back to my desk and start earning the money that I'm being paid, and let the CEO run the corporation."

McColl took the advice.

Hodges decided he would convert adversity into opportunity. His supporters commissioned a poll that showed him as a likely victor in a campaign against the Republican front-runner, a radio announcer from eastern North Carolina named Jesse Helms. Joe Martin counseled Hodges against jumping into the Senate race, believing Storrs was forcing the timing to the detriment of Hodges's political aspirations.

Shortly before Christmas, the die was cast. The *Charlotte Observer* declared, "Hodges to run for U.S. Senate—will leave bank in June."

The June primary date coincided with Hodges's fifteenth anniversary with NCNB, but once the departure was announced, it was to all intents and purposes a fact. Storrs relieved him of his principal duties with Banking Group I, turning it over to McColl. Although Hodges retained a token status at the bank, giving him a platform from which to conduct his campaign, McColl put Buddy Kemp in charge of the North Carolina banking operations. He watched in righteous satisfaction as Kemp "immediately turned the damn thing around. He got rid of people left and right. He changed the way it operated." McColl knew the consumer side of the bank was about to become as successful as the commercial side, and this time there was no side but his.

None of Hodges's previous responsibilities was placed in the hands of Bill Dougherty, who continued in charge of operations and oversight of the nonbank subsidiaries. Though McColl refused to regard Dougherty as a serious challenge to his ascendancy, Tom Storrs made sure the doubts were still there. To have an undisputed second-in-command as close to the common seamen as Hugh McColl was would be courting another mutiny. Storrs started working on a plan that would keep everyone guessing.

By the middle of 1977, Dennis Rash's Fourth Ward project had run out of gas. Rash himself was living in Fourth Ward, in the second Victorian house he'd managed to renovate. He had a few other houses and a few other neighbors, but by-and-large, the dream of a neighborhood in the midst of a business-centered uptown was still more dream than reality. Charlotte worshipped the suburbs, and so far this inner-city sanctum had drawn fewer than thirty people.

It was Joe Martin who found the new source of energy. The Bank of America in San Francisco had gone to the Federal Reserve with a proposed nonprofit subsidiary to build low-income housing. It was just a pilot project for BofA, but the Fed had approved. NCNB attorney Paul Polking suggested that by going to the bank's other regulator, the U.S. Comptroller of the Currency, NCNB might be able to take the idea one step further than the Fed allowed BofA. McColl agreed the California ruling might present an opportunity for NCNB.

Working with NCNB lawyers and city planners, Polking and Martin came up with the NCNB Community Development Corporation (CDC), a nonprofit company that would undertake general real estate development in the public interest, and the Comptroller agreed. They talked Rash out of his university job and signed him on as head of the new company, the first venture of its kind by any bank in America. Somewhat reluctantly, Tom Storrs approved all this, though he doubted it would go forward without costing the company money. "Other than not screaming and shouting when they came up with the idea," Storrs's participation would be minimal.

In the Fourth Ward, McColl and the bank could put to good use some of the painful lessons they had learned over the past three years in real estate, construction and mortgage lending. McColl went to one of his friends, Reitzel Snider, and got him to joint-venture with the CDC in a high-dollar townhouse development. Next door was a brick apartment building that the corporation would remake into condominiums.

The CDC needed a public partner to define the "public interest" to the satisfaction of the Comptroller. The city's first Republican mayor, Ken Harris, organized a committee that recommended creation of a Charlotte Uptown Development Corporation (CUDC), funded by an assessment on property in the designated uptown area. The CUDC would involve many of the city's corporate leaders, not just NCNB. But Mayor Harris had been a sheep-dip trainee with McColl back at American Commercial in the early sixties, so he naturally picked his old colleague to chair the new entity. Now all of the city's revitalization efforts would be at McColl's direction. This was the application of power he had imagined when he first asked why Charlotte couldn't be more like London. Martin saw another side of Hugh McColl, surprised at his ability to "play a delicate political game," and also "how much fun it could be to plot strategy with him, Polking and Rash—and especially how much fun it was to win and get exactly what we wanted."

With Hodges off running for the Senate, McColl realized that part of his desire to lead the city must have been driven by his pervasive love of competition. "Luther was a big player in North Carolina and in the city. And I had always just been a business person, had no reputation in the city at all. People didn't know me from Adam's house cat. And so somewhere in there were some of my personal ambitions. How much of it, I don't know. But I'm always a mixture of everything ."

McColl and Storrs each contributed the maximum four thousand dollars to Hodges's senatorial campaign, and everyone at the bank made a show of supporting him, but Hodges didn't get far. He was embarrassed in the Democratic primary by "Crazy John" Ingram, whom hardly anyone took seriously and who then lost handily to Republican Jesse Helms, a newcomer to politics. Hodges left North Carolina, and eventually wound up presiding over a bank in Washington, D.C.

At Mercy Hospital, the man who had willed the end of Wachovia Bank's stranglehold on the North Carolina economy lay dying. McColl stood at Reese's bedside in late August, shocked to see the towering totem of the mezzanine reduced to a pale, frail old man. McColl knew that Reese would be interested in news of NCNB's continuing effort to capture customers in North Carolina, so he told him the story of a bank in North Wilkesboro that was reeling after a barrage of allegations of fraud.

"What are you doing about it?" Reese asked in a hoarse whisper.

"We're going after their customers everywhere we can," McColl answered.

"Good." Through the bed railing Reese stretched out his arm, taped to an intravenous drip bottle, and patted McColl's hand. "Show them no mercy."

On September 1, 1977, Addison Reese died.

Joe Martin's responsibilities had grown considerably under McColl's leadership. He now was in charge of government relations and communications, training and affirmative action, reporting to Chuck Cooley. Martin felt "challenged by it all" but "not prepared for the managerial role—and I did not like it." His most cherished projects, Fourth Ward and the Community Development Corporation, were far too dependent on the involvement of Hugh McColl, which was "sporadic, unpredictable, and demanding and difficult for me."

When Billy Wireman, the new president of Charlotte's Queens College, offered Martin a job as vice president for development and college relations, he accepted. Before he left, McColl asked him to take a walk from the Tower to the emerging community of Fourth Ward. It was a warm spring day and the two men threw their coats over their shoulders. Despite McColl's acclaimed proclivity for being with the troops, this walk, Joe Martin realized, was "the longest time I had ever spent with him alone."

With no warning, McColl stopped on the sidewalk and said, "Look, Joe, we have rescued people before. If Queens is not everything you want, come back and talk to us."

Martin did not know what to make of the statement, uncertain whether McColl was asking him to stay or simply offering him friendship. They spent the rest of the walk "talking about all the things that might make Charlotte a better place and, for the first time, I wondered if leaving was a mistake."

McColl did not understand how Martin could want to abandon such opportunity for the seclusion of a small college. All he knew for certain was that he was losing a tiger. With both Hodges and Martin gone, the bank might find itself short in the area that could only be called its "soul." Though he did not realize it at the time, Martin would come to understand that "Hugh was committing unconditional loyalty to me long before I was willing to commit to him."

Equally unwilling to commit to Hugh McColl was Tom Storrs. In September 1978 Storrs told the executive committee of the board it should start considering its options. "I went to them around my sixtieth birthday and said, if they permitted me to serve to sixty-five, I'd be retiring in five years. It was time for them to start thinking about a successor."

Storrs, ever methodical, had prepared an evaluation form for his committee, "a set of qualities that could be backed up by fact." For the next five years, the executive committee would pore over these evaluation forms, compiled on some of the top people in the bank. Rather than the CEO-designate, or the finalist in a two-man race, McColl was "one of several" contenders to be judged on "what kind of experience people had in various aspects" of the chief executive officer's job.

Although he was unaware of Storrs's machinations, Hugh McColl still had five years to prove himself, five years to stay out of serious trouble.

"It's hard to believe I get paid $200,000 a year to get a good education but I do. The problem is of course what to do with it. Time really waits for no one and I only wish I were twenty-five and had my knowledge base."

Hugh McColl
Letter to his parents from Thailand, March 5, 1979

CHAPTER 9

Under Addison Reese, McColl had his marching orders clear: Beat Wachovia. In Tom Storrs's early chairmanship years the goal was even simpler: Survive. Now that McColl and his bank had come through both those campaigns it was his turn to help write the theme that would define NCNB in the 1980s: Expand Across State Lines.

That theme had one inherent flaw. Interstate expansion was virtually outlawed by the federal government. In 1927 with the McFadden Act, Congress put the power to regulate bank branching in the hands of individual states. The Douglas Amendment to the 1956 Bank Holding Company Act prohibited the acquisition of a bank in State A by a bank in State B, unless expressly permitted under the laws of State A. These two pieces of legislation neatly protected local banks from "big city bank" competition and kept small-town Americans safe from the clutches of those "big city bankers" who would otherwise suck away their savings from Main Street to Wall Street.

As of 1978, nearly every state, including North Carolina, had a law on its books forbidding bank incursions. Yet, as both Storrs and McColl saw it, the question was not whether the big New York and California and Texas banks would find their way into North Carolina, but when. NCNB's best hope was to get so big so fast it would make the other banks—say Wachovia and First Union—seem more attractive targets. The game was to find a way around the law before the money center banks did.

All around the country, the most aggressive institutions were sniffing like bloodhounds in the legal underbrush for the scent that would put them on the trail of interstate banking. Lead dog Walter Wriston, chairman of Citicorp, firmly believed the trail would have to be blazed by his banklike subsidiaries. Citicorp's money was on its Nationwide Finance chain, a St. Louis-based consumer loan company it owned. By 1974 Wriston's understudy John Reed had Nationwide writing loans in fourteen states, but it could not yet accept deposits or cash checks; it was not by any stretch of the imagination a *bank*.

That same year, 1974, two California giants, Bank of America and Security Pacific, graciously offered to buy up Franklin National's flotsam on the east coast, but Fed chairman Arthur Burns scuttled those deals. Interstate banking remained an imaginary sail on the far horizon. However, there was no federal law that could prevent the government of one state from *inviting* another state's bank in for business. If both State A and State B found it in their best interest, they might even *reciprocate*.

Tom Storrs first heard the idea of reciprocity in 1978, from one of his friends at a conference of the Reserve City Bankers Association in Palm Springs, California. Guy Botts, the sixty-four-year-old CEO of Barnett Banks of Florida, asked Storrs to get his top people together for a private meeting to discuss a "Southeastern Banking Compact." Hugh McColl listened with growing interest as Botts outlined a recent decision by the Federal Reserve to allow a Minnesota bank holding company to expand its subsidiaries in Iowa, since it had specific approval of the Iowa legislature. The Fed said, and the courts agreed, that Iowa could let one out-of-state bank in and continue to keep others out.

McColl got the point. A legislature in one state, say Florida, could admit a bank like NCNB. At the same time, the legislature in North Carolina could open its doors to a bank like Barnett in reciprocity. And the Georgia legislature could let them both in. Meanwhile, all three states could tell Citicorp and BofA, as McColl succinctly summed it up, "to go screw themselves."

"Precisely," said Guy Botts.

Assuming they could get the state bankers associations to lobby the changes, and assuming the state legislatures would go along with the idea, they could organize a "Southeast Banking Compact." If they played their cards right, they could craft the laws so that the big bankers in a state like North Carolina could graze in the green pastures of Florida while still maintaining the old fence that kept the Yankees out.

At first it was only talk. McColl brought it up in South Carolina with his friend Hootie Johnson at Bankers Trust, convincing Johnson he should make plans for a compact between the two Carolinas. Hootie Johnson jumped on the idea that interstate banking was inevitable. "I saw that we were going to be bought," Johnson said. "We would join hands with NCNB when interstate banking came. And my people saw it as having great opportunities down the road. There was no movement, no dream of legislation, but we knew it in our minds that it was coming."

Most Southern bankers were less genteel in their response to the NCNB-Barnett overtures. It was more like pistols at dawn. To non-predatory banks within the two states, the arguments in favor of reciprocity paled beside the fear of opening the hunting season. Wachovia and even First Union refused to join NCNB in lobbying Raleigh. In early 1979, the North Carolina Bankers Association rejected an NCNB-crafted bill. The small-town bankers delighted in thumbing their noses at Rude Hugh McColl, who had profaned their sacred traditions six years earlier by "buying" the election to their presidency. The association reported unfavorably on the bill, which assured it of a quick death in a state senate committee. There would be no "banking reciprocity" in North Carolina.

In Tallahassee, Botts's legal department met with the same treatment from the Florida Bankers Association and the Florida Legislature. Yet Storrs remained convinced that his bank's future lay outside the borders of its home state and that reciprocity was the key to territorial growth. NCNB had grown up in the security of a walled and gated neighborhood; it only made sense to open the gates and build a wider wall around the entire region.

In early 1980, Citicorp made another thrust. The state legislature of New York slapped a usury ceiling law on credit card interest, much as North Carolina's legislature had done on mortgage interest several years earlier. In retaliation, Citibank President John Reed and his lawyers took advantage of a law passed by Congress two years earlier. This allowed banks to charge credit card interest rates based on either the prevalent rate where the customer lived or the prevalent rate where the bank had its credit card operations. The law did not specify that those credit card operations had to be in the bank's home state. Citicorp decided it would pull its credit card operations out of New York and move them to South Dakota, where the legal interest limits were higher and where the bank could make a greater profit. Shortly after Citicorp's coup in South Dakota, Chase Manhattan dispatched representatives to Delaware, to promote legislation that would open that state to outside banks. They might be yet a long way from Charlotte, but at night Hugh McColl could hear the big dogs baying at the Carolina moon.

NCNB's chief planner Frank Gentry confirmed with charts and statistics what McColl knew in his heart: they had to grow and grow quickly, not just to keep from being eaten, but because growth was essential to NCNB's "corporate culture." McColl had been partly responsible for the conception of that culture. He had nursed it like a mother with his international operations and acquisitions and leadership building. Now, when Frank Gentry told his officers that "our corporate culture necessarily has significant implications on how we spend our resources and our energy," Hugh McColl barked, "Damned right." Nomads had to travel, Neanderthals had to hunt, McColl and his bank had to grow.

At meeting after meeting, on whiteboards and chalkboards and flipcharts, Gentry's strategy for the bank kept coming out the same way, and so did the tactics necessary to achieve their goals. The bank would "raise capital whenever we could; hire bright young people, even if we didn't know exactly what we were going to do with them, because by the time we train them we will need them; take a proactive approach to regulation, and try to make our own breaks by tearing down the regulatory barriers as quickly as we can."

Hugh McColl summed up Gentry's carefully laid plans on the fingers of one hand: "Get the money. Get the talent. Make our own breaks in Washington. Go for it."

Storrs prepared the board and investors with a position paper published in the NCNB Corporation Annual Report for the year just ended, 1979. "It is now clear that we have entered a period of fundamental change in our business." That change demanded "untraditional responses, some of which are contrary to the Depression-era regulatory environment that still governs our industry." To Storrs, there was no longer a question of whether interstate banking should be permitted. "Instead, the relevant question is, 'What is the way that will have the greatest public benefits?'"

No bush so thorny McColl would beat around it. He had a ready answer to the chairman's question: "Whatever way we can win."

Storrs directed McColl to put together "a little task force," to determine what that way should be. The task force would include NCNB's top strategist, Gentry, and its top legal mind, Notre Dame Law School graduate Paul Polking. Marketing vice president Winton Poole and marketing specialist Ken Reynolds were assigned, as was government relations officer Mark Leggett. Storrs's unexpected appointment was Joe Martin, lured back from his sabbatical in academia by Storrs and Chuck Cooley, who assured him that even McColl wanted him back.

Martin felt very much wanted, returning at twice his old salary, with corporate strategy and planning added to his responsibility areas, reporting directly to the chairman, not to the man he preferred to keep at arm's length, Hugh McColl. Specifically, Martin was assigned "to help create interstate banking," which Storrs warned him would be "both logically imperative and legally impossible." That challenge Martin found "irresistible."

The Interstate Banking Group—the IBG, they called themselves—took a hard look at Citicorp's strategy. Perhaps they too should use nonbanking subsidiaries to break into other markets. TranSouth Mortgage Company seemed like a good bet, since the housing market was picking up again. But, as Tom Storrs reminded the group, they had less than a perfect track record where mortgages were concerned.

Then the task force hit on an idea that had intriguing possibilities, that of creating an entirely new subset of subsidiaries. These would be *industrial banks,* also known as "Morris Plan" banks—after entrepreneur Arthur Morris, who devised them in the early part of the twentieth century. A Morris Plan bank was a hybrid, part credit union, part finance company, which sold investment shares to the public, then used that money to make consumer loans. Only in a few states, where bankers kept their feet sunk deep into the past, were Morris Plan banks still legal. One of these was Florida, the state that already was much on NCNB's mind, thanks to the friendly suggestion of Barnett Banks' Guy Botts. Attorney Polking told the IBG group that the old Morris Plan law could be hauled back into service as NCNB's vehicle to cross state lines. This caused the Interstate Banking Group to shelve all its other conjurings and focus strictly on Florida, bringing the glint of sunshine to Hugh McColl's eye.

McColl knew Florida was hot and getting hotter. Down the Atlantic coast, up the Gulf of Mexico side, throughout the interior and across the panhandle, businesses were moving in faster than retiring government workers. It could be a commercial banker's heaven. Yet most of Florida's banking establishment slept like old dogs after a big meal, each in its own kennel. Every bank had its borders marked and guarded jealously, and few strayed from their home county.

As for the legal side of banking, Polking reported that Florida's legislature stood ready to protect and to serve its money custodians, but to serve them ever so cautiously. Until 1977, Florida law had limited a bank to but a single main office; now they were allowed to open branches, but no more than two branches in one year. In recent years this change had enabled the breakneck growth, by Florida standards, of the state's few aggressive bank holding companies, such as Barnett Banks in Jacksonville and Southeast Banking Corporation in Miami. However, in distinct contrast to centralized North Carolina banks, whenever a bank headquartered in one Florida county bought or opened a bank in another county, the second bank always would have its own president and board of directors, each of which maintained close ties to local businesses, suppliers, families and politicians. This was thought to be good for business, although it fed a ravenous appetite for redundancy and unaccountability that few businesses outside of banking would find acceptable. For example, the Barnett holding company had sixty Florida banks with sixty presidents and sixty boards. Barnett thought such "unit banking" (rather than a unified bank) was far and away in the company's best interest. As a result of tradition, Florida banking relationships were tangled as an Everglades mangrove thicket, roots interlaced with branches thick enough to discourage a dragonfly, the air smelling faintly of decay. Every banker seemed to know every politician and, indeed, their families seemed inevitably intermarried.

The more he learned about the state, the more Hugh McColl realized that if NCNB wanted to move on Florida, it would have to get its shots in quickly. This deposit-rich unit bank state was a fat and happy target for the big New York banks, as soon as they found their way around the restrictive laws. When the new president, Ronald Reagan, eliminated controls on oil prices, McColl saw the era of Republican deregulation coming on fast. He was all for deregulation, in theory, but in practice his bank wasn't quite ready for it yet.

One of the things that puzzled McColl was the lack of enthusiasm for interstate expansion that he felt from Bill Dougherty and his people in operations. McColl was waving the interstate flag as wildly as he could, telling everyone in the company they were by damn going to take Florida before any damn New York bank got there, but he got nothing but cold stares from Dougherty. He wondered whether Storrs was putting that down in his reports to the executive committee.

McColl felt that he and Storrs were growing closer, accomplishing a lot together. He and Storrs "never really disagreed with each other about where we were going," despite the fact that they rarely saw eye to eye on how they should get there. "We didn't necessarily agree on tactics and we didn't necessarily get to the same place the same way—that is, our logic patterns didn't flow the same way—but we got there."

When McColl referred to his company in terms that reflected his convictions, as a family or as an embattled army, Storrs would smile. To others he would speak of McColl's "whimsy" in comparing the bank to the Marine Corps. Military metaphors were just "Hugh's little eccentricities." But whether or not Storrs admired the style, McColl knew he respected the results. "He used me, as you are supposed to use people. That is, he had the brains, I was the leader. He was the genius as to where we ought to go, I could get his people to go there. He was a brilliant thinker, strategist and planner. But he had no ability to rally the troops to the war. So I was Stonewall Jackson to his Robert E. Lee, so to speak."

The student of history may be hard-pressed to conjure up an image of lemon-sucking, battle-branded Jackson enduring from Lee the sort of treatment McColl took from Storrs. Recommendations from the IBG panel often were presented by lower-ranking executives, simply because McColl feared that if an important concept came from him, "Mr. Storrs will treat me like a kid and dismiss the idea out of hand."

When McColl went into Storrs's office, he either stood stiffly or, if invited, sat in a straight-backed chair, nervous and just on the edge of the seat, in case the professor called on him to write an answer on the board. From that chair, the view of the chairman was never straight-on, and Storrs's slightly ferretish face was always a bit in silhouette from the sunlight hammering through the wide bare window beyond. If there was another guest in the office, he or she took the second straight-backed chair, also on an angle to Storrs's carrier-deck desk. Between the two chairs, its face facing the chairman, was a highly prized ship's clock. McColl was ever being interrupted by the clock's seemingly random disturbances, little clangings and bangings that erupted at intervals that must have had something to do with the tides rather than the time. But the chairman could always see the clock's hands creeping, so he could weigh a meeting's anchor at his own command. "Are you having lunch with me today, Hugh?"

"Yessir," answered the fearless marine and president of the largest bank in the southeastern United States of America.

"Then block your tie."

When he was not in the company of the chairman, McColl slipped out of his sheep's clothing like Superman divesting himself of Clark Kent. He was an offensive-minded player in a defensive industry. In the setting of an advertising agency or a shipping company, his aggressiveness might have blended in, but in an industry of "very staid people who suffered through the Depression and were clinging to their jobs," McColl found himself feared and disliked. From his perspective, he was "just resolved to doing my thing and attacking."

Sometimes the attacker turned on his colleagues in what he himself referred to as "random acts of hostility." More than once, the random acts fell on McColl's secretary, Pat Hinson. Once Addison Reese's secretary, Hinson had gone to work for McColl in 1978, excited to be with someone who was moving up in the company and who would give her far greater responsibility than the take-a-letter Reese ever had. Hinson "wanted the job. I wanted to be his secretary, just simply because I believed in him and I liked him. It was a wonderful opportunity for me careerwise." As for the emotional outbursts, Hinson knew all about those from her days on the mezzanine. "I knew they were nothing personal. They were just something that came with the territory."

Storrs ultimately came to agree with Pat Hinson. What he considered overaggressiveness was a part of McColl he would have to live with in order to avail himself of McColl's more positive traits. In late 1980, using his executive committee to build consensus, Storrs recommended a promotion for McColl. The new position would add no responsibilities, but it would set him unmistakably above Bill Dougherty, who remained president of the holding company. The move was circumspect, in the style of Tom Storrs, awarding McColl the "anomalous" title of chief operating officer of the holding company, effective April 1981. Although the holding company had no "operations" of its own, Storrs figured the title "did make sense, because the holding company was an operating company." More importantly, it was a consecration from his board, the board's way of saying they would be electing McColl chairman as of September 1983, upon Storrs's departure.

In his announcement to shareholders Storrs wrote, "Since 1974 Mr. McColl has been president of the bank, an office he will retain. His banking experience has covered virtually every aspect of the business, including personal involvement in domestic and international corporate banking, correspondent banking and funds management. In recent years he has had supervisory responsibility for consumer and middle market banking as well."

Privately, Storrs told McColl the board would be watching closely to see how he handled the situation with Dougherty. He should take his time and use good judgment. Whatever McColl decided, Storrs said, "it had to be his decision. It couldn't be mine. I had found Bill a very useful member of the bank, but I realized that Hugh's relationship with him was different than mine."

Storrs had wrestled with this question for a long time. "One of the important things, it seems to me, about running a company is being able to use what people can bring to the company, at a price that you are prepared to pay. And my conclusion was that I could use what Bill brought to the company at a price I was prepared to pay. And Hugh's decision was that he was not willing to pay the price. . . . And the fact that Hugh and I came out with different answers does not prove that either one of us was wrong."

McColl saw it differently. Just as he felt about the long-ago "palace coup" aimed at keeping Tom Storrs from the presidency, he believed there was only one "right" way to proceed in the matter of Dougherty, whom McColl considered to be a negative influence on the company. McColl never understood Storrs's relationship with Dougherty, though he had "confronted him many times with it." In the late seventies, on a trip to Europe, he told Storrs, "I was going to leave if

Dougherty didn't leave. One of us was going." McColl said he understood Storrs to say he would resolve the issue, but nothing happened. "He finally resolved it by putting me in charge."

In April 1981, Hugh L. McColl Jr. became the heir apparent to NCNB Corporation and North Carolina National Bank. He was Tom Storrs's field general, the man who would lead the troops into battle. As yet he had no plan for getting his troops there, but McColl believed his theater of operations would be the state of Florida, one of the fastest-growing states in the nation.

As they were looking into the possibilities of setting up a Morris Plan bank, Paul Polking approached the Interstate Banking Group with the germ of a new idea. Polking was thinking about the time, nine years earlier, that he had prepared and filed with the Federal Reserve Board an application to acquire a little trust company in Florida. He recalled it distinctly, he told the group, because he'd been "actually upset that the Fed took forever to approve the damn thing. And I remember writing a nasty letter to them, as a matter of fact." McColl remembered that little trust company well. He and Hodges and Dougherty had bought it while Storrs was off at a meeting somewhere.

For nearly a decade the holding company had held on to that Trust Company of Florida. It had been Tom Storrs's stubborn personal decision not to sell it, despite Luther Hodges's recollection to the contrary. One of the principal shareholders of the Orlando trust was his old boxing coach at the University of Virginia, and Storrs would have felt bad about letting him down. He would have felt even worse about giving up what he considered an advantage, a privilege for NCNB in a highly regulated environment. So the Trust Company of Florida had sat on the books of the NCNB Corporation through the recession and the recovery, churning out its little profits and occupying a line in the annual report.

When Paul Polking looked at the Florida statutes, it occurred to him that there might be a way to use the Trust Company of Florida to buy one of the old existing Morris Plan banks. "The way they (the legislators) did it, they obviously screwed up. I mean they left an opening for us to jump into. And so, when that statute was passed in '72, theoretically we could have jumped on it right away, done it right away, if we had discovered it."

Polking dug a little deeper and a light went off inside his skull. The task force was on the wrong track. They shouldn't be looking at using the trust company to buy a limited-service Morris Plan bank at all. Instead, they should use it to buy a dyed-in-the-wool, full-service bank. The way the laws were written, even though NCNB Corporation was an out-of-state entity, it was grandfathered in. The Trust Company of Florida could legally buy a bank in any Florida county. If Polking's interpretation of the law stood up, ultimately, the owners of that little no-account trust company could buy many banks in many Florida counties.

Polking delivered the news first to McColl, who was ecstatic. Polking had found a loophole. No, a "unique legal authority," Polking corrected him. They took the news to Storrs, who was cautious. Maybe, maybe. Storrs directed Polking to engage outside counsel in Washington. The Interstate Banking Group held its collective breath as their lawyers prepared two briefs, one in support of NCNB's position, the other against it. Polking reported to the group that both positions were strong. Certainly there was as much going for them as there was against them. Hugh McColl liked those odds. He and his lawyers were looking at the very worst case the enemy could throw at them. They were prepared. "Shred that bad brief," he instructed Polking, "and go to work selling that good one. And find us a bank for sale in Florida."

The market data suggested that the hottest areas of commercial loan growth would be in Miami and Tampa. But in April, as the group trained its sights on those two cities, McColl received a phone call that diverted him to Jacksonville. The call was from Guillermo Carey, a smooth, elegant lawyer who had done business with NCNB's international group in Chile. By coincidence or kismet, Carey was seeking McColl's aid on behalf of his clients, a Venezuelan family that owned about 15 percent of the stock of a Florida bank that was thought to be "in play," or ripe for a takeover. It was the $2.5 billion Jacksonville bank, Florida National.

From Carey, McColl found out that a number of investors were flirting with Florida National, under the highly likely assumption that someone other than the current management could earn more money with the sleepy bank. The Venezuelan group was ready to file a Form 13-D, notifying the Federal Trade Commission of its intent to purchase another 15 percent of the shares. Carey said he could get nowhere with the Florida National board and wondered whether McColl might have any influence in Jacksonville. The board there had begun to view the Venezuelans as a threat for a hostile takeover. McColl said he'd see what he could find out.

McColl flew with Joe Martin to Jacksonville. They had lunch with a local entrepreneur, Raymond Mason, who was a protégé and confidante of Florida National's chairman, Ed Ball. From Mason McColl learned that Ed Ball was ninety-three years old and in failing health, confined to bed at New Orleans' Ocshner Clinic. McColl's instinct was to dispatch Joe Martin to the clinic with a briefcase stuffed with enough cash to buy the old man's bank just as soon as he woke up. Mason slowed him down. First, it was anything but certain that Mr. Ball would ever wake up. Second, if McColl wanted Florida National he would have to do business with Ball's and the bank's attorney, Fred Kent. Another piece of advice: to confront Kent in his Florida den he should hire a savvy attorney from inside the state, someone like Judge B. K. Roberts. McColl had learned in Nassau that no matter how true all those lawyer jokes might ring, the right one could make his deal. So he and Martin flew to Tallahassee to meet Judge Roberts, retired chief justice of the Florida Supreme Court.

Roberts surprised McColl by recommending that NCNB back away from Florida National. It would be too complicated, he said, too messy, would attract too damned much attention. Go after something quick, clean and simple, he advised. Show a small target, provide the state legislature with the minimum in time and the least ammunition for shooting down a deal. Go find an out-of-the-way nationally chartered bank, Roberts told McColl. Do a deal that would be subject to approval not by the State of Florida but by the Fed. And make it a bank in trouble, so the Fed might be inclined to look on NCNB as a friend in need. Finally, Judge Roberts recommended, put the deal to bed during the seven months when the Florida legislature was in recess. By the time those lawmakers returned to Tallahassee the following January, NCNB had better make sure every "i" was dotted and every "t" crossed.

"How soon can we get started?" McColl asked.

"Wait until the legislature's packed up and gone home," Roberts advised. "That's scheduled for Friday, June 5."

McColl grinned at the coincidence. They could move on Florida as of June 6, the thirty-seventh anniversary of the Allied invasion of

Normandy. A military metaphor dropped right in his lap.

"All right then. We'll call it Operation Overlord." Whimsy or not, there were times McColl just couldn't resist imagining himself the leader of men-at-arms.

He believed Judge Roberts was right about waiting until the legislature adjourned. Eisenhower waited to cross the Channel until the tides and weather were right and Hitler was distracted. Napoleon should have waited for spring. But McColl wasn't easy with the Judge's recommendation about backing away from Florida National. That Jacksonville bank looked like a dog that would hunt.

In fact, McColl saw Jacksonville as the perfect beachhead—near the state's northeast corner, closest to North Carolina, putting minimum strain on his supply line. Moreover, Florida National's commander-in-chief was off dying in Louisiana, which seemed like a whole different country. The bank was defending itself from siege by Caracas to the south, and Hugh McColl's army would be attacking from the north. Judge Roberts's recommendations notwithstanding, McColl instructed Joe Martin to set up a command post in Jacksonville, while an assault team of commandos went looking elsewhere for the Judge's target of opportunity, a struggling small-town national bank.

As Storrs gave McColl his head in Florida, the chairman continued pushing hard, in North Carolina and elsewhere in the region, the notion that the states must move quickly or else lose control of their banking system to New York and California interests. While as yet the state legislatures were united in disbelief, Storrs's argument won over the Southern Growth Policies Board, a regional planning organization. The board became the first nonbanking entity to officially endorse the idea of a "Southeastern Banking Compact." Then, finally, Storrs began to hear at least lip service from Wachovia and First Union; however, they continued to block NCNB's efforts within the North Carolina Bankers' Association. Storrs was not optimistic about winning his political battle in time, but he had high hopes for McColl and his Interstate Banking Group.

From the office in Charlotte, Storrs watched "Operation Overlord" capture the executive imagination. He was particularly gratified to see the CEO-designate calling on people in the bank who were different from McColl's gung-ho, handpicked workout crews—people like focused, meticulous Paul Polking; crisp, logical Frank

Gentry; academic humanist Joe Martin. Storrs began to recognize a blossoming in McColl's development, as "Hugh really became adept at using people who weren't like him." Storrs also noted that McColl had learned a lesson from their failed effort to strong-arm the South Carolina legislature with their American Trust proposal in 1973. No matter that his blood was up, McColl was forcing himself to lie low until June, to keep the Florida legislature from catching his scent. His man McColl was maturing.

Much to Joe Martin's surprise, he was enjoying working for Hugh McColl. The McColl approach was a far cry from Tom Storrs's analytic, methodical mind. Typically, Storrs reached acceptable answers to questions before his teammates were able to formulate suggestions of their own. Storrs's were decisions reached without options proposed. But McColl loved exploring the questions almost as much as finding the answers. There was as much gamesmanship as leadership in McColl's method and everyone could play. Even preposterous ideas were welcome. Nothing was too impossible. Anything could be laughed at.

McColl played the general in a way that Martin found curiously agreeable. He became "patient, sensitive, cooperative, encouraging. All those things I had thought he was not. More than anything else, I saw that he was having fun, that he loved the game." It was a war game. The executive officers brainstormed every possible move by the opposition, every possible countermove of their own, and out of the game came the plan for victory.

In Florida, Frank Gentry's next step was to engage the investment banking firm of Robinson-Humphrey. They made a quick and quiet check of small banks to find out which might be for sale, coming up with a dozen banks that fit the bill. Mostly these were one-office country-town banks struggling to make a profit, with deposits ranging from $4 million to $42 million.

While Gentry narrowed his search, McColl refused to give up on Florida National, a bank that already was in play, a big bank that would make the world take notice when he captured it. McColl pressed his suit with attorney Fred Kent, pointing out the advantages of doing business with a North Carolina bank as opposed to financiers in Caracas. Kent seemed to agree, telling McColl he would take the NCNB offer to his board, provided NCNB would "solve my Venezuelan problem first." McColl reminded him of Judge Roberts's concern about moving quickly, but Kent, eighty years old and well baked in the Florida sun, was not impressed. Instead, Kent did his best to slow things down. He expressed delight upon finding out that Joe Martin's father was the same "Piggy" Martin he'd played high school basketball with back in Savannah.

"You know, Joe, I believe my son turned out a bit taller than you did. Let me get him in here and see. . . . You fellows stand back to back now." Martin played along, he the magnolia, McColl the marine. As the old man measured his son against Piggy Martin's son, he learned that Piggy had gone into the ministry, which took the conversation in yet another unfulfilling direction, as far as McColl was concerned. He excused himself and left the office. When McColl was gone, Kent lolled, *"Joe, if you could get your boy Hugh to slow down we might be able to decide something here."* But the North Carolina bankers left the Florida National building with no more of a deal than they'd had going in. McColl reported back to Storrs that Kent was "stiff-arming us."

Annoyed, McColl set up a meeting in Miami with Carey and the Venezuelan group. One of them, Pedro "Luis" Vallenia, had been deputy governor of his nation's central bank and was one of the founders of the Organization of Petroleum Exporting Countries, OPEC. McColl believed he might be able to structure a deal that would get them off Florida National's back. The deal was that NCNB would contract with the Venezuelan interests to buy their shares at a premium, provided Florida National agreed to sell itself to NCNB. Carey was relieved. He was as frustrated as McColl with Kent and his board. Carey thought he could convince his investors to sign their shares over to NCNB, for a price, contingent on the buyout of Florida National.

McColl telephoned the good news to Kent. "Well, that's just fine," Kent said. "Appreciate it. Glad you took those people out."

"So do we have a deal?" McColl asked.

"I'll just have to run it by my board," Kent said, "and we'll see."

Chafing at the delay, McColl asked for a report from Gentry on the search for targets of opportunity. Out of the dozen low-profile banks on their list, the task force agreed their most promising target bank was Central Florida's Clewiston National, with $8.2 million in deposits, most of that from sugarcane farmers. With Florida National still dangling just out of reach, McColl decided they would reach for Clewiston's low-hanging fruit. Thursday, June 4, as the Florida

Legislature was rushing its last bills to passage, McColl drafted a half-page memo to Bill Dougherty, the first exercise of his new authority as vice chairman and COO. He wanted Dougherty to lead the acquisition mission so that any appropriate deal could be consummated on the spot. The memo was headed "Purchase of a Small National Bank in Florida."

> *As we discussed, you are to head a team including Mr. Gentry, Mr. Polking and the firm of Robinson Humphrey which will purchase a small national bank in Florida as soon as possible. While we have agreed that the Clewiston National Bank is our primary target, you are authorized to switch to any other available target which seems appropriate, if, in your judgment, we will be unable to conclude an acceptable agreement with Clewiston National Bank.*
>
> *We expect to pay in the range of twice book value for this bank in order to obtain it quickly. While we would hope not to exceed this amount, you are authorized to exceed it up to a limit of two and one half times book.*

It was not until the following day, June 5, that Storrs and McColl received permission from the NCNB Corporation's Executive Committee to spend as much as $7 million on the Florida purchase. Then, late that same afternoon, Joe Martin telephoned from Florida with the disconcerting news that the legislature would not be adjourning as anticipated. Their session would continue into the next week. Between the dalliance of Fred Kent and the foot-dragging of the lawmakers, McColl's patience was at an end. They would move ahead with the attack, maintaining the highest level of secrecy, taking their chances with the legislators.

McColl moved his command post to Suite 1901 of the Holiday Inn in downtown Jacksonville, where Joe Martin had booked the entire nineteenth floor for "the Martin Group," which would include all the IBG team—Poole, Leggett, Reynolds, Polking, Gentry—plus attorneys from inside and outside the NCNB family. As far as anyone at Holiday Inn knew, they were a lot of people named Martin. Suite 1901 consisted of three adjoining rooms. In the large central living room, the furniture was pushed back to the walls to make room for three fold-down tables draped with white linen, along with several flipchart easels. One of the bedrooms was converted to an office, complete with secure private telephone lines, the newest technology in magnetic-card typewriters, desk and file cabinet stuffed with supplies. The other bedroom was where Hugh McColl would sleep, if and when he could.

Joe Martin embraced the clandestinity of it all. He was the son of a preacher man, but he seemed born to the cloak and dagger. He had large quantities of cash flown in from Charlotte, so no one would need to flash NCNB-issue credit cards. He rented a small fleet of nondescript cars to be driven by one Martin or another. In the locked glovebox of his rental he kept the extra money. Since Jacksonville was an air force town, he located a secondhand military store that rented debugging equipment—just in case the Florida National people or some legislative lawyer got tricky. After all, the break-in and bugging of the Watergate was fresh in everyone's memory. McColl delighted in all this, but when Martin pointed to his cache of legal pads and rented typewriters, McColl asked where the secretaries might be. Martin hadn't thought they'd be needed. Proud of his own typing ability, he'd planned on creating a steno pool out of the officers on hand. McColl ordered him to bring in a couple of real secretaries.

Pat Hinson, along with Melva Hanna from the legal department, got to Jacksonville just in time to help Martin conduct an electronic sweep of the hotel walls and ceilings for eavesdropping devices. One of Polking's imported attorneys expressed surprise at encountering women. It was 1981, but most lawyers, like most bankers, wore their same old habits even longer than they wore their same old suits.

"Well, Mrs. Hinson," said the lawyer, "how does your *husband* feel about you being here?"

Pat Hinson, a quick study of the McColl style, shot back, "Probably the same way your *wife* feels about you being here."

Entering the master suite late at night, the secretaries found McColl in a T-shirt working at one of the cloth-draped tables. Instantly, Hanna and Hinson were caught up in the thrill of McColl's corporate battle-planning. Pat Hinson's pulse raced. It was all so "really, really exciting."

As other members of the NCNB SWAT team arrived, the meeting grew intense. There was much to be done before they could plant their flag in Florida. Dougherty would lead the sortie into Clewiston first thing Monday morning. McColl still had a few cards to play in his Florida National hand. Polking's bunch had to pick out some other likely players, just in case Dougherty couldn't deliver Clewiston. Judge Roberts's people had to keep tabs on the legislature in Tallahassee. By 2:00 A.M. McColl was ready to catch a few hours sleep. Hinson saw him yawn and expected the boss to simply get up and leave. The whole meeting he had not moved from his chair. Usually he paced, looked out windows, made bullet-lists on flipcharts.

Finally, the vice chairman rose from behind his cloth-draped table and walked into the bedroom. That's when Pat Hinson and Melva Hanna realized he was dressed only in his underwear.

McColl's first action when he woke up Monday, June 8, was to call for a large pot of coffee. His team would need it when they gathered to go over the day's plans. As details were questioned, tension rose. McColl wanted to bleed off some of the excess angst in the room by spreading around a little morning comfort. He liked to control the environment and he hated when some outsider's failure to perform ruined his plans. "Where the hell is that coffee?" McColl demanded. "Hell, I ordered that coffee a good half-hour ago."

Someone called down, but it was another long wait before they heard a knock on the door and the inevitable, "Room service." As the uniformed hotel worker entered, McColl blistered her as though she must be personally responsible for the delay. Did she work for the Jacksonville Holiday Inn or the Florida Bankers Association? He wouldn't stand for sloppy work like this; when he gave an order, he expected it to be carried out.

The others in the room were embarrassed at their leader's display. As they cautiously got back to work, Martin slipped out to a grocery store. Unwittingly, he was taking his cue from McColl: *Control the environment.* By doing that he could help the boss focus on what was essential to the operation. *If we can keep him cool,* Martin thought, *he'll make us invincible.* When he returned with a coffee maker and supplies, he found an opportunity to tell McColl, "Now if the coffee's late we have nobody to blame but ourselves. We can yell at each other, but not at anybody else." McColl simply nodded and asked Martin to brew another pot.

By mid-morning his caffeinated nerves were jolted by a call from Frank Gentry. Clewiston turned out to be a mistake, Gentry said. The board members were eager to sell, but they could not deliver their bank on a handshake because they simply did not hold enough of the stock. Buying Clewiston would be a long, drawn-out prospect, not the quick hit Judge Roberts had recommended and McColl had ordered.

McColl saw his Florida beachhead slipping away. What if the jilted bankers in Clewiston said something about the offer to the local newspaper? Would the still-convened legislature get wind of an attack and change the law? Finally, approaching noon, the team came up with a prospect almost as good as Clewiston. It was a bank in a town called Lake City, about an hour's drive west of Jacksonville. Controlling interest in First National Bank of Lake City was held by three businessmen who lived in Des Moines, Iowa, and who could be reached by telephone. The business day was an hour younger in Des Moines, and the Iowa investors could smell cash cooking over the long-distance lines. They agreed to charter a plane and be in Jacksonville in time for dinner.

Meanwhile, Tom Storrs joined McColl, and the two men left the hotel to pay yet another call on Fred Kent. Frank Gentry watched them leave, both "very optimistic that there was going to be some agreement with Florida National." Gentry and Polking were equally optimistic about reaching an agreement with the Iowans who owned First National Bank of Lake City, even though the lead member of their team, Bill Dougherty, was palpably unenthused.

From the Iowans they learned that the Bank of Lake City had more history than it had depositors. The bank helped bankroll the Confederacy during the Civil War, issuing its own gold certificates to pay farmers, who produced a lot of the food that was in short supply at the front. It was not unlikely that Hugh McColl's great-grandfather Duncan Donald had said battlefield grace over corn and carrots financed by the Lake City bank. In 1981, bypassed by time and Interstate 75, Lake City and its bank had fallen into quaintness. With but $22 million in deposits, First National was on the FDIC's "watch list" of tottering institutions. Consequently, the Iowans were ready in a heartbeat to pull out of Florida and they named their price, demanding for their controlling shares a sum that was higher than the total amount on deposit. Gentry and Polking gulped, ready to haggle, but Dougherty simply said, "Fine, but you don't get the money until the Fed gives us approval to go ahead."

Frank Gentry all but pirouetted into Suite 1901 with his good news. "I got mine," he chirped to McColl. "Did you guys get yours?" Only delight at the Lake City success kept McColl from throwing a water pitcher at Gentry's head. In fact, the deal with Florida National still eluded him.

"Where's Bill?" asked Tom Storrs, looking for Dougherty.

"He went home," answered Gentry. "Paul took him to the airport." Storrs's expression did not reveal his emotions.

Melva Hanna waited for Polking and spent the next several hours typing up the contract. The next morning Gentry was scheduled to fly the Iowa bankers over to Lake City where he would act as NCNB's ambassador, welcoming the bank's president onto a team he probably never had heard of, and to see the bank they were going to buy. Gentry had a surprise waiting for him at the airport.

"We've been thinking this thing over," began one of the Iowa investors. Gentry sensed that Dougherty had left him to juggle a hot potato alone. After having an evening to think over NCNB's offer, the Iowans had reached the conclusion that the Fed would never approve the purchase of a Florida bank by a North Carolina holding company. If they didn't collect something up front from NCNB, they might never get paid. So the sellers now demanded a fee for keeping their bank "off the market" for every month NCNB waited for approval by the Fed. The businessmen threatened to fly back to Des Moines if they could not get an answer immediately.

Gentry cursed Dougherty under his breath for leaving before the deal was consummated. The best he could do was get Storrs and Polking on the telephone, and he felt a bit like a messenger facing the firing squad because of the message he had to deliver. He could hear the fury in Mr. Storrs's voice. Attorney Paul Polking, used to settling disputes, took over negotiations with the Iowans. Polking said the only reason NCNB had agreed to pay the full asking price on the Lake City bank was that it was understood payment would be contingent on approval by the Federal Reserve Board.

Polking chiseled out a deal whereby NCNB would pay $19 million for Lake City Bank, with interest on the unpaid balance to be paid monthly, starting seven months from signing, until NCNB received regulatory approval. Polking did not mention to the shrewd Iowans his confidence in swinging a Fed okay at least thirty days before that interest bill would come due.

By Tuesday afternoon, NCNB had contracted to buy a full-fledged national bank in Florida. The rules of American banking were changed—subject to approval from Washington.

Tom Storrs was visibly, bitterly angry at Bill Dougherty for allowing the Lake City shareholders to "double dip," and for taking French leave. Dougherty would not be allowed to have anything more to do with Florida or with interstate expansion as long as Storrs was chairman.

Tuesday night Hugh McColl hosted a party in the lounge of the Holiday Inn. It was "stinger time," time to drink and unwind. When McColl found out that Pat Hinson and Melva Hanna had spent their teenage summers on Ocean Boulevard at Myrtle Beach, South Carolina, he knew they'd love to shag as much as he did. No matter that none of the other men could or would join in the dance. No matter that outside the sidewalks of Jacksonville had been rolled up since 6 P.M. McColl and the two women kept the Holiday Inn band cranking out beach music till the wee hours. Already Florida seemed a little more like home.

Joe Martin and Frank Gentry couldn't dance because they were already on their way back to Charlotte, to set the wheels in motion for filing with the Federal Reserve. Martin was forced to detour back to Florida because, in his euphoria, he had turned in his rental car without remembering to extract several thousand dollars in cash from the glove compartment. Martin had to convince the Hertz representative in Jacksonville to hold that specific car for him. "Don't clean it up, don't wash it or anything. I love that car and I want it just the way I left it."

The money was still there, but Joe Martin would be a day late getting back to his wife Joan. On his second plane ride to Charlotte, Martin thought over a McColl remark he'd overheard as the vice chairman was helping himself to a cup of coffee from the pot Martin had installed.

"One thing I like about Joe," he said, "is that he'll see a problem and solve it. No muss, no fuss."

Martin smiled at that. *Just like Hugh McColl to recite the brave deeds of his comrades. Makes us all want to defend one another to the death.* He'd seen it work the other way—a manager reaming out one employee in front of another, undermining the whole team. *I like Joe Martin because he solves problems.* Meaning: *Be like Joe Martin and solve problems.* Or: *Be like Frank Gentry and think out-of-the-box.* Or: *Be like Buddy Kemp and take charge.* Be like Hugh McColl, Martin told himself, and sing the praises of your troops around the campfire.

Ream them out in the solitude of your tent.

Wednesday morning, June 10, Tom Storrs and Paul Polking flew to Washington for meetings with attorneys for the Comptroller of the Currency and the Federal Reserve to discuss their application for the purchase of the Lake City bank by the Trust Company of Florida and its parent, NCNB Corporation. With the Florida lawmakers at last packed up and out of Tallahassee, the crucial thing was to get it filed, get it approved and get it over with before the legislature assembled for its next session. In Washington, the government lawyers could hardly contain their laughter over what the North Carolina bankers had in mind.

It took several hours of explaining and feather unruffling before the representatives of the banking industry's watchdogs agreed even to consider NCNB's application; its success, of course, was unthinkable. But on the flight back to Florida, Polking assured Storrs the law was on their side. There would be considerable legal fees involved in convincing all the necessary parties, but eventually they would win their case. He still believed he could get it done before the following January, when the bank would have to begin paying interest to the Iowans and when the Florida legislature would reconvene.

Hugh McColl's personal mission was to build on the Florida victory before the Fed had a chance to shoot it down. If he came away from Florida with nothing but little Lake City, he couldn't think of Operation Overlord as a success. He dearly wanted to add the big Florida National fish to his creel, and if he could get the Venezuelans to put something in writing, he might be able to force Fred Kent's hand.

June 18, McColl celebrated his forty-sixth birthday in the air on the way to Miami. Since he expected terms to be dictated and a contract to be drawn up, Pat Hinson was with him. She ordered a cake and served it on the flight down. In Miami she took notes through "hours and hours of negotiation," the first time she had been a party to anything like this. Much of the negotiating required lengthy translation. When it was done, there were handshakes and signatures and McColl believed he had put the finishing touches on the deal that was necessary to make the deal he really wanted. Finally, there was no way Fred Kent could keep stalling.

Back in Jacksonville, Kent thanked him, said he would need just a little more time. McColl seethed and smiled back.

Seven days later, June 25, Ed Ball ran out of time. The doctors in New Orleans could no longer keep him alive and the man who had built Florida National into one of his state's most successful banking fiefdoms was no longer a factor in its disposition.

June 26, Hugh McColl learned that his deal to buy Florida National was dead as Ed Ball. Kent either could not sway his board or he'd never had any intention of trying. He told McColl he admired "a person who has the intelligence to conceive such a plan and the guts to make it work out." Yet he doubted NCNB ever would be successful with its Florida strategy. From the security of his office, Fred Kent wrote:

"What you needed to do was, as I told you and Mr. Storrs, move slower. Florida National was like a maiden lady who no one had ever even tried to seduce! You rushed too much. You were a little too rough. And you withdrew too soon."

McColl flew into a rage. Other members of the team tried to calm him, but he paced Suite 1901 swinging his tennis racket and cursing. He wanted to hit someone. He hated being played for a fool and that's what had happened here. McColl had gone along with the lawyer's game, protecting Fred Kent and his board from those Venezuelan investors, only to be given the shaft. "Kent told me to solve his Venezuelan problem. I solved his Venezuelan problem. Now he tells me he can't do business with us 'cause we're dealing with the Venezuelans. Great guy." Damning the collective hide of Florida National, McColl vowed to stay in Jacksonville until he could dig more than a toehold in Florida. "One day," he told the room, "we're going to own this whole goddamn state."

To calm himself, he called Jane. It was well into the morning, but he knew he would feel better after he went over his problems with his favorite confidante. Jane listened and offered counsel. Hugh should get away from Florida as soon as he could and join her at Litchfield. Barefoot walks in the evening surf would soothe his soul. He agreed. A few days later Jane wrote to her parents from the South Carolina beach:

"The air conditioner is broken, but the breeze is back. And the breeze means that Hugh can sail and be happy. He finally got here for some vacation Thursday night and hopes to stay all this week. . . . He is exhausted and very disappointed and down that the Florida bank voted not to accept their offer, but on Friday another bank in Florida called Mr. Storrs and said they would be interested in selling to

NCNB, so I doubt that it is a dead issue."

There were indeed other banks in the Sunshine State and a few of them not so demure as Jacksonville's teasing Florida National. From the panhandle to the lower peninsula, eyelashes batted and petticoats lifted as word of the bold raiders from North Carolina swept across the state. Hugh McColl was not inclined to still Florida's fluttering hearts. Invited to speak to business students in Tallahassee, he told them—and the attendant media—"You have a good many banks in Florida with assets of $40 and $50 million. We call those 'drive-in branches' in North Carolina."

A local journalist posed the question, what if the Fed should do the unthinkable and approve the Lake City purchase? Wouldn't the Florida Bankers Association take NCNB to court to keep them out of the state?

McColl dared the association to do its worst. "We'll fight it with every dollar and resource available to us," he roared.

The leading business publication in the state, *Florida Trend*, heralded McColl's assault with a cartoon depicting NCNB as an armored car, barreling south under a Rebel battle flag with guns blazing. Joe Martin was afraid this might set McColl off. For one thing, he hated being pigeonholed. For another, his flag was the stars and stripes, not the stars and bars. Martin remembered his tactic of "controlling the environment" with the coffee maker at the Holiday Inn and decided his best move would be to give the boss a cartoon he could live with and laugh at. Martin raced to the Army-Navy store, a block down Trade Street from the bank, to pick up some props. He came back with marine fatigue caps for himself, Polking, Gentry and Leggett, and a general's helmet for McColl. In deference to Storrs, he found some pliers and snapped off one of the helmet's five stars. The flag he needed was the captured state flag of Florida. In the bank's fortieth-floor Reese Room, McColl grinningly donned the helmet and posed for a photo with Martin and the others, reminiscent of the statue of the marines capturing Iwo Jima. The photo-cartoon made the rounds of the twenty-third floor of the Tower, but Martin was careful to keep it away from the media.

As the weeks dragged on, McColl paced his office, awaiting approval from the Federal Reserve on the Lake City purchase. In August, he decided that if he could not move the Fed, at least he could take care of business at home. McColl went to Bill Dougherty's office in Charlotte and sat down. "I told Bill there was no place for him in the organization that I envisioned for the future."

According to McColl, Dougherty answered, "I don't blame you, I'd do the same thing, I would do the same thing if I was you." That's when McColl "made the mistake of being generous, and I asked how long he would like to stay. He said March, so I was locked into him staying till March." After firing Dougherty, McColl told the bank's controller, Bruce Beery, that his services were no longer required. Even while Storrs was still in charge, McColl got rid of the company's CFO and controller, with no designated replacements on board. He told Chuck Cooley to find him a CFO, quick.

Joe Martin distracted McColl with Dennis Rash, who had yet another Charlotte uptown development project in the wings. Rash's Fourth Ward revitalization was proving out. After a "land rush" of condominium buying by pioneer professionals who saw the advantage of escaping in from the suburbs, there were now several established developers involved. The Chamber of Commerce could brag about "redevelopment of the dilapidated Fourth Ward area into an attractive residential option for several thousand people." Even though it was a long way from becoming Soho or Covent Garden, Rash told McColl their work in Fourth Ward was over for the moment. Now the bank was being petitioned by residents, who wanted a better neighborhood—more police patrols, improved garbage collection, street repairs, a crackdown on drugs and prostitution, clean-up of a toxic dump and junkyard—and Rash himself was wavering on whether the bank should get involved with anything this extensive.

The difference between Third and Fourth Wards, Rash said, was that while the Fourth Ward project was chic, upscale, nouveau and involved replacing vacant lots with people, Third Ward was currently inhabited by "a significant neighborhood group," all of whom were black. The new plan called for relocating many of those residents to make way for industrial plants for companies like Duke Power and the *Observer* Publishing Company, which might otherwise be lost to the suburbs. Rash introduced McColl to the leader of the group with the greatest concerns about the plan, the Committee to Preserve and Restore Third Ward, and to its chairwoman, Mildred Baxter Davis, a former university professor with a doctorate from Columbia in New

York, who made a deep impression on the banker.

McColl listened to Dr. Davis's arguments and was forced to come to grips with a fact of which he was not proud: Southern whites still maintained ghettoes for their black help. Charlotte of the 1980s wasn't all that different from the Bennettsville of his childhood, where white kids went to play around the old "burnt factory," with its mill pond and wooden floodgates, and when the rains came and Crooked Creek overflowed you could bet there'd be floods down below, where the black people lived. Marian Wright Edelman grew up there, near the black church, and was famous around Bennettsville long before she founded the Children's Defense Fund. Heber Covington, Uncle D. K.'s chauffeur, was rich enough to be the first black man in the county to own a television set—put the antenna up on top of his big brick home, the first one in the county to house a black family—but the Covingtons had to live on King Street, where the training school was. Couldn't live in the white part of town. On the east side of downtown was "The Gulf," the black commercial district on Market Street. Cadell Chestnut, the barber, ran the county's oldest black business there, but he could only cut black people's hair. Dr. Toby Richardson and his wife, Sadie, would sell you a comic book or a soda at their drugstore even if you weren't black. Couldn't run a black business in the white part of town.

McColl was ready to try out his power on something challenging, any challenge that would build on the bank's Florida achievement. He decided to lead from the front. "Hell, Dennis, you've done it in Fourth Ward. This'll be a piece of cake."

Rash doubted that McColl could cite many examples of predominantly white banks and predominantly African-American neighborhood groups working in friendly cooperation. "It might be a lot of things," he grumbled, "but it won't be a piece of cake. It's not historic. It has an existing neighborhood. Those residents are African-American, and like it or not, the real estate people will have a certain bias against that."

McColl looked hard at Rash and spoke first with his eyes: *Dennis, this is the last damn time we're having this conversation.* Aloud he said, "We're making a lot of money in South Africa, and we sure as hell ought to be doing something good for the people in our own community."

"Yes, sir," said Rash.

In late September, Tom Storrs told Martin to leave Third Ward to

Rash. He had communication problems of a more pressing nature to be addressed. The Federal Reserve seemed about to issue its ruling on the Lake City, Florida, bank purchase. Even if Paul Polking was wrong, even if the story had a bitter ending, Storrs wanted it told the right way.

Paul Polking was optimistic. The Florida Bankers Association had flown a planeload of lawyers to D.C. to argue against NCNB's claim. The Floridians had made a number of reasonable arguments against the deal, but, Polking told McColl, "none were as good as the case we presented against ourselves and then shredded." NCNB's lawyers, with help from Judge Roberts's staff and the Washington consultants, had laid out a powerful case before the Fed. Polking didn't see how they could be turned down. Storrs and McColl hoped Polking was right, but they told Martin to be ready for the worst.

October 5, Polking called from Washington to say this could be the day. Martin pulled out the memo written and approved days earlier, circulating it to eleven key executives. The memo began: "We expect that notification of the Fed's decision will come late in the afternoon. There may be very little time for actions required by our objectives." Those objectives were twofold: "Internally, to create a sense of pride and victory in the successful result of aggressive and intentional risk-taking." And, "Externally, to create a sense of confidence in the company with the successful result of a lengthy and deliberate plan and to create a sense of expectation (without generating hostility) about further actions." The memo went out, the phones were covered.

The phones did not ring that afternoon, nor any afternoon that week. McColl fretted like a boy stood up on his first date. "We've got to buy this little bank," he said, "so we can prove our point to all the other Florida bankers, so they'll know that what we say is true." In fact, the Fed did not release its decision for another eight weeks.

December 7, 1981, Joe Martin's well-laid plan was finally triggered. McColl knew he would always remember that date, forty years after Pearl Harbor. Late that afternoon the call came through and was forwarded immediately to Storrs. Even before putting it through, secretary Mary Covington told Pat Hinson to notify Polking and Martin so they could contact the others. Communication specialist Betty Ledford was dispatched to the fortieth floor to activate the building's public address system. Attorney Jim Kiser's secretary began getting directors on the phone. Mary Covington pulled out two speeches from her desk drawer; Mr. Storrs would select one of them on his way to make the PA announcement, essentially the same as the statement to be read to the media. One speech was headed APPROVAL, the other REJECTION.

The "approval" speech was to be accompanied by the commercial jingle NCNB was using in its current advertising campaign, "We want to be the best bank in the neighborhood," implying that the neighborhood was about to get a whole lot bigger. In this speech, Storrs would congratulate his team and thank them for "a lengthy and deliberate planning process." The chairman would say, "All of us can take great pride in this achievement for our company." He would "look forward to our association with the people of Lake City." He would maintain an aura of mystery by hinting that "although we expect to have other opportunities to expand our service to customers in the Florida market, we do not have any definitive plans to announce at this time."

The other sheet on Mary Covington's desk held just a half-page of text. If the news from Washington was bad, Storrs would deliver his "rejection" speech, dolefully telling the team the news they would "undoubtedly read in tomorrow's newspaper." He would be "naturally disappointed at this decision" and would "continue to believe we had a sound legal case." What the bank might do next, "it would be premature for me to comment." There would be no musical accompaniment.

Only a few minutes later, throughout the NCNB tower in Charlotte, the music played. The people of NCNB cheered and hugged.

One of the first calls out of the tower that December afternoon was to K. C. Trowell, the president of Lake City Bank, now the newest branch manager of NCNB. The message was simple: "Break out the champagne!" Trowell had kept the bubbly iced for two months, ready to pop and pour for his people, to toast their new status as associates of the Southeast's first and only two-state bank.

In authorizing the bank to proceed with the acquisition, the Federal Reserve Board determined "that NCNB may, in accordance with Florida law acquire, retain, or own all the assets of, or control over any Florida bank or trust company." The order stated that "Florida law authorizes grandfathered out-of-state companies to acquire Florida banks and that this state authorization is sufficient for purposes of satisfying the Douglas Amendment."

McColl came up with a line that was quoted by the *Observer*'s Dick Stilley and that turned up in one article after another: "We have stolen a march on the world, into one of the fastest-growing markets—a hundred-billion-dollar deposit market."

"Stealing a march" implied that one's competitors were also on the move. McColl imagined every banking aggressor would be stalking Florida now to find its own way around the legislative fortifications. And Paul Polking had demonstrated clearly that any wall one lawyer could build, another lawyer could poke a hole in. For the moment, the advantage was theirs, but they had to keep seizing the moment.

First they had to close the deal in Lake City before the legislature could convene and write any new laws. True to its placid reputation, the Florida Bankers Association informed the press that it would not challenge the Fed ruling in court, unless it was requested specifically to do so by either of the other two banks doing business in Lake City's Columbia County. NCNB already had sold those bankers on the notion that neighbors from North Carolina would be less threatening than say, Venezuelans, so the Bankers Association gauntlet stayed where it fell.

At 8:30 A.M. on January 8, 1982, following a ceremonial breakfast with Governor Bob Graham and other Florida dignitaries, Tom Storrs and Hugh McColl officially took ownership of First National Bank of Lake City, their first piece of the territory of Florida.

They knew it needed company, and quickly. After his Lake City breakfast, Storrs had a lunch appointment in Miami. His mission there was to tell Chairman Phil Searle that NCNB had just purchased 360,000 shares of his Flagship Banks Corporation, about 5 percent of the stock, and to let him know they were ready to buy controlling interest in the bank.

Searle said no deal. While agreeing that mergers throughout Florida were inevitable, Searle intended his bank to be "an acquirer or survivor," or else he would wait to sell out after national interstate banking was legalized. That way he was certain to get the best price.

The bigger Florida banks declared themselves unafraid of the North Carolina threat. The state's largest bank holding company was Southeast Banking Corporation, based in Miami. Charles Zwick, Southeast's CEO, actually invited Storrs in for a friendly chat. He provided insights into Miami and other Florida markets and alerted Storrs to the fact that Florida National's Kent was "bad-mouthing" NCNB to other bankers. As for a "compact" or reciprocal banking agreement among Southeastern states, Zwick was mildly interested, but he did not feel the idea merited betting "big chips."

When he spoke to the *Miami Herald* about NCNB, Zwick came up with a quip worthy of Hugh McColl. Though not a tall man himself, Zwick implied he could look down on Storrs, on McColl and on their bank. "They're about five feet, six inches tall, and we're about five feet, six and three-quarters inches tall. And, no, we don't believe they can do anything better than we can. . . . We know the market better than they do."

Storrs, McColl, Gentry and Martin scurried around the state like beachcombers with metal detectors—probing, listening, scratching the surface, digging down. In Jacksonville there were even conversations with the Barnett holding company. Guy Botts admitted to Storrs he had been "thinking about" the possibility of merging with NCNB. That would make both banks "less vulnerable to takeover" and would provide "a good base for moving into Georgia." But Botts was no longer chairman of Barnett. The torch had been passed to Charlie Rice and, as Botts pointed out, "a CEO has a stake in the status quo." Botts floated the idea of a "confederacy" of the two banks, but Storrs insisted on one bank, one direction. "Were you and I in our fifties," said Botts, "we'd do it. Since we're not, we have management questions to consider."

In Orlando, Sun Banks of Florida's CEO Joel Wells insisted customers would see McColl and Storrs and their bank as outsiders. "People still want to deal with a local bank," he told the *Herald*. "If NCNB thinks they can manage Florida from Charlotte, maybe they can. But I would say the further away you get, the harder it is."

Yet even as Florida's big holding companies postured and huffed, small to medium-sized bank shareholders around the state were salivating over an anticipated landrush. After the Florida National "fiasco," Storrs told his people, NCNB probably would not be able to buy a large bank, but would have to string together a few little pearls quickly, creating a multicounty Florida bank before New York pried its way into the oyster.

Flagship's Searle had a lead. Gordon Campbell, CEO of Tampa's venerable Exchange Bank and Trust Company, appeared to have "a real desire" to merge with NCNB, he said. Storrs was onto Exchange already. He knew Campbell from the American Bankers Association and liked the growth potential of the Tampa-St. Petersburg-Gulf Coast market. As Storrs worked that area, McColl canvassed the south, including the cash-rich retirement community of Boca Raton. Gulfstream Banks, Inc., was there, and a few smaller prospects were in Miami.

On Washington's Birthday, McColl was in Miami, talking to the $10 million, one-office Downtown National Bank, when he got a call from Tom Storrs telling him there was a much bigger prize to be bagged back home. Storrs had learned that McColl's friend, C. D. "Dick" Spangler Jr., was talking merger of his $425 million Bank of North Carolina with their competition. NCNB had rescued BNC in 1972 in their typical "relationship banking" fashion. Now, ten years later, Dick Spangler was ready to get out of the banking business and get back to what he understood, construction.

McColl sprang to the offensive. If Spangler was going to sell his Raleigh bank, he'd be damned if it was going to First Union or Wachovia. That "relationship" worked both ways. By the time McColl tracked him down in a wee-hours phone call, Spangler was already in the West Virginia mountains for a long weekend of skiing with his family. He agreed to meet McColl at the nearest landing strip.

"It's 0200 hours. Pick me up at the Greenbrier Airport at 0900," McColl said, just before hanging up.

Late Saturday morning, Spangler and McColl pulled into the parking lot of the exclusive Greenbrier mountain resort, where neither one was registered but where they suspected they could find a quiet—and warm—spot to talk. In a large, empty banquet room, they sat in a corner and McColl began to jawbone the deal. NCNB had good people, a good future ahead. It was time for the bank to strengthen its presence in eastern North Carolina.

'Well, this all sounds interesting," Spangler managed to get in. "We ought to talk some more about this next week. I'll be back in Charlotte on . . . ."

"You don't understand, Dick. My board and my chairman have authorized me to make this transaction today, not next week."

Fifteen minutes later they had a deal and McColl scratched it out on a sheet of paper. He made a second original, all in longhand. Both men signed both copies. Then they talked about their families over hamburgers at the hotel's grill—paid for by Spangler, since McColl had left Florida without his wallet. In the parking lot, Spangler's car had a flat, so the two bank presidents, breath frosted and cheeks red in the Appalachian winter, wrenched lug nuts and switched tires. Then Spangler drove McColl to the little airstrip for his flight back to Florida.

On the road, they went over their simple agreement one more time: Spangler would trade his Bank of North Carolina interest for about two million shares of NCNB stock, worth more than $32 million. The two friends parted, shaking hands on the largest bank merger in the history of North Carolina.

McColl had no time to celebrate. Back in Boca he had a board of directors right where he wanted them—thinking they had Hugh McColl right where they wanted him. Gulfstream Banks had twenty-one branches and assets of $741 million. McColl agreed to buy it for $92 million. He wanted the world to learn about this deal through a carefully crafted message from Joe Martin, whom he had come to trust implicitly in matters of communication. But when he telephoned Charlotte, he discovered Martin was stuck in one of the Third Ward meetings with Rash. Not wanting to seem too excited or alert any outsiders of his success, McColl reached back into his memory and came up with the perfect hush-hush signal, a play on astronaut Neil Armstrong's first words from "Tranquillity Base" on the surface of the moon. To bankers in North Carolina, the southern tip of Florida might as well have been the moon, until now. "Take a note to Joe," he instructed the secretary. "Just write down, 'The martin has found a nest.' He'll know what to do."

Storrs gave McColl a modicum of congratulations. Gulfstream was "not a big deal, but there had to be a start somewhere."

The next step, and a somewhat bigger deal, was Storrs's. By the end of May he had a commitment from Gordon Campbell and the board of Exchange Bancorporation in Tampa. Their fifty-one branches in eleven counties gave NCNB a total of seventy-four offices in Florida. Storrs paid nearly twice the book value of the holding company's stock, $135 million, but he considered it a good catch nonetheless.

In the fall of 1982, Frank Gentry hooked and reeled in Miami's little Downtown National Bank for McColl. The rest of south Florida's financial establishment had paid little or no attention to the one-office company; now it had their undivided attention. NCNB got into Miami's Dade County for the paltry sum of $6 million, and nobody expected the North Carolina gang to settle for just one branch there for very long.

The more astute bankers and securities analysts in the state were beginning to figure out that NCNB had them by the short hairs. The Tarheel boys knew how to get bargain-rate money to buy banks. McColl had shown the way in London and now NCNB had a network of banking backup around the country. Success in the international trade, along with North Carolina's long-permitted policy of intercounty merging and branching, had given NCNB much deeper pockets than any Florida institution had. NCNB's credit limit to any single customer was more than $50 million, 25 percent more than any Florida bank could lend. That was an important consideration to the state's large businesses.

"Our corporate customers will no longer have to leave the local market for financing," McColl bragged to the mayor of Tampa on the day he formally claimed Exchange Bank and Trust for NCNB. It was significant that he chose the pronoun "our" rather than "your."

Tampa securities analyst Jerry Williams sounded the alarm for his state's bankers. They had grown fat, Williams observed in the *Miami Herald*, by paying low interest rates on long-term savings account deposits from well-heeled retirees. It did not take a genius to produce a profit out of that kind of raw material. NCNB, on the other hand, "knows how to purchase wholesale funds and lend them out at a profit. Florida bankers don't do that as well."

From New York, analysts looked south with mounting curiosity. McColl's "stolen march" enthusiasm was "by no means unjustified," commented Richard Stillinger, vice president at Keefe Bruyette & Woods. "They will be operating in a state that is more promising than their own. In the future their growth will be greater in Florida than in North Carolina."

During the Christmas holiday of 1982, McColl's swagger was intact as he walked into a conference room for an interview with Dick Stilley of the *Charlotte Observer*. In the space of just over a year, he and his bank had pulled off a coup that no one could have imagined possible. They had grown from absentee landlords of one little trust company in Orlando into the most feared aggressor in Florida banking. They were in sixteen Florida counties now, where nearly 67 percent of the state's ten million people lived. Adding up their Florida and North Carolina purchases in 1982, they had spent $200 million, a new one-year record for bank acquisitions. Anywhere.

But, McColl told Stilley, there was more money to be spent. They had to make the Florida operation efficient, make their Florida customers as satisfied as NCNB's North Carolina customers, make their Florida team members part of the NCNB culture. "We will not divert ourselves with casual mergers," McColl said. "Retained earnings is the greatest way to build capital. We will pay back the debt and get in good shape to start over when they drop the barrier to interstate banking."

Streamlining the operations of seventy-five more-or-less individual Florida banks into one smooth system—controlled from Charlotte— had all the earmarks of a daunting task. Neither Gulfstream nor Exchange had a unified operations department, so NCNB would have to invent something. McColl would need to call on many of the top people, including Jim Sommers, Jim Berry, Frank Gentry and Buddy Kemp—people whose leadership strengths McColl had bulked up in his national and international training days, people who had come through the fire of the mid-seventies workouts. As to the individual who would take the point and integrate all these Florida banks into the NCNB culture, Tom Storrs believed he had the perfect candidate.

The man Storrs chose to head up NCNB's Florida operations was Donald D. Buchanan, a Westerner recruited by Bill Dougherty in 1975, when the bank was past the worst of the workout crisis. Like Dougherty, Buchanan was a detail-oriented, control-minded individual who had captained the national champion debate team at the University of Denver. Dougherty hired him away from the United Bank of Denver to handle the bank's back-office and trust operations. For the past seven years Buchanan's responsibilities had included supervision of the Florida Trust Company. That, Storrs believed, should give him a better grasp of the Florida market than anyone else at the bank would have.

McColl was less certain of that. He put out a terse memo announcing: "Don Buchanan has been named Florida Group Executive for NCNB. . . . Mr. Buchanan's initial task is to help develop and implement the overall strategy for NCNB in the Florida market. He will report to me."

Buchanan clearly saw Florida as an opportunity for advancing his own career as well as an opportunity for the bank. In an interview with the *Observer*, he acknowledged that if the Florida operation worked the way Hugh McColl expected it to, much of the credit would accrue to Buchanan. "We believe this can be enormously successful," he said. "Some of us have bet our jobs on it."

Within just a few weeks Buchanan might have wanted to take back that remark. To start with, the Florida operations were in far worse shape than he or anyone else had imagined. The most advanced of the five new banks was Exchange. It was at least in the process of revamping its antiquated computer processes. But even Exchange had nine separate ledger systems. Bedford Boyce and Darwin Smith were called in from the Charlotte office to design and bring online a completely new operations center in Tampa, compatible with the one back in Charlotte.

Even more disturbing was the incompatibility of NCNB's new contingent of Floridians with the existing NCNB culture, so carefully crafted by Addison Reese and Tom Storrs, so personified in Hugh McColl. Buchanan asked for Chuck Cooley's help, and Cooley was horrified at what he encountered. "We found people who went to Florida because of the weather and because of the laid-back environment, not people who went there to do business the way we did. They weren't as serious as we were." Cooley, a physically imposing yet gentle man who wrote poems to commemorate NCNB victories and employees' retirements, was distressed to find himself labeled "arrogant" and "abrasive" by his new Florida teammates.

At Cooley's bank, executives got no frills, no new cars every year, no country club memberships, no Wednesday afternoons off to play golf with clients. In Charlotte, nothing mattered but the thrill of the chase, the glory of conquest. In Florida, as Don Buchanan put it, "you didn't let anything interfere with a good sunny weekend at the beach." Executives at the former Exchange and Gulfstream banks had so thoroughly mixed business and pleasure that even they had a hard time distinguishing which was which.

Cooley found expense reports listing such "business expenses" as golf shoes and bags, drivers and putters for bank officers' customers. "They just put it on the tab, had the bank buy this stuff."

NCNB's heavy hand fell like a lead blimp on the Florida sand. Bankers did not appreciate having their privileges revoked. The executive griping worked its way through the ranks into teller lines, where lower-level employees served up dissatisfaction to customers. One day Buchanan waited incognito in a branch office line and heard his direct telephone number being read out to a customer by a teller. "You know, this NCNB has come in here," the teller said, "and you probably aren't gonna like some of this stuff. It might be helpful if you'd call the president."

In his first months on the job Buchanan watched seven out of every ten of his Florida officers quit their jobs or get fired. Gordon Campbell, still using Exchange Bancorporation stationery, pleaded with McColl for help. "During the past five years we have recruited some very talented bankers," he wrote, "and it is certainly to the best interests of both of us to retain them. . . . These are precisely the same people who will be pursued by other banks during the uncertain months ahead."

McColl wrote back, saying, "I share the view that your people are important. . . . A healthy and happy marriage is very important to us. You can be sure that I am going to do everything possible to see that your good people have the same opportunity as if they had been in our family all along. One thing you will learn about me is that I love winning and that I like all my teammates, particularly those who help us win."

The image problem was not strictly an internal one. Frank Gentry's assignment in Tampa was to handle marketing, including deposit growth and customer relationships, reporting to Buchanan. Gentry observed that NCNB was quickly being perceived as "different from other Florida banks." This was a great help in attracting potential commercial borrowers, but was as threatening to existing customers as it was to most Florida employees. The changes being instituted by NCNB were undermining loyalty, internally and externally. "The most important key to overcoming the problems is *leadership* at all levels," Gentry wrote in answer to a question from McColl.

By summer's end, McColl was losing confidence in and patience with the leadership of Don Buchanan. "I want you to stop worrying about controlling everything," he wrote. "You need to worry about doing business—how to organize, how to create momentum, how to achieve results and how to do this fast." With Buchanan in charge, McColl felt "we were struggling, really struggling mightily. And I was having to fly in and out of Florida to talk to people, to motivate people, and to try and hold it together. I was tested in a different fashion than I had been tested ever before."

To help Buchanan look more like a good neighbor than Attila the

Hun, McColl sent Dennis Rash to Florida to see if he could come up with a community project similar to the Third Ward effort, some way that NCNB could help out and, in the process, generate a bit of positive publicity for the bank. Rash found his project in Miami's Liberty City, which had gone to seed since its devastation in 1968, following the assassination of Martin Luther King Jr. The bank put together a revitalization plan, and Rash went to Washington to collect a $17 million check from the Department of Housing and Urban Development to help build a hospital in Liberty City.

Meanwhile, Tom Storrs assigned Joe Martin the challenge of coming up with a new name for the bank. "NCNB" had evolved out of the merger of American Commercial and Security National of Greensboro. There was nothing sacred about it, and there was no reason a new name should not evolve out of this merger of two states. The generally accepted wisdom was that "North Carolina National Bank" would rankle old-time Floridians—even though most people didn't have a clue what "NCNB" stood for and half the old-time Floridians were from New York, New Jersey or Pennsylvania.

Martin took to the challenge and hatched: *NovaBank*. With his usual thoroughness, Martin put together arguments to beat back concerns of the science-minded, who might snicker that the bank was nothing but a nova star: big flash and quick burnout. He anticipated the concerns of linguists: *no va* would mean "won't go" to the Spanish-speaking residents of Miami and Tampa. After Martin's presentation, NovaBank got thumbs-up from Storrs, McColl, even the board. However, Martin could not settle the nervous stomachs of NCNB's law department. Out in California, they found a bank that was promoting a new account product called *Nova*. "They'll take us to court," warned the lawyers. "This will cost us plenty. We might even lose."

So Hugh McColl's new, fractious outposts united in mid-1983 under the red-white-and-blue banner of "NCNB National Bank of Florida." It was innocuous, redundant and unglamorous, but it was safe.

As the new name was being sold in Florida's newspapers and over Florida's airwaves, the Florida legislature considered a bill sponsored and liberally funded by Citicorp and Chemical Bank. This legislation would have let New York banks into the state, establishing *de novo* (start-up) full-service banking facilities, but the legislators voted it down. Walter Wriston gnashed his teeth and swore he would not long be kept at bay by Tom Storrs and Hugh McColl, who once had come begging to him for help.

But Wriston was diverted to California when the United States Supreme Court at last opened the door for him to buy Oakland's failed Fidelity Savings & Loans Association. For that one, Wriston got his picture on the cover of *Fortune* in a cowboy hat next to the head-line "Citicorp Goes West."

McColl was delighted at the help from the unlikely quarters of Tallahassee and Washington, but what about set him to shagging again at the Jacksonville Holiday Inn was word that the Florida Bankers Association had elected Gordon Campbell as its new presi-dent. His peers were honoring Campbell for long and distinguished service as chief executive of Exchange Bank, but now Campbell was in the employ of those North Carolina marauders the association had labeled as unwanted and illegal aliens.

Almost immediately, Campbell got the born-again Bankers Association behind the idea of a regional reciprocal banking agree-ment. Campbell, along with NCNB's Paul Polking and Mark Leggett and other lawyers from Miami, took the case to Governor Bob Graham. Since his own agenda included foundation of a "Southern Common Market," Graham signed on.

Suddenly the case for regional banking, which Storrs and McColl had been pushing for nearly five years, had a spokesman. Florida was the state whose banking establishment had the most to lose if the fed-eral government pulled up all the fences at once. Florida was also a state that bankers from every other state pined for. When Florida talked about opening its golden gates, bankers in other Southern states started rattling their own keychains.

Quickly pulling together a coalition of state bank associations, Polking and Leggett organized a regional meeting in the neutral city of Atlanta. Banking and government representatives from Maryland to Texas were invited. They brought in a speaker, the Bank of New England's chairman, who told them how banks in his region, under attack from the big New York banks, had begun exploring reciprocal banking as a device to keep Citicorp and Chemical out.

Bankers in Louisiana, Mississippi and Alabama rolled up like armadillos. They heard the jingle of spurs and the clomp of big Texas boots in all this "regional reciprocity" talk. The big Texas bankers snorted. No way they were about to let some bankers from

North Carolina into their state, where money flowed black and thick from the soil.

Buddy Kemp, leading the NCNB delegation in Atlanta, saw the main line of interstate banking interest running in a swath up the east coast: Florida, Georgia, Tennessee, the Carolinas, Kentucky, Virginia . . . . In those states there was a consensus building, slow, but coming.

McColl wondered: What if a Southeastern Banking Compact train left the station before NCNB had all its tracks laid? NCNB had started this train and now it actually had the most to lose, namely the Florida advantage. What McColl needed to do was secure Florida, wrap it up, before First Union and Wachovia and the big Atlanta banks got their hands on all that low-hanging grapefruit.

Meanwhile, Citicorp helped out again, slowing down the train with a lawsuit charging that any attempt to form an interstate compact would foster "divisive regionalism." Citicorp lawyers realized that the only way to stop regional compacts was to challenge them as unconstitutional. But the District Court denied Citicorp's arguments and the case was thrown out of Appeals Court.

The Florida bankers themselves were figuring out they had better start eating if they were going to grow big enough not to be somebody else's meal. Sun Banks announced a merger with Flagship. Florida National bought Royal Trustco. The *Miami Herald* thought it noticed "a heightened competitive fever among Florida bankers."

Storrs and McColl were well aware of that competition. Despite their promise at the end of 1982 to go slow and consolidate what they had already in Florida, they convinced the board that they needed to move even faster. In May 1983, the two men began traveling from Tampa to Tarpon Springs, just up the Pinellas County coast from St. Petersburg. They were meeting with Alpheus L. Ellis, a banker whose relatives had governed the states of Florida, Alabama and Georgia at one time.

Nearing eighty, Al Ellis was a conservative curmudgeon in the style of Ed Ball, the late Florida National tycoon. In fact, Ellis so admired Ball that he had an elaborately framed heroic painting of his Jacksonville mentor hung where he could admire it any time his office door was open. If there was one thing Ellis and McColl had in common it was the quick and fearless *bon mot*, though Ellis had a penchant for the malaprop as well.

"My father would never give one of us boys a nickel," Ellis groused to McColl, "but he would give us a job. Gave me one as a janitor of the bank when I was fourteen." Ellis's five brothers also had jobs at the bank. When their father, O. A. Ellis, reached the age of eighty-nine in 1960 they held a secret board meeting one Sunday and fired the old man, fearful of what he might commit the bank to when they weren't around. They never told him, though. The old man "continued to come to his office and promptly go to sleep in his chair," until he died eight years later. Now Al Ellis, born in 1906, was thinking about retiring himself, and there was nobody he wanted to leave it all to. He liked these fellows from North Carolina a whole lot better than he liked the New Yorkers who'd been nosing around.

From his Spanish colonial headquarters in Tarpon Springs, Al Ellis had built his Ellis Banking Corporation into the powerhouse of Florida's hot central west coast market, seventy-five banks in sixteen counties. All told, Ellis's banks were worth $1.8 billion, and the old man knew where every dollar was hiding. Ellis once told the *Tampa Tribune* he had presided over his empire for more than thirty years and lost less than nine thousand dollars in bad loans. He proudly showed McColl a 1980 report from the Comptroller of the Currency's office on his First National Bank of Bradenton. The report complimented the "ultra-conservative policies" of Ellis's holding company, "rigidly enforced in its subsidiary banks." The Comptroller noted that this conservatism "restricts individual initiative," but resulted in "the sound asset condition and good earnings of this bank."

On McColl's birthday in June, Ellis sent him a note wishing "for you to live to be a hundred and I a pallbearer." But business was business and Ellis would not give in on the matter of price, including maintaining his annual salary of $325,000. Ellis told the North Carolina bankers they could "appeal to Jesus Christ or whistle 'Dixie,' but I am not going to change my mind and opinions." Ellis wanted a voice in management of the bank, so they gave him the title of "senior chairman" of NCNB National Bank of Florida. In Tarpon Springs, on August 23, 1983, McColl worked out the final details of the deal on a scrap of paper. Wanting to make sure he had it down the way Mr. Ellis wanted it, McColl wrote:

"We the undersigned agree that the collar (breakaway points) on our merger agreement is $21.00 on the lower side and $31.00 on the upside. The price refers to the price of NCNB Corp. on the day of closing as defined in the agreement to merge." The paper is signed by

H. L. McColl Jr. and A. L. Ellis. Under those terms, Ellis would receive $68 million in cash and four million common shares, making him the largest single stockholder in NCNB Corporation.

The *Miami Herald* was impressed by NCNB's persistence and success. "Carolina's Pac-Man Bankers Strike Again," read the headline. That was an *au courant* reference to the then-ubiquitous Japanese electronic game that featured a little character with only a mouth and eyes, scrambling around a maze, frantically gobbling pellets and combating ghosts. It was St. Petersburg banking analyst Timothy Rayl who supplied the metaphor. "I think this is going to be a continuing trend in Florida," said Rayl. "You are in the early stages of a Pac-Man game here."

NCNB had eaten its way to become the fourth-largest bank in Florida, in terms of both number of offices and in-state deposits. Only Barnett, Sun Banks and Southeast Banks were larger. With more than $13 billion in assets, NCNB Corporation was far and away the largest bank in the southeastern United States.

September 1, 1983, Tom Storrs retired, leaving the company in the hands of Hugh McColl, the last man standing. McColl's salary as chairman and chief executive officer would be $320,000—exactly $315,500 more than his starting salary in 1959. It might be $5,000 less than the salary he'd promised to pay old Mr. Ellis, but that didn't matter. The money didn't matter. He'd keep his promise to Al Ellis because he always kept his promises.

Hugh McColl remembered another promise he made, back in 1960, when he was still wet behind the ears from his immersion in the sheep dip of bookkeeping and proof transit, a promise to his father, who'd said he wasn't smart enough to be a farmer so he had to go to work for a bank up in Charlotte.

"Some day, Daddy, I'm gonna run that bank."

Promise kept.

> *"People like me came along and very early in our careers we were treated like dirt by Wachovia people. We were aggressive because we didn't like being the little guys pushed around."*

Hugh McColl
July 14, 1983

CHAPTER 10

McColl was dead set on having people he trusted in every position of responsibility.

With Dougherty and his top people on their way out, McColl asked the bank's outside auditor, Price Waterhouse, to lend him on a full-time basis the man who handled the bank's account. This was James Hance, a lanky thirty-nine-year-old auditor from Missouri, a man McColl found direct and trustworthy. Hance handled details of the Gulfstream, Exchange and Ellis acquisitions until Dougherty left and NCNB got its new chief financial officer, Timothy Hartman.

Chuck Cooley found Tim Hartman working for a piano company. Actually, Baldwin-United Corporation was a piano manufacturer as NCNB was a Charlotte bank. Under Baldwin CEO Morley Thompson, Hartman had been instrumental in growing the company into a $7.5 billion conglomerate. He liked the corporate culture he saw in Charlotte, liked the fact that the executives of NCNB all owned stock in the company, which prompted them to work and work hard for its success. He also liked the fact that no one, including the new CEO Hugh McColl, had a contract. McColl seemed to trust everyone in the company to do his or her job, and he insisted that every one of them have the responsibility for getting those jobs done.

Hartman's perception was accurate. Under McColl, Tom Storrs's top concerns—precision and accountability—edged a bit lower on the priority scale. NCNB's new first and second commandments were: *Thou shalt trust as thou art trusted,* and *Thou shalt take responsibility.* "I'm not a perfectionist," McColl told the bank's former public relations man, John Jamison, in 1983. "And therefore I do not demand perfection of the people working for me." He enjoyed investing people with his trust since "in turn they seem to trust me. I've had a disappointment or two on that score, but on balance, over twenty-four years I've only had two disappointments and that's really not too bad. I don't plan to quit trusting."

Even though he always wanted to be in touch, to know what was going on, McColl wanted to "work through people," to "let them run with it and give them the authority to go forward." He figured that enabled him to attract and keep talented young people, to keep challenging them—"by far my greatest contribution to the growth of the company," he told Jamison. When he looked around the company, at the people in positions of influence, either he had recruited them or they had worked for him at one time. "I think I've trained a lot of people, helped develop them, helped keep them."

By the summer of 1984, that Orwellian milestone year, legislatures in both Carolinas, Georgia and Florida had blessed the Southeast Compact with their imprimatur. This was in spite of—or perhaps because of—the fact that McColl had withdrawn his troops from that campaign and left it to the banks that had snubbed NCNB's earlier efforts. There would be a one-year waiting period, to make sure the regulators and the courts approved, but Tom Storrs had successfully designed the widest pond in which his bank could start out as the biggest frog. It was one of those "clear advantages" Storrs prized so highly in his regulated industry. Now it would be up to McColl to make something of that advantage.

He had until mid-1985, when the Southeast Compact floodgates would officially open, to buy a bank in Georgia. For the moment his target of opportunity remained Florida, where First Union and Wachovia and Atlanta's Citizens and Southern already were knocking on doors, even though it would be a while before anybody could let them in. More than anything, McColl wanted to get into Jacksonville, where the Holiday Inn band could play decent beach music, where he could fire broadsides at defenseless Florida National and Fred Kent.

He started conversations with the number-two bank in town, Atlantic Banks, and he was encouraged by their response. His new CFO, Hartman, groused about how much money they wanted, but McColl thought he could lower Atlantic's demands, or perhaps raise Hartman's expectations of their performance potential.

While negotiations with Atlantic proceeded, he had a number of other pompano on the Florida grill. His Sunshine State troopers needed a headquarters they could call their own, and none of the buildings belonging to his already-acquired banks could meet current demands, let alone satisfy the business needs McColl saw in his crystal ball. He would erect something new and impressive in Tampa.

As 1985 laid George Orwell to rest, Hugh McColl and all the dignitaries Tampa could muster stood before television cameras and announced NCNB would build a thirty-story headquarters at a cost of $100 million. It would be round, like a lighthouse, with searchlights on the roof to summon borrowers and investors from everywhere. Somebody on the public payroll proclaimed this would be a "new day for Tampa," that NCNB's commitment would be good for every individual and business in the entire Tampa-St. Petersburg area.

"What about other banks?" asked a reporter of McColl. "Are they going to be happy about this news?"

"Hell, yes," grinned McColl. "Everywhere my airplane lands bank stocks go up. Next question."

He was starting to enjoy these news conferences. He thought he could play the media like his sister Fran used to play the piano. After a formal session, he enjoyed nurturing relationships with reporters. He invited a *Miami Herald* reporter up to his room for a drink and a chat. When the reporter asked him about the market for banks in other Southern states, McColl laughed and said he wouldn't be hunting on "every little pig path in Georgia."

He imagined himself becoming a Major Power in Tampa the way he was in Charlotte, maybe other cities too, Miami, Atlanta. That Charlotte Fourth Ward project had turned out to be the most rewarding experience he'd had, outside the bank, something "very ego-satisfying," he told John Jamison. And Fourth Ward had led to McColl's appointment as chairman of the Charlotte Uptown Development Corporation, NCNB's "unique power base in the city."

Because of McColl's involvement with uptown development, working through people like Joe Martin and Dennis Rash, NCNB had been able to influence the direction and personality of the city's growth, working steadily to make it more cosmopolitan, more like London and less like, well, Charlotte. Nothing else could come "within miles" of his involvement with uptown Charlotte.

But at a dinner party, McColl could only shake his head in disbelief when a woman told him, "I don't see why on earth anyone would ever want to live uptown."

"Haven't you noticed what's going on in Third and Fourth Wards?" McColl asked.

"Goodness, no. I haven't been uptown since . . . well. How long has it been since they built that shopping mall at SouthPark? Twenty years?"

That Old Southern Comfort, institutionalized ignorance. It always stunned McColl to butt up against it, made him see intellectual stars. How could a woman who contributed thousands of dollars to the United Way and bought her season tickets to the opera at Ovens Auditorium every year miss the news that Charlotte's investment in uptown had paid off at least fifteen times in property tax valuations alone? Uptown Charlotte was Hugh McColl's baby and Old-Money Charlotte wouldn't help it grow. "I'm extremely proud of that uptown development," he told John Jamison. "I don't know anything that I feel I'm more interested in or more proud of."

Within the bank, his baby was the international division. McColl had set it spinning around London, the office he personally had instituted, rather than orbiting around Charlotte. Now the U.K.-based group was financing the exports of not only of the United Kingdom, but of Italy, France and the Scandinavian nations as well, using the guarantees of those governments as partial protection against risk. They were doing business in Germany, in Japan, in Hong Kong. They were helping Australia, Brazil, South Africa and less-developed nations move raw materials into the ports of manufacturing nations. It was, he believed, a very sophisticated operation run by some of the company's most sophisticated individuals.

Jim Sommers had been one of the key international players. George Campbell started up the London office, bringing in Peter James and Van DuBose. Richards Roddy took over from Campbell and signed on other good people, like John Sheldon, the lawyer who helped them work out the subsidized financing for British exports. Interesting people. John Brimelow, historian-businessman, a right-wing anarchist, if there could be such a thing, opposed to all government except a dictatorship in which he served as dictator. Brimelow brought in his college roommate, Richard Gross, who was a South African. It was Gross who led them into Johannesburg, Cape Town and Pretoria in the mid-'70s. That was the period of Prime Minister Balthazar J. Vorster's attempt to appease neighboring black-ruled African nations with development loans and trade concessions, though his own republic maintained its policy of apartheid, strict segregation of whites from blacks and mixed races— "coloreds," they called them, which always made McColl wince.

Wincing became a daily occurrence at NCNB as racial tension increased inside South Africa, particularly in its black townships, piling much of the outside world onto a bandwagon of harsh criticism. NCNB, Citibank, Chase and other major American banks found themselves facing the music. McColl refused to go on the defensive. His people had financed creation and expansion of any number of South African industries—furniture factories, coal mines, railroads, power plants, breweries—and they had funded the movement of goods and raw materials between the Republic and the western world. Along the way, NCNB had established a $4 million line of credit in South Africa for the Urban Foundation's development of private housing for blacks. McColl's stance on South Africa created a degree of dissension within the ranks. Joe Martin urged "the grand gesture of withdrawing, primarily for the antiracism message it would send to our own region." McColl and Martin recognized validity in the other's position, but neither would budge. Martin admired McColl's determination to become informed on the subject, boning up on Andre Brink, Nadine Gordimer and other liberal South African novelists, then going overseas to seek out the major players on both sides of the issue.

McColl's first visit there came in 1978. Like so many first-timers, he was taken with the scale and diversity of South Africa's natural beauty, revolted at the degree of poverty in the black townships, offended by the absence of diversity among its business and political leaders. In 1979, the McColls entertained the South African Minister of Finance and his wife at their home in Charlotte. Amid the polite conversation was an undertone of uncertainty—how long could NCNB resist the pressure to "disinvest," as the news media were putting it? McColl was firm. He was not bowing to any pressure. He believed it was in the best interest of his company, and of all the people of South Africa, for NCNB to continue bolstering the Republic's economy.

In 1983 McColl made another trip to South Africa, this time accompanied by Bill Vandiver. Their express purpose was to determine whether NCNB should continue lending money in the Republic. From a hotel in Capetown, he wrote a letter home.

Dear Mother,

Arrived in South Africa yesterday. Had lunch at our local representative's home high on a hill over looking Johannesburg. Their home is a combination of Dutch Colonial with a wall surrounding it. The exterior is white on a stucco type surface. We cooked on a large patio overlooking the city. Took a sun bath and went swimming.

This afternoon at 4 PM we flew to Cape Town some 800 miles south for dinner with the U.S. ambassador. Tomorrow we visit the Minister of Finance and the governor of the Central Bank. Later we visit the leader of the colored people Dr. Boesak, currently head of the World Council of Churches. Then we fly back to Johannesburg for dinner with some of South Africa's business executives.

With so many problems in the world it is amazing to find things here much as I last saw them in 1978. Things are relatively peaceful even though they are having the same problems as everyone else in terms of economics.

McColl and Vandiver spent three hours at the home of Dr. Alan Boesak, an outspoken critic of apartheid and a loud voice in the call for disinvestment. They went to see Dr. Alan Makker, a white Presbyterian minister who had been imprisoned for condemning apartheid but who pleaded with them to continue investing in the South African economy. They heard opinions similar to Dr. Makker's from the mayor of the black township of Soweto, from the leader of the Black Labor Party and from American businessmen. By the time he boarded the airplane for the flight home, McColl had his mind made up. For now, NCNB would not be disinvesting in South Africa.

Pieter W. Botha became president of the Republic of South Africa on September 14, 1984. A new constitution replaced the old unicameral legislature with a three-chamber Parliament, racially divided to represent whites, Indians, and coloreds—people of mixed race—but not black Africans. Apartheid was South Africa's official government policy.

Until now, the bank's record of rehabilitating black neighborhoods and minority lending had been enough to insulate it from high-profile protests against its persistent South African presence. But in 1984 NCNB found itself the target of protests led by South Carolina's Jesse L. Jackson. Founder of People United to Save Humanity (Operation PUSH) and the first serious African-American candidate for president of the United States, Reverend Jackson led a parade of placard-waving marchers into the bank's main lobby in Greensboro. Jackson happened to be in Greensboro for meetings of the board of trustees at his alma mater, North Carolina A&T State University, to which NCNB was a significant contributor.

The bank's most visible African-American executive, Ed Dolby, found himself defending McColl and his policies as he made the community rounds in Raleigh, Durham and Chapel Hill. That gave him a chance to trot out one of his favorite stories about the chief executive. "Lemme tell you something about Hugh McColl . . ." Dolby would begin. "I'm working like hell one day, and all of a sudden from nowhere these files just literally fall out of the sky on my desk with this loud thump and I looked up and there he stands. And I am thinking to myself, *What is going on?* He says to me, 'Listen. I want to know how you feel about Dr. Martin Luther King.' And I said, 'Why are you so concerned about that?' He said, 'I'd like to know where you stand on the issues.' I told him. He said, 'Okay fine, we have been struggling for a couple of years to put Dr. King's statue up in Charlotte. We haven't had the leadership. If you would take this on, it becomes your responsibility to head all this up and raise the money.' And we're talking about seventy thousand dollars, which is a significant amount of money for an African-American cause in 1978, here in Charlotte, North Carolina."

McColl wrote "some very frank and candid letters to members and leaders in Charlotte. He talked about Dr. King benefiting *all* people and how he had made America better. And how someone had to take the risk and the initiative and somebody had to get us talking about it. Somebody had to get us focused on the fact that we were not using all of our talents, and he thought Dr. King had done that. And if nothing else you had to respect him for that. And we raised the money. We got the job done. The statue stands today in Marshall Park. Now you can't tell me Hugh McColl doesn't care about black people."

Still, statues and neighborhood restorations in Charlotte seemed insignificant in the face of news reports from the black townships of South Africa. Children were being shot in Soweto. Yet, despite the world's mounting outrage against apartheid, McColl's board of directors and executive committee supported his position. They agreed with him that the bank could help raise living and education standards for black South Africans, creating a black middle class that would, in time, create sufficient internal pressures for abolishing segregation. The board acknowledged that NCNB's more than $200 million in outstanding South African loans would not only prove to be a profitable investment, but would also hasten the end of apartheid.

The *de facto* national spokespersons for McColl's viewpoint were Citicorp's Walter Wriston and John Reed, who told the media their people in South Africa were spending nearly half their time working out race problems, almost like working out bad loans. Another often-quoted voice against disinvestment was National Urban League President Vernon Jordan, who visited American-owned South African plants and returned with the convictions that the banks and manufacturers should stay the course. Jordan declared he "didn't have the right to come back to New York and vote those kids out of work to facilitate my own moral orgasm."

McColl insisted that the apartheid issue was oversimplified by the media and misunderstood by religious and civil rights activists like Jesse Jackson, not only in New York but in Charlotte as well. So in February 1985, he agreed to an interview with a reporter from the *Observer*, so he could set the record straight about NCNB and South Africa. The interview lasted three and one-half hours; its effects would be around for considerably longer. According to McColl, the interview went something like this:

"What do you think of South Africa, Mr. McColl?"

"I love it. I think it's the most wonderful country in the world. It is breathtakingly beautiful and exciting. However, I find it tragic that its racist and police-state policies make it almost impossible for us to appreciate its natural grandeur. I think it's a great country, but it doesn't have a great government."

The *Observer* printed:

"I love it. I think it's the most wonderful country in the world."

"What about apartheid and segregation, Mr. McColl? Aren't you supporting that with your loans to South Africa?"

"It's a goddamn shame that the government over there doesn't see

how idiotic apartheid looks to the rest of us. I've told them that, tell them every chance I get. I've talked to the minister of finance about that, their ambassador to the United States, chairman of their central bank. And I've also told them what I think about their police state—arrest and detention without habeus corpus. Appalling. That said, I've lived in a segregated society and that doesn't kill people. What kills people is starvation, deprivation caused by being out of work. What kills people is the kind of revolution being incited by people sitting over here in America, comfortable in their living rooms, because thousands, maybe hundreds of thousands of people could be killed in that kind of a revolution. My position is that investment in South Africa is good for black people—little black people, big black people—children, mothers, fathers, everybody. Even revolutionaries."

The *Observer* printed:

"I've lived in a segregated society and that doesn't kill people."

"My position is that investment in South Africa is good for black people—little black people, big black people—children, mothers, fathers, everybody. Even revolutionaries."

McColl found himself quite suddenly in an ugly situation—treated like a head of state in countries like Guatemala only to be hoisted on his own petard in his "power base" of uptown Charlotte. He felt he had been "thrown into public life, before I matured completely as a person." He had studied business and banking under Reese and Storrs, but had paid too little attention to the subtleties of managing public opinion. "I didn't get to observe others for long periods of time before I was in charge." McColl felt himself "floundering a lot. I stumbled a lot in the early going." Stumbling in the persona he presented to the public, he nevertheless remained confident in his business decisions.

In the early months of 1985 McColl thought he had Jacksonville's Atlantic Banks ready for a buyout. They were to the stage of what he considered "social issues"—the name of the bank, location of headquarters. Those were issues McColl had no doubt of winning because, at the end of the day, it was really only the money that mattered to most other bankers. He took Tim Hartman to New York, where they sat down with Atlantic's investment bankers to talk them down on the price. They were asking fifteen times earnings, which his surly CFO insisted was too high.

McColl wasn't sure what he'd gotten into with Hartman. The man could be on top of the world one minute, ready to blow up the world the next. He seemed to look at life through dark gray glasses. Economic pessimism was his favored perspective. There were indications that Hartman's distemper might erupt in tantrums. But a bank needed a chief financial officer and he was McColl's choice. If Atlantic held its ground and Hartman said no to fifteen times earnings, he would just have to go with Hartman's advice, trust him with the call.

The investment bankers held their ground and Hartman held his. Once again, Hugh McColl was frustrated in his bid to buy a bank in Jacksonville.

Quickly, NCNB turned its attention to Atlanta. "From a market standpoint," McColl told his team, "Atlanta would make us so powerful in the Southeast that a company with any substance would find it difficult *not* to do business with us. We would increase the number of individual consumers we do business with by a staggering margin."

He had to march on Atlanta quickly. The U.S. Supreme Court was about to rule on the legality of the regional banking compacts, and Paul Polking assured him Storrs's dream was still on go. The banking grapevine had it that First Union—now in the capable hands of Ed Crutchfield, who by all rights should be working for Hugh McColl—was already talking to banks in Georgia and Florida. There was even a rumor that somnolent Wachovia might be waking up to the possibilities of interstate banking. McColl wanted not only a swift deal, but a big one.

NCNB's best target looked like First Atlanta, a $7 billion bank with more than a hundred branches throughout Georgia. First Atlanta and its CEO Thomas Williams seemed nearly as aggressive as NCNB and McColl. Like NCNB, they had jumped on the credit card craze before it hit, the first Georgia bank to issue BankAmericard—and now the seventh-largest issuer of Visa cards in the country. Like NCNB, First Atlanta did a lot of commercial business with Fortune 500 companies. "A perfect fit," McColl declared.

He found an ally in First Atlanta's largest single shareholder, Mack Robinson, who set up a meeting at the Sea Island resort off Georgia's Atlantic coast. Robinson was all for the deal. He told McColl he knew his bank was a peach ripe for the picking and he wanted it in Hugh McColl's basket. Robinson had invited one of First Atlanta's investment bankers to the meeting and even he seemed to like the deal. There was no question that First Atlanta was "in play," ready to be bought. Now the case had to be presented to the bank's CEO, Thomas Williams.

McColl was introduced to Williams by his old buddy Hootie Johnson, chairman of Bankers Trust of South Carolina. Johnson paid a call on Williams and suggested that, once the Southeast Banking Compact passed its Supreme Court test, "the logical thing for us to do is to get NCNB, your bank and my bank and put them together. We'd have three-state coverage. It's just a great concept." Johnson arranged a meeting as soon as he could, in Washington, D. C., where the three CEOs would cross paths on their international travels.

McColl was deliriously happy. Finally, his first big-deal opportunity as chairman, and it was a gimme. None of his advisors had any qualms about this one, not even Hartman. They would offer $855 million. *Hell, that's $33.50 a damn share,* McColl told himself. *They've got to think that's manna from heaven.* McColl and Hootie Johnson worked out the details in advance. Williams would be chairman of the board, Johnson chairman of the executive committee, McColl president of the bank. The game was afoot as McColl strode toward Tom Williams in the first-class lounge of National Airport in Washington on a chilly, gray day, overcoat thrown over the arm he extended in greeting.

"Tom, Hugh McColl." The grin flashed, the Carolina accent charmed. "I'm gonna buy your bank."

Williams shook the extended hand, but the deal never got any closer than that. McColl and his advisors all had missed the point that Mack Robinson, while he may have been the largest single shareholder, did not represent controlling interest in First Atlanta. In fact, he represented one of two factions, and the other faction had the higher stack of chips.

Tom Williams knew he couldn't stop his bank from being sold, but he did not have to sell it to this reprehensible Hugh McColl, the man whose "I won't go down every pig path in Georgia" line was push-pinned to half the coffee-room bulletin boards in his hundred and four Georgia branches. Thanks to an unnamed informant of the First Atlanta group, the downhill progression of the National Airport meeting was chronicled by the *Wall Street Journal:*

"Here was Hugh L. McColl Jr., the ex-marine chairman of NCNB Corp., trying to take over First Atlanta Corp. the way troops took Iwo Jima. There sat Thomas R. Williams, the genteel First

Atlanta chairman, listening impassively. Using military jargon and Anglo-Saxon expletives, Mr. McColl of North Carolina pressed for surrender to his buyout offer until Mr. Williams of Georgia finally interjected, 'Hugh, you're not being very friendly.' Through clenched teeth, according to a witness, Mr. McColl replied, 'I *am* being friendly, damn it.'"

The *Journal* story suggested that big mergers could be done in by big egos.

McColl blamed the failure not on his own ego but on Williams's. He was like a kid who "took his football and went home." Rejected and dejected, McColl flew back to Charlotte. "Nobody wants their company taken over," he told his teammates. "It's more fun running your own company."

Not for long. No sooner was he back in his Atlanta office than genteel Tom Williams was on the phone with another North Carolina banker, an old friend who was just as genteel as he was. Negotiations would be discreet, polite, pleasant. Williams's post-merger place in the company would be assured.

June arrived and with it the Supreme Court's anticipated rejection of the lawsuit against regional interstate compacts. From Florida up through North Carolina the merger game Tom Storrs had designed was about to begin. The starting whistle had been blown and the crowd was ready for the kickoff, but unless he counted Bankers Trust—and South Carolina was the least attractive of the Southeast Compact's states—Hugh McColl had no ball to play with, no big bank ready to let him take it over.

Ed Crutchfield had one. June 17 he announced that First Union would merge with Atlantic Banks in Jacksonville. That would bring First Union's assets to $14.4 billion, pushing it ahead of NCNB to make it the largest bank in the Southeast. The deal was substantially the same one McColl had cut, only to be talked out of it by Tim Hartman. "The biggest tactical error I've ever made," McColl told his teammates.

The day was long and the news got worse. Wachovia chairman John Medlin proudly announced to the world that his bank would now be the largest in the Southeast, with $15.5 billion in assets, because Wachovia was going to be part of an exciting new interstate banking company, First Wachovia Corporation, thanks to its "merger of equals" with that fine old Georgia institution, First Atlanta.

Hugh McColl had delivered the bank he wanted in the market he coveted to his worst enemy. And it all came out in the newspapers on June 18, his fiftieth birthday.

Everybody in the company knew how McColl felt about Wachovia. In fact, the final question of a long and rambling interview with publicity man Jamison had been: What was the origin of the general impression that Wachovia was more conservative, NCNB more aggressive? Speaking into Jamison's tape recorder, McColl answered that when he arrived at American Commercial Bank in 1959, Wachovia was not merely conservative but arrogantly so. "They looked down their noses at everybody. We were the Johnny-come-lately . . . . People like me came along and we were treated like dirt by the Wachovia people. We were aggressive because we didn't like being the little guys getting pushed around. There is a certain breed of cat that's been around here a while that won't ever get rid of that."

McColl was one of those cats. To him, The Wachovia was like the Soviet Union. "I may not dislike Russians individually, I don't dislike Wachovia people individually, but I don't like Wachovia any more than I like Russia." The entire NCNB game plan was to leave Wachovia in its dust, "so far behind that we can't remember who they are . . . . We don't like them. Mr. Reese didn't like them. I don't think Mr. Storrs likes them. I don't like them. Period."

Exactly one year and eleven months earlier, McColl had predicted that within the next five years First Union would become larger than Wachovia. He was certain Wachovia would finish dead last among the major banks of North Carolina. As of June 18, 1985, he was dead wrong and his own bank was dead last.

The taste of crow spoiling his birthday cake, McColl pushed ahead with Hootie Johnson's plans to sell Bankers Trust. At least that would give NCNB the distinction of being the first regional to operate in three states. Johnson tried to hold his friend to the price they'd agreed on earlier, but McColl said that without First Atlanta as part of the deal he would not pay a premium for $2-billion Bankers Trust. Johnson told him he was getting a hell of a bargain, at just 14 percent over market value for his stock. McColl told Johnson he was still paying too damned much. But Hootie was his friend and McColl respected his business judgment. He recommended to his board that Johnson be named chairman of the executive committee, the CEO's first line of upstream consultation when he had important decisions to make. Only four years older than McColl, Johnson was grateful. Being named chairman of NCNB's executive committee would be "probably the finest compliment that I've had in business."

Wall Street liked the NCNB-Bankers Trust merger. One analyst told the newspapers it was "a marriage made in heaven." McColl found himself wondering what hell would be like.

By the end of July he scratched his way into Georgia's DeKalb County by signing an agreement to buy Southern National Bancshares, a $93 million bank. The deal would cost only $11 million and give McColl at least a toehold in fast-growing north Atlanta. The same day, July 25, McColl announced the purchase of the $1.7 billion Pan American Banks in Miami and south Florida, in a stock transaction valued at $219 million. The deal, if approved, would make NCNB once again Florida's fourth-largest bank, with $7 billion in Florida assets and 228 Florida offices. Asked whether this would satisfy his Florida ambitions, McColl told a reporter, "I'm never satisfied with anything, clearly not at being number four."

That was number four in Florida. The Bankers Trust, Southern National and Pan American deals, if approved, would shoot NCNB back to number-one bank in the Southeast, with assets of more than $20 billion. By September, First Union did exactly what McColl had predicted it would do, outdistancing Wachovia with purchases of Central Florida Bank and North Carolina's Northwestern Financial. McColl's one-two-three prediction for NCNB, First Union and Wachovia was back on track. Ed Crutchfield announced First Union would build a new tower, taller than NCNB's, hoping this would fill one of the "gaps" in Charlotte's skyline recently lamented by CUDC chairman Hugh McColl.

The three North Carolina banks appeared to be leading the parade of what Wall Street was calling the "super-regionals." A senior vice president of Salomon Brothers declared, "Where investors have traditionally thought of NCNB and Wachovia as good regional banks, now they will be thought of as large major companies." However, John Medlin and Wachovia had no more stomach for the mergers and acquisitions game. It would be another seven years before Wachovia bought another bank. Just as McColl had promised, NCNB and First Union were leaving it in the dust as far as expansion was concerned.

NCNB's third-quarter earnings jumped 27 percent, setting a new record. McColl told a meeting of North Carolina securities dealers he had "no plans for any major acquisition over the next eighteen months. Instead our plan is profit improvement." Nonetheless, McColl wanted the dealers to understand that his company had "the marksmanship and the ammunition to win the interstate banking wars."

In November he handed out new titles and substantial raises. Buddy Kemp—the best person in the company as far as McColl was concerned—became president of NCNB Corporation. Jim Thompson, another who'd helped McColl save the bank from failure ten years earlier, moved up to vice chairman. Hootie Johnson, as promised, got the executive committee chairmanship. And to replace Don Buchanan— who simply was not getting the job done to his satisfaction in Florida—McColl selected Ken Lewis, who had been supervising commercial lending to medium-sized companies throughout the Southeast. Lewis would call on the services of Harris A. "Rusty" Rainey, now in charge of coordinating personnel in merger situations.

One of Ken Lewis's first moves in Florida was to put someone aggressive in Miami. He believed, and McColl concurred, that there was a lot of business that could be done there as they waited for approval on the Pan American deal, even though they had only the little one-office Downtown National to fly the NCNB flag at present. Lewis believed he had the right person for the job in Adelaide Sink, who was ready for a new challenge after three years of running the loan production office in New York. McColl asked Lewis whether he was sure he wanted a woman running the show, what with so many Cubans and Central American businessmen there, oozing machismo. Lewis said he was sure. If a woman with a Wake Forest degree and a North Carolina accent could sell loans in New York, she sure as hell could make it in Miami. Besides, she called herself "Alex," so her charm and good looks might take those Latins by surprise.

No sooner had Alex Sink got herself installed in the Miami office than McColl decided to pay her a visit. He was intrigued by the possibilities of Miami, where the number-one bank in town, Southeast, was a lot like Wachovia in 1959—asleep at the wheel. On the Monday morning of his arrival, Sink was ready for him with two weeks' worth of appointments over a stretch of five days. They called on customers and potential customers and community leaders and at night they merengue-ed at Miami's night spots.

McColl found his south Florida enthusiasm matched by Alex

Sink's. She had only twenty loan officers, with twenty more handling strictly international business, but she was determined to chase down Southeast. Most impressive were the new people she was bringing into her fold, dynamic, hard-hitting money lenders with great contacts and sound judgment. What surprised him most was that the majority of Sink's new officers were stolen from Southeast's payroll, and that they were women. Clearly the Florida competition didn't appreciate the talent of its best people, especially its female people.

There were still more than a few banks like Southeast that had failed to make opportunities for women, and as a result, many of the top-producing loan officers at those banks found themselves in dead-end jobs. When they heard about a woman running the show at the new bank in town, they were lining up to work for Alex Sink, bringing their customers along with them. One Southeast expatriate, Joan Tukey, introduced McColl, Sink and NCNB to three major new customers that week, including a high-rolling country club, an importer and a real estate developer. McColl was delighted. He wanted good loan officers, and who the hell cared if they wore skirts? In fact, he rather enjoyed the fact. Joan Tukey and the other women said they figured they weren't going anywhere at their old banks; he was going to make sure they went somewhere with his.

Friday afternoon Alex Sink dropped McColl off at Miami International. "You keep up the good work, hear?" he told her as he pulled his suitcase out of the trunk. "'Cause we're gonna have a whole lot more branches for you to run down here in another couple of months when we take over Pan American."

Sink smiled, suspecting how mixed such a blessing would be. A week with the chairman left her exhausted and ready for a weekend by the pool. "I was never so glad to see somebody leave in my life. He wore us out!"

As 1986 arrived, there was no resting for Hugh McColl. His legal department now was part of a consortium working to recruit the Washington City Council into the Southeastern Compact. D.C.'s local banks were certain it would be in their better interest to let in banks from North Carolina if it helped them to hold the dreaded money center banks at bay. But Citicorp had a lot of influence in Washington and a lot of money to spend. John Reed's lawyers convinced the city council it should do business with a solid Yankee outfit rather than that Southern Confederacy—or whatever they called themselves. Citicorp had to purchase little National Permanent, a fourteen-branch thrift, to make it official, but John Reed would beat Hugh McColl to the nation's capital.

McColl promised his shareholders he'd get them to the Washington area before the year was out. Most likely though, any buyouts would be small ones, because 1986 was going to be "a year of consolidation." McColl insisted he had "no plans for major acquisitions, period." True to his word, McColl quickly reeled in CentraBank in Baltimore, a mutual savings bank with eight offices; Prince William Bank in northern Virginia; and Ameribanc Investors Group, with thirty savings and loan offices in Virginia's D.C. suburbs. More "flagpole banks," as Frank Gentry put it, more push-pins in a map. Only now the map covered six states.

At the end of May, McColl resigned as chairman of Charlotte's CUDC, yielding the position to a resident and developer of Fourth Ward, Malloy McKeithen. Meanwhile, rumors were circulating—and McColl did nothing to scotch them—that NCNB would soon build a new tower, taller than the one Ed Crutchfield was putting up. But First Union, unlike Wachovia, would not go away. McColl knew Crutchfield was working on a deal with First Railroad and Banking Corporation, a deal that would get him a big leg up in Atlanta and another $3.6 billion in assets. McColl needed something like that, something big, not just more poles to fly his flag from.

Only in his third year as CEO, Hugh McColl was beginning to feel the weight of time. The '90s were just around the corner and they would dead-end at his mandatory retirement. End of the millennium, end of the road: sixty-five. Looking forward from 1986, McColl pictured himself growing old gracefully and he found the prospect repulsive. For years people had been advising him to mellow, take it easy, be at peace with himself and the world. Either he was taking their advice or else peace had him in a hammerlock. He was a fighter, a warrior, a predator. He had to hunt or die. On the wall of his conference room were twenty-five trophies, framed articles of incorporation from banks he had bagged. *Like mounting rabbit heads. Small damn game.*

And where now was game worth the hunting? All that passionate, desperate financial legerdemain of the sixties and seventies was gone, smoke and mirrors. President Ronald Reagan was America's sweetheart. Employment was on the rise. The dollar was stable. Hugh McColl was "mellow."

He picked up the *Business Week* Pat Hinson had left on his desk, opened to the finance page. There was his picture, hale and hardy in his NCNB workout shirt and running shorts, bare legs pumping along West Trade Street. The photo embarrassed him. Why was this leathery little man running? What was he running *from*? Did he have to prove his manhood?

He had enough trouble getting the Wall Street gang to take him seriously without this. And the headline—"HUGH McCOLL: JUST A GOOD OL' DOG-EAT-DOG BANKER." Bad dog? Junkyard dog? All you bankers out there watch out for ol' Hugh.

Quote: "A guy from a much larger bank can brag about how profitable his bank is, and I can say, 'Yeah, so what? I just bought you.'" *Did I really say that? Yeah, I said that.* And the trusty local rag, the *Observer*, made sure to reprint it. MCCOLL SOUNDS OFF IN *BUSINESS WEEK* ON BANK GROWTH. "Charlotte's own financial gunslinger" hip-shooting a few quips. At least he didn't sound *mellow*. Oh no. The article proclaimed him "unashamedly ambitious." Until now his ambition had been to stand in this office, looking out over the comfortable little skyline of Charlotte. *Some day I'm gonna run that bank, Daddy. You watch. Some day I'm gonna run that bank.* Run-run-run, but where to? Into the ground?

"Now there are no boundaries," he'd bragged to his board. Now we have banks in Florida, South Carolina and Georgia, with Maryland and Virginia in the wings. *Bullshit,* he told himself. All we've done is to hold off the big dogs for a while, New York and San Francisco and Chicago. How did he intend to run away from them if the only money he could get his hands on was the money in the old Confederacy? As soon as the high-paid Northern lawyers worked their fingers into the loopholes, Tom Storrs's wall around the Southeast would crumble.

"McColl's brash style," *Business Week* said, was what had cost him the jewel of First Atlanta. He really hated that. First Atlanta would have proven to his board that Tom Storrs picked the right man in Hugh McColl. Not that the board really had anything to complain about. Over five years the Florida expansion had more than doubled NCNB's holdings. But when he ticked off the nation's top banks—Citicorp, BankAmerica, Chase Manhattan, J. P. Morgan, Manufacturers

Hanover and so on—McColl knew there would not be a chief executive among them who'd take his little upstart bank seriously, if they even knew what the initials NCNB stood for. Yet there he was bragging in *Business Week* about his competition being not Wachovia and First Union, but Citibank. He skimmed over the article again until he re-read the backhanded compliment:

"While NCNB's financial performance has lagged behind Wachovia and First Union, its record is still impressive." He threw the magazine across the office. *Impressive? Screw impressive.*

Even his friends were starting to worry. Just the other day Henry Carrison had warned him that the business community was growing hostile. "They refer to you by a lot of names," Carrison said in his self-deprecatingly formal way, "with 'pushy' and 'arrogant' being among the milder adjectives. And most of those adjectives are used merely to modify the phrase 'son of a bitch.'" Carrison said he was having to defend the bank at parties. "Somebody asks you where you work, Hugh, and you suffer patiently through the 'Oh!' followed by silence."

Especially coming from the commercial side of the bank, McColl found that hard to believe. *It's still the customer I'm thinking about,* he told himself. *At the end of the day, when I go home, what I worry about is whether we took care of our customers today.* Maybe his bank was settling into the unresponsiveness of bureaucracy. He wouldn't have that, would not allow his people to forget that other people depended upon them. His problems were deeper, he knew, than satisfying his own ambition.

Three years he'd been in charge and still McColl felt the need to prove himself. He had assembled perhaps the most skilled group of hunters in all of banking history, but they found themselves sitting around the campfire, telling brave stories and dreaming brave dreams. *Three years of no real expansion, not in Florida or anywhere else. My team is as frustrated as I am. We've got more management than we have bank; that's the real problem here.* Hugh McColl saw his top management team as stumbling all over itself and dissatisfied. *Maybe they aren't happy with the CEO either. There isn't enough company for people like Tim Hartman and Buddy Kemp and Jim Thompson to run.*

He'd already lost Joe Martin. Again. That made him angry because he'd tried to hang onto the choirboy. "Joe, I'm not seeing enough of you and I'm not happy about that." Meaning I need you, I like having you around. Chuck Cooley told him Martin had taken it the other way, the boss being critical of his performance, wanting to keep him on a shorter leash. Sometimes you wear people out, Hugh, Cooley told him. Joe was feeling like he was trapped in a cage with a tiger looking for his next meal, Cooley said, and he didn't want to be it. Martin was taking a "sabbatical," to work on a book about Presbyterian churches in South Carolina, just about as far as he could get from Mammon's money counters.

McColl wondered who'd be next to leave. His "high drive, high energy culture," as the newspaper people wrote, couldn't be kept alive in a stagnant, sterile corporation. The bank had to expand or explode, and the fuse was burning down. His thoughts were interrupted by the intercom.

"You have a call from a Mr. Jerry Finger."

He barked into the intercom, knowing his secretary was used to his curtness. "Who?"

"You met him at the ABA in Dallas in 1974. He wants to talk to you about a bank in Houston."

McColl picked up the phone. Was that the scent of big game in Texas?

Jerry Finger turned out to be the controlling stockholder of a Houston bank called Charter. Finger said he believed McColl was a man to be trusted, so he let him on the secret that Charter Bank was going belly-up unless somebody strong came in with some quick cash.

How much cash? McColl wanted to know.

About $6 million, Finger figured. For that NCNB could own about 25 percent of Charter's stock, which would be made available. Was he interested? McColl put on his poker-face voice and said he thought he might be able to get someone down there to look into the Charter Bank situation in the next few weeks. He immediately placed a call to Frank Gentry. In spite of his temporary marketing job, McColl knew Gentry belonged back in his job as chief planning officer.

"Frank, whatever you're doing in Tampa, drop it. We need to see what's going on in Texas."

McColl knew his Texas history. His namesake, great-grand-uncle Hugh McColl, older brother of Duncan Donald, had lost himself in Texas after the Civil War, and that had prompted McColl to do some reading about the place. He knew it was exactly one hundred fifty years earlier, in 1836, that American settlers in the territory found themselves in deep trouble, about to be assimilated by Mexico. Newspapers around the United States put out the call for heroes to ride to the aid of the besieged underdogs. Ever since, Texans had been remembering the Alamo, that most famous of lost battles in a won war. McColl remembered what most Texans forgot—that many of their heroes hailed from North Carolina, men like Dolphin Floyd, Mial Scurlock, Joshua Smith, John W. Thompson, Claiborne Wright.

Now here stood Hugh McColl, a century and a half later, reading about the Lone Star State's problems in the *Wall Street Journal.* This time the war in Texas was economic and the invaders wore burnooses. Just about the time McColl took over as NCNB CEO, world oil prices started slipping. By 1986, the hole seemed bottomless. Saudi Arabia was adding more than a million and a half barrels a day to its gush. OPEC's crude glut had prices down from twenty-eight dollars a barrel to ten. Petroleum was the lifeblood of its economy and Texas was being measured by the undertaker.

At weekly meetings McColl was hearing a lot of small talk about big ol' Texas. Jokes about how Tom Storrs had been so careful to keep the Texas banks out of the Southeast Compact and North Carolina, and how now it was the Texas bankers who might be wishing they had some company down in oil hell. About how the oil market collapse was kicking every Texan in the balls, or at least the shins, and turning the state's financial institutions into paraplegics. Millions upon millions of dollars in loans were outstanding to individuals and businesses who could never pay them back unless the price of crude took a turn for the better. Many of these loans involved Texas real estate, where prices had been inflating into the blue, high Texas sky since the beginning of the decade. At NCNB they knew where too many real estate loans could get a bank. Somebody kept singing, "Mamas, don't let your babies grow up to be cowboys."

The unofficial Texas watch at NCNB had been on for two years, ever since the Federal Deposit Insurance Corporation's attempt to rescue Continental Illinois in 1984. Odd how a Chicago bank wound up the first major casualty of OPEC's price war. A heavy investor in Texas and Oklahoma, Continental Illinois had more than three-quarters of its $41 billion in assets tied up in oil-related loans. Rumors of bankruptcy started investors pulling their money out of Con-I,l and the FDIC felt compelled to step in. Let Continental Illinois go under and bank investors everywhere might panic, because Con-Il was supposed to be "too big to fail." Worse, more than 175 smaller banks had at least half their capital in Continental; they might be dragged under if the big ship went down.

There was no buyer for Continental Illinois, so the FDIC took control, protecting not only the bank's depositors but the bank's investors as well. That made the government look bad, like the patsy holding the bag. When the big Texas banks started to fall—and they would fall—the best brains at NCNB figured the FDIC would not let itself get trapped like that again. McColl suspected the agency would be looking under every rock for help, maybe even under rocks in North Carolina. Of course, the Texas legislature would be dead set against a bank headquartered outside of the state buying a Texas bank outright. The Florida legislature had felt the same way.

As weeks went by, McColl kept reading the gory tales of Texas in the financial press. Out-of-state banks were selling off whatever holdings they had in Texas. The state that was always bragging about being the biggest now led the nation in unpaid real estate loans—nearly fifteen out of every hundred bank loans in the state. The FDIC had its hands full supervising fifty different bank failures in Texas. Twelve more Texas banks were on the brink, cinched up by federal loans. The state's financial institutions were stitching together desperation mergers, looking to cut losses and consolidate what few strengths remained. From Texarkana to El Paso, banks and savings and loans propped each other up like beaten soldiers on a battlefield, wounded, out of ammunition, under relentless OPEC attack. Sooner or later, McColl had been thinking, somebody in Texas was going to realize their tradition of mulish disdain was only setting them up for the fall. Sure enough, that somebody turned out to be a Houston businessman named Jerry Finger, who swallowed his pride and called a fellow he remembered from a long-ago meeting.

After flying to Houston and going over the Charter books, Frank Gentry reported in. Despite the wisdom of the marketplace, Gentry told McColl, this might turn out to be a good investment for NCNB. Charter should be able to hang on, with the infusion of cash Jerry Finger had requested. McColl agreed and took his first $6 million bite of Texas. It was an amount NCNB could afford to lose and McColl knew well he stood to lose it.

McColl was looking for bigger game in Texas than Jerry Finger's bank, but to have a shot at it he would need more information, not only about Texas, but about the FDIC as well. McColl relieved his best advisor, Gentry, of all Florida marketing responsibilities so he could spend more time sniffing around Texas. McColl sent Tim Hartman down to help him. Whatever his personality idiosyncrasies might be, Hartman was McColl's "brain trust," a man who could "run his mind on five channels at one time." If anybody could track down the big game, it ought to be Gentry and Hartman.

Quickly, they identified a target: Allied Bancshares. It was not easy to find out just how deep a hole Allied had dug for itself in Houston, but Hartman thought he could put together a merger deal with what remained of, ostensibly, a $9 billion bank. McColl liked the sound of that. Nine billion, eight billion, whatever. Maybe his hunters at last were on the trail of that big game. With Buddy Kemp in tow, McColl hustled down to Houston for a meeting with the top brass at Allied. The arrangement they came up with involved NCNB buying a minority interest in Allied for eighteen dollars a share.

McColl was excited. His blood was up. At last he was working on a deal that would shake up the banking establishment and make them take notice of Hugh McColl's bank, not merely his quips. Leaving Kemp and Gentry to work out the details, McColl and Hartman flew back to Charlotte for a meeting with Tom Storrs and Hootie Johnson, both of whom had encouraged him to see what he could turn up in Texas. He was stunned by their response when he laid the Allied Bancshares deal on the table.

"Poor timing," said Storrs.

"Look what just happened to Texaco," warned Johnson. "America's eighth-largest corporation in bankruptcy court. That's what can happen to us if we put too much stock in Texas. It's quicksand down there."

McColl had no comebacks. Johnson and Storrs told him he must be crazy to take the sort of risk he was proposing, and they would be just as crazy if they let him go through with it. This might be the dumbest idea they had ever heard of, especially when McColl had so many problems to take care of in his own front yard.

Left alone in his office, McColl was chastened. So many problems in his own front yard. A fraud loss at NCNB Mortgage Corporation. Balance sheet slipping into the red unless he agreed to sell of a lot of the overseas investments. Trading the bond portfolio to wangle an

18 percent earnings increase in the second quarter. Personal image defaced and dismembered by the media. His people restless, sniping at each other now instead of the enemy . . . Maybe Hootie Johnson and Tom Storrs were right, maybe he should take care of the problems here in the Carolinas instead of building castles in the clouds of Texas. He told Gentry to go back to Tampa.

Jane convinced Hugh that he should get his mind off business altogether for a couple of weeks, so they drove down to the South Carolina coast and their new condominium at Litchfield. They'd continued to share the beach house with Craig Wall and his family long after Luther Hodges left, but with the kids grown up the condo seemed more practical. Besides, it was right on the water. He and Jane took long walks at twilight, looking for sand dollars and sharks' teeth.

Even at the beach McColl couldn't stop worrying about the bank. He wanted a company of leaders, decision-makers, take-charge types, tigers. Maybe all he really had was a company of little banks full of little bankers. He recruited his son John to drive him over to Pawley's Island, where NCNB had just opened a loan office in a strip mall. John circled the mall's parking area twice without spotting a red NCNB sign. Between the grocery store and the pharmacy was an unmarked storefront and maybe that was it. John pulled up in front to wait while his father went inside. NCNB brochures on a coffee table told McColl he was in the right place.

"Is this where I come to apply for a loan?"

"It certainly is," answered the smiling officer on duty.

"Well, I'd like to speak with the manager," said McColl.

"That would be me," the smile replied.

"If you're an NCNB office," he growled, waving the brochure in the man's face, "why don't you have a goddamn sign anywhere that says NCNB?"

"Oh, our sign is still being made," the manager shrugged, no longer smiling. "You know how that goes. Those things just take a certain amount of time, I guess. Now, how . . . ?"

McColl cut him short. "I don't think I want to do business with a company that can't even get a sign up to tell me who they are." He threw down the brochure and stormed out of the office.

"Find us a hardware store," he barked at his son.

By age twenty-three, John McColl had learned to act without questioning these impulses. Just up the highway from the strip mall, they bought four wooden mailbox letters—two N's, a C and a B—a length of ten-inch-wide pine shelving, a hammer, a box of finishing nails and two cans of spray paint. Crouched in the bed of the pickup truck, McColl sprayed the board white and the letters red. Without waiting for the paint to dry, he nailed the letters to the board.

Back at the shopping center, John held the tacky board while his father hammered it to the outside wall of the storefront, bringing the distraught manager on a run.

"Stop that right now! Who do you think you are?"

"I'm Hugh McColl and I'm your boss. And until whoever the son of a bitch is in this company who's responsible for putting up signs gets around to putting up yours, you've got one installed personally by the CEO."

Rather than firing the branch manager, McColl gave him a graphic lesson in responsibility. In Hugh McColl's company you didn't wait for things to happen, you made them happen. Even managers of little boondocks branches had to know they could do whatever it might take to get the job done.

"Don't ever let yourself be impeded by the bureaucracy again," he instructed the man. "You do what you need to do and I'll back you up. You are responsible. Be responsible."

It was a lesson not only for the Pawley's Island manager, but for McColl. He realized he had to accept responsibility for everything that went on in his bank. And for everything that was not going on. Yet one of his iron-clad rules was that "if you're not at a meeting, your opinion doesn't matter." That way he believed his company would "always keep charging ahead." Away from the office again later in the year, he received a call on his car phone telling him that his senior management team had come to an important decision. "We've been talking," Tim Hartman told him, "and we believe that we ought to sell all our foreign paper and take the losses. This year's blown away anyway, and we're going to do that unless you don't agree with it."

"Go ahead," McColl told Hartman. "Do it." There would be no bonuses that year, and McColl would cut his own salary by one-third.

As for Texas, board reticence be damned. He called Gentry, bunkered again in the Tampa lighthouse. "Get back to Houston, Frank. Find us a bank we can buy, like you did in Florida." It was time to make good things happen in Texas or else bad things were going to happen in North Carolina. *Something* had to happen before the end of 1987.

In October something did.

Frank Gentry telephoned McColl to say that for the first time the FDIC was asking NCNB for help, trying to figure out just what to do about Western Bank. Western was another $250 million Houston bank, roughly the same size as Charter. The FDIC recognized the role NCNB had played in rescuing Charter, Gentry said. "Now they want to know if we'd be interested in doing the same sort of thing for Western."

McColl forced himself to respond with caution. Tom Storrs and Hootie Johnson had been right to call him on the carpet over his pie-in-the-sky approach to Texas. Those Allied Bancshares stocks he wanted to buy at eighteen dollars a share were now almost worthless. He told Gentry to step softly into that Texas quicksand. It might be best to let their recently acquired Houston allies, Charter Bank and Jerry Finger, lead the column. Gentry should convince the FDIC to let Charter take over Western Bank. That would instantly double Charter's size and gain it some prime locations, including one in the prestigious Galleria area of Houston. Charter's stock would skyrocket, guaranteeing a good return on the $6 million NCNB had invested in Houston.

Gentry wasn't certain how that would fly. The FDIC might be less than thrilled with the notion of Charter buying Western. Had they wanted to hand over one crippled Texas bank to another slightly less-crippled Texas bank, they already had a decent offer from Texas Commerce. And while McColl was looking at NCNB's rescue of Charter as a done deal, the FDIC would argue that Charter was still a long way from out of the woods.

Hoping his notion would get as far as a discussion of the legal ramifications, McColl offered to dispatch Paul Polking to Dallas for the meeting with the FDIC. Gentry asked if McColl could come down as well. After all, this might be the deal they had been waiting for. McColl turned him down. He was scheduled to deliver a speech to Florida bankers in Miami. "You and Polking go ahead and handle it," he said. "I trust your judgment. Just keep it close to your vest."

Miami sunshine recharged McColl's spirit. He felt a battle brewing. At the conference, he laid the South Carolina drawl on heavy, suspecting that half the audience was from New York. *Let them strain to figure out what the hell I'm talking about.* At the end, somebody tried to ring his bell by asking him facetiously whether NCNB was interested in buying Jacksonville's Barnett, the largest bank in Florida.

"Hell, no," McColl shot back. "They want too much more than they're worth. I've got no intention of paying twice the book value for stock in another Florida bank when right now I'm busy buying a bank in Texas for next to nothing."

Just keep it secret, he told Gentry. *Right.* On the flight back he agitated over the possibility that financial reporters might have been in the audience. He'd probably put his foot in his mouth again and would read about it in tomorrow's *Wall Street Journal.* Heading out of Charlotte Douglas Airport into afternoon traffic on the Billy Graham Parkway, he picked up the car phone and called Pat Hinson.

"I'm back. Any messages?"

"You'd better go right to Mr. Kiser's office when you get here," his secretary said. "I think there's a problem. Something to do with Mr. Gentry and Mr. Polking."

Jim Kiser, a small and customarily reserved barrister, was laying into his Texas delegation big time when McColl walked into the office. Polking and Gentry were getting a full-scale lecture on "the rights and prerogatives of the board" from Polking's boss, the chief legal counsel for NCNB. As McColl entered, Kiser turned to him.

"Do you know what these two have done? They just signed away $7 million of NCNB's assets without board approval. And in Texas! I'm telling you, Frank Gentry here is as dangerous as Ollie North."

The reference was to Oliver North, the marine lieutenant colonel who'd been telling Congress about the illegal sales of military weapons to Iran in order to secure the release of American hostages there. President Ronald Reagan, supposedly never informed about the "Iran-Contra" affair, had been much maligned in the media for permitting underlings such broad and unconstitutional latitude. The comparison of Frank Gentry to Ollie North implied that Hugh McColl should be as incensed by Gentry and Polking's action as Reagan had been by that of North. Instead, McColl asked Kiser to just calm down and let Gentry tell him what had transpired in Dallas.

"It was just like we suspected," Gentry began. "The FDIC turned thumbs down on Charter single-handedly bailing out Western." Western would need capital to reorganize and Charter didn't have all it would take. Gentry, Polking and Jerry Finger came up with a plan for NCNB to sink another $7 million in Charter. That would more than double its investment in Charter and give it controlling interest. That way Charter could afford to bail out Western. If the FDIC said yes, NCNB would have a bank to call its own in Texas, and a pretty fair-sized bank at that when you put Charter and Western together.

On the other side of the table, the FDIC negotiators countered. Would NCNB agree to take full responsibility for the combined investments of Charter and Western, all the outstanding loans? And if so, would they put the NCNB offer in writing? Gentry asked for a piece of paper, handed it to Polking and told him to write something down.

"That's when I got to a phone and tried to call you," Gentry told McColl. "But Pat told me she couldn't reach you down there in Miami."

Hugh McColl smiled. Gentry's story was sounding like a replay of the one he liked to tell about Florida Trust in 1981. He wondered whether Frank's story would have the same happy ending. "So, what did you boys do next?"

Gentry told McColl how he had studied Polking's single fat paragraph scratched on the legal pad. It committed $7 million of NCNB's $19.7 billion in assets. That would be a lot of money to lose, but if the investment paid off, Hugh McColl would control a $500 million bank, deep in the heart of what might one day regain its position as one of the nation's most prosperous states. And it would cost NCNB a total commitment of only $13 million. Gentry reached for a pen and signed the paper. That's what had infuriated Jim Kiser. A commitment like that required board approval.

"We were sure you would be delighted," Gentry protested. "Henh-henh. You know, it never crossed my mind that you would not be delighted."

McColl put his arms around the shoulders of Gentry and Polking. "I *am* delighted," he said. Then, looking at Kiser, "Don't be such a Nervous Nelly, Jim. These two have just put us into the major leagues. Now we just need to find a way to hit a home run."

Perhaps the earliest existing photo of Hugh McColl,
taken in Bennettsville when he was two years old.

McColl with his bride-to-be, Jane Spratt, on the Fontana di Trevi in Rome, 1959.

Addison Reese (foreground) signed this photo to Tom Storrs (left) on January 1, 1974, the day Storrs took over as CEO of NCNB. Storrs, always wary of superlatives, kept his "best team in the business" – McColl, Luther Hodges, and Bill Dougherty – out in front, but kept their photo on the wall of his office lavatory.

The "Iwo Jima" pose was supposed to be an in-house joke. CEO Tom Storrs looked in and said, "If anybody sees this, you're all fired." Planting the Florida State flag in the NCNB conference room are (l-r) McColl, Paul Polking, Joe Martin, Mark Leggett, and Frank Gentry.

McColl, Buddy Kemp and Benny Shaw (three on right) sit with strategic planner Joe Holzinger (left) at Pat O'Briens on Halloween Night, 1972, during a conference of the American Institute of Banking in New Orleans.

CBS newsman Charles Kurault, once a Charlotte newspaper reporter, donned a hardhat in 1987 for a McColl-guided tour of some of the bank's efforts to reconstruct the "Queen City of the South."

When McColl met with President George Bush in November, 1990, he was on crutches after injuring his knee during his death-defying Alpine glacier hike.

After the most acrimonious merger battle of his career, McColl got Atlanta's top bank executive, Bennett Brown, to smile after agreeing to sell his C&S/Sovran to NCNB in 1991. Jane McColl snapped the picture in front of the McColl condo on Litchfield Beach, South Carolina.

President Bill Clinton invited McColl to join him in the White House Rose Garden for the announcement of $382 million in funding for the "Community Development Financial Institutions" for low-income neighborhood development. "You're gonna fix about this much of the problem with that kind of money," McColl told Clinton.

To set the stage for his invasion of Texas, McColl mounted a set of longhorn steer horns on the auditorium lecturn prior to briefing his transition team on July 28, 1988.

Charlotte's skyline in 1994 was dominated by the NationsBank Corporate Center, in the background, when McColl joined his old rafting buddy Jerry Richardson at the groundbreaking ceremony for Richardson's Carolina Panthers stadium.

W. W. "Hootie" Johnson – shown here with McColl on a hunting trip in the 1980s – once tried to hire McColl to help run his South Carolina bank. Eventually he became one of McColl's most trusted confidantes and head of his executive committee.

McColl and longtime friend Craig Wall were honored by Davidson College in 1993. Wall played a major role in uniting McColl's NCNB and Atlanta's C&S/Sovran in the merger that created NationsBank.

Personnel head Chuck Cooley and corporate affairs chief Lynn Drury helped put together an "instant news conference" August 29, 1997, when McColl hooked the biggest fish in Florida banking, Barnett Bankshares.

The management team that would never manage the first coast-to-coast bank in the U.S., at New York's Waldorf-Astoria, April 14, 1998: (l-r) Jim Hance, Mike Murray, McColl, Dave Coulter, Ken Lewis and Mike O'Neill.

The McColl boys at a family reunion in Bennettsville
in 1996: Hugh, Kenneth, and Jimmy.

The McColl boys, Part Two:
McColl with grandsons John McColl Jr. (right) and his little brother Duncan.

As Ben Long's fresco for the dome of Transamerica Reinsurance Building neared completion in mid-1996, McColl climbed the scaffold for a look at his portrait as a "homeless warrior whose time is forever running out."

"We're the only little bank crazy enough to be in this hunt."

Hugh McColl
Meeting of the XYZ Task Force, April 1988

CHAPTER 11

A North Carolina bank was now the principal shareholder of a Texas bank, Charter, which would absorb the assets and liabilities of the Western Bank. Hugh McColl suspected this was the defining moment of Frank Gentry's career. Immediately, McColl assigned him, along with Tim Hartman, to the Charter Bank board. He wanted two of his best people to spend as much time as possible in Texas. After all, NCNB now had a whole new pack of business competitors down there, and in Hugh McColl's "dog-eat-dog" world of banking, there was little difference between competitor and prey. McColl intended to be the dog that did the eating.

It was not Gentry or Hartman but corporate treasurer John Mack who sighted the target. At a routine meeting in March 1988, Mack casually asked if McColl was following the story of First Republic Bancshares. When McColl said no, Mack explained.

First RepublicBank was now quite simply the number-one bank in Texas, the product of one of those last-ditch efforts by two big, faltering Texas banks to shore each other up through a merger. In this case, the effort was sure to have a fundamental impact on the future of the state's economy, because these were the state's two largest bank holding companies, RepublicBank Corp. and InterFirst Corp., both headquartered in Dallas. McColl asked more questions and the answers were supplied by Gentry, Hartman, Polking and others who were by now on intimate terms with Texas, its airports and its highways.

RepublicBank had been the conservative, old-line "Texas Wachovia," the bank that condescended to extend Hugh McColl a $7.5 million line of credit to keep NCNB afloat back during the hard times of 1974. InterFirst was much newer, the flashy, expansion-minded gunslinger whose seventy-two-story, argon-lit edifice so dominated the Dallas skyline that the media dubbed it the "green pickle."

"You know," someone in the room suggested, "First Union's logo is about that same color." McColl threw an icy stare across the table and the subject never arose again in his company. Green was the color of money; that's all anyone had to think about that.

The saga continued. In the spring of 1987, the directors of InterFirst and Republic realized they both were about to go under. Together they had $4 billion in nonperforming loans, mostly tied up in overvalued real estate; in fact, nearly a third of their combined real estate loans were in some stage of default.

"How much were they losing at that point?" McColl wanted to know. He whistled: joint losses estimated at more than half a billion dollars.

So, the two captains tied their two sinking lifeboats together to see whether they had anything that would float, then christened their sieve First RepublicBank. They combined departments, closed overlapping branches, eliminated redundant positions. In the process they threw three thousand men and women overboard without life jackets. And in spite of all these efforts, First RepublicBank found itself taking on more water, total deposits down $3.6 billion since the merger. McColl was not surprised to learn that the Texans were sending up flares in the direction of the federal government. John Mack reported that the FDIC had just announced a guarantee of all the bank's deposits, even those in excess of one hundred thousand dollars, and had made a billion-dollar loan to First Republic.

"It ain't the FDIC those Texans need," McColl decided. What they needed was the same kind of help those Texans at the Alamo got, a few heroes from North Carolina. He looked around at the people he considered his best and saw heroes in the making. For more than a year now these "dog-eat-dog" bankers had been circling and snarling at one another. Not dogs at all—that was just media talk—but hungry wolves. He needed something to bond them together in a hunting team. They needed motivating, needed to know they were trusted, needed to perform. They required something big to hunt, and they required it fast, or he was going to start losing them the way that First Republic was losing its assets.

"All right," he said. "This is the largest damned bank in Texas? Let's make it ours."

In a matter of hours, McColl was on the phone with Jerry Finger, trolling for information on First Republic. Finger told him about a conversation he'd had with Marshall Davidson, a New York investment banker with Drexel Burnham Lambert. Davidson was talking with First Republic's management about restructuring and he seemed to have good insights into the bank's problems. McColl called Davidson, who told him he believed that a deal could be structured in which NCNB might buy First Republic outright, provided the FDIC could be convinced that the plan would work. Listening between the lines, McColl sensed that serious conversations were going on about First Republic, conversations his people didn't know about.

What McColl ought to do, suggested Davidson, was hire a well-known Washington attorney who had experience dealing with the FDIC, someone like Baldwin Tuttle. That surprised McColl. He would have thought a Texas attorney would be more help, the way Judge Roberts had been in Florida. It sounded to him like following the trail from Finger to Davidson to Tuttle was only going to lead him where he already knew he needed to go—to the FDIC. Maybe Marshall Davidson was trying to pinhook the deal, like some cheap hustler; somebody was going to introduce him to somebody who would introduce him to somebody who would make him a lot of money.

However, even though he wanted to believe he could simply call up the chairman of the Federal Deposit Insurance Corporation and say, "I'm a banker and I want to come see you." Hugh McColl had to face facts. He was still small potatoes to the banking establishment. If a big-name attorney could add to his credibility, he would just have to pay the price. Besides, his team needed a locker room where they could huddle before taking the FDIC's playing field, and attorney Baldwin Tuttle's office would provide that. McColl hired Tuttle and Tuttle arranged a meeting in Washington with the chairman of the Federal Deposit Insurance Corporation. Before he left for that meeting, McColl asked his staff to pull together some information on the man he'd be meeting with, L. William Seidman.

McColl learned that Seidman was a Republican from an old-money family in Grand Rapids, Michigan. Seidman had left his Big Eight accounting firm to enter the bureaucratic battlefield of Washington in 1974. He'd been summoned to help his friend Gerald Ford organize his new office when Ford unexpectedly took over from Spiro Agnew as vice president. Just a few months later, when Richard Nixon's resignation elevated Ford to the presidency, Bill Seidman became a White House insider. After Ford's defeat by Democrat Jimmy Carter, Seidman left Washington for Arizona. He spent nine years there, first as vice chairman of Phelps Dodge Corp. and then as dean of Arizona State University's Business School. He went back to Washington as chairman of the FDIC in 1985. For the past three years he'd been writing the agency's most turbulent and controversial chapter since it rose out of the economic ashes of the Great Depression.

Seidman stepped out swinging, taking the media punches after the FDIC's unprecedented and much-questioned bailout of Continental Illinois. Now Seidman was suffering with his own Texas-sized headache in the form of First City, a Houston holding company for sixty-one faltering banks across the state.

But Seidman's real battle was not in Texas; it was in New York, where Wall Street bond speculators had gobbled up nearly a quarter of First City's $225 million indebtedness at a heavy discount. These investors refused to sell for anything less than a dollar-for-dollar return. That was like holding Bill Seidman hostage. The FDIC's recovery plan for First City would only work with across-the-board markdowns of the bank's bonds. McColl could identify with Seidman, those big investor guns pointing at his head, Wall Street all set to score on Texas's misery. McColl figured Seidman was backed into a corner with First City. He'd have to shut it down altogether or give in to the hard-line speculators. If McColl wanted Seidman in his corner for the First Republic bout, the surest way to the FDIC chairman's heart would be over the toes of those Wall Street thugs.

The *New York Times* quoted Seidman's predecessor at the FDIC, William Isaac, to the effect that there were only four U.S. banks big enough to handle First Republic's collapse—Citicorp, Wells Fargo, Chase Manhattan and Security Pacific. Nevertheless, Baldwin Tuttle sent word that Seidman was quite eager to meet with a regional banker from North Carolina. The financial press had been stirred up by the imminent collapse of First Republic, Tuttle explained, and Seidman was smelling blood that could turn out to be his own. Rumor had it the big Japanese banks might move in, and Seidman would do anything he could to keep Japanese hands off Texas banks. The chairman had rearranged his calendar to meet with McColl in early April, less than three weeks after the NCNB hunting party's first hint of game in Dallas.

McColl called together his top people for some "out of the box" thinking. The road to Texas's financial collapse, he observed, had been paved by bankers who thought like bankers. "I'm not a banker," he told his team. "I'm a businessman. Let's think like businessmen."

McColl was serious about not being a banker. Traditionally, corporate flowcharts designated not individual men and women but operations, enabling the collective to function smoothly. In America's large traditional banks, assimilation by the collective had fostered a degree of isolation. Even when it did work well, a traditional bank could never be equal to the sum of its parts. Moreover, because the institution severely limited the value of individual contribution, individuals weren't ever allowed to become all that they could be. Thus the traditional banker could not begin to imagine his company achieving the *potential* of its many parts. A bank was an institution whose assets were deposits, loan customers, stocks, but never really people.

In his bank's culture, McColl's people were his most important assets, a team of people he could set to work on a plan different from anything the FDIC had ever seen. One of the people he wanted back on the team was Joe Martin, who had completed his history book and was looking for a job. Joe and Joan Martin lived about four blocks from the McColls, so on a Saturday afternoon McColl walked over to talk his choirboy-tiger into returning. He would not have to manage a big group or have his every move scrutinized by the CEO; instead Martin would be able to do what he enjoyed doing, working on projects.

"Okay," Martin said. "I'll come back."

Martin joined McColl's preliminary Texas advisory team: Tim Hartman, Chuck Cooley, Frank Gentry, Paul Polking, John Mack and Bill McGee. McGee was a retired Naval Intelligence officer who joined the bank as McColl's chief of staff—a new position necessitated by McColl's assumption that his company would be growing, creating extraordinary demands on the CEO's time. McGee had been a Naval

ROTC classmate of McColl and finished his military career as chief of staff to a Pentagon admiral. He fit perfectly into what was shaping up as a quasimilitary operation.

Hartman, Mack and Polking began by throwing out traditional thinking on bailouts, which would have NCNB ask permission to buy the FDIC's failed leftovers. In place of that, they began with the assumption that NCNB and the FDIC would act as partners. A fresh approach, partnership with the FDIC, but McColl wasn't sure they could carry it off. The deposit insurer was expected to stand aloof and suspicious of all bank management. The two sides would need to sit down like not-quite-allies in a loan workout, going over the entire First Republic portfolio, loan by loan, separating the wheat from the chaff.

The plan to rescue First RepublicBank began to take shape. In NCNB's imagination, the FDIC would absorb all the bad loans in a separate bank and then write them off as losses. What was left over would be managed by NCNB. In turn, NCNB would pump a substantial amount of money into the new-and-improved First Republic, perhaps as much as $200 million, and would supply the people and the strategy necessary to turn the bank around.

There was one other possibility, Hartman said, probably a crazy idea, but worth looking into. "It has to do with tax write-offs. Let me do some homework and I'll find out whether it's worth a battle with the IRS."

"Fine," said McColl. "Let me know."

On the afternoon of Wednesday, April 5, 1988, Hartman accompanied McColl to Washington, where they picked up attorney Baldwin Tuttle, then went to see whether he could talk the FDIC into giving NCNB a Texas hunting license.

Across from the Executive Office Building on Seventeenth Street sits the square seven-story office building of the Federal Deposit Insurance Corporation. Its design is modern, not federal, and, just looking at it, McColl could almost believe that the agency was part of the private sector, as it was intended to appear. But he knew he was in Washington, where appearances are just that. The FDIC paid its bills out of the insurance premiums it deducted from banks like his.

Up on the top floor, where the grand view swept from the Mall to the Potomac, McColl entered Seidman's office. He felt embraced by the Southwestern motif, the Navaho rugs, the Hopi kachina dolls. *He has an attachment to the earth, respect for traditions not his own.* Seidman stood up to shake hands and McColl smiled. *Plus, he's every bit as short as I am.* The accountant from Grand Rapids and the farm-boy banker from Bennettsville took to each other from the get-go.

After just a few sentences of weather-talk, McColl stepped right into the issue of bad loans. "You need to know that I'm not going to take your losses, Mr. Chairman. These are somebody else's losses. We didn't create them so we're not taking them. We'll come run this bank for you and save what you've got, and at the end of the day we'll help you make some money out of it. What do you say?"

Seidman said the approach was certainly different, an interesting notion. He told McColl he appreciated getting to the point. "It's quite apparent you didn't come up here on a wild goose chase." They would continue exploring a relationship.

As he stepped out of the FDIC's front doorway, McColl saw a bill scudding along the pavement, stooped, and came up with a ten-dollar note. Feeling extraordinarily lucky, he stepped into the next doorway, which happened to be a bookstore. "Let's buy *Texas*," he said. Michener's two-volume novel was available in paperback, but it still cost McColl something more than ten dollars.

"Good vibes," McColl told Hartman on the plane ride home, "from the moment I shook hands with him. He's a man's man, a very straightforward person. Very candid with us. Our styles go together well, I think. In other words, no BS, just straight talk. He liked me, I liked him. We understood each other."

Now the Texas team had to turn its notion into a full-fledged proposal, a stack of papers that lawyers could haggle over and secretaries could proof. McColl asked Hartman whether he was ready to pull that IRS thing out of his hat. "Not just yet," Hartman smiled, "but I can give you a peek at the rabbit."

Hartman told McColl about an experience with Baldwin United in Cincinnati, when he had found himself involved in the company's takeover of an Ohio savings and loan gone bankrupt. Baldwin's accountants learned about a then-new tax provision that could significantly enhance the value of the deal. It was called a "G Reorganization," a Tax Code amendment that would allow the newly restructured company to carry forward the losses and favorable tax benefits onto subsequent years' returns.

"So basically you're telling me that we could take a million-dollar bad loan from First Republic and convert that to a million-dollar loss for whatever we call our new bank . . . say, NCNB Texas?"

Hartman didn't see how the IRS could make a distinction between an Ohio savings and loan and a Texas bank. "If I'm right about this thing," he told McColl, "the tax benefits alone could off-set our total investment."

McColl's eyes went wide. "You mean we could get First Republic without paying a dime?"

"Maybe," said Hartman, his customarily dour countenance gone to glee. "Could be we'll wind up buying them with their own bad loans."

Hartman's obscure tax regulation only came into play because the FDIC operated independently of the government as a whole. Under the Banking Act of 1933, the Bank Insurance Fund (BIF) had been created to insure commercial and savings bank deposits up to one hundred thousand dollars. Tradition held that the FDIC was the steward of that fund. As long as it protected the BIF, the FDIC was unconcerned that money might come out of some other government agency pocket—say, the IRS. Unpaid taxes were dollars lost to the federal government, but not lost by the FDIC. While the IRS might not like handing out tax write-offs, it seemed to have set a precedent with its Ohio S&L ruling. And Hartman recognized that precedent, not possession, is nine-tenths of the law.

This was the first time McColl ever heard of anything as crazy as this, but Hartman had surprised him before. In his first year at NCNB Hartman had figured out how to use the purchase accounting method to buy all of an acquired Florida bank's subsidiary compa-nies. That allowed NCNB to write off any assets that had low "fair market value," at what were considerably higher tax-value prices. This created substantial losses on paper and substantial benefits to NCNB's bottom line. Hartman knew his taxes.

"Too good a trail not to sniff down," McColl said. He told Hartman to bring a few good people together to work on the IRS notion, but to keep it quiet. "No mention of this G Reorganization thing to anyone, not even to the FDIC. The last thing we need is for somebody like Wells Fargo to find out they could get Texas for next to nothing."

As Hugh McColl contemplated the task before him, doubts began to set in. Whatever he proposed was bound to be carefully scrutinized by his board. Hootie Johnson and Tom Storrs might talk a good game about moving on Texas, but they'd turned him down once already, on Allied Bancshares. And nobody, certainly not Hugh McColl, could say for certain how deep that hole in the Texas economy might be.

A few on the board still held him responsible for the bad press on South Africa. More than a few damned him for screwing up First Atlanta. Now, if word leaked out that McColl was trying to buy the largest bank in Texas, he'd look like the all-time horse's ass of the industry. Those same Wall Street investors who were holding Bill Seidman's feet to the fire on Houston's First City would be the first ones to sell off their NCNB stock. The bank's credibility would nose-dive in the marketplace and his own credibility at the bank would take a hit. In the boardroom his ability to lead might be lost for good. On the other hand, if this First Republic deal went through, if little NCNB and little Hugh McColl really *did* beat out the world's biggest banks, well, maybe then everyone would find out who they were.

McColl had never wanted anything so badly, but deep down he questioned whether he was the man for the job. In truth he was nothing more than a role player, an actor in a drama. *My role is negotiator, contact point,* he told himself. *I'm the guy who bluffs or pontificates or does whatever we need to get done.* McColl had never before written his own script. It might be best to bring back Tom Storrs to go after First Republic. Storrs was more organized, more disciplined. Tom Storrs was better than he was. McColl would bring his top general out of retirement.

"I need somebody to coordinate the planning," he told Chuck Cooley. "I think the best person to do that would be Tom Storrs."

Cooley was thunderstruck. He had spent the first thirteen years of his career at the bank waiting to work for Hugh McColl, and it was out of the question that he should go back to reporting to Storrs. But he couldn't convince McColl by knocking Storrs. Instead, he played two of McColl's favorite cards, responsibility and trust. "We don't need to call back Tom Storrs to coordinate the planning," he said. "We'd like to give that a shot ourselves, Joe and Tim and Bill and I. We'd like you to be the person who calls the shots and not get Tom between us and you. All you need to do is trust us. Let us give it a go, and if you're not happy with the way it's going, we'll try it the other way."

Cooley forced McColl to the realization that he was at a water-shed. For the first time he had the chance to do the thing he had promised his father. *Some day I'm going to run that bank.* The war was his to win or lose, and no one would be taking a step that Hugh McColl did not personally set in motion. Among the traits that differentiated him from Tom Storrs—and McColl suspected there were many—was his insistence on listening to the troops, seeking the advice of the people who worked for him. But he couldn't just listen; now and then he had to heed their advice or eventually they'd stop offering it. Chuck Cooley's advice right now was good.

"Fine," he said. "Let's go to work. Let's talk about duties and responsibilities. Let's talk about who does what to whom."

The fight for control of Texas would be a war with two theaters of operation, one in Washington, the other in Dallas. In Washington Tim Hartman would do battle on two fronts, assisted by Frank Gentry, Paul Polking, Treasurer John Mack and Baldwin Tuttle, the outside counsel. On one hand Hartman's group would try to convince the IRS to permit G Reorganization of an unnamed bank. On the other they would push through the thicket of banking regulation and contract negotiations with lawyers and accountants from the FDIC, to work out a mutually acceptable deal for saving First Republic. Seidman and two other FDIC directors would make the decisions, but Hartman's people would first need to satisfy an entire bureau-full of underlings.

The war in Dallas would be a covert operation, conducted primarily out of NCNB's Charlotte headquarters. Bill McGee, McColl's personal aide, would handle logistics, a natural for the former supply officer and admiral's aide. Joe Martin would be in charge of public relations, politics, crafting comments and managing the flow of information. Officially now, Martin's title was senior VP for public policy. To chief personnel officer Chuck Cooley McColl handed what might prove to be the most difficult assignment. Cooley would put together a battalion of NCNB officers to actually take over First Republic, assuming they got the go-ahead. He would need to do that without telling the battalion where they were headed or, for that matter, making them aware that their battalion even existed.

Cooley, Hartman, McGee, Martin, Mack, Gentry, Polking. Not one of them believed there was a chance in hell of really doing this Texas deal, but they would all march into hell if Hugh McColl led them there. They congregated in an unmarked, sparsely decorated conference room on the executive floor of the NCNB Tower, the twenty-third, and this would be their "war room." Anything that went on inside would be Top Secret.

Reason One for secrecy: Should word leak that NCNB was talking about buying First Republic, the big international banks would bully their way in and take over.

Reason Two: NCNB had enemies in its own camp. If certain members of the NCNB board of directors found out what was being planned before McColl was ready to tell them, there was a real danger that NCNB never would get to Texas. "In fact, you all might wind up working for someone other than me here in North Carolina," he told them.

Reason Three—and McColl lowered his voice for this one: "We cannot, *must* not, let Wall Street know we're snooping around First Republic." Investor panic might destroy not only the Texas project but everything that NCNB had struggled to build in the past twenty-five years.

With secrecy the sine qua non, the project needed a code name, so they could at least talk about it among themselves. Gentry offered "Operation Calcutta."

"What?"

"Henh-henh. Because it's probably just a black hole."

They settled on the more prosaic, more hopeful and less sinister "XYZ Corporation" and they were the "XYZ Task Force." Only a very few individuals would even know that the project existed, let alone its details. They would bring in other key people as they became needed. For the Dallas branch of the task force, Martin wrote an objective on a flip-chart: "Build a winning team in Texas while maintaining our momentum here in Charlotte."

McColl commissioned Cooley to start by gathering information on two fronts. First, they had to learn more about their erstwhile partner, the FDIC. "We need to know exactly what to expect from the FDIC when it closes all those First Republic banks and we take over," McColl said. "Then we can figure out where we go from there."

Cooley brought in Mike Clement, who had watched the FDIC fail banks in Florida and Texas. The XYZ group heard Clement tell of the FDIC's "intimidating process," with agents storming into branch offices on a Friday afternoon, locking all the doors and forcing all employees to stay in their places until the branches' assets could be itemized and tagged. This examination invariably took hours and went into the night, Clement said. Employees were allowed to call home, but they could not leave. "The FDIC examiners did order out for pizza," Clement acknowledged. In Florida, NCNB representatives had to be on hand to witness the whole proceeding. McColl found that prospect disturbing. *They make us silent partners of the executioners.* Once all the bank's assets were tagged, all branch employees would be told they were fired. If they wanted their jobs back, it would be at FDIC wages. Finally, one by one, they were released from their workplace-turned-prison.

Over the weekend, Clement went on, the FDIC inspectors would turn over each branch—including books, assets and thoroughly shell-shocked staff—to the acquiring company. "That way operations can start up as normal on Monday morning." The word "normal" generated a round of black laughter. To the government this apparently seemed just an efficient way to get dirty business done. McColl looked at it differently.

"Hell of a way to treat people who'll be working for us in two days."

When the task force finished questioning Clement—never telling him the reason for their questions—they pondered the fate of all those employees at more than two hundred First Republic offices in Texas, at least three thousand people. "That's going to be a really awful, really scary time," Cooley remarked. Especially scary for a personnel director. "How are we going to turn those people into our associates?"

"First we fire you," McColl said, "then we offer you your job back at lower wages, then we tell you we're your new employer. All the while you're held prisoner while you were planning on maybe spending a nice Friday evening with your wife or husband or maybe coaching your kid's Little League team. How are we supposed to earn the trust of someone who's been treated like that? We're going to need those people. We can't take over Texas without the people to run the banks. We can't just replace all of them with our own people because there'd be nobody left to run the banks we have now."

The task force decided they would write new rules for the FDIC. It would be up to Hartman to convince Seidman's people that an officer from NCNB must be assigned to each branch in advance of the failure. That officer would go to that branch on the Friday afternoon of the failing with an FDIC representative. Together they would go into the branch manager's office and introduce themselves by name. The government agent would ask for the keys to the bank, then immediately turn the keys over to the NCNB representative. That officer would then hand the keys back to the branch manager and assure the manager that she or he would remain in charge, even though there would be a different corporate name on the bank's door. The NCNB officer, accompanied by the branch manager, would then speak to all the branch employees, making sure they understood that:

1. Their jobs were secure;
2. NCNB needed them;
3. Their Texas customers needed them;
4. NCNB people were "the good guys";
5. From this point forward they all had a sound, restructured bank to run together.

The task force called that their "Reassurance Plan" and it would be crucial for the FDIC to agree to it. McColl would not step again into the ill will their heavy-handedness had created in Florida. NCNB had survived those culture-clashes because Florida's was a healthy economic climate. In Texas it would be a different story.

In addition to gathering information on the FDIC and its modus operandi, McColl wanted to know everything knowable about First Republic and its top executives. For that, the XYZ Task Force needed insiders. In Houston Gentry had developed two moles within the First Republic organization, disgruntled executives who could be trusted to provide names and profiles of the key people. Like everything else, the existence of the moles was top secret.

"We're going to have so many secrets it's unbelievable," McColl told his leaders. "We have to put together the organizational structure of a company we don't own, using some of our own people. We then have to develop a plan to replace the people we might be sending to Texas from six different states, and we have to do all this without the knowledge of any of the people involved."

And then, Chuck Cooley noted, there was the element of timing. All their plans would most likely have to be executed at a moment's notice, all the while pretending that nothing was going on.

Cooley covered packs of three-by-five index cards with information on every important First Republic executive. His cards were made to be positioned on an organization chart that set out an

"NCNB Texas" management structure on one wall of the war room. McColl was impressed by Cooley's deck of cards, but even more impressed when Cooley turned the cards over. There were the names and profiles of current NCNB people who could replace the First Republic executives should replacement be deemed in order. As April wore cruelly on, Chuck Cooley's index cards smudged and frayed, but their existence was unknown to anyone outside the XYZ Task Force, other than a few individuals very high up in the corporate structure.

Working with Joe Martin, McColl established "who would say what to whom," when and if the First Republic buyout received FDIC approval. And at that point he turned all the details of the operation over to Cooley, McGee and Martin. "Let Hartman handle Washington," he said. "You three, make all decisions that need to be made here and implement them."

Texas, Hugh McColl told his task force, would be their finest hour. Each of them would have to execute more sharply than they'd ever done before. "I know you will," he grinned, "because you're all going to be allowed to do your thing. You won't be told what to do. I'm not going to tell anybody what to do."

McColl did think he might have one personal card to play. There were only three directors of the FDIC (as of 1988), only three votes for or against their proposal. One of those was C. C. Hope Jr., the independent director appointed by the president and confirmed by the Senate. A former senior executive of First Union Bank, Hope might feel he owed a little something to Hugh McColl.

In their earliest encounters Hope and McColl had engaged in the banking equivalent of hand-to-hand combat. That was back in the 1960s, when they were scouring the Carolinas for commercial loans, Hope for First Union, McColl for American Commercial and then NCNB. Hope was retired from First Union and, in 1985, had been elected president of the American Bankers Association, thanks in no small part to the support of Hugh McColl.

"I believe my vote actually got him elected," McColl told his task force in the war room. "He had to get nominated and our vote was key to that. He won by one vote, and that vote was not something we gave lightly. He would not have become president without my help." After the election, Hope had maintained friendly relations with McColl. He just might be "the kind of person who might retain the appreciation that I voted for him when it mattered." McColl set up a breakfast meeting in Charlotte with C. C. Hope, then called the group together for a debriefing.

"He was very gracious to me and we had breakfast together and chit-chatted," McColl said, "but he didn't tell me anything and he isn't *going* to tell me anything about what the FDIC will do." However, McColl found out that Hope actually had spoken to the chairman already on their behalf. "He said he told Seidman that NCNB knows how to run a bank, that we know how to run a branch bank. And that we have a lot of good management."

While the task force was pleased to learn that C. C. Hope actually had put in a good word for NCNB, there was a modicum of concern that Hope might alert First Union to what its up-the-street rival was plotting.

"There's nothing we can do about that," McColl said. "We can't be worried about that." All he could do was hope against Hope's putting First Union onto the scent in Texas. "We need to spend our time worrying about the big banks," McColl insisted. "We need to worry about Citibank or Wells Fargo or somebody. We might not know who the players are, but if this Texas deal is as big as we think it is, we really don't need to be wringing our hands over another player as small as we are. We're the only little bank crazy enough to be in this hunt."

The task force knew something about Hope and something about Seidman, but they knew very little about the third vote on the FDIC, that of the Comptroller of the Currency, attorney Robert Clarke. Ironically enough, Cooley reported, while Hope hailed from North Carolina, Clarke happened to be a native of Houston, in the target zone. The task force conjectured that Clarke, being a Texan, would see little good to be gained from "outsiders" turning a profit on his state's misfortune.

Frank Gentry reported that Clarke was the FDIC director who had recruited Al Casey to take over as CEO of First Republic and manage it, with the help of the billion-dollar loan from the FDIC. Casey, a friend of Clarke's, was the former president of American Airlines, and a fellow Texan. While Tim Hartman groaned that Clarke's almost certain vote against NCNB was likely a deal-breaker, McColl downplayed Clarke's heritage and connections. Ultimately, Seidman, Hope and even Clarke would come to see things the way they were: the common enemy was Wall Street.

April 10, 1988, five days after their initial meeting with the FDIC chairman, McColl and Hartman sent Frank Gentry and a team of credit experts to Washington to review the agency files on First Republic. The FDIC had offered to order First Republic to open up its books in Dallas, but McColl rejected that offer. If his people showed up at First Republic on a Tuesday afternoon, the financial press would have his stock in a tailspin by Wednesday morning. So Gentry and his team spent a week in a D.C. storage room rifling through fifteen boxes of loan review reports and other documents that would give them a look at First Republic's true situation. Prohibited from photocopying or borrowing any of the documents, their only recourse was to enter information by hand into a portable computer. Later, back in Charlotte, they hoped to figure out what it all meant.

On only the fifth day of this examination, April 15, the charm of carrying out a massive plan in absolute secrecy was wearing thin. McColl took the company jet to Washington, pulled his team out of the file room and told them they were going to pay a visit on the FDIC's chief negotiator, Tony Scalzi. McColl shocked Scalzi by telephoning him personally and demanding to be seen. In Scalzi's office he said he was going to take his people home and submit a written offer for NCNB's purchase of First Republic. "I want your guarantee," he told Scalzi, "that the FDIC will respond to that proposal, give me a yes or a no, within ten days."

Scalzi blanched. No bureaucrat dared accept such a responsibility. He did not have the authority, Mr. McColl. That sort of guarantee could only come from Chairman Seidman. "Is he in?" asked McColl. "Get him on the phone." Seidman agreed to see McColl and listen to his arguments.

It was easy for McColl to play his part now, because he really was worried. The strain was beginning to affect his people and their ability to perform. With every passing day, he told Seidman, more company executives were required to learn more pieces of the operation. Sooner or later, somebody outside his organization was going to put those pieces together. If that happened, NCNB stock might be devastated. "Mr. Chairman, you could be dealing with a damn bank failure in North Carolina to go with your problems in Texas."

Even worse, McColl insisted, First Republic's value was wasting away hour by hour. Soon there would be nothing left for the FDIC to sell nor for NCNB to buy. Seidman was not swayed. He told McColl that it might be in the realm of possibility for the FDIC to reach a decision in four weeks, but *never* in ten days.

On the flight back to Charlotte, McColl consulted a calendar. He had acted his role well. He knew good and well that a ten-day deadline would never fly, but at least now he had Seidman committed to a finite period. One month they could live with. Because he was dealing with the government, it would be wise to add two weeks to the timetable. That brought him to Memorial Day weekend. It made sense. Memorial Day would be Monday, May 30. The three-day weekend would give the FDIC an extra day to go through the books and reopen all those branches on Tuesday the 31st.

"Seidman is planning to fail First Republic on the Friday before Memorial Day," he told his task force. "May 27 is our D day."

Before he could make a formal bid for First Republic, McColl had to tell his board of directors what was going on. A full board meeting was scheduled in Tampa in less than two weeks, but he couldn't wait that long. Instead he filled the executive committee in on the plan to buy First Republic. Prepared for the worst, he was hoping their reaction would be supportive.

They listened attentively while he stepped them through the facts and figures. The first one to speak was his chairman, Hootie Johnson. "By golly, Hugh," Johnson smiled. "it just might work." McColl let out his breath, maybe home free.

Then Al Ellis coughed and sputtered into cantankerism. Texas: too far, too big and too risky. He'd be damned if he'd vote for such a foolhardy scheme. A. L. Ellis, eighty-plus and still salaried higher than the CEO, was used to getting his way.

But McColl felt the dynamics shift in his favor. As Ellis tried to force opinion to the downside, blaming McColl for impertinence and poor judgment, Johnson and Storrs felt compelled to pull against the old Florida curmudgeon. The more Ellis argued, the more pig-headed he seemed and the less support he garnered. They took a vote and McColl left the meeting with instructions to proceed with caution. McColl had no problem with caution; he figured he'd be hearing from Mr. Ellis again when the full board convened in Tampa.

For his directors as well as for Bill Seidman, McColl wanted to get the right proposal down on paper. It had to make the case—and he was beginning to believe it was true—that First Republic had enormous profit potential, given the right capitalization and good management. The buyout offer had to read like a no-lose proposition for both the FDIC and NCNB. McColl also wanted his proposal to give Bill Seidman a clear opportunity to stick it to the "big money interests" on Wall Street.

"With us as their partner," he told his task force, "Seidman and Clarke and Hope need to be convinced that every banker and investor and customer out there knows that, by God, this is the Federal Deposit Insurance Corporation and they have the power of the United States government behind them. Now, how do we give them that power? What weapon can we offer them?"

McColl got his answer from Tim Hartman, who conferred with tax attorney Frank Blanchfield, NCNB treasurer John Mack, and others, then came back with a proposal for a relatively untried vehicle called a "bridge bank." The bridge bank concept had been authorized less than a year earlier, in 1987, as part of the Competitive Equality Banking Act. The new law allowed the FDIC to issue a special charter to a bank that would assume the deposits and secured liabilities of an insolvent bank. Hartman said the law provided a way for NCNB to hold onto the tax benefits resulting from First Republic's losses, even though the entity called "First Republic" would cease to exist. In essence, the plan would allow them to keep the old corporation intact long enough for the tax benefits to follow into the bridge bank.

McColl liked what he heard from Hartman. It was conceivable that there might be even more tax benefits if Hartman could get his G Reorganization plan to fly, though so far the Washington team was getting nowhere with the Internal Revenue Service. Even without G Reorganization, the proposed bridge bank would make good on Seidman's demand that the FDIC no longer be considered a safety net for big money interests who, in his estimation, took too many chances, made bad investments and weakened the national economy. The only interests served by the bridge bank approach would be those of bank depositors and creditors and, of course, NCNB.

If Seidman gave the green light in Texas, all two hundred offices of First RepublicBank's forty different banking companies would be delivered by the FDIC not to NCNB but to the bridge bank. Stock in the First Republic holding company and its twenty-two nonbanking subsidiaries would immediately become worthless. NCNB would then have ninety days to buy 20 percent of the new bank, at $1.07 on the dollar, or 7 percent above the fair market value. NCNB would have the option to buy the remaining 80 percent from the FDIC over a period of five years. All of First Republic's bad loans would be moved to a separate "special asset" bank, whose expenses would be covered by the FDIC.

"If I understand you correctly," McColl told Mack, "when it's all said and done we'll be buying the largest bank in Texas at about half what it would cost us to buy a bank that size in Florida or Georgia?"

"Right," answered Mack.

"And we'll be doing it on the installment plan," grinned McColl.

In his cover letter, McColl wrote Seidman that "NCNB will share a portion of the risk since the questionable assets will be on the books of a bridge bank in which NCNB will have an interest. Frankly, we believe that this division of risk is appropriate since neither NCNB nor any other party other than the FDIC has a current obligation to undertake that risk and since the full extent of the magnitude of the problems may be impossible to assess." McColl said he would appreciate a response to his proposal in six days, by April 25.

Whatever Seidman's response might be, no deal this large could be consummated without the approval of NCNB Corporation's board of directors. Just a few days before the full board meeting, scheduled for April 20 at the hotel on Harbor Island in Tampa Bay, McColl received a curious letter from Joseph Weintraub in Miami, demanding that he put an immediate halt to his designs on Texas. Weintraub had been chairman of Pan American Banks in Miami, bought out by NCNB in the summer of 1985. As part of that deal, Joseph Weintraub had been made a "senior chairman" of the board of NCNB National Bank of Florida, the subsidiary of NCNB Corporation. His son Michael, the number-two man at Pan American, was given a seat on the NCNB Corporation board. It was Al Ellis—a director of both the holding company and the Florida subsidiary—who had brought the Weintraubs to the bargaining table.

With the big game squarely in his sights, here was a sudden shift in the wind that could ruin everything. Handled improperly, this thinly veiled threat from a man he'd never met could spell the end of his career. This was still Tom Storrs's board, not Hugh McColl's. He was younger than any other member of the board. He had been in office five years and most of them were already sitting when he came aboard. He did not consider himself particularly good at "handling" the board. He felt on edge and under attack. The letter from Joseph Weintraub accused McColl of "plotting to destroy the wealth of your shareholders." The implication was that Weintraub meant to take any means necessary to thwart the Texas strategy. The curious thing was that this letter was written not by son Michael Weintraub, who had a vote on the holding company board, but by Joseph Weintraub, who had no voice at all and no legal standing in holding company affairs. He folded the letter in the pocket of his sportcoat and headed for breakfast with the executive committee in advance of the board meeting.

Even before the biscuits were passed around, Al Ellis went on the attack. He said he'd had a little chat with his fellow board member, Michael Weintraub. He'd let his young friend in on what Hugh McColl and his gang were planning. Did the others know what Mike had to say about that? The others did not know. Well, Mike Weintraub proposed that if McColl was going to drive them to ruin, he and Ellis would be better off flying to New York to sell the company first.

Expletives swirled around the orange juice. Studying the frowns of the men who controlled his destiny, McColl knew he was staring failure in the face. He decided his best shot was to take on the Weintraubs rather than go directly after Ellis, the elder statesman and principal stockholder. He pulled out the letter from Weintraub senior and read it to the committee, then played his only hole card, hoping it turned out to be an ace. "Mr. Michael Weintraub is trying to stage a palace coup," he snarled. "This company is not big enough for me and him. If the board gives in to this sort of tactic, I will tender my resignation immediately."

Leaving Hootie Johnson to calm down his executive committee, McColl went off to brush his teeth a second time before the meeting of the full board. The primary item on the agenda was the proposed merger with First Republic Bank of Texas.

McColl laid out the takeover plan he had drawn up for the FDIC, stressing the minimal exposure it presented for NCNB and the extraordinary value of the deal, once First Republic's bad debts were disposed of. He gave it his best sell. But around the room he saw doubt, fear, anger. *They're missing the point. They think I'm playing fast and loose with their money and they don't realize there's almost no risk for them. They're afraid of this deal.* He had no choice but to push out all the chips.

"Now before you put the matter to a vote," he said, "I feel an obligation to lay a few additional facts before you, because, in all fairness, this board should know that not everyone who has been privy to our proposal is a hundred percent in favor of it." Nervous titters as he unfolded the letter from his pocket. "I received this letter just the other day from Mr. Joseph Weintraub of Miami, who, as many of you know, is on our Florida board and whose, son, Mr. Michael Weintraub, is with us this morning. 'Dear Mr. McColl . . . '"

As he finished he looked up to see all heads turned in Michael Weintraub's direction. Director Bill Klopman, a "tough hombre" in McColl's book, was the first to speak. "What the hell? How does Joe Weintraub know about this already?" Klopman thundered. "This is supposed to be confidential, what right does he have to know about this?"

Hugh McColl felt the wind shifting again. The enemy within had made a critical error in judgment. Members of a board can be more obstinate than members of a clan—they'd sooner be wrong than have an outsider tell them what's right. *Wounded pride beats fear of failure every time, sure as a straight flush beats a full house.* In fact, by giving inside information to an outsider, Ellis and Mike Weintraub had violated SEC regulations. McColl knew he'd won, that his board would go along, however grudgingly, with him, Storrs and Johnson. One director he respected highly, Pete Sloan, seemed to speak for the majority when he said the board would "continue to monitor the risk." Should that risk go any higher, Sloan said, he would call for another vote and cast his against the First Republic deal.

McColl had made it over the first hurdle, but left some of his blood on the crossbar. His board definitely had missed the point that this would be the greatest banking coup of the decade, maybe the century, a huge gain with virtually zero risk. No matter. He had all he needed from them for the moment. Now, by God, he would lead them where he wanted to go, fears notwithstanding. Now he had to concentrate on the FDIC.

"Let us become single-minded," he told his XYZ Task Force, "about trying to get the transaction to happen."

The next week he heard from William Seidman. His answer was no.

McColl read Seidman's formal response. NCNB's bridge bank approach solved some but not all of the problems implicit in the failure of a bank as large as First Republic, a bank "too big to fail." The real story was between the lines. Seidman wanted more of the benefit and less of the risk than McColl was willing to provide. The good news was that the FDIC did not seem to question the North Carolina team's ability to manage the largest bank in Texas.

"He says he wants more 'upside potential,'" McColl summed it up for his task force. "He's telling us we should sweeten the kitty for the FDIC and then redeal the cards."

There was nothing sweeter than Tim Hartman's tax ploy. If they could get a favorable ruling from the Internal Revenue Service on the G Reorganization, the benefits would accrue not only to NCNB but to the FDIC as well. That was the beauty of the partnership arrangement: nobody had ever invited the FDIC to stay on as a partner after it shut down a bank. Unfortunately, even after weeks of meetings in Washington, Hartman reported no definitive answer from the IRS. He and his two teams were stuck in a seemingly endless round of meetings with five different groups of lawyers and accountants, including a set from the Comptroller of the Currency's office.

McColl felt uneasy. Could it be that the Comptroller, Robert Clarke, was stalling the engines of both bureaucratic machines? He had to leave the next week for a twenty-one-day trip around the world. He was finally going to put the finishing touches on listing NCNB on the Tokyo stock exchange—the first regional American bank ever to seek equity capital on the Japanese market. In addition, Hootie Johnson and the board expected him to return from the Far East and Europe with a cache of foreign capital to finance the Texas deal. But he still didn't know for sure that Texas was for sale or that his bank's money was good with the FDIC.

The sixth of May, McColl lost his patience again. It was time for him to send another strong message to the FDIC. Still convinced that the agency was planning to fail First Republic Bank on Memorial Day weekend, McColl flew to Washington to call on Seidman.

"I need to know," he demanded, "if the IRS gives us a green light, do we get a green light from the FDIC? Because if we're going to do this deal I need to know by fifteen May."

McColl looked Seidman in the eye as he awaited an answer. It was all just too much like a poker game and him with no high cards down. The question was, did the chairman realize he had nothing down? He studied Seidman for any hint of concern. The man was cool, smiling, unruffled as one of his kachina dolls. The government simply would not work like that, Seidman answered. There was no way he could guarantee an answer by mid-May. Nothing was going to happen in nine days.

McColl forced a smile of his own. He understood what his role demanded now, even though Seidman had rewritten the script. He rose and pushed back his chair against the grain of the Navajo rug. His South Carolina drawl thickened perceptibly, demanding more in the way of attention and patience from his listener.

"If you *cain't* give us an answer, Mistuh Chaiahman, ah'm vair' much afraid we'll have to withdraw our offer. Y'all bettuh find somebody else to he'p you out with First Republic. Thanks f'your tahm." McColl executed a Marine Corps about-face (like riding a bicycle, something he would never forget) and strode out of the office.

He thinks I'm bluffing and he's right, McColl thought as his plane left Dulles. Certainly part of McColl's Mad Scene was genuine, but even he was not certain how much was real and how much was acting. He hoped like hell his frustration hadn't led him down the same First Atlanta path. Once again, he'd parted on hard terms with the player on the other side of the table. And without Bill Seidman, Hugh McColl had no game. Now there was little to do but make good on his threat. From the airplane, McColl let his task force know that anyone not included in the inner circle should be notified that the "XYZ Corporation" deal was off. They should go back to business as usual. Chuck Cooley, juggling people around organization charts in four states, asked if that was really necessary.

"It is," McColl told Cooley. "We want to be sure that if their negotiating team comes and asks our negotiating team, 'Is Hugh really just posturing?' they will say, 'No. He's mad as hell. It's *over.*'" As far as the key NCNB people were concerned, McColl gave them clear instructions to stay in the hunt. Yet, as he talked to each of his lieutenants, he picked up tension, doubt. And it was not themselves they doubted, but their leader. McColl had set them up for it. "It's my job to will the thing to happen," he had told them, "to be the best game in town, to be there, and then to threaten to leave if they don't do a deal with us." Twice he had tried that tactic and twice he had failed.

On May 11, McColl left for Europe and the Far East, searching for capital that would let him consummate the First Republic deal, if there was a deal, not so sure he still deserved the support of his own team, never mind the FDIC and the IRS. McColl made sure Bill McGee and Pat Hinson knew how to find him immediately if anything changed in Washington. "Maybe I'll have better luck with bankers and lawyers on the other side of the world," he told McGee.

His first meeting, accompanied by Washington-weary Tim Hartman and investor relations specialist Rusty Page, was at the Regent Hotel in Hong Kong. They sat in the poorly heated suite of Knobby Clark, CEO of Australia's national bank, hung over from jet lag, fatigue, too many complimentary drinks in first-class and nasty weather. Clark and McColl were as short on patience as they were on comfort, irritating each other for the better part of an hour before they called it quits. If there was going to be an NCNB Texas deal there would be no Aussie capital to back it up.

Two days into Asia, the jet lag eased and the news perked up with the weather. Gentry and Mack called with "good information" that the FDIC was leaning toward accepting NCNB's bid. They confirmed McColl's conviction that Seidman was shooting for closure by Memorial Day. Feeling on top of the world, McColl bought Jane some freshwater pearls and linens at the Hong Kong market. He told the executives of Hong Kong-Shanghai Bank he would be most happy to attend the horse races with them on Sunday. The way his luck was running, he looked forward to placing a bet or two. Did they play the trifecta in Hong Kong?

Before the horses even left the starting gate, all bets were off. Hartman's FDIC team called from Washington with the devastating word that the following Monday Seidman would be going public, seeking immediate bids from banks around the world that might be interested in taking over First RepublicBank of Dallas. Seidman was dealing himself a new hand from the deck he owned and marked.

McColl blamed himself. His petulance had provoked a response bitterly different from the one he'd hoped for. He'd succeeded in forcing quick action all right. McColl had pushed Seidman to invite in new players, bigger players. As soon as he let them in on the big tax advantage—the one that NCNB's Hartman had sniffed out and that would likely be a done deal before long, now that NCNB had worked its butt off for a month to make it happen—Chase or Citi or Chemical or Wells or BofA would be slicing through Texas like a bowie knife through a porterhouse.

For weeks Jane had been telling him, *Don't be so dang paranoid, Hugh. Quit thinking about losing First Republic to one of those "big boys."* Maybe it was fear all along, that same fear that had kept him awake during their first years of marriage, that underbelly of his macho Southern crust. Finally his fear was justified. Damned FDIC, sending out the signal to every big bank in the world. Ringing the dinner bell and hollering *"Y'all come and get it!"* Texas is served.

McColl was feeling anything but lucky when he, Page and Hartman met for breakfast Monday with the Hong Kong-Shanghai bank directors, but he had to go through the motions. He bragged limply about NCNB's success in regional expansion and how the bank intended to become one of the major forces in U.S. banking. He did not mention Texas or First Republic. Amazingly enough, the Hong Kong bankers seemed to buy it. His audience was energized and interested in what he had to say. McColl felt as though lightning had gone off in the room. Their interest swept up his spirits and swirled his imagination into the Hong Kong-Shanghai bank showering him with all the gold and silver he needed, $200 million to buy his way into Texas. But the schedule called for him to leave that afternoon for Japan, and on the other side of the world, the FDIC was putting First Republic on the auction block.

In Tokyo he had to be careful not to stir the oil specter. It was a listing on Japan's stock exchange he was after here, not funding, Tokyo investors might skitter like Wall Street at the notion of NCNB hunting in Texas. Even without Texas in the mix, Japanese investors projected economic jitters through their relentless smiles. McColl's timing in Tokyo was poor. Prime Minister Nakasone had ordered the Bank of Japan to lower its interest rates, then broken off talks with President Reagan without ever addressing the colossal trade imbalance. Japanese investment brokers considered the moment unpropitious for a moderately successful, capital-lean bank in North Carolina. Careful deliberations were necessary, tedious as tea ceremonies to McColl.

On his second morning in Tokyo, Wednesday, May 18, McColl returned to his hotel room deep in thought following his six o'clock jog in a nearby park. There was a message from Gentry waiting for him. Seidman wanted to talk with McColl. Because of the time difference, McColl was advised to be in his hotel room at ten that night, when the FDIC chief would telephone.

This is it, McColl told himself. *This has to be it.*

After a nerve-wracking and unfulfilling day of Japanese brokerage-hopping, McColl was relaxing with scotch and gin rummy in his room. He had Hartman and Page excited as he was, thinking maybe at last the chairman had blinked. Just after ten the telephone rang. McColl let it ring twice, projecting patience over the ocean. It was merely an FDIC underling, not Seidman himself. Gentry evidently had garbled the message. The underling in Washington said that, yes, Mr. Seidman wished to speak with Mr. McColl, but *this* call was simply for the purpose of setting up a conversation between the two chiefs. Yet again McColl had underestimated the complexities of FDIC protocol. He made an appointment to speak with Seidman when he reached London, the following week.

At that moment McColl wanted badly to be in Washington, to walk into Seidman's office again and this time refuse to leave until he had an answer. He would plant his feet in that Navaho rug. He would snap the head off one of those precious goddamn kachina dolls. Seidman could only be stalling, fishing around in his deck for another card, anything to strengthen his hand. But . . . another delay, another maybe. Time weighed heavily on Hugh McColl and squeezed the power from him. *A man with so much money in his control should not feel powerless.* Yet here he was, half a world away from the hunt that never ended, only dragged on and on. Perhaps he had made the hunt his only purpose, not the bringing down of game.

There were more airplane rides, more gin rummy, more meetings. From the world's investors, there was considerable curiosity about NCNB stock, even interest, but no money was changing hands. In Geneva they met with Salomon Brothers. More curiosity, more maybes. In Paris he felt a tingle of genuine interest from Bruxelles Lambert, a major investment house in Europe keen on strengthening its presence in the United States. At last, with Lambert, McColl might have something positive to take back to his board. Still, it was the telephone call in London he was waiting for. He had trouble concentrating on anything else.

Instead of keeping his appointment, Seidman let McColl chafe for an extra day before placing the call. He was McColl's equal at gamesmanship, perhaps his better. By the time the hotel room telephone rang, McColl and Hartman had resigned themselves to the idea that this would not be the final word they had hoped for.

They were correct. Seidman had been advised by his outside attorneys that he was required by law to follow the bidding procedures of the Competitive Banking Act. That was his reason for calling for bids from other banks. Citibank, Wells Fargo and a management team from First Republic were in the process of getting their proposals together. Seidman assured McColl, however, that he doubted any newcomer's bid would improve on the NCNB proposal as it stood.

That last part was sweet to hear, but not sweet enough. Over the phone lines McColl pressed for an end to the delay. Time was working against the tax benefits, he pleaded. Time was sapping the energy of his management team, the people upon whom the citizens of Texas were going to depend to get their bank out of its hole. And time was surely eroding the confidence of those Texans in their state's economy and banking institutions. How could the FDIC wait any longer?

Be patient, Seidman soothed, the FDIC was moving as quickly as it could. There could be no errors or somewhere down the road the deal might be challenged in court.

"Hell, Mr. Chairman," McColl nearly shouted, "the Allies invaded Europe in less time than you're taking to make up your mind about Texas. We need a date and we need it now."

All right, Seidman sighed. May 31, there was a date. If anybody else brought in a better offer, he would let McColl know by Memorial Day. If McColl had not heard differently by May 31, he should consider NCNB the front runner. That was the best he could do. They would talk again in a few weeks. They would *talk* again. More talk, still no action. In the world according to McColl, he'd be celebrating his new Texas empire by Memorial Day. Yet McColl felt for the first time that his team's efforts really might be rewarded in a very big way.

The Friday of Memorial Day weekend arrived with no word from Washington on the other bidders. A good sign. Hartman reported mounting concern among his group that FDIC director Robert Clarke might be engineering a Texas-based alternative to the North Carolina takeover. A bad sign.

Hartman might be a pessimist, but McColl had to face the facts that Hartman brought to the war room. Texan Vice President George Bush was looking like the heir apparent to Ronald Reagan's presidency. Now all Texas's Republicans were muttering that this rumored failure at their state's biggest bank could put the Out-of-Business brand on every Texan, even Mr. Bush. Hartman's theory was that Robert Clarke was working behind the scenes to hold off action by the FDIC while his handpicked Texas management team at First Republic struggled to mend fences to keep out those North Carolina rustlers. Hartman had another fact for McColl to face. One of the key stockholders in First Republic was Jerry Fronterhouse, a major force in Texas Republican fund raising. NCNB's deal would

hit Texans like Fronterhouse hard, adding the injury of huge investment losses to the insult to their ten-gallon pride.

"What can they do to us?" McColl asked. "Does Clarke believe the
people who caused the problems can really pull themselves up by
their own bootstraps?"

Hartman didn't think so. But he feared that Clarke might force a
delay until after the November presidential election. That at least
would protect the vice president's home base of support. In the mean-
time Clarke's personally selected management team of Al Casey and
company was digging an ever-deepening hole, out of which First
Republic—or NCNB-First Republic—might never be able to climb.
According to Hartman's best information, their big Texas bank had
shrunk by more than a third, down to $26.8 billion, since the two
Dallas banks pooled their resources and their debts. McColl saw the
quarry he had pursued for three months shriveling away as NCNB
looked on helplessly. Yet at least two other banks wanted to get their
hands on First Republic, so there must be something worth waiting for.

Paul Polking reported that the negotiators on the other side of the
FDIC table claimed to be dividing their time among several banks.
"We were at it until three in the morning last week," Polking said,
"and the FDIC people led us to believe they're working just as hard
with two or three other banks and they don't know yet which one of
us is going to be the winner. But you know, Hugh, I'm coming to the
conclusion that there's no way, I mean no way physically, that they
can be spending this kind of time with any other bidder. I am just
positive we are going to get this son of a gun."

Memorial Day brought hamburgers, beer and potato chips, but
no call from Seidman about a bid from Citibank or Wells Fargo that
had theirs beat. To keep his key players focused, McColl gave them a
new target. Fourth of July weekend became "the FDIC's logical
moment to fail First Republic." Maybe, said the ever-glumming
Hartman, but what about Clarke and his Texas bunch? Were they
supposed to just sit around and hope there wouldn't be another delay
while Clarke lobbied against NCNB?

Hartman's pessimism gave McColl an idea. True, Seidman had a
Texan whispering in one ear. What if McColl could put a different
Texas voice in his other ear, singing Nothing Could Be Finer than a
Bank from Carolina? It happened he'd gotten to know a Texan not so
long ago. Fellow at the head table with him at one of those obligatory

high-profile junkets, some event sponsored by the Belk Department Store chain just a couple months back.

"Anybody I know?" asked Hartman.

"Fellow named Ross Perot," his boss smiled.

Hartman was impressed. Henry Ross Perot, Texarkana, Texas, one-time IBM salesman, billionaire at forty after selling his Electronic Data Systems company to General Motors, folk hero status achieved 1979 by launching a private raid on the United States embassy in Tehran. Where the U.S. military failed, Perot had succeeded in rescuing his EDS employees held hostage by the Ayatollah. Hartman had to believe Perot and Hugh McColl were kindred spirits.

"Ross, I'm going to talk to you about something," McColl began the phone call. "You know that First RepublicBank's gone busted?" Perot was forced to admit that he knew that. "Well," said McColl, "we're bidding for it."

Perot's response was the one he had hoped for, high-pitched support. What could he do to help?

McColl began with a side issue, albeit an important one. The merger of InterFirst and Republic Bank had resulted in an intricate and unwieldy hybrid structure. First Republic's operating company was owned not by the bank, as in most large institutions, but by the holding company. It remained an unresolved question how NCNB was going to deal with this management problem. McColl asked Perot if he would first join NCNB's board of directors and then buy the independent operating company in Texas.

Perot declined the offer to become a director. Too many wealthy Texans had become a lot less wealthy of late thanks to their investments in bank stocks. And Perot felt no need to take that risk. Although his sentiments might have been with Al Casey and his group, Perot's logic suggested that McColl and his bank were the best option available for the state of Texas. "I was impressed with the man when I met him. Also, I was impressed with the work his bank was doing with small businesses. I believed that was just what Texas needed to get us out of that recession."

He'd met McColl only once, but on the telephone Perot said he would immediately call Bill Seidman and let him know that he would guarantee NCNB's Texas bid, in the amount of $210 to $240 million. Perot believed that if he didn't agree to back McColl, "hundreds of thousands of people in Texas could be adversely impacted. How many people do you know who'd put up $240 million of their own money for a fellow they'd only met one time?"

Seidman, who at the time thought of himself as "sort of a combination garbage man-IRS agent-undertaker," was not surprised that the Texas billionaire would throw his support to McColl. "I thought it was pretty typical of Ross. He told me the state and the country needed this to happen." Perot also agreed to intercede on McColl's behalf with Texas senator Lloyd Benson, "who could kill the deal if he wanted to."

The next day, June 10, McColl reported his good news when the task force gathered in the war room. The jubilation over Perot's support was exceeded only by the roar of delight at Tim Hartman's report. Finally, the IRS had ruled in their favor. They could take the big tax write-off on the bad loans in Texas.

There were cheers all around. McColl broke out a bottle of expensive Japanese liquor he had picked up at the Tokyo airport. The IRS was going to let them use First Republic's losses to offset what they assumed were going to be future profits for NCNB. That was going to mean a lot down the road, and it ought to sweeten the FDIC pot by at least a billion dollars right now.

"Let's move on Texas," McColl said.

The first advance would be the responsibility of the Cooley-Martin-McGee team. Based on the Florida experience, they would set up telephones, office space and temporary accommodations around the state for the two-hundred-plus NCNB people who would have to be airlifted in as soon as the FDIC accepted their bid. McColl just told the team to do it. Only after the fact would he learn how it got done.

This time there really was a major security concern. Rather than chance being spotted, they called in one of Martin's old college friends, Tom Drew, from Durham, North Carolina, who had served as finance director of the Democratic National Committee in the failed 1984 election bid of Walter Mondale and Geraldine Ferraro. Martin knew Drew had strong connections in Texas. After swearing a blood oath to secrecy, Drew began renting hotel rooms, sixty in Dallas alone, fifteen thousand square feet of office space, hundreds of thousands of dollars in communications equipment. He paid for it all with his NCNB VISA card, its customary five-thousand-dollar limit increased to one hundred thousand dollars, zeroed out as needed.

The task force believed it would be necessary to send an NCNB officer to every one of First Republic's two hundred branch banks and offices, including its one overseas office in Singapore. Chuck Cooley's index cards became the building blocks of a complex organization chart of 250 NCNB names, including 50 reserves, all "warm, friendly, extroverted, sales-oriented" men and women, grouped in teams headed by senior vice presidents. With the presumed "D day" only three weeks off, these group leaders were placed on alert every Wednesday, anticipating that the FDIC would make its move to close First Republic on a Friday afternoon.

McColl could walk through his bank and feel the tensions rise as the end of each week approached. Friday afternoons the task force and a steadily building auxiliary would sit in the war room, waiting for a call from the FDIC that wouldn't come, ordering out for dinner, hoping Seidman's people were working late in Washington. McColl kept reminding his team they were the only game in town, that it was only a matter of time. But around the conference table he saw eyebrows raised and shoulders shrugged, knowing glances and smirks when they thought he wasn't looking. He could feel the mood shifting again. Maybe Seidman actually felt cornered by Hugh McColl. Maybe Tim Hartman was singing the true blues this time, about Seidman and his people just dragging and dragging until they found a better game.

The paranoia hit the fan when Hartman stormed into McColl's office and handed him his resignation. Cooley had showed Hartman his scotch-taped and thumb-tacked organization chart—which had been drawn up for the purposes of communications planning, not post-takeover operations of "NCNB Texas."

"You've got me reporting to Buddy Kemp," he raged. "After all the work I've done for you on this deal."

Unaccustomed to being the calm in a storm, McColl assured Hartman that he was mistaken. This was nothing but a communications flowchart, showing who would give information to whom, just to make sure the information was shared. But Hartman insisted McColl was using Cooley to float the idea of a post-merger pecking order. This could only be viewed as a demotion for Hartman. McColl again told Hartman he was mistaken. True, Buddy Kemp would be giving up his job as president of NCNB Corporation to head up the Texas operations, but Hartman would report, as always, directly to the CEO.

"You cannot resign," he said, tearing up the envelope without opening it. He explained that he had brought Buddy Kemp into the picture because "he is the best business manager and the best leader that we have. The best banker, clearly the best one. And I felt he could command respect and turn the ship around, Tim. Buddy's job will be to run the banking side of the business, and yours will be to run the FDIC side, the operations in all the legal and credit side. I have to have you and I have to have Buddy. I need you both."

Soothed, Hartman returned to Washington, where he hoped the IRS resolution would lead to a quick wrap-up with the FDIC.

Not only his closest advisors, but McColl himself was feeling the tension of the long, clandestine operation, so focused on the Texas deal he could think of nothing else. For days at a time he would disappear from the bank or else just sit in his office and wait for the telephone to ring. The role he had written for himself was the most difficult he'd ever played. The seat of his chair was a pincushion. He fretted about his organization, brooded like Hartman about his own future in it. If the First Republic deal fell through, he was dancing his last dance. And yet, when he drove home to Colville Road at the end of the day, he felt sure Texas was unquestionably the opportunity of Hugh McColl's lifetime. He talked about the opportunity with Jane, who could coddle his fears back into excitement.

"This will separate NCNB from our competition," he told her. "I mean, all that is in the water. It could be an upper-deck homerun." Jane never got lost in the swirling metaphors of his emotions. "It will allow us to escape this Berlin Wall we built, Jane, this Southeast Banking Compact thing. And escaping is tremendously important to me. You know what really happened to us when we missed out on First Atlanta? People started to figure that they can just say no to me, and there's nothing I can do about it. But if this deal goes through, Texas could be our launching pad to expand across the nation."

Jane McColl understood the implications. Her husband had invested so much emotional energy into the Texas project that, if it failed, he might never completely get back to what he was before. Neither, perhaps, would his bank. She'd never seen Hugh walk so fine a line between euphoria and despair. He was spending more and more time at home, too preoccupied with Texas to manage the day-to-day affairs of NCNB. He trusted his people at the bank, went to them for business advice, but when it came to Hugh McColl the man, the only advisor he had was the girl from York County he'd chased around Europe the summer of '59. Telephone calls came in at all hours and Jane always hoped for the best, braced for the worst. She heard the frustration in his voice when, as usual, there was no news at all.

The phone even rang at the retreat they owned now on the shores of Lake Norman. "Fort Defiance," McColl dubbed it. June 17, Friday afternoon, he ended his weekly letdown early, beating the rush-hour traffic up to the lake. On the drive he confessed to Jane that he was not really looking forward to the combination birthday-Father's Day weekend, even with the kids there. He woke up Saturday morning with a premonition of déjà-vu disaster: three years ago his birthday had been ruined by the newspaper account of Wachovia's capture of First Atlanta. Now when Jane handed him the telephone and he heard FDIC director C. C. Hope's voice on the line, his heart sank. *They've turned us down.*

Instead, Hope was phoning in reassurance. He gave McColl a signal that the FDIC was "getting close." It was not beyond the realm of possibility, Hope said, that the FDIC would come to a decision "as early as June 24." McColl sensed that Seidman had assigned his Charlotte connection to keep the fish on the line. "Hope springs eternal," he told Jane, winking at his own bad joke. "Let's have a birthday party."

June 24 turned out to be just another Friday disappointment, but the Independence Day weekend was up next. Another three-day weekend, perfect for a bank failure. Surely Friday, July 1, would be the day they'd been waiting for these four months. Then, on Thursday, the last day of June, Hartman and Baldwin Tuttle told McColl to hit the brakes. Their sources in Washington claimed the FDIC was working overtime, but would not be ready for a closing on Friday. This time, their information called it "a sure bet" that First Republic would be failed the following Friday, July 8. "All right then," said McColl, "I'm sending in the troops. We can't wait on these fucking bureaucrats any longer."

On Wednesday, July 6, McColl put his entire transition team on alert. McGee, Cooley and Martin called in the group leaders and went over the organization charts. Names of people who happened to be on vacation were crossed out and replaced from the list of fifty standbys. The group leaders began calling each of the two hundred transition team members, telling them to bring packed suitcases to the office the next morning and be ready to leave town for a week.

"Don't ask any questions. Don't tell anybody where you're going." Those were the orders Alex Sink got from Ken Lewis. She hung up the phone in Miami, brimming over with excitement, knowing she was part of something very big and very secret. Even her husband, Bill McBride, couldn't be told.

Late Wednesday afternoon, McColl got word that Seidman had learned of his plan to airlift two-hundred-plus NCNB people to Texas. He went straight to Cooley's office for a consultation. "The FDIC is really upset with us, Chuck. They say this is too presumptive on our part and they don't want us to do it. What do you think?"

Cooley frowned, leaned back, tugged at his lower lip.

McColl sat down. "Well, what's the worst case?"

"The worst case," said Cooley, "is that we have people who have been taken away from their jobs for a couple of days. They are disappointed that whatever this was, it didn't come across. But they are going to be so excited about being asked to do something like this that the thrill is going to last them for a long, long time."

McColl smiled. "They are going to appreciate being asked."

"So the worst case is that we're going to spend fifty grand or so and we're going to have people who are excited about being picked. At least we take a shot at it. And if it does turn out to be D day, then we're rolling, and we've done it the right way."

"So, you think we should go against the wishes of the FDIC?"

Cooley did not hesitate. "Yes I do," he answered. "I think we ought to pull the trigger and maybe have to tell a lot of people to have another Pearl Beer and spend the night in a Texas hotel and come on home."

The responsibility was not Cooley's, McColl knew, but his own. If he was wrong, there would be consequences with the board, far worse than anything Cooley imagined. Directors like A. L. Ellis could use embarrassment like a torpedo. But this was the responsibility he'd worked for since 1957. "Okay, let's do it," McColl agreed. "Damn the torpedoes. Full speed ahead."

The following day, Thursday, Joe Martin was planning a mock news conference, a rehearsal for the press barrage he anticipated once they took over in Dallas. McColl, Hartman and Kemp face video cameras and take telephone questions from "out-of-town reporters." All the questions would come from Martin's staff, prepped with both accurate and bogus information. McColl, Hartman and Kemp stayed up all night Wednesday readying their answers.

The next morning the plot took an unexpected twist. For four months NCNB had kept the outside world in the dark as to what was really going on in Texas. Now the Thursday *Wall Street Journal* was quoting Citicorp chairman John S. Reed to the effect that his bank was one of two "principal bidders" for First RepublicBank, the other being Charlotte's NCNB.

The cat was finally out of the bag, and the first response was the one Hugh McColl had feared the most from the very beginning: NCNB stock began falling and continued falling all day. NCNB executives walked into their offices in North Carolina, South Carolina and Florida that morning with bags packed. By afternoon many of them had heard rumors about Texas, but still no one had called to tell them officially where they were supposed to be going, if this was the week to go. They could not talk about it with their coworkers and their only orders were to have their suitcases with them again on Friday. This could hardly be good internal relations. Externally, it was worse. By the close of business Thursday NCNB stock was down 62.5 cents.

Friday, a pall settled on the NCNB Tower at Trade and Tryon Streets. Around the war room conference table, the best guess was that Citicorp would not have made its intentions clear unless Reed had a signal from Seidman that he was getting First Republic. The big New York bank must have won and could not resist rubbing the little Southern bank's nose in its own sniffly self-importance. The normal end-of-week anxiety turned into deep depression. After such hard work, to lose on the final lap was a disappointment that sucked the air out of the team. After all the planning, the packed bags, the media rehearsal, this would not be their D day. McColl was slouched in a chair in Cooley's office when he got word that someone from the FDIC was on the line. McColl's frayed nerves jangled.

It was one of the FDIC lawyers, Ross Delson. He told McColl he was notifying NCNB—and all the other Texas bidders—that it would be another thirty days before they reached a decision on First Republic. McColl flew into a rage. "Fuck you!" he screamed at Delson. "You're just jacking us around and I'm not going to be jacked around anymore."

McColl slammed down the receiver and caught his breath before he spoke to Cooley. "They have delayed us out of this game," he said. "They've got other people who are coming into the game. We're out of it. Turn in the troops. We're not going to Texas."

Cooley threw his red "XYZ" binder across the office and papers went flying. He had tears in his eyes and only expletives on his lips. Cooley was a gentle man, but he felt like hitting someone. They would have to let Joe Martin's people know about the decision. Heads bowed, they took the stairs up one flight to the twenty-fourth floor and found the communications team gathered together in a conference room, waiting for pizza to be delivered. "We are out of the game," McColl said in a sober voice. "Joe, tell everybody to stand down."

There were audible sobs. One communications staffer, Mary Waller, came up to McColl and told him she had never believed it was right for a woman to hug her boss, but this was the moment to make an exception. She still had her arms around the chairman when a telephone rang.

"S-someone from the FDIC," a voice whispered, handing the receiver to McColl.

McColl recognized once again the voice of C. C. Hope, the man assigned to keep Hugh McColl on the hook. Hope told McColl that Seidman was "affected by the strength of your response." He begged McColl to stay in the chase, assured him that his efforts would not go unrewarded, despite the possible thirty-day delay. McColl set down the receiver and told the others what he'd heard.

"They blinked!" Cooley shouted. "The fuckers blinked!"

Incredibly, the blink lasted yet another three weeks. The FDIC negotiators insisted on more information, more meetings, before they could make the unretractable decision to fail First Republic and create a partnership between the FDIC and NCNB. McColl breathed deeply, willed himself to be patient. After all, he had people like McGee, Cooley, Martin, Hartman, Kemp—all self-motivated, action-oriented decision makers—Seidman had government lawyers, Washington bureaucracy. He had codirector Robert Clarke, delaying at every turn, protesting that the Comptroller of the Currency needed more time, that his office had never closed more than six individual bank corporations in one day and in Texas he would be failing forty banks in sixty-three communities, the way First Republic was set up. *Ain't life a bitch*, thought Hugh McColl. *Get on with it.*

In Charlotte, McColl no longer had to practice media confrontation; now he had real live reporters to deal with. Thanks to Citicorp's leak, both Wall Street and Tryon Street were buzzing with rumor and commentary on NCNB's bold-slash-foolhardy move. "Texas-Sized Gamble," blared the Charlotte *Observer's* front-page headline. Analysts everywhere turned grim-reaper cards and read ominous risk in their morning entrails. NCNB was rashly betting the ranch that the Lone Star economy had bottomed out. Hugh McColl's bank was just not big enough to swallow First Republic's bad loans. NCNB should concentrate on birds in the hand, closer to home.

McColl gave terse interviews, read most of the lengthy speculation. "If they knew about your IRS ruling," he told Tim Hartman on the phone, "maybe all those analysts and reporters might be giving this story a different slant." But the G Reorganization was still a secret.

In the last week of July, Hartman's Washington team told McColl that the deal seemed to be wrapped up at last. There was nothing official, nothing in writing, but the FDIC would be doing the partnership deal with NCNB. McColl decided, with secrecy no longer an issue, to gather his entire transition team in Charlotte for the charge into Texas. He personally wanted to be in Dallas when Seidman delivered First Republic.

The evening of Wednesday, July 27, Hugh told Jane he'd be sleeping in Texas for the next few nights. He told her about his plans for rallying the troops the next morning and they came up with the perfect dramatic touch. Where were those big horns that Willy Korf had sent him as a thank-you when the bank rescued his Beaumont steel mill back in '71? Jane knew exactly where they were, down in the basement. Hugh had to go right down there and bring them up. They'd be perfect. He wrapped them up in a couple of big garbage bags and got Jane to drive right down to the bank so he could get them set up before anyone came into the auditorium the next morning.

On Thursday afternoon, July 28, Adelaide Sink found a seat in the charged, chattering conference room on the twelfth floor of the NCNB Tower in Charlotte. She'd caught the first flight up from Miami and checked into the Marriott next door, only to learn she'd be flying out again that evening. Sink's luggage would be picked up in the bank's lobby and would be waiting for her in a hotel room, location undisclosed. People from the North Carolina bank told her they were glad to see her, hadn't spoken to her since her wedding. So many old friends from the National Division, the New York office, everywhere, and it would be good to catch up with them, but not now. Right now she couldn't wait to find out what in heaven's name was going on. As she sat down, she opened the bright NCNB-red ring binder that had her name on the front. It held 146 pages of detailed instructions. There was an airline ticket for Dallas in the front pocket, along with a hotel reservation and a confidentiality pledge she was supposed to sign and turn in. There was a name tag inscribed "Alex Sink, NCNB Texas National Bank."

So it is Texas. Sink had worked Texas for NCNB in the mid-'70s. Texas, Oklahoma, Kansas, Arizona, Colorado. Just selling loans to the big companies out west. She had wondered what it would be like to work for a bank out there. Looked like she was about to find out.

At 3:00 P.M., McColl stepped out to the applause of 217 NCNB officers. He stood behind his Korf Industries Texas longhorn steer horns, mounted on the front of a lectern. He wore a ten-gallon white cowboy hat.

"Ladies and gentlemen," McColl began. "We are going to Texas!"

For an hour and forty-five minutes the transition team sat through a briefing and inspirational messages from McColl, Kemp and Cooley. Just as rush hour arrived, they were loaded on buses at Charlotte's busiest intersection for their ride to the airport. No one from the media took notice.

Thursday night McColl and his key team members gathered in their command center, room 2207 of the Dallas Sheraton, less than a block from First Republic's headquarters. McColl studied the plan of the First Republic Building that Tom Drew had for him. It showed the route he should follow from the main entrance to CEO Al Casey's office, so he would not have to stop and ask for instructions. Beer and booze were flowing, but McColl was taking it easy. Alex Sink wasn't drinking at all because, though nobody else but her husband knew, she was pregnant. Her assignment would be in Tyler, just outside Dallas, so she found herself welcome in the command center.

Sink sat against a wall, away from the chalkboards and corkboards and telephone banks. She felt wonderfully inconspicuous, a rare thing in the career of a woman in an overwhelmingly male industry whose customers were 95 percent male, and almost always the hormones flowing because there were big macho deals going on and because all these men had to let each other know they were man enough to recognize Alex Sink as the Company Knockout. Here she was, early enough in her pregnancy that it added nothing to her shape, casually stunning in her shorts and golf shirt, hair down, and nobody's eyes on her. Nobody's. They were all looking just where she was looking, at Hugh McColl. He was Clint Eastwood in a saloon of supporting players. Where else could you look?

McColl paced, prowled, consulted, complained. He sweated bullets, changed shirts twice. "Get Hartman on the phone." *I'm in a movie,* Alex Sink thought. *I am in a movie.* "San Antonio? I don't see our people in San Antonio yet. I don't want to hear about goddamn airline schedules."

Phones rang incessantly. Through the night, transition team members reported in from across the state once big enough to be its own country. One by one, red dots got stuck on a wall map of Texas, over green dots indicating a First Republic branch, meaning the local assault team was in place. McColl stared at the map with a growing sense of awe at the sheer size of what they were attempting to pull off. When First Republic failed, NCNB would be managing branches in every corner of this enormous Texas, instantly the largest bank in the largest of the contiguous states. Red dots stuck up everywhere. Texas was a land mass twice the size of North Carolina, South Carolina and Florida *put together.* Add up all the people in both Carolinas and you'd have only about half the population of Texas.

The red dots kept going up. Since some branches were in towns located long automobile drives from the nearest airport, the last call did not come in until 2:30 A.M. All the green dots were covered. A little while after that McColl went to his room and slept, hoping the next telephone voice he heard would be that of William Seidman.

The call did not come until Friday, July 29, 1988, at 6:10 P.M. Central Daylight Time.

It was C. C. Hope, who immediately put his chairman on the line. "Mr. McColl," said Seidman, "we have decided to go with you."

William Seidman knew well what he was saying. He understood his decision would ultimately affect every individual in the United States who keeps his money in a bank, uses a credit card, makes a loan or pays a check.

Hugh McColl knew his dancing days were only just beginning.

"You choose me as an enemy, you get me as an enemy."

Hugh McColl
Interview with the author, April 1998

CHAPTER 12

In the week that began at 6:30, the evening of July 29, 1988, Hugh McColl compiled enough memories to fill most business executives' entire careers.

There was that moment of sublime justification when McColl, unrecognized, approached the surrendering generals in their plush, Gainsborough-hung command post. Tall, bespectacled Al Casey, patrician as Addison Reese, brought in by Bill Seidman and Robert Clarke at a salary of six hundred grand with another four-fifty signing bonus, at the center of his frightened disciples, like an asp arched to strike, hissing: *"Who is he?"* McColl wanting to say, but resisting: *"I'm the son of a bitch who's about to throw you out."*

There was the Sheraton lobby, jammed with reporters when he got back, and Ross Perot joining him in the glare of their Frezzi lights and sun-guns, Perot telling the world Hugh McColl and his bank were heroes for saving Texas, then the frantic rushing-out of television people in time to make their ten o'clock news.

There were the breathless telephone calls—to Storrs, to Jim Thompson, to his fraternity brother Paxson Glenn who lived in Dallas now and who knew how good NCNB was going to be for Texas, and to some of the key NCNB people now in place around Texas—but forgetting *(How in the* hell *did he forget . . . Hell to pay for forgetting*) to call Jane, who had taken all those middle-of-the-night calls for him and held his hand and soothed him to sleep.

There was the first meeting of NCNB Texas, one-thirty in the morning, after the FDIC had finally failed all the First Republic branches around the state. Chairman Buddy Kemp, vice chairman Tim Hartman. Jim Berry would go to Houston as senior banking exec. Rusty Rainey, personnel, in charge of the merger, sworn to prevent the Florida fiasco from reoccurring in Texas.

There was the 3:00 A.M. party at Love Field, champagne as Hartman and Baldwin Tuttle flew in from Washington, McColl now in the "Don't Mess with Texas" T-shirt his aide-de-camp intern John Hill had come up with. All over the highways, those signs, like "Keep Out," like "No Girls Allowed," threat implicit. To McColl, at this moment, the slogan meant, *"We messed with 'em. Now we'll save 'em."* And back at the hotel, the party continued.

McColl had about a half-hour sleep that morning, aroused by room service to a steak-and-eggs Texas breakfast and a Saturday Dallas *Morning News* headline that was better than Alka-Seltzer. There were McColl and Perot grinning like the Winston Cup winner and his crew chief. There was Perot saying: "Tomorrow we start rebuilding Texas."

Well, they wouldn't be needing any new buildings to do the rebuilding. McColl, Kemp and Hartman took a quick look around their posh new office space—four skyscrapers in Dallas alone, two each built by Republic Bank and InterFirst, including the seventy-two-story green pickle and a fifty-story headquarters building. In Florida they'd had to design their own lighthouse.

Somewhere, in one of those buildings, he remembered to phone Jane in Charlotte. She called him a jack-leg for not phoning her last night. She had to find out about it from Jim Kiser's wife, Nancy, and then Toni Hartman called because of course Tim had remembered to call *his* wife, but Toni was at their Litchfield-by-the-Sea condo with her mother and couldn't get any news on TV at the beach, so Jane had switched it on and turned up the volume real loud so Toni could hear it over the phone, and now Tom Roboz had sent Hugh over this *humongous* bottle of champagne, almost as big as she was, and she'd got somebody to haul it into a bathtub for her and go buy a bunch of bags of ice at the Circle-K, because by God she wasn't going to wait for him to get home to drink it. "I'm gonna get right on the phone and get some of the girls from the bank whose husbands are all down there in Dallas celebrating to come over here and *we'll* celebrate."

Jane had more to tell him, but he had to cut her short, because First Republic's Dallas people were expecting to meet him at noon.

Al Casey had called in a couple hundred of his top executives for an emotional farewell-and-hail ceremony in First Republic's headquarters auditorium. Casey led off and McColl could hear the bitterness in his quivering voice, letting his people know he believed he'd been set up and ultimately spurned by Seidman and his FDIC. Casey clearly thought that, instead of handing over his sword to these people from Charlotte, he should be standing on this stage explaining how he had just saved Texas. He'd had it all lined up, with Drexel Burnham Lambert and Michael Milken, the "junk bond king" under investigation by the SEC. Milken had the deal worked out that would have put the government's white hats on him and Al Casey, and salvaged the investment for First Republic's stockholders to boot. But Seidman turned him down, claiming he, Seidman, was "trying to solve the problem at the lowest cost possible to our limited resources," and that meant McColl and his *deus-ex*-IRS. When Seidman called him that morning to apologize, to sell him on the idea that he did what he thought was right, Casey told the chairman of the FDIC to get lost. Now, after assuring the First Republic executives that he was their "good friend and one who enjoys you and who wants to stay in touch," Casey left the hall to a standing ovation, then turned at the door and tossed a hand grenade into the crowd: "Get your résumés up to date."

Damn. McColl couldn't believe it. The one thing he couldn't stand, after all their careful preparation, was a repeat of the Florida personnel exodus. There was no way his Charlotte bank could replace the people in this auditorium, let alone all the officers at all the First Republic branches.

No script, no notes, McColl started talking. He explained that he had brought in one or two persons for each branch, just to help the managers through the transition. As soon as the dust settled, the Carolina and Florida people had their own jobs to do and would be out of Texas in short order. The NCNB Texas permanent contingent, he said, consisted pretty much of the people they saw in the auditorium, minus him, because as much as he might like the place, he had a wife who preferred Carolina barbecue to Texas-style.

"What we need is you and your teammates," he said, and no matter how bad the economy might seem in their state right now, Hugh

McColl and NCNB wouldn't be here unless he believed it was going to start getting better real soon.

Buddy Kemp picked up on the theme. Most of the North Carolina transition team would be out of their hair—and Kemp was bald—by Tuesday. "We're going to run our own bank here in Texas and Hugh's going to fuss at us if we don't." McColl scribbled a note to himself: "Don't Mess with Texas" would become official policy in Charlotte. He'd get John Hill to buy those T-shirts for all the senior staff.

Questions came from the floor as the ex-First Republic executives loosened up. What would their legal lending limit be, come Monday? McColl fielded it on one hop. "About $280 million on top of what you could lend on Friday."

Should they be aggressive lenders in spite of the miserable Texas economy? "We turned the bank around at one o'clock last night," Kemp barked. "You won't find anybody who likes to do business more than I do."

Was NCNB really as tigerish as the media reported? McColl got into his role. "That's true. I don't like my competitors. I don't eat with them." If another bank got business that by rights should have been NCNB's business "that's like taking bread off my children's table." He wanted to see his kind of aggressiveness at every branch in Texas, as of Monday. "I want you to come out attacking. That's what I want, walking tall."

Now he was primed for his news conference back at the Sheraton, the one Joe Martin and his people had rehearsed him for back in Charlotte. No merger like this had ever happened in American banking, and news assignment editors around the world were whipping each other into a frenzy to cover the story. The AP, UPI and Reuters wires all were plugging the news conference. (It didn't hurt that this was a Saturday and nothing ever happened on a Saturday.) All around the walls of the hotel meeting room, past the bobbing heads and fluttering palms of reporters, past the tripod-mounted cameras and popping flashguns, Hugh McColl saw his friends. Joe Martin was there. There were Bill McGee, Chuck Cooley, Pat Hinson, Paul Polking, Bob Kirby, Pat Phillips, Judy Bratton. Baldwin Tuttle, Alex Sink . . . and, hell, there was Pax Glenn, his fraternity brother. McColl couldn't help grinning when he looked at all those winners, arms crossed every one, trying to be inconspicuous with their thumbs-up and victory Vs.

"We are excited to be in Texas," he started, and quickly cut to the heart of it. "The biggest change is: there's going to be money available at NCNB Texas National Bank. The first thing you're going to notice is that we're going to be back on *offense*. People who are quite capable bankers are going to be out there lending money again."

And here was Ross Perot again, stepping up to the microphone, something no one could have rehearsed. "First thing Monday morning," Perot promised McColl in front of the world, "I'll be putting my money in NCNB Texas."

"And we'll be expanding the vault," McColl shot back. Even the reporters laughed.

Perot wanted the world to know Texas was about to "turn a corner," now that NCNB Texas was here. "Those small- and medium-sized businesses that are starved for financial lubrication are going to get it." That was the secret of Hugh McColl's success, Perot told the press, "grinding it out the hard way by making thousands of loans to medium-sized businesses." McColl spoke his gratitude in words he would later put in writing to Perot: "Without your confidence and support, I don't know that we would have been successfuk in entering Texas."

Ross Perot's caricature was one of the hundreds on the walls of the Dallas Palm Restaurant, where some of the hungrier NCNB invaders wound up for dinner Saturday night. They were wondering how long it would take before Hugh McColl's mug went up, or maybe Buddy Kemp's, when the first bottle of champagne arrived, compliments of Big-D business people who were mighty pleased to welcome them to the Lone Star State. Above the bar, the TV news was on and there was Perot telling Texas that there was no finer banker in the USA than his friend Hugh McColl. Then came the next bottle of champagne, and the next. By dessert, grateful Dallas diners had contributed a half-dozen bottles of bubbly to Sunday morning's hangovers at the Sheraton.

Back in Charlotte, Jane McColl was deftly tilting Tom Roboz's ten-gallon bottle into a large iced tea pitcher, which she carried from the bathroom to the women gathered in front of the TV set in the family den. She poured it into her best crystal glasses and passed it out to Debbie Phillips, Pat's wife, who was there with a cast on her foot, to Bonnie Cooley and Sarah Gentry, to Ginger Kemp, who lived right around the corner, to Nancy Kiser and Jane Berry, to Donna Covington, Bill's wife. Then she poured a glass for herself.

"We are going to toast to those who also serve and sit and wait," she said, raising her glass to cheers, then sipping with the others. "Say, you know, this stuff tastes right nice. You wouldn't think they'd put up good champagne in that big old huge thing. Girls, we are going to have a grand time and we are going to finish that bottle, because I'll be damned if I want anything left in there when Hugh gets home. I want to show him an empty bottle in that bathtub." She toasted herself again.

Hugh McColl was with the troops at the Cadillac Bar & Grill, standing on a table with his best friend in the company, Buddy Kemp, toasting him with some exotic tequila drink that had to be set on fire before you could drink it. Alex Sink wished this could have happened a few months earlier, before the baby came along, so she could have tried one of those flaming margarita concoctions, but this much excitement made even a club soda taste heady. Working for Hugh McColl was more fun than she'd ever imagined business could be.

Stories were told that night that would take on mythic status, like corporate Norse legends to be retold around flaming margarita goblets and sterno-blazing pu-pu platters and mountain lodge fireplaces until Valhalla went up in smoke.

Ken Lewis would relate the one about his ride around Dallas suburbs that afternoon, learning he was to be yanked out of Florida to run the Texas operations. Watching the For Sale signs slide by on verdant mansion lawns, McColl chortles of the fabulous real estate bargains awaiting his teammates in the economic wasteland: "Look at that one, Ken. You know, people here have been sliding down into a depression. I'll bet you can get that house for six hundred thousand now." "What?" Lewis is astonished. Even the house behind the house doesn't look like it would sell for six hundred thousand dollars. But he memorizes the number and calls the realtor from the hotel. "I understand the price may be depressed," Lewis tells the woman on the telephone, trying not to sound too eager. And the realtor answers, "You're exactly right. This house has not sold and we have just reduced the price to only $6 million. May I make an appointment for you to come and take a look, Mr. Lewis?" And Lewis cannot wait to see the boss that night and set him straight, and when he does, McColl shakes his head. "You know, these are just about the goddamn richest broke people I have ever seen."

If you could hear Bob Kirby over the country-western din in the Cadillac Bar & Grill, you'd hear him relate the tale of his new assignment, direct from Hugh McColl, the man he nearly didn't hire back in 1959. "And so Hugh says, 'Ken's gonna come out here and Buddy's gonna come out here and Hartman is going to stay out here. But I want you to replace Ken in Florida.' And, hey, I haven't thought about that at all. I figured maybe I would be running Trust, 'cause don't tell anybody but I'm fifty-eight years old, not planning on moving any more. But sure enough I said, 'I guess I'd better call Jackie?' And he says, 'Hell, no, Jackie's gonna want whatever you want, you know that.' He had a little beard on, you know, and that 'Don't Mess with Texas' T-shirt. He was hungover. I was too, but I had on a suit, a coat and tie. So he says, 'Bob, I'm not going to have much time to spend in Florida and I need to put it into somebody's hands that I trust.' I said, 'How long have I got to stay?' He said, 'Ah, I don't know. Talk about that later.' I said, 'When do you want me to go?' He said, 'Well, the board's meeting Tuesday morning. I'll send our vice chairman, Jim Thompson, down there to ensconce you as president in Florida. So you go whenever you want to.' And I'm thinking, *Right. As long as it's between now and Tuesday morning.* Then he said, 'Now, Bob, there's one thing I forgot to tell you.' You know how he talks. 'Just one thing I forgot to tell you.' I said, 'Well, what's that, Mr. Chairman?' And he said, 'I want you to know I'm giving you a bigger bank than Storrs gave *me* when I became CEO, so don't screw it up.'"

And if you could hear that punch line above the country music at the Cadillac, you'd be sure to laugh over Kirby's final "Yes, sir."

Nobody partied harder that weekend than Francis "Buddy" Kemp, leading candidate for Mister Nice Guy of NCNB Corporation and most-likely-to-succeed Hugh McColl as CEO in the year 2000. Veteran of the mid-seventies workouts, rescuer of Luther Hodges's North Carolina Banking Group I in the early eighties, Kemp had hit the wall at age forty-five. His father died in his mid-forties of heart failure and Kemp raised his blood pressure over worry that he would follow in the family tradition. As it turned out, he was right, but after quadruple bypass surgery and a quick recovery in 1985, he was walking three miles a day and convinced he had dodged the bullet. Kemp would be fifty soon, out of what he thought of as his inherited danger zone.

Buddy Kemp was like McColl in his adrenaline-rush approach to the stickiest, trickiest banking deals and in his ability to inspire and

motivate. McColl actually considered Kemp his superior in organizing and attending to details. After all, Kemp was a Harvard Business
School graduate, in the mold of Tom Storrs. McColl was ready to
turn over Texas to him and let Kirby take charge of Florida while he
went looking for new worlds to conquer.

But McColl did not intend to consign his key people to distant, disregarded outposts, like Roman commanders forgotten in Gaul and
Carthage. He gathered his generals to reassure them of their ultimate
rewards. "I don't want you, or any of our people for that matter, but
especially this group, to have to stay around here till you're sixty-five
and go away with a pitiful little pension." Bob Kirby felt a warm glow
as he heard the chairman say, "I want you to go away with something
in your pockets. If you make me look good, I'm going to see to that. I
want everybody that works here to be special and to be treated special."

There would be twenty-one NCNB executives assigned to Texas,
not to replace the culture but to seed it. Chuck Cooley confirmed
what McColl already knew: wholesale replacement was not an
option. The Eastern bank would fall apart if the bulk of its leadership
was lopped off and sent West. It would be up to the twenty-one—"a
mountain of talent," McColl mused, "a hell of a team"—twenty-one
who might never return to North Carolina, to convert the Texans to
their new corporate culture.

"Given all of the problems of this state," Cooley told McColl, "the
people we're taking over from First Republic are here either because
they have no other choice, or because they have so much pride that
they're going to stay around just to make sure it comes out right."
McColl knew it would not take long for Cooley, Hartman, Lewis and
Kemp to separate deadwood from firebrands. At any rate, that would
be their job, not his, because he had to start raising money to pay for
Texas. Sunday afternoon McColl flew to New York where he would
explain it all to Wall Street Monday morning. His future and his company's would be riding on Wall Street's thumbs, and it was his job to
make them turn up.

He left his bags and aide-de-camp John Hill at the bank's apartment on East Sixty-first Street, then taxied uptown to his son's place.
Hugh McColl III was a twenty-eight-year-old investment accounts
manager for Bear Stearns. His sister, Jane, was there with him. Twenty
years old now, Jane was between semesters at the University of North
Carolina and working as an *au-pair* for a family in nearby Bronxville.

She happened to be spending Sunday with Hugh in the city, so McColl took them both to dinner at Juanita's, a Mexican restaurant on the Manhattan's Upper East Side.

The night was hot, the beer cold, the salsa spicy, almost as though he'd never left Dallas. This was the first telling of the Texas tales, and to share them with his children meant a lot. Hugh, the investment banker, wanted to hear all about the Deal and its details. Jane, the risk taker, wanted to be swept up in her father's emotional high.

McColl was prouder of his children that evening than of anything he'd accomplished in Dallas. Hugh had his B.A. from Carolina, his M.B.A. from Virginia, three years of traveling for Manufacturers Hanover around the Midwest. His father's son. And now Hugh was getting on in the investment world. Jane was aggressive, tough, a girl who sat around hunting camps in her long underwear playing poker with her father and brothers and other men, taking them all to the cleaners, taking them to the tune of twenty-four hundred dollars one November night on the South Carolina coast. Wiry little Jane, more spunk than sense, her father's daughter, hauled her own trunks up to Oldfields Prep, north of Baltimore. Now she was working summers, plowing through her courses at Chapel Hill. Looking after three young children would teach her things about life and responsibility, McColl suspected, better than anything they could teach her at UNC.

They're sharing my adventure, he thought. *Everybody excited about it as I am, high fiving and hugging. Jane can get way up. She's got those McColl genes, those manic genes. She's skying. The people who really love you are your family. That's what makes moments of triumph so extraordinary, being with people who genuinely, honestly share your joy, people who can hear you talk deeply about it and never be uncomfortable, people who will never judge your right to that joy.*

They sat at a small table, drank Mexican coffee, talked into the night. At the end, because Jane had to catch the last train to Bronxville, they left Juanita's, hugging and kissing, even the men, because in the McColl family everyone kissed everyone else, and in New York they weren't sure how that would look but they wouldn't let that stop them. At Eighty-sixth Street the father kissed his children one last time, turned left and walked down Park Avenue into the bright hot night. His running shoes stuck to the pavement, his jeans stuck to his legs, but he would feel it all only in his memory. He needed sleep because he hadn't slept but maybe ninety minutes in three days and, his mind still spinning in the wonder of it all, he wasn't sure when he'd sleep again. Even the simple arithmetic of blocks-to-go eluded him. Twenty? Forty?

"Only $210 million. The price is right," McColl told a Monday morning ballroom packed with investment analysts at the Intercontinental Hotel. "We have walled off the credit risk, and the rewards are substantial." The analysts' eyes dewed with wonder, their smiles broadened as he reminded them how well NCNB stock was doing, thanks to its good management of acquired banks in Florida, South Carolina and elsewhere, asked them to imagine for a moment how much more perfectly that stock would have purred along had they bought up all those other banks for such a song. Imagine if they'd had two years' grace to pluck out any questionable loans in Florida. Imagine how delighted their shareholders would be today if, since that first Florida acquisition, NCNB had been holding hands with the FDIC in an unprecedented partnership. Such was "the opportunity presented to us with this investment" in Texas.

McColl borrowed Ross Perot's optimism for the Texas economy, but vowed that even if the state's slump continued, the FDIC's willingness to let them restart the bridge bank without the albatross of First Republic debt all but guaranteed success. "With the burden of today's bad loans removed," he proclaimed, "we are highly confident that we can manage a healthy Texas bank, even through a period of slow economic growth."

Suddenly the notion of a "healthy Texas bank" sounded less like an oxymoron. Analysts bolted to their buy phones just as they had scurried to sell NCNB stock on the black news of 1974. In print, on television, on radio, economic pundits glimpsed brilliance in the deal. Goldman, Sachs & Company sang hosannas: "This marks a new era, in our judgment, for regional expansion." Smith Barney cheered: "Unlike most acquisitions, this will add to earnings per share right away . . . . NCNB got a great deal."

Not that the deal was universally admired. Martin Mayer, writing in *American Banker*, called the FDIC's decision "amateur hour in Texas." The FDIC did not truly understand the problem, Mayer declared, because William Seidman was "only an accountant, after all." Paine Webber cautioned that all the euphoria might be "too much too soon," and Dean Witter soft-pedaled the North Carolina-Texas management shifts and culture blends as "stretching credulity."

But Salomon Brothers pulled out all stops: "This will go down in the annals of bank history as one of the finest transactions ever consummated . . . the right bank, the right people, the right deal."

The deal very nearly collapsed, due to the keen computer eye and unimaginative computer brain of CHIPS, the Clearing House Interbanks Payments System in New York. McColl got the bad news in a frantic telephone call from Tim Hartman.

"They're going to kick First Republic out of the Clearing House," Hartman shrieked. "They won't let us clear up there, because they don't have the net worth."

McColl calmed him down and found out what was wrong. As far as the computer was concerned, First Republic had failed and the Charlotte institution called NCNB was not sufficiently capitalized to cover its own international transactions and First Republic's as well. CHIPS, which cleared all dollar-payments between domestic banks and their counterparts in other countries, was the same computer that had thrown out Germany's failed Bank Herstatt in 1974, just after McColl's Fourth of July rescue operation of NCNB.

Telling Hartman he'd take care of the problem, McColl began with a telephone call to the Clearing House assistant director. He summed up the conversation as follows: "I said, 'What the hell are you talking about? This is owned by the United States Government. What the hell do you mean, it doesn't have any capital line?'" The assistant director's response was less than satisfactory. "I got a chickenshit answer. Got a yik-yak answer, essentially, 'No, we are not going to accommodate you.' It was sort of a New York way of sticking their finger in our eye. It would have made things impossible for us. Literally it would have put the bank the FDIC just saved out of business. It was just people in New York being obtuse."

While CHIPS is operated by the New York Clearing House Association, its accounts are maintained at the Federal Reserve Bank of New York. CHIPS member banks—essentially any large American bank doing business overseas—send and receive large-dollar, time-sensitive payments over the "Fed Wire," which is owned by the Federal Reserve System and the United States Treasury Department. In McColl's mind, one branch of the government, the Fed, was attempting to kill something to which another branch, the FDIC, had just given birth. McColl decided to do something he'd never done before. He put in a call to the man he considered the most powerful individual in the United States,

Federal Reserve Board Chairman Alan Greenspan. To McColl's total disbelief, the chairman took his call immediately.

"Dr. Greenspan, this is Hugh McColl. I'm—"

The chairman politely cut him off. "I know who you are."

"Well, I've got a problem." McColl explained the situation, careful not to tell Greenspan what he *really* thought of his New York clearinghouse people. Then he said, "I need your help. I need you to get them to not throw us out of the Clearing House. We have to be able to clear or we can't run the bank."

"I don't think I can tell them to do that," Greenspan replied.

"No, sir," said McColl, like a quarterback calling an audible play at the line of scrimmage, "I understand that you can't tell them to do it. But you all have had no problem explaining to me when you wanted me to do something that you wanted me to do it. So I assume you all can handle this one the same way."

Greenspan laughed. "I'll see what I can do."

In a matter of hours, the problem was solved. That came as no surprise to McColl. What did surprise him was that this "most powerful individual in the United States" knew his name and, obviously, understood that NCNB was his most important ally in a period of crisis for the nation's banking system.

Unaware of the backstage confusion, Wall Street rose to its feet and cheered. Before Texas, McColl's company's stock had hovered around eighteen dollars. On the first day of trading after the merger, NCNB common closed at twenty-five dollars. McColl immediately went to market with convertible preferred shares and placed them at thirty-five dollars, raising $250 million. He set the wheels in motion for another private sale, to be held in the spring of 1989, of subordinated notes, which held a lower claim on the bank's assets than either common or preferred stock, and anticipated raising another hundred million or so from those. Tim Hartman issued NCNB Texas certificates of deposit and marketed them nationally through Merrill Lynch. All the national publicity over the Texas rescue triggered the investment equivalent of a ticker-tape parade and CD orders rained down from everywhere. In just six weeks, people bought more than $1 billion in CDs, by the end of the year, more than $4 billion.

In the fourth quarter of 1988 McColl saw "money pouring in over the barricades in earnings." The Texas strategy, he told his executive committee, was going "like gangbusters." He looked at the foreign investors, the Australians, the Japanese, the Hong Kong bankers, the Swiss, the French, the British—the ones who had listened politely and then rejected him during his long struggle to bake the Texas deal into something sweet—and McColl felt a bit like the Little Red Hen. Now they all wanted to do their part, whatever friend Hugh wanted. But outside help was no longer required. NCNB could manage to eat its cake alone, thank you very much.

On November 22, Frank Gentry put up $210 million of NCNB's money for 20 percent ownership of NCNB Texas National Bank, still considered a "bridge bank" under terms of the agreement. The FDIC put up $840 million for its 80 percent, with NCNB receiving an exclusive option to buy out the FDIC at any time within the next five years.

Reflecting on what his team had accomplished in Texas, Hugh McColl told Joe Martin, "Sometimes we lapse and are not at our best, but this time we were at our best. There is a bonding that took place among the people who all made it happen. There is very little our people will be faced with in the future that will be as challenging as what we did here. Reputations were made here. We operated seven days a week. We developed a team in the Texas deal who, given just forty-eight hours, can do due-diligence, who can analyze contracts, look at leases, look at credit, look at *everything*, not just loans. We learned and we learned to trust each other. We trusted the lawyers to do their thing, we trusted the logistics people to do their thing, we trusted the corporate communications group to do theirs."

The man who had made his career by feeling his way, always hands-on, now understood he must take his hands off. Whatever happened in the matter of NCNB Texas would be very much the doing of his teammates.

Paul Polking, Baldwin Tuttle and the other attorneys would be putting out fires in Washington, where the House Banking Committee—chaired by Texas Democrat Henry Gonzalez—wanted some quick explaining. Harry Grim, the hired-gun attorney who fought alongside McColl in the workout wars of the seventies, went on the NCNB Texas payroll as general counsel. Tim Hartman would be responsible for finalizing the finances and engineering the cash flow in Texas. Winnowing off the uncollectible loans would fall to a cadre of credit officers headed by Fred Figge II, chairman of NCNB's credit policy, and Bill Kelly of Texas. Ken Lewis was president of the bank, so bringing in the new business and managing the old would fall to him. Over it all, watching the forest along with the seedlings, was NCNB Corporation's heir apparent, Buddy Kemp.

On his first day as Texas chairman, Kemp made a decision that impressed even McColl. He had a yellow rose delivered to all seventeen thousand Texas employees as a gesture of courtship. Project Yellow Rose was as big a hit in Texas as young Hugh McColl's cartful of flowers had been in Jane Spratt's Brussels hotel room. Nearly half the employees sent thank-yous to Kemp, including a florid, yet businesslike card from the trust department of the bank in Lufkin that read: "Just as the Yellow Rose of Texas reaches its full bloom, may our relationship reach full bloom, so that we as individuals and members of a team may encourage the growth of NCNB Texas National Bank. Thank you for the roses."

The sweet scent of success wafted north on every breeze from Dallas. Before the buyout, First Republic had been losing $20 million a month. McColl watched the numbers turn 180 degrees, with NCNB Texas showing a $20-million-a-month profit. He let Hartman and Kemp know they were "doing a fabulous job."

The directors of NCNB thought McColl was doing a pretty fabulous job himself, awarding him bonuses that effectively doubled his $530,000 salary for 1988. As *Fortune* magazine interviewed him for a cover story on 1988's "25 Most Fascinating Business People," McColl became the first North Carolina banker to earn more than a million dollars in one year from his primary employer, salary and bonuses totaling $1,137,500.

Others at the company came in for big raises too as their responsibilities increased. McColl had uprooted twenty-one of his most important people out of their positions in the "eastern bank" and moved them halfway across the country to the "western bank." In Charlotte and Tampa, he had good people to put in their places, but they were completely unprepared for the new jobs they were called upon to fill. One of the most critical repottings was that of Jim Hance, former outside accountant for the bank, who suddenly became CFO of NCNB Corporation. Hance stepped right into Tim Hartman's running shoes, responsible for financing the parent company while Hartman financed NCNB Texas National Bank.

"NCNB Texas National Bank"—the advertising and public relations people began to beg McColl for something better than that.

Yearning to simplify their marketing efforts from Maryland to Florida to Texas, they restated the obvious point that "NCNB" was not the perfect name. "NC" meant "North Carolina" and "NB" meant "National Bank," so in Texas you could call them "North Carolina National Bank Texas National Bank." It was no less absurd in Florida and their other states. The title adopted only reluctantly by Addison Reese a quarter-century earlier had outlived its usefulness. But McColl told Joe Martin to forget it. Changing the name would be like surrendering the flag.

What the chairman wanted was not a new name but a new building. When he found out the Belk family was going to give up on uptown for its department store chain, McColl looked across Trade Street, on the other side of Independence Square, and realized that would be the perfect place to set down a sky castle he'd been painting in his imagination. Something tall, elegant, reminiscent of the Empire State Building. It could have a crown on top, the king building of the Queen City. It could house an arts complex, too, a way to keep the city alive at night in spite of the Belks' pullout. It could have restaurants and shops and places for people to gather, much the way London's multi-use districts worked. His company had grown enough already to fill big dreams. Besides, Ed Crutchfield had just announced that First Union would be putting up a forty-six-story building. McColl couldn't let himself be one-upped by number two.

As Addison Reese had done in 1971, McColl called his top executives together and shared with them his vision. He laughed at himself, remembering how he'd felt then. *A bigger trophy, a taller flagpole. I'll give you an environmental statement: It's gonna blot out the sun!* "You know, y'all are really gonna have to *want* this thing," he said, remembering Reese's words, "because I'll be gone, and you'll be the ones to have to pay for it." Unanimously, they wanted it.

Jim Berry, Buddy Kemp, Tim Hartman and Jim Thompson were among the teammates who made the decision to move ahead with the plans. Something new and bold: NCNB Corporate Center. Only maybe it would be called the Something-else Corporate Center. "You ramrod it through," McColl told Vice Chairman Jim Thompson. "Let Buddy and me worry about the design, come up with the architect." They settled on Cesar Pelli, whose team got right to work on the project, although they agreed to keep the plans secret for the time being. McColl distracted public attention by spearheading another construction project, a new convention center for the region. He took charge of a committee reporting to Charlotte Mayor Sue Myrick and began looking for ways to finance the center.

He also wanted a way to finance an early purchase of the FDIC's 80 percent of his Texas bank. McColl hated not to be in control of whatever he was involved in. He was the sort of leader who told drivers which route to take, pilots which angle of ascent they should fly, and he wanted to tell Bill Seidman's people when to let go of his bank. NCNB had five years to buy out the FDIC, but in early 1989 McColl asked Jim Hance how soon they could "accelerate our purchase options."

Hance agreed the acceleration made sense, since the buyout was based on net asset value, and therefore would rise in cost over time. To the rest of the financial world, Hance told him, Texas looked like "the third rail of banking," but if the NCNB team could really believe their risk in Texas was minimal, they should also be able to keep Wall Street convinced of that. The worst-case scenario, Hance suggested, was some sort of management foul-up that would cost them the $210 million they had invested in Texas so far. "Operational embarrassment?" Not a chance, McColl assured Hance, not with Kemp, Hartman and Lewis in charge of Texas. In that case, the two agreed, the sooner NCNB could own it all, the more profits they could bring in.

Hance believed that even though the company might be able to raise everything it needed simply by selling shares of stock, the bank's current shareholders would be better served if they used their capital on-hand to buy another healthy bank. If the acquired bank was sufficiently large and sufficiently profitable, it would give them a strong enough equity base to buy the rest of Texas with debt rather than with cash. Since Georgia was a relatively well-off Southern state, and since NCNB still had no branches of substance there, it might be a good time to reconsider Atlanta.

Hance's argument made sense to McColl for two reasons. For one thing, First Union was reportedly close to a deal to buy Florida National in Jacksonville, the bank McColl had sweated blood over, the bank that had spit in his eye after he negotiated the deal with the Venezuelans. He didn't want Ed Crutchfield to savor that success without tasting just a little bitterness along with it. For another thing, NCNB could afford it. In the space of one year, NCNB stock had doubled in value, up to $35.50 a share. His company was stronger than he had seen it since he started work in 1959. McColl believed it was time to march on Atlanta again, and this time he had no doubt he would win.

In early March 1989, as First Union prepared to announce its Florida acquisition, McColl got on the phone with Craig Wall in Conway, South Carolina. The two old friends started talking about the biggest, most prestigious bank in Georgia, C&S. An Atlanta acquisition like that would put Wachovia's First Atlanta merger in the category of small potatoes. Wall liked the sound of it. He had been a director of C&S for the past three years, ever since the Southeast Banking Compact opened the doors for Georgia banks to do business in South Carolina. Wall observed that he was not typical of C&S directors in his warm embrace of Hugh McColl. However, he agreed to pursue the idea, quietly, in Atlanta while McColl did the same in Charlotte.

Hootie Johnson, intimate with C&S operations in South Carolina, led the executive committee in support of McColl approaching C&S. "We were excited about the prospect. And we encouraged Hugh to pursue it."

McColl's senior executives agreed. Frank Gentry, who sat in on the executive committee meeting, said that of all the acquisitions NCNB could have pursued, C&S looked to be "the best fit." When he went over the map of the eastern seaboard with McColl—who had begun collecting maps—Gentry saw that the C&S acquisition "would help us in Florida, would help us in South Carolina, would make us number one in Georgia. There was no other bank that would have been a better fit for us than C&S. So that should be our number-one target."

The target, Citizens & Southern Bank, started out in Savannah, Georgia, in 1887, the New South family enterprise of Mills B. Lane. One of Lane's sons took over the Georgia operations and eventually moved its headquarters to Atlanta, where it became the city's leading bank. Another Lane son started up his own Citizens & Southern bank in Charleston, South Carolina, later relocating to Columbia.

When the states ratified the Southeast Compact, nearly a century after its founding, aggressive C&S Georgia moved quickly into Florida, acquiring one of the early rejecters of NCNB's advances, Landmark Bank Corporation. The following year, 1986, C&S Georgia married its sister, Citizens & Southern Banks of South Carolina.

Among the South Carolina executives who found themselves working for C&S Atlanta was Hugh McColl's brother Jimmy, who became chief financial officer of the South Carolina banks. One of the three South Carolina bank directors given seats on the Atlanta corporation's board was Craig Wall.

By 1989, C&S was a three-state bank with $21 billion in assets. Its chief executive was sixty-year-old Bennett A. Brown, tall, loping, jut-jawed vestige of the Palmetto State's gentleman-planter class. Like Hugh McColl, Brown started out as a correspondent banker in South Carolina in the 1960s. In those early days the two crossed paths and swords on occasion, but for the most part their rivalry was distant and friendly. Twenty-five years later, CEOs McColl and Brown were seen sharing the occasional drink at a monetary conference or waving to one other on the Litchfield beach, where Bennett and Mary Alice Brown owned a house and Hugh and Jane McColl now owned a three-story townhouse condominium. Craig Wall—sole owner of the Litchfield house once shared by the Walls, McColls and Hodges—suggested a meeting at the beach between the CEOs of NCNB and C&S.

Bennett Brown guessed exactly what Craig Wall had in mind. Only recently some analyst had mouthed off in the *Wall Street Journal* that his bank was ripe for a merger, perhaps with the Virginia-Tennessee holding company known as Sovran. Brown wasn't interested in merging with anyone. He told Wall, politely but coldly, no thanks.

McColl was puzzled. Much had been made in the financial press of NCNB's delicious solvency, how it could buy anything it wanted in the South. Didn't Bennett Brown understand that? Could it be his fellow traveler on the Lowcountry backroads was feeling resentment, even fear?

McColl's board was summoned to a meeting on the last Thursday of March. The topic for their consideration would be a possible merger between NCNB and C&S, to create the nation's sixth-largest banking company. Certain he could convince Bennett Brown, he sent him a special delivery letter, helping him understand what a natural fit their two banks would be. Brown's answer came two days later. It was short and negative.

March 30, with his board scheduled to meet in only a few hours, McColl telephoned Brown from the privacy of his office. Mindful of the mistakes he'd made with First Atlanta, he put on his most cordial voice. *"Don't tell him you're going to buy his bank,"* Jim Hance had warned him. *"You ever think how it feels to have somebody tell you he's going to buy your company?"* He wouldn't make that mistake. Gently, McColl let Brown know that NCNB was too far along this road to drop its pursuit of C&S and turn back. Surely Bennett had to see this was a match made in heaven. But, if Bennett was just going to keep on stonewalling, the NCNB board might have to be told the people in Atlanta were thumbing their blue noses at Charlotte. And that could result in someone's nose getting bloody. Brown told him to "do what you have to do."

In the board room, what McColl had to do was both simple and easy. He had to get his board to approve the biggest buyout in all the history of banking. He began by informing the board that their success in fund-raising would allow them to buy up another chunk of the Texas bank from the FDIC, bringing the NCNB ownership to 40 percent or more. The directors applauded that news. After his success in Texas, McColl could do no wrong. The directors then gave their enthusiastic approval to the Atlanta deal proposed by McColl, Hance and Gentry. It would be a stock swap, 1.075 NCNB shares for one C&S common share, nearly 62 million of which were outstanding. Altogether the deal was worth about $2.4 billion. The offer was drafted in a letter from Hugh McColl to Bennett Brown and copied to key C&S directors and stockholders, so that they would all know the offer was on the table. The C&S annual meeting was scheduled in just two weeks, and McColl hoped Brown would allow him to present the offer formally at that time. To make sure the letters reached their targets quickly, young NCNB associates from Charlotte would be assigned to deliver them in person.

Disregarding the lessons he should have learned from Florida and Texas, McColl was attempting to do a deal without pulling together his full team of advisors. With cash and brass supplying firepower, he neglected to call on his brain-power. Chuck Cooley knew nothing about the plan to buy C&S until he received a call that afternoon from Lynn Drury, a junior public relations executive recently transferred from the Columbia office. Drury announced she had been instructed by Mr. McColl to direct the messenger service. She needed Cooley to assign people to her immediately, and to assist her in getting the home addresses of the C&S directors and drafting the letter. When Cooley balked at the timetable, Drury informed him that Mr. McColl had told her to "attack and win." She needed those people now. Cooley considered her attitude "snippy," but he did drop everything to assemble the message and the messengers.

Craig Wall got his letter by hand-delivery about 10:30 that night in a Durham hotel room, where he was spending the night before a physical next morning at Duke University Medical Center. Wall wondered whether any other director was going to share his enthusiasm over the offer from Charlotte.

At the Brown home in Atlanta, the doorbell rang shortly before eleven. Bennett Brown's youngest daughter answered the door and told the person outside he could not come in because her father was already in bed.

"Well, it is really important I see him," said the voice from the doorstep. "I'm here representing NCNB."

Upstairs, the girl pushed open her parents' bedroom door and said there was "a gentleman from NCNB" with an urgent message for her father.

"Is he short with a big grin on his face?" Brown rumbled.

"Short, yes."

"Well, it's got to be Hugh McColl. Tell him I'll be down."

It was a young man named Tommy Shealy, not McColl, but to Brown it was the first shot of the war. Suddenly, the antique-encrusted C&S executive offices took on the aura of a command HQ. In downtown Atlanta the good guys were "Peachtree," the bad guys "Tarheel." Brown brought in one of the highest-paid and best-known anti-takeover lawyers in the country, Rodgin Cohen of New York's Salomon Cromwell firm, and put him in charge of the counterattack. Cohen put Brown before a video camera so he could speak to his officers in three states, letting them know he was in charge of the company and that they had nothing to worry about. He told them they were fighting for a heavenly cause against the hellion known as Hugh McColl, and, just in case they hadn't heard of McColl, Brown would tell them all about their enemy.

One of these videotapes was delivered to James McColl, who was personally injured by the attack on his older brother. Jim offered to resign, since his company held a McColl in such low esteem. But he was persuaded to stay. No one at C&S would bring up the hostile takeover in Jimmy's presence or "say anything bad about Hugh around me. They were very circumspect." The brothers agreed to have no contact until the issue was settled.

Bennett Brown, Southern gentleman, was less evasive in his

interviews with the local, regional and national media. "I like Mr. McColl," he told the *Wall Street Journal*. "I just don't want to do business with him." To *Business Atlanta* he warned that any city that permitted itself to parlay with the ruthless and terrible McColl could expect to be treated ruthlessly and terribly. "If anybody thinks he's going to change, then they don't know Hugh McColl," he said. While McColl persisted in telling the media the NCNB offer was "friendly," Brown called it "uninvited and undesired."

To protect its flank against C&S's anti-takeover attorney, NCNB called on the services of Ed Herlihy, from Wachtel, Lipton, Rosen & Katz in New York. Herlihy, who had helped the bank in Florida and again in Texas, looked at the numbers and the history, then told McColl, "You can win this fight." That was all the encouragement McColl needed. He had started out friendly enough, going through Craig Wall, asking for a nonthreatening meeting at the beach. It was Bennett Brown who'd turned it into a gunfight. Now he had lawyers telling him it was a fight he could win, because in all likelihood C&S would roll over if he persisted.

"Let's go for it," McColl ordered.

Thursday, April 13, with the current *Business Week* featuring his smiling face in its annual "25 Executives to Watch" story, Hugh McColl took his case to Atlanta. He was not invited to the annual stockholders meeting, five days hence, but he would be available to anyone from C&S who wanted to understand the virtues of the NCNB offer. Around the country, McColl's message was delivered to the CFOs of fifty-two institutional shareholders—companies and pension funds that owned at least one hundred thousand shares of C&S. Ultimately, McColl believed, both banking and investing were about money. C&S and NCNB could make more money together than either or both of them could make separately. With the nation's economy facing an uncertain future, this would be money in the bank for every C&S shareholder, right now and in the future, and, as McColl was fond of observing, "cash has no enemies."

It seemed, however, that Hugh McColl had an enemy in Bennett Brown. Even the Charlotte *Observer* began taking gentleman banker Brown's side against the "aggressive" Charlotte "ex-marine" and his "expansionist" bank. McColl was knocked for a loop when he read the morning paper. "They're painting us as the bad guys," he told Jane. "This is our hometown paper. What about how important the banking business is for this city? What about rooting for the home team?" McColl telephoned *Observer* publisher Rolfe Neill, the former business editor, but got nowhere.

In South Carolina, the most influential newspaper looked at the two expatriate native sons and came down on the side of Brown. Should McColl succeed in his buyout bid, the Columbia *State* editorialized, "the strong likelihood is that this state would lose more than it would gain . . . . Any merger would reduce decision-making capability at the local level."

The C&S shareholders met April 18 in Atlanta, with only one of the opposing armies represented in the hall. Reporting on the meeting, the *Observer* called Bennett Brown, "a preacher whipping up his congregation," who "drew sustained applause from nearly seven hundred shareholders by personally taking to task NCNB Corp.'s chairman." April 19, readers throughout the region had their eggs, grits and coffee with such anti-McColl rhetoric as: "The people of Savannah, of Macon, of Augusta absolutely resent Hugh McColl saying he did not want to go down every pig path in Georgia."

Brown got that ammunition right out of McColl's hometown paper. After hearing the "pig path" line from a Miami reporter who remembered it from four years earlier, the *Observer*'s banking writer published it as though it had come from a news conference. No matter that McColl remembered the remark as the tail end of an informal hotel-room conversation, over drinks, after badgering by the reporter about whether NCNB would go chasing down a lot of one-branch banks in rural hamlets of the Southeast. "Every little pig path in Georgia," he explained to anyone who'd listen, was a South Carolina expression from McColl's childhood. Never had he intended it as an insult to Georgians.

Bennett Brown, well coached by Rodgin Cohen, made repeated references to McColl's telephone call the afternoon he presented his C&S buyout proposal to the NCNB board. According to Brown, McColl had responded to rejection of his offer by saying, "You've got three hours to answer or I will launch my missiles." That was unmistakably a declaration of war, Brown said.

McColl had no witnesses, but he halfheartedly denied the remark. "I was thinking about sending letters to Bennett's directors," McColl told his team, working up a smile. "I must have said we'd be launching our *missives*. Somebody must have been taping our conversation and, what with my accent, they got it wrong. Maybe that word's not in their vocabulary in Georgia." Another slur, perhaps, but no reporter around to report it.

At Brown's impassioned urging, the C&S directors rejected the NCNB proposal. The $2.4 billion of NCNB stock was "clearly inadequate" and involved "a substantial amount of speculation" that the stock value would hold up, despite the huge risk NCNB had taken on in Texas. McColl immediately told Brown his bank was prepared to make a "substantial price increase." But C&S attorneys said no NCNB offer could amount to a hill of beans; there were too many unanswered legal questions, surrounding NCNB's relationship with the FDIC in Texas, that prevented their board from accepting, even if a majority of shareholders wanted to do the deal.

McColl offered to make Bennett Brown chairman of the merged bank, but Brown observed that McColl would insist on staying around as CEO, and the chief executive would always call the shots.

C&S president Robert Royall, CEO of the South Carolina bank and another Marine Corps veteran, went on the attack. "C&S is not for sale, has not been for sale and will not be for sale," said Royall. The *Observer* and the Atlanta *Constitution*, once cooperating midwives in the birth of the New South, now egged on the combatants. "Bloody Battle" headlines lured readers into lurid prose. It now was a "bruising takeover fight," with "arrogant assumptions" and "both barrels blazing." Accusations from both sides grew "increasingly nasty."

C&S put together a coalition of Southeastern banks united in their fear and loathing of NCNB in general and Hugh McColl in particular. Among these banks were Sovran of Virginia, Maryland National and, inevitably, Wachovia. The banks' lobbyists and lawyers carved out a piece of legislation, to be cosponsored by the senators of Georgia and five senators from other Southeastern states. It did not make matters easier for fireman-choirboy Joe Martin that the leader of the anti-NCNB bomber squadron was his friend from college, Georgia Senator Wyche Fowler.

The Fowler amendment to the banking law would make it illegal for any "acquisitor bank" to use a "government assistance program" to purchase other banks. In plain language, NCNB would not be allowed to use its IRS-assisted Texas profits to buy a tax-paying bank like C&S. McColl told NCNB lobbyist Mark Leggett to hire any help he needed to kill the Senate bill. Leggett promised he would get the job done. McColl swore he would get even with the other bankers who were "sticking their noses into our fight."

Behind the scenes, it was nastier than either the *Observer* or the *Constitution* editorial writers imagined. As the anti-McColl coalition gelled, word went out from Maryland National that they were considering ending their relationship with investment counselor Bear Stearns, as long as any son of Hugh McColl worked there. This was all too personal for the McColls. Jane especially was angry that anyone would try to hurt her son. She expected this would cost "Little Hugh" his job.

Jane McColl felt snubbed by so-called friends, who read the things the papers printed and yet did nothing to console her. "They don't call," she complained to Hugh. "They just want to stay out of it. They are just damn glad it's not their husband, I'm sure." Then there were those who felt obliged to make a wisecrack when they saw her. *"Well, that man of yours sure is marchin' through Georgia, Jane."*

It got worse. Personally damaging rumors about McColl and his family began circulating through anonymous phone calls. Chuck Cooley, as empathetic as anyone on the NCNB team, felt a degree of anguish. "It's an old labor-union tactic," Cooley told his friend and chairman. "They want this to cause so much pain for you and your family that you'll just back off."

"I'm worried about what they might try next," McColl said. "Maybe I'm getting paranoid." Cooley tried to bring a laugh with a line he'd used before. "Just because you are paranoid doesn't mean that they aren't trying to get you."

"Yeah, I can deal with paranoid," McColl said, "but this other stuff, this is not fair play."

Cooley knew he was right. He also understood that C&S felt cornered. Bennett Brown probably never instructed his people to play dirty; he just told them to do whatever they had to do to beat Hugh McColl. And, once again, McColl was beaten in his quest for a bank in Atlanta.

Friday, April 21, exactly three weeks and one day after he fired the first shot at C&S with his "missiles" or "missives," McColl sat down in the NCNB board room with Tom Storrs, Hootie Johnson, Ed Herlihy and Herlihy's boss. Marty Lipton had flown in from New York after an anxious telephone conference, to explain his firm's reasons for changing its recommendation. Lipton and Herlihy now advised NCNB to back off.

C&S, Lipton said, had adopted the "classic just-say-no strategy." He said there was still a strong possibility that McColl could force shareholders to vote a second or third time, and in that event he might eventually collect the votes he needed for the buyout. But that tactic would result in such carnage that there would be little company left for NCNB to buy. McColl would be taking over a bank in which everyone from the chairman to the janitorial crew hated him. Whatever "tigers" there might be in C&S would escape before he had a chance to talk them into staying.

McColl bridled at first, accusing his legal advisors of "showing the white feather." Then he admitted they were right. On Monday he would release a brief statement declaring that the bid to buy C&S was withdrawn.

First he had to talk to his teammates. He called them together in the penthouse, the fortieth-floor reception area, the way he did when it was time to pass out congratulations, spread credit around. This time there was only blame and no one to share it. He stood next to Cesar Pelli's drawing of the building-to-be and he smiled. It looked as though he'd be staying right here in Charlotte, putting up this new tower, after all. Maybe Buddy Kemp would get to Atlanta—Buddy or whoever else came after him—but not Hugh McColl.

"Well, this one has not worked," he said. "We have to throw in the towel on this one. But there will be another day and another opportunity somewhere else."

Martin summoned the media so McColl could break the news. He stood in the same penthouse reception area, but the easel with the Pelli drawing was gone and so was the emotion. He kept it simple. "Atlanta is a very important city in America, not just the Southeast. One of my successors will sooner or later try to get into Atlanta." He still had his vision of a national bank, headquartered in Charlotte, but very likely NCNB's next important expansion would be in Texas, and he introduced Buddy Kemp, chairman of NCNB Texas, to tell them all that good and happy news.

In Atlanta, Bennett Brown poured expensive champagne for his team. In the main lobby of the C&S building downtown, a stage was set up, so the victorious Brown could address his cheering workers.

Did Hugh McColl have a company of tigers? Did Hugh McColl feed his executives tiger meat? Brown held up a stuffed toy tiger, choked it ... *"Here's the tiger Hugh McColl!"* ... swung it by the tail above his head ... Did Hugh McColl want to have a little *tête-à-tête* at the beach? ... *"Let's go for a little sail, Mr. Tiger!"* ... The crowd roared. Brown let the tiger go. Somebody caught it. Brown thought there should have been a band playing "Hold That Tiger."

The Carolina beach keeps its winter cool deep into April, especially in the evenings, so you might require a jacket for a walk after supper, or maybe your UNC sweatshirt, which fully half the people in Litchfield owned. On an almost-May weekend you could still enjoy the beach the way it was before it got crowded in the summer, before Craig Wall started building his Litchfield-by-the-Sea "gated community" extravaganza. You could remember how it was when the McColls shared the big house with the Walls and the Hodgeses.

Walking with Hugh, waiting for the stars to come calling, Jane loved to talk about those times, playing Remember When. *Remember when we had our house, and the children were little? All of this was empty, totally empty beach. And we had that one little dirt road through it and it had a little rickety gate? We were down at North Litchfield, and you teaching Little Hugh how to drive on the little dirt road down there. And you and Craig would send the kids through that dirt road alone in the car, even though they weren't supposed to be driving, and then you two would walk to the inn and buy the newspapers, and then bring them back to the house?*

Jane is talking still as they walk, talking about how the beach has changed so much. "You know, Hugh, it is a crime. A quiet, sweet, peaceful little beach, and now everything is . . . ." Jane snaps her fingers in the sand-peppered wind. "They build everything like that. I keep thinking they won't be able to sell something and it will all fall through, you know? I mean, nobody in their right mind would pay so much money for a lot. Hugh, do you think these people know about a hurricane? I mean, look at all these fabulous houses—they are absolutely wonderful. And maybe the hurricane won't hit them, maybe it'll hit our condos, who knows? Anyway, if the hurricane comes, we don't have any more in this condo than one of those lots cost. They are selling those lots for a fortune!"

She is talking to keep his mind off his failure, but she is thinking: *He used to have his sailboat and he loved it. He would stay on that beach all day long. Maybe he's bored with it now. He doesn't like to play golf that much any more, doesn't give two hoots about fishing really, so he doesn't do much when he's here. Doesn't stay like he used to. Hasn't been for a whole week in years.*

Hugh is answering her softly, not his usual argumentative self, squeezing her hand now and then. Jane knows she has to keep the words flowing.

"Did I tell you what my friend Ida told me the other day? She said, 'Jane, what you do is you keep Hugh *normal*.' But she doesn't understand how I can keep you in a good mood down here when we have so many people to stay over at the condominium. I told her, we just do what we can."

Jane is making him think of what family is for. Curiously, out of nowhere, he remembers the time he stood as best man for Sol Salerno.

He was a junior at Bennettsville High when Mr. Salerno came to teach and coach basketball. A good coach, from up north somewhere, New Jersey, Pennsylvania maybe. No family anywhere nearby, so Hugh took him in, treated him like a big brother, even though it was always "Mr. Salerno" or "Coach" on the court. So when Coach Salerno announced he'd be getting married, to the pretty teacher who was the daughter of the Baptist preacher, he asked Happy McColl to be his best man. He'd never been in a wedding before, so Hugh said sure. He'd be a senior by then.

Trouble was, Coach Salerno was not only a Yankee, but a Catholic Yankee, the first Catholic Hugh McColl had ever known. The bride's family disowned her, said they wouldn't go to the wedding at the Catholic Church. It was all in Latin, with lots of candles and genuflecting, and Hugh only half-rehearsed. But that wasn't what he thought about that Saturday afternoon in June 1953, that wasn't the part he didn't understand. What he didn't understand was how a family could desert one of its own, the way that Baptist teacher's family deserted her. He just never could have any use for people like that.

Family was family. It was just like his little brother Jimmy to say he'd resign if Bennett Brown's people had to keep bad-mouthing his big brother Hugh. *Mess with one of us, you have to mess with all of us.*

Point of fact: when it came to size, little-brother Jimmy was the tallest at five-nine, Kenneth in the middle at five-eight, Hugh five-seven in crew socks. But Hugh could outrun either of the others. Only one time he could remember Jimmy beating him, and a good thing, 'cause if he'd caught him it would have meant the other kind of beating. *We're lobbin' corncobs, Jimmy, and you throw a goddamn cottonwood branch at my head. If I catch you . . .* But for once Jimmy ran for his life, two and a half miles before Hugh finally gave up the chase.

Okay to fight among the family. Like that time in front of the entire town, at the baseball field. Jimmy the terror of the Pony League, Hugh home from his freshman year at Chapel Hill, Kenneth a junior in high school and both of them umpiring. And Jimmy comes up to bat in the seventh and this time instead of his usual home run he bounces one off the right field wall and tries to beat the throw into second and Hugh yells, *Yerrrr out!* And bang, slap, Jimmy's up from the dust and throwing punches and Hugh throwing them right back and they're swinging and rolling and staggering over to the track that runs around the field. Now the fans are screaming and cheering on the McColl brothers, half the town there watching, on account of what else is there to do on a July afternoon in Bennettsville? Kenneth decides it's up to him to break it up, so he wraps his arms around big brother and says, "Hugh, you got to stop that." And Hugh says, "You want some, too?" And Kenneth can't resist the dare, so he says, "Why not?" Now it's the two umpires and the homerun king in a rhubarb. It ends in the mean, spiky gravel of the track, with Hugh sliding four or five feet on his back with his two brothers on top of him. And it's not until they're all seated around the dining room table, sweet as three McColl lambs, that Mother lets out the scream. *"Hugh McColl, your back is bleeding through that T-shirt!"* And he says something like, *"Oh, shit,"* and, college boy or no college boy, he is in deep trouble for that, 'cause it was the bad language, even more than the fighting, that drove his mother to distraction. *"You will go to the kitchen, Hugh McColl, and you will wash your mouth out with Octagon soap."*

The last big fight, if he remembers correctly, was the Oldtimers Game at the Bennettsville High gym. He and Ken both in college then, and Jimmy the basketball hero as a senior. The score was lopsided, in favor of the Oldtimers, due partly to the tendency of Hugh and Kenneth to grab their brother any time he made a move toward the basket, thus keeping the varsity score to a minimum. With only one referee, it wasn't hard to get away with a foul. *Lost your cool there, Jimmy. Turned around and popped me good, your own brother. Right many fine punches thrown then. Bloody noses all around. And this time mother in the stands, embarrassed half to death there on the bleachers.*

Through all the fighting, they were family. Fifty-three years into his life, Hugh McColl knows for a fact that family is more important than business, knows that he'd back away from a business fight to protect his family, even when the enemy came at him with lies. His family trusts him, maybe even more than his bank family does.

Only once he'd ever failed his family's trust, forty years ago or more, just a boy telling a boy's lie. Riding in the back seat of his mother's car, heading home after some dress-up occasion, next to Kenneth with Jimmy in the front. Mother said she'd be stopping just a moment at the hospital to call on a sick friend. Three boys waited in the car, waited and waited some more, boys getting hot and restless, getting on each others' nerves, looking for mischief to make. Hugh, oldest but not wisest, took decisive action: leaned over the front seat and blew the horn. *Quiet,* Kenneth said, *that sign there says Hospital Zone No Noise.* But no don't-do-it sign was ever meant for Happy Hugh McColl. He leaned over and let it rip, held his hand down, loved the long *aaawwwnk* of it. Still, the mother failed to appear. No succor for her hungry child. *Aaawwwnk* again. Again. This time it worked. Furious mother slammed the door of her car and demanded the identity of the culprit. "Wasn't me," said Jimmy, truthfully enough, so Hugh got the next line in: "Wasn't me, it was Kenneth." *"Was not, it was Hugh!"* But the first ace played wins, even if it's drawn from a sleeve. Kenneth got a switch cut from the privet hedge.

Only later did Mother investigate further and wring the truth from her oldest son and by then the lie had already done its work, killed the trust. Would the Swiss Family Robinson ever lie against one another? *No, ma'am.* Would John Geste ever bring shame and punishment down upon his brother? *No, ma'am.* Truth, trust, family, Hugh McColl. Be true to these and nothing else will matter. Your family is counting on you.

Jane breaks in on his thoughts.

"You know what I found the other day, Hugh? I found two cookie tins full of sand dollars, in the closet up there in the house, and I thought, 'Oh my god, I wonder how long I've had these.' I had big intentions of doing something, you know, making all this artsy-craftsy stuff. You remember when Hugh's friend from school, Addison May, was down here with us and he would get in the water with his toes and he would find them? I bet you can't find them like that anymore. But we had hundreds of them that summer. And I remember Addison and

Hugh really got into it. Even you. Then your nephew Patrick taught you how to find shark's teeth. I don't for the life of me know how you ever see those little-tiny things."

He answers her, but hardly hears himself above the pounding of memories and regrets in his head, louder than the evening waves coming in.

Kenneth had trundled off to the First National Bank of South Carolina, just like Daddy wanted him to, though Hugh helped him land the job. *Too conservative a company for you, Kenneth, staid as old Wachovia.* Jimmy maybe was better off at C&S, *though you'd have been happier working for me than for Bennett Brown.* All of them, the three brothers, never but one job in their lives, loyal, committed, their companies like extended family to each of them. *Oddballs in a world where people change jobs every six or seven years. Throwbacks.*

And Frances, poor, unhappy Frances. Her nice Roy Covington dead of cancer now, leaving Frances more despondent and guilt-ridden than ever. Her six pregnancies in seven years yielded four children she couldn't deal with. Anti-depressant drugs, washed down with alcohol, the same stuff that made him whoop and sing and dance the shag. She was the depressive, Hugh the manic. Two halves of one malaise.

How talented you are, Frances, how brilliant. Brightest of all the McColls. A writer, she should have been, or a singer, a musician. But she had to embrace the one career she just wasn't cut out for, motherhood. Frances had the other side of her mother, the talent side. The *Saturday Evening Post* published one of her short stories when she was only sixteen. And what was it about? A girl dying at age sixteen. *Why so morbid, Sister Frances, sweet Pal o'mine, brilliant at basketball, beautiful diver, graceful swimmer. Straight-A super woman.* Now she is back in a hospital again: Institutionalized. The word disgusts him. Frances's illness had sapped their mother's strength, defeated her in the end. Years of caring for her daughter had kept the mother from attending to her sons and to her grandchildren. No matter how loud his own horn blew, Hugh could not distract Mother away from the hospital, from sad, lost Frances.

And now his mother is gone, dead one year. He could have used her comfort, because he finds losing very, very hard. Even on the Litchfield beach, even holding Jane's soft hand and hearing the lilt of her Carolina voice above the crush of waves, losing makes him so damned angry.

CHAPTER 13

Truth was, NCNB never did have any missiles to fire at C&S. All the missiles were incoming, and they were coming still. Grenade-slinging, pig-path Hugh McColl might be short in real life, but as a media caricature, he was just too big a target to miss. Once Bennett Brown's skillful public relations people got the coordinates, Joe Martin sighed, "they ruthlessly cut us to shreds in markets where we were most vulnerable—not with Wall Street and the national media, but in the weekly papers on the Main Streets of C&S communities, across Georgia and South Carolina. We had been caught flat-footed, unprepared."

Truth was, Hugh McColl had a right serious image problem.

This came as no surprise to him or to the people at NCNB who'd been working on that image since Tom Storrs's day. Joe Martin had been onto a solution, meeting with legendary New York publicist Roger Ailes in the summer of 1988, when he was diverted to Dallas by the FDIC-First Republic deal. After that experience, with the Texas conquest grandly gushing publicity, like Jane McColl's big bottle of champagne, the NCNB team reckoned it could win the image war without any help.

Former *Observer* reporter Dick Stilley was now in charge of the NCNB publicity artillery, and his staff was fielding story and interview requests from around the world. Thanks to Texas, the NCNB publicists could plant all manner of seeds about McColl. His Marine Corps experience? That wasn't training in grenade lobbing; it was a virtual M.B.A. program in leadership, motivation and team-building. Tired of that two-dimensional, Southern stereotype of McColl? Trade it in for a visionary civic leader, responsible for Charlotte's inner-city revitalization. It was working like a charm, because reporters inevitably walk through open doors and go for fresh meat.

Then came C&S. The Atlanta *opera buffo* constituted a serious setback, but McColl and his team went to work to make sure nothing like that would happen again. "Operation Image" evolved into a joint venture among several divisions at the bank—corporate communications, personnel, government relations, contributions, the Community Reinvestment Act and Community Development Corporation teams—with McColl himself the well-rehearsed on-stage performer. As fall hit the North Carolina Blue Ridge, the turning of Hugh McColl's new leaf began in earnest.

An easily engineered McColl speech to the local Rotary Club, backed by a Stilley news release, stoked headlines across the South: "Our Schools Are Not Good Enough." Overnight, McColl was cast as a champion of public schoolchildren. The bank followed with an unprecedented $2 million commitment to the Southern Regional Education Board for training of educational leadership, then invited all employees to take two hours of paid time per week to volunteer in the schools.

Having achieved positive results with Fourth and Third Wards, NCNB now announced a plan for rebuilding yet another Charlotte central-city neighborhood. Northwest of the Fourth Ward was the century-old Greenville neighborhood, where about a hundred families lived. NCNB proposed to refinance those existing mortgages for renovation and then build another hundred new homes in Greenville. Community reinvestment was central to McColl's belief that a bank could thrive only in a thriving city.

Looking beyond Charlotte, there were newspapers and magazines eager for positive stories on matters dealing with women's rights. Feminism had foundered with the states' refusal to ratify the Equal Rights Amendment in the eighties. By 1989, the target of feminist opportunity had become the so-called "glass ceiling," an invisible yet impenetrable barrier that prevented women from advancing beyond a prescribed level in a traditional corporation. For McColl, and for those who understood him, the culture of growth and aggression at NCNB was no less willing to embrace women than men, providing those women were aggressive and growth-minded. The men who occupied the executive floor of NCNB's Charlotte headquarters wanted the world to know that their company, under the leadership of Hugh McColl, was clearing the way for women to advance to the highest levels of management. They believed this was something they did better than other banks.

But how to *tell* the world? Propaganda concerning aggressive women was a challenge for Dick Stilley and his people to promulgate. They seized on the concepts of "Select Time" and company-supported day care for the children of mothers who worked in the bank. Those were stories they could sell, and true stories. Stories like that would make Hugh McColl feel better about letting the team down in Atlanta.

Perhaps because of the personal battles waged by his mother and sister, McColl had made a personal issue of women's rights. In the "management-by-walking-around" style he had practiced since the sixties, McColl learned first-hand how women would stay with the bank for six to ten years, becoming very good at their jobs, only to leave in their late twenties or thirties to have children. These were not "women" as a class or sociocultural group, but female individuals, people he knew, each with special talents and skills that could be put to work for the betterment of his company. McColl wanted these women to be able to care for their families, but he also wanted them to become high-level executives, and that meant putting in long hours for long years.

Sometimes he found out about situations he could influence directly, like getting Alex Sink transferred from Miami consumer manager to Tampa Bay Region consumer manager, so she could quit dragging her baby through Florida airports three or four times a week because her home now had to be in Tampa with her new husband. Sometimes he could take his "walking around" insights and carve out new company policy. That was how Select Time came about in the fall of 1988. Using Select Time, a working mother could take an extra day off in the middle of the week, or she could come in each day from eight to noon, whatever it took to balance the needs of the home with the needs of the company.

One of the first women to take advantage of Select Time was Trudy Nix in Florida. Once senior management removed the obstacles,

Trudy Nix was able to outproduce several male counterparts, earning the first of what McColl suspected would be many promotions.

At lower-paid levels of the company, the problems of being a working mother were exacerbated by the inflating cost of day care. As the bank's new Corporate Center inched upward on the Square, NCNB announced that in Fourth Ward it would erect another new building, this one to house the program Hugh McColl had growled down in 1973 in his battle for supremacy with Luther Hodges. Sixteen years later, but still way ahead of most American corporations, NCNB would begin providing company-subsidized day care for its employees.

When the bank announced a new low-interest loan program for day-care centers in South Carolina, Joe Martin ordered a photograph of the CEO on a playground jungle gym, surrounded by bright-eyed, smiling children of several races. Martin offered a bounty of two hundred dollars to anybody on the staff who could place that photo on the cover of a magazine or the front page of a newspaper. Editors found the picture so appealing, Martin discovered, "the reverse image of the missile-hurling Hugh," that he "had to pay up more than half a dozen times."

All around the country, Select Time and employee day care made good copy and bore immediate fruit. *Working Mother* magazine sang NCNB's praises in its September issue, ranking the company in the nation's top sixty employers for working women, based on pay, advancement opportunity, benefits and child care support. In its centennial edition, the *Wall Street Journal* selected NCNB as one of sixty-six companies in the United States "positioned for success." According to the report, the bank's most outstanding characteristic was not its breakdown of barriers to interstate banking in Florida and Texas, not its unparalleled performance in the stock market, not even its record-breaking profits. The thing that made Wall Street appreciate the vision of Hugh McColl was his leadership in providing child care. "In essence," reported the *Journal*, "NCNB is addressing productivity by looking at the lives of its employees."

Like the rest of the media, the *Wall Street Journal* missed the real story. McColl wasn't "addressing productivity," he was addressing the needs of the people he cared about. "None of these things was an artifice," Joe Martin insisted. "Hugh actually had all these interests, had always been more multidimensional than he had been seen to be.

And, with his knowledge of the issues in any of these areas, he could hold his own with skeptical reporters. All we had to do was to find—or build—new stages on which he could showcase those interests. The whole Hugh."

Other companies in America were beginning to throw around phrases like "winning through teamwork" and "family of associates," but McColl had been building a team modeled on his own family for nearly thirty years. Building, coaching, managing a team, no different than he'd done at Bennettsville High School. Even more remarkably—perhaps because his childhood "teams" inevitably included his actual brothers, and sometimes his sister—to be a member of McColl's team was to be a member of his family. Occasionally, McColl seemed to take that company-as-family concept to extremes, as when he embraced a prodigal cousin of whom the rest of the family was quite ignorant.

That happened at a meeting of the NCNB construction committee and the associates of architect Cesar Pelli, when everyone was excitedly discussing how the interior lobby of the NCNB Corporate Center was going to look. Windows along Tryon Street, doorways here and here, elevator banks . . .

"I want a fresco," McColl declared, out of nowhere.

"A fresco?" asked Pelli.

"I want a fresco and I want Ben Long to do it." And the family turned as one to its patriarch and asked, "*Who?*" Which launched McColl into his Ben Long Story.

It was all Jane's doing. She was the one who saw the wonderful portrait of Charlie Wickham at her friend Ida Wickham's home and just had to have one like that made of Hugh for his fortieth birthday. The artist was Ben Long, whose studio was in Blowing Rock, in the North Carolina mountains. Long drew in charcoal, painted in oils and, when he could find a commission, created frescoes. Hugh and Jane McColl let Long show them two frescos he and his associates had created on the walls of mountain churches. They learned about the grinding of pigments, the suspension in water, the application to freshly plastered walls. It was like a conversation with Giotto, who seemed to enjoy his whiskey just about as much as Hugh McColl did. Sitting three long days for bearded Ben Long in his dark, drafty studio, talking, eating and drinking for two nights, McColl and the artist developed a deep friendship. And why not? Long had been a combat artist for the Marine Corps in Vietnam.

"We talked about college, the Marine Corps. We talked about art. We talked about North Carolina. We talked about politics. And we found that we shared a lot of views about what some people would think of as soft issues: human rights, suffering. We were instantaneously friends. We made a connection."

The connection was strengthened when the McColls made a trip to Europe and took a long detour through the wine country near Lyon, France, in search of Ben Long and his mobile studio. They found him in a tiny village, in a loft over a cattle pen, living with another artist who also framed Long's paintings. She pleaded with McColl to buy some of them, and he selected four, writing a check for five thousand dollars.

"They were broke as billy goats," smiled McColl. "It was like the Lord had sent us there."

They walked the countryside together, drank wine, ate cheese, talked.

When McColl got back to Charlotte he helped raise money for Ben Long to do a fresco at St. Peter's Church on South Tryon Street. Long and his fellow artists created there a mystic triptych across the entire wall of the chancel. On the left panel is the Agony in the Garden, on the right is Pentecost. The centerpiece depicts the Resurrection: Christ, arms outspread, floating upward, a block of light—perhaps the opened shroud—separating him from the open tomb. The image is cruciform, but without a crucifix—most unusual in a Catholic Church.

Long finished the work on St. Peter's in early 1989, just in time to plan his next triptych. This one would span the nave of Hugh McColl's cathedral, going up just five blocks away.

Several attempts were made to talk McColl out of this somewhat unconventional, even radical approach to lobby art. Perhaps a nice mural—much less expensive. Wouldn't he rather have something that could be moved if he didn't like it? Eventually, McColl settled the issue "like I settle everything. I explained to people that we were going to have a fresco and that Ben Long was going to do it. At which point Joe Martin took over and got it to happen."

To Joe Martin it was all part of the job, repainting Hugh McColl's image to remove the horns and pitchfork. The details of the work were of no small concern, since the fresco would be designed to last upwards of a thousand years. When Long unveiled his preliminary drawings they included a group of business executives. Martin told him the group should not be all white or all male. When Long insisted on including a hooded Ku Klux Klan figure in the central panel crowd scene, Martin nixed it. When Long proposed including images of McColl and his Texas team, Martin's thumb turned down. McColl would have his portrait done for the board room, to hang alongside those of Addison Reese and Tom Storrs. The building itself was going to be a monument to McColl's vision.

The sixty-story NCNB Corporate Center could be billed as "the tallest building in the Southeast," a fitting home for the number one bank in the Southeast. First Union had a new building going up three blocks up South Tryon Street, and down in Atlanta, C&S was celebrating victory with a planned new tower, but NCNB's edifice would top them all. And the Corporate Center would have another distinction. Thanks to a major donation by Herman Blumenthal, one of Charlotte's most generous philanthropists, the building would be home to a new North Carolina performing arts complex, the Blumenthal Center.

When the bank's audiovisual specialist, Betty Ledford, orchestrated the Corporate Center unveiling to newspapers and television stations, she had commissioned a photo-mural of the city skyline, in front of which McColl stood to make the announcement. Computer artists had "enhanced" the photograph with architect Cesar Pelli's lifelike drawing of the new NCNB building towering like Mount Olympus over the minor peaks of the city. To be fair, Ledford made certain to include an equally realistic drawing of the completed First Union headquarters. But, as every artist knows, perception is at the mercy of perspective. Ledford's virtual skyline made Ed Crutchfield's bank seem almost to grovel at the feet of Hugh McColl's. Overnight the publicity gimmick turned into the "official view" of Charlotte—on the television evening news, at the Chamber of Commerce, in the newspaper, everywhere. First Union had the second-tallest building once again, before NCNB's ever came out of the ground.

Joe Martin, Betty Ledford, Dick Stilley—every bow he took, McColl figured he was taking it for some other member of the team. He realized that they were writing the scripts, taking the pictures, orchestrating the score, choreographing the media. Nothing made sense for McColl but to pass on accolades to those members of the family who continued to play well despite his letting them down on C&S. So, everywhere he spoke, he credited the corporation's success to the great job Kemp, Hartman, Lewis and their people were doing down in Texas. It was their handling of the Texas bank, McColl insisted, that was insulating NCNB from the ravages of the national economy.

All around him, lending institutions were screaming like brontosauruses stuck in OPEC's tar pit, but he was safe, untouchable, thanks to his people. Or maybe it was simply because he'd been here before, at the rim of extinction, that Hugh McColl assumed NCNB would live forever. It was the real estate cycle, just like in '73–'74. This time it started in Texas and Oklahoma and Louisiana, where the price of oil and gas had sent real estate prices gushing, then shut them down at the wellhead. And now all of a sudden (only it wasn't all of a sudden at all) the problems that started in Texas were spreading like an oil slick and the entire United States economy was threatened. The Northeast real estate market sounded as bad as the Southeast had been in 1974, and the Bank of New England might be facing a hard winter. Even the big New York banks were in trouble, domestic problems compounded by their uncollectable loans in foreign countries.

Savings and loan companies, which lived and died by the real estate sword, were in worse shape than banks. Forces in Congress wanted the FDIC to absorb the destitute Federal Savings and Loan Insurance Corporation, or FSLIC. President George Herbert Walker Bush—New England aristocrat converted to Texas oilman—signed into law the Financial Institutions Reform and Recovery Act, abolishing the FSLIC and transferring its liabilities to a new agency, the Savings Association Insurance Fund, managed by the FDIC. The Recovery Act—referred to in headlines and on TV news as "the S&L bailout bill"—raised $50 billion to keep some of the S&Ls alive. For the hopeless cases, the FDIC had to find financially sound institutions to take them over.

In Texas, where S&Ls were truly an endangered species, the most financially sound institution was NCNB. McColl cheered as Tim Hartman rounded up lowing S&Ls from Texarkana to Brownsville and put the NCNB brand on them. Their lead attorney in Texas, Harry Grim, had to work nights and weekends to keep up with the volume, accusing Hartman of joining a "thrift of the week club."

In New England, on the West Coast, in the Midwest, banks were going down in flames, but if trouble threatened a Texas bank or a thrift, it was NCNB to the rescue, thanks to its one-of-a-kind deal with the FDIC. If thy bad loan offend thee, pluck it out and placeth it in the special asset division. Give Buddy Kemp a bank with no bad loans and he'd make money all day long. McColl vowed to leave Buddy and Tim and Ken alone, trust them, give them the glory.

"Don't be bothering people down there," he told the rest of the senior executives in Charlotte. "You have no authority to give them an order. Run the damn eastern bank and Don't Mess with Texas."

There was only one thing Hugh McColl could do to help his Texas teammates: buy the rest of the bridge bank for them, ahead of schedule. That would reassure Kemp and Hartman and Lewis of his trust. That would let them see that he believed they would continue to succeed. He gave Frank Gentry and Paul Polking his blessing to go ahead with negotiations in Washington. Working out the deal with the FDIC was their responsibility.

Jim Hance told him he'd need to replenish the capital supply before the bridge bank buyout could be finalized, so McColl let Hance set up presentations to money managers in Boston and New York. Young Hugh's company, Bear Stearns, brought together insurance firms, pension funds and other institutional investors, who were so impressed that NCNB stock jumped immediately to yet another new high. Hance told McColl they would have the capital they needed in short order. McColl trusted Hance, believed he was correct. If there was one thing McColl had done right, he told himself, it was choosing up sides. He had the best goddam team in the business, maybe in any business. Even if he was in a slump, the team could carry him, no matter how rough things got.

Except things were getting a bit too rough.

Buddy Kemp was back in the hospital. There was a tumor in his brain, serious, but operable. McColl was all set to go down to Dallas, to be with Buddy for his surgery, when he got a call from Bennettsville.

It was more bad news, about his childhood friend, Bill Kinney, publisher of the Marlboro *Herald Advocate*. Kinney's only son had driven his car off the road and into a pond where he drowned. McColl got the call late Thursday and left Charlotte at midnight. Driving as fast as he could, he arrived at the Kinney home in Bennettsville an hour later and stayed up with his friend through the night. He and Bill had been close, though they didn't see each other so much these days. After McColl's knee surgery in the marines, Kinney had spent a lot of time at his bedside, back in 1958. They'd been two young men from a little country town, sharing their dreams. They had talked about all the important things, about how Bill would be a doctor and Hugh would be a gentleman farmer and cotton broker. They had talked about the need for friends and the way friends wouldn't let you down.

McColl stayed with the Kinneys through the funeral on Saturday, drove back to Charlotte, flew out Sunday morning to Dallas, where Buddy Kemp would undergo surgery Monday morning.

McColl was there when Kemp went into surgery and he was there when Kemp came out. He was there to celebrate with Buddy the news that the doctors believed they had got rid of the cancer. That was a good thing, McColl said, because he was about to make Buddy a present of the rest of the Texas bank. Soon he'd have 100 percent of it to run and he damned well better get up and run the thing.

McColl flew back to Charlotte in a state of agitation. His plan was for Buddy Kemp to take over when he retired. He had no backup plan.

In Atlanta, Bennett Brown had a backup plan for his bank, and it looked like a pretty good one. Alerted by McColl's bungled attack, Brown recognized that C&S was not really large enough to defend itself against a hostile takeover. He needed to merge with another bank quickly, and he found his partner in Norfolk, Virginia, home of Sovran Financial Corporation. The new bank would call itself Avantor Financial Corporation, "a bank for the '90s" and would maintain dual headquarters in Atlanta and Norfolk. In the Southeast, Avantor would be second only to NCNB, but they hinted of plans that might soon reverse those positions. Every financial analyst on the East Coast understood this was Bennett Brown's way of kicking sand in Hugh McColl's face. By pooling their resources, C&S and Sovran thought to make themselves too big to be bought. Avantor would be McColl-proof.

It was a bitter pill, the swallowing made only slightly easier by reports that both C&S and Sovran were being challenged for failure to lend money in low-income neighborhoods. Paul Polking believed the merger would be delayed for the better part of a year by hearings in Washington, to determine whether one or both of the banks had failed to comply with provisions of the Community Reinvestment Act.

CRA, passed in 1977, was Congress's attempt to keep depositors' money at home, rather than being pumped away to the vaults of distant holding companies. If a bank was deemed to be unresponsive to the loan needs of its hometown, including low-income neighborhoods, it would not be allowed to merge with another bank in some other locale. Polking predicted the Feds would not act on the C&S-Sovran merger any time soon. "They'll be in limbo for a year," he gloated.

Right down the street, First Union had its hands full with challenges from African-American and Hispanic neighborhood groups, complete with protest demonstrators shouting "Stop the loan sharks!" in Charlotte and Jacksonville. The protesters, led by northeastern activist Bruce Marks, wanted the Federal Reserve to deny First Union's application to merge with Florida National, McColl's dream-acquisition in the Sunshine State. That merger, too, would likely be delayed several months, while hearings were held to determine whether First Union was in fact "seriously deficient" in its services to low-income neighborhoods.

McColl actually sat down to meet with Bruce Marks and found he had constructive ideas about low-income lending. Marks had no intention of picketing NCNB. He agreed that initiatives like the low-interest loan program for day-care facilities and the Community Development Corporation's inner-city housing plans put McColl's bank well ahead of Congressional expectations on CRA. McColl was convinced the Fed would give swift approval to an NCNB merger, if there was a bank willing to be merged with Hugh McColl.

For the moment, there was only the remaining piece of the First Republic deal. Frank Gentry, Paul Polking and the Washington attorneys hammered out a final agreement for NCNB to purchase the Texas bridge bank from the FDIC, more than four years ahead of schedule. The contract called for NCNB Corporation to pay $800 million, netting the FDIC a $270 million profit on its investment. NCNB's assets now were around $60 billion, more than double what McColl controlled when he first set eyes on First Republic just eighteen months earlier.

Thanks mostly to the achievements in Texas, 1990 arrived with all the birthmarks of a very good year for NCNB. January–March profits were $140 million, an 85 percent improvement over the same quarter of 1989. Shareholders' applause continued.

Although Buddy Kemp's future with the bank was uncertain, McColl still pinned his hopes on the Texas executive corps. He decided it would be in the bank's best interest to end the "Don't Mess with Texas" strategy and instead allow the people who had done so well down there to "mess" with some other parts of the company. To make this plan work, McColl created a new group called the NCNB General Bank, which would include all consumer banking, credit cards, small- to medium-sized business customers, mortgages and investment management—representing about 70 percent of the company's profits. Since NCNB now owned all of its Texas operation, the methods that had been working in Texas could be fully integrated with the rest of the company.

The General Bank concept grew out of McColl's long conversations with Buddy Kemp in Dallas. There was no getting around the fact that Kemp's health would not permit him to continue in charge of the entire Texas operation. Tim Hartman was vice chairman, but neither McColl nor Kemp felt Hartman was a potential leader for the entire company. Kemp joked that there just were not many people in the country who could be trusted to run their bank the way they wanted it run. Kemp suggested Dick Rosenberg, but McColl pointed out that Rosenberg was already CEO of BankAmerica in San Francisco and probably would not resign that position to be chairman of NCNB Texas.

Within his Texas operation, Buddy Kemp felt he had a good, perhaps even great working relationship with Ken Lewis. In Florida, he had taken his hands off operations and trusted them entirely to Lewis. In Texas, Kemp was confronted by a huge and complex community relations challenge, so he needed someone he could trust completely to manage the organization. Once again, he called on Lewis, a Mississippi-born, Georgia-bred son of a regular army sergeant. To Kemp, Lewis was a capable leader, a strong motivator. Now Kemp and McColl agreed that Lewis was the best person to put in charge of the General Bank.

Immediately, the rumor mill cranked up, from Wall Street to Tryon Street, that forty-three-year-old Lewis was being groomed for CEO. Lewis had "steamed to the head of a pack of talented baby-boom bankers at NCNB," exuberated the *Observer*. McColl marveled at the perspicacity of the pundits, to see so clearly what continued to elude his own vision. If Buddy Kemp did not get well, he really had no idea who, if anyone, in the company was qualified to take over. The more he traveled to Dallas, watching Kemp's condition worsen, the queasier McColl became.

Back in Charlotte, McColl was late arriving at the City Club, where a group of his loan salespeople and managers were gathered. It was supposed to be a cheerleading, backslapping session that would pump up the spirits and let the bankers know it was time to get back to lending money. McColl played his part, congratulating his people and listening to their success stories, but he couldn't hold back his emotion. Without warning, he walked to the center of the room and said: "I need to tell you all something. I've just been with Buddy in Texas and . . . ." McColl's eyes teared up and emotion rose in his throat. ". . . And, he's, he's not going to make it."

Henry Carrison, one of the executives in the room, watched as the supposedly hard-boiled, bellicose marine broke into tears. "Hugh wept openly, unashamedly," said Carrison. "He knew he was among friends who understood, and he was right. There wasn't a dry eye in the room." Carrison turned to a friend and told him, "This is what makes our company different, and great. Our company has heart."

McColl's pain was not purely personal; he grieved also for the future of his bank. He found himself tensing up, particularly in the late afternoon, when the slightest aggravation could tighten his stomach and jangle his nerves. Working into the evening, he would feel his heart palpitating, even get dizzy when he stood up, disoriented. Usually a scotch would get him back on track, but he hated feeling old.

McColl wanted to scream when he got word of Bennett Brown's decision to put an extender on his new building in Atlanta, just so Charlotte would not be able to boast the tallest structure in the southeastern United States. Brown had arranged for his builders to add a 280-foot-high roof and spire to his erection, currently under construction. Charlotte's Taj McColl might have five more floors, but the fifty-five-story Citizens & Southern Plaza at 600 Peachtree Street, would top out at 1,020 feet. C&S's glory would swell 145 feet longer than the Taj. And of course the pundits could not resist the headline, "Mine's Bigger Than Yours."

McColl heard other bankers gaining on him. After nothing but a wrist slap from the Fed on its community reinvestment shortfall, Ed Crutchfield's First Union took over Florida National, out of which McColl still felt cheated. C&S—loved and lost by McColl—survived scrutiny by the Federal Reserve, the Comptroller of the Currency and the FDIC. By summer's end it would be allowed to consummate its McColl-proofing marriage with Sovran of Virginia. Bennett Brown of C&S would be chairman and CEO, Sovran's Dennis Bottorff would be president and chief operating officer. In the course of the year, the "Avantor" name had been dropped in favor of the less mellifluous "C&S/Sovran." The thirteenth largest bank in the nation, operating in six states and the District of Columbia, C&S/Sovran would dominate the Atlanta and Richmond markets.

McColl's publicists found their own numbers to spin. According to *Business Week*, NCNB stock was among the five most valuable in the country. NCNB now was the seventh-largest bank in the nation, with assets of more than $66 billion. Put that together with the $32 billion of First Union—the nation's seventeenth-largest—and Charlotte, North Carolina, was up to fourth place as a seat of banking power. Only New York, San Francisco and Los Angeles controlled more of the nation's money than did the little trading-path town of the Piedmont.

None of that gave McColl nearly as much satisfaction as it should have. It was more fun to bend somebody's ear on the subject of his daughter, just graduated from the University of North Carolina, commencement address delivered by her old man. He drew immense pleasure from passing around snapshots of his new grandbaby, little John Junior, son of John and Lee McColl. *"I'm a goddamn grandfather, if you can believe that! Do I look like a grandfather? Honestly?"*

A grandfather at fifty-five. McColl was not ready to think about a gold watch and a pension. He still could beat out a throw from right field, still could dribble rings around young Hugh and John. He was ready for a physical challenge to prove he yet had it all going for him. When his neighbor, Reitzel Snider, invited him on a little hike in Switzerland, McColl first made sure there was no mountain climbing involved—"Because I'm afraid of heights, Reitzel. Acrophobia. No mountain-climbing, okay?"—and then he told Snider to count him in.

Reitzel Snider was founder and president of Synco, Inc., a very successful REIT, and a member of the Charlotte Athletic Club. McColl figured Snider could be trusted on matters of real estate and physical activities. He lived just around the corner from McColl, which was about the only thing they had in common, other than a passion for competition and for winning. They hammered each other regularly on the Athletic Club racquetball courts.

To get ready for the trip, the two men visited a local outdoor adventure store and bought the very best, most expensive hiking gear they could find. They bravely laced up their boots and broke them in, striding the streets, lanes and sidewalks of Eastover and Myers Park.

On these walks, McColl learned he would be meeting a group of Swiss businessmen who regularly enjoyed outings like this—good contacts for McColl as well as good company. McColl admitted he didn't know too much about Switzerland, except that there were a lot of bankers there. They were to meet the men, Snider told him, in a little town called Wengen, on the Jungfrau.

At 13,667 feet above sea level, about eighty miles southeast of the Swiss capital of Bern, the Jungfrau is one of the highest peaks of the Swiss Alps. About halfway up the Jungfrau is the village of Wengen, one terminus of the *joch,* or pass, through which a traveler may make his way to the other side of the region of the Alps known as the Bernese Oberland. The Jungfraujoch, or "young woman pass," presents a manly challenge to daredevils like McColl and Snider, a glacier of ice covered with snow.

Near the summit of the Jungfrau is a restaurant carved into the side of the mountain, where the less adventurous tourists can sit warm and cozy behind a wide plate glass window to watch the adventurers set out on their transglacial trek. Not more than a dozen steps into that trek—roped to Reitzel Snider, to two large and young and powerfully built Swiss businessmen, and to a tall, steely guide—the CEO of America's seventh-largest bank feels his feet go out from under him and slides on his backside for nearly a hundred feet before the others, being pulled down by his clumsiness, manage to jerk him to a halt. McColl's grin, generally lupine, turns sheepish. The guide says something in German, translated by one of the Swiss businessmen as, "You must step only in his footprints."

One hour later, McColl is still walking, *homo erectus,* gaze glued to the guide's footprints. When he dares glance up, the scene reminds him of what he sometimes sees out the window of his NCNB airplane, a sky thick with cumulus clouds, God's high cotton thick to the horizon. He's wondered more than once what walking on those clouds might be like, and now he has some idea: monochromatic, monotonous and unsettling. Cloud counterpanes, glacier glades, both unencumbered by points of reference, no way to gauge distance traveled or distance yet to go. McColl knows only that he is one of five, that his team is one of three. Altogether, thirteen men, an unlucky number.

"*It's no problem, you'll see.*" One of the Swiss businessmen, Ernst, certified at the start. "*We hike on the glacier, that's all. Just like a road.*

You'll see, ja?" By this time McColl knows that Ernesto (as they call him) simply does not believe in the existence of problems. And the Swiss businessmen are how old? Thirty-five? And Hugh McColl is twenty years past that. His investment in Reitzel's "good hiking shoes" has been multiplied at least fifty times over by the Swiss at the Wengen outfitter. *"You'll need one of these. How does this ax feel? Take three of these, ja?"* Most of the items McColl has never seen, let alone mastered.

But he is thinking how wonderful it is just to be away from the business, completely out of touch, when suddenly the cloud gives way beneath his left foot. No cloud at all down there, only air. He feels himself pitching forward, his knee hyper-extending. Behind him, Reitzel tightens the rope and yells. Just to his right McColl sees the footprint of the guide, in which he should have stepped. Instead, he has stepped onto a snow bridge, covering a fissure in the ice. But for the ropes he is a dead man.

They pick him up. "How does it feel?"

"Knee hurts like hell. Can we go back?"

"There is no going back, only forward."

"Well, I can make it." Manhood demands much of a man.

But the knee grows more painful by each step, and his backpack grows heavier. *"Why do we need water? Can't we just drink the snow?"*

"Nein!"

Turns out that's another romantic illusion down the tubes, pure as driven snow. Pollution, acid rain. Alpine snow will make you sick. Don't eat the yellow snow, nor the white.

Hours later, he is still walking. The pain is there, but not in his conscious thoughts. Little else there but the instruction of his leader. *"Step in my steps."* The sky is turning from battleship gray to charcoal gray. A once-distant murmuring in his ears has somehow grown to a very proximate roar. They come up against a river, six feet across and ragingly impatient for the sea. Deep, gelid, menacing, the river is black beneath its froth. The guide throws his rucksack across, takes two steps back from the edge and leaps. Somehow, he makes it to the other side. He reels in the slack rope until McColl feels it tighten at his waist, then shouts in English, "Okay, yump."

He is fifty-five with a left knee that could give way at any moment, and he feels that tension-dizziness coming on, but he has no choice. Imitating the guide, he heaves across his thirty-five pounds of supplies, then he leaps, pushing off with his left foot so that his good right knee will bear the weight of landing. His foot barely clears the edge and he would fall back into the torrent but for the guide's quick tug on the rope, pulling him face down into the snow. Trust the leader.

All thirteen men make it across, pick up their rucksacks, hike on. The sky is darkening. Trust.

All at once they are facing a sheer cliff McColl swears wasn't there last time he looked up from the guide's footprints. The guide points up toward a postcard-perfect Alpine lodge. What, McColl asks, is it doing so far above them? It seems the lodge has served travelers over the *joch* for one hundred years, but over the course of those years, the glacier has sunk lower and lower, so that now the chalet sits high above their path. Regrets of ozone depletion and global warming rush into McColl's consciousness, but he cannot hold onto them, try as he may. There is climbing to be done, fear to be faced. His nerves are tightening up, he is sweating and ravenously hungry.

A long, rusty steel ladder is affixed to the side of the mountain, but even this must have been put here years ago. In the intervening time the glacier has melted down another twenty feet, so there is a rickety wooden ladder propped up from the ice to the first rung of the steel ladder. The feet of the wooden ladder are planted impossibly near the edge of a precipice. The sun is setting and McColl is freezing, but he feels the sweat soaking his sweater and eiderdown. He looks up at the little chalet. The top of the sheer cliff must be fifteen hundred feet above him, he imagines, half again as high as his sixty-story tower-to-be in Charlotte. There is no way his acrophobia will let him make this climb. But the guide insists. To stay below is to freeze to death. He begins climbing, untethered from his companions because if one should fall there is no need for all to die. Knowing he should never, never, never look down, he cannot resist the urge. To the acrophobic, this glance is like pulling the trigger in Russian roulette. Below, just past the feet of the rickety wooden ladder, is the crevasse, which he swears is *thousands* of feet deep.

How did I get here? Hand over hand, rung by rung, he makes it to the top, clambers sweating over the edge into the avalanche rubble called scree, boneyard of a mountain that chews itself. A friendly mittened paw steadies him, rights him, keeps him from slipping in the scree and sliding back over the edge. One more victory over acrophobia. *God, but I'm hungry.*

The lodge is one big warm room, exposed beams and a fireplace.

There is a hot meal: potato soup and cheese fondue, bread and schnapps, surely the Norse equivalent of ambrosia. Afterwards, merciful sleep, with sleeping bags laid side-by-side in long wooden troughs that line the wall. Should nature call during the night, one must use an open-hole facility that empties into the bottomless crevasse. McColl can wait until morning.

At first, sleep won't come and he can only fight back the anger at his own male ego. *What are you doing here? You're a fool, McColl. There are things in this world you cannot do and this is one of them. You'll die here and you'll never make love to your wife again, never see your kids, never be able to play with that little grandson of yours.* He fixes his thoughts on little John, imagining building a treehouse for him, showing him how to dribble, how to hit a baseball. *Choke up on that bat, John. Now put your shoulders into it. Ready? Here it comes.* Family, he feels, is everything. *I'll never see my grandson grow up.* He has always been a risk taker, but perhaps some risks must not be taken, not when the gamble could be a loss to someone he loves.

And then they are waking him at five in the morning, still dark, the guides preparing breakfast. Now it is time to return to the glacier, and that means going back down the ladder. McColl makes it only as far as the scree and falls shivering to his knees. Someone tells him he must go down, but he cannot. It is another American, Billy Wren. McColl is petrified, enervated. Wren sits down beside him and confesses that he is also frightened, and that gives McColl the ounce of courage he needs to stand again and inch forward. One of the guides takes his hands and walks in front of him, facing backward so that he can talk McColl down, but McColl is even more frightened that he will be responsible for this other man's death.

"Turn around and I will follow you."

The Swiss guide turns and continues the ten yards to the edge of the cliff, McColl fixing his eyes on the guide's brown rucksack. Finally, he squats, places his foot over the edge, onto the ladder's top rung, and lets himself slip down in the loose shale. Hugging the face of the cliff, learning its every wrinkle and smudge, he makes it to the bottom. Alive.

Now the hikers must cross what is called the Long Glacier, a full day to the other side—now and then stopping so the guides can huddle, reconnoiter, because melting has wrought so many changes in the glacier since their last crossing—doubling back, finding a new path. McColl, slogging, knee aching, keeps up. Toward day's end the clouds break and the sun empties itself out as they reach another cabin. McColl feels warm for the first time since cognac after supper at Wengen, stretches out beside the chalet to catch every ray. Without warning, agony seizes him, every muscle in his body cramps, excruciating pain takes his very breath away. There is no air, no breath. Now there is a paper bag cupped over his mouth and nose.

"Breathe, Hugh. Breathe slowly." Etienne, a very pleasant Swiss boy on one of the other teams, "E. T.," they call him. *"High-altitude cramps, hyperventilation. Breathe."* The air returns, the cramps leave his body like ectoplasm exorcised. He bends and moves and sees Reitzel Snider, also breathing into a paper bag. *A little hike in Switzerland, no mountain climbing.*

Another good meal, salt, fluids. Burning wet socks and power-bar wrappers in the fireplace, anything to lighten the next day's load. Dreamless, exhausted sleep in the little womb of wood, zipped into an eiderdown placenta. McColl jerks awake during the night to an awful clatter. Just a little avalanche, Ernesto's voice assures, no problem. *Falling, freezing, drowning, suffocating, crushing. How many ways to leave your life on a mountain?* No problem.

The third day they must start out before dawn. They must beat the sun to the ice banks so they can climb down to the bottom of the glacial fissure without their toeholds melting away. McColl and Snider are in the five-man team that always goes first, because they are the oldest and therefore are the ones to set the pace. The big guide shows them how to hold the chrome-plated ski poles and ice axes, two tools to a hand, then begins the steep-pitched descent. McColl chips, props, steps, hears the guide call to him. He has forgotten to put his gloves on and his hands are in danger of freezing to the metal. He cannot balance himself against the ice, hold on to his tools and pull the gloves on all at the same time. He becomes frustrated, curses, tears well and he must wipe them away quickly or they too will freeze. The guide is there to help him.

"Here." The gloves are on, the guide begins to move away, then says in his stiff English, "You know, these boots of yours are wrong kind. They are worst for this." A fine time to find out.

Hours later—though he can measure time no more accurately than distance here in the cloud—his improperly shod feet are on what the *jochmeisters* consider solid ground. Exhausted, the two Americans beg for a little rest. Let the others go first this time. They sit, eat power bars and sip water. After forty minutes the guide mushes them off in single file. As the path curves along an outcropping of rock, for the first time McColl can see something dark far ahead, something that takes on, in his imagination, the color green.

"The forest!" he exclaims, clapping Snider on the shoulders. "Dear God, we are out of here." Again the tears well, because he begins to believe he will see Jane again.

More hours later, the forest has disappeared in whiteness and still he is placing his feet in the prints of the guide. His left knee is on fire. The tension that has no name is building inside him again. At the next opportunity, unless there is a St. Bernard dog with a vat of single-malt whiskey—he will eat another power bar and that may make it go away. At the crest of a rise, he sees just ahead the eight who should still be forty minutes in front of them. McColl's heart sinks. Something is wrong, a river where no river should be.

When they come up to the others, their guide unclips himself to huddle again with his two counterparts. McColl hears them, shouting in German over the unremitting thunder of the river that blocks their path, ten yards wide or more, a rushing wound across the glacier's surface. The water pummels down from the mountain just ahead, in a waterfall that would be beautiful back in the Smokies but seems terrible here in the Alps. Of course, the river was not here on the guides' last trip. They believe the travelers must now make their way down the ice canyon wall, curved like the inner surface of a highball glass, to the foot of the falls.

"Why the hell do we need to do that?" McColl demands. A guide answers in German and a Swiss businessman translates. "We go down."

Each step must be hacked into the crystal face, used, then quickly hacked again for the next man, lest the spray coming off the waterfall fill it and freeze solid before the second climber's foot can reach it. McColl hears the river in his bones and this time he will not permit himself to look down. Falling, freezing and drowning all at once are too much for a man to fear. He tells himself it is time for him to act like a leader, to take charge of this little hike in the woods. So, in the well of the canyon, leaning against the curved wall like an ice cube in the bottom of a nearly drained glass, McColl demands answers.

"All right, what's happening here? How are we going to get across this goddamn river?"

"Across, no," says the guide who put on McColl's gloves for him.

"Up."

McColl looks up the sheer rock face, pockmarked by no more than a few months under the assault of this new waterfall. He suddenly is reminded of something from fifteen, no seventeen years ago. He is sitting on the curb at Trade and Tryon in the aftermath of rush hour, little Hugh and John beside him, looking up at crane operators and girder-walkers atop the forty-story tower Addison Reese decreed. "*How high are they, Daddy?*" He believes a man at the top of this waterfall would seem at least as small as those construction workers then had seemed. "*Oh, at least five hundred feet, Hugh. Be six hundred when they're done.*" Five hundred, six hundred feet of bare-knuckle clambering as tons of water explode past you. No thanks.

"I'm not going," McColl says.

"I'm not going either," says Snider.

The big guide shrugs like a bear done with a honey pot, turns and starts to climb. Roped to the guide, McColl can only climb too, cursing. Roped to McColl is Swiss businessman Max, who climbs, laughing. Roped to Max is Snider, who swears as he picks his way up. And behind Snider comes the Swiss named Herbie. The cataract buries all their comments, stings all their faces, chills them all with icy spray. Halfway up the waterfall, the guide finds the place he wants to cross, points to a thin ledge stretching across the falls, under a convex boulder that acts as a bumper in a pinball machine. The water caroms off the rock, then resumes its free fall, providing a pocket of airspace around and beneath the boulder for crossing.

McColl looks on in disbelief as the guide steps out onto the ledge, wrapping his arms around the big boulder. The guide *is* a young bear, burly, long-limbed, a foot taller than Hugh McColl. He hugs the rock like a Greek wrestler, arching his back out. The Bear seems not to feel the ton of water tugging at his rucksack. He claws and grunts his way across, pulls himself clear beyond the spray, signals to McColl.

"I can't do that," McColl shouts, "I'm not tall enough. My arms won't reach around the damn rock."

He is correct, but no one can hear him and no one cares anyway. This is the place to cross. The Bear pulls his lead rope taut. Behind him, Max climbs level with the ledge and pulls his trailing rope taut as well. McColl understands. They know his arms will not compass the rock. He is overcome with nausea, struggling to hold it back, wet everywhere from sweating that will not stop, as though there is a waterfall inside him too. He looks at Max: perhaps twenty-eight, already lionized in Swiss investment banking circles. Max is sturdy as a chalet, 240 pounds, useless weight of a camera slung round his bull neck.

The Bear, who has helped him before, signals McColl to come. He must trust his life to these two men. Trust.

Left foot first. McColl dances cheek-to-cheek with the boulder, a slow dance. Water pounds down on his head, his back. *Here is the real power—ice to water to air.* He could yield to it and be done with it, simply end the struggle. *Right foot.* He wonders what the rope is made of. Nylon? Carolina cotton? What gauge? He has not bothered to look, and now his life hangs on this rope. *Left foot.* Life is precious to him. He is not a bank chairman, he is a person, a small man whose life means a great deal to many people. They do not want him up here making love to a rock. Whose dreams will fall with him if he falls now?

"Komen zie, Hugh!"

Life, even his own, is nothing to risk. He could have killed a man once, in the Marine Corps, when he came across those drunk gyrenes about to molest the Puerto Rican girls and he shoved his shore-patrol pistol under the biggest guy's chin, but he relaxed the trigger and let the bastard drop in a faint. There is no power in him now, nothing threatening. *Right foot.* He concentrates on Jane, waiting at home, maybe down at the beach, fixing up the condo so it'll be ready for Labor Day, getting rid of Hurricane Hugo's last traces. Pulled the tub right out of the wall and Jane, God bless her, said at least we'll get a clean bathroom out of this. He feels himself slipping, leaning back, but the rope supports him. *Left foot.*

"Gut, Hugh, gut!"

There. He wants to let out a scream, but no air comes. Instead he buries his ice ax into a patch of soil and pushes his forehead into the side of the mountain. He may be sobbing, but he cannot be sure. His acrophobia has sent him spinning into a complete panic. And again, there is that palpitating hunger. Max is calling now, starting across.

"Pull the rope tight, Hugh."

McColl cannot hear anything but his own heart pounding. He is unaware that Max is teetering, separated from the boulder's embrace by his ridiculously unimportant Zeiss camera. The guide, the Bear, lurches up beside McColl, shakes him, forces him to grab the rope, and together they steady Max as he finishes his crossing, laughing all the way like a good sport.

"Okay, Reitzel, your turn," Max calls back.

McColl sees the panic in his friend's eyes. Snider is a half-foot taller than McColl, longer arms and legs, but he does not trust himself to make this crossing. McColl sees the words form, though he cannot hear them: "I'm not coming across." *Reitzel, you can do this. You're the fierce competitor. I only play racquetball with you because you're so damned determined to beat me. Don't give up on me here.*

All at once Snider is climbing, on his side of the waterfall, carrying his end of the rope that is attached to Max, standing next to McColl. Herbie, the other Swiss banker, climbs behind Snider, trying to talk sense into him, but up Reitzel goes. As the length of rope across the falls begins to tighten, Max must climb, must keep pace on this side with Reitzel on the other side. Behind him climbs McColl, then the Bear, three on this side, two on the other. McColl sees the length of rope dangling in the waterfall, snagging on outcroppings, clawed at by the rushing water. They all could be pulled to their death.

"Cut him loose, Max," McColl shouts. "To hell with him." No one pays any attention because McColl is not the leader now. "Cut the damn rope!" His orders mean nothing on the side of a mountain in Switzerland.

Just beneath the summit, the waterfall splays out over another jutting boulder. Only this time there is a ledge wide as a movie aisle and Snider sees his way clear to cross, followed easily by Herbie. McColl can only shake his head.

Now, having crossed the unexpected river, they must make their way back down to the glacier, along a goat path. Understanding McColl's terror, the Bear walks shoulder-to-shoulder with him, pressing him to the inside, against the mountain wall, so that McColl will not spend too much time staring over the edge of the path into the abyss. On the way down, McColl realizes how much he loves the Bear, and the others who have helped him. There is no machismo in his achievement, more like humility. Importantly, he realizes that for the first time since 1959, he has spent three days and nights without a thought of business. In fact, that thought is his first, and for some time yet, his last.

Hours later—he supposed it was hours—McColl felt the path widen from two feet to four. They crossed a friendly little stream on rocks that were not covered with ice and there, on the other side, was the forest. Beyond the forest was a road and on the road was an inn and in the inn was water and fire and whiskey and food. There was life.

But back in Charlotte, death.

Frances Carroll McColl Covington—Frannie, Pal—was finished with her fight. She died at her home at the age of fifty-eight on August 14, 1990. The obituary called her a homemaker, the one name her brother never would have applied. It was his father at the funeral who affected Hugh McColl the deepest, standing over the grave in the swelter of midday, small and old and unfamiliar in his wool business suit, lost in the big city between his boys. "Son, I never thought . . . ." His voice stuck, worked its way loose, "never thought I'd bury one of my children."

Hugh McColl never thought he'd bury his sister, nor his best friend in the company, Buddy Kemp.

As the cancer broke down Kemp's life functions, McColl increased his flights to Dallas. Pat Hinson helped arrange his schedule and tried to lift her boss's spirits the way she knew he would do with Mr. Kemp. It was in times of stress, Pat Hinson said, that people in the company knew they could count on Hugh McColl. She reminded him of how he'd arrived at the hospital just after daybreak on the morning her husband Doug was scheduled for a coronary operation.

"You got there just as they put Doug on the gurney to be wheeled into surgery. You took Doug's hand and held it and said, 'How you doing, buddy? I'm thinking about you.' That's one of those things you don't forget. You were a busy man, you didn't have to do that. We would have known you were thinking about us." That was the Hugh McColl that Pat Hinson and Buddy Kemp knew. That was why Kemp and so many others would "walk through fire" for him.

Buddy couldn't walk anywhere now. About all McColl could do for him was to bring Buddy a good meal, good conversation. Sometimes he found Kemp lying in a Dallas hospital in the company of those grim tubes and blinking lights and electrodes known ironically as life support, other times he would be at home. More often than not, Kemp's family would be there in the room.

"Barbecue? Hell, Buddy, if I'd known you wanted barbecue I'd have brought you the real thing from Carolina. What do they know about barbecue in Texas?"

Then McColl dashed out to the nearest barbecue joint he could find, ordered six of everything on the menu, tossed the cashier a hundred-dollar bill and hurried back to Buddy Kemp's room. They never talked about dying. Instead, it was more jokes, more reminiscing about old times, like breaking into Tom Storrs's liquor cabinet after that unbelievable workout in '74, like Mr. Storrs's Parthian shot of the Xeroxed sections on pronouns from his 1939 grammar textbook just because Bill Dougherty couldn't stop saying "him and I'll get right on that."

Then it was time to fly back to Charlotte, because business had to go on.

"See you next time," McColl said.

Eventually, there was no next time. Just before Thanksgiving 1990, Buddy Kemp died. Newsmen never saw Hugh McColl sit with Bill Kinney, hold Doug Hinson's hand or joke with Buddy Kemp to keep his mind a while from death. To the world, McColl remained the hard-hearted money merchant, the Shylock of Charlotte. He was "this powerful, driving and driven man" as the *Observer* would have it.

McColl's experience on the *Jungfraujoch* had proven to him that it was people who counted, not business. Yet the business would not let him go. It was like a game that needed to be played out, had a certain time to run, or a certain number of innings. This game he'd got himself into had ten more years before the final gun. If he'd made it up that waterfall, down that mountain, he could make another ten years.

In this game, though, one's chief opponent could be the playing field. The national economy heading into 1991 was as soggy and unplayable as it had been back in 1974, the year of NCNB's worst crisis. Down in Florida, Bob Kirby was talking about a "tsunami" headed his way. Real estate values dropping like a barometer before a hurricane, too many loans outstanding on dubious development. It sounded a lot like '74; only the repossessed mobile homes were missing. As the numbers came in during the last quarter, McColl learned that his bank had more than $1 billion dollars in questionable loans, mostly in Florida, but some in Virginia and in North and South Carolina as well.

Taking a page from his Texas book, McColl created a "special asset bank," a bank-within-a-bank, and parked the bad loans in there for workouts or write-offs. He couldn't stop the bleeding. Third-quarter earnings were posted at fifty-one cents a share, little more than one-third what they had been in last year's third quarter. As a bad year stumbled toward the exit, it became apparent that earnings overall would be nearly $100 million below their peak in that banner year of '89.

McColl and CFO Jim Hance believed the bank would be somewhat sheltered from Kirby's tsunami by its huge bond portfolios. "When the economy is rocky and headed for recession, which is what is driving the real estate losses for the most part," Hance explained, "you end up with a lower interest-rate environment." That would provide profits in NCNB's bond portfolio, where interest rates on the receivable side were considerably higher than the current rates the bank had to pay. They could take big gains on the bond portfolio and match it against the loan loss reserves on the problem real estate portfolio and come out, as Hance put it, "flush." It would not be necessary to "damage our capital." The greater threat was pressure from Washington to increase the bank's loan loss reserve to $505 million, more than double the amount set aside for 1989.

Not that NCNB was the Lone Ranger of loan losses. The FDIC was anticipating nearly $32 billion in 1990 loan defaults for banks around the country, more than any time in the past eight years. Real estate loans nationwide were going bad at a rate that was 84 percent higher than that of 1989. One of the victims was Luther Hodges, who had become chairman and chief executive of Washington Bancorp, holding company of the National Bank of Washington. His bank went under in August, costing the FDIC $300 million in insurance payments.

Bad real estate loans finally sank the Bank of New England, and the FDIC awarded the big Northeast salvage operation to Fleet Financial of Rhode Island. On the West Coast, Security Pacific was on the shoals, looking for help from BankAmerica. In New York, the future of Manufacturers Hanover was in question. Citicorp was anticipating losses of $400 million for the year. Chase Manhattan was cutting back its workforce and its dividends. By fall the FDIC insurance fund was down to $4 billion, and chairman William Seidman warned that if many more banks failed, his agency could fail along with them.

Republican President George Bush called an economic summit meeting in Washington, to include the heads of all the regulatory agencies, along with the CEOs of the nation's most powerful banks. On the way to the summit, McColl stopped off in New York for a meeting. He was hustling across a street against a flashing Don't Walk sign when his left knee gave out and he slipped. The knee—the one he'd injured on the *Jungfraujoch*—came down on a chunk of asphalt and McColl could not get up. He'd made it across a glacier in Switzerland only to be felled by a street in Manhattan. He was rushed to a hospital for emergency surgery, but the next day he put in an appearance at the White House.

The president was between his own rock and a hard place, with the Federal Reserve's chairman Alan Greenspan at odds with Richard Breeden, chairman of the Securities and Exchange Commission over how banking regulations should be reformed to put the economy on the road to recovery. One of many points of contention was the accounting system that was causing banks to expand their loan loss reserves with capital that might have been put to other uses. The SEC's Breeden, along with Comptroller of the Currency Eugene Ludwig, wanted banks to place the value of their loans at the market value of the property that secured those loans. This approach had the comptroller's agents poring over bank records, looking for ways to write down loan portfolios to reflect what banks might actually collect on those loans at the time of the inspection. Federal Reserve chairman Alan Greenspan sided with McColl and other bankers, arguing that "paper" must be assumed to be "good paper." Any promissory note should be carried at face value until it was either written off or repaid at maturity. Write-downs, they argued, were causing banks to fail.

Because McColl was on crutches, he was given a more comfortable seat on the administration's side of the table, next to the secretary of the treasury, two seats to the left of the president. In a conference room in the west wing of the White House was gathered the most powerful group of individuals McColl had ever encountered. He was across the table from John McGillicuddy, CEO of Chemical Bank; Carl Reichardt, chairman of Wells Fargo; the leaders of several Midwestern banks; and two of the country's most successful real estate developers. In addition to the president and secretary of the treasury, Vice President Dan Quayle was there, along with the president's chief of staff and director of the Office of Management and Budget. McColl found himself surprised by the president's firm and effective control in a business meeting. Until now, "I'd only seen George Bush on television and, frankly, I didn't think much of him on television. Here he was very much in command and very articulate and very easy to be with."

Bush began by going around the table, starting with Wells Fargo's

Reichardt, asking each businessman to describe the state of the economy in his part of the country and to offer suggestions as to what the government might do to help. The last one to speak was McColl, who said things were getting better in Texas and that the Carolinas were "not doing as badly as the rest of the country."

When it came time to offer suggestions, McColl warmed to the task. "The problem you all have is that you think you are running the country, and you are not. There is only one man running this country and he is not in this room."

A murmur of surprise ran around the table before treasurer Nicholas Brady asked McColl to state his meaning. He looked Brady in the eye and said: "Well, he works for you. He's the chief national bank examiner on real estate, and he is destroying the banks all over America by forcing marked-to-market accounting. Carl's bank, my bank, everybody else's bank. He's the man who decides who gets credit in this country. And he works for you."

Chief of Staff John Sununu, sitting to the president's right, leaned over to make eye contact with McColl and said, "What's his name? What's his name?"

McColl found it remarkable, even funny, that this piece of information should be coming from him, a fellow who had barely passed his college economics courses. "Hell, he's famous," he said, deciding not to blurt out the name of the chief bank examiner, Joseph Hooks. "He's the grim reaper. He comes into the bank. He marches into banks' real estate divisions and shuts them down. And as long as that is going on, this country is not going anywhere."

Rather than going after Hooks, he decided to give the Bush Administration a banker's-eye view of the national economy. As he saw it, "This rolling recession is crushing the banking industry. Billions and billions and billions of dollars are being wiped out," he said. "And much smarter men than me—Paul Volcker, a much smarter man than me, said, and I was with him when he said it, that what we are doing as bankers is the very antithesis of what we are supposed to do. Bankers are supposed to be here to help bridge the gap when the economy gets disorderly. And we are supposed to help borrowers work their way through their problems so they can get to the other side of their problems."

Instead, "By forcing us to write down the loans and take it to our earning stream, all the incentive to work with people goes away. Our incentive becomes just to get rid of the bad loans." He admitted that real estate prices were seriously inflated, "but it doesn't have to be done all at once, we could have wandered through this."

McColl told the assembly that the banking industry was itself in danger of being crippled if the federal inspectors did not ease off. The regulators were "beating on us and everybody else, trying to put the pressure on us." McColl claimed the comptroller's people were "absolutely dead flat wrong" in their wholesale marking down of real estate loan portfolios. He echoed the observation of his CFO, Jim Hance, that the government's negative attitude toward the economy was causing the banks to be "overly harsh" on themselves, by pumping up the loss reserves. This, in turn, served to grease the skids of recession.

Already the United States was seeing the negative effects of domestic restraint of trade, with unrestrained foreign banks financing unprecedented foreign investments in the United States. The Japanese, in particular, were buying Hollywood film production studios and huge chunks of major American cities. What was needed was not more regulation but less. McColl suggested that the White House begin chipping away at the artificial barriers to interstate banking erected after the Depression. It was time, he insisted, to end interstate compacts—which merely moved back the fences—and open up the nation to free-market banking.

At the end of the White House meeting, McColl's leg was still in pain, but he felt better, having gotten a lot off his chest. He had "said something pretty impressive to the president of the United States and to his entire financial staff. And meant it. And was right. And everybody knew I was right. And they agreed. There were a lot of yesses. A lot of amens from the bankers at the table."

Back in Charlotte, McColl told his key executives about the meeting, doubting that anything would come of it. The president seemed to feel his hands were tied. If he fired the chief bank examiner, "the press would go bananas." But if Hugh McColl had been president, "I would have sent him to Alaska. You know, I'd have seen that he had gotten a good job where he couldn't have done any harm. I would have promoted him."

Within the Bush administration, McColl had a number of eager listeners. But the question remained, what could anybody actually *do* about banking deregulation? At the moment the president had his attention distracted by hostilities in the Middle East. Since August,

Saddam Hussein's Iraqi army had occupied Kuwait, and a United Nations-sponsored trade embargo was not making it let go. There were those who thought Bush should do something—anything—to divert America's attention from its domestic problems, even going so far as to suggest a military invasion of Iraq.

Domestically, the Republican White House was incapacitated on major legislative issues because of a Democratic majority in both houses of Congress. One Bush advisor told McColl he should put together a piece of legislation, and then, "Hugh, we will be for it or against it, whatever helps you the most." McColl and a few of the other bankers agreed to get their legislative people started on a deregulation bill, but he doubted the administration could "get it off ground zero."

In McColl's estimation, the United States required a few truly nationwide banks, deep-pocketed entrepreneurs that could borrow money from an economically thriving region and use it like fertilizer to enrich the soil of an economic Dust Bowl in another part of the country. Even the comptroller of the currency could get behind an idea like that. "But if you can't have interstate banking, you can't get there from here," McColl opined.

And one of the sticking points of interstate banking was that most of the big bankers tended to be territorial. Achieved on those bankers' terms, interstate banking would involve a multibank holding company that could own one bank in Illinois, another in Texas, another in California. What McColl wanted was something very different—interstate *branching*. One bank, one centralized system, extending its branches into many different parts of the country.

Yet, in the final quarter of 1990, McColl wondered whether his own bank might already be overextended. Like a Monopoly player, making his way around the board while other players' gamepieces languished "in jail," McColl's Texas players were jumping into a new city with each roll of the dice. As the regulators put them out of business, Texas banks and S&L's were up for grabs in every cranny of the republic, and NCNB always seemed to be the first to land on them. Trouble was, NCNB was running out of cash for buying banks.

"Chewing up capital," McColl called it. "No matter how much capital we raise, we keep chewing it up by growing." At summer's end he had considered going to the market with preferred shares, but let himself be talked out of it by Tim Hartman, who was convinced that the national economy was on its way to hell in a hand-basket and that his successor as CFO, Jim Hance, was giving Hugh McColl bad advice. The picture was changing too rapidly, warned the ever-pessimistic Hartman. He was frightened the company would be selling promises on which it could never deliver.

Negativism from his chief advisors tended to sink McColl's spirits. Desperate to force a change, McColl took Hance calling on investment and bond houses, hoping to find a new cash-rich partner. They would sell a quarter of the bank for $300 million in capital. Only one bond firm in New York even nibbled at the NCNB preferred stock, then swam away after looking at the loan loss reserves and the questionable real estate loans. "Nobody has any clue where the bottom is," Hance told him after that. The situation was "stunningly depressing, unnerving."

McColl's funk was worse than the economy's.

He was even beginning to lose confidence in his management team, the team he had put together. Buddy Kemp's death had thrown everything into imbalance. McColl felt like he was back in Switzerland, climbing that damned waterfall, with Reitzel Snider going up the wrong side—or was it the right side?—and he himself yelling *cut the rope, cut the rope.* Where was this management team taking him? Exactly whom was he supposed to trust and how the hell was anybody supposed to trust him?

Part of his problem came from the forced integration of the Texas leadership into the corporate team. He'd assumed those hard-driving Texans would imbue the rest of the organization with their against-all-odds winning attitude. Instead the entire company now seemed to be infected with the paranoia that all the odds were stacked against them. Tim Hartman, genetically predisposed to pessimism, was hunkered down in the face of what he termed "the terrific write-downs and the constant deterioration in real estate values." There were people who worked for Fred Figge in credit whom McColl identified as "gloom-and-doom" people. Because they'd seen the bottom fall out once before, they assumed that all loans in the Carolinas, Florida, Virginia and Maryland would behave as the loans in Texas had. What really bothered McColl was that he was starting to feel gloomy-and-doomy himself.

Not only McColl, but most other senior executives in the Charlotte office had been spooked by this it-could-happen-to-us thinking. There was just no escaping the fact that the oil-imploded

Texas economy had sucked the rest of the country into its seemingly bottomless pit. "The negative vibes going on in the bank," as he assessed the situation, were caused by "very senior men who believe the worst and predict the worst." Only recently depicted as the company's heroes, the Texas bunch seemed to be "poisoning the thinking of senior management and the board." McColl wondered if NCNB would ever get back to its old self.

He welcomed an opportunity to escape with Jane to San Francisco for a few days, to an International Monetary Conference, where bankers from around the world could slip behind rose-colored glasses and sip California wines and assure each other that nothing was as bad as it seemed. At functions like these, McColl had noticed, old enemies found opportunities to bury hatchets.

One of these was Charles J. Zwick, CEO of Miami's Southeast Banking Corporation, who had once balked at signing over his company to Hugh McColl. Back in 1982, Zwick had told the *Miami Herald* he wasn't afraid of the big bad bankers from NCNB. "We know the market better than they do," he said, issuing a personal warning to McColl to stay out of his bank's business. Yet, in 1990 San Francisco, Zwick seemed a changed man, friendly, all handshakes and sweet introductions. From one of Zwick's buddies, Paul Volcker, McColl learned Zwick now was of a mind to talk merger. McColl told Volcker, former chairman of the Federal Reserve, and himself, to get real. They both knew damned well NCNB wouldn't be buying anything any time soon.

It was a bit harder to shake hands and exchange smiles with his old Litchfield Beach chum, Bennett Brown. Yet, at the Monetary Conference supper dance, the McColls found themselves seated across a round table from Bennett and Mary Alice Brown. Insulated from the Browns by three other couples, Jane McColl was happy enough with the seating arrangement. It was "really a cute group of people, and everybody was feeling good, and everybody was teasing each other. So it worked out fine." Fine, that is, until Brown leaned forward on the table, West to Jane McColl's East, and began telling her how he really couldn't help all those things he'd done the previous year. A man in business had to do what a man had to do. Still smarting from the personal attacks on her family, Jane tried to ignore him, but Brown heard the orchestra begin to play, so he walked behind her chair and asked Jane to dance.

"The first thing I said to him as we walked out on the dance floor was, 'I don't want to talk about it, it gives me a hot flash.' And I didn't say anything else to him. I had my chance. You know, I could have said, 'Look you two-faced skunk . . . .' But I had my chance and I kept my mouth shut and didn't say anything."

Brown led her in a swaying foxtrot, tall and tuxedoed, smiling as he spoke, "trying in his South Carolina gentlemanly way to cut up and be cute with me and apologize. Then I just looked right at him and said, 'Bennett, I don't want to talk about it. I just want to dance and have a good time.' And that was it."

Hugh McColl heard Bennett Brown kept that little stuffed tiger on a shelf in his office, the tiger he'd swung by the tail and thrown to the crowd the day NCNB retreated. *Hold that tiger, Bennett,* McColl thought. Maybe it was McColl's turn to smile. Brown had escaped the tigers and stepped into a swamp full of alligators with his new sweet-hearts at Sovran. The real estate market in Washington, D.C., was in a tailspin, and a fat portion of Sovran's portfolio was tied up in D.C. real estate loans. The nation's capital was supposed to be one of those can't-lose investment propositions, but C&S/Sovran was losing its wrestling match with the real estate gators, looking at fourth-quarter losses of a quarter-billion dollars.

Hugh McColl bore all that in mind as he sipped his chenin blanc and watched the CEO of the bank that wouldn't be bought dance with the wife of the CEO of that bank that ought to own him. *Hold that tiger, Bennett.*

Back in Charlotte, the band was playing a dirge. Well before the year was out, McColl knew there would be nothing but a lump of coal in NCNB's Christmas stockings. He scheduled meetings around the company so that he could speak personally with his top executives and give them the news that 1990 would be a year of no bonuses.

At the Tampa Bay session, Alex Sink was prepared for the worst. It seemed as though half a dozen of her customers were declaring bank-ruptcy every day. McColl made the no-bonus announcement, then closed by telling his executives that if they wanted significant bonuses next year, they would have to provide the company with something more than profits. Sink could tell by that no-prisoners edge in his voice that McColl was serious. "We don't have enough diversity in this corporation. All you have to do is stand up here where I am and look out at this audience, and you'll be as embarrassed as I am. The only way we can make things happen is for each one of you to take personal accountability for creating more diversity in your own organization. And when bonus time comes around next year—and there will be bonuses next year, I promise—your success in building a more diverse team is going to be a very important part of determining the size of your bonus." *When the going gets tough,* Sink reflected, *the tough get tougher.*

McColl didn't mind sharing his displeasure with the troops. Everyone else at NCNB should be just as unsettled as he was. Certainly, the directors conveyed their concerns to him. His heretofore supportive board had become "very uncomfortable with losses," second-guessing his every decision. Where was all that company boosterism, all that shareholder applause that helped McColl pick himself up from the wreckage of his C&S missiles exploding on the launch pad a year ago? He needed a Billy Wren here to lift him from the scree, a Bear (better yet, a Bull) to help him climb.

Nineteen-ninety was turning out to be a very tough year, the most depressing of his life. What with the suffering morale of his senior people, the pressure from regulators, and now even the second-guessing of his board, it was awful. The CEO desperately required a vote of confidence.

That vote came from C. D. Spangler, the man who played touch football with newlywed correspondent banker Hugh McColl back at Selwyn Village, the man who sold his Bank of North Carolina to NCNB president Hugh McColl in the West Virginia mountains, pulling off what was then the biggest bank merger in North Carolina history.

By the close of 1990, Dick Spangler thought he must have engaged in "probably thirty different transactions with Hugh, where he said, 'We will do this together.'" He had learned that when McColl said he would do a thing, the thing was as good as done. Spangler had served on the NCNB Executive Committee until shortly before the Texas incursion, when he left to become president of the University of North Carolina. In 1986 his wife, Meredith, was elected to the board. While Meredith was prohibited from talking with him about what went on in board meetings, she let him know that Hugh McColl was promising he would get the company back on its feet. Despite what he knew about the nation's economy and about the bank's recent stumbling, Spangler believed McColl would deliver on his promise. Spangler was convinced that NCNB was a company of destiny, and that McColl would be the man to achieve that destiny. He knew that without even consulting his backyard stars.

And so, with NCNB losses up and NCNB earnings down, consulting no accountant or investment broker, C. D. Spangler bought $100 million worth of NCNB stock, making him the largest single shareholder in the company of destiny, with a total of eight million shares. He bought most of his new shares at twenty dollars or less.

McColl got the message. There were people who knew him and trusted him, people who were willing to step out on uncertain ledges just because they were following him, as he had followed the Bear across the waterfall. On their own—no ropes tethering them to their leader. On the slippery, cataract-pummeled slopes of banking, his lot was to lead. He might praise his teammates, but he could not lean on them. They had their responsibilities and he had his. Nor could he simply lay the blame for NCNB's sluggish performance on the economy or on the pessimism of his Texas bunch. Tim Hartman might be Doctor Doom in Dallas, but he was doing what he was supposed to do, rounding up those faltering banks and S&Ls. McColl and Jim Hance had to do their job, which was to round up some cash for Hartman.

As McColl had looked to London for money in 1974, this time he and Hance flew to Edinburgh for a meeting with Scot investors. Exactly two hundred years earlier, in 1790, the first Hugh McColl of his line, a thirteen-year-old boy, had left the Scottish Highlands village of Appin for America.

McColl was delightedly surprised at the willingness of the Scotsmen to part with their money. They believed it was a good time to invest in a United States bank, especially one with a McColl at the helm, and they opened their purses to purchase 1.2 million shares of NCNB stock. "Apparently," McColl told Hance on the ride to the airport, "Europeans see the turnaround coming before we do, kind of like the sunrise."

Time to stop in the airport lounge for a drink before boarding, with McColl well aware he must order a single-malt whiskey, never "Scotch." Amusingly enough, the bar had American pop music going, not the brave keening of pipes.

"When times are mysterious, serious numbers speak to us all . . . ."

Paul Simon, singing about Jim Hance. Serious numbers. McColl believed numbers spoke only seriously to Jim, and when Jim *spake o'numbers,* as they might say in Scotland, *ye maun gie ear.* Jim Hance, son of an insurance man, born in St. Joe, Missouri, nine years younger than McColl. Brought up from Price Waterhouse, like bringing up a cleanup hitter from the minors, only you couldn't call P-W the minors.

"When times are mysterious, serious numbers are easy to please . . . ."

Some people read numbers like tarot cards, McColl knew, telling you what you wanted to hear. Hance read numbers and told you how they add up, period.

"When numbers get serious, you see their shape everywhere . . . ."

Hance, Mutt to McColl's Jeff, sloping, lanky, with a long drop between hairline and chin. Hance of the cautious laugh, held back like loan loss reserves, but a good sense of humor for a'that. And humor, McColl concluded, was precisely what this situation called for.

"I'll be damned if I can figure out what we're doing here in Europe," he began. "It ain't like we need to buy Scotch at the duty-free shop."

Hance was aware that, strictly speaking, they were not in Europe, nor could his chairman be anything short of crystal-clear on the purpose of their visit to Scotland. He recognized Hugh in his circuit-riding-preacher mode.

"I mean, hell, we ought to be back in Charlotte lighting fires under certain people's butts," McColl continued. "Dammit, Jim, you know it and I know it and everybody over here in a kilt knows it. We've turned the corner on this economy. You know what I feel like? I feel like that old saw—the cat that sits on the hot stove and won't ever sit on it again. But he also won't ever sit on a cold one either."

"Once burned, twice shy," Hance summed up.

"Yeah, kind of. We've got a battle going on between people in the company who are spending every waking minute worrying about the examiners overreacting to the credit problems and other people who are worrying that *we* are overreacting to the credit problems. This has been going on for nine months now. Jim, you and I just a few weeks back tried to sell off a big part of this company for a measly $300 million. What the hell are we thinking about? What are we crying for?"

Hance leaned forward over the bar, raising his eyebrows and stretching his long upper lip, a bit like a turtle sunning on a log. McColl's question, when he jotted and tittled the implications, was a legitimate one. NCNB's financial situation was better than almost any other bank in the country and, as the Scot investors already knew, the economic processes were cyclical. It was not a question of whether things would get better but how quickly.

"I'm sick and tired of retreating, Jim. You know what I think we ought to do?"

"Attack?"

"Hell, Jim, that's who we are. It's just part of our mental set. We're not like those other belt-and-suspender bankers. You know what the marines say: When in doubt . . . "

"Attack."

"So what do we have to do to buy another bank?"

Hance's answer was clear and simple. Instead of issuing more stock, they should expand their bond portfolios, thereby leveraging their assets. Hance recommended this be done quickly, while most of the marketplace was still of a bearish mentality.

NCNB had assets in the form of residential mortgages, leases and credit card receivables, which would serve as security for bonds. In essence, this allowed the bank to collect cash now, on money due sometime in the future. These bonds would be marketed as attractive fixed income to more conservative banks and investors. Hance believed it would be safe to "run bond portfolios" supported by as much as 30 percent of the corporation's total assets. "That will give us really big gains to marry against our losses," the CFO said. When they were ready to go after another bank, they would be able to offset its bad loans "without diluting our shareholders' earnings by going out and issuing a bunch of new stock."

By the time McColl and Hance got back to Charlotte, the decision had been made. McColl declared the NCNB recession ended. His team would go back on the attack, restore their reputation as the bank that wouldn't stop shooting. Instead of selling themselves piecemeal, they'd buy somebody else, whole hog. Somebody had to jumpstart the stalled economy, and it might as well be Hugh McColl. Drive the economy or be driven by it.

He'd felt that cloak of responsibility brush his shoulders at the White House conference. *"Hugh, we will be for it or against it, whatever helps you the most."* That was a very different kind of power than what he felt in Charlotte, merely shaping a city. Here was the president's top man asking Hugh McColl what to do about banking deregulation.

Well, McColl couldn't wait for Washington, couldn't wait for the laws to change. He had to grow his bank again. They'd done the impossible in Florida, then in Texas, and they could do it again if that's what was required. His tigers, his wolves, were just restless, that was their trouble. They just needed something new and exciting and big to go after.

The only question was, where?

Briefly, they entertained the possibility of "filling in the holes" between Florida and Texas, buying a bank in Alabama, Mississippi or Louisiana. To McColl, there was a certain supply-line logic in that. However, Frank Gentry said that of those three Deep South states, only Alabama could be considered having reasonable growth opportunities. Unfortunately, that state was carved up equally among four dominant banks, none of which seemed ripe for acquisition. Mississippi, Gentry believed, was simply not the place for a hit-the-ground-running company like theirs.

Louisiana had a lot of banks that needed rescuing—the second largest bank in New Orleans, Hibernia, was on the verge of sinking into the swamp, with nearly twice the total of its equity capital committed to nonperforming loans. But Gentry warned that Louisiana was too much like a foreign country, complete with Napoleonic Code instead of English Common Law. Its bankers seemed concerned with little other than gas wells, offshore drilling and Mardi Gras. And then there was the quagmire of Baton Rouge politics.

McColl agreed. Filling in the supply line was not an option. He told the others about his conversations in San Francisco a few months earlier, concerning Southeast Banking Corporation of Miami. NCNB still controlled less of Florida's money than did four other banks, which did not sit well with McColl. Since one of those four was Southeast, it was decided that he would approach Charles Zwick, who had been so friendly at the monetary conference.

Only that wouldn't work, because Zwick had got himself fired by his board. So McColl got in touch with Zwick's friend, Paul Volcker, now with the New York investment banking firm of James D. Wolfensohn, advisors to NCNB. Volcker said he could help set up a meeting with the new Southeast Bank leaders. McColl suggested they meet in New Orleans, where even a former Federal Reserve Board chairman was unlikely to be recognized.

At the French Quarter meeting, McColl, Hance and Gentry worked out a preliminary deal to buy Southeast. They left it contingent on

NCNB board approval and on Gentry's ability to talk the FDIC into a First Republic-like arrangement in which they would cull out what appeared to be about $1 billion worth of bad real estate loans.

The NCNB contingent also had some private discussions with Paul Volcker, who posed the question: What if there was a better deal on the market than Southeast? McColl said he was not wedded to the Miami deal, so the conversation continued. McColl became fascinated with the suggestion that NCNB just might be able to buy Chase Manhattan Bank!

That was a fantasy to be indulged in for at least a little while. They imagined the drawling kid from Bennettsville and his team of Southern kamikazes taking over the big money center bank of the Rockefellers. The image was entertaining, but there were too many stories of infighting and poor management at Chase. The culture seemed terminally aloof, not at all a fit with NCNB's.

So the question still nagged: Where? Was Southeast of Miami really the bank acquisition NCNB was looking for in 1991?

"Southeast is about to collapse," McColl said to Hance and Gentry. "Why in hell are we buying these guys instead of somebody stronger?"

"Well," said Gentry, "Southeast has a billion dollars worth of bad loans. That's the same amount that Barnett's got, and Barnett's much bigger, so why don't we buy Barnett?"

"Somebody get Charlie Rice on the phone," said McColl.

Rice, the same age as McColl, had taken over Barnett from Guy Botts, the old friend of Tom Storrs who hatched the notion of a Southeastern Banking Compact. Rice controlled about a third of Florida's retail market from his headquarters in Jacksonville, and nearly a quarter of its deposits. Unlike Southeast, Barnett was in no danger of failing. Yet Rice readily acknowledged to McColl, when they met in New York, that his bank was in a lot of trouble with bad real estate loans.

Talks with Barnett progressed. McColl and Rice had a second meeting in New York. Flying back from that session, someone on the NCNB jet asked the innocent question, how did Barnett's problems compare with those of C&S?

The answer was that C&S/Sovran was in much worse shape than Barnett. Thanks mainly to the real estate mess in the Washington, D.C., area, Bennett Brown's stock was performing at less than half its value of a year earlier. That about matched the C&S/Sovran drop in earnings. Since almost one-third of his bank's assets consisted of real estate loans, the worst assets possible at present, Brown's immediate future looked bleak.

"What the hell?" McColl declared. "With a hundred percent of Texas we're a tremendously viable company. This time, we're dressed for the party. So, let's go buy C&S."

Somebody cheered.

Somebody groaned.

CHAPTER 14

Craig Wall was hardly surprised. Of course Hugh McColl wanted to talk with him about C&S. Ever since Bennett Brown's decision to merge with Sovran, Wall had been betting NCNB would be back. The very day the Atlanta board approved the deal he laughed at them, told them they were painting themselves into McColl's corner.

As a developer, Wall figured the C&S/Sovran merger was built to collapse. Sovran was a little larger than C&S, so Sovran got the tie-breaker seat on the board. Clearly C&S was better managed than Sovran, but C&S would not be able to call the shots. Now it turned out that Sovran's so-called assets were significantly weakening the combined bank. Fourth-quarter '90 earnings were down to a piddling penny-a-share. By the spring of 1991, Craig Wall knew there was only one way out of the mess. C&S/Sovran "really needed to be acquired."

But before McColl took off after C&S a second time, he had some work to do. This time around he would use his brain, not simply his instincts. He discussed strategy with Frank Gentry, and they decided on the divide-and-conquer approach, since their target was already split down the middle like a rack of ribs ready for the grill.

C&S/Sovran was still two different banks. Bennett Brown had his bank and his headquarters in Atlanta; Dennis Bottorff had his bank and his headquarters in Norfolk. Discomfort with the merger stiffened every corporate joint. The right hand's fingers didn't even want to claim the left hand as a distant relation.

Moreover, who was allowed to do what with whom was very much open to debate, Gentry reported, because Bottorff was named in the merger agreement as CEO-apparent. He would assume command as soon as lame-duck Brown stepped down at the end of the current year. Only weeks earlier, the board had shocked Brown with a vote of no confidence. There were fifteen votes (all former Sovran directors) against Brown, fourteen votes (all former C&S directors) in his support.

From everything he learned, McColl got the idea that Brown would rather sell the company than turn it over to Denny Bottorff on January 1, 1992. NCNB's best bet might be to offer Brown a way to save "his" company from the clutches of the Virginia partner. Clearly, the window of opportunity was open, McColl and Gentry agreed, but only until Brown retired or the bank collapsed, whichever came first. NCNB should move quickly and decisively.

McColl set up "a little war room," near his office on the twenty-third floor. He invited Craig Wall in for a tête-à-tête and Wall agreed to function as a conduit. But because Wall's partiality toward McColl was hardly secret, there would be a safety valve on the other end. Wall would relay messages not to Bennett Brown but to Hugh Chapman, C&S/Sovran's vice chairman. McColl would speak to Wall, Wall would speak to Chapman, and Chapman would speak to Brown. It would all be what-ifs and just-supposes, nothing concrete, nothing that could be construed as negotiations. When both men were ready to talk, both would know they were ready.

As he conducted these oblique "peace talks," McColl proceeded to mass his artillery. In the wake of the previous C&S debacle, Joe Martin's communications people had developed a series of corporate "image ads" based on the interests McColl was beginning to project. The ads said things like: "Somebody has to pay for day care. It shouldn't be the children," and "Our best bankers still spend time in second grade." Martin kept them "filed under antiterrorism, for future use, in case anybody like the C&S public relations team should ever appear on the horizon." In another file was a carefully tended list of influential leaders in towns across the South—newspaper owners and editors, civil rights leaders, legislators, political kingmakers, arts advocates. Martin was determined that "nobody would find us unprepared again."

By the time they were ready to go after C&S/Sovran, that list numbered more than five thousand. The image ads came out of the drawer and were placed in just two newspapers, for the sake of expediency and also to save money. "Courtesy copies" of the ads were mailed directly to the list of five thousand local leaders, with a cover letter from Hugh McColl. It was, Martin said, "just a cautionary inoculation."

To make sure nothing went wrong in the final stages, McColl wanted investment bankers who were "big and tough," with a reputation for making things happen. He engaged not only Morgan Stanley, but Merrill Lynch and Salomon Brothers as well. Since those bankers would have to be paid hefty fees, even if the deal fell through, McColl and everyone else would understand there was no retreating this time.

But outside of those allies and his key advisors, not a soul was to know anything. No information was to leak out. No hints of acquisitiveness, no missiles, not even missives. McColl told his shareholders only that he would "continue to seek additional capital for the company," without giving them a hint as to why that capital was being stockpiled.

On that fragment of information alone, Wall Street's ears pricked up. Looking at NCNB's potential earnings picture, one analyst concluded that "maybe the despair that dogged the industry last year is beginning to lift." That gave McColl something to smile about. Simply by snorting and pawing the ground in a vaguely bullish way, he had the power to generate a chorus of "Olés!" from the national economy-watchers.

But this time around, he told himself, Hugh McColl would not act like some out-of-control hero on a mission. He could be a bull on Wall Street, but not in the china shop of antiquarian Bennett Brown. Dick Spangler had given him Sun Tzu's *The Art of War*, and McColl believed the Chinese classic was directing him to concentrate on "doctrine." The good general must organize, control, assign specific officers to specific jobs. This time around, McColl would use the talents he had assembled, the talents he believed to be the best in the banking business. Jim Hance would handle finances, Bill McGee logistics, Paul Polking the legal end. Joe Martin would be in charge of communications and Chuck Cooley would be McColl's personal trainer.

"What did we do wrong last time?" he asked Cooley.

"Everything but walk away from it," Cooley answered. "Last time we let C&S cause people to believe that we were the Huns, that we were brutal and people of low character."

As in all caricatures, McColl mused, there probably was a grain of truth in that. Naturally, he must not show any brutishness this time around. More important, before Brown and Bottorff started labeling him, he wanted some labels he could put on them. He asked Cooley to develop a profile of each of the men. Not just a resume, but a psychological profile. Cooley could hire whomever he needed to get that done, but McColl wanted the information ASAP. Cooley went back to his office and found a number for an industrial psychologist from whom Cooley had learned "a lot about how to look at people." But the doctor was unavailable for several days. "Hell, I don't have time to wait for him to call me back," Cooley told himself. "Let me just do it myself."

Dick Stilley's people brought him everything ever written by or about Bennett Brown and Dennis Bottorff. He closeted himself with the clippings in his office for a couple of days, like a photographer in a darkroom, painstakingly developing pictures of two men upon whom his own future now seemed to depend. Slowly, images emerged.

Bottorff was looking to Cooley like the best candidate for villain of the piece. The role, as performed, suggested a man who was acquisitive, or else not up to the job. Perhaps someone had craftily concealed the extent of Sovran's problems from a savior-searching Brown in 1989. Perhaps, instead, Bottorff's people were not good enough to know what was going on in their own company. The playbill called C&S/Sovran a "merger of equals." Now Denny Bottorff seemed intent on pushing Brown off the stage, even as Bottorff's bad loans were about to bring the final curtain crashing down on C&S/Sovran.

On the other hand, Bennett Brown was emerging as Chuck Cooley's designated good-guy. He was the closest thing to a hero that C&S/Sovran could claim: "very, very nice . . . a gentleman . . . honest . . . highly left-brain-oriented." Cooley's profile of Bennett Brown was that of a man who cared about his company, about his people and about his customers. In this regard, Cooley believed, Brown closely resembled Hugh McColl. Brown's primary motivation at this stage of his career, Cooley concluded, was to retire "with honor."

Cooley's profiles suggested to McColl and Frank Gentry a strategy based on acknowledgment of Brown's heroic posture, his commitment to leading a team. McColl must erase his old images of Brown as the vindictive, personal attacker, the slinger of toy tigers. In 1989 Brown was being attacked by an outsider. Now, two years later, Brown and his team were threatened by the enemy within. If McColl could convince Brown he could (A) retire with honor and with the respect of his followers, and (B) defeat Dennis Bottorff in the bargain, then Brown would very likely agree to the merger with NCNB. At that point it would be up to McColl to convince the Norfolk board members, and perhaps Bottorff as well, that the merger was also in their best interest.

Now that McColl knew everything about Bennett Brown, what did Bennett Brown think of him? Cooley had a paper prepared on that, too. McColl was: arrogant, overbearing, conceited, disdainful, presumptuous, crude, ungentlemanly, militaristic, power-driven, ambitious.

After accusing Cooley of spending his time copying a page of *Roget's Thesaurus*, McColl had to admit that he had a little image work to do. But, whatever it took, he would do it. This was the merger his bank needed if it was to grow. This was the direction in which he was destined to lead his people. He had failed them once and did not intend to fail them again. Even if he had to submerge his entire personality, he would get the deal done.

If he was to seek inspiration from ancient sources, he must turn not to *The Art of War*, but to the *Tao Te Ching*, in which the long-bearded Lao-tzu wrote that a leader who follows the Tao "has no need to resort to force of arms to strengthen the Empire, because his business methods alone will show good returns." Lao-tzu advised McColl to be "resolute, but not boastful; resolute, but not haughty; resolute, but not arrogant."

It fell to Chuck Cooley and Joe Martin to coach him, to take turns being Bennett Brown while they taught him how to be gentler, less aggressive, less abrasive. For weeks they worked, like a boxer and his trainers, going one-on-one with a surrogate Brown.

"Lead with a left," Cooley said. "Talk grandfather talk." Both men had grandchildren, so talk about the great company they could build, even the great country they could build, for their grandkids. Throw a togetherness jab: if there was a way to make a great bank work, two men as accomplished as they were could find it. In fact, they could lead arm-in-arm, in the clinches, Brown as chairman, McColl handling the CEO grunt work, equal salaries, equal limelight. A little fancy footwork to make it seem like the other guy's idea: McColl was delighted that Brown had seen fit to reconsider and to make NCNB his choice. As for the last time around, what had Bennett himself said to Jane? Just business. A man does what he has to do in business. Weren't they still friends, after all?

Shortly after that session, on April 24, McColl walked into the annual shareholders' meeting. If they were not up for a standing ovation, at least his shareholders were breathing easy again. The company's first quarter earnings were up to $1.16 a share, four and one-half times better than its performance the previous quarter, when it had netted a paltry twenty-six cents a share. McColl promised shareholders their bank would be "growing" again. He did not say just how it would be growing.

Jim Hance patiently explained the wisdom of the bank's huge bond portfolio—now worth $17.6 billion. He told shareholders this had resulted in a "paper profit" of $151 million for them. Hance was applauded also, even though he didn't say how all that money might be used.

The first week in May, Hugh McColl was ready to talk to Bennett Brown. According to the Wall-Chapman grapevine, Brown was ready to listen. The initial call was short, but not terse. Polite, but not stilted. McColl was pleased with the tone. Brown seemed to agree with his old friend—because, after all, 1989 had been "just business"—that together they just might be able to build a mighty fine company for their grandchildren. But Brown's executive committee had grandchildren, too. He would get back to McColl after he consulted them.

McColl chafed. He knew he had to let Brown set the pace, but McColl's engine had only one gear. He had to get his mind off C&S/Sovran. He spent time with Jane, spent time with grandson John, started a few new books.

He talked to Mark Leggett in Washington, asking him about the banking reform bill the White House had fashioned. Leggett, not sounding extraordinarily hopeful, said the House Banking Committee would be taking up the bill in the next couple of weeks. McColl said maybe he'd be up there for that. *Right*. He figured he had as much chance of selling Congress on Mr. Bush's bill as he had of selling Mephistopheles an igloo condo.

The better part of a month went by and still Bennett Brown didn't call. McColl complained to Craig Wall about the delay, but Wall assured him he was not getting jerked around. Brown would be calling.

Meanwhile, there was a curious nibble from an anonymous individual who claimed to be a "large C&S/Sovran shareholder" in Tennessee. Independently of Brown and Wall, this Tennessee investor had engaged a lawyer. The lawyer called to determine whether, by any stretch of the imagination, NCNB might be willing to buy C&S/Sovran.

Quickly, another tug at the line came from the direction of Richmond. It was another large shareholder looking for a solution to his sinking stock problem.

McColl told his team they would "go to the mattresses, like the Mafia does. Close down the twenty-third floor." Every bit of business that could be halted came to a halt. They nicknamed the Tennessee lawyer "Deep Throat," the pseudonym of the informant who leaked the story of the Watergate break-in that brought down Richard Nixon's presidency. NCNB's Deep Throat whispered intriguing tidbits about the goings-on in the C&S/Sovran boardroom. The directors seemed to be dividing into two warring camps. The more McColl heard, the more anxious he got about that long-anticipated call from Bennett Brown.

The call came the morning of May 30, and McColl wasn't in the office to take it. Instead he was playing on the living room rug with little John Spratt McColl Jr., age one. When he bounced into the office about nine-thirty, Pat Hinson told him he'd missed Mr. Brown's call and he cursed, very gently, before calling him back. As McColl waited for Brown to come on the line, he realized that "Sorry, Bennett, I was home playing with my little grandson" was not a half-bad way to start the conversation.

Sure enough, Brown ate that up. Good news, Bennett said. The executive committee wanted him to go ahead and talk with ol' Hugh. Bad news, though, was that they wanted him to wait until after the committee let the full board know what was going on here. McColl bit his tongue. And, oh-by-the-way, when would the board be getting together?

Well, not for a couple of weeks, in fact not until June 18. Bennett would get back to him just as soon as he could after that board meeting on the eighteenth.

June 18, McColl's birthday again, maybe a good sign. Maybe not, because it was on his birthday in 1985 that John Medlin of Wachovia snatched First Atlanta right out from under his nose.

With nineteen days to wait, McColl decided to go to Washington after all, go say hello to his brother-in-law, Congressman John Spratt, maybe talk Rep. Henry Gonzales's Banking Committee into passing the biggest overhaul of the industry since the Depression and incidentally legalizing interstate banking. That took up a day of his time. McColl gave the committee his best shot, then left Tim Hartman and Mark Leggett to carry on. None of them believed the Democratic Congress was going to pass what it could so easily dismiss as just another Republican attempt to give Big Business yet another advantage over The Little Guy. For once, McColl shared Tim Hartman's pessimism.

But his spirits were buoyed by what he learned in Washington about C&S/Sovran. For one thing, Bennett Brown's legal team was in a potentially fatal battle with the comptroller of the currency over the handling of certain loans in the D.C. area. For another thing, the infighting at C&S/Sovran was worse than it seemed. There were not two warring factions, but at least three. Brown's Georgia-South Carolina-Florida people were on one side, but Bottorff's Virginia camp was still split from the 1983 merger of Virginia National of Norfolk with First and Merchants Bank of Richmond. Hard times were opening old wounds.

McColl could only compare it to his early days at NCNB, when the vestiges of four different banks in Greensboro and Charlotte erupted in the "palace coup" against Tom Storrs. He was feeling better and better about his chances. On the other hand, with so many rival camps, McColl knew he could be subject to a sniper attack from an unexpected direction.

He decided to forget the banking reform bill and put his every effort into willing this merger into being. He sealed off the war room and his office on the twenty-third floor. Only his takeover team would gain admittance. He searched for inspiration in a book of Latin phrases, a gift from his London colleagues, and came up with: *Aureo hamo piscari*. He had it blown up and taped to a wall. Joe Martin knew that it meant, freely translated, if you want a big fish, use a golden hook.

McColl's hook was NCNB stock, glittering, golden. Martin, an occasional fly fisherman, observed that fishing demanded considerable patience, even more so than their big game hunting in Texas. If McColl understood the difference, that was a good sign. He confirmed that understanding with the second slogan he posted on the office wall: *Vincit qui patitur*. The one who endures, conquers. Martin did not mention to McColl the fact that his Latin dictionary listed an alternate translation for the verb *patior*. It could mean "to endure" or it could mean "to prostitute oneself."

Essential to McColl's enduring the wait was his ability to talk things over every night with his wife. In many ways Jane McColl seemed to be the direct descendant of her husband's grandmother, the wife of the "first Hugh." In 1909 Gabrielle had written that her "first object in life" was to "take care of Hugh. . . . It is on my mind day and night that I must be a tower of strength to him and a pillar of comfort, that I must keep him well and make him happy." In 1991, nearly a century later, Jane McColl helped her Hugh to refine Chuck Cooley's profile of Bennett Brown. She was certain that Bennett would respond to a sincere offer of friendship. She felt his determination to keep their friendship alive at the monetary conference in San Francisco.

McColl suspected that unfriendly directors and executives were taking potshots at Brown, blaming him for the company's problems. Brown was seeing his power to run the company draining away, drop by drop, like blood from a thousand insect bites. All the better to apply soothing friendship, Jane advised. Bennett would reckon Hugh as a friend in need.

"You know, Hugh," she said, "sometimes you take friendships for granted. You need to nurture a friendship. It takes work."

Jane could read her husband even better than she read other people. Getting to the top of his company had cost Hugh McColl dearly in terms of friendships. Yes, he took friendship for granted, and when friends transmuted into business associates—which they almost always did, in his experience—he tended to the business part and let the friendship part lie fallow. A bad habit, she figured.

On June 10, his best friend Jane left for her summer holiday at Litchfield, reminding Hugh he'd better not forget to keep in touch. "I don't want to have to hear about it on the six o'clock news, like I found out about Texas," she said. "This time you call me when you get your little banks bought." Hugh kissed her and promised he would call her. As she pulled away, he smiled at the bumper sticker he'd given her: "Behind every successful man is an exhausted woman."

McColl's birthday fell on a Tuesday. June 18 ten years ago, he'd blown out candles and made a wish on a plane, flying to Miami. His wish was to pin down the Florida National deal, but it didn't come true. This year he was safe in his office, waiting for a call from Bennett Brown, hoping like hell he'd have better luck this time. It wasn't until late afternoon that Pat Hinson buzzed him with the call he'd been waiting for.

Brown started on a cautionary note. He was sensing hostility from some of his shareholders. A few of them were even talking to the press, he said. They were blaming Brown (and McColl smiled but said not a word) for "picking the wrong suitor" two years earlier. The very same people who had cheered Brown's defiance of Hugh McColl now questioned how in the world he had ever let McColl's $2.4 billion deal get away. Finally, Brown got to the point: Yes, he had permission to carry on with discussions of a possible merger with NCNB.

It was all McColl could do to hold back a whoop. Calmly, sympathetically, he assured Brown that Hugh McColl and NCNB could be counted on to provide the blaze of glory Bennett required for his career finale in Atlanta. His words were the very balm Brown's bruised ego required.

There remained only that question of the *aurum* on the hook. How much gold would it take to buy Brown's glorious *coup de grâce*? Not so fast, cautioned Bennett; before he could talk price, his board wanted to understand just what sort of merger McColl had in mind. How soon could he come to Atlanta? McColl wanted to say he'd be there in about two hours, but remembered that Latin word *patitur*. Put up with it. Grin and bear it. He settled for two days. Brown said he'd be waiting for McColl at Atlanta's private airport, Peachtree-DeKalb, about noon on the twentieth.

"I'll be there at oh-twelve-hundred, *sharp*," McColl said. "See you then."

McColl immediately stepped over to see his chief of staff, Bill McGee. "I'll need the plane Thursday to go to Atlanta," he said. "Make sure the pilot knows I want to hit the ground at 11:59:59."

The next thing he scheduled was more coaching from Martin and Cooley. "It's not going to be about money," he told them. "And that's too bad, because we always have an advantage when it is purely about money."

It would be about friendship. The three plotters agreed that McColl would harken back to the old friendship, to morning walks on the South Carolina beach, to sharing good times, to volleyball games with their families and the Hodgeses and the Walls. Being grandfathers, Hugh and Bennett now had even more in common than before.

"Just be warm and caring," Cooley told him. That should be easy, he observed, because McColl was in fact a caring man. True, but McColl reminded his coaches that he harbored a certain resentment against Brown and his people for the personal attacks of 1989. "You don't just forget those things."

"No," Cooley said, "but this deal and this friendship must mean so much to you that you subordinate whatever those feelings might be."

"Everything you say has to be positive," Martin added. "And always there has to be an underlying promise that, with you at his side, Bennett can win his personal battle."

As the role-playing sessions went on, Craig Wall worked his pipeline, phoning in word that Bennett Brown wanted reassurance from McColl, before they went forward with a merger. Brown needed to be satisfied that a merger with NCNB would have a positive, not a negative impact on C&S/Sovran's communities, employees and stockholders.

As for communities, McColl would tell Brown he could anticipate no less a commitment than the one C&S had shown in its Georgia and South Carolina communities. A recent fifteen-page ruling from the Federal Reserve Board made the case, he explained. The Fed had labeled unfair lending charges against NCNB as ridiculous. The report sang NCNB's praises for making loans to poor and minority neighborhoods in North Carolina, Texas and Florida. Why should Brown expect a lesser level of commitment in Atlanta, where the C&S name meant so much to the company?

To satisfy Brown's concern over what would become of his employees, Cooley ordered up a mock corporate structure of the merged banks, similar to what he'd done with index cards for First Republic, only this time in a more presentable fashion. On the reverse of his chart—just in case that subject of *aurum* came up—was a theoretical stock exchange ratio. So much C&S/Sovran stock would be worth so many shares of NCNB stock, worth X number of dollars. McColl made certain it was all very hypothetical, nothing like negotiation, nothing like an offer to buy.

McColl ordered up a map of the combined franchise and rankings of banks by assets, showing NCNB-C&S/Sovran's impressive status as number two in the nation. It all went into McColl's briefcase, his "sales kit on the wonder of it all." As he was packing his kit, he remembered something. "Joe, where's that name you came up with last year? Maybe Bennett would like it."

Martin had to smile. Not last year. It was almost two years ago, right after the Texas invasion, that he first approached McColl with the idea of a new name. It was the head of marketing, Brad Iverson, who forced Martin to face the fact that "NCNB" as a name, in places like Texas, Florida and Virginia, was "somewhere between unmemorable and unintelligible." But McColl cut off the discussion immediately. "NCNB" was the company's flag and no one could think of desecrating it. Then, unwittingly, McColl himself had furnished Martin with the spark he needed to burn the old flag.

He passed to Martin a letter from one of his boyhood friends, Lee Ballard. McColl said they had camped together back in the North Carolina mountains. Ballard was writing to ask if McColl would be interested in the services of his new company in Dallas, the Naming Center. McColl wanted Martin to compose a friendly response, telling Ballard thanks, but no thanks. At first, Martin shrugged off the coincidence, assuming Ballard's company was one of those high-tech computer services where geniuses in lab coats fabricated nonword names that would never hurt anybody, as, for example, "Avantor," bought and trashed by C&S/Sovran. But as it turned out, the Naming Center employed the services of poets, writers, scholars of Latin and English—right up one of Joe Martin's favorite alleys. Without asking anyone's permission, Martin found a spot in his budget for the Naming Center's services.

One of Ballard's first recommendations was the word "Nation." Out of this grew the German-like compound "NationsBank," which would strike the ear as "Nation's Bank." Brad Iverson's public opinion research raised a startlingly favorable response to the name. Linguistic investigation found that nowhere in the world did "NationsBank" carry any negative connotation, nor did it require translation. Martin enlisted Paul Polking to conduct a legal review and, to everyone's astonishment, the name was virgin. Quickly, Polking registered "NationsBank" as a trade name, so that no one else could use it.

Next Martin prepared a rough-draft logo. "Nations" in blue, "Bank" in red, on a white field. Before he showed it to McColl, he ran it by terminally ill Buddy Kemp, because he knew McColl would consider nothing as sweeping as a name change without seeking Kemp's counsel. Kemp liked it. "NCNB's been a great flag," he told Martin, "but this one is better. And it's time to move on."

Martin finally sprang his name on McColl at a gathering of the bank's top executives. "You know, we've done some interesting market research," the choirboy sang sweetly, innocently. "I wonder if we'd be better off with this wonderful old set of red initials"—as he gestured to an NCNB logo mounted on the wall—"or with this dynamite red-white-and-blue word?" Martin pulled the logo from a file folder. He had been preparing for this battle according to Hugh McColl's manual: know the enemy, get your facts straight, cover your flanks, attack from the front. In this case the enemy was the CEO's obstinacy.

McColl picked up the logo, held it at arm's length.

Martin never stopped talking. "Because, if you agree with the research that says nobody can remember a set of initials and nobody knows what our initials stand for anyway, then you might be interested in the fact that we already own 'NationsBank.' It's ours, just as 'NCNB' is ours."

"We own it?"

"We own it."

Just to show he wasn't a dictator, McColl asked the others whether they thought Martin's notion was worth pursuing. Bill Vandiver spoke passionately against abandoning the grand old name. Ken Lewis, fresh from the front lines in Texas, said he disagreed with Vandiver.

"How long you been around here?" McColl sniped.

"Nineteen years," Lewis replied bluntly, "and NationsBank is a goddamn *great* name."

McColl remained unconvinced, but told Joe Martin he could keep working on it. He could hire one of those corporate identity specialists, to develop a graphic look. But for now—and forever as far as Hugh McColl was concerned—the name of his company was *NCNB*.

All that had happened when the only consideration for a name change was one of marketing. Now, as he prepared for his meeting with Bennett Brown, McColl wanted every card he could lay on the table. He could only imagine how ready Brown would be to get rid of that

"Sovran" dog tag. Here was a name that sounded important, almost majestic. It was Hugh McColl's gift to Bennett Brown. He asked Martin if he could have a "NationsBank" logo done up on foam-core board, as large as he could make it and still have it fit in his briefcase. Martin said he'd have it for McColl on the plane the next morning.

In the few hours they had left in the evening, Martin and Cooley drilled McColl and coached him on responses to anticipated questions and comments from Brown. When it was McColl's turn to lead the dance, they decided, he would use the "open probing technique," always asking questions, never pushing his own conclusions. He would be like a doctor with good bedside manners. *"Does it hurt here? What about this? Have you been sleeping well?"*

After a night and a day of that drill, McColl was exhausted. The evening of the nineteenth, since Jane was off at the beach, he stopped at a drug store for some low-attention-span reading material. Nothing deep, because he just wanted to get his mind off Bennett Brown and catch a little shut-eye. In the paperback rack he picked up a spy thriller by a British novelist he'd read before, Gerald Seymour. This one was called *Condition Black*, and the cover said it would be about somebody trying to build a nuclear missile for the Iraqis. Perfect.

At 2:00 A.M., he was still reading. Here was a bank harassing a poor nuclear physicist. Why were bankers always the bad guys? At 3:00 A.M., the hero, Erlich, was remembering his FBI training, "the six big P's." Sounded like something lifted from the marines. "Prior Planning Prevents Piss-Poor Performance." Boy Scout motto: Be Prepared. McColl felt as prepared as any man could be, but would that really Prevent Piss-Poor Performance, *à la* 1989? He really didn't want to come out of this one feeling lower than a snake's belly again. He had to keep himself under control. This novel was *not* taking his mind off his meeting with Bennett Brown.

At 4:00 A.M., Erlich was going in, guns blazing. "Condition Black" was supposed to be FBI jargon for a lethal assault in progress. This was not the book Cooley and Martin would have chosen for him. McColl was supposed to be thinking about a kinder, gentler NCNB, a company that cared for its communities and its customers and its people and its shareholders. He was not supposed to be thinking about war and gunfighting. Come to think of it, at 4:00 A.M. he was not supposed to be thinking about anything. Why was he still awake? Sometime after five he turned the last page, set the book down on the night table and thought about turning out the light. There seemed to be little point in it, sort of like Mr. Seymour's plot. The most important meeting of his life and he was about to face it without even one hour's sleep.

McColl got up, made himself some coffee, took a shower.

Shaving, he caught himself smiling in the bathroom mirror, thinking about Buddy Kemp. He often thought about Kemp when he shaved, about how tightfisted Buddy used to be. It was because of that time they'd been traveling together—who could remember where?—and McColl had forgotten his shaving cream at home and he went down the hall to Kemp's room and said, "Hey, could I get some shaving cream from you?" And Buddy said, "Hold out your hand," and went *spzzzt* with the Foamy can and out came about a dime's worth. "Buddy, give me some shaving cream, dammit." The man could squeeze more shaves out of a can than a stray hound dog in the summer had fleas. McColl lathered up extra-thick, thinking about Buddy Kemp, about what Jane said about nurturing friendships. It was time to be a friend to Bennett Brown.

He pushed aside his corporate-power blue pinstripes and found a kinder, gentler suit in the closet. A soft gray-blue plaid. Tie? Bennett was a University of Georgia alumnus and weren't their colors red and white? He found a red and white tie (also NCNB colors, but maybe Bennett wouldn't think of that.)

Cooley and Martin had agreed that only Martin would accompany McColl to Atlanta, since, as Cooley put it, Joe would be "more calming than I would be." Chuck was right. Joe just had that effect on people. They reconnoitered at the office briefly, checking and double checking that they had what they needed. The morning was dreary, so McColl and Martin left for the airport a few minutes earlier than they really needed to. They always raced each other to the airport, because everything at NCNB had to be a contest. On the way, the rain started. Martin made sure McColl pulled in ahead of him at the NCNB hangar.

As they settled in aboard the NCNB Cessna Citation, Martin worried that McColl did not seem to be his usual wired self. He seemed down, almost sleepy. Well, maybe Bennett Brown would interpret that as a positive sign. The Citation taxied out to the runway and got in line behind a big USAir jet, then went nowhere. The minutes on the runway dragged by. McColl was looking through his notes, studying his script, hearing radio gibberish from the cockpit. Finally, he lost his composure. "What the hell are y'all doing up there?"

The pilot turned around to face him. "A little trouble on the runway, sir."

"What does that mean? Does that mean USAir's afraid to take off just because it's raining cats and dogs?"

"No, sir. Geese."

"Geese?"

"On the runway, sir. Nobody can take off because a flock of geese have landed on the runway."

"Well, you're gonna have to goose this plane when we do get off, because you need to get me to Atlanta by noon."

At last the USAir flight took off, then it was their turn. The geese were gone, but the cats and dogs only got worse as they neared Atlanta, about an hour southwest under normal flying conditions. Flying directly into a strong headwind, the pilot had to run the engine full out. He would make it, because he was slightly more willing to crash the plane than to disappoint McColl.

The Citation hydroplaned on the flooded Peachtree-DeKalb runway, sliding to a stop near the C&S/Sovran hangar at one minute before noon. Martin, who would remain on board, gave him the V-for-victory sign as his CEO stepped down the ladder under a red and white NCNB umbrella.

McColl's wingtip shoes came off the ladder into a foot of water. His socks were soaked. He should have worn those boots he'd picked up in Texas. The water was osmosing up his pants legs. *Terrible start,* he thought, wading to a waiting golfcart. The man in the cart puttered him over to a nearby canopy. Under the canopy, standing beside a sedan, stood Bennett Brown.

McColl shook hands with Brown, got into the car and started off like a grandfather, talking about the weather. Small talk, all the way in, not to Brown's office, but to his home. *Interesting. Taking Thursday off to meet with me. Doesn't want anyone at the bank to know.* At the house, Bennett took him in through the back door, like they were good friends.

"Hugh, so good to see you!" Big hug from Mary Alice. *Much better start.* "How *is* that sweet wife of yours? Now you come right in here and take off those wet shoes and socks. Bennett, you go get Hugh a pair of dry socks." *It is going to work.*

They sat down at the breakfast room table for more small talk and lunch. Mary Alice Brown served homemade ham and cheese sandwiches with pickles on the side and a pitcher of iced tea. Talk about the beach, about Jane, about the children, about fishing. Talk about anything but business. *Ball's in your court, Bennett. Always, in your court.*

Mary Alice began to pick up the lunch things and that was Bennett's cue to say, well, he knew Hugh had some ideas he wanted to talk about. Which was Hugh's cue to say, as a matter of fact he'd brought a few things Bennett might like to take a look at. Which was Bennett's cue to say, why didn't they just go on into the dining room where they could spread everything out on the table.

They took their iced tea glasses and McColl opened his briefcase. Rather than sit across the table, he pulled out a chair right beside Brown, the way Cooley and Martin had rehearsed him. Side by side, they talked now about the importance of supporting communities and they talked about severance pay and they talked about return-on-investment for shareholders and they reached not a single conclusion.

What did Bennett think about leading such a big company as they might be forming?

Well, what did Hugh think?

Well, maybe it wouldn't be such a good idea for Bennett to resign at the end of the year, the way Bottorff wanted him to.

Funny, but Bennett had been thinking much the same thing.

And Hugh sure as hell would hate to lose everything Bennett brought to the company, sure as hell would hate to try to run that big damned company all by himself. Say, how about Bennett agreeing to stay on as chairman—just till he was ready to retire—and Hugh would handle all the CEO work? How about that?

Bennett could see how that made a certain amount of sense, provided the chairman got to take off and go fishing whenever he wanted to, heh-heh-heh. And, say, Hugh, by the way, what in the world could they call this new company, supposing they could do the deal?

Funny Bennett should ask that, because Hugh was hoping to get his opinion on something his people had come up with—just an idea, mind you, nothing cast in stone. He knew he had it somewhere . . . Oh, yeah, here. *NationsBank.* Had a certain ring to it, didn't Bennett think?

Well, yes. *NationsBank.* That was something to kick around now. Not bad.

And, oh, yes, look here, on the other side of this organization chart. We could do something like this for the shareholders. Give them, say, three-quarters of a share of NCNB stock for every one of their C&S/Sovran shares. Came to, let's see . . . $3.99 billion.

For perhaps the first time in his career, McColl sat through an entire buy-sell meeting without negotiating a single point, without making an offer, without reaching an agreement. It was more like a meeting of two college professors than of two corporate CEOs, like two men contemplating the origin of the universe.

After more than three hours, he shook hands again with Brown, thanked him again for the lunch and the dry socks, and boarded the Citation. The universe was done with rain for a while.

Martin asked him how it went and McColl answered, "Great. He's gonna get back to us after he sits down with his board. Let me just call the office before you debrief me."

McColl picked up the telephone, dialed Pat Hinson's number. But before she could pick up the phone at her desk—and she was always quick to answer—Hugh McColl was sound asleep. This was something Joe Martin had never witnessed in his career.

The takeover team had a weekend to recover, so McColl went to the beach to spend a little time with his wife, making sure to give her Mary Alice Brown's regards.

Monday, word came in from Deep Throat that both Brown and Bottorff were moving in their own heavy artillery. C&S/Sovran investment bankers, First Boston and Robinson Humphrey, were put on alert. Then in Norfolk, Denny Bottorff took the unusual step of hiring his own investment banker, Dillon Read.

"Unheard of," McColl declared. Nobody trusted anybody at C&S/Sovran. The target was beginning to leak information to the media. A bank analyst in Little Rock, Arkansas—perhaps another confidante of the Tennessee investor who'd hired Deep Throat—volunteered that he was "hearing more every day" about the likelihood of an NCNB-C&S/Sovran merger. At least no one had told the big boys yet. The word from Wall Street on that rumor was "unlikely." Tuesday, June 25, the cat scratched its way out of the bag. The merger talks were on the WBTV six o'clock news in Charlotte, as reported by the local *Business Journal*. The next morning, everybody who read the *Wall Street Journal* knew about it. A megadeal of megabanks was in the offing.

June 27, Charlotte readers woke up to a headline screaming; "NCNB GOES FOR NO. 2." If it was really going to happen this time, a merger with C&S/Sovran would create the second-largest bank in the United States. If McColl could pull it off, only John Reed's Citibank would be larger than his bank in Charlotte. Journalists everywhere realized that, for the first time since those New South pioneers dreamed their dreamy dreams, the United States' banking power was about to be divided more or less equally between the two sections of the nation. Even the *Atlanta Journal* bought into the idea, declaring the merger would be "a big banking boost" for the region.

That same day, a major print advertising campaign hit the newspapers and magazines, not only in NCNB's markets, but in those of C&S/Sovran as well. They were the ads Joe Martin had kept hidden in drawers that played the sweet music of community volunteerism. There were NCNB's "best bankers," still spending time in second grade as school volunteers. To make certain the message got through, tear-sheets had been delivered the day before to Martin's list of five thousand political and community leaders throughout the Southeast. Included in the mailing were all twenty-nine directors of C&S/Sovran.

Those directors came together the afternoon of the twenty-seventh, big wheels pregreased to mesh at last. Yes, said the board, Bennett Brown would be permitted to continue his merger talks with NCNB. The word "negotiations" at last was spoken aloud. After the meeting, Bennett Brown issued a brief and boring statement: "We are trying to determine from information obtained from NCNB and further discussions whether a combination of the two companies is in the best interests of the C&S/Sovran stockholders."

That "information" would be obtained over the upcoming weekend. Each bank would send a delegation of credit analysts, financial wizards and law viziers to the other bank, where books would be opened and files unlocked, in a ritual known as due diligence. Even the status of individual borrowers could be delved into, much as loan officers might investigate an applicant's creditworthiness.

From Dallas, Tim Hartman dispatched a posse of his best analysts, whose two years of work in Texas had seasoned them into perhaps the best in the industry. At NCNB Texas, they could round up what they called "dead horses"—loans that weren't ever going anywhere—like nobody's business. Working under the direction of Jim Hance, more than a hundred NCNB specialists converged on C&S/Sovran's major offices on Friday afternoon, June 28.

As the numbers came in to Charlotte, Hance confirmed that they were "serious numbers." His report to McColl divided the target bank's problems into three areas: bad real estate loans, a dysfunctional management structure—both of which came as no surprise—and the area of "nonintegrated systems," which McColl had not anticipated.

Hance reported that C&S/Sovran had "serious, extensive loan problems, centered in Florida and the mid-Atlantic states." Their management structure was poorly defined, in a "sort of loose confederation," with uniformly poor execution at every level. "They have huge market shares," Hance said, "and great customer bases, but they are getting along really poorly internally."

Mismatched systems were something else again. Because both C&S and Sovran had "just cobbled themselves together" out of multiple banking systems in six states, said Hance, none of their accounting, reporting and computer systems meshed properly. It was "unbelievably bad," Hance said. "Even the banks of the old C&S, in South Carolina and Florida and Georgia, don't talk, don't do anything together." Nor did the Sovran banks in Virginia communicate well with those in Maryland and Tennessee.

Fred Figge's analysis was that, essentially, they were dealing with not one bank but many banks in many states of disrepair. Curiously, the Atlanta bank actually had a "one" rating from the regulators, the equivalent of an "A" sanitation rating for a restaurant. Figge found that "quite interesting for essentially a bankrupt corporation."

Hance's prognosis: the combination of problems was fatal, imminently fatal. Only the immediate surgery of merger with NCNB could bring it back from the grave. Factor in NCNB's assets, bleed off the bad loans, and the numbers should work.

There was a minor setback on the public relations front. The Monday following the due diligence weekend, the South lost the potential of gaining the second-largest bank in the country. In New York, Chemical Bank announced it would buy Manufacturers Hanover Trust, and THAT would create a new number two, much larger than the proposed southeastern megabank. McColl would have to settle for third place, which wasn't so bad.

Joe Martin ordered up a batch of white baseball caps with the NationsBank logo in crisp red and blue. They were supposed to be secret, but he wanted McColl to have one, to give to Bennett Brown.

McColl liked it so much he wore it to work Tuesday morning, July 2, looking rather jaunty and causing something of a stir among his associates. "Whoever was in charge of blurt control," Dick Stilley groused, "has failed miserably."

To McColl, nothing mattered but that Bennett Brown was ready to talk again. The two CEOs would meet at Litchfield Beach over the Independence Day weekend.

Wednesday the third, McColl drove his Ford pickup truck to the beach, four hours of country music along the still-disreputable South Carolina highways. He bounced through Darlington and Florence and Conway, slipping south on South Carolina 544 to avoid Myrtle Beach, turning off U.S. 17 just north of Winyah Bay, where the Waccamaw and the Pee Dee dumped their drops into the great bucket of the Atlantic.

Jane was full of news about her high school reunion.

"Can you believe this? There's this girl who was in my class who works for Sovran in Virginia, who has told all these people she works with, 'I know Jane McColl. I grew up with her.' And now she says to me, 'I heard all about our merger. Isn't it going to be exciting?' And I looked right at that girl—I probably was very rude to her—and I said, 'Oh, yeah?' I said it, and I meant it, too. She looked at me real funny, and I wanted to say, 'Honey, you never lived through a merger. You don't have a clue what it is like. Not a clue.' I wanted to tell her it's not all big money and excitement. You know, that kind of stuff. It is damned hard work, and every time it's a balancing-personalities act.

"But, you know, Hugh, I really am excited for you. I am real, real excited about this."

Hugh McColl was pretty darned excited himself.

The phone rang about sundown and it was Bennett Brown, wondering whether they could get together first thing in the morning. Breakfast at our place, McColl suggested. No, said Brown, better just to take a walk together on the beach. He'd be by about seven.

"Oh-seven-hundred," McColl said. "I'll be waiting."

Next morning he stood on the third-floor porch, sipping the latest in a long line of cups of coffee, when he spotted Brown coming toward the house, picking his way through the shore grass and the picket fencing the state put up to slow Nature's reclamation of the sand. Brown had on white shorts and a striped shirt with the tail hanging out, black Bass moccasins, no socks. He was wearing an Atlanta Braves cap. McColl had on purple shorts and an inoffensive white golf shirt he'd picked up at some meeting or another. He decided to stay barefoot, so he could feel the warm morning beach. Downstairs, he gathered up his sunglasses as he went to the door, heard Jane saying, "Bennett, if you all think you're going to be inconspicuous walking up and down the beach on the fourth of July weekend, everybody and his dog out here is going to know who you two are."

"Oh, I don't know," Bennett answered. "It's still pretty early."

"By the time you get back it'll be going on eight, and that isn't early."

But Bennett seemed to be right. Perhaps on Independence Day people were getting a late start, anticipating fireworks later. McColl let Brown pick the direction and he gestured south. McColl took the surf side, since he was barefoot and could enjoy the occasional pleasure of an overreaching wave. The surf was calm though, with only a few wisps of white over in the west. Because the beach sloped toward the ocean, McColl had to look up more than usual to make eye contact with head-taller Bennett Brown, but eye contact was not what Brown was looking for. On the beach they could meander, like two men with nothing much on their minds. They could walk side by side, looking down at the beach ripples, the tidal pools, the raucous gulls, the sandpipers, the micro-crabs darting from the retreating surf to burrow out of harm's way, the shards of seashells in all their shades of brown that make the occasional Carolina beach find so celebratory.

McColl felt the unstated purpose in Brown's selection of turf. *Side by side, showing ourselves we are not in confrontation. Conversation, but no eye contact, no physical intimidation, no body language, just walking.* There was no need even to glance up at the occasional passerby, to note whether it was a stranger or a friend—morning exerciser, shell gatherers, fellow ruminants. Had Bennett read Sun Tzu himself? One of the five fundamental factors in winning a war was weather, the interaction of natural forces, like sun, sea and wind. Another was terrain, whether ground could be traversed easily and with what danger.

"What about the communities we serve, all those little towns?" Brown was asking. "Could we do as much for them if we move all the decision-making to Charlotte?"

McColl threw the question back at him. "Why would we do less?" He acknowledged that C&S had a reputation as a "great corporate citizen," was tempted to say that NCNB's reputation was even better, but said instead, "together we'll be able to do even more for our cities and our towns and our neighborhoods."

Brown began to talk about possible job losses and, for the first time, McColl found himself sounding a bit like Tom Storrs, a bit circumspect. He had to be careful not to promise what he couldn't deliver, because he was pretty certain they would need to eliminate some jobs, perhaps even close a few branches, once the buyout—merger—happened.

As he listened, it became clear to McColl that the principal concern was Brown's own people, the ones who had cheered him two years earlier, when he rallied them in the Atlanta lobby, when he threw them the stuffed tiger that was Hugh McColl and invited them to tear it limb from limb. It was the people who had taken it upon themselves (he must assume) to spread vicious rumors about Hugh McColl, to create anxiety for his family. McColl needed now to set Brown's mind at ease about the fate of these people once they pledged allegiance to their former enemy.

They were coming up to the inlet that cut off Litchfield Beach from Pawley's Island, so they had walked precisely a mile and five-eighths. McColl was always taking the measure of things, and of people, making note of details. He knew the distance from his condominium to the end of the beach.

"I would need to be sure about my people," Brown was saying. "I couldn't abandon them."

On a chance wave, breaking just at the shoreline from an almost glassy ocean, a large shell tumbled. It was one side of a saw-toothed pen shell, about nine inches long, shaped like a quill, with a point at one end. McColl stooped down and stopped the shell from rolling back out with its receding wave. He fit the convex surface against the palm of his right hand. When he wrapped his fingers around the edge, it became a perfect stylus.

"Let's outline the company," he said.

With his left hand he smoothed out a section of the beach that was still firm from last night's high tide, and McColl began to draw. An organizational chart of "NationsBank" took shape in the sand. At the top, furthest from the ocean, initials "BB/HM," side by side, equal, nonconfrontational. Short line down, long line across. More initials. What about Brown's top credit man? He'd need to be protected.

"You don't need to protect him," McColl said, scratching his initials into the sand. "I need him, I want him. That is not an issue, so don't even think about it."

They talked about who would go where. McColl knew the names of Brown's key players and what Brown would expect for them, because Chuck Cooley had provided him with that information. All the players, like his charts of New York Yankees and their opponents, forty years ago. What do you say we put this one here? No, maybe he'd be better over here. Right . . . Everyone had a place, everyone fit in. Look up at Bennett Brown and see the big face almost smiling, thinking: *I win.*

McColl was thinking the same thing: *I win.* Because when the conversation got down to organizational structure, they already were talking details. Once he was into details, he was selling, and for McColl, selling was winning.

As the men started back, ready for another cup of coffee, McColl felt Brown's arm around his shoulder. One important thing about that chart in the sand, which did not have to be said, was that Denny Bottorff's name was not on it, anywhere.

Jane McColl knew the merger was on when they opened the door of the condo and she heard the two men being cheery and cute. When Bennett Brown said that maybe they should preserve the moment and wondered whether anybody had a camera, Jane remembered that her daughter-in-law, Lee, had brought one along, so she ran up and got it and walked back out to the beach and Hugh took off his sunglasses and Bennett doffed his cap and she snapped one off. Then Hugh had an idea and said to wait while he ran back to the house, and when he came back he had that white cap with the NationsBank name on it and he traded it with Bennett for his Atlanta Braves cap— which was too big for Hugh and Jane told him so—and the NationsBank cap was way too small for Bennett, but he put it on anyway, and the two men shook hands and Jane didn't even have to tell them to smile, so she was pretty sure they had done their deal and Hugh had bought his little banks.

It was a four-day weekend and there were other meetings to endure. McColl was on pins and needles the entire time, with Jane trying to pull him down to earth, down to the water to play with little John, maybe build sand castles instead of sky castles. But Jane couldn't distract him from brooding about personalities.

His gnawing uncertainty was the personality of Dennis Bottorff. On Friday, as arranged by Craig Wall and Hugh Chapman, Bottorff flew in from Norfolk to meet at Wall's house. McColl and Brown arrived at the house early. There was no one at home, but McColl knew where to find the key—the same place it had been hidden since the Walls and McColls and Hodges owned the house together—so they went on inside to wait. When Judith Wall came back from grocery shopping she heard the two men deep in conversation. Because she knew what they were talking about, Judith decided to sit on the steps and wait for Craig to arrive rather than disturb them. McColl was delighted to be meeting in Wall's house, which everyone but he and Craig Wall would perceive as neutral territory. He felt a little like Brer Rabbit in the briar patch, right at home.

Wall and Chapman were on their way back from the little air field at Georgetown, about twenty miles southeast, with Bottorff. On the drive, Wall primed Bottorff for his first head-to-head encounter with Hugh McColl, assuring him that the notorious barking and snapping was just a ruse, that McColl was really a pretty friendly little dog, once he got to know you.

By the time the other three arrived, McColl and Brown had worked out a strategy to satisfy Bottorff, concentrating on the technical details. Bottorff knew about the difficulties with integrating management and systems, and he was painfully aware of the loan problems, so McColl could talk about how they would organize and manage the company, how NCNB's technology would help bring the disparate banks together.

Finding McColl on his best behavior, Bottorff let his guard down, reminding McColl of a player he'd beat in poker games long ago. Bottorff was confident he could get the upper hand. His tactic here was to study the enemy—and to Bottorff, every other player in the room might seem like an enemy—then go back to Virginia and work out his plan. He most likely would see himself as heir apparent. McColl thought, *He believes he's clever enough to take me on and come out the winner. He won't even make it to the starting line, much less the finish line.*

By the end of three hours, Dennis Bottorff seemed satisfied. He had explored every part of the deal he intended to explore. From his perspective, as from McColl's, everything but the price had been agreed upon. McColl volunteered to drive Bottorff back to his airplane.

Saturday, Brown invited one of his Atlanta investment bankers from Robinson-Humphrey for dinner at the Brown home on the marshy banks of the Waccamaw River. McColl knew this meeting was important, since anonymous executives from Atlanta and Norfolk were quoted as being "skeptical of NCNB's financial strength."

The fact that the meeting was a success, Jane attributed to Mary Alice Brown's skills as a hostess. Six people, including analyst Jon Burke and his wife, mixing conversation about families and fishing and weather in with high finance, and it all went smoothly. On the way home she told Hugh he was "damned lucky, because only Mary Alice could have pulled that off. And it was a magnificent dinner."

To Hugh McColl, the deal was the thing, and it was beginning to look magnificent indeed. If he succeeded he would be heading up a company unlike anything the United States had ever seen. It would be a unified nine-state system, eighteen hundred branches controlled from Charlotte, stretching from Maryland to Texas. He would be in charge, with Bennett Brown in the largely symbolic role of chairman, with Dennis Bottorff forced out, with six of eight senior positions held by his people. The board would be McColl's, since all eighteen NCNB directors would be stepping up to the NationsBank board, to be joined by only eleven directors from C&S/Sovran. McColl had only two more hurdles to clear and it would be a done deal.

The first hurdle was in Norfolk, the morning of July 16. The C&S/Sovran Board would consider a merger and would need to hear from McColl. He arranged for Ed Herlihy to join him from Wachtel, Lipton, just in case somebody wanted to negotiate price. Otherwise he would be alone. He would be the peacemaker, walking unarmed into the divided enemy camp. The C&S/Sovran directors would be sick of fighting each other, weary of explaining to their shareholders, frightened of losing to the economy.

As Lao-tzu put it in the *Tao Te Ching*, "Briars and thorns grow rank where an army camps." Hugh McColl, the warrior-banker-taoist, would play the conciliator. Again, Brer Rabbit in the briar patch.

They kept Brer Rabbit stewing outside the board room for four hours while the C&S/Sovran directors argued among themselves. There was a move to scuttle the deal, but Craig Wall convinced the opposition to hear from the man who had traveled so far to meet with them and to answer their questions. When at last he went in, McColl was hungry and agitated, feeling tense and balled-up inside, as he'd felt facing that waterfall on the *Jungfraujoch*. He began his pitch, like some tenor launching into his big aria, anticipating bravos and applause throughout. But someone left the lights on in the opera house and he could see all the blank stares, read the uncomfortable body language. Only Ed Herlihy, standing in the back of the hall, seemed to catch McColl's drift.

Craig Wall wanted to tell him he was doing a great job because, with this audience, sitting on their hands meant they weren't lobbing grenades. What Wall was thinking was: *Great job! You're selling them.* It was the new name, NationsBank, that put them over the edge. And Wall thought, *He's some kind of genius to come up with a terrific name like that!*

McColl finished his aria, took some questions, thought he might have answered them too aggressively, then was asked to wait outside for a while. He found a telephone and called his office, reporting rather solemnly that he had nothing to report. His nerves were jangling. He was finding it difficult to focus and he just prayed no one came out with more questions. He couldn't understand why they had jerked him around with all that waiting. He wanted something to eat.

The door from the boardroom opened and Bottorff came out.

"Okay," he said, "We'll move to the next phase, we'll go to negotiations."

We'll go to the mattresses, McColl thought, dismissing the passivist Lao-tzu and returning to Sun Tzu, where he felt much more at ease. Those who master the five fundamental factors win; those who do not are defeated. *If all they're looking for is money, we've got them by the short hairs.*

"We probably ought to get together later this week in New York," Bottorff was saying. "Say, Friday?"

"To hell with Friday. I'm leaving for New York right now. I'll meet you there tomorrow." *Keep pressing. Give them no time to reconsider.* New York was where the legal teams were, the place where the merger contract could be drawn up within a few hours after an agreement was reached.

Negotiations began Wednesday, July 17, at the offices of First Boston Corporation, C&S/Sovran's investment brokers. There actually was but one point to be negotiated, and that was the true value of a share of C&S/Sovran stock in the months ahead. If Jim Hance and his advisors were correct, especially in their prediction of a continuing drop in D.C.-area property values, then one hundred shares of C&S/Sovran were worth only about seventy-five shares of NCNB.

On the other side of the table, Hance's counterpart, Jim Dixon, maintained that his hundred shares ought to be worth at least ninety-five shares of NCNB. Considering that there were nearly 150 million shares of C&S/Sovran stock outstanding, and considering that NCNB stock was trading at over thirty dollars per share, the distance between the two sides of the table was a gulf of several hundreds of millions of dollars.

After two days the two sides were no closer than they had been when they started. McColl's spirits were hissing out like air from a punctured tire, so he kept telephoning Jane, who now was back in Charlotte. His friend Jerry Richardson always told him he could count on Jane to "ground" him, keep him in touch with reality. By Thursday night, he figured he could use a little more grounding, even if it had to be long-distance.

"You sound like you're about to jump out of your skin, you really do," Jane said.

Hugh told her the lawyers from C&S/Sovran were getting on his nerves. He'd think they had the deal done, they'd go across the hall for a conference and they would come back with changed minds. But he agreed with her when she said, "You just need to calm down."

He decided to suggest that he and Bennett leave New York and slip down to Washington Friday, for a talk with Bill Taylor, senior staff member at the Federal Reserve, about the way the economy was going. Taylor was "a regular guy," he told Brown, "one of the most intelligent, the most logical, and the toughest people in government." Taylor might give Brown a more realistic view of the future than the one he was getting through the rosy bifocals of his attorneys. Maybe Taylor could also help him follow his wife's advice to calm down.

The next day McColl was pacing the floor of the Wachtel, Lipton office, waiting for Brown to call so they could fly to Washington. Hance, Figge and Cooley did their best to ground him, but he was a live, sparking wire. Convinced Brown was standing him up, he personally phoned Taylor at the Fed to apologize and cancel the meeting. "I'm pretty sure the whole damned deal is off," he said to his teammates, hanging up the phone. "The hell with this. We're not going to sit around here any longer."

Cooley suggested they walk down the street to Brooks Brothers. They each could buy a necktie to commemorate the occasion. Since there was as yet no Brooks Brothers store in Charlotte, the trip shouldn't be a total loss. McColl thought that was a grand idea. Just let him stop at the men's room first. These days, he never passed up an opportunity to empty his bladder, because he could never be sure how soon it would feel full again. Hance, Cooley and Figge went with him.

Thanks to the visit to the men's room, the four were still in the lobby, waiting for an elevator, when one of the Wachtel, Lipton secretaries opened the office door and announced that Bennett Brown was on the phone. McColl went back in to take the call. Brown was excruciatingly cheerful. Maybe they should just go down to the beach and relax for the weekend, forget all this and start over on Monday. McColl felt his teeth clench. "Bennett, I'm not going to the beach. I'm staying right here and I'm going to make you an offer even if you're not around to hear it."

At five-thirty Brown and Bottorff arrived at Wachtel, Lipton, sans lawyers and investment counselors. Exactly one hour later, they had the deal that was acceptable to all three men. One hundred shares of C&S/Sovran stock would be exchanged for eighty-four shares of NCNB stock, which would be valued at the closing price that day, July 19, of $31.08 per share. The deal would be worth more than $4.5 *billion*. Somebody joked that maybe it wouldn't have happened if Hugh hadn't stopped off at the men's room.

Lawyers would work through the night completing the paperwork. Directors of both corporations would be summoned to special meetings on Sunday, first in Charlotte and then in Atlanta. McColl would attend both those meetings. Monday morning he and Brown would be back in New York to tell the world. Then they'd leave Hance, Ken Lewis and Hugh Chapman to answer investment analysts' questions while they flew south to meet the press in Atlanta.

Determined not to repeat his faux pas in Texas, McColl telephoned his wife from the small lobby of Peachtree-DeKalb Airport. The C&S/Sovran directors had convened there for a special emergency meeting and approved the merger twenty-eight to one. "The only 'no' vote," he told Jane, "came from this old gentleman who just couldn't bear to say goodbye to the C&S name," Hugh said. He wanted to tell her he was now CEO of a brand-new company, NationsBank, the third-largest bank in North America, with assets of $119 billion and nearly sixty thousand employees, but Jane wanted to tell him *her* news.

"The nicest thing just happened," she said, "Morgan Stanley sent me the most beautiful arrangement of flowers. Isn't that sweet?"

McColl couldn't hold back a laugh. He said, "Those flowers cost me $11 million."

He was not exaggerating about the cost of that floral arrangement. Morgan Stanley was due to collect brokerage fees of $11 million. Six other investment and brokerage houses would be sharing in almost $30 million more. McColl had that figure in mind when he told the media that the South would at last have a bank capable of "meeting financial needs from Main Street to Wall Street."

As far as "Main Street" was concerned, McColl's teammates brought him a brash idea, something that would protect his big buy-out from the costly delays being caused by so-called "neighborhood groups" and their challenges based on the Community Reinvestment Act. The idea initially came from Cathy Bessant, who was heading up Ken Lewis's efforts to invest in the struggling communities of Texas. Bessant had started her banking career with First Republic, moving to NCNB in 1982, where she was assigned to develop business among large corporations. When Lewis switched her to community reinvestment in 1989, she found her niche, considering herself "fortunate to have found a place where vocation meets avocation." Given a free hand in Texas, Bessant was convinced she had the support of both Lewis and McColl for her commitment to supporting the towns and cities where the bank did business. "We've got to matter," she felt. "Communities have to be better for our presence than they would be without us."

When Lewis learned he was going to leave Charlotte—having been reinstalled there only recently—to take charge of the new Atlanta office, he asked Bessant to join him at the NCNB Tower for a meeting with Joe Martin. Bessant arrived armed with figures illustrating the current community reinvestment and minority loan programs of both NCNB and C&S/Sovran. She pitched the notion that the new corporation should start out with a commitment then unheard of in American business. NationsBank, the bank with the widest-ranging geographical reach in the United States, would invest $5 billion in its communities over the next ten years.

Bessant's proposal had merit for several reasons. For one, Lewis had picked up considerable concern among neighborhood groups, particularly in and around Atlanta, that a bigger bank, headquartered two states away, would be less sympathetic to their needs. Those disgruntled locals could delay or even derail the merger in Washington. The bank's stated position was that the only way to build its business was neighborhood by neighborhood, and that the larger it became the stronger those foundation building blocks needed to be. But Cathy Bessant's experience allowed her to look at the new merger through the eyes of people who had grown up and invested lifetimes in those communities. For her it was "very easy to see where that cynicism and that skepticism and those fears, real fears, about our dedication to local markets would be coming from." The $5 billion commitment, she argued, would "immediately and in a very big way make a statement about how we intend to be important in neighborhoods."

Bessant's second point was one she had heard McColl deliver on more than one occasion: the company's long-term prosperity must always be dependent on the prosperity of the markets it served. "A key to that success," she told Lewis and Martin, "is what happens in low-income areas, in central urban areas and in other places that people generally think of as underdeveloped." The firm commitment to spend money in the economically depressed segment of the market would drive business in the thriving neighborhoods.

Finally, the unprecedented announcement would "make a statement to our employees about what kind of company this is, a company that believes in doing the right thing." That statement would be amplified many times if the community reinvestment effort was not placed in the hands of a small cadre of specialized lenders, but spread out through all parts of the team. Every employee—or "associate," in the newly decreed NationsBank vernacular—would be responsible for and rewarded for helping the corporation to fulfill its $5 billion commitment. "We wanted to say to every one of our associates, 'Each of you had a hand in this because it goes directly to the soul of who we are as a company. And we are so committed to this that we are willing to set the biggest goal ever for community-development lending and investment.'"

After they had discussed Bessant's arguments and considered her figures, the two senior executives agreed it would be no challenge for them to sell the notion to McColl. But Lewis raised another question. If the company could comfortably do $5 billion over ten years, would it be too much of a stretch to double the amount, to a billion a year for ten years?

Bessant laughs when she remembers the ease of answering that question. "We all looked at each other and said, 'Do we have the power and the capability to do ten billion?' And I don't want to make it sound like it was totally without intellectual substance, but we really basically concluded, 'Okay, five sounds good, but ten—ten *says* something. Ten says what we really want to say.' So we then had to build the infrastructure to deliver on our hyperbole."

At a news conference, McColl announced that over the next ten years NationsBank would commit $10 billion to low-income areas. "It's clearly the biggest number I've ever committed to anybody," McColl told a reporter. His number captured the imagination of the national media and made it virtually impossible for any disgruntled neighborhood association to challenge successfully the biggest business deal ever contemplated in the southern United States.

Cathy Bessant was promoted to head up the new companywide Community Development effort. Her first task was to make sure NationsBank had "products and programs and the right kind of people in place to do the internal motivation, and to do the internal road-mapping." Her object was to engage the industry's largest work force, more than sixty thousand men and women, "to do their jobs, just to do them in an expanded way and with a heightened sense of urgency, particularly about low-income areas and low-income people and minority borrowers." She quickly instituted the LEND Award—an acronym for Leadership Excellence in Neighborhood Development—to be awarded annually to a hundred or more individuals in different jobs and different markets who would have contributed substantially to the corporate community investment initiative. The awards would become highly visible and highly prized and they would bear witness to the commitment not only of the senior executives and loan officers, but of everyone in the company.

The ten-year CRA pledge was such a captivating gesture that Dick Rosenberg of BankAmerica Corporation copied it almost immediately. In August he announced a pledge of $12 billion in low-income loans over the next ten years, provided the Federal Reserve approved his bank's acquisition of Security Pacific. The BofA-SP deal would create the nation's new second-largest bank, dropping NationsBank from number three to number four before it could even be officially born.

But McColl got a public relations leg up on Rosenberg. He decreed yet another community commitment in the amount of $40 million to

Atlanta's 1996 Olympic Games, the first to be held in the South. At the same time, he extended a $300 million line of credit to Olympics organizers. This immediately endeared NationsBank to the city of Atlanta and to the state of Georgia. It also gave McColl a vehicle for spreading the word about his new bank. As the only banking sponsor of the Olympics on television, NationsBank looked to be winning the gold medal of name recognition.

To further solidify the company's hold on the city—and on the former C&S faithful—McColl declared Atlanta headquarters for the new General Bank, to be directed by Ken Lewis, who, with his wife Donna, would be moving down Interstate 85 to Atlanta.

Jane decided she would talk Hugh into buying the house into which the Lewises had just settled and now would have to sell. Like the McColl home, theirs was in Eastover, but it was a little nicer, a little newer, and a lot bigger than the house on Colville Road. She *had* to talk Hugh into it, because she just would *not* go along with his plans to build a house. While Donna and Ken were off in Atlanta, looking for a new neighborhood, Jane could spend some time there with her friend and decorator, Morrison Brown.

"Hugh is about to be dead to *build* a house," she complained to Brown. "I don't want to be building in the public eye. I mean, they'll be having pictures in the paper about how much the woodwork costs and everything else. I am just tired of being everybody's conversation point."

Jane was worried the Lewis's house might be too fancy for her and Hugh, "all that molding and all," but Brown set her mind at ease. This would be a perfect house, once she got her things in, her earthy colors, her simple lines. There was an airy, sunny den, where Hugh could stretch out on the sofa and fall asleep watching an old movie on television. There was a wood-paneled study in the front where he could keep his books and some of his favorite mementos.

Jane agreed. It would be a good place for her to keep him grounded, when grounding was what he needed. Besides, he was bound to like the name of the street. How could her Hugh McColl ever turn down an address on Scotland Avenue?

CHAPTER 15

At fifty-six, the man in Hugh McColl's bathroom mirror had a face on
the downhill slope of middle age: deep lines, pouches under the eyes,
brown spots in the tan skin, gray hair streaked with black now, instead
of the other way around. McColl found out he had onset diabetes—
which helped explain some of the difficulties he'd endured on the glacier climb, those afternoon agitations and hunger pangs as he dealt with
the C&S/Sovran merger—and doctors were telling him to take it easy.
His standard retort about stress was: "I don't have it, I give it."

Nevertheless, he took charge of his body like he took charge of his
company. Diet and exercise for the diabetes, no medication. To help
with the stress, he bought the vacant lot next to his new house and
took up gardening. He bought a lot of fancy bird feeders, too. He
started learning about dahlias and rufous-sided towhees. He got himself a Spanish tutor, because he believed Spanish was the language of
the future. During the fall and winter months he booked every weekend at a hunting camp in the South Texas coastal plain so he could
hunt quail. Nobody down there in the mesquite desert gave a damn
about his bank, and a lot of them spoke Spanish.

"Everything's done," he said, watching a customer cash a check on the
first day of business at NationsBank. He was quick to add, "Of course,

it's a beginning, not an end." But a beginning of what, exactly? The warlord of American banking found himself wearing a purple stole, like Caesar back from the Gallic Wars. Tribute was flowing from conquered enemies, conquered hearts. He heard his praises sung by *Newsweek* and *Business Week*, by *Fortune* and *Institutional Investor*, by even the *New York Times*.

Like it or not, McColl seemed to have built an empire, maybe too big to get any bigger. NationsBank was the fourth-largest bank in deposits. It had assets of $113 billion. McColl controlled twice as many branches as any other banker in the country, nineteen hundred of them. In geographical reach, NationsBank dwarfed the competition, stretching from Baltimore, Maryland, to Brownsville, Texas. It would take three days to drive that distance. "An awesome network," *Business Week* called it, one that could be "a model for other banking combinations in the 1990s." McColl had designed the template; now, it was suggested, others would use his template to carve their own empires.

Charlotte, whose six-county metropolitan region held just over half a million people, was home now to a bank bigger than First Chicago, bigger even than Chase Manhattan. When his shareholders arrived in Charlotte for the first annual meeting of NationsBank in 1992, McColl couldn't hide the truth. "We have achieved our strategic vision," he told them. Hugh Leon McColl Jr. had built himself a company unlike any other in America.

It was a big company with some big challenges, and the biggest, in McColl's mind, was how to keep growing. All his other challenges were nothing but toeholds to be carved, as he made his way up the face of that grandest challenge. He remained convinced that any company choosing not to grow sooner or later would become unimportant. Hugh McColl simply could not stomach the idea of ever becoming *unimportant*.

His first step was to chip away at resistance to his corporate culture. McColl had himself a brand new flag and about twenty thousand new soldiers who had precious little idea what that flag stood for. He had people in Atlanta and Columbia who openly referred to the troop leaders up in Virginia and Maryland as "those idiots." He had loan officers in Norfolk and Richmond and Washington who refused to take orders from "those rednecks" from Atlanta. Step one to solving that problem was to get rid of Bennett Brown's nemesis Dennis Bottorff, which McColl did by summoning him to Charlotte for a brief conference. The conference ended with Bottorff gone.

Step two was more complicated. McColl agreed with Chuck Cooley that people from C&S and people from Sovran had to start seeing each other as competent and capable. Their so-called "merger of equals" had left both sides equally stultified, equally immobilized. "They haven't been able to get anything decided," McColl said. "Everybody knew what needed to be done, but they wouldn't pull the trigger, so we come in and pull the trigger. I think they'll all be thrilled to hear the gun go off."

The job of firing the starting pistol went to H. A. "Rusty" Rainey, whose first merger experience had come with Dick Spangler's Bank of North Carolina in 1982. Rainey had learned from mistakes in Florida and from success in Texas. Now he went to work with Jim Thompson and Hugh Chapman to smooth out the "people transition" from Brown and Bottorff's C&S/Sovran to Hugh McColl's NationsBank.

McColl was impatient. He felt that baptism by cultural immersion had to come swiftly, relentlessly, leaving no place in the pond for agnostics. A few months after the merger, he placed a handwritten memo on Chuck Cooley's desk:

When the Mongol horde conquered China they appeared to be headed for world dominance. This did not happen for an interesting reason. They lost their power due to losing their fierceness. This was caused by intermarriage with the Chinese. The old NCNB horde is in danger of doing the same thing.

The major threat to McColl's dream of world dominance was that his company might "go soft." NCNB's intermarriage with C&S/Sovran must not produce a NationsBank so fat and complacent that its only means of crushing the competition would be to roll over on it.

McColl had to trust Cooley, Rainey and a lot of others to deal with the horde. This new company was too big for his old "management by walking around" style. To ward off some of the stress, he put a hand grenade on his desk. The grenade was labeled: "COMPLAINT DEPARTMENT. Take A Number." The number "1" was firmly attached to the pin and, with Hugh McColl, you just couldn't be sure the grenade wasn't live.

There was a personnel land mine McColl had to defuse personally. It was that old, negative "can't-do" attitude. He could still smell it, wafting up from Texas like road-kill armadillo left too long on the asphalt. It seemed to be coming from the office of Timothy Hartman, principal architect and chairman of what was now known as NationsBank West.

Not that McColl was forgetting Hartman's role in his own success. In interviews and conversation he gave Hartman credit for putting together the numbers that made the whole First Republic buyout work. If it hadn't been for Hartman's IRS ploy, McColl's grand adventure in banking would have ended toes-up in Texas. But Hartman now seemed to have grown increasingly pessimistic about the outlook for the industry. After hearing his objections to the C&S/Sovran merger, McColl felt that Hartman had lost interest in the business and was standing in the way of further expansion of the company.

When he found out Tim Hartman was selling off his NationsBank stock, McColl's eyebrows, antennae and bile rose as one. The financial press picked up the sale and Dick Stilley's people had to respond. "Part of a strategy to diversify his personal investments," said NationsBank spokesperson Beth Ulinger. *Bullshit*, said NationsBank CEO Hugh McColl. He was paying Hartman a million a year and Hartman was dumping 116,573 shares just because the stock was up to forty-nine dollars?

Tim Hartman seemed out of harmony with Hugh McColl's *tao*, and, according to Sun Tzu, that would indicate that McColl no longer exerted "moral influence" over his one-time chief financial officer. *The Art of War* warned him that without moral influence and its resultant harmony, a follower would no longer fearlessly accompany his leader into battle. McColl didn't see how his "old NCNB horde" would be pillaging any economic countryside as long as its commanding generals were selling their stock and squatting in a stockade.

During one of their conversations, the subject of early retirement came up, and McColl decided that would be the best way out of a touchy situation. At the next annual meeting he would stand up and, with suitable regret and gratitude for years of service, McColl would announce that Hartman would be leaving the company on his fifty-fifth birthday. No one would be more surprised at this news than Tim Hartman.

As this little drama played out, Ken Lewis, once Hartman's right hand in Texas, was demonstrating in Atlanta the kind of leadership McColl wanted to see. Using the bank's Olympics commitment as his passkey, Lewis opened all the doors to Georgia's heart. NationsBank instantly achieved name-brand status, almost as familiar as Atlanta's most famous company, Coca-Cola. The animosity of 1989's failed coup disappeared more quickly than C&S/Sovran billboards. Even the Atlanta Chamber of Commerce had no complaints about the city's largest bank now being headquartered in Charlotte.

As president of the NationsBank General Bank, Lewis was a strong presence in Georgia community gatherings. Once snubbed by country clubs in Dallas, Lewis told McColl that in Atlanta he was "instantly accepted, instantly put into the power base." That quickly, NationsBank had made its point in the city that Bennett Brown once thought he could make McColl-proof.

Much of Lewis's success in the old C&S stronghold was due to McColl's unswerving commitment to investing in all of the bank's communities. McColl actually believed that the corporation would not thrive unless it helped its communities to thrive. Whatever pond he found himself a big frog in, he had to keep that pond from going stagnant or choking with apathy.

McColl's $10 billion commitment to low- to moderate-income lending had surprised even his own people. Dennis Rash, who had first opened McColl's eyes to the reciprocal possibilities of community development, was moved. "Surely nobody thought that $10 billion was what the regulatory requirement would have been," Rash said.

Ed Dolby, head of the North Carolina Consumer Bank, was no less impressed. "It's a commitment which is absolutely unheard of in the banking industry," said the company's highest-ranking African-American. Dolby accompanied McColl to meetings of neighborhood groups eager to learn about this new largesse.

"And of course, everybody shows up and says to Hugh McColl, 'Now, if you have $10 billion, how much of that do I get?' But he told every one of them, 'I'm not committing the money to any organization. What I am saying is that $10 billion has to be used by people in low economic areas and underserved neighborhoods. That's who is going to get the money and that's what I mean.'"

At meetings up and down the Atlantic Coast and all around Texas, McColl heard his sincerity questioned. Cynics opined from newspapers he'd never read. Newsletters poured the thick gravy of righteousness over their simple greed. Ed Dolby saw his CEO present the same face to each and every one: "He was very blank and very frank. 'Do you want to tell me how I am going to spend my money? I tell you I'm going to do that, that's all you need to know. I am going to do that.' Then he'd walk out of the meeting and leave the rest of us there to say,

'Well, let us sort of explain to you what he meant. He meant what he said.' And then we'd tell everyone how we would work with them."

McColl discovered that his $10 billion commitment was a big stick he could shake in a lot of different ways, not only to raise eyebrows, but to open doors as well. Invited to address the 1992 Emerging Issues Conference, he informed the region's leaders that the South would be unable to compete in the decade ahead unless its workers could be set free from their dependence on low-paying manufacturing jobs. Up to one-third of the Southern populace, he lectured, was "undereducated, under-rained and rapidly becoming unemployable." The cynical view of that statement would be that workers who earned more money would be able to put more money into his bank, but McColl's own money seemed to be where his mouth was, or so his people believed.

Joe Martin's new corporate contributions officer, former C&S executive Veronica Biggins, introduced McColl to the only other native of Bennettsville who might be as famous as he was. Marian Wright Edelman, a few years younger than McColl, was the black Bennettsville preacher's daughter who founded the Children's Defense Fund. The two finally met at Edelman's home in Washington, where she was hosting a dinner for the Children's Defense Fund board of directors.

One of the guests that night was Hillary Rodham Clinton, wife of the governor of Arkansas who was seeking the Democratic nomination for the presidency. McColl spent a great deal of time with Mrs. Clinton, discussing children's issues. He enjoyed her company and found her ideas stimulating. The conversation turned to community reinvestment and McColl took the opportunity to speak about NationsBank's $10 billion commitment. When Marian Wright Edelman heard McColl's sentiments, she invited him to speak at her organization's annual meeting in Atlanta. That became another national pulpit for McColl's gospel: banks owed it to their shareholders to strengthen the communities in which they did business.

Because, to McColl, the most important business community was still Charlotte, he delighted in receiving the "World Citizen Award" from the Charlotte World Affairs Council, for "turning global attention on the region." And certainly in mid-1992, the worlds of banking and architecture took note of the opening of the NationsBank Corporate Center.

The country's fourth-largest bank now boasted its third-tallest concrete structure. Visible from thirty-five miles on a clear day, the obelisk-with-windows had a crown that lit up a shimmering diamond-blue at night. McColl and his architect Cesar Pelli had produced a crown for Charlotte. The city had been named to honor the bride of England's George III, just two years before the Revolution. Now McColl was doing his part to justify the city's nickname, "Queen City of the South." Thanks to his castle, the title seemed a bit less pretentious. McColl's friend Ben Long had produced three frescoes that were awe inspiring, towering over visitors to the pink-marbled lobby. One man, a magazine editor from Washington, remarked: "This can't be a bank. It looks almost . . . *comunista*." The editor, whose office was surrounded by some of the nation's most prestigious museums, spent the better part of an hour studying the serious construction workers with their gilded picks and shovels, the black-robed boy in front of the burning bush, the business circle that includes a white woman executive but leaves a black male on the outside looking in, the manacled black man raging against some unidentifiable injustice, the all-seeing nun, the whirling fireball of nudes reminiscent of William Blake. The visitor searched the face-filled triptych in vain for any representation of Hugh McColl; Joe Martin had won his battle for humility.

Other visitors gawked at the enormous atrium called Founders Hall on the back side of the building. Sunlight poured through a high arched ceiling of glass into a cavern of space for art exhibits, musical performances, lectures, special events and milling around. Shops, restaurants and theaters lined the walls of the ground floor and of the promenade, an escalator ride above. At the rear of the hall, a double stairway wrapped around a stage, rising to a covered walkway that spanned College Street, one of three over-street connectors to the Corporate Center's nearest neighbors. The only reminder that this was a bank was a small teller's window and ATM tucked into a cranny of the promenade. The "bank lobby" remained in Addison Reese's "NationsBank Plaza" building across Trade Street.

There was another building McColl wanted to see in Charlotte, one that would take considerable doing to pull off. This one was not his own dream, but the dream of his friend Jerry Richardson, former football player, successful hamburger slinger and navigator of the Grand Canyon. Richardson's wish-building was a stadium that would cost in excess of $150 million. His plan was to bring a National Football League franchise to Charlotte. When he shared that vision with his banker buddy, McColl snorted, "You've gotta be crazy." Then he said, "Okay, I'll help."

Richardson never would have dreamed his NFL dream had not Hugh McColl helped another local sports entrepreneur, George Shinn, to secure a franchise from the National Basketball Association in 1987. It was McColl's eleventh-hour telephone plea to the owner of the Houston Rockets that got Shinn the final vote he needed to create the Charlotte Hornets. Only days after the NBA vote, McColl attended a meeting with Jerry Richardson, his son Mark, attorney Richard Thigpen Jr. and accountant John Lewis to discuss the possibility of seeking an NFL expansion franchise for Charlotte.

McColl believed in Jerry Richardson, who, for the first time in his life, was free of personal debt. If Richardson could really pull together all the other pieces required to get an NFL team, then he believed Jerry could make it pay off—not only for the city, but for his bank as well. NationsBank—still NCNB at that time—already the bank of the Charlotte Hornets, would become the bank of the Charlotte Panthers, which was Richardson's favored name for his team.

McColl said he would lend Richardson whatever money he needed. But first he had to go "buy Texas," as he put it. And then, not long after that, he had to buy C&S/Sovran. As those deals and others went down, McColl managed to stay in touch, go to meetings with Richardson, and make phone calls as needed. Now, nearly five years after that 1987 meeting, the NFL owners were on the verge of expansion and Charlotte was, *mirabile dictu*, in the running for a franchise. The four other cities in the hunt were St. Louis and Baltimore—which had lost their old teams, the Cardinals and the Colts—Jacksonville, Florida, and Memphis, Tennessee.

If Charlotte could win one of the two franchises to be awarded, the stadium would be built right smack in the middle of uptown, in Third Ward, on land the city would lease to Richardson at a dollar a year for ninety-nine years. However, the gift land would not have a stadium on it. Whereas competing cities were planning to build stadiums for their prospective franchises, Richardson would have to build his own, at a cost of something like $150 million. McColl said not to worry, his bank could finance 100 percent of that and Richardson would own the building. Of course, the downside of ownership would be a mortgage note in excess of $10 million a year, payable to NationsBank.

Hugh McColl, the man credited with bringing world attention to Charlotte, cheered his friend on. He knew there were still a lot of maps that didn't show the "Queen City of the South," and an NFL team could well make the difference. There were only twenty-six existing franchises, and Jerry Richardson believed he could put a team in Charlotte. The actual vote to award the franchise would not happen until sometime in 1993, but by mid-'92 Richardson noticed he was still encountering smiles of skepticism around the league. "If you want to know the truth of the matter, people we are talking to really don't know where Charlotte is," he admitted to McColl. "They can't get Charlotte straight from Charleston. I mean, it's amazing."

And there was another problem. Richardson told his friend that some of the cities were putting out the word that Charlotte did not have the "full support" of its corporate citizens. "Hugh, to make this work, in my opinion, we need First Union and Wachovia to be as enthusiastic about this as you are."

McColl was cool to that idea, assuring Richardson that "we can do this without them."

"I know," said Richardson, "I mean, yes, we can do it financially. We could put the structure together. We can get the money from Japan or Europe or wherever. But we need John Medlin and Ed Crutchfield to step up and say they are supportive of the Panthers, that they really want this franchise."

Richardson got no more than a grunt of grudging assent. He decided his best bet would be to seek advice from Tom Storrs, who could tell him the right way to approach the other bankers. He gathered his friend Hugh McColl was just about out of patience with other bankers.

Indeed, after losing his bid for interstate bank branching in the 1991 Congress, McColl was ready for some of those "other bankers" to get into the game. In 1992, McColl threw down the gauntlet. He began by threatening to pull NationsBank out of every state banking association to which it belonged, unless he received the association's support for interstate banking. He knew that threat would not be taken lightly, since NationsBank was the largest or near-largest member of those state associations, which depended on McColl's financial and lobbying support to win their intrastate battles.

In February, McColl addressed the annual meeting of the American Bankers Association and made it clear he would not hesitate to pull out of that group if its members continued to posture and temporize on the one issue that should matter to them. Two weeks later, the three hundred members of the ABA's leadership council voted to back full interstate branching, the way McColl demanded.

Almost immediately, McColl asked the CEOs of the other large banks to join a "Coalition for Interstate Banking & Branching." BankAmerica Corporation, Fleet Financial, Citicorp, Bank One, Norwest, Wells Fargo and First Interstate were among the first to climb aboard NationsBank's bandwagon. At the same time, NationsBank's twenty-five thousand shareholders received letters from McColl urging them to write their congressmen on behalf of interstate banking. Form letters were enclosed. Within weeks, offices on Capitol Hill were peppered with thousands of letters. Congressional aides reported the mail was overwhelmingly in support of interstate banking.

While he had help on the Hill from several experienced banker-politicians—notably Terry Murray, from Providence, Rhode Island's Fleet—the name that now came up most frequently in Washington conversations about banking and finance was that of Hugh McColl. The Independent Bankers of America Association—perceiving itself as directly threatened—sent a plaintive plea to its five thousand members: "Don't Let Hugh McColl Control Congress."

This "lobbying alert" by the association's executive vice president, Ken Guenther, was the first clear recognition that the battle for interstate banking was being led by one man: McColl of NationsBank. The small banks were terrified that McColl and his ilk would come into their towns with *de novo* operations. It made no difference how much McColl assured them this was unlikely. Expansion, he said, made no sense unless it brought greater efficiencies, and the only way to achieve those efficiencies was through mergers and acquisitions.

By May, Mark Leggett and Paul Polking delighted McColl with news that they, along with their supporters from a few other banks, had taken out one of the strongest enemy positions. The Coalition for Interstate Banking & Branching had cut a deal with the Independent Insurance Agents of America. The insurance industry would support interstate banking, so long as the enabling legislation included a provision that banks not be allowed to sell insurance.

McColl had to personally endorse the agreement, asserting: "I don't need to sell insurance. Give them whatever they want, but give me interstate branching." Senator Terry Sanford, the North Carolina Democrat, told reporters that the deal made him "fairly optimistic" about passing an interstate banking bill in 1992, since it had been the insurance industry's provisions that killed the bill in the previous session. This time around, the vote would not be taken until after the fall elections, which included a race for the White House. That vote—and the fate of NationsBank—could well depend on how Americans would vote in November.

With the economy climbing out of the recession, McColl thought President George Bush might deserve a second term. Despite his life-long Democratic Party loyalty, inherited from generations of one-party South Carolina voting, McColl was drawn to Bush's centrist tendencies. After all, Bush had abandoned New England for Texas, which by now McColl thought of as his second home. He'd never met the Democratic front-runner, Arkansas governor Bill Clinton, though he found Clinton's wife engaging.

But there was a second Texan in the race, maverick Ross Perot, who didn't mind taking on the big boys. Though McColl had his doubts about more than a few details of the Perot plan, in many ways Ross Perot was a man after McColl's own heart. Besides, Perot was a member of the NationsBank team. His company was handling data processing for NationsBank West. McColl contributed to Perot's campaign and figured he might as well vote for him. When he read that Perot, a man supposedly worth $3.5 billion, had sold $1 million worth of NationsBank stock, McColl had second thoughts about that decision.

On the other hand, this was an unpredictable time for the company on Wall Street. NationsBank earnings were up an astonishing 22 percent from the same period in 1991, yet the bank's stock was declining. Investors apparently believed the company's profits would never be any better; therefore this could be the best time to sell and take their gains. McColl and Hance went to work on a deal that might show the market that NationsBank wasn't quite finished growing after all. The deal involved Maryland National Bank of Baltimore, largest bank in the state of Maryland. Mired in the same D.C.-area real estate bog that nearly swallowed C&S/Sovran, Maryland National was desperate to be bought.

Instead, McColl and Hance threw a lifeline to MNC, as the parent company was known. NationsBank would invest enough capital to keep MNC's head above the waterline, in exchange for an option to buy the bank at a fixed price. Fourth of July weekend, McColl, Hance and Paul Polking met MNC's top executives in New York, at the office of Wachtel, Lipton's Ed Herlihy, to negotiate the details. The amount of NationsBank's investment was fixed at $200 million, the buyout price at approximately $1.3 billion, the option at five years. Under the terms of the deal, MNC felt it had the capital necessary to survive; NationsBank had the exclusive right to buy, with potential losses limited to $200 million. If the rescue plan worked, then MNC executives would hand over a healthy bank for a relatively small amount of money. It was a deal everyone could feel good about.

As the MNC negotiations wound down, a Wachtel, Lipton receptionist interrupted the meeting with a telephone call for McColl. It was Ross Perot, calling to say he had learned one of the major parties was about to launch a "dirty tricks" campaign that could damage members of his family. The presidency simply was not worth that much to Perot, so he was going to pull out of the race. He just wanted his friends to know before they heard about it on the evening news. McColl thanked him for the courtesy and hung up, finding himself suddenly politically uncommitted.

Then, only a few days after Perot announced his withdrawal, McColl was invited to meet one of the Democratic candidates, Bill Clinton. The call came from Charlotte's most successful investment banker, Erskine Bowles.

Bowles had impressed McColl from their very first encounter, in 1973. That meeting only came about after Bowles's first NCNB contact, Luther Hodges, made him feel that no one at the bank was interested in his ideas. Erskine Bowles—whose father, Hargrove "Skipper" Bowles, was then vice chairman of First Union—had a notion that North Carolina needed an investment bank. This would be a bank devoted to selling and distributing securities, on behalf of corporations attempting to start up or expand through public stock offerings.

Since his own company, a commercial bank, was prohibited by the Glass-Steagall Act of 1933 from the risky business of securities underwriting, McColl told Bowles, "I think that is a great idea. I think you will be enormously successful, and NCNB wants to help you in any way we can."

Bowles went on to found Bowles Hollowell Conner & Co., and he retained a debt of gratitude toward McColl, who continually "referred people to me. He spoke highly of me. He gave credibility to somebody who didn't have credibility. And he went out of his way to do nice things for me, with, near as I could tell, no ulterior motive. He did it just because he thought it was a good venture, because it would be a good asset for Charlotte, because it would help the community grow. And he just liked the cut of my jib, I guess."

As Bowles's company and stature expanded, he tried to pay back McColl by supporting his efforts to improve the city, make it a bit more Londonesque. In the process, Bowles learned something about McColl and his dreams. As he came to know the Arkansas governor, Bowles suspected that Clinton's "socially progressive but fiscally conservative" approach to rebuilding American cities was compatible with that of Hugh McColl. Bowles believed Hugh McColl and Bill Clinton "would get along immediately," but that they would have to get to know each other quickly, before they were overly impressed by what Bowles considered to be their media caricatures.

"I've met zillions of politicians," Bowles told McColl in early July of 1992, "and this is the first guy who really hit me over the head with a real vision." He thought McColl would agree, and that Clinton could benefit from McColl's advice "from a business viewpoint, from a financial viewpoint, that he might not be able to get from any other source." Impressed by Bowles's conviction that Clinton would attempt to restore "fiscal discipline" to the nation, McColl agreed to attend a Democratic fund-raiser in Charlotte the following week.

Amid a wine-and-cheese crush of politicians, cause-pushers and hand-shakers, McColl found himself in the company of Hillary Clinton, who remembered him from the Children's Defense Fund dinner. She maneuvered the two men together in a quiet corner.

McColl had read somewhere that Bill Clinton was "the best one-on-one politician in America," and he was inclined to agree. Most politicians he'd met shook his hand while looking over their shoulder for the next hand to be grabbed. Not Clinton. From the moment they made eye contact, Clinton instantly shut out the rest of the room to focus on him. He wanted to know whether he could have McColl's support.

"Well, you know, I'll have to think about it," McColl answered, "but, to be candid, I need to know where you stand on interstate banking."

Clinton said, "Talk to me about that."

The candidate listened intently as McColl delivered his argument and what he believed to be the facts in support of nationwide branching. Clinton said he wanted to hear more. He also wanted to find out what McColl thought about banks helping to restore the nation's central cities. To McColl, it sounded like the start of a deal. They arranged to meet a few days later in Valdosta, Georgia, on a day when McColl could fly in and spend some time with Clinton after a campaign stop.

McColl arrived at the Valdosta courthouse along with the rest of the crowd, in hundred-degree swelter, in time to hear the town's mayor announce that the Clintons would be "just a tad late," because their bus had gotten stuck on a back road. Two hours dragged by before the band played, the bus arrived and the tent meeting got underway. The sun was well down by the time the speechifying was done and the campaigning couples invited McColl into the bus for a chat, a Diet Coke and some air conditioning. While Clinton conferred with aides, McColl found himself engaged in a lively conversation with Hillary Clinton and vice presidential candidate Senator Al Gore over their proposal that salaries over a million dollars not be entitled to standard deductions.

"Why should you give a damn about me earning a million dollars?" he asked. "How illogical can you be? I make just one-tenth of 1 percent of the after-tax profits of my company. It earns a billion dollars, I earn a million. But it's all right for you if a guy earns four hundred thousand dollars in a company that only makes $4 million, even though he's getting 10 percent of the company's profits. He'd be eligible for the deductions and I wouldn't? That is simply illogical."

After more heated discussion, the would-be First Lady abandoned logic. "A million dollars is just too much," she said.

McColl was laughing as Bill Clinton passed his portable phone to somebody and announced he was hungry. The bus was pulling into the parking lot of the Holiday Inn. "We're gonna be spending the night here," Clinton said, "so let's have something to eat together." McColl said that would be fine. He phoned his pilots at the Valdosta airport and told them to grab some supper.

It was quickly determined that by 10:00 P.M., most restaurants in Valdosta were closed. Dispatching his aides in search of food, the Clintons led McColl to their Holiday Inn suite, which was no more than two single rooms with an archway cut into the connecting wall. In one room there was a king-sized bed, in the other a sofa, chairs, table and television. Hillary Clinton excused herself and, after a quick shower, turned off the bedroom light and went to bed. For the next five hours she slept through a discussion of interstate banking and community investment.

Clinton let McColl know he was fascinated by minority-owned Shorebank Corporation in Chicago, which since 1972 had specialized in rebuilding deteriorated neighborhoods. He wanted to learn more about a subject about which McColl had practically written the book—how banks could make capital loans available to minorities and small businesses. Clinton said he was interested in getting money into the hands of less advantaged people. When (never "if") Clinton got elected, could he count on McColl's help in getting other bankers committed to that kind of lending?

About that time the food arrived and McColl got a first-hand look at the already-storied Clinton appetite. The aides had what seemed to McColl like "a ton of food" from a ma-and-pa country restaurant, "rice and butter beans and tomato and okra. And we had a mountain of corn bread. There were pork chops, and there was this huge basket of fried chicken." McColl had never been one for fried chicken. "In fact, I never eat it unless it is cold and out of the refrigerator, probably don't eat but one piece a year. So I didn't eat any. He ate the entire basket of fried chicken. I ate some vegetables."

What appealed to McColl about Bill Clinton was that "he struck me as being genuinely interested in trying to rebuild the central cities, in making credit available to people who couldn't get it. But he was not *blindly* interested. He wanted to know the specifics: 'How do you get money to small business? How do you get people to invest in center cities? How do you bring jobs to central cities?' It was a pretty broad-ranging discussion, in which he showed a lot of intelligence and thought. My impressions were that Bill Clinton was committed to trying to help people from less advantaged economic circumstances, and he would like the banks to work with him. I thought that he was a centrist, who had very good liberal instincts, about civil rights and social equity. And, you know, I found that we were not in disagreement."

McColl agreed with Clinton's position that so-called "development banks," small, minority-focused institutions, in the central cities might be helpful. But banks like Chicago's Shorebank could only be "Band-Aids on a gaping wound. Those inner-city development banks don't have enough capital. It really is going to take the

Chases and the Citis, and the NationsBanks and the BankAmericas and the First Unions. It's going to take huge banks to make any dents in the problems we have."

As Clinton went from chicken breast to drumstick to wing, McColl pledged his commitment to community reinvestment, provided that "President Clinton" would promise to support his efforts on behalf of interstate branch banking. Unimpeded megabanks, he said, would be the most likely institutions to move America's capital around. A multiregional NationsBank, with billions of dollars in assets flowing from the wealthiest segments of the nation, could afford to invest more of those assets in loans to the less affluent sections.

After considering McColl's points, Clinton agreed that interstate banking would help him in his own cause, and it also might help keep the United States in a leadership position in global finance. He also agreed that the cornbread was good, and was Hugh sure he didn't want a piece of this delicious fried chicken?

It was after 2:00 A.M. when McColl finally stretched himself up from the Holiday Inn upholstery and said, "I've got to go." They had been talking since nine-thirty. It was nearly 3:00 A.M. by the time he found the NationsBank plane on the dark, deserted tarmac. He had to pound on the fuselage to wake the pilots, long ago locked out of the Valdosta airport lobby. McColl stretched out on the flight back to Charlotte, smiling at the unlikelihood that any of this would amount to anything. Dark-horse Bill Clinton would never get nominated, let alone beat a sitting president. He simply needed any support he could get, and, because most bankers were Republicans, he'd come a-courting Democrat Hugh McColl.

But by the end of July, Bill Clinton was the candidate of the Democratic Party, nominated by a Madison Square Garden crammed with delirious delegates who believed Clinton could actually lead them back to the White House after years of crushing defeats. Clinton's acceptance speech attacked Bush's "failed economic policy." He called for the backing of supporters of Ross Perot. He had a plan for rebuilding America's cities. Much of what he said echoed the sentiments of Hugh McColl, now referred to in the press as "Bill Clinton's banker."

Nationally, Hugh McColl was "hot." The National Association for the Advancement of Colored People honored him with its Corporate Social Responsibility Award. In his acceptance speech, McColl told the NAACP his bank was "ahead of schedule" in meeting its $10 billion pledge to low- and moderate-income borrowers.

In August NationsBank launched a new ad campaign in all its major markets to attract poor and minority borrowers. In English and Spanish, in print and on radio, the ads let people know there was a huge pool of available funds to help finance their dreams. This campaign led into another, in which NationsBank solicited advice from residents of low-income neighborhoods on how the bank could better serve them. Even the bank's post-merger layoffs provided "positive spin." Instead of simply laying off seventeen print-shop employees in the Richmond office, NationsBank financed the creation of a new, minority-owned printing company in a low-income neighborhood of Richmond, then awarded the new company its Virginia printing contract and secured jobs there for the former C&S/Sovran employees.

In Charlotte, Hugh McColl's team succeeded in breaching the walls of one of the city's bastions of white male conservatism, Myers Park Country Club. Twenty years earlier McColl had told his people to tear up their memberships in organizations that discriminated, but Chuck Cooley had convinced him it would be better to press from within for radical change. Finally, the club extended invitations to NationsBank (formerly Sovran) executive Eileen Friars, its first female member, and to two African Americans. These were Bill Simms, who had moved his Transamerica Reinsurance Company to Charlotte from San Francisco, and NationsBank executive vice president Ed Dolby. In a speech at Dolby's alma mater, Shaw University in Raleigh, McColl let it be known that his own board would be taking on its first minority director within a few months. Although he did not reveal the name, McColl's candidate was fifty-one-year-old African-American Ronald Townsend, president of Gannett Television, a unit of Arlington-based media giant Gannett Company.

On Veterans' Day, 1992, Bill Clinton won election as president of the United States. No sooner were the results tallied than rumors about his cabinet began to fly. According to *Business Week*, Clinton's choice for Secretary of the Treasury was Hugh McColl of Charlotte. Dick Stilley spent days on the telephone putting out that fire. His standard response to reporters' queries was the truth: the two men had met only twice. Clinton selected Senator Lloyd Bentsen of Texas to lead the Treasury Department.

But another Charlottean would soon be packing his bags for

Washington. Clinton selected Erskine Bowles to head the Small Business Administration. More important to McColl was the news that a congressman from Winston-Salem, North Carolina, Democrat Steve Neal, would head up a new Financial Institutions subcommittee of Rep. Henry Gonzales's House Banking, Finance and Urban Affairs Committee. Neal's thirty-member subcommittee would begin the tedious process of moving an administration-backed interstate banking bill onto the floor of the House of Representatives. "Now the real work begins," Neal told a news conference in January. Hugh McColl told Paul Polking and Mark Leggett to hunker down in Washington, because this time around he intended to win.

With so much national attention focused on its CEO, it was hardly surprising that NationsBank's name came up whenever and wherever talk of bank mergers cropped up. Throughout 1992 the rumors kept coming, despite the fact that without interstate banking, there were very few actual opportunities out there. In New Mexico, Albuquerque's Sunwest Financial Services was said to be a NationsBank target. In Florida, where NationsBank was still only fourth-largest—languishing in the shade of number-one Barnett, number-two First Union, and number-three SunTrust of Atlanta—rumors grew like grapefruit. August brought speculation that mighty Barnett Banks might someday soon sell itself to NationsBank.

In California, went the Wall Street buzz, Wells Fargo and First Interstate Bank were on the block. Asked whether NationsBank might be "interested in California," Joe Martin told a business writer, "That would be an understatement. Hugh and others have said our strategy is to gain a presence in large, growing markets. If you look at the growing markets, they're on the West Coast."

To McColl, the gossip was just that. It afforded a few laughs at the executive dining room, where the salad bar was always fresher than CNN's lunch-hour *Business News*, pontificating from a TV hung from the ceiling. Come November, the Wall Street reporters were almost too preoccupied with the election to take note of NationsBank's daring decision to buy Chrysler First, the Detroit giant's nonautomobile consumer credit division. Acquisition of the $2 billion credit company came when other banks were getting out of the appliance- and furniture-financing business. Among the country's banks, only BankAmerica Corporation (still sporadically referred to in California as Bank of America, or BofA) now had a larger consumer financing operation than did NationsBank.

By the end of 1992, Jim Hance brought McColl some cheery numbers. With $1.15 billion in earnings, NationsBank was the first Southern bank in history to top $1 billion in a year.

More good news came from Baltimore, where the injection of NationsBank capital had enabled MNC to get-out-of-jail in just six months. Rather than waiting five years to become the largest banker in Maryland, McColl authorized his people to go ahead and exercise the option, buying MNC for $1.36 billion. The acquisition, said McColl, "moves us a large step toward our objective of building the foremost retail banking establishment in the United States." At least for the moment, it also made NationsBank the *third*-largest bank in the country.

But—also for the moment—McColl wanted to scotch any more rumors of wanton expansion. Despite Joe Martin's honest answer about heading west, McColl told his shareholders that he doubted there would be any opportunity to buy a bank in California anytime before his retirement in the year 2000. He chose his words carefully, yet the Charlotte *Observer* ran an article headlined, "McColl Rules Out California Foray," in which "McColl said that as long as he is chairman the bank will not plant its flag in Golden State soil." On the contrary, McColl was never one to say never. He simply understood that his best hope of growing—or of "surviving and prospering," as he continued to say—was to concentrate his weapons on Washington, where interstate banking could be cajoled into being.

The elections of 1992 had put McColl's man in the White House. Now McColl believed that banking's support of Clinton's inner-city lending program would elicit Clinton's overt support of interstate banking. He also believed the president could deliver a significant number of votes in Congress, where the Democrats still held the majority of seats in both houses. As for the Republican side of the aisles, McColl had the Coalition for Interstate Banking & Branching, whose membership included some of the nation's largest banks, to help satisfy GOP legislators that interstate banking must be "good for business."

It didn't hurt that business was finally getting better for his banking allies. By the start of 1993, Citi, Chemical, Chase, Wells Fargo, and Banc One all were able to report troubled loan levels headed down. Lower interest rates in 1992 were helping them clean up their lending disasters of the 1980s. McColl—who had no more loan disasters of his own to clean up—served as point man for the group, calling on senators, members of the House, and often the chairman of the House banking committee, Henry Gonzales.

His chief concern in Washington was Secretary of the Treasury Lloyd Bentsen. McColl knew that Comptroller of the Currency Eugene Ludwig was in favor of NationsBank-style interstate branching, but he could not be sure he had Bentsen's support. He worried that some of the former Texas senator's business dealings had suffered in the failure of First Republic and the formation of NationsBank West. In addition, he learned that Bentsen had a niece whose husband had parted company with NationsBank under unpleasant circumstances, or, as McColl put it, "on mutually agreed terms." There could even have been a friction caused by the post-election rumor that McColl, not Bentsen, had been Clinton's first choice for the cabinet position.

"Worried that Secretary Bentsen would hold that against me personally, and therefore against the company," McColl took his case directly to the Treasury Department, where he received a welcome so warm it took him by surprise. Bentsen appeared to be supportive and McColl realized his fears were unfounded.

Not so unfounded, however, that McColl forgot to protect his flank. In February he publicly proposed that the nation's biggest banks replace the Treasury Department's $30 billion line of credit to the FDIC for bailing out failed banks. Since this would represent an enormous budgetary saving, McColl's recommendation was cheered by the administration and Capitol Hill. The only cynicism came from other bankers, who labeled this simply another grandstanding play by NationsBank and Hugh McColl.

In fact, McColl believed that the large banks could not only handle the $30 billion guarantee, but that they never would lose any of the money they put up. "I call it being your own grandpa," he argued. Under the current system, if the FDIC should have to borrow any of the money, it would then be required to pay back the Treasury for the loan. In order to do that, the FDIC would have to increase its assessment on major banks. "So we can essentially be the guarantors of our own loan," explained McColl.

While he got a number of his fellow bankers to agree with him, the offer was never taken up by the administration. Nevertheless, it may have helped to quell any negative vibes from the Treasury Department on the subject of interstate banking. "Whoever was unhappy with it quit being unhappy with it," said McColl.

The second front of McColl's interstate branching war was the dismantling of the Southeast Banking Compact. Willed into existence by NCNB, first through the efforts of Tom Storrs, then of Buddy Kemp, Frank Gentry, Mark Leggett, Paul Polking and Joe Martin, the compact had finally been blessed by the Supreme Court in 1985. By then, the compact had seemed to McColl a bit like a four-lane interstate highway: outmoded by the time it opened to traffic. To get to Texas he'd had to build his own road.

Now, more than three years after the fall of Communism in East Germany, the big regional banks of the Southeast found themselves still "behind our own Berlin Wall." McColl told other Southern bankers that, "you know, we locked out the Yankees because we were scared of them, but we forgot that walls run in two directions, that they have two sides, and we got caught on the other side. We're trapped."

Perhaps fortunately, the banks he called "our big friends" felt trapped as well. They were big, but not yet big enough to feel safe. McColl's NationsBank got help from the very bankers who had fought against Storrs's compact from the first time the idea was floated. In April 1993, both Ed Crutchfield of First Union and John Medlin of Wachovia followed McColl before a committee of the North Carolina state legislature, asking for a repeal of the compact and the lifting of barriers it had set up against encroachment from New York and California.

That meeting in Raleigh was public, but only a few weeks afterward, the same three bankers, Crutchfield, Medlin and McColl, attended a secret meeting that had nothing to do with interstate banking. It had everything—at least in Jerry Richardson's estimation—to do with the future of Charlotte. McColl considered the meeting unnecessary. It also could become awkward, he reasoned, since Crutchfield's bank had recently replaced his as "official bank" of the only big-time sports franchise in the region, the NBA Charlotte Hornets.

Hornets owner George Shinn was the self-anointed lord of professional sports in Charlotte. Because Richardson's NFL bid was "competition" for his own dynasty-to-be, Shinn told McColl he could not do business in both camps. McColl told Shinn "to shove it. I told my men to throw him out."

McColl found out that attorneys at Moore and Van Allen—Harry Grim's firm—had been issued the same ultimatum and were actually considering Shinn's demand. McColl told the lawyers, "This isn't between Shinn and Jerry Richardson, this is between Shinn and NationsBank. In other words you are making a choice between George Shinn and ever doing any more business with NationsBank and its clients. Because Richardson is my client. We brought him to you. You leave him for a nonclient, then you leave all my clients, and you don't come back."

The Moore and Van Allen meeting, as McColl describes it, was "a short conversation."

Shinn tried to bury the hatchet with McColl, bearding the lion in his own executive dining room, but made the mistake of beginning the conciliatory conversation with, "I realize we've both made mistakes . . . ." McColl stood up from his chair and said, "Stop. Right there. We're done again. *We* have not made a mistake, *you* have made a mistake. Now, if you want to come and apologize and acknowledge that mistake, fine. But no, we have not made a mistake and I will not sit here and have lunch and talk about making mistakes, because we haven't made one." McColl walked out of the dining room and First Union inherited the mantle of "official bank of the Charlotte Hornets."

Now, in early June 1993, McColl was feeling a bit testy at sitting down to lunch with First Union's Crutchfield and Wachovia's Medlin, to let them into a deal he really would have preferred to do by himself. But that was how his friend Jerry Richardson wanted to play it, convinced the NFL owners felt a need to see spiritual agreement among a franchise city's business leaders. McColl believed they really wanted to see the color of Richardson's money, and NationsBank had all the green the Panthers would need.

But the meeting had to happen, so Jerry Richardson convinced Medlin and Crutchfield to sit down with Hugh McColl. For dramatic effect, they met atop the Duke Power Company Building, overlooking the land where the stadium would be built, supposing the National Football League did the unlikely and awarded Charlotte a franchise. Richardson had set the stage by floating large balloons around the site to suggest the height and shape of the stadium. Roger Milliken, the textile mogul from Richardson's old home of Spartanburg, was there, indicating solidarity from business interests in South Carolina. William States Lee, the CEO of Duke Power, hosted the meeting, following up Richardson's presentation with a promise that his company would lease the stadium parking garage.

The only real question of the day was whether Richardson would be able to go to New York the following week and assure the league owners that he had the unqualified support of each of these men. Medlin and Crutchfield demanded that Richardson tell them exactly how much financial backing he was going to require. Richardson insisted that the target continued to move. The franchise fee had doubled from $50 million to $100 million in the six years he'd been hunting it. The projected stadium cost had started out at $85 million and now looked more like $140 million. Crutchfield asked for a "round figure," but Richardson said he couldn't even give him a ballpark for the ballpark, let alone for the team.

The discussion grew heated, with suggestions that it might be Jerry Richardson's ego at stake, rather than the future of the region. Finally John Medlin asked, "Jerry, at what price will you say no?"

"There is no price that would make me say no," said the big man, showing the scowl he wore since retiring his Baltimore Colts helmet and facemask.

"There is no price at which you'd release us from our commitment?" Medlin persisted.

McColl looked at Medlin. "You release yourself by saying no, any time you want to. But, as far as our bank is concerned, whatever it takes, we are going to figure out how to make it work."

Those were some of the sweetest words Jerry Richardson had ever heard. "I suppose if he hadn't said that, it would have been all over. Because we had to have them. It was critical."

Before they left the rooftop, Richardson had the financial commitment he wanted. McColl believed the other bankers were simply worried about being left out, but, whatever their reasons, Medlin and Crutchfield did agree to back Richardson. The following week McColl accompanied Richardson to an owners' meeting in New York and helped him sell the Carolinas. He assigned Ed Brown to work closely with the Panthers' financing team—which included Richard Thigpen and John Lewis—to do whatever it might take to bring a team to Charlotte. When the Richardson group came up with the concept of selling "permanent seat licenses" to help finance the deal, McColl wound up guaranteeing not only NationsBank's share of the PSL sales, but, since Crutchfield seemed to think this was a limb too far, First Union's share as well.

It would take another four months of arm twisting and nail biting, but Jerry Richardson's six-year dream would come true. On October 26, after a last-minute withdrawal by the group from St. Louis, the NFL's twenty-eight owners would vote to award one franchise, to Charlotte. (Later, Jacksonville would get the second franchise.) And in every interview he gave to every publication and talk show, the first person thanked by the new owner would be Hugh McColl.

For much of 1993, McColl found himself in the spotlight. As *Working Mother* magazine went to press in July, the *Wall Street Journal* pronounced the magazine's awaited list of pro-family corporations "one of America's hottest competitions." The winners were *Working Mother's* Family Champion of the Year, Hugh McColl, and NationsBank, ranked Number-One Company for its $35 million program to assist its employees in caring for their children and elderly family members.

In other publications, business writers were discovering that NationsBank had taken a bold, unprecedented step toward corporate democracy. For the first time in the banking industry, employees at nearly every level, not just top executives, were offered NationsBank shares at a fixed price. "Ownership makes a difference," McColl declared.

Outside the bank, McColl's influence was being felt in dozens of inner-city neighborhoods. In Columbia, Maryland, NationsBank formed Nations Housing Fund, a $100 million program to finance as many as four thousand low-income homes in the Washington area. By this time, NationsBank already was using up its targeted $10 billion in CRA lending at double the projected rate of a billion dollars a year. Even outside the corporation's territory, McColl's people were looking for opportunities to make money while scoring points as good citizens. Thus, in Mobile, Alabama, NationsBank bought 46 percent of a small minority-owned bank. An investment of only $350, 000 would give the Mobile bank the strength it needed to expand and prosper, at a time when big oil companies were pouring billions into Mobile Bay, the site of the nation's largest natural gas drilling operations.

Although these actions, apparently motivated by something other than profit, had their critics among his shareholders, McColl insisted that "NationsBank has stood right where we were on the day we made the commitment. We said, 'Yes we believe in affirmative action. Yes we believe in the Community Reinvestment Act.' We are committed to doing not our fair share, but doing *more* than our fair share, trying to build houses and bring credit to people who historically have not been able to get it."

The ultimate argument against nay-saying was that the company actually was making a profit out of low-income lending. "NationsBank really is a funny company," said McColl. "We like it. We've made a business out of it. We don't do it because we have to."

Once again, McColl found himself out of step with other big bankers, some of whom were lobbying to get rid of the Community Reinvestment Act as hard as he was lobbying for interstate banking. So, in July 1993, McColl found himself the only major banker in a line of celebrities standing behind the president in the White House Rose Garden as Clinton announced new legislation allocating $382 million to fund "Community Development Financial Institutions" for low-income neighborhood development. This was to be modeled on the Chicago development efforts of Shorebank, which Clinton and McColl had discussed over fried chicken in Valdosta.

"Peanuts," is what McColl honestly thought of the Clinton plan. In his judgment, the administration did not appreciate the magnitude of the inner-city problem. "Three hundred million dollars. So what? I mean, you've got to have $300 *billion*." He told that to Paul Polking and Mark Leggett, but he merely thanked the president and said he would be happy to work on behalf of the community development bill. Bill Clinton meant well. "In my Democratic heart," McColl believed, "I had the president I wanted, a centrist, with a human touch—not a leftist, not a radical right-winger, but a centrist with good instincts toward other human beings."

Secure in his company's commitment to pro-family and pro-equality issues, McColl did not hesitate to speak his mind at the August convention of the National Urban League in Washington. The "freight train of diversity" was barreling down the track at corporate America, he said, and that "means changing the way we act and think." Back in Charlotte, Ed Dolby watched the address carried live on the C-SPAN cable network, astonished at his CEO's frankness.

"I thought, huh? Did I hear what I just heard? I believed him, but here he is publicly putting this on the line in front of all these African-American leaders at the Urban League. And they were just absolutely surprised. There was this shock that here is this white man, Southern, from a conservative industry, standing before them and extolling the virtues of diversity. And a diverse work force. And his vision for America. And what he is planning to do. And I thought, *Wow!* And I was proud."

It was hard not to feel pride in the fall of '93 if you worked for NationsBank and Hugh McColl. The Federal Reserve authorized the company's formation of a capital market unit, which would raise money for its corporate customers by placing short-term debt paper and selling stock in those companies. NationsBank became the first bank outside of New York, the first nationally chartered bank and one of only five banks in the country to achieve this status. The unit was called NationsBank Capital Markets, Inc. Its initial deal was a $150 million debt offering for Dallas's First USA Bank, put together with J. P. Morgan and Merrill Lynch & Co. Up until this moment, it would have been unthinkable that a bank from Charlotte, North Carolina, could play in the same league as Morgan and Merrill Lynch. Even bigger deals were in the offing for NationsBank Capital Markets, including Quaker Oats' $2.4 billion buyout of the Snapple Beverage Corporation.

As image-builder Joe Martin continued to come up with new stages to showcase what he considered the "true image" of his CEO, McColl found himself making a lot of speeches to business schools. He enjoyed imprinting impressionable young minds even more than he had in 1970, when he first looked over Ed Dolby's shoulder. But when Rock Hill's Winthrop University invited him to address its business school, McColl would only agree to speak at the campus if Winthrop would reinstate his mother's name as valedictorian of her class. It worked. More than sixty years after the fact, Frances Carroll's airplane ride peccadillo was stricken from the Winthrop records.

In Charlotte, McColl was chairman of the board of trustees at Queens College, a Presbyterian women's school grown into a coed liberal arts college. When McColl's old banker-friend from Florida, A. L. Ellis, wrote Queens a check for $2 million, the Hugh McColl Jr. School of Business was born. At its dedication in October, McColl said, "I'm humbled. And, you know—it's hard to humble me." But what he really felt was pride. The young man who seemed to his father "not smart enough to be a farmer," who struggled to pull Cs in his college business courses, was grown into an icon, with a business school named for him.

The extent of McColl's influence became clear a few days later, on October 24, when the Clinton administration formally endorsed the interstate banking bill. Treasury Secretary Bentsen spoke for the administration, saying, "We have anachronistic, inconsistent and sometimes excessive legislative and regulatory restrictions on our financial system. This is too critical an element of our economy to have its potential held back."

That was an unusual position for a Democratic president to take, and Clinton might easily have given himself reason to oppose the legislation. "In his heart of hearts," McColl assumed, "Bill Clinton would love to be able to tell us bankers what to do. As would almost every politician, so I wouldn't want to blame him for that."

Instead, Clinton had bought McColl's arguments, and McColl believed NationsBank had "acted out our *quid pro quo* for the bill" with his support for community development banking. "And in fairness to President Clinton, he didn't ask for anything for himself. There was nothing the president wanted, except that money be made available to the inner cities of America, where we have so much poverty and crime. He wanted to give the bankers something on one hand, and he wanted some commitments back on the other. He certainly had my commitment."

The legislation became known as the Riegle-Neal Interstate Banking and Branching Act of 1994, named after its two sponsors, Senator Donald Riegle and Representative Steve Neal. There were those in Charlotte who smiled when they said it should be called the Hugh McColl Act. There were those in Washington and New York who sneered when they said the same thing. The Independent Bankers Association's Ken Guenther credited McColl with—or blamed him for—"delivering the president and the administration." The legislation's passage, Guenther told the *New York Times,* "is in good part due to McColl's tenacity and work."

Part of that work consisted in maintaining the industry's impression of Hugh McColl as "Washington's favorite banker." It did not hurt that the White House received a box at the NCAA basketball finals in Charlotte that March. McColl and his brother-in-law, Congressman John Spratt, accepted the president's invitation to be his guests at the Charlotte Coliseum. Since one of the teams in the Final Four turned out to be the University of Arkansas Razorbacks, Bill Clinton was in his glory. The Razorbacks' opponents in the championship game were the Blue Devils of Duke University, perennial arch-rivals of McColl's alma mater, UNC. When the cameras showed Clinton enjoying the game, yelling "Go, hogs," there was McColl at his side, rooting for those hogs.

It was, McColl believed, in their "mutual benefit" for him and Clinton to be viewed as friends. "People believed that I had access to the president, which is good for the company. And he in turn needed the support of big business, and to have the support of one of the largest banks in the country was important to him. And so therefore I did what it took to maintain those appearances."

Arkansas did what it took to win the championship, beating Duke 76-72, and the administration did what it took to get the Riegle-Neal bill through both houses of Congress. Provisions of the bill would forever free United States banks from old laws that had severely restricted their geographical expansion since before Hugh McColl was born. The regional compacts, along with NCNB's evasive incursions into Florida and Texas, had weakened the government's resistance to change. Now most states were out of the compacts. On June 1, 1997, when Riegle-Neal was scheduled to take effect, there would be nothing on the books to prevent a bank from operating coast-to-coast.

Perhaps predictably, McColl was *American Banker*'s choice as "Banker of the Year." The magazine cited the "deal-making prowess that enabled Mr. McColl to build his empire within an astonishingly short period of time," and the "unrivaled ability to act on his visions and turn them into reality."

Until recently, that vision had been expressed in what McColl termed "a little litany that we loved." The litany was: "We want to build the dominant financial institution from Baltimore to Miami." He had built that. As for what his vision of the future might be, McColl told the *American Banker* he now planned for his company to be "the preeminent financial institution in this country." He wanted "a nationwide company that was perceived as the best place to do business in America." More than anything, perhaps, "We want to be masters of our own fate."

The Independent Bankers' Ken Guenther, whom the *New York Times* called "an outspoken critic" of McColl, suddenly sounded more like a fan. "He has outcompeted the big money center banks of New York and built one of the premier banks in the world," said Guenther. With church bells instead of howitzer blasts ringing in his inner ear, McColl felt curiously off-balance.

In his modest office on the fifty-eighth floor of his skyscraper, he faced an oil painting bought in Texas, a dramatic scene of an old-west bank holdup in progress. The painting, by Dan Mieduch, was entitled

"Take the Money and Run." McColl liked to see himself as the leader of that outlaw gang in the painting, six-guns blazing, mounting his mustang, making off with the loot. He'd even paid the artist to change the name on the bank's window from the innocuous "Commercial Bank" to "Republic Bank." On a shelf behind him he kept the stuffed tiger captured from Bennett Brown after the C&S/Sovran merger. McColl enjoyed being feared by other bankers and wasn't sure he really enjoyed being their friend.

Despite the occasional need to associate his company with those of other bankers, McColl wanted his people to continue seeing other banks as "the enemy." Whenever someone in NationsBank went above and beyond the call of duty to inflict damage on the enemy—including peaceful actions that simply might make the enemy envious—he wanted to hold that person up as worthy of special merit. He needed something like a Congressional Medal of Honor. He came up with the notion of hand grenades, real grenades, plated in gold, silver and bronze, a combination of marine machismo and Olympic spirit. A local dealer in china and gifts, the Gutman Company, caught wind of the plan and placed a rush order with Tiffany in New York for a hundred life-sized grenades in hand-cut crystal. A sample arrived on McColl's desk without an invoice, but with a note suggesting that this might be a more attractive alternative, especially since some of his award recipients no doubt would be women. McColl immediately bought all one hundred.

The first grenades were given to the people he considered largely responsible for his success in capturing C&S/Sovran. They were Chuck Cooley, Joe Martin, Jim Thompson, Paul Polking and Fred Figge, along with Marc Oken, who had come in from Price Waterhouse to serve as Jim Hance's principal accounting officer. As the merger proceeded, McColl handed out two more grenades. One went to Catherine P. Bessant, whose handling of the Community Reinvestment program had made her a hero in the company. The other went to senior credit officer Bill Kelly, who, like Bessant, had come out of the First Republic merger, just in time to clamp down on lending during the credit crunch of 1990.

The grenades exploded in internal goodwill. "My people think it's magic," he said. "You can pass by their offices and see them prominently displayed. Some of them have even had special stands made to hold them. I'll keep giving them out as long as I'm here, no matter what the press may think. My people love it."

Yet in spite of this evident corporate enthusiasm for bellicosity, McColl worried that the company might be going soft around the edges. More and more, the media—the same reporters who used to wave his "ex-marine" image at other bankers like a red kerchief at Pamplona—were portraying him as a Mr. Nice Guy. The *Times* actually started out a McColl profile with a reference to his puzzle-making skills, then let the bank's new president, Ken Lewis, gush: "He is the most inspirational, charismatic person I've ever known." Instead of being rude and fierce and militaristic, this nouveau-McColl was "a gifted consensus builder and concerned leader who cares about his people." Maybe Joe Martin's image campaign had gone too far. Maybe his people were thinking the fight was over, that it was time to stack arms and take some well-deserved R-and-R. Nothing could be quite so disarming as hubris. McColl dashed off a memo to his team commanders: *The biggest risk is to believe we have arrived, because once you think you're there, you won't be there long. Somebody will take you out.*

McColl's emotional attachment to his corporate family exploded one afternoon in mid-October, when a grim-faced Joe Martin walked into his office, sat down in one of the chairs in front of the big Texas bank holdup painting and said: "I have ALS."

McColl wasn't sure he'd heard correctly. "What's that?"

"Amyotrophic lateral sclerosis. Lou Gehrig's disease."

McColl felt his eyes tear over, but he steeled himself and said, "You do whatever you need to do, Joe. Take whatever time you need to take. Just give me access to your brain. It doesn't matter where you are, so go wherever you need to go, just be sure I can get to you."

Without asking Martin's permission, McColl instructed Pat Hinson to phone a neurologist he knew. The doctor was out on the golf course, but not safe from McColl. According to the neurologist, there probably wasn't anyone in Charlotte who knew much about amyotrophic lateral sclerosis, but he promised to find out who and where the top expert in the field might be.

Like racing to the airport, finding the best specialist turned into a competition between McColl and Martin. Later that week, the CEO charged into Martin's office with the name of Dr. Stanley Appel in Houston. Martin already had Appel's name written on a card, but McColl ignored that, instructing him to take a company plane and get to Houston right away. When McColl learned that Reitzel Snider and his Swiss friends were planning to climb Mount Kilimanjaro the following summer, he insisted Martin make plans to go along with him.

McColl's determination to take action, whatever that action might entail, provided Martin with a stronger sense of purpose. "It helped take my mind off ALS," he said. "I started looking more outward and less inward."

Perhaps it was the prospect of taking Joe Martin along that gave McColl the strength he needed to face another mountain with Snider. Or perhaps his troops simply had infected him with their attitude of invincibility. Living on the fifty-eighth floor could give a man the idea he was atop Mount Olympus, and surely that was higher than Kilimanjaro.

At any rate, shortly before Thanksgiving, both McColl and Martin had their full attention diverted by Jim Hance, who'd picked up the signal that BankAmerica was ready to talk turkey—in this case, that griffin-like creature of myth, a "merger of equals."

It turned out to be a case of Merrill Lynch "talking up the deal." Hance brought them in for a show-and-tell and they laid out all the numbers, just the way McColl had done for Bennett Brown at Litchfield Beach. The Wall Street team said the merger made sense, and McColl had to agree. They told him that Richard Rosenberg, the CEO of BankAmerica, also thought it made sense, and they said he would like to arrange a meeting with Hugh McColl. And that made sense to the NationsBank team. What the people from Merrill Lynch did not say was that they were assuring each team that the other was ready to be bought out.

Months dragged by, and still no word from San Francisco that Rosenberg was ready to meet. But in the years since his agitation over C&S, then C&S/Sovran, McColl was seasoned into a more forbearing man. He trusted now in the Arab proverb Jane had found and framed for him: *Have patience, and the funeral procession of your enemy shall pass in front of your tent.* That was on the wall of the little conference room behind his office.

In March 1995, he and Jane were forbearing in the Florida keys when the office reached him to say his presence was requested in San Francisco. On the way back to the plane McColl patiently stopped at a roadside flea market, where his patience paid off in a tent filled with military treasures. As she waited for Hugh to poke through the helmets and bayonets and medals, talking to the vendor like he always talked to everyone, as though they had gone to school together, Jane noticed that the dealer's tent was partially constructed of tank camouflage netting. She didn't know exactly what the stuff was, but it gave her an idea.

Hugh and their neighbor, Bill McGuire, had just finished building the cutest tree house for the grandchildren and now Hugh was insisting it needed a roof, so the kids could sleep out there, even though she kept telling him a roof would ruin the look of it. She called his attention to the camouflage material and said, "Hugh, I believe you could put that on the tree house."

Jane knew she'd hit a home run. "He was like a child at Christmas. He got so excited." After coming to terms on a price, the flea market vendor cheerfully dismantled his tent. McColl bought one of his two rolls of netting, then decided he'd better go back and buy the other one. Jane's only regret was that she didn't have a camera with her. "If you could have seen him coming back through that flea market with that thing on his shoulder, and this grin"—and she stretches her lips wide with her fingers—"this big. So playful! Nobody would have thought that something this simple could make this man that happy."

McColl would have been even happier had his trip to San Francisco netted the deal he wanted. Unfortunately, the Merrill Lynch brokers were only trying to "pinhook" that merger—trying to sell a deal they really didn't own. Dick Rosenberg was just plain not interested in selling his bank to Hugh McColl. And, of course, vice versa.

About the only thing to come out of the six months of posturing and sub rosa conversations between NationsBank Corporation and BankAmerica Corporation was an agreement that both companies wanted very badly not to be put out of business by Bill Gates's Microsoft. The Internet was looking like the drive-up teller of the future, and Microsoft, with access to nearly all the nation's computer users, was already selling checking account software. The two banking giants would team up to buy MECA Software for a shared investment of $35 million. Together, they hoped to create a nationwide on-line computer banking service.

Months would pass before Wall Street picked up the McColl-Rosenberg scent, but there were plenty of other rumors to hunt out. Which bank was Hugh McColl planning to buy next? Was it First Fidelity Bancorp, New Jersey's largest? In fact, First Union turned out to be the buyer of the Philadelphia-Newark bank. First Fidelity's $5.4 billion price tag made this the largest corporate merger ever. The new and expanded First Union would be the United States' sixth-largest bank.

In April, McColl's favorite rumor so far rolled out of the mill: NationsBank was buying Chase Manhattan. He assigned Jim Hance the pleasant task of responding to the breathless media. Why, yes, Hance said, NationsBank indeed would be interested. Thomas Labrecque, Chase Manhattan's CEO, bristled at the suggestion. His bank was not for sale and never would be. McColl finally acknowledged that the talk was merely "silly rumor." What NationsBank actually was up to in New York happened to be the opening of a private banking office, for clients whose net worth, excluding their primary residence, was at least $10 million. Sort of a tree house for the rich and famous.

In June, just about the time Jane McColl proposed that Hugh celebrate his sixtieth birthday with breakfast in the Scotland Avenue tree house (camouflaged) with his two sons and three grandsons, NationsBank proposed to scale new heights in southern Florida. It would buy Miami's Intercontinental Bank for $208 million and Citizens Federal Bank for $516 million.

A few weeks later, NationsBank was said to be poised for a purchase of the 211-year-old Bank of Boston. Indeed, McColl did have talks with Boston's retiring CEO, Ira Stepanian, but the conversation led nowhere. The rumor mill kept rolling, and McColl, Jim Hance and Frank Gentry kept fielding calls from Wall Street types who were trying to use NationsBank to make their fortunes. In fact, *Fortune* magazine got an unnamed "Wall Street security analyst" to admit: "Our investment bankers fly down to Charlotte with deal ideas once a week. Their only directive is, 'Bring us something big.'"

One important hill taken by McColl's army during the summer of 1995 was the United States Army. In August, while McColl was off climbing Africa's highest mountain (without Joe Martin, as it turned out, since the doctor thought the trek might subtract too much from whatever his reservoir of strength might be), NationsBank's Washington cadre was negotiating a contract to set up banks at the army's 125 overseas bases in Europe and the Pacific. The five-year exclusive contract, beginning in October, would bring in nearly $900 million in deposits, along with a captive, constantly rotating market of 425,000 soldiers and Defense Department employees.

And when McColl came down from the mountain, there was another call from Dick Rosenberg. This time, Rosenberg wanted to meet at a neutral site, somewhere closer to Charlotte, and this time he said he would present "some new ideas." He was ready to "look at our two organizational charts and see how we can merge them." He suggested the CEOs meet in Pensacola, Florida, at a hotel in the center of town that was built out of an old railroad depot. The notion of a secret meeting in an old railroad station appealed to McColl, putting him in mind of his great-grandfather, Duncan Donald, who had started up a railroad in Bennettsville after the Civil War. He agreed to fly to Pensacola the next day.

The railroad depot was as advertised. McColl had not been in a hotel room so small since his early days traveling the rural byways of South Carolina, drumming up commercial loans for NCNB. But instead of laying on the coffee table his current organizational chart, as McColl had anticipated, Rosenberg unrolled a hand-drawn chart of the proposed coast-to-coast bank's corporate structure. McColl studied Rosenberg's vision of the merged companies calmly, almost disinterestedly. Why were so many of NationsBank's strongest people, some of his closest advisors, left out while David Coulter, Rosenberg's chosen successor at BofA, had a prominent position in the proposed new company? The chart made precious little sense to McColl.

Perhaps the most troublesome part of the new plan was that Rosenberg insisted on moving the company headquarters to Chicago, where BankAmerica recently had bought Continental Illinois. McColl and his team had taken a look at First National Bank of Chicago, with its valuable credit card business, but abandoned the idea. For a moment, McColl let himself wonder whether it might not be best to play along with Rosenberg. He could agree to the new terms, relocate to Chicago, then move again once he had the merged company under his control. But he knew he might be forced into retirement before he could pull that off. Time and distance would be against him. In Chicago he would lose touch with his own people back in Charlotte, and yet be equally out of touch with the people he really needed to influence, the new team members in San Francisco. *So, maybe Dick knows what he's doing,* McColl thought.

"If we'd wanted to be in Chicago, we could have been there already," he said. "But who would trade our weather in Charlotte for, what, two months without snow?" Half-seriously, to test the boundaries of Rosenberg's offer, he suggested a headquarters in Dallas, NationsBank's westernmost capital. Like Chicago, Dallas could be thought of as "centrally located." In short order, Rosenberg shot down Dallas, then Atlanta. Those cities were not sufficiently "important" to serve as the headquarters of America's largest bank.

For McColl it made little difference. In his mind it would be extremely difficult, even impossible for his company to move out of Charlotte. "The company's culture would be very hard to keep alive," he told Rosenberg. "Culture does not reside in the top executives, it resides in the people at all different levels of the company—the tellers, the secretaries who've been there for so many years. They can't move with you."

That a corporation could have its own culture, worth preserving, seemed a new concept to the California banker. Rosenberg told McColl he was "crazy for wanting to stay in Charlotte. It's nowhere. It's small-time."

Instead of letting his anger take control, McColl decided he would try to make Rosenberg see reason—the way reason was seen from his side of the table. He talked about what it had been like to grow up in the South. He told Rosenberg how—before NationsBank and First Union—Southern bankers had always been forced to go north to borrow money. McColl explained how Addison Reese and Tom Storrs had built a company that could stand tall, a company that deserved respect. This was not just another bank, it was a *Southern* bank.

"You must understand, Dick. After all, you were a Jew in Massachusetts, where the Irish ran it all."

Now it was Rosenberg who grew irritated, insisting that McColl was "thinking small."

"Actually," McColl smiled, "more often, people accuse me of thinking too big."

"I can't understand this provincial attitude of yours," Rosenberg fumed. "You're pissing away an overwhelming opportunity here. There is simply no way you can achieve your personal ambitions with a company headquartered in Charlotte, North Carolina."

The backward, corn-shucking, watermelon-eating South. North America's unofficial third-world country. McColl kept thinking the stereotype would go away, but there seemed to be no end to the assumption that his company's success was a product of some blind twist of fate. Whenever you managed to scratch and claw your way out of the past, there was always someone waiting to speculate on how lucky you were or what kind of unfair advantage you must have wangled. This had become McColl's bond with African-Americans.

Sitting in the little railroad depot hotel room in Pensacola, Hugh

McColl felt undone by his own lack of pretense. McColl just never rose to that "Southern gentleman" standard his grandmother had worked so hard to set for him. No matter how often Cooley and Martin stropped his image, they couldn't hone down the rough edges. His style was still nick-and-scratch hyperbole, not gentle understatement. He was competitive in a profession where compromise was valued. He was as pushy as he was short, cocksure of himself because he never, ever doubted he would win. All of those character traits fit him as naturally as his black cowhide boots, custom-cobbled now in Raymondsville, Texas. Ergo, other bankers could only assume he must be the beneficiary of some cosmic quirk. And why not? They'd been misjudging Hugh McColl for about thirty-five years.

McColl ended the meeting. Once again, he was noncommittal: "Interesting offer, Dick . . . a lot to think about." Neither man took any joy nor read any hope in the weak handshake.

On August 9, 1995, returning from Pensacola, McColl wrote a memo on his meeting with Richard Rosenberg. With coded reference to the initials of the two principals, he headed the memo "HLM/R2." Half-printed, half-cursive, the memo took up three pages of lined paper imprinted with the Merrill Lynch logo. McColl would hold on to it for five months, then give it to Pat Hinson, to photocopy for Chuck Cooley and Joe Martin. The first page of the memo reads as follows:

I had but to reach out my hand to become the most important banker in the world. I could not do it. Why? Sitting in front of me was the chairman of BankAmerica. In exchange I must move HQ to Chicago, change my name and guarantee that my successor would come from BankAmerica.

I was being asked to surrender my army which had not lost to our foe who had the upper hand but had not won.

NationsBank has wasted vital time on the defense and now must surrender or attack. The issue for me is whether to sell out my team and my region for personal glory. The issue for my team and my town is "do they merit the personal sacrifice."

The second page of the memo appears to be McColl asking himself what it would take for him to agree to a merger with BankAmerica, or perhaps with another giant.

I have no interest in a titular job only. I am willing to agree to leave (surrender the CEO title) at the 1999 annual meeting—approximate-

ly 3 years & 3 mos from the time we merge.

I am not willing to be CEO but have no power. I want to make clear that I will not be inhibited in taking decisions or making recommendations to the board in the best interest of the new co.

No director of the new company should have loyalty or commitment to the old companies that will cease to exist upon merger.

Any CEO would need the authority to move on organizational and executive matters free of interference.

In the top margin of the second page, McColl appears to have added:

I want a straight salary—(No Bonus)—and significant stock participation. i.e.—$20/40 million

The final page appears to be McColl's synopsis of Rosenberg's main points at the meeting.

(1) No real belief that HLM means anything except way to get the deal done.
(2) Chicago because Dallas is an unimportant city.
(3) BofA important in Asia.
(4) Wants 3 yrs & out with HLM—Coulter to follow. I suggest 5 years Board to pick Chairman.

In a remarkable coincidence, the Pensacola meeting happened just as *Fortune* writer Linda Grant was completing her seven-page article-with-sidebars on Hugh McColl. The August 21 issue of one of the nation's most respected and sophisticated business magazines had McColl holding his Bennelli shotgun on its cover, finger on the trigger, smiling like a man who knows exactly where the next covey of quail will rise, black felt western hat pulled down so the brim barely cleared his ever-pricked ears.

OPEN SEASON ON BANKS, the fat Helvetica letters spelled out over McColl's chest and gut, and just to the side, "Hugh McColl started the hunt. Now he's aiming to make NationsBank No. 1."

Open the magazine to its table of contents and there is another McColl photo, this time a casual head-shot. "You lead from in front," the cutline reads, quoting the subject. "Nobody wants to follow someone who doesn't know where he is going." And the synopsis of the story (*Here Comes Hugh*) reads: "Over the past 12 years, CEO Hugh McColl has grabbed up 49 banks, taking NationsBank from the 29th largest in the country to No. 3. He's aiming to make it No. 1." And: "McColl's reputation as a skin-you-alive dealmaker makes other big bankers sweat."

On page 42, the article began: "He's tough. He's predatory. He's aiming to make NationsBank No. 1." The article talked about NationsBank being the "800-pound gorilla," about managers of other banks fearing McColl. And McColl, keeping the Rosenberg meetings to himself, said ("confessed ruefully," as Grant wrote it): "Nobody wants to merge with us." As for the future, the article asked, was it true that NationsBank had its list of preferred targets, just waiting for one of them to stumble? "McColl responds with the deadpan stare, 'It's hard for me to believe that my industry will not make an error again.'"

The article rang bells on Wall Street. Buy orders went in and NationsBank stock rose to nearly sixty dollars, a fifty-two-week high. Not far from the floor of the stock exchange, the executives of troubled Chase Manhattan Corporation were, after all, making a deal to sell their company. John D. Rockefeller's institution, the cornerstone of money market banking, would be merged into Chemical Banking Corporation, headed by Walter Shipley. If the Fed and the shareholders approved—and no one doubted they would—the new company would take over bragging rights as the number-one bank in the United States, dropping NationsBank to number four. As for First Union's "largest merger in U.S. banking history," that $5.4 billion First Fidelity deal fell to a distant second. It would cost $10 billion for Chemical to eat Chase Manhattan. It was interesting for Hugh McColl to observe that the new money center bank would be managed by the Chemical team, that the culture would be Chemical's, even though the name would be Chase Bank. The memory of Salmon P. Chase, Lincoln's secretary of the treasury who authorized the funding of the Civil War, would live on, simply because "Chase" was a better flag to march behind than "Chemical."

"NationsBank" was a damn fine flag, he decided. What he needed now was to get some more good troops behind it. According to *Fortune*, there was "a horde of McColl watchers around the country . . . analysts, consultants, and bankers waiting for the next NationsBank shoe to drop." The Miami acquisitions, even the Maryland National deal, those were small potatoes in the stewpot McColl had single-handedly stirred.

The magazine puzzled: "Has McColl lost his nerve? Has his board reined him in? Is he hiding another ace up his sleeve?"

Said McColl: "I rule nothing out."

CHAPTER 16

In the mid-'90s Charlotte had serious competition for McColl's attention. The NationsBank-sponsored Olympic Games were turning Atlanta into his second home. The company's persistence in low-income lending was strengthening neighborhoods around Texas and Florida, and even in economy-flattened cities like Washington, Richmond and Baltimore. Multiregion expansion provided him with one urban power base after another, yet it was still Charlotte that held first claim to McColl's heart and energy. He identified with the little Southern town that had no business being big, just like his bank, just like him. Charlotte could never quite be good enough, big enough, prosperous enough to suit Hugh McColl.

Since he first set eyes on architect Gouldie Odell's plans for uptown Charlotte in 1971, McColl had been waiting for the city to build a public transportation center. Now that his bank owned three of the four corners of The Square, plus much of the surrounding turf, McColl was weary of watching the city's buses disgorge their passengers into the weather, and onto his doorstep, each morning, where they waited for other buses at the only transfer point that would allow them to move from one side of the city to the other. No matter how the city campaigned for upscale bus commuters, the overwhelming majority of public transportation riders continued to be people on the lower end of the income scale. Afternoons they gathered along Tryon Street again, waiting for buses to take them home. There was nowhere for them to go, to get out of the rain or the heat or the cold.

At least in McColl's mind, if not on paper anywhere, there was a promise from city government that if his company would build its $300 million complex at The Square, a public transportation center would be constructed nearby. By 1995 the carpets in his building were starting to show signs of wear and McColl was tired of waiting for a bus stop that never came. At a party he confronted Mayor Richard Vinroot: "When are you going to deliver on your promise to me?"

A few days later, the mayor—a white-haired Republican lawyer nearly seven feet tall—invited McColl to a breakfast meeting. The main course was that peculiar Charleston delicacy, shrimp grits, and the topic was a transportation center for Charlotte.

McColl was looking for a commitment from the city, but, "We got into the same kind of counterproductive discussion of how they didn't have the money and dah-da-dah. And I got infuriated. I stood up and said, '*We'll* build the damn thing. *We'll* put up the damn $10 million. If we can design it, and if you can cooperate, we'll build it.' And I stalked out, leaving one or two of my lieutenants to pick up the pieces."

Actually, McColl anted up a mere $3 million that morning; only after the scope of the project expanded did the price, and NationsBank's commitment, get up to $10.5 million. But his lieutenants, Jim Palermo and Dennis Rash, understood the decision had been made, regardless what the eventual price tag might be. They picked up the ball and the breakfast bill and told the mayor they'd be back to him the following week with a contract.

If McColl expected cheers on his free bus pavilion, he was disappointed. No sooner did Mayor Vinroot put out the story of NationsBank's "generous pledge" than anti-McColl charges began to fly in the newspapers and on the nightly news. The gift prompted rather outrageous outrage: It must be a racist plot to force unwanted African-Americans off the public streets. It could only be the greedy McColl's way of clearing riff-raff from his steps. It was power-mad McColl, throwing money at whatever he didn't like to make it go away.

This helped force McColl to come to grips with the fact that there were new forces at work in his city. Charlotte's old Chamber-of-Commerce boosterism was giving way to media-masticated cynicism. Chief spokesman for the so-called "leadership revolution" was Republican County Commissioner-at-large Tom Bush.

"Elected officials used to operate at the beck and call of the big banks and corporations," Bush railed. "Now many of us have been elected whom the economic powers in Mecklenburg (County) didn't know or weren't interested in."

When the city commissioned a Ben Long fresco for its new police headquarters building, the cynics had railed against $180,000 of tax money being spent on "worthless art." McColl had wound up footing half the bill for that one. Now, even a gift transit center had to be examined from the mouth out.

Prosperity had provoked a smallness in Charlotte's civic soul. Having attained what they considered their rightful portion, the righteous were easily roused to defend their claims against anyone labeled as a threat—which might come either from the have-nots or from the have-mores. The most frequently applied label for any such threat was "Uptown Business Interests," seeming to imply a privileged cadre leading the unwashed and out-of-touch against the "majority." The personification of the Uptown Business Interests, of course, was Hugh McColl.

McColl counterpunched. He insisted he was more concerned with protecting the underprivileged than with "removing" them. He memorized an alliterative theme, suitable for print or broadcast media: "We're trying to get rid of the pimps and panhandlers, the pushers, pickpockets and prostitutes, the people who prey on the pedestrians and the public transit riders."

The bank commissioned an independent survey of those transit riders, seeking opinions as to what they really wanted at their uptown bus transfer site. The answers were: bathrooms, shelter, someplace to get a bite to eat and drink. McColl read the survey results with predictable pleasure: "Just like anybody that had to stand out there for hours waiting for a damn bus, they wanted a place to sit down. They wanted to get something to eat or drink. They wanted police protection from all the people preying on them."

When the survey results were published, the complaints drifted away.

Mayor Vinroot had nothing but praise for his benefactor. "It was typical Hugh McColl cut-to-the-chase, get-on-with-it, do-the-right-thing-for-the-community," he told Charlotte's *The Leader*. "There's not a city in the country where the mayor has that kind of citizen sitting at the other end to get a project done."

Meanwhile, McColl knew the citizen he wanted to design "his" transportation center, former mayor and architect Harvey Gantt, first African American to attend a white public college in South Carolina (Clemson) and the Democrat who came within a whisker of beating Luther Hodges's one-time target, Republican Jesse Helms, in the 1990 Senate race.

Gantt joined McColl in his glass-walled conference room on the fifty-eighth floor. "We looked north, up Tryon Street, and I said: 'You know, you are a city planner by trade. You and I have been talking about this city for a long time, and I decided to fix North Tryon Street, and I'd like you to do a master plan for me of North Tryon Street. Would you be interested in that? I am going to build a new building up there and I'd like you to design it for me. Would you be interested in that?'

"He said, 'Are you kidding? What does an architect dream of? Being able to design the whole north side of town and build a new building for you!' I said, 'Well there is a catch. That's not all of it. It's a package. I want you to design the new transportation center for me too. These are inseparable.'

"He's very smart, does not need a guardian. I am too. And he said, 'You make it hard. You drive a hard bargain.'"

There was an instant understanding between the two men. As one of the most visible African Americans in the region, Gantt's involvement in the transportation project would shield McColl and the bank from charges of racism. But this only was possible because, as McColl knew, Gantt could get the jobs done. "He did both, and did them both well. In other words he designed the north side of town. He did the Transamerica building and he did the Transit Center. And he got paid. A big number. But in fairness, we got what we paid for. I am so damn proud of that transportation center. I'm proud of my tower, but I really think that the transportation center may be the best thing I ever did for this city. I say I did it, but that's not fair, the bank did it."

Charlotte, North Carolina, fancies itself "a city of trees." It has more oaks, maples, dogwoods and Bradford pear trees than it has Baptists and Presbyterians. People may be taken to court there for cutting down trees. Lawns there are lush and beloved, fertilized every spring and aerated every fall. Charlotte's Piedmont climate, nestled between the blizzard-killing Smoky Mountains and the usually mild-mannered Atlantic shore, is perhaps as near to perfection as Mother Earth offers. All of which may explain Hugh McColl's passion for escaping to that least-blessed land of all American geography, the Wild Horse Desert of the South Texas coastal plain.

On old Mexican maps, the region Texans know as the Wild Horse Desert was labeled "Desert of the Dead." A United States cavalry officer, Phil Sheridan, crossed the scrubby territory with General Zachary Taylor's army in 1847 and wrote home that if he happened to own both Dante's Inferno and the Wild Horse Desert, he would most likely live in Hell and lease out the Wild Horse. In Hugh McColl of NationsBank, Sheridan would have found an ideal tenant.

McColl had to admit the Texas brush country might seem like "the ugliest, most drab, worst-looking place you have seen in your whole life," nothing but mesquite and cactus. But, "then it grows on you. It is my favorite part of the world. And it makes no sense that it should be."

Taking every opportunity to visit his leased happy hunting grounds, McColl learned everything he could about the land. He learned about the goatweed that grows thick along cattle trails and dirt roads, releasing seeds all winter long, the staple of the quail diet. "Birds are just like the rest of us," McColl discovered. "They do what is the easiest thing to do, go where they have to move the least to get the food." The goatweed plants were strut-by McDonald's for quail.

He learned how to pull the disk tiller, with its round blades that chew the sand-clay soil and somehow bring the goatweed to life, so that, four months later, the coveys will forage along the trails, where the men with their dogs and guns can flush them and watch them rise of an instant and, if they are quick and understand how to sight without aiming, and if they pull the trigger in one motion with the birds, fill their bellies and sticky their fingers with tender flesh grilled that night over the hard, heat-packed mesquite.

He found "a good pair of dog men" who would hunt with him upwards of forty days a year, during the fall-winter season. It meant a lot that these men would accept him. "That means that they think a lot of us, otherwise they wouldn't do it. They can hunt with anybody they want to, because they are the best and they are in demand. And in the field you want the best man, the best dog. In the field you can't lie about shooting, you either can or can't."

There were times in South Texas he couldn't have had anywhere else on earth, memories he never could have made in any other surrounding. Off in the middle of a cactus- and mesquite-studded prairie, grazed by Santa Gertrudis cattle big as rusty buses, rose a huge oak. "That's Jane's Tree," he would say proudly. The first time he brought his daughter to the desert the dogs raised about forty quail near that tree. "Jane was firing so much, she was firing through the trees and out at everything else. She was about ready to shoot me." He would always laugh at that. "So all the guys call it Jane's Tree."

By the 1995–96 season, McColl decided he needed some more Texas to hunt in, so he moved south of Falfurrias into Kenedy County—all of which was comprised of two ranches, the Kenedy Ranch and the Armstrong Ranch. He signed a six-year hunting-rights-only lease on tenty-five thousand acres, and he bought lots of maps so he could show his teammates where it was.

"The place that I lease lies along the line right here across Armstrong, thusly." The map is spread out on the floor of his study and he is squatting over it, drawing lines with his finger. "And I rent about tnty-five thousand acres right there." The spot is just south of the dot labeled "Sarita," which, he explains, "is a little town populated by Mexicans who are the ranch hands for the Kenedy Ranch. When you're in Kenedy County you are in a sort of separate nation, because the judge, the jury, the sheriff—everybody works for the Kenedy Ranch. So you don't screw with the Kenedy Ranch."

McColl had his picture taken on a sailboat in the Gulf of Mexico, with the flat South Texas shoreline just behind him. In his right hand he holds a tumbler of single-malt scotch on the rocks, elbow bent, ready to raise that glass as if it were his 30/30 rifle. The smile on his face is sure, confident. The thick black letters screened onto his white T-shirt spell out: FUCK YOU WE'RE FROM TEXAS.

The ranch was a fine place to bond with his like-minded directors, old banking pals like Hootie Johnson and Alan Dickson, the Ruddick Corporation CEO. Both of them loved to hunt. Both of them were also on his executive committee. "We've made a lot of decisions about policy," he acknowledged, "riding along on the back of the truck, sitting and talking about it. Strategic moves, plans to have mergers, long-range plans." Nights in the Spartan bunkhouse, or "camp," were filled with "long hours of philosophizing" that spilled into the dreams of wealthy men.

And, occasionally, McColl could use the ranch to consummate a deal. Toward the end of the '95 quail season, he invited Jerry Finger to fly down from Houston for the weekend. It had been eight years since Finger pointed the way into Texas, yet NationsBank still owned only 40 percent of his Charter Bank. Over afternoon drinks, McColl explained how that was going to change. "I told him that I had an investment in the bank for some time, NationsBank had. We had put it in there in the '80s when he was in trouble to help save him. It was getting to be a problem. It had gotten pretty big, and we owned less than 50 percent of it. I sat out there and told him I had made up my mind and it was time for us to exercise our option to buy his bank. He told me he liked it the way he had it. I essentially told him it was right now or never, and it was *now*."

In the final week of January 1996, the deal was announced. NationsBank would pay $94.7 million to buy the remaining 60 percent of Charter Bancshares of Houston. Ten years earlier—and clearly they had been good years for Charter—NCNB had paid $13 million for 40 percent of Finger's bank. McColl was much happier owning all of something than he was with just a piece of it.

In February, Ken Lewis, who now was president of NationsBank, declared that the Charter deal was just the sort of thing Wall Street could look for in his company: conservation of energy, strengthening its hold on territories where its flag was already planted, solidifying its base of operations. NationsBank was in no rush to buy banks outside its current domain. Lewis said NationsBank was waiting for some sort of "serious disruption" in the economy that would force certain "desirable" banks to sell at lower prices than they could demand in the current marketplace.

But in the NationsBank Planning Office, where Frank Gentry held sway, there was an open file called "Project Atlas." The Atlas (because it was based on a map of the United States) had begun with a listing of the two hundred largest bank holding companies in the country. That list was whittled down to the fifty companies NationsBank—at the time, NCNB—viewed as potential takeover targets. "When we first started doing this we had to struggle," said Gentry, "because, generally speaking, we weren't on anybody's list of people to be invited to a party."

By 1996, Gentry was on all the lists and Atlas was into its "Phase

Six." Each quarter Gentry got the numbers on the affordability of each prospective target bank, analyzing boards to see if there were relationships that could be enhanced or exploited. Like Caesar's Gaul, McColl's Atlas was divided into three parts: "in market," "out of market" and "adjacent market." When any bank was "in play," Gentry would get a call from at least one investment banker, asking: "You want a book? You want a look?" If the bank was on Gentry's current list, his answer would be yes and yes.

The most obvious "adjacent market" in the NationsBank Atlas was the Midwest. Hugh McColl had been eyeing that flat breadbasket of America since he closed the C&S/Sovran deal. Not interested in the Louisiana-Mississippi-Alabama connection, he viewed the Midwest as the logical linkup between his eight-state East Coast market and his western republic of Texas. In an interview with *American Banker*, he had asked himself the question, "Are there any other places that we'd like to go?" The answer he gave was the Midwest, "a very stable part of America, with good people and good businesses." He said he was attracted to the region because of its "diversification of risk," in states "not given to the boom-and-bust of the two coasts." From the cornfields of Nebraska to the oilfields of Oklahoma to Marshall Fields in Chicago, the midwestern United States had an economic base so broad it could "protect us against the next round of—whatever." Consequently, at the very time Ken Lewis was scoffing at rumors that his bank might be getting acquisitive again, McColl was sending out feelers to the chairman and CEO of St. Louis-based Boatmen's Banks, Andrew Craig III.

The largest bank in Missouri, Boatmen's was a well-managed company, with assets of $41 billion, operating in nine states that stretched across the southern tier of the region into New Mexico. Jim Hance suspected that Boatmen's could be looking at the cost of retooling for the next technological revolution and perhaps doubting that they had the capital to get through that process. "Boatmen's is further behind than we are," he said, "and they are going to dilute the earnings too much to make that technology commitment. They want to protect their shareholders, and get a good price for their stock."

McColl, resisting the temptation to fire any missiles, hoped his missives would find their way to Andy Craig's heart. He was sure that NationsBank and Boatmen's would combine to make a better NationsBank. He could only wait.

In May 1996, with buses rolling into the new Transit Center and work nearing completion on Transamerica Square, the working-and-living space that would be headquarters for Transamerica's Reinsurance Division, McColl spoke with a reporter. Looking out on Charlotte from the same fifty-eighth-floor conference room where he had twisted the arm of Harvey Gantt's imagination, he said: "I'm going to finish everything before I leave here, and I have to leave here by the time I'm sixty-five."

Shortly after that interview, NationsBank rolled out its plans to develop a ten-level uptown parking garage-cum-market, where somehow the aroma of fresh produce and prepared foods would waft untainted by the exhaust of bankers' BMWs. Meanwhile, McColl was working with a group of private developers to visualize a half-billion-dollar uptown entertainment "megaplex." It would complement the new Panthers football stadium—now sponsored by a cellular communications company and called Ericsson Stadium—with a new arena for George Shinn's Hornets, shops and restaurants, an entertainment complex and park, along with economic development initiatives on the city's west side. If the politicians did not shoot it down, this would be the largest public-private venture in Charlotte's history, a new "heart of Charlotte." McColl hoped the megaplex eventually would include a major league baseball stadium.

It came as no surprise to his lieutenants that McColl should insist on taking a personal hand in the design of Transamerica Square, once again "suggesting" a fresco by the Ben Long studio. This time he wanted a dome. Michelangelo had his Sistine ceiling, Giotto had his bell tower, Long should have a dome in Charlotte. Harvey Gantt complied, designing an overhead "faux dome" in a breezeway entrance to the offices and restaurants, which took visitors through the office building to a greensward and condominium building beyond.

There, two blocks up North Tryon from their Corporate Center triptych, Long and his troop of artists went to work on their backs from scaffolds, the greatest technical challenge of their career, to create a mystical amalgam of North Carolina symbols, from the mountains to the shore. To the passerby, the fresco presents a number of challenges—not the least of which is how to spend enough time looking up without causing pain to one's neck. The view is worth it.

There is a child reaching helplessly out a window as his papers (containing the secret of life?) are carried away in the wind. A man climbs a tall wooden ladder to reach a woman perched on the crumbling edge of an elevated highway to nowhere. There is a group of musicians whose instruments were never played as a group—hurdy-gurdy, banjo, cello, tambour. A stern young man in a smock seems about to pounce down from the plaster. A man on a dying tree throws a rope to the outstretched hands of his comrades. There is a serenely out-of-place bevy of nude sunbathers, gathered under a beach cabana. And, 180 degrees around the circle from the beach cabana, a solitary figure looks down from a rude lean-to. He wears, perhaps, a French army greatcoat, World War I vintage. He might be homeless. Beside him is an hourglass, sand fixed at three-quarters emptied for the projected thousand-year life of the fresco. The homeless warrior whose time is forever running out is Hugh McColl.

McColl wasn't sure how he should respond when Joe Martin told him that Long proposed to include him in the fresco. What was it his grandmother had said? *"Fools' names and fools' faces often appear in public places."* But he was in his sixties now and the sand really was running out. Looking at it honestly, he had to admit he liked the idea. He'd spent his entire adult life in the city. "And, immodestly," he told Martin, "I think I have a lot to do with it. Maybe I'd like to be buried up there, uptown somewhere." Memorializing McColl in a fresco seemed to Martin a better option than adding a crypt to one of NationsBank's buildings.

By mid-1996, McColl's face was almost as well known in Atlanta as it was in Charlotte. He believed that the bank's commitment to the Olympics, coming immediately after the announcement of the C&S buyout, had "really given them the impetus to go forward." NationsBank had raised the Olympic Committee's credit line to $800 million, although the bank never had to lend out more than the originally pledged $300 million. Under Ken Lewis and CRA expert Cathy Bessant, NationsBank had become a partner with Habitat for Humanity throughout Georgia. The bank had improved Atlanta's downtown parks and neighborhoods. It supported the symphony, the ballet and the art museum in Atlanta, and created a pool of money for a leadership program in the city's schools. With African-American universities and colleges an important part of the region's higher learning, NationsBank's Atlanta office made major contributions to the United Negro College Fund.

"We poured our energy into that city," McColl boasted. "We have been sponsors of Tom Cousins's very brilliant idea of the Bobby Jones Golf Course, restoring former public housing, turning it into nice housing around the golf course for the same people who had lived there before."

With all of that, and with its work in the Washington area, in Texas and Florida, McColl's 1991 promise to make $10 billion in low-income loans within ten years proved to be a very conservative bet: NationsBank had met its ten-year CRA pledge in just four years.

In June, as he prepared to visit Atlanta for the pre-opening festivities at the Olympics, McColl got his first response from Boatmen's Andy Craig. The timing was not propitious. McColl honestly hoped not to get into another spending spree until after a projected stock split at the end of the year. At long last, NationsBank stock was going up, and word of an expensive buyout would be sure to scare off investors. Nevertheless, he invited Craig to join him in Atlanta.

Craig met McColl at one of NationsBank's apartments at Park Place on Peachtree Street for a game of Let's Pretend—all very friendly, no pressure, no specific offers. But McColl learned for a fact that in a matter of weeks, Boatmen's would be in play and NationsBank would be one of the players. He and his advisors agreed that they dearly wanted to own Craig's bank, "but if we had picked our time for Boatmen's to come available it would have been the next year. They became available to us before we were ready for them. But we weren't willing to *not* do them. We would not walk away."

On August 12, after the Olympics, Craig called McColl to say that he was ready for serious talks. There would be a bidding process and NationsBank would be in competition with Banc One Corporation of Columbus, Ohio, along with two Minneapolis banks, Norwest Corporation and First Bank System. Jim Hance sent an accounting team to St. Louis to conduct a due diligence review, just to make sure there was nothing for the *emptor* to *caveat*. Hance brought back a good report. Boatmen's books were clean, with no liabilities that would kill the merger. Having grown accustomed to buying banks with deep problems, this would be a departure for NationsBank. "We joked that it was the first time we ever tried to buy a healthy company," McColl said. "We didn't know how to act."

On Tuesday, August 27, McColl took his deal-making team to Washington, where they'd won their wrestling match with C&S/Sovran. At the offices of Boatmen's lawyers, McColl laid on the table an offer the Boatmen's side could not turn down. Craig had been expecting something on the order of two times the Boatmen's "book value"—which is determined by first deducting the number of outstanding shares of preferred stock from the number of outstanding common shares, then multiplying the remainder by the current trading price per share. Instead of 2x book, McColl was offering 2.7x book, or $9.46 billion. That would be one of the highest premiums ever paid for a large bank.

In a matter of a few hours, the two sides shook hands across the conference table and the third-largest banking deal in United States history was consummated. Next to his purchase of the Bank of North Carolina from Dick Spangler at the Virginia ski resort and the more recent Charter purchase over scotch in the Wild Horse Desert, this was one of the quickest, easiest deals of McColl's career.

Going in, NationsBank was the country's fifth-largest bank, with $192 billion in assets. Adding the $41 billion of number-twenty-four Boatmen's, it would rank just behind BankAmerica Corporation as number four, moving well ahead of the new number five, J. P. Morgan ($198 billion), and number-six First Union ($140 billion). At this snapshot of time, Chase—Chemical in disguise—was number one with $321 billion, and Citicorp was number two with $267 billion.

To its nine-state empire, NationsBank would now add Boatmen's branches in seven new states: Missouri, Kansas, Arkansas, Oklahoma, New Mexico, Iowa, Illinois. The two banks overlapped only in Tennessee and Texas. Geographically, no other bank even came close to the combined territories.

Wearing a St. Louis Cardinals baseball cap for the cameras, McColl joined Craig at an early-morning analysts' meeting in New York. He told the analysts that the Boatmen's buy signaled a shift in NationsBank strategy. In the past few years the company had emphasized a "global strategy," specializing in investment banking and Wall Street-style services. The Boatmen's network was strong because it was grounded in the basics of banking, lending to consumers and small- to medium-sized businesses, the same strategy that NCNB had used to grow into NationsBank.

But to McColl the warlord, there was something else at least as satisfying about the deal. He was "putting a wall around our large Texas enterprise, where we're number one, and making it more difficult for our competitors in Texas to gain economies of scale through a southwestern operation." Based on deposits, NationsBank would now be number one in the four states sitting above Texas to the north, as well as in New Mexico to the west. In recent years Ohio-based Banc One, California-based Bank of America and New York-based Chase-née-Chemical had made forays into Texas. McColl believed that he had effectively prevented those challengers from any substantial growth in his adopted Lone Star home. The merger "also comes close to permanently stopping new players like Norwest, which have small investments in Texas and down that way. And it provides in a classic strategic sense—and you can use 'military' or otherwise—it provides a buffer around our big number-one position there. Our Texas franchise cannot be replicated and this franchise that we acquired cannot be replicated."

After his Wall Street pep rally, McColl flew to St. Louis for an afternoon news conference. He answered Missouri reporters' "what next?" questions with: "It would be impossible for me to suggest that I don't have ambitions. Do I have time? Not much. I'm sixty-one."

Scheduled to close January 7, 1997, the Boatmen's merger became the fastest yet for NationsBank, just four months from handshake to hand-off. The regulatory agencies approved the merger, as did the shareholders of both banks, so 1997 began with Andy Craig's twenty thousand employees joining Hugh McColl's sixty-two thousand troops, all marching under the banner of NationsBank.

The first step in getting all those people pulling together was what McColl had come to call his annual "road show." It was one of his favorite times of the year, turning a usually dreary week in January into a round of surprises, encounters with old teammates, win-one-for-the-Gipper speeches and the handing out of coveted crystal grenades. He and some of his top advisors would hit some of the bank's principal cities and face an auditorium filled with eager top-level management folks. Now and then came a year—1990 had been one—in which the road show had all the fun of a funeral cortege, but most years it was exciting, giving McColl the chance to set a strong, positive tone for the business year ahead. This year would be both exciting and challenging, thanks to the quickly executed Boatmen's merger.

One of the key figures in the annual road-show drama was McColl's chief of staff, responsible for getting the chairman into and out of each venue on schedule. That position, first held by Bill McGee, was filled now by Vick Phillips, a tenacious detail man who earlier had headed up the bank's call centers, where customers phoned in their problems and expected quick response. He considered this to have been excellent training for his current position. Phillips was tight as the head of the bluegrass banjo he loved to play and he could snag loose details like a bullfrog stabbing flies.

The NationsBank hangar at Charlotte-Douglas Airport was one of Vick Phillips's responsibilities. About the area of two football fields laid side by side, it seems high-ceilinged enough to handle a space shuttle. Phillips loved to walk visitors through that hangar, eat-off-the-floor clean and lit up like heaven. He would smile at the Citation 5 Ultras, once the pride of NCNB's fledgling fleet. He would admire the still-impressive Hawker 800 XPs. But it was the new Gulfstream G4 that really turned him on. More comfortable than any commercial airliner, able to cross large oceans at a single fueling, built to be worth the $25 million and change it cost the bank. "When you're flying," Phillips would say to a first-timer in the G4, "look out the window and remember that the winglet at the tip of the wing is six feet tall."

All his airplanes were gleaming white with pinstripes of red and blue. The tail identification numbers all included the letters "NB"; however they sported no NationsBank insignia. "There are occasions," Vick Phillips explained to the curious, "when we don't want people to know we're in a particular city. People who are trying to track when you're going to buy something don't need to know when you land."

On the twenty-sixth of January, a Sunday afternoon, Phillips arrived at the airport thirty minutes early, just to make sure the Gulfstream was ready for its flight to Dallas, the first stop of the 1996 road show. Anything that happened aboard that aircraft was his responsibility. Airborne, the pilots wrote the rules and the chairman reported to Phillips.

As was his habit, McColl arrived precisely on schedule. Everyone else was ready to step aboard, luggage stowed. The chairman's arrival was the signal to board the plane and taxi to the runway. Phillips watched them mount the stairs, one at a time: McColl, Jim Hance, Chuck Cooley, Lynn Drury, and then he stepped up. They were greeted by captain Gary Self and copilot Marvin Knecht from the cockpit. Flight attendant Sherri Settle settled them into their seats.

The flight to Dallas was relatively smooth. A weather front was pushing down from the Great Lakes, but their flight took them south of that and the front presented no problems. McColl and Chuck Cooley sat at the fold-down table at the rear of the cabin and talked about issues and insubstantialities. Hance sat in the center, ferreting through figures. Drury and Phillips held down the forward area, just talking and reading. Flying down on a second plane was Ken Lewis— because Phillips had a strict rule against the chairman and the president of the corporation ever being aboard the same aircraft. Bill Vandiver, president of global finance, was with Lewis, as were Fred Figge, chairman of risk policy, and Betty Ledford, in whose mind alone resided the intricacies of the slide projectors and audio systems required to make the road show bells ring and whistles blow on cue.

When the two teams gathered together in Dallas, there was disturbing news. NationsBank director Tom Belk had died and McColl would need to return to Charlotte for the funeral. Tom Belk had joined the board of American Commercial Bank in 1960. His first action as a director was to cast a vote in favor of the merger with Greensboro's Security Bank that would create NCNB, North Carolina's second-largest bank, with resources amounting to more than $650 million. His retirement in 1995 took him out one year before the vote that created the $233 billion fourth-largest bank in the United States.

McColl turned around and headed back to Charlotte, leaving the Dallas meeting, at the Hyatt Hotel Monday morning, in Ken Lewis's hands. He would rejoin the group in St. Louis in time for the Tuesday session, his first face-to-face meeting with his new management team from Boatmen's.

By the time McColl landed in St. Louis, the winter storm had moved well down into the Mississippi Valley. There was snow on the runway. He was pleased to notice how well the plane handled the snow, but a rattle had turned up in the door frame, so the new G4 was dispatched on a quick repair trip to Gulfstream's assembly facility in Savannah. It returned in time to make the scheduled 3:00 P.M. flight that would get them to Washington by 4:45.

The midday temperature had turned the runway snow to something the consistency of a frozen daiquiri, but the big G4 rolled right through the slush into the takeoff queue behind its larger Boeing and Douglas cousins. McColl hoped the weather wouldn't delay them. The funeral and travel had worn him out and he was looking forward to a good night's rest at the Capitol Hill Hyatt.

The passenger cabin of the NationsBank Gulfstream was divided into three sections. The first section, immediately aft of the pilots' compartment and main cabin door, could seat four individuals, two on each side of the central aisle, with one seat facing forward and one seat facing rear. The second compartment was the same as the first, except that instead of bucket seats on the right-hand side there was a couch-like bench with armrests, comfortable for three. The couch was upholstered in cloth; all other seats were soft padded leather.

McColl told Cooley to join him again in the third, most private and roomiest compartment, just forward of the galley and restroom. Here there were no seats on the right side. Protruding from the left bulkhead wall was a card table. Its padded leaves could be folded up for conversation and drinks, folded down for card-playing, meals and spreading out work papers. The legs of the table were actually two hydraulic pedestals that allowed the surface to be lowered to the height of the four passenger seats that flanked it. If someone—say, the CEO—wanted a nap, the flight attendant could bring out a specially made mattress that turned the table-and-seats into a comfortable bed.

CFO Jim Hance kept to himself in the center section of the plane, studying figures, making notes, his method of preparing for anything. Meanwhile, McColl used Cooley as an iron to stoke the embers of ideas that might burn themselves out if left untended. McColl asked Sherri Settle if she would bring him a glass of Lagavulin and a slice of toast with melted cheese. His dietitian prescribed the poor man's Welsh rarebit; he prescribed the rich man's Scotch tea.

"Join me, Chuck?" Cooley shrugged a why-not. Flying through clouds, who could tell whether the sun was yet below the yardarm? Settles, charming and effervescent as any stewardess from Central Casting, brought place mats, turned down the table leaves, and served McColl and Cooley their drinks in heavy crystal tumblers.

They spoke of the extraordinary opportunity they had fallen into with Boatmen's. Like NationsBank, Boatmen's had a better-than-average record in supporting their communities. He wanted to make certain they built on that record. "If you have a healthy community, you have a healthy bank," he preached to his onboard choir. That would be an important part of his sermon to Washington-area managers the following day.

They moved on to the subject of generating savings through the economics of size. How much did Jim Hance think they were going to save between the two banks in operating expenses? Hance heard the question, called over his shoulder from the midsection of the plane: "We're talking about $335 million. Could be more." McColl echoed the figure, did the math in his head. It could be 20 to 30 percent of combined expenses.

"A lot of Post-it Notes," Cooley smiled. He reminded the CEO of a lesson they had learned long ago, in Florida: in each Boatmen's community there would be relationships that would need to be severed before the combined culture could be made strong.

McColl agreed. "We are creating a cultural disruption in relationships," he said. "The more banks they have, the more relationships are disturbed."

"People who supply checks," Cooley elaborated, "local advertising agencies. Just by consolidating our check supplies we've probably saved more than $100 million over time in the banks we now own."

Vendor relationships were not the only things disturbed when one company takes over another. "These are good people," McColl said, looking at the "20k Boatmen's" he had written on his small, yellow, lined crib sheet—the number of former Boatmen's employees now working for him. "Their experience was that they were winning. They thought they knew how to run a bank. We've destroyed their experience, all their accumulated knowledge in one fell swoop. In some cases that's twenty years or more of experience, worthless, or so they think. At age forty-five, maybe even fifty-five, they see themselves starting over, as trainees."

McColl admitted he'd handled this improperly in the past. "In the '60s, when we were buying all those banks in North Carolina, Statesville and places like that, we had no respect for the people. They didn't want to think our way. What we thought of as normal was to them radical. But it was like that old saying, 'Lead, follow or get out of the way.' We were the leaders. They didn't want to follow. So we got them out of the way." There was neither regret nor cruelty in his tone, simply resignation.

Some of their associates from Boatmen's, Cooley conjectured, were going to feel betrayed. "Right," said McColl. "They've had the ultimate failure of trust. They went to work for a company, they were loyal to it, they fought for it, they were winning, and it got sold. Now how would you feel about that if you were a middle-level manager who had been doing your job well? All along you've been told, 'We're kicking butt. We've got it right and those other people have it wrong.' And now 'those other people' just went *poomp!*" His right hand came down like the jaws of a lion, covering his left fist. "That's what we're dealing with. It is big time."

McColl nodded, leaned back in his seat, finished his Scotch, listened to Cooley comment on the persistence of the glass ceiling at the bank. "You've diminished its influence," he smiled, "to the point where it might be considered a high-level semipermeable membrane."

Sherri Settle, maneuvering in ways known only to flight attendants, brought in two slices of whole wheat toast covered with melted cheddar, served on good china plates with sterling silver forks and knives. There was also a bowl of sliced fruit to complete the afternoon snack. She thought of it as high-altitude high tea.

No sooner had McColl finished his toast than the plane began to rock and kick against the weather. Imperturbable Sherri arrived with china cups and saucers, somehow steadying herself to pour coffee from a black carafe. Cooley was not certain he could manage even to get the cup to his lips. The plane dropped violently and McColl covered his coffee with a folded linen napkin, pressed down tightly by the palm of his hand. He was practiced in foul-weather dining.

The attendant came to reclaim the impossible coffee cups and McColl decided he would wobble up front for a while to see how the others were doing. He took his customary seat, facing forward on the right side of the cabin, where he had a clear view into the cockpit. Drury and Phillips were across the aisle. On the wall to McColl's right was a tiny video monitor, the "Air Show" viewscreen going through its cycle: altitude 1000 feet . . . temperature 28 degrees . . . current time 4:33 EST . . . 16 minutes to destination. . . . Then a map came up, showing Charlottesville, Virginia, just to the northeast of a tiny airplane-shaped icon that represented their current position. About two centimeters to the northeast was a circle representing Washington, D.C. Almost there.

McColl fished through his stack of papers for the list of D.C.-area

Crystal Hand Grenade Award recipients. Had he misplaced them? "Lynn . . ." he began, instantly cutting off the conversation between Drury and Phillips. Then, "Never mind, I got 'em."

He remembered a story he'd been wanting to tell someone. "Did I tell you I had a teller the other day who wanted me to give her my driver's license? I had to give it to her before she would cash my check. I did ask her how long she had been here and she said since the first of the month." Drury and Phillips laughed. "Just to show you what our turnover problems are, there was nobody on that teller line who knew me, and that's in the main office. At least the manager waved to me. But you know, that teller was right. I had a thousand-dollar check made out to cash. She responded to her training perfectly."

McColl wondered if he should get used to showing identification. "I need to be prepared for, about sixty days after retirement, not anybody knowing if my check is good. I've been chairman fourteen damned years. I feel like I just got here. I think, how did I have time to do all that stuff?"

"One minute you join the bank and fifteen minutes later you're at your retirement party," Lynn Drury joked.

"Sort of sad, really," said Vick Phillips. "But maybe it's the natural order of things."

"The time has just, just flown," mused McColl.

Drury said: "And the reason is, it's been so full every day. Building is a lot of fun."

"Building is fun," McColl agreed, "but nothing gets close to winning."

McColl looked up to see the copilot, Marvin Knecht, come out of the cockpit with a serious look on his face. If there was anything he hated it was a serious-faced pilot in a plane he was on. Then Knecht did something McColl had never seen a pilot do. He went down on one knee in the aisle to look the chairman straight in the eye.

"Mr. McColl," said Knecht, "all the news is bad."

McColl was vaguely aware of his executives stirring through the cabin, Hance and Cooley coming forward. "What does that mean?" he asked.

"We don't have our nose gear, we can't get it down. We have thought of everything. We tried to blow it down with the nitrogen cartridge. It doesn't work. I'm afraid we are going to have to land without our nose gear."

McColl was still calm. He trusted his pilots. "Well, you have done that before, haven't you?"

"No sir, but we know how to. I've done it in a simulator."

"Well, that's good."

Knecht rose and walked slowly back to the cockpit. Phillips quietly went back to the galley. There was a telephone there he could use without being overheard. He punched in the number for the NationsBank hangar in Charlotte and got the company's chief of aviation on the line. Dropping his customary reserve, Phillips demanded to know: *"What the fuck is going on?"*

As he suspected, Charlotte was well aware of their emergency. The best guess was that the frozen slush in St. Louis had somehow affected the coupling releases of the nose landing gear. Engineers from Gulfstream's facilities in Long Beach, California, and Savannah, Georgia, were on the horn with pilot Gary Self right now, trying to talk him through some possible solutions. Unsettled and unsatisfied, Phillips returned to his seat as Captain Self stepped forward into the cabin.

"Here are our options," the pilot said. "First, we are going to try and dive and try to jerk it loose. By dropping five hundred feet, then pulling the nose up, we may be able to use the G-forces to drop the landing gear. If that doesn't work, one other option we are discussing is taking it in bouncing, slamming it into the deck hard, going in at 200 mph and banging on the main wheels. That might knock down the nose wheels. Then we'll go back up and come back and do it again. But I'm not sure about that idea." Before he tried anything, Self wanted his passengers strapped in. He told them to listen to Sherri Settle and she would tell them what to do.

McColl could not resist an opportunity to take control. He might never have another opportunity to give an order. He said he wanted Lynn Drury to have the safest seat, the one in the back of the aircraft, facing the rear.

"Wrong," said Vick Phillips. "That's your seat. You don't get to be chairman again until we're out of this plane." Phillips and Settle took charge, showing Jim Hance to the theoretically second-safest seat, with Cooley and Drury placed forward of them. Phillips and Settle would be nearest the cockpit.

Strapped in, they endured the gut-wrenching sensation of plummeting five hundred feet, then pulling suddenly out of free-fall. The plane screamed down a second time, then a third, before Self came back to tell them that the G-force idea was not going to work. What they must do now, he said, was fly around Washington for about two and a half hours, to burn up their fuel reserves. As he went back to the cockpit, someone asked why they had to do that. McColl knew the answer. "It's so we don't turn into a ball of flame when we hit," he said.

There were three telephone receivers on the G4, so the passengers took turns trying to reach their spouses. Cooley's wife was traveling in France, so there would be no way for them to talk. Lynn Drury got through to her husband and Vick Phillips reached his wife. Phillips managed to convince his wife that nothing out of the ordinary was going on. He just had some extra time and wanted to talk. They each spent a half hour on the phone, managing not to sound desperate or terrified. McColl reached Jane on her car phone. She was shocked by the news and burst into tears, unable to talk or to drive. She pulled over to the side of the road and began to ask questions, but McColl had to hang up, since the pilot was coming out to speak with him.

The phones kept ringing, because now there were people who thought they could help. Even Ken Lewis and his group, waiting at the hotel bar in Washington, wanted to know what they could do. McColl tried to put it all out of his mind. He found himself remembering the nights on the glacier in Switzerland, alone with his thoughts. They were, none of them, about business or banking or big deals or power; they were about Jane and the children and the grandchildren, about how they would go on without him.

Gary Self returned to the cabin. "Well, we are not going to try and bounce it," he said. "There seem to be two schools of thought about how to land this plane without nose gear. Some people think that you should go in and land on your two rear wheels, hold the nose up as long as possible, and then try to put her down softly. I don't favor that. There is too much risk. The plane is too tall. It could break in two while we are still going fast. We're going to do it the other way. We are going to make a normal approach, as if we had a nose wheel. There will be a lot of noise and a lot of sparks, but don't worry. We'll be landing in ten minutes."

"Sherri," McColl said as Self returned to his place. "I'd appreciate it if you'd get all of us a drink of that Lagavulin . . . in a plastic cup."

They drank to each other then, in spite of the phones ringing, each saying some fine words about the others. They spoke softly, over the fortissimo monotone of the jet engines. Their eyes teared up. Settle instructed the men to take off their ties. Everyone should get rid of any loose clothing that might get caught in debris. She went over the exit procedures, all the safety instructions they'd heard before and never thought they'd need. Then she said, "You know what I do every time before we land—I mean every time, not just in emergencies? I go over in my mind exactly what I am going to do if the plane catches fire and the cabin fills with smoke."

McColl worked on focusing his "muscle memory." He memorized how it felt to raise his hand up, reaching across the aisle to the T-intersection of the window latch. He followed Sherri's instructions on checking how his seat belt opened, right to left. He heard the sounds outside change as the plane slowed for its final approach. *Final approach.* It sounded like the title of some adventure novel he might have read on some flight somewhere.

"When we get outside," Settle continued, "go immediately to the front of the wing and jump off the front of the wing, not the back, because you don't want to get sucked into the engines. The engines will still be running. A lot of people get killed getting sucked in the engines." *Great stuff to be talking about now,* McColl thought, wondering if he'd be able to tell the front from the rear with smoke everywhere. He imagined the headline: *Bank Chief Sucked In.*

Suddenly Lynn Drury blurted: "I need to take off my panty hose."

"What?" asked Phillips.

"I remember reading that if it burns it sticks to your skin." She began trying to wriggle out of them without unstrapping herself.

"No," said Settle. "We're less than a minute from touch-down. You don't have time. Leave them on."

The telephone in the galley rang and Settle jumped up to answer it. "Sit down," McColl said, happy to be giving any order. "Whoever the hell that is, they can't help us now."

The television screen on the wall of the galley, at the rear of the cabin, suddenly lit up with the picture from the video camera positioned in the nose of the plane. They were going to watch their own crash on television! There were flashing lights everywhere against a black field—blue, red, yellow, white lights—like an electronic painting on velvet. Some of the lights were mounted on fire engines.

McColl was transfixed. The rush of air was like a soundtrack to a movie. Then he heard that little screeching sound that airplane wheels always make when the plane touches the tarmac. *Beautiful. Three-point landing.* Only it was two-point. An instant later the lights and the firetrucks disappeared from the monitor and they could see only a white line, white painted on black, rushing, rushing past. He recognized it as the center line of the runway, the nose pointing almost straight down at it now. A scrape, a screech, metal grinding. A glow of red around the rushing white line. Out the window, sparks were flying over the wing. His body pressed into the leather—since he was facing aft—as Gary hit the reverse thrusters. The nose of the plane lifted slightly, lessening the deafening screech, slowing the spark shower. McColl had his first conscious thought during the landing: *We are going to make it.*

After a brief eternity, the plane stuttered to a stop and Sherry barked a command: "Out the front." She was throwing her slender, five-foot-ten body against the door seal, muscling it open, as McColl swung out of his seat. Lynn was struggling with her seat belt. Chuck reached into her lap and yanked it open. Jim stepped aside to let Lynn out ahead of him.

Moments later, they were running across the runway, slippery with ice and snow. Settle was in the lead, suddenly stumbling to a stop. "I lost my shoe!" "Screw it," McColl shouted. "We'll get you some new ones." But Cooley was retrieving it, and the run resumed. Any minute McColl expected to hear an explosion, but there were only the sirens, the shouts of emergency workers, the pounding of his feet and heart together, the staccato gasps, the panting words: *Come on . . . Keep moving . . . Almost there . . .*

The five bankers and three crew members collapsed against a police car, gasping, sobbing, hugging, and looked back at the emergency crew hosing down their new G4 with foam. Nothing caught fire, nothing exploded. The police asked them a lot of questions, then took them to their hotel. They rode the whole way in silence.

It was a time of raw emotion for Hugh McColl. From the fear of losing his life and family as that airplane turned wide circles in the Washington air, he turned to celebration of success: a NationsBank two-for-one stock split in February, his salary moving up to $4.2 million. ("Even after the government takes half, that gives me two hundred thousand dollars a month to spend," he joked. "How can anybody spend two hundred thousand dollars a month?")

Not long after that, McColl flew to St. Petersburg, Florida, to take part in a neighborhood revitalization project put together by Cathy Bessant's Community Reinvestment group. The LEND awards had turned into weekend festivals built around activities that supported the bank's CRA efforts. The hundred-plus LEND honorees gathered once a year, with McColl, Lewis and other executives, in a rush of energy and enthusiasm for the sake of some worthy cause. The previous year the chairman had put on wading boots to help clean out a marsh near Annapolis, Maryland. The St. Petersburg project involved refurbishing a run-down basketball court, painting new foul lines and keys, hanging nets on bare hoops.

As soon as the paint dried, McColl rounded up a group of neighborhood kids for a game. Bessant was cheering on her boss when she saw him fall to the ground, clutching his left side in pain. Her first thought was that he was having a heart attack and that she would be held responsible. "Ninety-nine percent of me was saying 'Oh, my God, Hugh is hurt!' One percent of me was saying, 'Please God, not at *my* event. Don't let me be forever known as the person who caused the demise of Hugh McColl!'"

It turned out to be no worse than a separated shoulder, and the chairman made it back from the emergency room in time to finish out the day with the 125 associates who had won the right to go one-on-one with him. Straying from his loosely prepared remarks, McColl said, "I look at what you have accomplished today, what we have accomplished together here, and I look at what you accomplish in your everyday work, and . . . and I love you all." That word, "love," was coming up more and more in the company, as though McColl's confusion between business and family had become infused into the corporate culture.

Bessant was even more pleased by his words than by the sight of the CEO getting up from the basketball court. "Maybe it sounds hokey when I say it, but if you are one of 125 and you just had this really amazing experience of helping to change the face of a neighborhood in a physical way, and then the chairman of your company, who has an aura that is very powerful, says, 'I love all of you,' well, it was stunning stuff. And that is how he really feels about the people who work for him."

The emotional roller-coaster ride continued. In the first week of March, his best friend, Craig Wall, suffered a heart attack and died.

Suddenly McColl was forced to come to grips with the fact that friendship meant nearly as much to him as family did. "I trusted him totally," he said of Craig Wall. "I would trust him with my children and my wife. And he was a very honorable person." His dying left McColl "lonely, in a lot of ways. I don't have a lot of friends, a lot of close friends," he told another friend.

Friends begot friends for McColl, people connected. Luther Hodges had been at Harvard Business School with Craig. The three young men came together to form a partnership to buy raw land in South Carolina. When Hodges's part of the friendship broke up on business rocks, the other two gave him the company and let him go. McColl and Wall kept on playing tennis, going to the beach together, hunting together, doing business together. In the slump of 1989–90, Hugh helped Craig out of some serious financial trouble. The very next year, Craig paid him back with help on the C&S/Sovran merger. He thought back on how he'd been introduced to Craig by Craig's daddy, down in Conway, South Carolina. It was Wall's father who sparked their friendship, tended it like a traveler fanning a campfire to life before he moved on, just to warm the next generation of travelers.

In much the same way, Hugh's own father had set his career in motion—and he'd lost his father by now, the day before the Fourth of July, 1994. His father, the man who owned only what he needed. "He believed there was no need to add value to yourself. Anything you didn't need you didn't buy. His whole life he only owned three different cars. Most of the time he drove an old truck. I bought him his last one because I thought that old truck he was driving was going to fall apart underneath him." It was because of his father that people in Bennettsville thought McColls hid their money under mattresses.

Not in Charlotte though. When it came to spending money there, Hugh McColl Jr. and his bank were notorious for their generosity. So, two days before the Fourth of July, 1997, McColl stood behind a phalanx of potted calla lilies in front of a burned-out church on North Tryon Street and announced that his company would be donating $7 million to renovate that old shell of gothic-arched bricks, reeking in the morning sun of fortified wine and its urinary byproduct, instead of tearing it down. McColl had simply decided—and got the city's Arts and Science Council to agree—that the old church would make a great *artists colony*. Right on Hugh McColl's favorite street to do business, just ten blocks from his Taj, he wanted a place where master painters could teach apprentice artists, who, in turn, could hold classes for the city's schoolchildren. Meanwhile, eight blocks closer to The Square, NationsBank purchased a prime piece of North Tryon real estate, the old Montaldo's—an upscale women's emporium abandoned in the exodus to suburbia—and handed it over to Charlotte's art museum as a second home. Interestingly, the Mint Museum already housed its main collection in a relic of Charlotte's gold rush days, the old United States Mint building.

McColl saw North Tryon Street as a place to exercise his territorial imperative; he felt much the same way about the state of Texas. There, in the capital of Austin, certain Lone Star legislators saw McColl as an invader of *their* turf. It started two years earlier, in 1995, when the Legislature of Texas joined that of Montana as one of two states to "opt out" of his—technically, Riegle and Neal's—interstate branching act. That meant that NationsBank and other out-of-state banks could do business in Texas only so long as they treated their Texas bank as a wholly owned subsidiary. It was required to have its own separate board of directors, on which certified Texans were in the majority.

McColl considered this a desperate attempt by protectionists, prodded by the state's Independent Banking Association, to keep NationsBank from doing what McColl had no intention of doing in the first place: "bleeding" money out of Texas to fill vaults in North Carolina. From his perspective, Texas was simply costing NationsBank enormous, unnecessary operating expenses, negating the efficiencies of scale he wanted to achieve. He believed centralized control of his entire company was a prerequisite to becoming the best bank in the United States.

Paul Polking brought McColl a plan to undermine the Texas Resistance. Down in the west Texas town of El Paso, as Marty Robbins once sang, was a little bank with the big name of Sun World. Quietly, without asking the Texas legislature's permission, NationsBank bought Sun World's three branches. Unlike other Texas banks it bought, NationsBank did not immediately change the bank's name; Sun World remained curiously independent.

Then little Sun World filed a routine application with the office of the comptroller of the currency in Washington. Would it be all right for Sun World to move its headquarters just up the road a piece, to the little town of Santa Teresa, a New Mexican town that wasn't even big enough to make most maps?

The comptroller's office had no problem with that. There was a time-honored exemption to the old federal banking laws known as the "Thirty-Mile Rule." This allowed banks to move their headquarters up to thirty miles in any direction, even if that meant crossing a state border. However, this raised the hackles of the state's brand-new banking commissioner, Catherine Ghiglieri. In August 1996, Ghiglieri got a Texas court to rule against the headquarters shift, but Sun World—which by now everyone recognized as NationsBank—got the injunction overturned in federal court. As Polking interpreted the law, it would now be possible for all the NationsBank branches in Texas to become branches of the bank headquartered in Santa Teresa. The entire NationsBank Texas operation would no longer be subject to the banking regulations of the State of Texas.

By mid-1997, NationsBank of North Carolina owned Sun World of New Mexico and its three El Paso branches. Coincidentally, thanks to the Boatmen's merger, NationsBank also happened to be the largest bank in the state of New Mexico.

McColl enjoyed sparring with Banking Commissioner Ghiglieri, making certain people understood he didn't take her too seriously. "She's very intelligent and very attractive, kind of cute, really." Like McColl, Ghiglieri was a Texan by conviction rather than birth. At least in her public statements, however, she did not find McColl as cute as he found her. "I cannot stand by and watch a trampling of the state's decision to opt out of interstate branching," she proclaimed. "It seems like a game to me." To McColl, it was indeed a game, one with very high stakes and one he intended to win. As he walked into the Adobe Gallery in Albuquerque, where he planned to negotiate for a painting on display there, he was thinking about his team's next at-bats.

First, there would be a bunt to advance the runner: Sun World of Santa Teresa, with the comptroller's permission, would be "rolled into" the parent company. This would give his North Carolina bank—as opposed to his Texas bank—three branches in El Paso. There would not be much Ghiglieri could do to prevent that, though she probably would try. Then—and this would be the home run—NationsBank Texas would seek the comptroller's approval to merge all its Texas operations into the El Paso branches of Sun World/NationsBank. That would be considered an "intrastate merger," perfectly legal under Texas law. McColl felt quite sure that would travel clear into the upper deck of the U.S. Supreme Court. He also knew down to the pointy toes of his black cowhide boots that it would win the game for him. Like Tinker-to-Evers-to-Chance, command of NationsBank would flow Charlotte-to-El Paso-to-everywhere in Texas. Assets, quite naturally, would flow in the other direction. McColl would gain complete control of the $44 billion Texas operation, no matter how much time and Texas taxpayers' money the banking commissioner spent to stop him.

He had all that on his mind August 20, 1997, in Old Town Albuquerque as he talked art dealer Alex Anthony down from his asking price for *Young Cottonwoods Shedding*, so he couldn't be certain just which cellular telephone in which NationsBank jacket pocket went off. It was the next thing he heard that got his attention, from his lieutenant Efrain Lopez: "It's your office, Mr. McColl. They want you to call Charlie Rice."

Someone in the party asked, "Who's Charlie Rice?" But McColl's response was, "Excuse me a minute. Efrain, hand me that phone."

On a rough-hewn bench inside the Adobe Gallery, surrounded by Cochiti Pueblo figurines, Tohono baskets, Zuni jewelry and Navajo paintings, Hugh McColl sat to hear the words he'd been waiting sixteen years to hear. Charlie Rice's Barnett Banks, the far-and-away number-one bank in the state of Florida, was for sale. Rice wondered, would NationsBank be interested?

"Damn right, we're interested."

The next call was to Barnett's investment banker at Morgan Stanley, Dean Witter in New York. McColl learned that the Jacksonville bank would be selling itself to the highest bidder in a "Dutch auction." Sealed bids would be accepted from invited banks only. All bids would be final offers. There would be no negotiation on price. Other banks invited to bid would be Banc One of Columbus, Ohio, SunTrust of Atlanta, and NationsBank's neighbors, First Union and Wachovia. The necessary documents would be sent to McColl by overnight carrier.

Art trading in the gallery came to a standstill. Everyone in the NationsBank group, McColl's ever-present coterie of road warriors, huddled and tried to pick up a little bit of what was going on. The CEO leaned against a two-foot-thick terrones wall and placed another call, this one to Frank Gentry. He went into command mode, speaking in code. It didn't matter that anyone monitoring the call would already have the same information he had.

"This is an unsecured phone, Frank." Gentry understood.

"Remember that city where we launched Operation Overlord?" How could Gentry ever forget? Jacksonville, 1981, the Holiday Inn, shagging in the lounge. "Do you know what's left there?" Gentry had to think a moment to get his drift. First Union had the old Florida National that Hugh had worked so hard to get. That left . . . *Barnett?* Gentry allowed himself only the verbal equivalent of a nod. "Right. Well, that man called me. . . ." Gentry understood McColl was talking about Charlie Rice. ". . . and here's what's gonna happen. There's a letter coming to my office in the morning. You get hold of it and put everybody on alert." Gentry thought: *Wow!*

McColl could not get back to the office until the following afternoon. Until then, he would stick to his agenda. He would also buy that painting of the cottonwoods.

McColl's policy committee—including Ken Lewis, Jim Hance, Fred Figge and Bill Vandiver—met with Frank Gentry and Gentry's new boss, Greg Curl, who had come in through the Boatmen's merger. By the time they gathered in the small conference room behind McColl's office, Gentry and Curl had already "run the numbers," playing all the what-ifs they could think of, analyzing what the other players might bid. They knew it was going to be expensive and very likely would preclude whatever other merger opportunities might be out there. Barnett had assets of $44 billion, $3 billion more than Boatmen's. As Ken Lewis put it, "We're talking about acquiring the number-one franchise in the number-one market in the greatest country in the world." Whatever it might take, they had to go for it.

On Friday, August 22, McColl spoke again with Charlie Rice, this time on a "secure line." They had begun this conversation once before, in 1991, until McColl decided to make a second run at C&S/Sovran. McColl had a good deal of respect for Rice and for his bank. It was Rice's predecessor, Guy Botts, who had first proposed to McColl's boss, Tom Storrs, that something like a Southeastern Banking Compact might be feasible. In large part, the two companies were responsible for breaking the logjam that finally opened the flow of banking across state lines. McColl had a sense of destiny about all this.

When he found out Rice would be in New York all the following week—the week that would culminate in the sale of his bank and leave Charlie Rice a far, far richer man—McColl suggested they get together there for a face-to-face meeting. McColl's face was already due in New York the following Monday; he was sitting for an oil painting to be hung in the NationsBank sixtieth-floor boardroom alongside portraits of Addison Reese and Tom Storrs. Rice agreed to meet him Monday afternoon at NationsBank's Midtown apartment.

Saturday, while his people worked on the customary "wonder-of-it-all-charts" and graphs that would convince Charlie Rice that the marriage of their two banks was already written in the heavenly registry, Hugh McColl went out to spend a little money and maybe ease the tension of the merger. But when he spotted a model railroad store, the business connections just wouldn't stop coming. He and Charlie Rice both sat on the board of CSX Railroad Corporation. McColl's great-grandfather had started a railroad. Ed Ball, the Florida National banker who died before McColl had a chance to buy his bank in Jacksonville, owned a railroad, and the name of it was—McColl had to think a minute to remember—Florida East Coast Railroad. Florida East Coast was headquartered in Jacksonville, the same as Charlie Rice's bank. By chance, fate or destiny the shopkeeper had a red-orange die-cast Florida East Coast double-diesel and four passenger cars he'd be willing to part with. McColl did not even bother to haggle. He loved trains. The shop even had an old-fashioned cash-register that went *ka-ching*. He loved that sound, too.

Monday morning McColl sat for his portrait by John Howard Sanden and was back in the Midtown apartment in plenty of time for his 3:00 P.M. appointment. Charlie Rice was late arriving, but McColl didn't even mind. They talked about art and they talked about family. When they got down to turkey, McColl was ready to share with him the wonder of it all: Did Charlie realize how much better his portfolio would look if he traded his Barnett shares for shares in NationsBank?

Check out this ten-year comparison of his bank's shareholder returns and the stock performance of those other banks: Banc One, SunTrust, First Union and—What's that little bank you're talking to? Heh-heh. Oh, right—Wachovia. The numbers don't lie, Charlie. Now look how sweetly our two banks fit together on this Florida map. Hardly any overlap. Hardly any room left for anybody else. Why, look here, all we need to do is divest a little here and a little there and we'd control just under 29 percent of Florida's deposits, Charlie. And, hell, the law says we can't own more than 30 percent. First Union? They'd be way back in second place with 17 percent. We've got a way-better franchise than First

Union, what with Texas and Boatmen's, plus, our price-earnings ratio is better than theirs, meaning we have less vulnerability and more upside potential. Not only that, you merge with them and you'll be fighting tooth-and-nail over Jacksonville.

It went like that for two hours and Rice seemed in no hurry to leave. That was a very good sign to McColl. Rice said he'd look forward to opening the NationsBank bid at 5:00 P.M. Wednesday. Maybe they'd talk again on Thursday, he said, but McColl shouldn't forget there were other players in this game.

McColl reported back to his teammates the next morning. They agreed that now it would come down to simple arithmetic: how many dollars-per-Barnett-share a bank would be willing to put up. Jim Hance suggested that the top bid might come in around sixty-eight dollars per share. However, they should bear in mind that First Union currently was boasting a higher price-earnings ratio than NationsBank's. Ed Crutchfield might well come in with a bid as high as seventy dollars, even seventy-two. If they wanted to be sure, the NationsBank bid had better ratchet up to, say, seventy-five dollars a share.

"That's going to be around $15 billion," McColl said, raising eyebrows around the table. "It seems an extraordinary amount of money to pay for a $44 billion company. That's eighteen to twenty times earnings." There was a round-robin mumble about paying too much and leaving money on the table and whether they really could afford this right on the heels of the Boatmen's deal and maybe they should pass because their resources were stretched so damned thin. But Ken Lewis cut off the mumble and McColl loved him for it: "The question is simple. Would you want to wake up Monday morning and find out that First Union had bought them?"

At which point the universal sentiment was expressed by McColl: "Hell, no, I wouldn't."

McColl got the executive committee of the board to buy into the seventy-five-dollar proposal. They even granted him a little leeway on the price, up to seventy-six dollars a share. Nobody wanted to be beat out by First Union in Florida.

To put their bid together, Hance had lined up some of the nation's top investment bankers and lawyers: Chris Flowers from Goldman Sachs, Herbert Lurie from Merrill Lynch, Ed Herlihy and Craig Wasserman from Wachtel, Lipton, Rosen & Katz. Dotting all the i's, crossing all the t's and adding up staggering rows of numbers took all of Tuesday and Tuesday night. Wednesday morning, as they were about to send a courier to the NationsBank hangar for a flight to New York, Flowers and Herlihy suggested that McColl deliver the bid in person.

It was almost noon by the time he got Rice on the phone. "I'd like to talk again, bring the offer to you," McColl said. "I'll hand-deliver it."

Rice almost unnerved McColl with his calm demeanor. He poured ice water through the copper lines. "Well, I wouldn't want you to come up here, you know, unless it is worth your while."

McColl tried to match his attitude. "I'll tell you, Charlie, I think I have a number you might-could be interested in."

"Well, why don't you just give me the number and I'll tell you whether I'm interested—whether you should come or not."

McColl didn't even hesitate. Instead of the seventy-five dollar per share his advisors thought would win, he laid down the other dollar his executive committee authorized, all his chips. "My number's seventy-six," he said. He hoped that would bring a vocal blink, but Rice gave him no reaction.

"All right. Well, I think you should probably come on, then."

When McColl worked on a merger, he did it in a style that was all his own. He was dressed in a black T-shirt, jeans and boots. In his office closet were a suit and a change of underwear. He grabbed those and headed for the airport. Somewhere over New Jersey, he put them on. His pride of investment bankers and lawyers in tow, McColl arrived at Morgan Stanley about four. Everyone shook hands. Charlie Rice—five-eleven, blond, starched and pressed, a man who looked as though his tan was ironed on in a sweat-free environment—ushered his short, slightly wrinkled friend Hugh McColl into a conference room and shut the door.

McColl lost track of the time. He reassured Rice that his people would be taken care of. There would be no wholesale replacements the way NCNB had handled things back in '81 and '82. That was many big mergers ago, he said, and he was a wiser man. Rice's other major point was inclusion of Barnett directors on the NationsBank board. McColl conceded five seats and Rice thought that was fair. For two and a half hours, while some of the highest-paid lawyers and investment bankers on earth read back issues of *Barron's*, the two men did their deal.

All points covered, Rice rose. "I think I could get more money out of you on the price," he said. "but I'm not going to negotiate any further with you on that. I'll do the deal at your price, because I want to be a big shareholder, and I don't want to do anything to hurt the stock." They walked out of the conference room and advised the advisors that there was a new number-one bank in Florida.

Back in Charlotte, they were waiting by the phone. "We were right about one thing," McColl told them. "Three other banks bid above seventy dollars. They tell me two of them called in while we were meeting, wanted to rebid, put another offer on the table, but the Barnett people said no dice. So we were not wrong. We had it figured dead-flat perfect, because there was at least one bid in there at seventy-two or seventy-three dollars. So our seventy-five dollars were needed. Maybe seventy-six was throwing away a dollar, but we got it."

For McColl, "got it" was only half the fun of the Barnett deal. The "Gotcha!" to First Union could be a day-maker for the rest of his career. He believed Crutchfield's biggest reason for bidding high on Barnett was to keep McColl from getting it. "It would have precluded us from ever being number one in Florida," he reasoned, "which, of course, is a big part of any war. You have to put some defensive thought in it. You do some things to deny the enemy."

The Barnett deal, he believed, was his end-game, his "show stopper, kind of Stop-the-Music in Florida." Ken Lewis was 100 percent right. If Hugh McColl had to wake up August 28 and read in the paper that First Union owned Barnett Banks, "I would have been permanently nauseated."

CHAPTER 17

Friday, August 29, 1997, before he left the office for the day, McColl sat on the sofa beneath his bank robbery painting, leaned forward onto the coffee table and wrote a memo to himself, the businessman's equivalent of John Henry Newman's *Apologia Pro Vita Sua.*

> *At about 11:00 a.m. today the Board of Directors approved our merger with Barnett Bank, bringing to a closure a process that began in June of 1981. I have very powerful, emotional feelings about this transaction, as it will make us the number 1 bank in Florida, something we set out to do in 1981 but were unsuccessful in doing.*
>
> *It has long rankled me and has caused me to have a sense of failure that we got into Florida well ahead of others but were never able to land the big one. We missed Florida National, Atlantic National and Southeast Bank. We were turned away by Landmark and Flagship and we chose not to buy Southeast Bancshares. We struggled for probably the first 10 years we were there but have been making good money lately. However, I have continued to believe that my greatest single mistake was turning away from Atlantic in 1985, so, for me, I have today washed away that particular sin; and now I own the state.*

It is interesting that we will pay $15 billion for this franchise,
an amount of money that is twice as much as our assets were when
I took over as chairman in 1983. We have really come a long way.

As I thought about this morning, I decided to call Tom Storrs
and invite him to the meeting. It was very important to him, and
he thanked me, because for him it is a closure of the process
begun by the Martin Group in 1981.

McColl was a man getting his affairs in order, a man at the end of a
long and prosperous voyage. As for growing his little North Carolina
bank, he believed he had gone about as far as he could go. In his final
three years as CEO, he expected to spend most of his time perfecting
what he'd already built. "I will have seemed like a failure if after leaving the company disintegrates in terms of its culture," he told his people. "I don't think that will happen, but it's not something you can
take for granted."

McColl's corporate army now numbered more than one hundred
thousand people, from several hundred different organizations.
Getting all those different people in all those different cities to function as a dynamic, interlocked, interdependent team of independent
thinkers—now *that* was a challenge. His pep-rally chant became: *We
are bound together by our desire to win with our friends.*

"Winning" depended on everyone in the company looking on former rivals and in-house competitors as "friends." Men and women
who had once regarded each other as targets for missiles and
grenades were now required to invest in each other that same sublime
trust that a circus flyer must invest in her faraway partner, to get that
trapeze to that exact spot where her fingers should be when she came
out of her triple somersault a hundred feet up in the air. Nobody but
McColl could set the standard of trust, to show that his company was
a meritocracy which insisted on "doing the right thing."

That was clear in his decision to name Alex Sink, a woman, to
head the entire Florida operation, which he considered one of the
most important positions—if not the most important—in the company for the next several years. The standard would be reinforced by
his decision to name Ed Dolby, an African American, to head up
banking operations in the Carolinas, where all this had started. To
replace the implicitly trusted Joe Martin as head of corporate affairs
and communications, McColl selected a woman, Lynn Drury, fresh

from the public relations challenge of the Olympics. Martin, whose personal communication faculties were being tested by the advance of Lou Gehrig's disease, would retain his office and his position of trust, becoming special counsel to the CEO, notwithstanding the "handicapped" designation on his wheelchair-accommodating van.

For McColl, there was no symbolism in decisions like these, simply a recognition of success and the expectation of greater success to come. He couldn't help wondering what his great-grandfather would have made of all this diversity. Duncan Donald, who nearly died defending the Old South, then committed the rest of his life to building the New South—what would Duncan Donald think of his great-grandson's bank?

Just two blocks up North College Street from the rear entrance to McColl's bank, The Museum of the New South had an exhibit on banking, in which McColl addressed that very question. By pressing a finger to the smiling face of the NationsBank CEO on a computer touch-screen, the museum visitor could see and hear McColl say that he "grew up in a banking family. My great-grandfather was president of a bank, my grandfather was president of a bank, my father was president of a bank. So it never occurred to me that I wouldn't be. I see it as a very natural order of things. But, having said that, those were very small banks that they were presidents of, and I could never have imagined that we would be where we are today, even though I think I dream a lot."

McColl's great-grandfather had been part of a dream that built a "New South" out of the ashes of the old. As the New South century drew to a close, it might well be time to relegate that dream to a museum. Hugh McColl's own visions had helped create something different, something more like a "Super South," proclaimed in cities like Atlanta, Miami, Tampa, Dallas, and now Charlotte. Hugh McColl could claim at least a minor role in shaping each one of those cities.

As 1997's months rolled by, Charlotte continued to look less like a New South crossroads town and more like a Super South metropolis. It became the corporate home of a major investment banking concern, a major player in stock underwriting, when NationsBank bought San Francisco-based Montgomery Securities for $12 billion. The city thumbed its nose at Wall Street in September when NationsBank became the first U.S. bank to issue bonds—more than $4 billion worth—backed up by its own commercial loans. Then, when First Union announced its plan to buy the Philadelphia banking giant, CoreStates Financial for $16.1 billion, Charlotte became the nation's number-two banking city, topping San Francisco.

The Queen City was NationsBank's City. On the fringe of uptown, a project called Gateway Village was on the drawing boards for West Trade Street. With the help of Atlanta developer—and NationsBank director—Thomas G. Cousins, the bank's Jim Palermo unveiled plans to convert a run-down, seedy area between Interstate Highway 77 and a railroad track into a $250 million living-and-working complex. The project would realize the vision McColl shared with Dr. Mildred Baxter Davis in 1981 of revitalizing Charlotte's Third Ward. Gateway Village would be completed just in time for McColl's scheduled retirement, giving NationsBank claim to more than six million square feet of Uptown Charlotte.

Though he genuinely believed NationsBank's geographical territory would expand no further during his tenure as CEO, McColl was certain he had set the stage for a coast-to-coast banking empire. "If you come back here in a few years," his interactive digital image smiled at visitors to the Museum of the New South, "whoever is sitting in my seat will be running perhaps the *largest* bank in the United States."

Now it was up to McColl to make sure "whoever is sitting in my seat" proved to be the right person at the right time. His money at the moment was split between two candidates, Ken Lewis and Jim Hance. Both Hance and Lewis felt qualified to take over when McColl left. Both could speak eloquently about the corporate culture and corporate values.

They were two different types—each with something of Hugh McColl in him, but each very much his own man. At fifty-three, Jim Hance was methodical, sure of his facts, a great negotiator, a man of thoughtful understanding. Hance had played a critical role in putting together the C&S/Sovran deal. Ken Lewis, three years younger than Hance, tended to fly a bit more by the seat of his pants, but his instincts rarely failed him. In working out tough issues with his teammates, Lewis shone. He, more than anyone, had achieved the daunting goal of folding the C&S/Sovran people into the NCNB culture.

In the fall of 1997, McColl got his board of directors to add two seats, for Hance and Lewis, so that both of them would have a chance to be involved with policy-making on the highest level. This was a somewhat different approach than the one Tom Storrs had used in

1978, when he gave his board an evaluation form with which to rate McColl, Bill Dougherty and anyone else they might be inclined to consider as his replacement. McColl preferred having everything out in the open, preferred to give Lewis and Hance a chance to demonstrate their leadership from very exposed positions, in front. His expectation was that both men would succeed, making it all the more difficult to choose between them before he left in June 2000.

There was every indication that his directors might be sailing into some choppy waters come the millennium, provided the wave beginning to show itself in the Far East didn't prove to be a tsunami. By November 1997, the trend of "globalization"—which had linked the United States economy to those of fast-growing countries in Asia, Latin America and Central Europe—looked as though it might have a few U.S. banks over their waists already. Especially vulnerable were banks that had financed huge real estate development and construction projects in Asia.

In China and Japan, in Korea, Thailand, Malaysia, Indonesia and the Philippines, manufacturers were producing more automobiles, chemicals and semiconductors than consumers were likely to buy. Currencies in Asia were being devalued, by as much as 40 percent. That not only hurt banks which had traded heavily in those currencies, assuming their value would go up rather than down, it also made it difficult for Asians to purchase any significant percentage of their gross national products. The result was that all these troubled economies were looking to the United States for life preservers, while American banks were searching for ways of cutting the losses they'd suffered already. Word out of New York was that J. P. Morgan had the largest exposure, and it could be facing fourth-quarter profit reductions of 30 percent or worse.

Federal Reserve Chairman Alan Greenspan—McColl's "most powerful man in America"—told Congress he worried that Americans had lost control of the nation's economy by spreading too much of America's wealth and influence around the globe. It was too soon to panic, said Greenspan, because "the market" was in command of the situation and economic Darwinism would be proven true once again: the fittest would survive.

McColl was in full agreement there. Since NationsBank had minimal exposure in disoriented Asia, he would be sure to heed

Greenspan's directive: Americans should not waste their time worrying about lost control and lost profits, but instead should learn how to "capture the benefits." The message he would take to his board would be along those very lines. NationsBank should be hanging tough and looking for opportunities.

Yet, from Hugh McColl's vantage point, there did not seem to be many more opportunities on the horizon, no low-hanging fruit. Ken Lewis brought the point home in a direct and merciless fashion, when he sat on the sofa under the bank robbery painting and told the CEO, "You know, you probably only have one more Big Deal left."

McColl didn't like hearing that, but he caught Lewis's drift. He was close to the end of his ability to convince the board that they should continue doing deals while their stock was becalmed in the marketplace. What Ken Lewis meant was that sooner or later—and probably sooner—his directors were going to tell him no. If they did let him merge with another bank, it would undoubtedly be the last purchase of his career.

Chief planning officer Greg Curl brought in his Atlas so he and McColl could consider their options. In New York, the only likely target was Morgan Guaranty, and McColl considered Morgan "a Little League company." His hubris forced a chuckle. "Would you ever think somebody from a little country town would ever turn down Mr. Morgan's bank?"

What about a combination of, say, First Chicago, to nail the upper Midwest, and Wells Fargo in California? Better yet, Curl suggested, what about cutting to the chase? What about going after BankAmerica? "Wells Fargo doesn't come close to them in market share," he explained to McColl, who required no explanation. "Wells Fargo is damaged goods, and they are too expensive for what they are worth."

McColl thought he was paying Greg Curl an awful lot of money just to suggest something he damned well knew could not be done. *Why would I pay you for that?* he almost said. But he kept his irritation down and agreed, for the moment, that he would "work on just two things. And that's the Bank of Boston and BankAmerica." Then he let the matter drop.

There happened to be an appointment on McColl's calendar, three days before Christmas, with David Coulter, the man Dick Rosenberg had picked in 1995 as Hugh McColl's eventual replacement in BankAmerica's first attempt at a merger. But McColl decided he would not take this opportunity to ask whether BankAmerica was in the mood to be merged. He'd been down that road once already and had not enjoyed the scenery.

The December meeting was only the second time ever that he'd been with Coulter. They were joined by the CEOs of several other top banks in the country around a conference table in New York, for what McColl had labeled a "get out of Visa meeting," since the credit card company had been "screwing us for the past twenty-five years."

The bankers' ire had been provoked by the decision of Visa International Services Association (the heirs to the BankAmericard empire McColl had helped create in the mid-sixties) to form a relationship with Microsoft for credit services over the Internet. If the relationship was not nipped in the bud, it would threaten the nascent network called "Integrion" being put together by several banks in cooperation with IBM. "Consorting with the enemy," was McColl's description of Visa's proposal. The New York meeting was one of those rare occasions when other bankers permitted themselves an appreciation of Hugh McColl's jugular decisiveness. Most of the time, they wanted to be as far away from him as possible.

The end of 1997, New Year's Eve, fell on a Wednesday. Since there wasn't much to do at the office, McColl went home early for a drink and some conversation with a couple of friends. Instead of spreading out in the living room (Jane's living room, he always called it), he brought the visitors into his study, where the chairs were mismatched but comfortable. He picked the armchair under the side window with the wooden venetian blinds. Changed to his favorite pair of old jeans and a faded blue T-shirt, he propped up his boots on an ottoman and found himself attempting to put some hard feelings into soft words. He was in a mood to verbalize his hopes for the company he'd all too soon be leaving.

"I think together that we've built something pretty wonderful and we've proved we can do something," he told his friends, lifting his glass. "And no one person did it. All of us did it together."

But, someone suggested, there was always coach-quarterback-general Hugh McColl setting the direction. He had to give himself credit for that, didn't he?

"It is factual that large egos end up in a lot of high places," he agreed, "because one has to believe in what one's trying to do. But I would have thought that confidence is something you develop over time, not something one is born with."

McColl's eyes fell on an oval-framed photo of his mother posed with her first two children. Fran was standing, Hugh sitting on her lap, listening to their mother read. He thought of one of his favorite childhood books, *The Little Engine That Could*, the Golden Book edition, with its bright drawings of the sturdy little steam engine struggling to pull a heavy load up a steep hill. "*I think I can, I think I can*," had been chugging along in McColl's private thoughts for a long time. On the downhill slope now, coasting, he heard: "*I thought I could, I thought I could, I thought I could.*"

"Nobody ever let me go around with *I can't do this, I can't do that*," he said. "In fairness to my mother, my father and my grandmother, I was taught to believe that we could do anything. I got a lot of confidence from my family. I think I was the beneficiary of a lot of love and encouragement. I was encouraged to be confident."

He was on a roll now, into his subject and ready to jawbone till somebody's ear went to sleep. He expressed concern that maybe American kids weren't getting the same kinds of nurturing and encouragement he'd had as a child.

"One of the most important things for us to consider in our planning for the future of our company," he said, "is that we have broadened the game. When we were growing up, you could look around you at the kids in your town and see who would be running the bank or the grocery store. Today, everybody's in the game. Today, some kid who's being born in Shanghai could one day take over the entire computer industry. We don't know him—or her. We don't know his momma and daddy. But we know he's out there. There are kids in other countries who have dreams, and they're dreaming of the kind of success that we here take for granted. But it's only because we made it happen."

So, was he saying that American children were destined to become second-class citizens in the global village?

"No, maybe not. But how are today's kids going to be able to do what I've done, and other people like me? Nobody today is willing to work somewhere for thirty years to achieve success. It's hard to develop good leadership without developing good followership, and that only happens over a period of time."

Time. There it was, the bugbear that was really haunting the CEO. Ben Long's painted hourglass would retain its allotment of sand for a thousand years, or until a wrecking ball sent Charlotte's Transamerica Center to the same grave Rex's Pool Hall occupied. The real Hugh McColl could feel the sand slipping away. His body was not what it used to be. Conversations without reference to his diabetic diet were growing scarcer.

"So, maybe you're just feeling your age?" someone asked.

"Well, no," he insisted. "I didn't much like being in my late fifties. Fifty-six to fifty-nine, I had to face the fact that I was getting old. When I hit sixty, though, I had no more problems. I stopped worrying about it and in fact I don't really feel old at all. But, I have to admit, I do think back on how invigorating it was to be one of the 'Young Turks' at NCNB. You knew you could just *outlast* other people around you. Today I find there are some penalties for being old in business."

Penalties, perhaps, but also enormous awards to be reaped. After all, who would have thought in those early days that one of the "Young Turks" would be earning $4 million a year? McColl kicked off his boots and wriggled his toes, thinking he might be ready for a trip to Armando's Boot Shop down in Raymondsville, Texas. Beneath the frayed cuffs of his twenty-year-old jeans were double-layered socks, which made the boots tight, but made his feet feel better. He took a moment to jot a note on the ever-present yellow lined pad. The note consisted of three words: Money. Power. Freedom. The first two were connected by an equal sign. "Freedom" had a circle around it and a slash-mark through the word.

"More than money," he told himself as much as his friends, "I have always wanted freedom, nobody telling me what to do, an absence of power over me. The most sensible thing I did was to realize that I needed to work and earn money to live before I could ever have anything else. Then, the harder I worked, the more power I accumulated. And I assumed that with the power would come freedom. Today I have a lot of power, but not a lot of freedom. I have too much responsibility to be free. I have responsibility to one hundred thousand associates, to all our shareholders, to my board. I have accumulated more and more responsibilities, not freedom. When I retire I'll have the freedom, but I will have lost the power."

He paused, tapped the end of his ballpoint pen. His own thoughts surprised him. "Curiously, I feel ambivalent about that. I'm not sure how I feel." He tilted his head, gave a half-smile. "But I feel good about my ambivalence."

McColl stood up, leaving his boots on the ottoman. He padded three feet across the oriental rug on his double-thick socks to his leather desk chair, where he looked up at the built-in corner bookcase that formed the backdrop to his desk. He was thinking about retirement, although he did not mention the word.

"I'm not going to wait until my sixty-fifth birthday. One day I'm going to pick up a book from this shelf and open it to a page at random and say: 'This page number is the number of days till I retire.' Don't know when I'll pick up that book, though." He smiled, hedging his bet. "It'll be a thick book. Or maybe I'll just announce that I'll retire on the first Tuesday following the next quail season. Got to fly down to Texas one more time on the company plane to hunt quail."

But what about all those months, those springs and summers, early falls and late winters, when the quail were out of season, when the goatweed was growing and the eggs hatching?

"I don't really know," he mused. "I'll be able to devote more of my time to helping to build this city. Of course, I can't really build it, only help build it." His eyes scanned the shelves for remembered inspiration. Books about soldiering. Spy novels. Biographies. Nothing came to mind, no General Douglas MacArthur speech, no *Beau Geste* grand gesture.

"I know there will be days when I get a sick feeling that I'm not in the hunt anymore. I know that."

His listeners understood that McColl was not speaking of quail.

The second week of January was the start of his 1998 Road Show, featuring, for the first time, a command performance in Jacksonville, Florida. At the headquarters of what, until a few days earlier, had been Barnett Banks, McColl would be introduced by his new chairman, ex-Barnett CEO Charles Rice. McColl flew to Florida in the same Gulfstream jet that had nearly crashed the previous January, with the same contingent on board. This time, there was no snow.

The themes of the road show were "Back to Basics," and "No More Mergers."

"We're on all the battlefields we're going to be on," McColl told his managers, "and this is where the war is going to be fought, right here in Florida. We're going to emphasize blocking and tackling, no new bells and whistles." He told them he would focus 1998 on savings and restraint throughout the company. NationsBank was entering the first quarter with "the strongest balance sheet we've ever had. We took in $40 million in profits the first week of the year. This is a good world."

Hugh McColl's world appeared stable, defined, manageable. It continued that way for about one month after his return from the road show tour of NationsBank capitals and outposts.

Then, toward the end of February, Jim Hance came in for an afternoon chat. He had just been on the telephone with Michael E. O'Neill, vice chairman and chief financial officer of BankAmerica. After a routine discussion of what was going on in Washington and how they needed to cooperate in their lobbying efforts, the two CFOs talked some serious numbers. They both noted the curious polar reversal their big West Coast and big East Coast banks had recently undergone. NationsBank earnings for 1997 would be posted at $1.2 billion, BankAmerica's at just $800 million. "So we're making 50 percent more than they are," Hance said. This was almost exactly the lead BankAmerica had held over NationsBank at the end of 1995, the year Dick Rosenberg attempted to buy Hugh McColl.

McColl was stunned, almost numb at this development. If he read conservative, cautious Jim Hance correctly, Hugh McColl was going to get one more chance to build the company he and Joe Martin had named, the Nation's Bank. All the old, long-buried possibilities rose up and formed instant, glittering sky castles in his imagination. Once again, he imagined himself the colossus of American banking, one foot on the East Coast, the other on the West, CEO of the world's most important financial institution.

But he couldn't let his imagination take charge this time. He instructed Hance to continue his contacts with O'Neill, but to tell no one about the call. "I don't want to start a stir in the company that would cause us to be disappointed," he said. "I'd have to answer a lot of the old flack, brought up again. I'm not even going to tell my aides." To keep his own lip from slipping, McColl adopted code names. NationsBank became "nickel" and BankAmerica "bronze," just because those metals began with the same letters as did the company names.

Hardly a week went by before McColl broke his own rule of silence, dashing off an e-mail message to Joe Martin. Now getting around in a motorized wheelchair, Martin relied on a computer operated by eye movement to communicate, either by e-mail or computer-generated speech. From the computer in his study at home, McColl typed out a message regarding "new developments on the western front." Remembering the "Martin Group" in Florida and "XYZ Company" in Texas, and wasting no time pressing the "shift" key for capital letters, McColl wrote: "THE HAND THAT WAS EXTENDED AND NOT TAKEN MAY WELL BE PROFFERED AGAIN. MY GOAL WILL BE TOTAL VICTORY BUT WE ARE A LONG WAY FROM AGREE-MENT. NO ONE—REPEAT NO ONE KNOWS . . . SEMPER FI—HUGH." Joe Martin knew exactly what he was referring to.

For the next three weeks, by telephone, Jim Hance and Mike O'Neill conducted what McColl termed "clearing away of debris" discussions. Meanwhile, in San Francisco, the BankAmerica board of directors convened to consider putting the bank in play. Officially, according to bank publications, the BankAmerica directors were deliberating "a review of changes in the industry, the industry's financial performance, the financial services consolidation trend, characteristics of recent mergers and acquisitions of banks and non-bank entities, the status of BankAmerica as a competitive acquirer and as a desirable partner in a business combination."

The BankAmerica board looked at five "business combination" partners—Chase, Citicorp, NationsBank, First Union and American Express. That field narrowed quickly to Citicorp and NationsBank. CEO David Coulter's first choice was Citi, which, like BankAmerica, had a reputation as an international powerhouse. Coulter believed it would be a natural match. However, he received only a chilly response from Citicorp CEO John Reed, and that shifted the breeze back in NationsBank's direction.

Since the CFOs of BankAmerica and NationsBank were developing a telephone rapport, O'Neill was assigned to continue his discussions with Hance. Also assigned to the case were BankAmerica's investment consultants, Goldman, Sachs & Company, as well as its seasoned outside attorney, Ed Herlihy. Herlihy's long relationship with McColl and his company was a fortuitous coincidence.

From San Francisco, Hance reported that BankAmerica seemed hung up on the same old issues—whether a combination with NationsBank would be considered a buyout or a "merger of equals"; whether the headquarters would remain in San Francisco, where BankAmerica had such a "rich tradition"; whether the treasured, though frequently misused, "Bank of America" name could be retained; whether the BankAmerica board would be fairly represented; whether

David Coulter would be assured of following McColl in the CEO's chair.

What did not seem to be a sticking point was the issue of money. From their earliest conversations, the two CFOs agreed that neither bank would be expected to pay a premium for the other, and that whatever deal was done, it would be constructed in the best interests of the stockholders of the two companies.

By the second week of March, McColl knew he had become the dancing partner of choice, and that BankAmerica was "seriously, really going after us." On March 11 he sent another e-mail message to Joe Martin, its subject labeled "showstopper":

> do not wish to overstate current situation BUT target is in fact exploring options as they like us feel they are in an end game. what we MAY do affects the reasoning of others as much as what we do. ergo no one can explore options without including us as a potential partner or competitor. the issue then is which is worse. our current strategy is to wait and see where this leads us. food for thought: assuming we get to talks the issues will be the same: succession, name, headquarters, board makeup. the latter will drive the former issues. talk to no one!

McColl's line in the sand was the headquarters location. He reminded Hance that "the first time, we broke up over it, if you remember. That was the show stopper for me the first time. I wasn't going to move the bank out of the South no matter what." When Hance told him, "They don't want to be a Southern bank," McColl answered, "Well, that's fine. They don't have to, because we're not going to do the deal." Hance let O'Neill know that if BankAmerica wanted to do business with NationsBank, it must agree to become a "Southern bank."

Thursday, March 26, Greg Curl took the CEO by surprise when he asked to see him regarding some materials Jim Hance wanted on the BankAmerica deal. McColl got on the phone, ready to chew out Hance for leaking the information, but Hance calmed him down. He was scheduled to meet in San Francisco the following day with O'Neill, and Hance needed Curl to supply the requisite "show and tell" pieces.

On Friday, while Hance was in San Francisco, McColl brought the two other members of his policy committee, Ken Lewis and Bill Vandiver, up to speed. Along with Hance, these men might stand to lose, in terms of personal advancement, from a merger with

BankAmerica. At the very least, David Coulter and Mike O'Neill would need to be inserted into the chain of command somewhere near the top. McColl was delighted with their response—that the opportunity to be part of the dominant bank in the nation was more important that any of their personal ambitions to dominate NationsBank.

Hance visited McColl at his home on Saturday, bringing word that his three-and-a-half-hour meeting in San Francisco had marked the official starting point of negotiations, in what could become, far and away, the largest merger in the history of banking.

McColl listened to Hance describe how he and O'Neill had laid out all their serious numbers—balance sheets, earnings, credit quality—and then moved on to anticipated benefits and cost savings, to be garnered by pooling resources and people. Apparently, Hance reported, the BankAmerica executives understood that McColl must be named CEO for the deal to go through. All that was good news. On the negative side, Hance said, BankAmerica seemed to be demanding that Coulter be designated CEO crown prince, to be enthroned at McColl's 2000 retirement party. They also could not get over their insistence that San Francisco was a far better location for the merged banks' headquarters than was Charlotte.

Hance said the next move would be for McColl to fly to San Francisco and woo David Coulter, show him "the wonder of it all." Then, after winning Coulter's heart, McColl would have to undergo the personal obloquy of prostrating himself before the board of directors of BankAmerica, begging permission to lead them. None of this, in 1998, was Hugh McColl's idea of a swell time. He had been all those places and done all those things, with this very same bank, only two and a half years earlier. As he got Jim Hance's jacket out of the hall closet and saw him to the door, McColl was making up his mind to call his key people together Monday morning and tell them what was going on, then tell them it would go no further.

Saturday night brought him no rest. He kept thinking about his people and the trust they placed in him. He kept thinking about what it would do to them—and to him—if Coulter took over the company in 2000 and moved it to the West Coast. And what about Charlotte? NationsBank was now one of the tectonic plates on which the city was constructed. What would happen if that plate suddenly shifted, or dematerialized? He'd be damned if he sold out to BankAmerica on their terms. Better not to travel to San Francisco at all.

Sunday morning Jane was up with the sun. "Let's go to early church," she perked.

He'd napped for maybe two hours and his brain was anything but clear, so McColl agreed to make his first appearance of the year at Covenant Presbyterian. They arrived in time for the eight-thirty service, with the choir singing something that had a certain soporific charm. He decided he'd better take copious notes or he might embarrass Jane by falling asleep.

There was a line in the first hymn he liked as it went past, something about surrendering one's sword in order to conquer. He jotted that down and looked at it, thinking that just maybe there could be something predestined about his landing in this particular pew on this particular morning. As a Presbyterian he was supposed to be a believer in predestination. Maybe he was here to rethink the BankAmerica merger. Maybe, as the hymn suggested, he should go to San Francisco in a nonthreatening way, swordless, and come back to Charlotte with a company twice the size of what the city had right now.

The pastor, Reverend John Rogers, seemed to McColl to be doing a particularly fine job delivering his sermon that morning. Rogers, who had grown up in Bennettsville with McColl's younger brothers, was preaching on the last five commandments, the "thou shall nots." McColl made it through murder, adultery and stealing before he found it useful to take any more notes. There was something in "Thou shalt not bear false witness" that got him jotting. *Not even kings can take away your good name,* he wrote down. And he wondered: *What's in a name? McColl's good name, NationsBank's good name?* It was not the name itself that mattered, but what it stood for. Even if he had to take on BankAmerica's "good name," he could make it stand for the things Hugh McColl believed in. There were worse flags to march behind.

Then the pastor said—and McColl jotted—*Lying: the worst sin.* If we cannot trust each other, the pastor preached and the banker agreed, then the community of men would be doomed to failure. McColl believed he had built what both he and the preacher termed "a community of trust." If he could manage before he left to spread that trust, from one side of the nation to the other, through America's largest bank—*bank and trust, they used to say*—then perhaps, before he was through, he could leave his imprint on the community of men.

One more note. "Thou shalt not covet . . ." He wrote: *Desire to profit from anything not reason to do it.* That only worked for McColl if he defined profit in terms of money. *It's not the money. It never has been and it isn't now.*

After the sermon, more music, Big Music. McColl suspected that he was the only one in that congregation who failed to appreciate Big Presbyterian Music. Truth be told, he didn't know an anthem from an oratorio, so he referred to anything that wasn't a Christmas carol as a "dirge." During the dirges he generally read from his Bible. Not that he was expecting a religious experience; rather, he was fascinated since boyhood by Old Testament history. He had been thinking that one way to fill the time during his retirement might be to enroll in a Bible history class. Perhaps he would even get interested in the theology of the Old Testament—he particularly enjoyed what he thought of as the "eye-for-an-eye, tooth-for-a-tooth thing."

In the pew, he found himself ruminating through one of the Old Testament's earthier pastures, the book of Second Samuel, perhaps unconsciously heading for Bathsheba's rooftop nude scene. But his eye stopped at Verse 1 of Chapter 11: "In the spring, when the kings go forth into battle." Spring, Hugh McColl's battle-time. He remembered the spring of 1982, hunting banks in Florida, bagging first Gulfstream in Boca Raton, then Exchange in Tampa. He spent the spring of 1988 waiting for William Seidman to signal the attack on Texas. The spring of 1989 was the time of his ill-advised assault on Atlanta, and the forced retreat. He remembered the spring of 1991, a tiger waiting in the brush for the C&S/Sovran game to show itself at last in May.

He told himself that coming upon that line from Second Samuel was not divine inspiration, simply happenstance. But it did force him to think a little deeper about his decision to walk away from BankAmerica again. As he shook the pastor's hand at the door of the church he was thinking: *I'll go have a talk with my special counsel before I play out this hand.*

Sunday afternoon he walked around the corner to Joe Martin's house. Joan Martin welcomed him with a hug and opened one of the bottles of wine she brought back from France on a trip the McColls and Martins had made together six months earlier. Sipping the wine, McColl shared with Joe Martin his "wonder-of-it-all" charts, the status of Jim Hance's preliminary negotiations, even notes he'd made in church. As Martin listened, McColl's voice became steadily more despondent. Finally he said, "I don't want to give away our name and I don't want to give away who we are. This single transaction could create the greatest bank in the world. But it could also destroy everything we set out to build. And we won't know for a long time whether we did the right thing."

The lips and tongue are some of the muscles disabled by amyotrophic lateral sclerosis, so ALS had robbed Joe Martin of gab, one of his most prized gifts. It could take him agonizing seconds to form syllables. He had to force his lips into shapes he couldn't be certain they were forming; he aimed his tongue, but could never sure he was hitting the target. It was not quite as difficult, but almost, for Martin's listeners to decipher what he was trying to say. Usually, one repeated each word as it was spoken, just to make certain the meaning was grasped. Yet Hugh McColl had become adept at understanding his special counsel's speech, valuing it all the more highly because it required so much of his concentration. When Joe Martin spoke, Hugh McColl listened.

"Will . . . we . . . have . . . any . . . options . . . later?" Martin asked. "Other . . . than . . . to . . . stand . . . still?"

This was the same conundrum McColl had puzzled over with Greg Curl. Other than BankAmerica, what possible merger partners remained? He went over the short and shortening list, pointing out, for his own sake as much as Martin's, the rotten spots on each of those prize apples. By the time he got to the end, he could anticipate his counsel's advice. Without waiting to be told McColl said, "I agree with you. This is our last chance."

Martin asked to hear again the language McColl and Hance had fashioned regarding David Coulter's succession to CEO. "It is our present intention," McColl read. Martin smiled, one of the voluntary muscle moves he could still make. McColl saw that Joe Martin remembered the phrase they'd both learned from Tom Storrs. It was not misleading, just precisely limiting.

What about the board makeup? Martin asked. McColl said preliminary indications were that BankAmerica would agree to a minority position on the board, but that details were to be determined. Again Martin smiled. He was ready to give counsel.

"The . . . name . . . is . . . not . . . important," he said, aware that his boss and friend would be concerned about his emotional investment in *NationsBank*. "And . . . to . . . make . . . this . . . merger . . . happen . . . every . . . one . . . of . . . your . . . teammates . . . would . . . trust . . . you . . . to . . . trade . . . away . . . anything . . ." McColl thought the sentence was over and lifted his finger to protest, but Martin was still speaking. ". . . except . . . control. . . . Just . . . one . . . CEO."

Joan Martin walked back into the room, jubilant because her husband was smiling. She wanted to pour another glass of wine. McColl felt like celebrating. He telephoned Jane and asked her to join them. The four friends spent the afternoon going through Joan's photo albums, reminiscing about France, and drinking excellent Beaujolais. As he rose to leave, Hugh McColl said, "You know, pretty soon we'll have to switch to California wine."

On Monday, Hance set up a meeting for McColl in San Francisco with BankAmerica CEO David Coulter. The other side suddenly was projecting a sense of urgency, so the tête-à-tête must happen in just two days—April Fool's Day. McColl couldn't help wondering what that might portend. As he had done with Bennett Brown, he asked Chuck Cooley for a profile of the man with whom he'd be dealing. Cooley came back quickly. "Your number-one ammunition," he said, "is this: you are going to be talking to Tom Storrs."

That told McColl that in David Coulter he would encounter a cool, logical, analytical man. There would be no place in their discussions for emotion, Cooley said. If, for example, McColl wanted headquarters to be in Charlotte, then he'd have to show Coulter that Charlotte was the logical location, not simply the place where Hugh McColl and his bank had their roots.

Among the tidbits he picked up from Chuck Cooley was the fact that Coulter was something of an outsider to his fellow BankAmericans. Even though McColl had learned in 1995 that Dick Rosenberg wanted Coulter to succeed him, it was not until the following year that industry experts, along with most people at BankAmerica were let in on the secret, and some of them expressed surprise at Rosenberg's decision. Coulter had been the company's head of corporate and international banking for the previous three years, but he tended to remain out of the spotlight, seemingly preoccupied with the possibilities and impositions of technology. Coulter was known to believe a bank could be expanded more efficiently through expanding electronic banking than through acquisition of other banks' customers and territories. Coulter's two-year tenure as CEO yielded huge gains on Wall Street for BankAmerica stock—a 57 percent increase at the end of his first year—and a fine gain for David Coulter's salary as well. His paycheck for 1998 was said to be more than $21 million, better than four times what Hugh McColl would earn.

There was much in David Coulter's portfolio that McColl liked. He was the son of a Pennsylvania long-haul trucker who'd had to talk his way into a high school honors program, then managed to finish first in his class, playing football and baseball along the way. McColl thought that sounded a little bit like himself. Coulter had started working on a doctorate in economics at Carnegie-Mellon Institute (very much not like McColl) when he quit to go to work for BankAmerica as a financial analyst in 1976.

Salomon Brothers' report on BankAmerica in 1996 featured a cartoon of Coulter as "Mr. Fixit," complete with a wrench and tool chest. Yet, from what he learned, McColl deduced that Coulter might well be a visionary, someone who knew where he wanted to take his company, yet someone who actually had trouble accomplishing the small tasks necessary to reach his goals. The cartoon might have it wrong.

"He's very much playing the long game," McColl said to Cooley, "and having trouble playing the short game. I think he sees where he wants the company to be, but he's having trouble getting from here to there, and he might be having trouble communicating his vision."

It could be simply that Coulter had an overabundance of something McColl lacked: patience. David Coulter was a fly fisherman, wading cautiously into a stream to find just the right spot, willing to stand for hours there, flicking his wrist, waiting for a trout he could try to outsmart. Hugh McColl was a quail hunter. He leased the hunting rights, paid the best man he could find to train the dogs to flush the birds. The birds rose, *boom!* McColl fired. He seldom missed.

If the run-and-gun style for which NationsBank had become famous—or infamous—was a reflection of McColl's style, perhaps the style of BankAmerica also took a cue from its CEO. While McColl's people kept their eyes on the game ahead, Coulter wanted his troops well drilled in the bank's long history, expected reverence for founder and corporate hero A. P. Giannini. As McColl's company was building its huge domestic franchise over the previous twenty years, BankAmerica had encountered more than its share of slippery rocks in international waters. Now, some analysts painted BankAmerica as reluctant to make any sudden moves; to many outsiders, the bank seemed mired in a kind of executive sludge, in which words like "swift" and "decisive" had little relevance.

After two days of intense study, McColl believed he knew his man.

Though he'd met the fellow but twice, once on Integrion, once on Visa, he was ready to talk merger with David Coulter. McColl thought he held the better cards; if he played them correctly, he could put together his second Biggest Deal of the Century, bigger even than the one he'd pulled off in Texas.

The schedule was tight. Tuesday, March 31, McColl had to deliver a speech to business students at the University of Kansas. Two days later, Thursday, April 2, he was scheduled in Phoenix for the annual meeting of the Bankers' Round Table. In order to meet with David Coulter on Wednesday, he had to leave immediately after his Kansas speech for California, still running on Eastern Standard Time, eat a meal on the plane, then collapse into a Mandarin Hotel bed for a few hours of sleep before getting up, having breakfast, showering, shaving and dressing in time for David Coulter's appearance at 0900 hours.

Seven minutes late, Coulter knocked on the door of his room. McColl detected nervousness on Coulter's part as he wobbled into the conversation by admitting it had been difficult for him to press the elevator button in the lobby. McColl gripped his hand firmly, putting on the drawl. "Well, I had a pretty hard time convincing myself to come out here." He started off trying to empathize with Coulter, thinking of him as a potential teammate rather than as an adversary. This would be a different kind of merger, because McColl would not have the luxury of enticing the CEO with a chairmanship, good until the next merger. This time Coulter expected to stick around long after Hugh McColl would be gone.

Since his ill-fated charge at Atlanta's C&S, McColl had learned to steer conversation toward its destination indirectly, more like a sailboat tacking to catch the wind than a torpedo slicing through the waves. He wanted to take his time with Coulter, determined to get to know this man who considered himself qualified to take the tiller from the hands of the most feared, most aggressive banker in the United States. After several minutes of this, McColl got in the hard question. "Why would you merge your bank, Dave? Hell, you don't have to."

Coulter seemed to have thought that one out. He said the entire banking industry was shuddering with apprehension about how to maintain a sufficiently broad revenue base, in order to keep up with the escalating cost of business in a technology-intense, global economy. Candidly, he admitted his company was far from prepared for the computer challenges posed by the rapidly approaching Year 2000. By itself, BankAmerica might not be big enough to spend what Coulter believed would be needed to compete in the decade ahead.

Coming out of a corporate banking background, Coulter explained, he tended to think in global terms, with the fortunes of banks resting on huge transactions. McColl's company was much less dependent on earth-shaking loans and investments, more deeply involved with small- and medium-sized domestic businesses and personal relationship banking. Coulter admitted his predisposition to do a merger with Citicorp, since they did so much retail business offshore. But when he looked at the figures Jim Hance had given Mike O'Neill, Coulter could see that the bigger picture was one of payments dominance, and he liked what he saw in that picture.

Put together, BankAmerica and NationsBank would clear *25 percent* of the payments transactions in the entire United States. One out of every four checks, credit card charges or electronic money transfers would be, in banker talk, "on-us items." They would be both drawn on and deposited in—or paid and received by—the new, merged superbank. Instead of collecting one fee on each of these transactions, they would collect two. That alone should provide the revenue base for investment in future technology, Coulter believed. Together the two banks would have the power to go forward.

"Stunning," McColl agreed simply. "All the power we need."

Then Coulter gave his other reason for the merger. In his two years as CEO, he said, he had replaced his entire senior management team. Coulter had spent one-fourth of his time evaluating his top two hundred people. He had determined that his senior managers could be divided into three groups of about equal numbers, the pretty good, the average and the below average. Across the company, decisions were often debated rather than made, and answers to questions could be a long time coming. It was a tiring, less than fruitful process. "My people are fatigued," Coulter admitted.

He said he had decided, ultimately, that NationsBank had the best franchise and McColl had the best management team. Had David Coulter been coached by BankAmerica's equivalent of Chuck Cooley, he could not have picked a better card to play against Hugh McColl's hot hand. Consequently, McColl found himself in a giving mood when the subject turned to the question of a name. The "brand" value of their respective companies' names was pretty well determined by which side of the Rocky Mountains one happened to be on—with the exception of New York and Wall Street, where the dividing line remained (as McColl saw it) a bank's location, either in New York or anywhere else. They agreed that, since both names were good, they might be successfully combined into, say, "Nations Bank of America," or perhaps "AmericasBank." But McColl did not rule out the conversion to BankAmerica's flag, so long as it could stand for Addison Reese's and Tom Storrs's bank as well as A. P. Giannini's. "The power of this franchise, by any name, will be palpable," he concluded, giving himself good marks for rational behavior.

The talk was not strictly business, except for the fact that even the slightest loose tie might have derailed the train. The two men spoke of their wives and how much they confided in them. Coulter said his Susan was a crackerjack businesswoman. He wanted McColl to meet her and thought the three of them might have dinner that evening. McColl offered to take them to their favorite restaurant, but Coulter said Susan was expecting him for dinner at their house. McColl wondered how much this had to do with avoiding the paparazzi, but he didn't ask. He also knew the purpose of dinner was not so much that he would have an opportunity to meet Susan Coulter, but that she would have an opportunity to form a judgment about him.

It was noon when Coulter rose from the chair he'd occupied for three hours, explaining that he had another appointment. As he shook hands with McColl he said he felt a lot better than he did when he came in. McColl said he felt a lot better too, about everything.

In Jim Hance's suite one floor down, McColl joined Hance, Mike O'Neill, Ed Herlihy and another lawyer, Adam Chinn. They ordered lunch and spent three and a half hours going over details. McColl got in touch with Pat Hinson, recently gone into semiretirement, and asked her to join him in Phoenix. He had a feeling he was going to need her to type up a few finer points of the understanding between him and David Coulter, the way she had done back in Florida.

At 7:00 P.M.—1900 hours McColl time—he pulled up in a rented car to the entrance of a luxury condominium on Steiner Street in Pacific Heights, just about three blocks from the Presidio. It was the only building in sight taller than two or three stories. The doorman was a surprise; he thought all American doormen lived in New York. This one directed him to the elevator and the ninth floor, all of which, it developed, was occupied by the Coulters' penthouse.

After an awkward moment with a Chinese butler (McColl thinking he must have the wrong apartment) who stepped him into the living room, Dave Coulter—he was "Dave" now—gave him a warm handshake. The apartment's glass wall provided an inspiring view of the city and the Golden Gate Bridge, but McColl's eyes were drawn to Mrs. Coulter, who extended her hand. "I've heard a lot about you," she said, the way many people did when they met him.

"I hope some of it was good," he answered, the way he answered most people he met.

"It was *all* good." He liked that, something different.

If Dave Coulter was a $21 million man, McColl thought Susan Coulter looked every bit his mate. Dressed in a fetching pantsuit, she was blonde and an inch taller than McColl. His mental note: aggressively gracious. She said she had so looked forward to meeting him. He made a joke about hoping he's not so tired that he fails her inspection. She missed the hint and, instead of inviting him to sit, she insisted on walking him around the room, playing tour guide, pointing out the attractions of San Francisco at sunset. McColl explored her taste in books and discovered she was an avid mystery reader. Had he read something-or-other by so-and-so, the Australian? He had not. He must. She would send him her copy when she finished it.

Hors d'oeuvres and wine came out, served by the butler. McColl was struck by the difference between the Coulters' lifestyle and his and Jane's back in Charlotte. Jane might have put out some crackers and cheese, he would have poured the drinks. They would have sat down somewhere and put their feet up on the furniture.

Before McColl finished his glass of wine, the butler announced dinner. It was served at a table nestled in a bay window. McColl had a clear view of the BankAmerica and Transamerica towers. He expected to hear Tony Bennett, but there was something tinkly and oppressive in the background. New age dirge. McColl complimented Susan on the dinner, but she demurred. The only thing she'd had to do with it was the selection of their house man, who did all the cooking. They talked about children. McColl learned that the Coulters had been married for twenty-five years, but had no children together. Susan's two sons from her first marriage were grown up.

Like a second shoe long dangled over the edge of an upstairs bed, the M-word, merger, at last thudded onto the table. It all seemed so . . . *exciting*. Susan Coulter did most of the talking. She wanted to impress upon him the fact that "Bank of America is a proud name." There was no question in McColl's mind that both she and her husband considered the name to be of paramount importance when the merger agreement was drawn up. *When, not if. Ha!* McColl sensed that he had the game won.

The name was somehow more than a name. To the Coulters it was like one of those historical markers a Hugh McColl drove right past on the way to Litchfield Beach. Did McColl realize, they wondered, how important the bank and its founder, Amadeo Peter Giannini, had been in the history of California? With a sigh he hoped had not been audible, McColl let himself be drawn into the Giannini Legend.

Born in San Jose, California, in 1870, A. P. Giannini was a first-generation American. He started out as a child on the family farm, picking cherries, apricots and strawberries, until his father was killed by an angry farmhand over a two-dollar debt when Amadeo was six years old. By age fifteen, A. P. was selling other farmers' produce in San Francisco. He was dark, tall and handsome and he knew how to sell. He also knew his customers. They were Italians—immigrants, first- and second-generation Americans—many of whom, Giannini believed, could succeed in business if they could just get started. However, they often were forced to borrow money from loan sharks, since banks did not consider them trustworthy.

At the age of thirty-four, with a fortune of nearly half a million dollars, Giannini started his own bank, the Bank of Italy. According to the legend, he used his salesmanship to convince the Italian families of San Francisco's North Beach neighborhood to "take the money out of their mattresses and put it into his bank." Two years later, when the 1906 earthquake and fire destroyed the city, the Bank of Italy set up an outdoor "office" on the Washington Street wharf—a plank laid across two barrels. A. P. Giannini, the little fellow's friend, made loans with no paperwork.

By 1920, Bank of Italy had offices all over California and enough money to buy out the bigger Bank of America in Los Angeles, even to open offices in London and Tokyo. During the Depression, Giannini lost $138 million, but nevertheless he agreed to finance construction of the Golden Gate Bridge. It was partly to prevent Giannini's omnivorous bank from overrunning the country that Congress voted into law the Glass-Steagall Act of 1933, requiring commercial banks to dispose of their nonbanking affiliates.

Giannini struck more gold in Hollywood, supplying the money MGM and David O. Selznick needed in 1939 to finish *Gone With the Wind*. When Mussolini and World War II made the Italian flag a less than propitious banner, the man whose ambition was to run the largest bank in the United States usurped the name of the company he had bought in Los Angeles; Bank of Italy became Bank of America. By the end of Giannini's life in 1949, Bank of America was the largest not only in the nation, but in the world.

The history lesson dragged on and on. McColl believed it all, took it on faith, didn't need proof: Amadeo Peter Giannini was a great man. A great *dead* man. He wanted to understand the past, but not wallow in it. McColl's pride needed to flow from his own sense of having built "today's bank," and working to build "tomorrow's bank." He could derive no satisfaction from a connection with "yesterday's bank." He thought: *Makes for great press, but Mr. Giannini didn't get it done. I'm going to get it done.*

Perhaps because he was bone-weary, McColl resisted the urge to recite the history of NationsBank, beginning with Duncan Donald McColl in the Civil War. Indeed, there was much about Giannini's accomplishments that appealed to him, but he was far more impressed by the fact that Hugh L. McColl was now in line to be CEO of the first coast-to-coast bank in America, a dream that had eluded A. P. Giannini. "You know, Dave," he said, "you and I weren't hired to run Mr. Rockefeller's Bank or Mr. Giannini's Bank. The prime reason that NationsBank is different from yours is that yours is steeped in tradition, while ours is: 'Hey, man, this is *our* company, *we* built it.' There is a difference. There is a huge difference. We are not in love with somebody who was there yesterday."

Somewhere along the way, McColl was convinced, A. P. Giannini's bank had missed a beat, if not the boat. BankAmerica had taken far too much risk in Latin America during the 1970s, resulting in huge losses during the late 1980s, just as NCNB/NationsBank's star was rising. Now Coulter, a native Pennsylvanian, had been replacing many of his predecessor's key people with executives like Mike O'Neill, from the Continental Bank of Chicago, even as he expounded the Giannini myth. And now a merger was about to sever Giannini's California umbilical cord, which had sustained BankAmerica for more than ninety years.

When Susan Coulter excused herself, the two men returned to the living room. Talk turned to identifying the top-level management team, those whose positions must be established for the deal to work. McColl considered CFO Jim Hance and President Ken Lewis essential. To go beyond those two would open the door so wide that it would be impossible to bar many of his teammates. Coulter wanted his CFO, Mike O'Neill, and his president, Michael Murray, another Continental Bank transplant. Coulter would claim the presidency of the new corporation, with McColl as chairman and chief executive officer. They agreed to a six-person executive team. Then Coulter hemmed a bit. What about the risk management executives? Shouldn't they be included? McColl reminded him that they had to draw the line. He would explain that to his teammates and Coulter would have to do the same. They agreed once again on six. Then Coulter hawed. Was six really the logical number? McColl assured him that it was, that any larger group would be unwieldy. McColl was developing a keen appreciation of the difficulties of decision-reaching at BankAmerica. He wondered how long it would take to put this question to bed, because he needed to get to bed himself.

"So, it's decided," McColl said, making his move to leave. "We go with the six-man team of McColl, Coulter, Hance, Lewis, Murray and O'Neill."

"Right," Coulter agreed. "You know, all along I intuitively knew that six was the right number."

Showing McColl to the door, Coulter repeated the sentiment he'd expressed upon leaving the hotel room. He felt "so much better at the end of the day than I felt at the beginning."

Outside, the spring sky showed a fair number of stars, never mind the ambient glow of the spread city. At 2230 hours, 1 April, 1998, Hugh McColl smiled, slapped the roof of his car and looked up. *All the stars are aligned for us. I believe we have a deal, if we can sell our boards.*

Shortly before eleven, he was back at the Mandarin Hotel, stretched out on Jim Hance's bed as he told Hance, Herlihy, O'Neill and Chinn about the evening. He wanted desperately to go to sleep, but there were yet a few details that had to be worked out. O'Neill was not sure the BankAmerica board would be willing to move quickly, but McColl left no doubt that it had to be either a quick deal or a no-deal. Already too many people knew BankAmerica was in play. Coulter had talked to John Reed at Citi.

"We'll announce on April 13," McColl said.

"That's the day after Easter Sunday," O'Neill complained. There was no way they could pull everything together with Good Friday and Passover and . . . *everything*.

"Yeah, and I'll probably have to miss the Masters at Augusta," McColl quipped, unaware of and unconcerned over his irreverence. "We're about to create the largest damned bank in the world and you all will just have to forego the Easter Bunny this year."

He won his point, as he knew he would. There would be executive committee meetings of both banks on the following Monday, April 6, followed by a two-day period of due diligence. On Thursday morning, April 9, McColl would be in San Francisco for a meeting of the full BankAmerica board. Friday morning, he and Coulter would be in Charlotte for a NationsBank board meeting. Immediately after the NationsBank board approval, all parties would fly to New York, where the papers would be signed. Monday morning, at a media festival arranged by Lynn Drury, the world would learn about the new bank.

About 2:00 A.M.—having had less than six hours sleep over the past forty—McColl went to his own room and turned out the lights. He had to be up again at 5:25 to make the scheduled flight to Phoenix.

America's best-known bankers flocked into Phoenix by the hundreds, ready to consider momentous technological changes, to cluck at one another's weighty opinions, to agree on how to convince the government that the banker's way is the right way, to have a few drinks and tell a few lawyer jokes. The convention was being held at the Arizona Biltmore, where McColl had booked a self-contained "cabaña" behind the tennis courts, away from the main hotel, so his comings and goings would be less conspicuous. He didn't mind showing up at these functions, but he'd be damned if he was going to spend any more time than necessary with the people he considered on good days his competition and, at times like this, his enemies. Pat Hinson had booked two more rooms at the Ritz-Carlton, clear across town. She would take a room on the eighth floor, with Room Number 940 the rendezvous for McColl and Coulter, to finalize their plans, out of sight of the conventioneers.

The convention started out with afternoon gatherings at the Biltmore, to be followed by a reception and cocktail party. McColl and Coulter had agreed to forego the party and meet in the Ritz-

Carlton Room 940 at 7:00 P.M. Right about six, McColl got the keys to the rental car from Hance and told the rest of the NationsBank contingent to wish him luck. As he was standing under the front canopy, waiting for a bellman to bring the car around, he heard a woman's voice calling.

"Hugh McColl? Hugh? It's Ann Fudge. What are *you* doing in Phoenix?"

Fudge was the head of Philip Morris's Maxwell House Coffee Company, a powerful young African-American businesswoman whom McColl had tried to recruit for his board of directors a few years earlier. She was in Arizona for a different convention, headed for a different cocktail party and dressed to kill. McColl did not want to be late for this meeting, but he couldn't avoid making conversation. Fudge was running late herself, concerned that she might not be able to find a taxi.

That's when a limousine pulled up and Ed Crutchfield got out.

"Hugh! Good to see you. Didn't expect to find you at one of these things. We could have flown out together. How about a drink?"

McColl had to think quickly. "Have to take a raincheck, Ed. Ann here—You two know each other? Ed Crutchfield, Ann Fudge—anyway, Ann's got to get to some big shindig across town and I said I'd give her a ride. I'll have to catch you later on that drink. Here's my car now." He couldn't help but wonder what Crutchfield was thinking as he watched McColl speed off in the company of the attractive Ms. Fudge. Whatever it was, it wouldn't be anywhere near the truth.

Since Fudge's event was in yet a third part of far-flung Phoenix, McColl had his turn showing up late for a meeting with Coulter, maybe the most important meeting of his life. Pat Hinson had shown Coulter into the room, where McColl found him famished and wondering if they might order something to eat. Coulter said he'd take care of the order while McColl got comfortable.

"Order me a cheeseburger and a couple of Lagavulins," McColl said. When he came back into the living room, Coulter seemed to be in an argument with the room service person, but he hung up, assuring McColl it would all work out.

As for the deal, that seemed to be worked out too. As had been agreed to prior to the Phoenix meeting, Coulter accepted the precisely worded language referring to his position after the merger: he would be president of the combined company and it was "the present intention" of McColl and both boards that he become chairman and CEO upon McColl's retirement. There would be no guarantee of succession chiseled into a tablet next to the bust of A. P. Giannini. McColl would be chairman and CEO; Coulter would be president and member of the board. The only positions stipulated in the merger would be theirs and those of the other four men previously named—Hance, Lewis, O'Neill and Murray. They were about to move on to other matters when room service arrived.

Even McColl was impressed by the tab, over two hundred dollars. The bellman explained that the hotel policy did not permit the delivery of mixed drinks to guests' rooms, so they had sent the entire bottle, at the Big Hotel Price of $180. McColl, Scotsman even where Scotch was concerned, was about to send it back, but Coulter poured his twelve-dollar bottle of beer and told him to just go ahead and sign the chit. "What the hell?" McColl figured. "You're right. Here we are putting together a $570 billion company and I'm worried about a hundred-eighty bucks."

They had a drink, took a few bites of their burgers, and Coulter said, "Would you like to talk about the hard things?"

"Sure. That's why I'm here."

Coulter bit into what McColl referred to as "the social issues."

Item 1: headquarters location. Coulter agreed with McColl that headquarters would be in Charlotte. The global wholesale bank would be located in San Francisco, since BankAmerica's international commitment was primarily in Asia and the Pacific Rim.

Item 2: name. McColl agreed that the corporate name, the holding company, would become BankAmerica Corporation. He felt that Coulter was ready to accept his stipulation that the brand name be a combination, such as "NationsBank of America," but he decided to leave this one on the table. He knew from experience that there were marketing and legal considerations to a brand name, and that one could be chosen after the fact of the merger. They agreed to "preserve both names" for the time being.

Item 3: board of directors. Coulter believed he should go to his board with an offer to split the new board down the middle—ten directors from NationsBank, ten from BankAmerica. McColl reminded him that the CFOs and lawyers had agreed on a greater representation for NationsBank. Perhaps Coulter would agree to ten-ten, plus the CEO as swing vote. Coulter named nine directors with whom he felt personally comfortable. Almost ashamed of his brashness, McColl said, "Well, Dave, why don't we just split the damn board eleven-nine? I mean, that's consistent with the shareholder makeup. NationsBank shareholders will wind up owning 55 percent of the stock."

Coulter considered the proposition and found it logical.

McColl thought this might be a good time to cash in his chips. "I believe in clarifying what we've agreed to, something I learned from my predecessor, Tom Storrs," he said, dialing Pat Hinson's room. Into the receiver he said, "Mrs. Hinson, I think we're ready for you up here, if you'll bring your pad and pen."

Then to Coulter: "I'd like you to listen as I dictate what we've just said to Mrs. Hinson. If you want to make a correction, just go ahead and do it. We'll call it our Memorandum of Understanding."

It was about 10:30 P.M. when McColl started dictating. The Memorandum of Understanding was a plain-language document, consisting of five bullet points. The first concerned the positions of McColl and Coulter, concluding that it was "the present intent of the boards of directors for Mr. Coulter to succeed Mr. McColl."

Second came the list of six executives who would manage the new company. Third, the matter of location was settled—headquarters and CEO in Charlotte, global bank office and president in San Francisco. "It is our intention," McColl dictated, "that the senior management team will be located in the principal cities within the franchise."

The fourth bullet point was the new company's name. "Both banks have good, patriotic names which will be retained in one form or another," Hinson wrote down. There would be a careful study before the brands were converged and a permanent name selected. "In any case, our colors will be red, white and blue and will take advantage of the greatest franchise in American banking."

The final bullet point made it clear that the new board would be made up of twenty directors, McColl and ten others from NationsBank, Coulter and eight others from BankAmerica.

Pat Hinson read her shorthand back and the two executives approved. Coulter returned to the Biltmore and Hinson went back to her room, where she would type the notes into her laptop computer. After that, she telephoned McColl's room and read it back to him again. He signed off on the memorandum and told her good-night. He slept soundly.

He spent most of the next morning trying not to look at

Coulter, across the table at a heated technology symposium. McColl was flanked by the CEOs of Wells Fargo and BankBoston and wondered what their reactions would be when they found out. He joked with them about getting their pictures taken with him, so their stocks would go up. McColl was playing out his dream, his "end-game" of American banking.

Back at his Biltmore cabaña, McColl had to sit around an hour waiting for Coulter to show up and look at the printed memorandum. Finally, he arrived and approved. The two men signed four original printouts of the Memorandum of Understanding, Hugh L. McColl Jr. on the left side of the page, David A. Coulter on the right. McColl wanted to give one of the originals to Jim Hance, to frame and hang on his office wall, because Hance, more than anyone, had made the deal happen.

Later that evening, McColl arranged to meet with Mike Murray, the only member of the new executive team he didn't know. Over what remained of perhaps the world's most expensive bottle of Scotch, the two men discussed what they intended to be the world's greatest bank. McColl found Murray "an enthusiastic, fired-up sort of person," who lifted McColl's already buoyant spirits. *We are doing the right thing*, he told himself.

Flying home the next morning, McColl ordered up a champagne breakfast for everyone aboard the Gulfstream. He was exhausted but jubilant, convinced he had come out of the negotiations with more for his stockholders and his teammates than he had thought possible. Headquarters would be Charlotte. He would be unencumbered and unrestricted as CEO. Every other important decision would be left to the board of directors, whose membership would be weighted eleven-to-nine in favor of NationsBank.

When the door of the aircraft opened outside the NationsBank hangar in Charlotte, McColl thought he heard someone, or something, playing the Marine Hymn. It was, by God, a bagpiper! As he started down the stairs, there was Joe Martin, sitting in his wheelchair, laughing. There were Chuck Cooley, Vick Phillips and Lynn Drury, applauding. There was his new secretary, Kathie Rice, and his young aide-in-training, Bob Zeigler, and various spouses. Joe Martin had on his Atlanta Olympics jacket, with a red-white-and-blue Uncle Sam hat and an American flag draped around him. The kilted piper was wailing away and McColl knew the words by heart: ". . . We will fight our country's battles, on the land and on the sea."

Inside the hangar, champagne, more champagne, and hugs.

The morning of Monday, April 6, McColl woke up on top of the world, ready to share the Good News with his executive committee. But when he turned on the television, there was a big story that gave him a big headache. Travelers Group—the huge insurance company that now owned Salomon, Inc.—was going to merge with Citicorp. It was going to be an $80 billion deal, creating what was touted as "the world's largest financial-services company."

McColl hated to have his thunder stolen, and here it was happening to him for the second time, a repeat of the Manufacturer's Hanover-Chemical merger that had one-upped his buyout of C&S/Sovran in 1991. Instead of becoming the second-largest bank in the country that year, he had been dropped to fourth. Well, at least *that* wasn't going to happen this time. Travelers wasn't a bank. They could cross-sell products like crazy with Citibank, but it would be NationsBank of America—or whatever they decided to call it—that would come out on top of the banking world. Still, he told Jane, the news made him feel low down as a rattlesnake's belly.

Before leaving for the office, he e-mailed his new teammate, Dave Coulter, who would be waking up to much the same emotion in a couple of hours. He typed, "trumped before we kick off," in a mixing of metaphors that somehow summed it all up. When he got a return message later, Coulter agreed the news was tough, but it didn't change the fact that their deal would still result in the number-one bank. The new Citigroup, as the merged companies were to be called, would simply make it easier for their two boards, the regulating agencies and the public to swallow the NationsBank-BankAmerica merger. McColl added: "It's also a wake-up call, to remind us that the game is never over."

McColl noted another interesting point about the new Citigroup. According to the announcement, Citibank CEO John Reed and Travelers CEO Sanford I. "Sandy" Weill were planning to cochair the merged companies. McColl considered that decision to be a hand grenade with a cardboard pin. Inevitably, there would be a power struggle and the grenade would go off. At least he and Dave Coulter could agree on who was senior. McColl felt that success in a corporation depended on being absolutely truthful with one another. Truth begat trust and trust begat teamwork; he believed that.

McColl's meeting with his executive committee was a smooth success. He read them the Memorandum of Understanding and was roundly cheered. Executive committee chairman Hootie Johnson took on the task of contacting Charlie Rice in Jacksonville and explaining to him why his tenure as chairman of the board was about to be cut short. After considering the potential impact of the merger to the other directors and shareholders, the executive committee agreed to recommend the merger to the full board when it convened on Friday.

As McColl worked out directorial issues with his committee, wheels were churning in other parts of his company and in BankAmerica as well. NationsBank engaged Merrill, Lynch, Pierce, Fenner & Smith to render an opinion as to what the exchange rate of stock should be so that neither bank paid a premium for the other. Jim Hance's people and Mike O'Neill's people—along with their respective accountants and lawyers—flew to Dallas, to go over each other's books without arousing suspicion. Texas and New Mexico were the only states where both banks maintained branches, which made Texas a good place to conduct due diligence and negotiate the merger details, stock options and payments to key executives.

One of the key "due diligence" questions was the extent of BankAmerica interest in Asia. Even though Hugh McColl might believe California, Oregon and Washington contained BankAmerica's most important "Pacific Rim" assets and liabilities, the company did have a significant presence in a troubled segment of the global economy. Moreover, BankAmerica had a history of making huge investments in foreign countries without fully appreciating the risks involved—as in Latin America during the 1970s.

Now Japan, whose economy was twice the size of all other Asian economies combined, seemed politically paralyzed. Whatever happened to the yen, the Tokyo market and Japanese factories was being felt in Malaysia, Thailand, Indonesia, Singapore and China. There were analysts who believed Japan was on the brink of a collapse worse than anything the world had seen since the Great Depression. Despite the fact that BankAmerica had Asian nonperforming loans in the vicinity of $1 billion, Hance's analysts felt that Michael O'Neill had the proper risk management strategies in place and that corporate-global executive Michael Murray had held currency trading losses to acceptable levels. For its part, NationsBank had almost no exposure in Asia.

By Wednesday afternoon, the due diligence process had turned up nothing to prevent the deal from going forward. Wednesday night, McColl was booked as the opening act at the NationsBank Performance Place at Spirit Square, which was being renamed in honor of Loonis McGlohon, a Charlotte composer and jazz pianist who worked with many of the biggest names in popular music. McColl wanted to stay, to enjoy music he understood and to bask in the warmth of a hometown crowd, but he had to slip out backstage.

His twenty-six-year-old assistant, Bob Zeigler, drove him to the airport, where they boarded the Gulfstream jet and headed for San Francisco. Aboard "Six November Bravo"—his name for the big plane with the letters NB and the number 6 stenciled on its tail—McColl fell asleep. Somewhere over the Midwest he woke up and decided to read the Australian mystery that David Coulter had brought to him in Phoenix, a gift from Susan. She had also sent the biography of A. P. Giannini. He would wait on that one.

Thursday morning, April 9, McColl was pacing his hotel room, half-listening to morning news reports he'd heard half a dozen times already, when, precisely at nine, the telephone rang. Zeigler reported that the car sent by BankAmerica was waiting downstairs. There was an administrative assistant along who would take him into the BankAmerica building through a loading dock and up a freight elevator. Once at the appointed floor, McColl was hurried into a vacant office, where he would await the pleasure of the board. The office afforded a hell of a view of San Francisco on a rainy day.

The first person he saw was Ed Herlihy, who came in with a long face. It looked as though the board was intent on crushing the entire deal. McColl asked what parts of the deal they objected to. Herlihy said it seemed to be every part: Coulter's future, the eleven-nine board split, San Francisco losing out to Charlotte. Everything.

"How about Dave?" McColl asked.

"Coulter is holding strong," said Herlihy. But the directors were fuming over getting out-traded. Herlihy advised McColl to stay calm, to "go in there and do your thing" and maybe everything would turn out all right.

Herlihy left and Coulter came into the office, confirming what McColl already knew. McColl reminded him they had a deal. Coulter agreed and promised his board would come around. Coulter exited and was replaced by attorney Adam Chinn, sent by Herlihy to calm down McColl.

At last McColl was summoned to the boardroom. He started talking, but afterward could not remember what he said. Whatever it was, when he stopped, the BankAmerica directors were ready with their questions.

"Mr. McColl, did you and Mr. Coulter consider the option of twenty-one directors? Ten, ten and you the swing vote?"

"Yes, I did think about that," McColl answered. "Even suggested it at one point. But Dave and I felt that the eleven-nine relationship was consistent with the respective ownership of the merged company."

To the question of whether the executive committee of the new board might be divided evenly, McColl made the point that "Dave and I will need the support of the entire board." There could not be a fifty-fifty split at any level of decision making, because that would set up a rift, similar to the one his company had encountered with C&S and Sovran. "That company destroyed itself in '91 because of a split board. The split enervated the company. If you want to go that route, I'll just go back to Charlotte."

One of the directors expressed appreciation for NationsBank's capitulation on the issue of a name, at least for the holding company. But someone else snorted, "Making this company BankAmerica Corporation? They can change that later in about twenty seconds."

"Right," McColl agreed, "so let's call it NationsBank Corporation. We can change that in twenty seconds, too. You know, that cuts both ways."

What about some stronger language regarding his successor? Couldn't McColl at least agree to guaranteeing their man the job?

"I've never seen that work," McColl answered. He decided to give this board a slightly sharper picture of the man they were dealing with. "I don't have a damn contract," he said, "Never had one. Nobody in my company has a contract. My job is good for the day. The board of directors decides how long I stay there." He saw some shifting in their chairs, hands reaching up to remove reading glasses. He saw good signs in their body language. "In a perfect world, I'd stay to the annual meeting of 2001. If you'd like to know the reason for that date, I think it will take that long to know whether we've got a winning combination, and if we do, then I'm going to end up with the reins of this company that I built before I hand them over to someone else. I want to be the one to do that. It's like show business. I'd like to do that."

The men and women around the table seemed to like what he was saying. He was neither giving an inch, blowing smoke or throwing bull. He left the room feeling good about his performance, believing he had deflected every objection. He sat down in his holding pen and waited, looking out the window at San Francisco in the rain.

Forty floors below where Hugh McColl sat was Portsmouth Square, landfill that once had been San Francisco Bay, perhaps about to become part of his domain. In 1846, just about the time young Duncan Donald McColl moved with his parents to a farm at Shoe Heel, North Carolina, a detachment of U.S. Marines landed, right down there, where BankAmerica stood today, and claimed the territory of California for the United States of America. Marines raised the American flag over San Francisco for the very first time. Marines from the sloop-of-war *Portsmouth* brought the two coasts of the nation together. Here was Hugh McColl, still a marine, trying to bond the economies of the same two coasts, 152 years later. He thought: *I've come this far. I don't want to blow it. But I can't be forced into making any concessions.*

He was just a trifle unsure where Dick Rosenberg stood. McColl was afraid that Rosenberg, who had tried so hard to put this merger together three years earlier, might still be angry with him over those 1995 negotiations. Never having understood McColl's ingrained determination to stick with the South, Rosenberg might feel simply disrespected, not taken seriously. *Dick is mad at me 'cause I didn't say yes to him,* McColl fretted. Perhaps more to the point, Rosenberg was a man justifiably proud of his horse-trading skills. His anger over being out-traded could cloud his judgment so that he might not appreciate the perfection of the deal on the table.

In the end, McColl's fears proved unjustified. Not only did Rosenberg not block the merger, he led the vote on its behalf. The board of BankAmerica approved the merger with NationsBank. McColl could have stepped out of the fortieth-floor window and never hit the ground till he got back to Charlotte. He had everything he needed to become the first coast-to-coast banker in the history of the United States.

At the NationsBank Corporate Center, Bill Vandiver, Chuck Cooley, Lynn Drury and Vick Phillips were together when the call came in from the car in San Francisco. McColl told them they now worked for the United States' first coast-to-coast bank. The fifty-eighth floor of the Corporate Center erupted in whoops. Phillips said he'd contact the pilots and tell them to start the engines. McColl's schedule called for him to get his own board's approval the following morning, then fly to New York for the Easter weekend finale.

A few moments after that call, Phillips took the phone again. It was McColl.

"Vick, call the pilots back and let them know we'll be about an hour later than we thought. I just found out Bob Zeigler's never seen the Golden Gate Bridge and we're going to take a little drive across it."

The following morning, in the sixtieth-floor boardroom of the NationsBank building, McColl stood to speak to his directors. "Addison Reese once said when you have something important to say, you should write it down and read it. Heeding that admonition, I would like to read you a statement."

McColl stepped the directors through the five-week sequence of events, the telephone conversations among Hance, O'Neill and Herlihy; the Hance-O'Neill meeting in San Francisco; the McColl-Coulter meetings in San Francisco and Phoenix.

"During the course of our conversations," McColl read, "Mr. Coulter explained to me the logic that had led him to consider this course of action. He outlined the benefits of merger, which are enormous and consistent with our own research on the matter. He advised me that he had made an assessment of his management team over the past two years and had concluded that he did not have the depth or strength to go it alone. The combination of NationsBank's powerful franchise, technology advances and strong management led him to us."

That led him to the Memorandum of Understanding. "As an aside, it should be noted that one can learn a lot from one's predecessors. Tom Storrs had always taught me to get all understandings in writing so that there could be no misunderstanding between parties." As Jim Kiser passed out copies of the signed memorandum, McColl neared the end of his prepared statement.

"While this Memorandum of Understanding deals with the so-called social issues, it is the financial issues that we should examine. It is, however, important to note that during my meeting with the board of directors of BankAmerica Corporation yesterday that they attempted to negotiate each point again. The Memorandum of Understanding signed by both of us and honored to the letter by Mr. Coulter, turned out to be pivotal.

"Before I turn the meeting over to Jim Hance to walk us through the transaction, I would like to take note of the fact that Jim is, in fact, the father of this deal. His skillful negotiations and careful structuring gave us an opportunity to play the last important card in the end game of bank consolidation with zero dilution."

After Hance went through his numbers, McColl introduced his board to David Coulter, who found his reception far less contentious than had been McColl's in San Francisco. Coulter told the directors about BankAmerica's strengths and how he anticipated them complementing the strengths of NationsBank. Sometime later, two of the board members expressed their satisfaction with the merger as described. Director Jackie Ward, CEO of Computer Generation, complimented Coulter on giving "one hell of a presentation." She praised his "directness and candor."

John A. Williams, chairman of Post Properties, who had come on the board only recently from the Barnett merger, was impressed with the overall calmness of the meeting. He observed that McColl, Hance and Ken Lewis managed to keep their elation "well contained," despite having fulfilled their dream of building a nationwide bank. For his own part, Williams believed this would be the merger "that changes the playing field," making it difficult for other banks to get to a size that would make them relevant. "It's the mother of all mergers," said Williams.

Saturday morning, April 11, an auburn-haired woman stepped up to the registration desk at New York's Waldorf Astoria hotel carrying an armload of dossiers and documents that would have shaken the financial industry to its roots, but for the fact that most of the industry was taking the weekend off. She had, for example, a set of twenty-eight overhead projector transparencies that graphically illustrated the power of the bank to be announced in less than forty-eight hours. One set of figures showed that the new bank would operate 4,800 offices and 14,700 ATMs, with household customers numbering 29 million and 2 million business customers. Most impressive, on transparency number seven, was the number "8.1," representing the percentage of domestic deposits that would be controlled by the new bank. The closest competitor, when it completed its merger with CoreStates, would be First Union, with 3.8 percent. According to the official numbers, this new company would have a relationship with nearly one out of every three households in the United States of America.

The woman with the numbers registered at the Waldorf as "Elizabeth Lynn," but her real name was Lynn Elizabeth Drury. With her was "David Kenneth," better known as Kenneth D. Lewis. McColl's battling bankers were moving into position, eighteen strong. And because his commanding officers had things so well under control, "Leon Hughes" could check into his room, then mosey over to Fifth Avenue to do a little shopping. New Yorkers looked at the short fellow in jeans, black T-shirt, black cowboy hat and custom-made boots and figured the rodeo must be in town at Madison Square Garden.

Easter Sunday, after going over the speech he would deliver twice the following morning, McColl called to order the first executive management meeting of the soon-to-be largest bank in the United States. "Our first attempt at the six of us sitting down at a meeting," McColl shook his head, "and this is pretty grab-ass. This is a mess." It did not help that all six men were entranced by the final round of the Masters Golf Tournament being telecast from Augusta.

In spite of this distraction, they managed to discuss technology and how to bring BankAmerica "up to speed." The San Francisco management team was actually operating its three merged companies in California, Seattle and Chicago on three stitched-together computer platforms. They determined that upon completion of the NationsBank "model bank" installation in Florida, they would immediately begin switching the West Coast banks to the model-bank platform.

About the time Mark O'Meara putted in a birdie to win the Masters by one stroke, the meeting broke up and the group headed out to dinner. McColl found it interesting that, after having "a drink or two together, it was fun, we really enjoyed each other. It kind of fired us up for the next day." There was a sense of relief that the chemistry was good. McColl couldn't be certain it would always be that way, but for the moment, he decided, "it's going to do all right. It's not going to be perfect, but it'll hold."

Monday morning, April 14, in Charlotte, the earth shook. Coincidentally, perhaps, but literally. Just before 6:00 A.M., as newspaper route carriers were making their rounds, an earthquake woke people up, rattling windows and creaking floorboards, but causing no serious damage. It was only 3.9 on the Richter scale, too small to be noticed in California, with an epicenter just about exactly halfway between Charlotte and Bennettsville, South Carolina. For those who were awakened enough to go outside for their papers, the front page of the *Observer* provided the morning's real shocker.

Headlines screamed "NationsBank's giant deal," "BankAmerica

merger keeps headquarters in Charlotte" and "McColl realizes his view of destiny." Under direct orders from McColl, the story had been given in full to *Observer* business writers Melissa Wahl and Pamela Moore. Elsewhere, Monday morning headlines were based on the hints and vagueries that Dick Stilley and his media jugglers were tossing into the air. The *Wall Street Journal* indicated a big deal between NationsBank and BankAmerica would be announced "in the next day or two." The *New York Times* told its readers the merger would be disclosed "today."

Almost amazing as the earthquake in Charlotte was the coincidence that the CEOs of two other banks—Banc One and First Chicago NBD—were also planning a news conference, also at the Waldorf Astoria, that same morning to announce the $30 billion merger of their Midwestern companies. But they were mightily upstaged. The really big show was across the hall, where Lynn Drury—with the aid of Melba Spencer and Sheryl McAlister—was setting up her double dog-and-pony show, first for financial analysts, then for reporters.

Back in Charlotte, Drury's associates, led by lanky, gritty, growly Dick Stilley, were already playing catch-up, fielding telephone calls from analysts and reporters in places far from the carpeted Waldorf halls. NationsBank's public relations staff, abetted by people with good communication skills from other parts of the company, lined the circumference of the thirty-by-thirty conference room on the eighteenth floor of the Corporate Center. Folding tables were jammed up against one another from the middle of the conference room outward. Telephone cables, papers and pencils streamed toward the walls from the tables' center, where an industrial-size plastic bottle of Tylenol rose up like the glowing red hub of a cyclotron.

Since very early morning the calls had been coming in to the war room. McColl's speechwriter John Cleghorn had been awakened at his home at 3:30 by Reuters calling from London. Tokyo Broadcasting, *American Banker*, the *Chicago Tribune*, television and radio stations from Florida, Georgia and the Midwest had checked in already. Cleghorn had started out keeping a list, but he was falling further and further behind.

At 9:00 A.M. Eastern, five telephones and eight styrofoam coffee cups were in use. A television sat on a roll-about stand near the doorway, emitting a CNN interview with Stephen Brobech, president of the Consumer Federation of America, who was waxing ecstatic about the benefits the Big Merger would bring to consumers. Brobech envisioned easier credit card and ATM access, business banking from coast to coast, absolutely "no downside" for consumers.

Cleghorn cupped his hand over a receiver to hear what CNN was saying. "It doesn't get any better than this," he grinned, slapping a high five with Dick Stilley. "Did you write his speech, John?" Martha Larsh asked from across the war room.

Sheets of flip-chart paper were taped on the war room walls, on the trophy case, on framed magazine covers and awards that fill the room. The sheets bulleted key information to be given out:

- 22 states and D.C.
- 180,000 associates
- capabilities and convenience
- earnings growth to make investments for the future—but the industry leader today.

The sheets of memory-joggers only partially concealed the wall-mounted trophies to Hugh McColl, in his many manifestations. One entire section of the conference room was devoted to NationsBank's efforts on behalf of the family, dating back to a 1989 cover of *Working Mother* magazine. A corner glass trophy case contained awards and commendations not easily mounted on walls, such as the 1997 Diversity Leadership Award from the National Summit on Hispanic Women in Business. A crystal flame, inset with a bronze likeness of Dr. Martin Luther King Jr., awarded the King Center's 1996 "Salute to Greatness" to Hugh McColl. And on other walls, the history of NationsBank in the McColl Dynasty was framed.

From *Forbes* magazine, November 7, 1983, there was a photo of McColl as NCNB's new chairman and CEO, and a simple headline: "Breakthrough." The article below included a quote from brash Hugh: "I won't allow an opportunity to elude us because we are busy doing something else."

A striking magazine cover from July 1988 showed Tampa's big bank buildings lit up by dozens of lightning strikes, a photo taken a few days before NCNB's invasion of Texas. "Blitzkrieg," the cutline proclaimed, suggesting that the lightning bolts could be "merely the emanations of McColl Power."

A yellowed front page of the July 30, 1988, Dallas *Morning News* featured a photo of McColl with Ross Perot and Reece Overcash of

Associates Corporation of North America. Below was a quote from the city's international real estate developer Trammell Crow: "This is daybreak. This is sunrise. This will be good for Dallas and good for Texas."

The *Wall Street Journal*, of Monday, August 1, 1988, read: "Hard charging NCNB seizes a large share of banking in Texas. Bail out of First Republic Bank will make CEO Hugh McColl a hero or a bum. Good enough for Ross Perot."

From the 1991 C&S/Sovran acquisition, there was an unsigned, hand-executed map of Atlanta in the style of a Civil War military chart. It showed the city being "invaded" from four directions by the forces of McColl, Hance, Thompson and Figge. "General Bottorf's" troops are beating a retreat to the west, along the Tennessee River.

The *Business Week* cover of July 15, 1991, featured McColl against a red field and the edge-to-edge headline: "Super Banker." Below the headline were the words: "Hugh McColl is going after his biggest deal yet. It would make his NCNB the second largest bank and change the face of banking in the US."

A cartoon in the *Financial Times* of London, July 24, 1991, depicted McColl waving a cowboy hat and holding the reins of nine "horses," representing the states of Maryland, Virginia, North Carolina, South Carolina, Tennessee, Georgia, Florida, Texas and the District of Columbia.

A large gold medal named "Financial World's CEO of the Year, Hugh McColl, Jr., NationsBank Corporation, 1993," thanks to his "executive excellence and outstanding corporate leadership."

The *New York Times*, of Wednesday, October 2, 1996, declared, "NationsBank finds riches in plain vanilla banking. With Boatmen's deal NationsBank returns to its roots." And the article began: "Ever since it was a pipsqueak bank here in central North Carolina, NationsBank has always thought big."

The front page of the May 3, 1997, *St. Petersburg Times* featured a color photo of McColl working on a Tampa Bay Habitat for Humanity house, perched on a rafter, hammering away. The June 1997 cover of *America Economia*, Latin America's financial monthly, exploded in "NationsBANG!!" The November 9, 1997, *Chicago Tribune* headline asked, "NationsBank out to live up to its billing . . . Perhaps Chicago?"

Soon there would be a bale of new headlines to frame.

At 9:20 A.M. the TV was switched to MSNBC, where McColl and Coulter were being interviewed live from McColl's suite. In the war room, Dick Stilley was summoning more help. "There's a guy from *Time* magazine due any minute and I'm afraid he's going to walk in here and I'll have my underwear around my ankles," he barked into a phone.

The TV graphic read "Merger Monday" as from the floor of the New York Stock Exchange a reporter was predicting NationsBank stock would open, after a delay, at between eighty-one and eighty-six dollars a share, up at least seven dollars. None of the war room staff heard this news, because they were all on the telephone.

Cleghorn rang off his call and looked up wide-eyed at the television. "When you think about being bigger in net earnings than IBM, Philip Morris . . . Wow!" Laura Hunter and Mary Waller agreed that *wow* was the operative expression for the day.

Terri Phillippi switched the television channel. Now CNBC was doing a live interview and Coulter was saying, "Mr. McColl is in charge, and I have a lot to learn." From the coffee-and-doughnut table off to the side, Peter Davis shouted his agreement.

A CNBC reporter asked how the government would be able to "handle such a huge bank in the next economic downturn." McColl answered by citing the strength of the two banks involved. "We're running about $8 billion per annum in earnings," he said, "cash flow well north of that. We have huge reserves. And most important—and different from other banks—we are the largest depository bank in the United States, by some staggering margin. So we are funding our loans with basic American deposits and we are not dependent on any indifferent money in the marketplace. So that's a very real backup strength. So what does the government do? I don't think the government is worried about that. They still have control of us through many different regulations. And Dave and I are not going to mess up something that we've created. That's just not going to happen."

Dick Stilley rushed back into the room, waving his arms and wearing an uncharacteristic, McCollish grin. "Our stock's trading at eighty-four and an eighth," he shouted. Ellison Clary answered, "I feel rich!"

Minutes later, with the television volume turned down, the voice of Hugh McColl was heard from a multidirectional telephone speaker set up near the Tylenol vat at the center of the war room folding-table array. It was a live audio feed coming from the Waldorf meeting room, where the nation's top investment analysts were gathered to get the news first-hand and to pose the questions they believed only they could be qualified to pose.

McColl was speaking of "the company Dave and I have agreed to create." It would be "the premier bank of the twenty-first century" with a "coast-to-coast" presence, focusing on "the country's largest and fastest-growing states." Left up to him, this premiere bank would, for the time being, remain unnamed. "Our company will be unmatched in coast-to-coast market presence," McColl continued, "but, perhaps most important, our franchise will be unmatchable. Our market presence, our franchise, will indeed be unique. . . . This is a watershed event in the financial services industry, and the *customer* is the defining element."

When it was David Coulter's turn to speak, he immediately raised the flag of "the new BankAmerica Corporation." Emphasizing that the projected population growth in the markets served by the combined companies "represents 80 percent of the projected population growth in the United States," Coulter declared the new bank would be number one in support of the fastest-growing industries, including technology and entertainment. "Even I was surprised by the data," he told the analysts. Coulter said the new bank would process far more checks each day than the Federal Reserve system.

Asked how he would handle the "execution risks," a term popularized only the previous week with the formation of Citigroup, McColl responded, "How are we going to handle the execution risks? We're going to *do* it."

Shortly before noon, the rest of the media team left the war room telephones in charge of Terri Phillippi and some newly recruited help to troop across College Street. In Charlotte's Trade Center building, the Palmetto Room had been converted to a teleconferencing center where about 250 executives from NationsBank Charlotte gathered to watch a satellite feed of the news conference at the Waldorf Astoria on a ten-by-twelve-foot screen.

The news conference began with McColl and Coulter shaking hands in front of banners bearing their two banks' logos. McColl and NationsBank screen left, Coulter and BankAmerica on the right. Still cameras flashed wildly. Lynn Drury stepped to a microphone and established the "ground rules" for the news conference. McColl would speak first.

He began with the same speech he had given to the investment analysts. McColl was proud to announce formation of "the leading bank of the twenty-first century." When he got to the part about anticipating first-year earnings in excess of $10 billion, there were audible gasps from the Charlotte crowd, only now beginning to feel the implications, the wonder of it all.

Then McColl diverted from his prepared text to deliver a line he had penned for just this moment, something he'd read in the biography Susan Coulter sent him. He spoke of a 1930 Congressional hearing, "five years before I was born," in which BankAmerica's founder had testified concerning his dream of nationwide banking. "It is coming, gentlemen. And there is nothing you can do to stop it," said A. P. Giannini.

McColl then ticked off six points he wanted to establish concerning the merger:

"This is for the customer. We are going to have the most diverse workforce in America. Business success in a worldwide marketplace would hinge on available capital—capital power—we're going to have *lots* of it." His new bank would have "stability unmatched in the history of U.S. banking." Both banks had demonstrated unequaled concern for the communities they served, and together they would continue their "100 percent commitment to building strong communities." Finally, he promised that as federal banking restraints disappeared, they would establish a true "nationwide brand," a unified image that would reflect "the greatest franchise in America banking."

McColl concluded with a quote from Victor Hugo: "An invasion of armies can be resisted, but not an idea whose time has come."

Coulter's job was to excite the media with the statistics of the merger, but he began with a comparison of his bank's founder and McColl—clearly the individual he identified with NationsBank's success. "A. P. Giannini's dream was the same as Hugh's," Coulter proclaimed. "Today we are creating America's bank."

Coulter was beginning to sound like McColl without the accent. Calling the leadership assembled on the dais "a world-class team," he observed that "philosophically as well as financially, this is a great marriage. . . . We've got a lot of genuine respect for each other's organizations . . . the whole will be greater than the sum of its parts."

The questioning began with a reporter handing McColl a perfect opportunity. How had they decided who would be chairman? "How did we decide?" He shot a glance at Coulter. "We figured out who was the oldest and would get out of the way quickest. And I won."

Coulter played straight man. "I think I can learn a great deal from Hugh McColl, and I am looking forward to it."

In response to a question about location of headquarters, Coulter began a long explanation. McColl pulled out two caps. He donned a red San Francisco Forty-Niners cap and handed Coulter a blue Carolina Panthers cap. Photographers jumped up in front of the television cameras and flashed like runaway disco balls.

When a reporter compared this merger to the one announced the previous week, between Citicorp and Travelers, McColl said his merger was different. "We're not in any businesses either of us does not fully understand," he said. Coulter added that the Citigroup merger "is a good idea on paper" and wished those two companies well.

Most of the media seemed to ignore the one hot-potato question, thrown out by a reporter telephoning in a question from San Francisco. He pointed out that BankAmerica's insurance policy extended "family benefits" to couples of the same sex, and he wondered whether these liberal benefits would now be available to NationsBank employees as well. Coulter's cautious demeanor suggested that this subject somehow had not surfaced in the previous five weeks of discussion and negotiation. He tried to take the edge off the question by explaining that these benefits, in fact, included "all members" of an employee's "extended family." But as he was digging an explicatory hole, McColl broke in.

"Yes," he said. "The answer to the question is: Yes."

Asked what had finally cleared the hurdles to the long-considered merger, McColl asked Coulter to respond. "We talk a lot," he said. Coulter told the room of reporters that when discussions heated up "about three weeks ago," both sides had realized that this was "the right time, the right place, the right group of people."

"Amen," said Hugh McColl, who thought the final prayer of his career was answered.

"It's only when you get to be the lead dog that you start enjoying the view."

Hugh McColl

CHAPTER 18

The events of the next six months, following that Easter Monday merger announcement, would write one of the more bitter chapters in American banking. They would be months filled with secret meetings, with charges and countercharges, and with media leaks that produced both misrepresentation of facts and misinterpretation of events. Before the end of 1998, some NationsBank shareholders who had cheered the buyout of BankAmerica would think of McColl as the villain in a nasty power struggle that cost them dearly.

As this book went to press in the spring of 1999, there would be in the U.S. courts more than thirty lawsuits, either pending or in progress, enough to make the principals in the drama wary of saying too much or, in some cases, of saying anything at all. As a result, much of what follows has been assembled out of scraps of information, newspaper accounts and shards of evidence. Certainly it contains a great deal of the truth, although it may well not be "nothing but the truth" and certainly is not "the whole truth." Where dates are certain, they are given. Otherwise, the sequence of events—critical to some potentially expensive lawsuits—is a reasonable reconstruction, but no more than that.

May 18, McColl boarded the Gulfstream for a flight to Atlanta, wearing a suit, because he had an important appointment, but carrying a change of clothes in a duffel bag. The real purpose of this trip was to spend a little time with his grandchildren, John and Lee's kids, who lived in Atlanta. And what was on his mind was a third thing entirely, the matter of merging two distinct management teams.

McColl carried like a St. Christopher medal the mental picture of Dave Coulter, bald, spit-and-polished in his blue-striped shirt with starched white collar and cuffs, his polka-dotted tie, standing up to address the NationsBank managers for the first time at the Charlotte Marriott. "Every one of us wants to work for a leader," Coulter told his new teammates that day, "and, in the end, that's what we're going to be—a leader." And later, echoing McColl's phrase, Coulter named the three cornerstones of what now would be their joint corporate culture: "Winning, teamwork, doing the right thing." McColl grinned, asked his NationsBank teammates, rhetorically: "Y'all see why I like this guy?"

Despite the talk of teamwork and commitment to a common cause, the new company would find itself committed to more than a thousand "golden parachutes" for BankAmerica executives with change-in-control contracts. In corporate America, change-in-control contracts mean what their name implies; they insure individuals against loss of income and job equity in the event that their company is sold or merged. McColl had outlawed such self-protection devices at NationsBank. Yet at BankAmerica they were in place and they became part of the cost of doing the deal. According to the proxy statement to shareholders, the merger would not be considered a "change of control" for NationsBank, but would be considered such for BankAmerica.

David Coulter's change-in-control contract would now be renegotiated as a "retention agreement," to provide protection should he part company with the merged bank. The *San Francisco Chronicle* (October 21, 1998) dug into the proxy statement to distill for its readers the details of Coulter's new contract, which the newspaper called "one of the most generous golden parachute packages in American business history—severance pay, stocks and benefits worth as much as $100 million." McColl would not consider a contract for himself. He did his best aerial work without a net.

Everywhere he looked, McColl could find opinions regarding his relationship with the executives of BankAmerica. Most of these opinions were from "financial analysts," who talked more like psychoanalysts when they conferred over telephone lines to the media. One of the notable quotes in the pile of clippings Dick Stilley circulated came from Gerald C. Myers, former CEO of American Motors, who told the *Washington Post:* "These 800-pound gorillas (NationsBank) don't allow anyone else in their territory. A day will come when they'll have a major conflict, and then they'll find out who the boss really is."

One potential source of conflict lay in the perception that BankAmerica leadership was all wrapped up in numbers. They were like generals trying to marshal their troops with the data: miles traveled, rounds fired, enemy positions sighted. McColl had a simpler way to get his troops' hearts pounding and their feet stomping. *"There is only one number you really need to understand. And that is number one. If you can remember ONE you go to the head of the class."* Simple, declarative and eminently quotable.

Coulter wasn't that sort of a speaker. In fact, he eschewed the soapbox in favor of company-wide videotaped messages or site-targeted electronic voice mail recordings. The *Washington Post* contrasted Coulter's understated leadership style with that of McColl, "arguably the most powerful man in North Carolina . . . self-appointed leader of the revolution that has transformed banks into full-service financial institutions." McColl believed the bank—the combined bank—needed someone who could create a little public attitude adjustment out in California, because out west the merger was being raked over a slow-burning charcoal fire by the media.

The *San Francisco Chronicle,* in its news articles, columns, editorials and letters to the editor, bewailed the selling out of its trademark financial institution, the one-time largest bank in the world. The county supervisor was "stunned and disappointed." The city archivist lamented that "part of our unique San Francisco is going down the drain." A columnist sneered that while San Francisco was "home of the 49ers, *haute cuisine* and culture," podunk Charlotte could claim only "the Panthers expansion team, stock car racing and pork slathered in barbecue sauce." The merger was "so frightening on so many levels that it's hard to grasp." No blow was too low. "What a concept: pickled pigs' feet—the San Francisco treat," commented one commentator.

McColl held his tongue, at least in public. Reporters seeking a response to the bilious West Coast upchuckery were turned away. Flying to Atlanta, McColl looked through the day's newspapers and was happy not to find any more anti-big bank articles. He remembered the red "Six November Bravo" stenciled on the tail of the Gulfstream. Vick Phillips might have to change the aircraft registration and perhaps even the lettering, once they added BankAmerica's three-plane fleet to their seven and agreed on a new name. He felt bad about the possible name change, because it was a concession he really hadn't been required to make. Uncharacteristic of him, leaving something on the table like that.

"Fine, use BankAmerica's name," Lewis had said. But McColl couldn't help thinking how that might hurt a few of the eighty thousand people in his retail bank who'd been fighting under that other flag. Of course, nearly all his NationsBank troops had fallen in at one time under a different name: American Commercial, NCNB, C&S, Sovran, Maryland National, First Republic, Barnett, Boatmen's—the company was like a family tree where all the offspring were daughters and the surname changed on every branch. And yet, part of his company's mystique derived from having made "NationsBank" stand for something special in the big vanilla vat of American banking. None of that would matter, as McColl always put it, "at the end of the day." Ken Lewis believed—and McColl suspected he was right—that NationsBank could lead its one hundred thousand people under any flag. "Whatever our name ends up being," he told his managers, "we will all like it. It's the people in the other banks who won't like it."

Underlying McColl's concern over naming his company "BankAmerica" or "Bank of America" was his reluctance to continue rattling the chains of A. P. Giannini's ghost. McColl's appreciation of Giannini grew with each chapter he read from the biography given him by Susan Coulter. Yet McColl had become convinced that the founder's current favor at BankAmerica was due almost exclusively to the company's need to find some maypole around which to dance. Now some of the San Francisco media were trumpeting the merger as the "fulfillment of A. P. Giannini's dream." That truly galled McColl. The mere mention of "Giannini's dream" got him angrier than the sight of a roadrunner sucking up quail eggs. "This will not be the bank that attains Giannini's dream," he'd say, putting a sharp edge on his voice. "It is *our* dream that has made it all happen. There is no nice way to say it: Mr. Giannini is dead. He doesn't have a damn thing to do with this merger."

McColl suggested that Ken Lewis begin venting the veneration of history that hung heavy as lead incense in the San Francisco halls of

BankAmerica. The PR people should sell the idea that the new, merged bank would not be "a company of yesterday." In his bank, "the only people who can make it" would be people who cared not about yesterday but about tomorrow. "The challenges are too great to be sitting around being satisfied with where one was," McColl said. "Where one *was* has nothing to do with where one must now *be* and what one must *become*."

One opportunity, McColl believed, was to become the most diversity-conscious bank in the world. For the first time in McColl's merger history, the acquired bank seemed to have made greater strides in social diversity than had NationsBank. He had looked out over assemblies of officers from First Republic, C&S, Boatmen's and Barnett and realized those mergers meant taking two steps backward in equal opportunity for the sake of forward progress in corporate growth. But at BankAmerica's Los Angeles office he had encountered "the most diverse workplace I've ever seen anywhere on the face of the earth." Ken Lewis told him about his tour of the BankAmerica call center in San Francisco. After a visit to what Lewis called "the normal section," where telephone operators spoke English, he had been shown around other hubs at which customers could communicate in Mandarin, Cantonese, Vietnamese and Spanish.

"Now *that* is diversity." McColl told Lewis. The following January, when the road show made its first stop on the West Coast, McColl would look out at last on an auditorium of faces that showed the true colors of the United States. There might be five or six aging white men on the stage, but they would be talking to an honest representation of the future. The men and women of BankAmerica gave him a new, heterogeneous gene pool from which to draw his leaders of the twenty-first century.

"When we come together in October, we are going to be America's bank and we must reflect America," he had told one reporter. "We will make it that way across our company, and the way we will do that is by opportunity, opportunity, opportunity, opportunity. That's what we are going to do. And we are committed to that as a team."

He intended to begin with his new board of directors, creating "the most diverse board in the United States." That was the first part of his mission in Atlanta this warm May day, to begin a relationship with one of the BankAmerica directors who would be offered a position on the new board, Walter Massey, the African-American president of Morehouse College. Visiting campuses had taken on a new importance for him since his election as chairman of the board of trustees of the expanding Queens College, home now to the McColl School of Business.

Because he had twenty minutes before his appointment at Morehouse, McColl asked his driver to take him to the NationsBank branch located in the predominately black neighborhood around the college. It was a one-story, squat building with a drive-through window and an ATM. McColl strode in, a short white man in a business suit. Careful not to disturb the customers, he stepped up to a teller's position, read her nameplate, and addressed her personally.

"Sandra, Hugh McColl. How y'all doin' today?"

"Mister Muh-caw-ull!"

The branch manager rushed out to the lobby from her nearby office. "Mr. McColl! What a surprise." The manager's smile seemed as genuine as those of her tellers. The customers continued cashing their checks and making their deposits. What might have been mistaken as a round of small talk was actually McColl pumping the manager on her perceptions of the subtle shifts in clientele, the changing neighborhood, the need for more security at the ATM and a larger parking lot. It was his old "management by walking around," learning from the frontline troops. Mission accomplished, he told them to keep up the good work and he left the branch.

Just a few blocks further, the driver pulled into a roped-off VIP parking space near the main entrance to Morehouse. Upstairs, in an anteroom, Dr. Walter Massey greeted McColl warmly and led him into his private office. They discussed how Morehouse and the other black colleges in Atlanta had benefited from the building program of the 1996 Olympics—and Massey recognized the pivotal role McColl had played in that. McColl explained that it was "probably inappropriate" for the two to meet, since Massey had not yet been nominated for the new board by the BankAmerica nominating committee. "But I'm willing to take the risk that you will be," he said.

It was an easy first step by McColl. Massey was in Atlanta, to which McColl could refer as "my city," just as he could in nearly every city from Baltimore to Santa Fe. After this, the job would get harder, because the other new board members were located in locales less convenient to Charlotte, where he was largely unknown. On the West

Coast were former Nestle USA CEO Timm Crull, former PacTel CEO Donald Guinn and Stanford business dean Michael Spence. US West Communications Group CEO Solomon Trujillo was in Denver and General Motors VP Shirley Young in Shanghai. Economist Kathleen Feldstein lived in Boston. Then there would be Dave Coulter and Dick Rosenberg, completing the BankAmerica nine.

The ten members of the new board coming from the NationsBank side would not require personal visits; it would be the noninvited directors he'd have to face. Creating unanimity on this board would be one of the most important and potentially explosive tasks of McColl's career. The new company could not achieve greatness unless he could lead it out of the past and into the future, and nobody knew better than he did that the future keeps its own counsel.

After his Morehouse meeting, McColl stopped off at NationsBank Atlanta headquarters—former C&S headquarters. Someone was parked in the space reserved in perpetuity for the CEO, so he told the driver to park in Jim Dixon's space. There was a secret code for pressing the elevator buttons so that one could disembark on the executive floor, but McColl could never remember the sequence. He had to get off at the floor below and take the stairs up.

The bank executive offices still looked like a private club, a yacht club, judging by the nautical prints, etchings, oils and bronzes that were a legacy of Bennett Brown's maritime mania. After a conversation about how Hootie Johnson had just been voted in as chairman of the Augusta National Golf Club, McColl ducked into his office to change into comfortable jeans, T-shirt and boots, to spend the afternoon with his grandkids.

Wearing nothing but his boxer shorts, McColl folded up his suit pants onto a hanger. His physique was more trim and athletic than it had been in the sixties and seventies, when he was a hard-drinking, diet-unconscious young executive. Looking out a broad expanse of window glass, he acknowledged the irony of his standing there, just a fig leaf short of naked, overlooking the freeways of Atlanta.

"You could argue that I'm not really suited to the job I have," he smiled. "You could argue that I'm not suited to be chairman of a $570 billion company. And my wife is not good at her job, either. You could argue that we are not good at pomp and circumstance, that we don't care about it. In fact, don't care about it to a fault." He slipped into his jeans, not the twenty-year-old pair, but almost as comfortable, a little worn around the pocket seams where his thumbs dangled over. "But I will tell you that I don't think I've done a lot different from what I did as a kid on the playground. In other words, I was always in charge of putting the teams together. You know I think leadership is a function of standing up and saying: this is what we are going to do. If you can articulate for people why it is we need to do this, and here is what we are going to do, they tend to follow you."

His shirt was a white knit with a NationsBank logo, soon to be a collector's item. He pulled it down over his head, then tousled his hair back into place, commenting on the fact that when he bought this Atlanta building and the bank that owned it in 1991, the people who worked here understood they needed a hero. Their company was in trouble and could go out of business unless the business could be sold. That had been the same in Texas. As for the St. Louis and Jacksonville banks, the invitation to buy had been extended by the directors of those companies. In 1998, it was a different story. Most of the people who worked for BankAmerica assumed their civilized West Coast bank was doing just fine and required no help, thank you, from Hugh McColl, San Francisco's idea of a cross between Genghis Khan and Attila the Hun with a Carolina drawl.

McColl simply couldn't understand why he was so misunderstood. "I think my father gave me a strong business code," he mused, "a your-word-is-your-bond sort of business code that makes it impossible to take advantage of people who are weaker. People who have had unpleasant experiences with me would say that I am a vicious sort of enemy, you know, that I fight very, very hard for whatever. And that would be true. But I have never fought unfairly; I've always behaved properly. You could say that I forced somebody to sell to me who maybe wished he didn't have to. That's possible. No, not 'possible,' that is true.

"People who don't like me in business don't like me because we—the company and me as an individual—are perceived as being arrogant. When we announce we are going to do something, we do it. That annoys the living hell out of everybody, because we have been successful at it. And we are then not modest about having done it. We are guilty of all of those sins: pointing at the fence, hitting it over the fence and then being gleeful as we round the bases."

McColl's point was clear as a crystal hand grenade. Babe Ruth could do that in baseball and be revered as a hero. When Hugh

McColl did the same thing in business, at least in the business of banking, he was perceived as villainous. Of course, maybe the pitchers on the teams that played against the Bambino hadn't been such admirers of his heroic gestures.

"People like structure, and structure means staying in your place, doesn't it? And we refuse to stay in our place. We not only do not stay in our place, we do things that are dramatic and we sort of shove it to you, as a side deal, just to be sure you didn't miss it. Ha!"

From his briefcase he extracted a video camera the size of a pound-of-coffee bag that wasn't really a whole pound. "Remember, we took over everybody's company and we made no secret of taking over those companies. I mean, if you said what is your worse trait, *being* arrogant or *appearing* arrogant? I don't know. They have the same effect."

He had picked up the camera on Forty-second Street in New York to carry on a trip of Eastern Europe he and Jane would be making in a few weeks: Vienna, Budapest, Prague. Today he wanted to try it out by taking some shots of his grandchildren, John, Duncan and Virginia. He turned it over in his hand as though it might have instructions engraved on it somewhere, perhaps in Japanese Braille. "This is sort of an idiot-camera, but I can be a sort of idiot-person," he admitted.

Don Lee, the driver, was a former Atlanta police detective who felt comfortable with the *capo di tutti capi* riding shotgun. McColl talked about the different guns he was packing up to take down to his place in Texas, where his son John was building him a fine new camp—no more roughing it on quail hunting trips—where he'd have a big old bank safe in which to lock his rifles, shotguns and ammo. Don Lee noted that all the guns McColl listed fired single rounds. Correct, said the boss, not automatic weapons. He felt automatic weapons were of absolutely no value to hunters and that the National Rifle Association was way off base in defending their use by anyone except law enforcement officers and the military. Lee grunted agreement: automatic weapons were mostly used to fire at policemen, in his opinion.

That led them to a conversation about bank robberies, high on the list of McColl's existential banes. Did Don remember that one in D.C. last year? "The son of a bitch came in shooting and our guard took him out." McColl was angry at himself for not recalling the guard's name. "I wanted to give him a crystal hand grenade for that, but my

PR people wouldn't let me." Lee shook his large fedoraed head in sad comprehension. "I was proud of the guy," said McColl. "I don't want people coming into my banks shooting at my customers."

After some winding detours through tree-cluttered neighborhoods, Don Lee located the country club where McColl was to meet his daughter-in-law Lee and her three children. He pulled the gray sedan into the parking lot just as John Junior, Virginia and Duncan were tumbling out of the family four-wheel in their swimsuits. McColl hugged them all, then opened a crumpled brown paper bag he was carrying and extracted "gifts" for the children. They were baseball caps, shirts and key chains, all bearing the NationsBank logo. The kids didn't know they were last-minute pickups on his way out of the building in Charlotte. All they cared about was that Granddad had brought them presents.

At poolside, McColl took what he hoped would turn out to be video pictures of John and Duncan and their swimming lessons, then he sat down in the shade with three-year-old Virginia on his knee. There were any number of important subjects to be covered, mostly dealing with Virginia's experiences in kindergarten, at Sunday school and as the lone female sibling. Don Lee stood off to one side in the shadow of his hat brim, arms crossed, policeman's shoes spread apart for balance, banker's suit as out-of-place as an Eskimo parka in the afternoon Atlanta sun. He was there in service of the CEO, who was there to be a grandfather to kids who were there to learn how to survive in pools of chlorine before they had to swim with the sharks. When the lessons were done, it was off to Frankie Allen Park, where little John's softball team, the Thunder, was due to go up against the Lookouts.

On the way to the ballpark, McColl reminisced about his high school summers, when he and his brothers played in the Border Belt League, mostly on teams from the mills along the border of the two Carolinas. He played for a mill in Lancaster, South Carolina, then another in Anderson. "Had a cousin, Dick Swetenburg, who was a good first baseman and a good pitcher. I used to catch Dick. I was a good hitter, could usually get the ball into the outfield. As I fielder, I could cover a lot of ground, but just couldn't throw. They tried me at several positions. Played second base some, but my brothers were better at baseball than I was."

He knew his grandson, John, was a big fan of the Atlanta Braves.

McColl had been working behind the scenes to bring major-league ball to Charlotte, but so far had been unsuccessful. He thought Charlotte might be ready for baseball, but he had his doubts. There was talk of the Minnesota Twins moving there, but he had his doubts about that, too. At Frankie Allen Park, McColl's son John joined the rest of the family. They talked about John's Atlanta business, about the plans for the camp in Texas, about the merger. Then little John came up to bat and they became prototypical Little League father and grandfather.

"Keep your eye on the ball, son. Just get the wood on it. No need to hit it out of the park."

"Choke up on that bat, John."

"Good swing."

"Choke up on that bat," little John's grandfather repeated. "Boy's got a good stance. Just needs a little practice."

After four innings, John had one hit, one put-out, one assist and two errors. His grandfather had one hot dog, one soda pop and one case of heartburn working. The score was Lookouts 9, Thunder 4. It was time to head back to Charlotte, where McColl had an obligatory evening social function on his calendar. Behind the bleachers, he gave each of the kids a hug. He got one back from Virginia that left something sticky and sweet-smelling in his five-o'clock shadow. To little John he said, "You keep choking up on that bat now. I'm going to buy us one of those pitching machines."

Flying back to Charlotte aboard the G4, McColl was thinking about how he enjoyed being more trouble to other bankers than they could possibly be to him. He still remembered the irritation from the early days: *"Well, that's a house account at Wachovia, so you don't want to call on them."* He wondered if there were other American businesses in which it was considered bad form to go after a competitor's customers. *"Oh, I'm sorry, ma'am. Since you're a Sears customer we'd prefer that you didn't shop here at Wal-Mart."*

One of his earliest media mistakes was the time he said he'd rather go to dinner with a Soviet bureaucrat than with a banker from Wachovia. Arrogant, certainly, but honest. After all, there might be something he could learn from the Russian. He wasn't interested in making friends with his competitors, because he enjoyed having enemies he could beat. He believed that attitude had paid off in spades for the bank, making it externally focused and therefore free of the infighting that can sap a corporation's strength. "All of our hostile energy is focused toward our competitors," he said, "which is where it ought to be."

This was the attitude he hoped to instill in his new associates at BankAmerica. From one merger to another, it had taken some of McColl's newly grafted teammates a bit of time to accept that they were accepted, but more often than not, they came around. One of McColl's favorite lines was that there were only about a thousand people in his company who came out of the old NCNB, while there were close to ninety-nine thousand who came in from "somewhere else." So obviously, he would shrug, precluding debate, "we have done *something* right, 'cause we have a hundred thousand people who *chose* to work with us. People tend to focus on the few who don't like it and don't work for us, but you talk to most of the hundred thousand and they like it. They like the attitude. They like the straightforwardness of it. They like the trust everybody gets."

Shortly after the trip to Atlanta, McColl was off to the British Isles and then to Europe, his annual meetings with European investors, followed by the International Monetary Conference in Vienna, where he would be joined by Jane and, this year, by Dave and Susan Coulter. The conference was scheduled from May 31 to June 3, after which the McColls planned to spend two weeks in Prague and Budapest, places they had read about but never seen.

McColl reached Vienna feeling good about taking a vacation. He and Hance had made a strong impression on their European investors. In Glasgow, in Edinburgh and in London, they had people who understood history and understood maps. They talked about the inexorable rise to prominence of the Carolinas, that part of the colonies settled by the Scots and the English; about the alliance with one of the United States' bastions of banking across the continent; about the claiming of vast territories under one flag. The investors were delighted by what they heard, and their response was a welcome change from the doubts and cynicism that echoed yet in the hollow canyons of Wall Street and Market Street. McColl was looking forward to the conference and to touring Eastern Europe. First, he had to make it through some unexpected sessions with David Coulter in Vienna.

Details of the Coulter-McColl meetings in Vienna are sketchy, because neither principal will speak openly about what was said. If we are to believe any of what was later published, one issue had to do with Gene Taylor, NationsBank's former president of the Florida bank, moving to San Francisco to take charge of the Western Region.

The San Francisco media had assumed that BankAmerica would have a great deal to say about which executives would head those parts of the bank that would have the most contact with the American public. Yet, as appointments were announced, it seemed that in virtually every key area of customer relations, Coulter's people would be reporting to McColl's people. Consumer and Commercial Banking, the "retail bank," would be run by Ken Lewis and would be divided into three regions: East, West and Southwest-Midwest. Each one of those regions would be headed by a former NationsBank executive, and only seven of the twenty-six positions in the upper echelon of the three regions would be going to BankAmerica people.

According to unattributed newspaper accounts published after the fact, umbrage was taken over what the press called the "unilateral decision" to move Gene Taylor to San Francisco. Coulter was depicted in the newspapers as having been bitterly disappointed at his failure to change McColl's mind about putting Taylor in charge of the San Francisco office when, the press maintained, there were more qualified candidates already in San Francisco. Reading these unattributed newspaper reports, McColl blistered. He said he had instructed Ken Lewis not once but three times to make sure the BankAmerica team was satisfied with the Taylor appointment. Only after Lewis reported three times that there were no objections did McColl make the appointment official.

Perhaps the Taylor appointment was one of the items discussed by the CEO and the president of the soon-to-be-largest bank in the United States when they met privately in Vienna, Austria.

If the Vienna meetings succeeded in uniting the two men, that was not apparent from later reports in newspapers on both coasts. While the apparent disagreement was mentioned in a number of publications, it was given the greatest attention by the *San Francisco Chronicle,* followed close behind by the *Charlotte Observer.*

Neither the disagreement in Vienna nor the events that followed would be revealed until several months had passed. The story broke in the *Chronicle* November 10. Those who went public with the tale were identified by the media as anonymous "informed sources."

According to the newspaper accounts, McColl and Coulter had

"clashed" or "had a run-in" in Vienna. Reported the *Chronicle*, "People close to BofA said that they didn't know the details of what McColl said in Vienna, but that he apparently treated Coulter as a subordinate rather than an equal." A "lawyer who knows Coulter" was quoted as saying, "McColl said things privately and publicly in Vienna that shocked Dave, and they had a major falling out. He came back wanting to break the deal and consulted various people." According to a "senior person," everyone at BankAmerica felt "under siege," and, rather than the imagined merger of equals, Coulter believed his associates would suffer "death by a thousand cuts—that his people weren't going to survive very well." The *Observer* obtained an internal memo circulated at BankAmerica that suggested that the company had hired an outside consultant to "help managers cope with their feelings about the merger." The senior managers were so low, according to this memo, that "there was worry their dark mood would spread." The press reported an acute attack of "seller's remorse" at BankAmerica. Finally, members of the old BankAmerica board were depicted as looking for a way to back out of the sale.

Whatever the content of their Vienna meetings may have been, McColl left Austria ready to sightsee and shop with Jane. However, instead of traveling from Prague to Budapest as planned, McColl was aboard the G4, headed back to the United States, on Sunday, the seventh of June. The aircraft touched down long enough to drop off Jane, her luggage and her disappointment, then continued on to San Francisco where the CEO attended more than one meeting, seeking to reassure Coulter and members of the BankAmerica board.

As the summer wore on, McColl wanted to believe the troubles were behind him. The concerned executives and directors finally seemed to be at ease with the Memorandum of Understanding, which gave him ultimate authority and made Coulter one of five senior executives reporting to him. As he had said more than once in the past. "You can't have but one philosophy at the end of the day. There is not room for two philosophies, ever."

Yet, even with a single philosophy, there were distinct thought patterns that sometimes clashed. The problem can be illustrated by the decision regarding what the name of the new company would be. At the recommendation of his consultants, McColl was convinced that the most profitable brand name would be "Bank of America." Not NationsBank of America, not BankAmerica or BofA, but "Bank of

America," which was the flag Giannini had picked up in 1920s Los Angeles. As McColl explained it, the studies had determined that "*Bank of America* is powerful and *BankAmerica* is like a finance company. It is not powerful. It loses something. The 'of' does bring something to the party. So we will have a new look, a new logo, a new color scheme. The whole thing."

Coulter was pleased with the recommendation, but wanted to take the matter "under consideration." Instead, a vote was taken. By unanimous consent of the Policy Committee, the new company would be called Bank of America. Next up at the same meeting was the matter of a logo. The marketing group had a distinctive emblem and McColl liked it. Coulter wanted to think about it, insisting they should show the logo around to the company, to their consultants and friends. This was something they and their successors would have to live with for years. "No, we are not going to sleep on it," said McColl. "If we decide to change the name of the company, we sure as hell can decide on a logo." Another vote taken, another case closed.

The company McColl had built would go on under a different name, as it had done before. There might be different ways of doing business, but: "We have been doing it our way for forty damn years, and it ain't goin' to change." McColl made no bones about his policy. "It is very simple," he said. "First, facts are king. Second, we always say what we think. That's a rule internally. You'd best say what you think, because if you don't it doesn't matter what you think. And if you say something that you don't think, and then go and try and act in a different way, people will take you out. In other words, you have to believe what you say and say what you believe. And then, third, once a decision is arrived at, it is expected that everybody will come to the party. If you say you will do it, then you will do it. Period. Not do it halfheartedly. Not passively resist. We make a decision, and then we are in lockstep. And there is no room for somebody to not do that. You are not allowed to lose a decision, let's say five to one, and then continue to be a 'clubhouse lawyer.'"

The debate was over, but McColl sensed that issues remained unsettled in the minds of some at BankAmerica, and that disturbed him. He recognized that he and Coulter were "quite different people. I'm sure I frustrate him, and he for sure frustrates me."

Perhaps even more agonizing to McColl was the continuing refusal of the news media to look at what he believed to be the "big picture" of this merger. The press occasionally got into a dueling banshees' wail about whether the big losers would be consumers—who *obviously* could expect paying higher fees for fewer services—or the employees—who *obviously* could expect to be pink-slipped by the thousands. But hardly anyone bothered to write about the joint NationsBank-BankAmerica announcement that, immediately following the merger, the nation's largest bank would pledge a total of $350 billion to low income lending and to projects in poor urban and rural communities, a commitment to be met within ten years.

It may have simply been the high-decibel level of cynicism blaring at the moment, due principally to President Bill Clinton's unprincipled display of lying to hide his extramarital sex in the White House. Had he been less distracted, Clinton could have seized the opportunity to trumpet the good news of private industry acting in the public interest, much the way he and Hugh McColl had planned it back in 1993, standing in the White House Rose Garden to proclaim the government's Community Development commitment of $382 million. This time, just five years later, the banks had to take out full-page newspaper ads to tell the story of the largest private commitment to neighborhood reinvestment ever imagined.

The $350 billion CRA pool was another idea born in the brain of Cathy Bessant, hatchery of the 1991 $10 billion-over-ten-years commitment that came out of the C&S/Sovran buyout. Bessant summoned together a group of community-focused bankers from NationsBank and BankAmerica and personally typed their ideas into her laptop computer. "It was a small group of people from both banks who wrote it," she said. "We proposed it to Hugh and to Ken, and they bought it." It would be, she acknowledged, "a huge challenge" and a "really exciting one, because we stuck a lot of things in that commitment that are programmatically innovative. We've got a rural initiative, a Native American or 'Indian Country' initiative, an economic development initiative. Some things that are really going to push us. So this one is about more than the number. The number was shocking to many people, though, including us."

McColl liked the statement that number made. There was nothing halfhearted about $350 billion. It would become *the* standard for community development across the country, maybe even around the world. It would take a team of more than six hundred just to oversee the program, with a commitment from management and line-level associates that no one else could touch. McColl lived by the maxim attributed to Texas financier Clint W. Murchison, that money is a lot like manure. One could do considerable good by spreading it around, but could achieve nothing more than a mighty stink by piling it up in one place. From this day forward, any corporation's commitment to its community would be judged against this commitment, he believed.

And others would follow. As McColl had instructed Cathy Bessant, "the goal is to lead, but not to be alone." The $10 billion pledge, met within four years of the NCNB-C&S/Sovran merger, had over-achieved on this score. Following BankAmerica's acquisition of Seattle First in 1991, Dick Rosenberg had upped the CRA ante to $12 billion. That underscored the irony in 1998, when the two most community-committed banks in the nation found themselves challenged by activist groups who claimed that their merger would be harmful to minority borrowers and minority-owned businesses.

July 9 and 10, Cathy Bessant seethed in the hearing room of the Federal Reserve Bank of San Francisco as, one by one, the charges of unfair lending practices piled up. African Americans, Hispanics, Vietnamese, Mexican Americans, Filipino Americans, Native Americans, disabled Americans—each minority group fielded its complainants. And if the Federal Reserve believed there was a pattern of discrimination, the Fed had the power to block the most impor-tant deal in Hugh McColl's career, and maybe write an unhappy end-ing to Bessant's career as well.

Then she heard a familiar name called out, that of Bruce Marks, the New England activist who had taken on Fleet and then First Union, organizing "Stop the Loan Sharks" pickets in 1995. NationsBank actually had adopted a number of Marks's suggestions on using the banks' influence to develop run-down inner cities. In San Francisco, Marks had with him a contingent of low-income men and women who told how NationsBank had taught them how to become homeowners. Bessant listened in amazement as "each one said, 'I never knew home ownership was a possibility and this bank and this community group came together and made me realize that I could achieve it and now I have.' It was hugely powerful stuff. I sat and I cried. I pride myself on not being a wimpy banker, but I sat and cried in the audience when I heard these stories."

More than sixteen hundred organizations and individuals had

submitted comments pro and con. The issue never really was in doubt, because the Federal Reserve Board played by the numbers, and the numbers were very much in favor of Bessant, McColl and the merger. Less than a month after the hearing, on August 16, the Fed voted six-nothing to give final regulatory approval to the formation of the largest bank in the United States and the third largest in the world. Only in three New Mexico markets—Albuquerque, Clovis and McKinley County—were overlaps of the two banks sufficient to merit the sale of branches. Seventeen BankAmerica branches in New Mexico would have to be sold, none in Texas.

Under happier circumstances, the Fed vote would have repercussed in the popping of corks in Charlotte. But this was August 1998 and the world's knock-kneed economy was rattling the teeth of banking's tigers. Suddenly, the Russian economy became Chernobyl, joining those of its Asian neighbors in meltdown mode. Television news footage showed Muscovites waiting in line to barter their clothing and jewelry for bread. Not a few United States banks had converted dollars to rubles, placing heavy bets on President Boris Yeltsin's conversion of communism to capitalism. On Wall Street, analysts were making educated guesses that American banks had something north of a billion dollars at risk in Russia, though no one could be sure which banks had lost how much in what markets.

In the last week of August, BankAmerica issued a news release, announcing it would write off $220 million in the current quarter, "primarily to cover securities and currency trading losses in Russia." Within the next three weeks, those loss estimates, including some from "other emerging markets" had risen by 50 percent to about $330 million. As the *Chronicle* reported, "BofA's trading losses since Russia's financial meltdown are the largest recorded by a U.S. bank."

McColl had no delusions about the global financial market's stability. Yet, ever since his staving off disaster in 1974 by paying ten cents on the dollar for shares of the Israel-British bank, he had trusted himself always to make the best of a bad situation. As word of the BankAmerica losses spread, financial analysts predicted McColl's position of control would be strengthened and Coulter's future with the company could be in doubt. The *Chronicle* blamed Coulter, now "in charge of risk management for the combined bank," for failure to control its high-risk exposure. "No one stands to lose more from the losses than David Coulter, the once-lionized chief executive of the old BofA," the newspaper predicted. "Apparently the old BankAmerica lacked proper risk controls," said Thomas Theurkauf, an analyst with the New York brokerage firm of Keefe, Bruyette & Woods. "There will be pressure applied to some of the old BofA managers."

At this point, McColl's assumption was that the Russian losses represented the worst of what the media considered to be BankAmerica's poor decision-making. But there was also the matter of an unsecured loan by the bank to D. E. Shaw Company, a computer-driven hedge fund, in the amount of $1.4 billion.

In gambling, investing and other speculative enterprises, the tactic of "hedging a bet" can be traced back at least as far as the mid-seventeenth century. It refers to building a barrier or "hedge" against the loss of one's total investment by making a transaction on the "other side" of the risk. One might lose on one side of the hedge, but win back at least a portion of the loss on the other side. Even better, by jumping quickly from one side of the hedge (where prices are up) to the other side (where prices are down), one may earn a few pennies on one's transactions.

Financial market hedgers buy futures contracts and options on futures; they sell interest-rate contracts for future delivery; they deal in exotica such as arbitrage and derivative mortgage-backed securities. When a vast pool of capital is amassed from a number of different sources to make investments like these, it is called a hedge *fund*.

Hedge funds typically use the otherwise idle money of very wealthy individuals and institutions, many of whom do not trust their own instincts or have sufficiently immediate and accurate information on the traditional stock and bond markets. Several large and highly respected universities have great chunks of their endowments in hedge funds. Because the sophisticated hedge fund managers use arcane, computer-compiled "models" of future interest rates, foreign currency values and commodity prices, they provide much the same aura of authenticated security that soothsayers and necromancers once peddled. There is an element of fear, a scent of greed and an air of black magic about it all, considering that "to hedge" may also mean "to prevaricate."

Investment opportunities in hedge funds are by invitation only, so their activities are scantily publicized. The government's regulatory agencies don't pay a great deal of attention, trusting billionaires not to do anything wild and crazy with their money. There is, however, a regulation preventing hedge funds from advertising, which only adds to their aura of gothic mystery. The typical hedge fund is a limited partnership, with the limited partners supplying the capital, the general partners supplying tactical genius and operational savvy. For this the general partner is entitled to 20 percent of the net profits it earns with the limited partners' capital.

Like a sheet of flypaper, the bigger a hedge fund gets, the more profit will stick to it. So hedge fund managers like to partner-up with bankers, who have more money to play with than almost anybody. With a banker on your team, you might take a few hundred million dollars from your endowment and trust fund partners and borrow against that—leverage your fund up—until you have a few *billion* to play with. For David Shaw, a one-time computer science teacher at Columbia University, the perfect banker partner would be one who shared his fascination with computers, one who understood the potential of the Internet, with its speed-of-light connectability, to switch from one side of a hedge to another in the blink of an eye. In late 1996, D. E. Shaw Company, which *Fortune* then considered "the most intriguing and mysterious force on Wall Street today," found BankAmerica.

In March 1997, BankAmerica and Shaw announced a "strategic alliance," which would provide Shaw with "long-term financing, credit enhancement for certain client transactions" and access to the bank's "receptive global customer base." In making the announcement, neither side would provide details of the financing aspect. *Investment Dealers' Digest* reported that "both sides were tightlipped," but noted that Shaw "has been expanding rapidly in the venture capital arena, which requires a steady cash flow."

Shaw's strategy had been to trade on the slight variations from one securities market to another, buying where the price was a few cents lower, selling where it was a few cents—or even fractions of cents—higher, using Internet communications to turn a virtually instant profit. But, by the middle of 1998, stock, bond and foreign currency markets were collapsing simultaneously and willy-nilly. There was no safe side of the hedge.

On Tuesday, September 15, less than three weeks after its first announcement of the $220 million in Russian losses, BankAmerica issued another news release, acknowledging that there might be additional third-quarter losses from "interest from equity investments" and a loss of $12 million "from buying and holding securities."

Thursday, September 17, McColl needed a break from the merger and its continuing headaches. With two traveling companions whose only connection to the bank was their mortgage, toting his favorite guns and all the quail-hunting art he'd bagged in ten years of gallery tracking, he loaded up one of the NationsBank Hawkers and took off for the new camp his son John had built in the Wild Horse Desert. There was one week to go until the shareholder meetings. Jane was preoccupied with little Jane, who would be having her second baby any day now, and said she'd be glad to have him out of the house. It was a good time to give himself a long weekend.

The South Texas coastal plain had just come out from under weeks of rainclouds. From the air, the desert was greener than McColl had ever seen it, and the view from his new all-terrain vehicle was spectacular with wildflowers. At Corpus Christi airport, the safari was met by Don Strubhart, the builder and now manager of McColl's camp, *Cielo de Cazadores de Cordoniz*, which translates to "Quail Hunter's Heaven."

After checking in at the Kenedy Ranch gate, Strubhart drove over a road that was distinguishable from the rest of the ground only because it was lined by goatweed and free of mesquite trees, through two cattle gates and onto the fenced-in camp property. Quail Hunter's Heaven consisted of roughly three acres, with the new house stretching impressively across the grounds. Don Strubhart had assembled the hunting lodge lovingly, painstaking as a man building a ship in a bottle. Each cedar plank, the same color as the earth, had been fit in place by hand.

The design of the house was bi-aliform, like two hands joined at the wrists, open to receive whatever blessings might come their way. Front-and-center, wooden stairs led up to a breezeway that took the visitor past the common area to the left, sleeping wing to the right, onto a porch. At the rear, the house embraced an ancient, gnarled mesquite that long ago had split into a pair of trunks, grown their separate ways, like a compass laying down the angle of house wings for a human architect to someday discover. There was an extraordinary fit of structure to nature, neither interfering with nor unfriendly toward the other.

Although McColl was a hunter, he was committed to killing only what would be eaten. The only "trophy" in the house was his old longhorns, Georgetown Steel's thanks-for-the-rescue gift that he'd mounted on the NCNB podium the night before he sent his troops to Texas in 1988. The horns hung high on a beam in the great room, though he was thinking about moving them over the door to the gun room. There were some expensive lamps with bases that featured former quail, but his son John had bought those in Corpus Christi. McColl was not a personal supporter of taxidermy, preferring to bankroll artists who specialized in paintings of quail and of men hunting quail and of retrievers with fallen quail cradled gently between their jaws, no matter that one picture looked very much like another. (While there are several different species of quail, with interestingly varied markings, all men who hunt quail appear to be middle-aged, white and clad in red-orange hunting vests. Only careful scrutiny can distinguish among them.) McColl planned to decorate his lodge with quail art. He and his traveling companions would study which paintings should go together and which groups should hang in which rooms. That was his only "purpose" for this trip, since quail hunting season was still six weeks off.

Of course, his hope was to get away from the merger, but it was filling too many synapses of his brain for a great many thoughts to make it across without falling into a viperous merger pit. Even when Don Strubhart talked about the recent explosion of Mexicans coming across the border, McColl could turn the conversation to BankAmerica.

"Some of them came right into the yard the other night. The leader had a cellular phone." Strubhart was a large man, next to McColl. Except for a tour of duty in Vietnam, he had spent his entire life between Corpus Christi and Brownsville. He and his wife Dee would not live anywhere else. "The guy pulled out a roll of hundred-dollar bills," he went on. "Offered me six hundred bucks to drive them across the check-point."

McColl laughed. "There's no way in hell to stop those border crossers." On a more-or-less weekly basis, men, women and children waded the Rio Grande and wound up walking cattle trails across the Kenedy Ranch until they were safely past the Border Patrol's checkpoint, just two miles up Route 77 from *Cielo de Cazadores de Cordoniz*. He greatly admired these Mexicans for taking their lives into their own hands rather than settling for their dismal birthright. They simply wanted what he wanted for his people and his company: to survive and prosper. And that triggered what was really on his mind.

"You know, that's kind of my problem at the bank now," he said to Strubhart and his guests. "We've got six hundred companies at least that went into making up this bank. Most of the people who now work for me once worked for companies that did not survive and prosper. They did just the opposite, they were absorbed by this great machine that comes along. This Pacman that just comes along and eats you."

And what was eating Hugh McColl now was this: people who worked for large corporations were used to hearing their CEOs promise that theirs would be the company that would survive and prosper, a promise that sometimes failed the test of time. As he put it, "Really, I am trying to sell them something that the other guys didn't deliver to them."

He didn't want to be like all those quail hunters in all those paintings, just another guy with a gun. To the employees of a potential merger partner he might seem even worse, because he was always riding in from some distant horizon, a Hun or a Mongol or a Visigoth, rumors flying ahead of his horde: McColl takes no prisoners; McColl permits no deviation from his law; McColl will burn your icons and demand your conversion and carry away your firstborn. And when McColl arrived, the old, trusted leaders of the people took McColl's money, McColl took their company.

"That is the cold-bloodedness of the capitalistic system," he mused, "that I put enough money on the table where nothing else matters but the money to the sellers." After each merger, part of the challenge was to convince new members of the group that they were part of something stable and inviolable. "I have to make this merger work so that all of us, new teammates as well as old, survive and prosper, so that I have not failed on my promise. That would bother me to no end. I'd never get over it. So we will succeed, because I can't have it any other way."

His guests were quiet. Don Strubhart nodded and excused himself to go check on the corn feeder out beyond the fence. He was expecting the wild hogs in just a few minutes, because they were regulars in the late afternoon.

"You see, I've given everybody my word. 'You fight with me and I'll give you victory, and you will survive, and you will never have to worry about being merged again. You had this trauma happen in your life, but it won't happen again.' You see?"

But who could believe a businessman? Truth was too rare a commodity in this age. The nation was wringing its hands over its president's perverse rupture of the marriage vows, turning the Oval Office into a five-dollar motel room; but somehow the public expected Bill Clinton, once caught with his pants around his ankles, to then lie about it. The news media—their way made crooked by the baptism of advertising agencies—had convinced Americans that everybody lied to everybody else. Especially untruthful were politicians and big business leaders.

As for dissembling about one's company and its intentions, a corporate CEO was assumed by the press to be guilty until proven innocent. When Hugh McColl promised his new company would remain in Charlotte, local reporters asked the man-on-the-street how Charlotte would survive without NationsBank. When McColl promised $350 billion to improve the lot of America's underprivileged, he had to buy advertising space to tell people about it, and then, because it was paid advertising, the gesture acquired a second layer of assumed duplicity. When McColl said he would cut expenses by eliminating eight thousand positions through natural attrition, San Francisco columnists converted that to the perceived and oft-replicated "truth" that McColl's intention was to put eight thousand San Francisco men and women on public assistance.

In his treatise on heroes and hero worship, Thomas Carlyle wrote, "No sadder proof can be given by a man of his own littleness than disbelief in great men." That was in the nineteenth century. It had taken another hundred years for little men and women to so overwhelm the public imagination that even the possibility of greatness would be hooted down by disbelief.

"The hogs are here."

Don Strubhart pushed open the glass door and summoned the first visitors to Quail Hunters' Heaven out onto the back porch. Boars, sows and shoats, nearly a dozen animals pushed and grunted around the gunmetal feeder suspended from an oak branch out beyond the back fence. Each time a boar butted the feeder with its tusked head, a few kernels of corn would sprinkle to the ground.

"Good eating," McColl said. He was talking about the hoofstock, not the corn. "Once you taste it, you'd never want pork from the supermarket again." He raised a rifle to his eye and adjusted the scope, using it to get a closer look, then passing it to his guests. He could bag one of the hogs now, because it was always open season on them and coyotes, both indiscriminate breeders. But cleaning a hog was hard labor and McColl was here to rest. He'd let the cook Strubhart hired plan the meals without any help from him. Later that evening, wild turkeys and quail came to feed, and Santa Gertrudis cattle, big as red rhinos, to wallow in the pond Strubhart had dug for the animals, and deer to drink splay-legged at the pond's edge. Nothing got killed.

Next morning McColl went for a walk, rifle on his shoulder, marine-style, and he talked about the ranch. He said he could not own anything here, because the owners wouldn't sell and because nobody was sure who owned it, anyway. The land paid big dividends in terms of its cattle and its drilling rights, leased to Exxon, but the property ownership had been tied up in the courts for years, with descendants of the original ranchers claiming their lawful inheritance had been denied.

The ranch's story, as McColl told it, started right after the Civil War, the very time his great-grandfather was starting to rebuild Bennettsville. Two enterprising riverboat pilots named Mifflin Kenedy and Richard King, their fortunes made from hauling first U.S. ordnance, then Confederate cotton up the Rio Grande, bought vast tracts of coastal plains wasteland from the descendants of Spanish land-grantees for just pennies an acre. They saw the desert as an immense beef factory, with the added advantage of being space through which the railroad would have to be built. They cleared, fenced and built the million-acre King Ranch, then moved south to establish the four-hundred-thousand-acre La Parra Ranch, which eventually became known as Kenedy. Established side by side, the Kenedy and King Ranches were the two largest in Texas.

From what McColl had been able to glean, out of books and old library files, the Catholic Diocese of Corpus Christi had the strongest claim to the land on which his new six-hundred-thousand-dollar "camp" was built. As a sign of good grace, he had instructed Strubhart to make sure the Bishop got invited to the first party at *Cielo de Cazadores.* Not that he expected the invitation would buy him any indulgence beyond his six-year lease. To McColl, the land's value lay in the sanctuary it afforded the quail. He was somehow more content here without the delusory burden of "ownership." Like the condominium at Litchfield, no more permanent than the sand it was built on, his desert retreat was temporary. McColl enjoyed an element of uncertainty in his life. Perhaps that was why he refused to strap on a golden parachute before jumping into a merger.

"No one knows why the goatweed grows wherever we turn the soil," he said. "But it does. And the quail love the goatweed, so we try to turn a lot of soil. It drops its seeds and the quail eat the seeds."

An oversize pickup came along, horn blowing and arms waving out open windows. It was his "dog men," Danny Duff and Dudley Marschal, come to train a new hound in the art of flushing birds. Their truckbed was crowded with kennels, two stories high. Atop the kennels were two swivel chairs, like the fishing seats on deep-sea boats, where McColl and another hunter would perch, come November.

"How are the birds looking?" McColl asked.

Marschal, sun-dried as a sulfured apricot, squinted out the window, "Well, Mr. McColl, I b'lieve they're looking good. We're seeing a few more eggs than last year. But, you know, you never know."

As the dog men and their truck dusted away into the mesquite and tasajia cactus, McColl observed that just as young dogs could be taught to assist hunters, so could young birds learn to avoid those same hunters. As the season wore on, he maintained, it became more and more difficult to correctly predict the quails' angle of ascent.

"The bird who's lived through five or six covey rises has learned not to go up right away, and not to go up straight," he said. "I swear, by January, the smart ones are listening for you to fire off the second barrel before they go up." Having survived and prospered, the smart quail were unwilling to end up on a spit over a mesquite grill. "The way I see it," McColl said, "the dumbest birds get shot first."

That afternoon, the CEO of what was about to become America's largest bank haggled over the price of a blanket in the Mexican border town of Progreso, about sixty miles due south of his rough-hewn rental palace. It wasn't the money. After all, he had two high-priced pilots hanging around Corpus Christi, not to mention the Hawker and its hangar fees, all coming out of his own pocket. He haggled because the dignity of the vendor demanded it.

"*Quanta costa?*" he asked. When the attractive, hard-smiling young woman answered in passable English, "Twelve dollar," he responded by saying he would take two at ten dollars each. "Okeh, ten," she answered, pleased to turn a decent profit.

McColl figured he needed some bright colors to break up the unrelenting woodiness of the lodge John and Don had constructed. Having loaded up the Jimmy with rugs, blankets and a new cowboy hat, McColl found himself ordering lunch at Garcia's, Progreso's fanciest restaurant, located on the second floor above the Canada Curio-Gift Shop-Liquor Store-Farmacia, Best Prices In The Border. He ordered the luncheon *bisteca,* hoping it would be something better than the cobbler-reject skirt steak served up by Mexican restaurants in Charlotte. It turned out to be quite tender, as was the music played on Garcia's hammond organ over by the dance floor.

Out the window, one could see the tops of buildings in mostly stairless Progreso. Into the air above each building protruded dozens of metal rods, like the bones of dead cattle picked clean by vultures that would be back for more after their siesta. "You know why all these buildings have re-bars sticking up?" he asked. No one knew. "It's because of the way the laws are written. As long as your building is still under construction, you don't have to pay taxes." Every building in Progreso was still under construction, which meant that few citizens here were paying property taxes, which accounted for the lack of progress in Progreso. The schoolyard gym consisted of old truck tires nestled in a mosquito miasma. With the added international strength of BankAmerica, McColl was thinking, maybe his company could play a greater role in upgrading the standard of living for people in less developed countries.

"Banks control money and the access to money," he said. In many nations of the world, the big American banks controlled access to capital not simply for corporations or individuals, but for entire governments. He, Hugh McColl, would be able to wield "immense power" upon the completion of this final merger of his career. The big banks could either provide capital or deny it, he said. "And if you are the biggest player and you don't play, it sends a signal to everybody else that they had better not be playing. Because the elephant has moved off." Power, and with it, enormous responsibility. He felt the pressure of that responsibility, believed "we have to learn to handle it judiciously."

The decision to lend or not to lend could make or break the economy of entire nations. "If BankAmerica-slash-NationsBank decided tomorrow morning to get out of, say, Brazil, it would cause a panic in the Brazilian market, because the biggest player in that market decided they are not playing anymore. The other people would be trying to get out the door behind us."

That was power that even the United States Congress did not possess. "And that's why they don't like banks. Now Dr. Greenspan can make us do something, never lose sight of that. He can call me up and say, 'Hugh, it would be nice if you'd stay in Brazil.' And implicit in that is: 'or next time you come to see me, you won't get what you want.' But, if the government could have everything their way, Congress would fix it so that they could control the money, rather than the banks. As you know, there are members of Congress who don't particularly like banks."

Notwithstanding what might happen in Brasilia or in Progreso, McColl's policy for the new Bank of America would be "America First." He wanted to use his influence on behalf of people in the United States, where he considered his business constituency to reside. He valued relationships with customers who maintained three-hundred-dollar checking and savings accounts, not just the big international conglomerates. "Now, my teammate, Dave, would say, 'on behalf of our customers globally.'" McColl smiled, sipping his orange juice. "And he would mean that, because we have multinational customers. And certainly I would agree with helping out multinational customers. I believe in that. But I guess, I believe first and foremost in America. So, first American customers, and then our other customers."

Flying home to Charlotte, McColl was still thinking about customer relations. He understood that he could not personally deal with every bank customer the way that woman in the market had dealt with him over the blankets, but he needed to know that for every customer, there was an individual in his organization who took responsibility for that customer, some individual who could reach out and touch that customer, in person or over the telephone. He could not bear the thought of all those customer-persons, with their personal mortgages and business loans and deposits, globbing into something called a "customer base." That was nothing more than a data base wearing a mask.

He pulled the paper napkin out from under his cup of coffee and began to draw on it with a felt-tipped pen that sent its ink wandering in every direction along the bulky fibers. He drew dots for customers and little boxes for customer-service people and big boxes for high-paid executives. "Look," he said, "NationsBank is organized so that the people who deal with the customer have the top line. And the people supporting those groups are down below them, furnishing service to them as requested. As opposed to driving down opinions—which can get in the way of doing business—and not being held accountable. We make this guy (He circled one of the little boxes. The napkin was looking as though it had been attacked by a slow-moving squid.) responsible for the customer's business, and accountable for it. These people (big boxes) have only one thing they are supposed to do, and that is whatever *these* people (little boxes) tell them they need to get the damn job done. So it is a hundred-eighty degrees out from a lot of banks.

"Chuck Cooley tells me I use the military analogies too much and it doesn't go down well with a lot of people, but I don't really give a damn because in fact the military analogy is the best one. You can see it more clearly when you understand the difference between an infantry division in attack mode (little boxes, dots) and a supply officer (big box, again) back here. That supply officer doesn't *want* to attack. So you can't let the Supply Corps run the business." McColl looked at his watch, then went for the air-to-ground telephone, located in a drawer under his seat. "I'd better find out if that baby's on the way."

His daughter and her husband, Luther Lockwood, were expecting their second child today, which was Saturday, September 19. Since they already had a Jane ("Baby Jane" Lockwood was born on her grandmother Jane's birthday in 1996, McColl remembered, because it was "right after the Atlanta Olympics."), they were hoping for a Little Luther this time. Hugh and Renee had given him Hugh IV and Tanner. John and Lee had John, Duncan and Virginia. This second Lockwood progeny would be his seventh grandchild, a propitious number. He couldn't get anyone to pick up the phone at his home, so he punched in Hugh's number.

"Renee? We got a new baby in the family yet? . . . Fantastic . . . Everybody okay?"

Little Luther and his mother were doing fine. So was the grandfather. He would change out of his ranch gear into a more maternity-ward-appropriate outfit as soon as the plane touched down, then he would drive his new black BMW straight to the hospital. There was absolutely nothing like a family happening to get his mind off his troubles.

Four days later, Wednesday, September 23, the sky began falling on hedge funds. While D. E. Shaw Company was not mentioned by the media, another hedge fund called Long-Term Capital Management took it squarely and publicly on the skull. LTCM had rewritten the Wall Street mythology of greed by leveraging up its $4 billion of capital through bank loans until it had about $1 trillion—*a million million*—to bet on its assuredly sure things. In a colossal display of chutzpah, a pool of money equivalent to the gross domestic product of China had been overseen by LTCM's 150-member staff, working out of a cozy harborfront office in Greenwich, Connecticut.

When the Dow Jones index plummeted 15 percent, the entire LTCM $1 trillion was in danger of being devalued like a trillion week-old bagels. Just like one of the nation's major banks, Long-Term Capital was considered "too big to fail." Consequently, Federal Reserve Chairman Greenspan took matters into his own hands, fearing that if he did not, the entire international banking system might collapse. Greenspan told the House Banking Committee that letting LTCM die its natural death could trigger "the seizing-up of markets." That, in turn, could imperil "the economies of many nations, including our own."

Admitting the "moral hazard" in protecting this billionaires' pyramid scheme, Greenspan nevertheless got the message to those bankers and investment houses that had enabled the LTCM capital leveraging: it was up to them to quickly shore up the hedge fund, rather than let its investments be auctioned off at fire-sale prices. As McColl had observed over lunch in the dusty border town of Progreso, "Dr. Greenspan can make us do something." Once again, the "most powerful man in America" lived up to Hugh McColl's billing; the sinking hedge fund was bailed out.

Europe's largest bank, UBS of Switzerland, one of the big losers, wrote off $700 million of its total investment in LTCM. Barclays of Britain was into the fund for about half a billion dollars. First Boston, Credit Suisse, Merrill Lynch, Bear Stearns and other big Wall Street names were badly stung. Both the old NationsBank and the old BankAmerica managed to escape the torrent of bad publicity surrounding the LTCM deal, which exploded just one day prior to the synchronized shareholder meeting of the merging corporations.

As in most big mergers, the overwhelming majority of shareholders had mailed in proxy ballots, and the overwhelming majority of those would have awarded their proxy votes to the directors of their respective corporations. That meant there was almost no chance this merger would not be approved. Still, the meetings had to be held, the shareholders heard from.

Across College Street from NationsBank Corporate Center, at noon on the twenty-fourth of September, about three hundred shareholders, many of them associates of the bank, packed the International Trade Center to hear outgoing chairman Charles Rice call the meeting to order and turn the floor over to Hugh McColl. Everyone in the room was aware that, far up the Eastern seaboard, the mood on the floor of the New York Stock Exchange was one of fear and nausea, but here hearts could be buoyed by McColl's insistent ebullience.

"In the second quarter this year," he barked—and even though "year" was "yee-uh," its crease was razor-sharp, its surface brilliant as a first lieutenant's dress shoes on parade day—"NationsBank was the most profitable bank in the United States. With operating earnings of more than $1.1 billion. Let me repeat this: No bank in this country, not one, made more money than *your* bank in the most recent quarter on record." The people understood, applauded as though they were listening to Pavarotti rather than Patton.

McColl acknowledged the applause. Then he acknowledged the trying tenor of the times. "Performance of stock around the world over the past month has focused all of our attention on the need to plan for the future very carefully. But we should not fall into the trap of basing long-term strategy on short-term turbulence. The past few weeks have been tough for all of us. After all, I own more than a few shares of our stock myself." The crowd's laughter rang sweet, but it left a bitter aftertaste. By day's end the Dow Jones Industrial Average would have careened down a 152-point bobsled run.

"Our long-term strategy however, remains sound. We are building a bank that will blanket every significant high-growth market in the strongest, richest country on this planet. And those markets will attract new customers, retain existing customers and deepen all of our relationships, by offering unimagined convenience, value and expertise in geographic reach to individuals and businesses." He concluded his pitch to shareholders by telling them there was "no question in my mind that this is the right deal and the Bank of America is the right partner. The wisdom of this strategy will be clear for many years after we have all forgotten Wall Street's rough ride of 1998."

The applause was strong. The believers believed. When it came time for questions, the floor was monopolized by a self-proclaimed eccentric, a seventy-ish woman of baroque background who lived in Washington, D.C., Evelyn Y. Davis. She spoke in a thick proto-European accent perfected over many years of bothering the CEOs of a number of the nation's largest corporations. Davis was a devoted fan of Hugh McColl's, and told him so, always addressing him by his first name, but Evelyn Davis was distrustful of the leadership of BankAmerica.

"I must tell you, Hugh," said Shareholder Davis, "you are paying a very high price for this under very poor management." She would feel much better about the merger if the BankAmerica executives would "promise to get out of the company as soon as possible." She warned McColl that he was being "taken advantage of by BankAmerica, and they are not telling you the truth, nothing but the truth and the whole truth. And maybe these losses—of course, I don't know, but they may only be the tip of the iceberg—they are not telling you everything. They are not straightforward with you." The audience tittered. McColl forced a smile, answered the little woman at the floor microphone. He called her "Miss Davis," but she corrected him. "Hugh, I've had three husbands!"

"We have been told everything," McColl assured Mrs. Davis and the crowd. "We have done due diligence. We understand the risks inherent in the business we are in. Banks are mirrors of the economy around them, and because we are the largest banking company in the United States we are going to be the largest mirror of the United States. If the United States does well, we'll do well, and if it doesn't we won't. Mrs. Davis, I am afraid that you have been affected by living in Washington."

She refused to let him off the hook that easily. What about the retirement issue? What about the succession issue? "We have to get rid of the top level of the Bank of America people. They are being operated like a 1950s bank." Even Jim Hance, seated next to McColl, was working overtime on his smile. "I'm telling you, Hugh, you have to get rid of these top people there, the sooner the better."

Rather than address that issue, McColl said, "I want to make sure all the shareholders understand that I suspect we will take more losses. One of the things we know is that there will be losses." He did not specify where these additional losses might arise or how heavy they might be, but insisted that the company would be prepared for them. "Our job is to see that the losses are not actuarially important. And that's the way we run the company." The new bank would have "the financial power to deal with whatever comes up."

After another half hour of this exchange, with input from two other shareholders opposed to the merger, the votes were counted. As expected, nearly three-quarters of all outstanding shares were voted in approval of the merger and reorganization plan.

Simultaneously, David Coulter was leading the BankAmerica shareholders' meeting in the Masonic Center on Nob Hill. Six San Francisco policemen were posted outside the auditorium, but the meeting was peaceful, with not a demonstrator in sight. Coulter told a mostly friendly crowd of about six hundred that shareholder dividends would rise to the level of NationsBank, which was about 25 percent higher than the BankAmerica payout. That generated warm applause. As in Charlotte, a majority of attendees were Coulter's employees, or "associates," as he had been instructed to call them now. The morning's loudest cheer, however, went to Catherine Paul, who had worked as a BankAmerica teller for eighteen years, when she ended her question to Coulter about retirement benefits with the quip, "I know you've checked *yours.*"

And when, as proof of the importance of size and scope, Coulter cited the recent mergers of Citicorp and Travelers, Banc One and First Chicago, Wells Fargo and Norwest, Paul drew another laugh. "Just because they're jumping off the bridge," she snipped, "we don't have to *join* them."

BankAmerica shareholders voted overwhelmingly in favor of the merger.

A few hours later, outside the NationsBank boardroom at the top of the sixty-story Corporate Center, Lynn Drury had a party going, complete with sushi, barbecue and brut champagne. Tom Storrs was there, as were Ken Lewis, Frank Gentry, Paul Polking, Ed Dolby, Pat Hinson, and a lot of others who had been through the fits and starts of the company's history. The party was not just for corporate brass, but included the people who had done the work—secretaries and assistants and junior analysts and communications officers—who would carry the memory and the culture into the future.

McColl had a good audience and did not even try to resist making a speech. He talked a little bit about the history, about Florida and Texas and Atlanta. He marked the memories of many who had not made it to the far side of this bridge, which now seemed as though it might not be a bridge too far. He remembered Buddy Kemp and Tim

Hartman and Bennett Brown and others, without whose efforts he would not be standing in this spot. It was a time of deep reflection. He told the crowd of about seventy-five what he had said just a few nights before to his board of directors.

"I made the point then that no man has ever had the opportunity that I have had, which is to actually fulfill your ambitions. Really fulfill your lifetime ambitions. There are few people that I know who have ever been allowed to do that. But I have been allowed to do that, by my board and by you. You carried me on your backs and I appreciate it."

Chuck Cooley's eyes teared up. Pat Hinson used her champagne napkin for a handkerchief.

"I think that we have reached an end to this journey that we have been on, that journey across the country. And we have begun a new one. I don't think it is over. I just think that we have got to the end of the first chapter. And we are getting ready to start a second chapter. And my goals are that we really become the leading bank of the twenty-first century. And I sum that up by saying that I want this to be the very best place to work, to have everybody say they have very best company in America to work for. I want to be the best place to do business. I want our customers to say that. And I want to *matter* more—to be the most important company to our communities and to our country."

Finally, he addressed the fact that hardly anyone in the room had been told of the decision to adopt BankAmerica's name. "I know there is lot of curiosity about what banner we will be fighting under," he said, "and we have just simply decided . . . not to tell you." They laughed. "But I think it really doesn't matter, because we have fought under so many. It has always been the same heart, and the banners haven't mattered."

Cooley had a poem for the occasion. It gave him the opportunity to list a number of now-NationsBank cities that more-or-less rhymed: "Up to Omaha and down to Wichita, Albuquerque and L.A. and finally, the City by the Bay." Cooley wrote that "no one but one" could have imagined that Hugh McColl's dream of a nationwide bank could ever be achieved. He concluded his verses:

> But no matter the name, and no matter the pain,
> the pride and the spirit and the will to win
> will live forever in the hearts of Hugh McColl's women and men.
> So here's to you, Hugh, thank you.

The attributes of "pride" and "spirit" were much on the mind of Amy Brinkley, the bank's executive vice president of marketing. Rather than simply announce the bank's new name in a news release, Brinkley wanted to make a dramatic statement. Perhaps she had learned something from history—from buying advertising space in select newspapers to proclaim NCNB's good intentions prior to the C&S/Sovran merger and, more recently, from placing full-page ads to announce the $350 billion CRA pledge. This time the company would spend its money on television time, forcing the principal newspapers to give it front-page space at no cost. The bank bought ninety-second time slots, equivalent to three regular-length commercials, on two prime-time programs that were heavily viewed by business people on both coasts, ABC's *Nightline* and CNN's *Moneyline.*

Brinkley and her people shot expensive 35-millimeter film footage of BankAmerica and NationsBank facilities around the United States and in visually identifiable cities around the globe, then they combined those pictures with arresting shots of men, women and children, along with original music reminiscent of an Aaron Copeland ballet score. By feeding the curiosity of the employees of both banks, making sure everyone knew about the commercial broadcasts, Brinkley hoped to plant the same message in the minds of all employees at one time. Aired that night only—because the two organizations would not be ready for many months yet to market their products under a single umbrella—the commercial deserves to go down as one of the most effective uses ever of an external advertising medium to achieve strictly internal communication goals.

The night of September 30, Hugh McColl delivered the message personally, in his accent that nearly everyone in the banking industry had come to know:

Today something remarkable happened.

It happened without fanfare in neighborhoods across the country, and in cities around the world.

Hundreds of thousands of people found themselves united, connected by a new bond.

Two great organizations have come together, merging the strength and talents of some of the brightest, most resourceful people on earth.

We come from different backgrounds and from many different places, but we are one team.

We share a vision. We share a future. And, starting today, we share a name.

Together we are the new Bank of America.

If the goal was to achieve a "positive spin" in San Francisco, the commercial succeeded. The next morning's *Chronicle* led its business section with the headline: "New BofA Will Keep Old Name. Nation's largest bank still Bank of America." The article began: "And the winner is . . . Bank of America." That could be considered a major victory. The headline in the *Observer* all but breathed a sigh of relief, using a local zip code to reassure readers that the new bank would remain firmly planted in Charlotte. The front-page banner headline proclaimed: "That would be Bank of America, Charlotte, NC 28255." Another victory.

Both newspapers included the new logo that had waved itself in public for the first time ever the night before. It was a red-and-blue parallelogram on a white field, perhaps a diamond but, on second look, perhaps a flag. The single blue quadrant was in the upper left, reminding one of Old Glory's star-field. The colors were not the muted, distinctive red and blue of BankAmerica, but the primary, patriotic red and blue of NationsBank, and of the USA.

Thursday, October 1, was the first day of business for the new Bank of America, trading under BankAmerica's "BAC" ticker symbol on both the New York and Pacific Stock Exchanges. Both McColl and Coulter spoke with reporters, announcing that the Bank of America Foundation would be making grants of ten thousand dollars in each of one hundred cities across the country, with the money going to causes selected by bank associates in those cities. Also, on Saturday, thousands of their employees would turn out to work on community projects in what the bank called "one of the biggest grassroots volunteer campaigns ever."

But once he got past the feel-good announcements, Hugh McColl's frayed patience revealed itself. One reporter asked whether he could give San Franciscans some assurance that he would keep his word and not move the corporate banking headquarters out of their city. As Peter Sinton reported it in the *Chronicle*, "McColl got testy." His reply was: "You are asking a question we Southerners take as an insult. When we give our word on something, we keep it."

A potentially more explosive question was whether either bank had significant exposure to hedge funds such as LTCM. Coulter responded only that the old BankAmerica "was not a lender to Long-Term Capital Management in any significant way." There was no mention of D. E. Shaw.

Monday, October 5, McColl learned the Shaw losses were potentially huge, in excess of $370 million to the company that now was Hugh McColl's to run. Two things appeared to be certain. Added to the bleak picture in Asia and Russia, the total losses for 1998 might overwhelm the current loan loss reserves. McColl and his senior executives decided to bite the bullet and put an additional $500 million into the loan loss reserve fund.

At the beach on Wednesday, McColl received a call that disturbed him more than any information he had received up to that point about Shaw. The BankAmerica investment of $1.4 billion had been leveraged by a factor of fifty or more, meaning that the total number of dollars at risk, should D. E. Shaw collapse, was between $50 billion and $75 billion. Furthermore, with the market collapsing, Shaw's downstream lenders were demanding collateral from Shaw, which had no cash. It was becoming clear that in order to salvage even a part of the loan, the new Bank of America was going to have to "step into D. E. Shaw's shoes," as McColl put it. As the lender of last resort, the bank would have to guarantee the principal of the downstream lenders.

Thursday, October 8, McColl arrived in Seattle for a speech, anticipating a call from Coulter in reference to the Shaw problem. Instead, he got a call from his old friend W. W. "Hootie" Johnson, chairman of the executive committee of the new company. One of the things they discussed was Coulter's position with the company, but they got off the telephone with the issue still unresolved.

The following Monday, October 12, as the combined bank and its auditors put together the new Bank of America's first quarterly report, the extent of the Shaw problems began leaking out. Two days before that report was due to be posted, "people close to the bank" started talking to the media. The October 13 *Chronicle* headlined its article: "Huge Loss Expected For BofA. Hedge-fund stake may cost bank $100 million." In this article, staff writer Sam Zuckerman for the first time made public BankAmerica's relationship with Shaw. That relationship, Zuckerman wrote, would prove "embarrassing to executives of the old

BankAmerica." The Shaw loss "could undermine former BankAmerica chief executive David Coulter, who is president of the combined bank and has risk management as one of his main responsibilities. Corporate banking chief Michael Murray is also on the spot, analysts said."

The article quoted a West Coast analyst as explaining that, "in essence, Shaw manages a private hedge fund for BofA." That supported McColl's contention that his bank and its shareholders were really the primary at-risk parties if Shaw went under. Also quoted were "people familiar with the arrangement," who let the cat out of the bag: the BankAmerica loan to Shaw was "about $1 billion."

October 15, financial journalists all over the world had a field day at McColl's expense. "BankAmerica Profits Take Huge Drop. Bad quarter may cost S.F. executives," was the way the *Chronicle* played the story. The *Observer* headline writer found a certain black humor in it: "Bank eats crow off hedge." As though to rub salt in the blackbird pie, First Union earnings were reported in the very shadow of the hedge line; they were up 35 percent because, according to First Union CFO Robert Atwood, "our strategy really insulated us" from the market problems. Jim Hance could have made a similar claim, had not the NationsBank strategy included a merger with BankAmerica.

The news kicked another 11 percent out of BAC stock when it was already down. It closed the day at $48.06 a share. Back in April, before shutting down for the Good Friday holiday and the Easter Monday merger announcement, Wall Street had blessed NationsBank stock with a price of $76.44, BankAmerica, $86.50. Hance, the man credited with engineering the merger, had hoped back then to top $100 a share before the year was out. He would be short by nearly forty dollars a share.

Wall Street analysts, who expected to predict such grim tidings before they were published, reacted as though they were personally injured. "People in business hate surprises," said Korn Ferry International's John C. Wilson. Lawrence Cohn of Ryan, Beck & Company, put his fellow analysts' feelings into words when he told the Associated Press he was "astonished at the size of the D. E. Shaw exposure." According to the quarterly report, the bank had written off $372 million—about one-fourth—of its $1.4 billion loan to Shaw. In order to help Shaw stay afloat, and thereby insulate itself from even greater hedge fund losses, the new Bank of America would purchase from Shaw $20 billion in U.S. Treasury bonds and other debt securities. The bank would be able to sell the portfolio slowly, at more attractive prices, whereas leaving the portfolio in Shaw's shaky hands would have forced a fire sale that would have done further damage to the nation's economy, not to mention the bank's net worth.

Concerned about reaction from shareholders, McColl's communication staff put a zipper on the corporate lip. However, an enterprising San Francisco reporter did get one "NationsBank employee" to speak under the promise of anonymity. "People here are very disappointed," this employee said, adding that the top executives appeared to be "furious" and ready to ride the responsible parties out of town on a rail.

News hounds and Wall Street wolves bayed loud and publicly for vengeance. From the New York mountaintop of Keefe, Bruyette & Woods, analyst Thomas Theurkauf proclaimed, "There will be pressure applied to some of the old BofA managers." An analyst who preferred his apocalypse to be published anonymously confided to the media: "No analysts will now cry when Coulter takes his big severance package and leaves. That's the reality. McColl can now do whatever he wants." Bank analyst Lawrence Cohn, sounding like Jeremiah summoning the women skilled in keening, waved his gold Cross pen and admonished, "If BofA were still an independent company, Wall Street would be after blood." And, "Now we have NationsBank management sweeping up after BankAmerica management's mess."

What McColl did not want was a lawsuit from angry shareholders. But, in New York, he got one, from a law firm that accused him personally of concealing the Shaw losses from investors. It was only the first of many lawsuits to be filed.

McColl had not imagined it would come to this. Just a few weeks earlier, he had received a letter of appreciation from a man who was retiring from NationsBank, Raleigh Hortenstein. In 1988 Hortenstein had managed First Republic's trading operations and was considered a candidate for CEO. McColl's own appreciation of Hortenstein, through Buddy Kemp and Tim Hartman, had been that Hortenstein was an excellent salesman but did not have the skills required to run the company. Yet he proved to be a "loyal, wonderful teammate," who agreed to move his family to Charlotte and worked for the company for ten years. He had requested a meeting with McColl, but, because of the merger frenzy, could not find a place in the CEO's schedule. So he wrote McColl a letter, thanking him for allowing him to become "personally independent" rather than being wiped out, had First

Republic been allowed to fail.

"Everybody with First Republic would have lost everything," McColl said, proudly showing off Hortenstein's letter. "A lot of them had worked twenty years and had nothing to show for it, not one thing. We reinstated all their pensions, gave them stock in the new company, paid them a lot of money, helped them get back on their feet. All of them prospered out of it. Raleigh was man enough to thank me. Not just thank me, but thank me profusely, and thanked me for the leadership." That was the sort of relationship McColl wanted with people whose companies he had made part of his own.

Friday, October 16, Hootie Johnson met with Dave Coulter in San Francisco. Johnson, who would suddenly find himself labeled in the press as "McColl's hatchet man," had flown to the West Coast on his own, with no urging from McColl. His mission was to convince Coulter he should remove himself from the roster of the company.

Tuesday, October 20, David Coulter announced his resignation. He would end his association with Bank of America on October 30. Bill Vandiver took Coulter's place on the six-man policy committee and accepted full responsibility for managing risk from that point forward.

The bank released a short statement announcing the resignation, which included a few words from Hugh McColl. "The decision was extremely difficult for me, both personally and professionally," he declared. "It is very painful to me personally to accept his resignation. We wish him well."

On the polished oak surface of McColl's study desk, next to the antique inkwell, sits his well-thumbed copy of *Nil Desperandum: A Dictionary of Useful Latin Tags and Phrases*, by Eugene Erlich. The page marked permanently with a paper clip contains the old motto of the warrior kings of Scotland. *Nemo me impune lacessit*, reads the Latin—"No one provokes me with impunity."

McColl's bellicose reputation was not lost on San Francisco's newspaper writers and columnists, who provided their readers with what they claimed to be the real story. All along, they insisted, it had been Hugh McColl's plan to purge Coulter and run the bank his own way, in defiance of the people of San Francisco and their interests. The *Chronicle*, whose Zuckerman described McColl erroneously as "crew-cut" and "blustering," now published reports of Coulter "taking the fall for the D.E. Shaw incident."

The *Chronicle* and the *Examiner* claimed to have sources at the very top of the old BankAmerica organization to feed them lines such as: "Dave was feeling more and more that the promises upon which the deal was agreed to were not materializing." Hugh McColl, "who is known for his military ardor and is famous for keeping a hand grenade on his desk, had a different philosophy about how to manage the combined company and was growing increasingly uncomfortable with anointing Coulter as the heir apparent." San Francisco columnist Ken Garcia, who had stirred local merger resentment since April, called Coulter's pension agreement an "obscene payout."

The story now in San Francisco was that Dave Coulter had never been part of the team. He had only been paid to hang around "to oversee the sellout of one of the city's oldest institutions." Garcia suggested that the black granite "banker's heart" sculpture in the plaza at Bank of America's San Francisco headquarters be engraved with names, starting with that of David Coulter and, of course, of Hugh McColl, "a Southern shark who likens himself to General George S. Patton."

The military metaphor persisted into the *Chronicle*'s long Sunday recounting of the "execution-style layoffs." In this piece, quite oblivious to actual circumstances, staff writer Edward Iwata wrote: "The military strike would have made the Pentagon proud. Last week a corporate general named Hugh McColl completed his assault on San Francisco's Bank of America. The 62-year-old McColl [actually, sixty-three on the date in question] is a steely former marine and head of the old NationsBank in Charlotte, N.C. By most accounts, he and his lieutenants blew away the trusting BankAmerica folks, who forgot that war can be brutal."

McColl was accused of trying to "bamboozle the media" by swearing he would "keep his promise to Coulter," notwithstanding the uncontested and almost unreported fact that the only "promise" had been expressed as a "present intention" in the memorandum of intent. Now "gloom has fallen over BankAmerica's offices in San Francisco. Thousands of layoffs are looming. Friends say Coulter is devastated." Swimming back to the shark concept, Iwata quoted "one local banking executive" as saying McColl was a predator and predators never rest. "There's blood in the water, and it's not his."

Perhaps to hedge his bet in case the Bank of America communications staff might have an opening, journalist Iwata concluded: "You've got to grudgingly respect McColl and his martial skills. You'd want him on your side in a street fight or a military campaign. He may not have many friends in San Francisco, but he stalked The City's most valued corporation with deadly and frightening ease."

Chuck Cooley and Joe Martin had warned McColl more than a few times: you live by the sword metaphor, you die by the sword metaphor. Martin shot him an e-mail message. "Don't flinch. We will get through this if you will just be you."

When Hugh McColl was contemplating his imminent retirement in early 1997, he agreed to be interviewed for a biography, believing such a book might hold some regional interest. When he asked what he hoped readers might learn from the story of his life, McColl replied, "I'd like people to see that I'm not just a one-sided, flat character."

McColl was weary of being seen through the glass of journalism, darkly. It is inevitable that journalists feed off each other's material, like that old game of rumors, where players whisper a story into each other's ear around a circle. The more times the story is repeated, the farther it gets from the truth. Thus one journalist's "ex-marine" might easily devolve into another journalist's "crew-cut," "blustering" parody of George C. Scott playing U.S. Army General George Smith Patton. While McColl never apologized for his brief stint in the Marine Corps, he'd had more than one occasion to regret the easy caricature it provided his detractors.

In fact, McColl spent a mere two years as a marine and the only action he saw was around the poker table. The only wound he received came on the basketball court and earned him no ribbons. To McColl, the old USMC slogan, "The Marines Build Men," suggested that one brought the skills and determination of youth into the corps and there received an opportunity to put those skills and determination to work, in adult ways.

Curiously, the single most important thing he took from the marine experience, the one *new* thing, had to do with the value of human life, not with the taking of life. In the marines McColl encountered, for the first time in his Southern youth, the reality that the color of an individual's skin made no difference to that individual's ability to perform. He took that information, combined it with what he knew about women's abilities, learned by observing his mother and sister, and used it to create one of the most intensely diverse companies in the United States, certainly the most diverse company in Southern banking.

The Marine Corps became his frame of reference because it was the place he became an adult. He would speak of leadership and teamwork in terms of war and esprit de corps, but, in fact, those were skills he had honed on the playing fields of his boyhood in Bennettsville. The Marine Corps was actually his "French Foreign Legion," a romantic, desperate, escapist refuge for a lovelorn young man.

Since the latter-day McColl was a student of history, instead of limning his BankAmerica merger as a military conquest, pundits might have likened it more appropriately to that moment of astonishment for Vasco Nunez de Balboa, first looking out from that peak in Darien and seeing the ocean that would be known as the Pacific. Far from planning a military strike against BankAmerica, McColl had been no less flabbergasted than Balboa to find himself standing in David Coulter's apartment looking out to sea.

There was also a certain pride in successful mischief-making about Hugh McColl, another character trait journalism never seemed to trip over. Like a kid throwing a frog into the girls' locker room, he just enjoyed stirring up excitement. Speaking of the history that flowed to him through Addison Reese and Tom Storrs, he said, "We disturbed the order of things in North Carolina, and then we disturbed the order of things in the South. We disturbed the order of things in the United States. And if we live, that will be true of the world too. Because we believe that the natural order of things is for us to be in charge, not somebody else."

He could make a statement like that and break into a grin, just like the boy listening to the locker-room shrieks. He knew damned well how many people his remark would offend and he did not mind in the least offending them. Despite everything his grandmother had taught him, McColl simply could not bring himself to be "polite."

In May 1992, Tom Storrs, Chairman Emeritus of NationsBank, introduced Hugh McColl as guest of honor at the annual meeting of the prestigious Newcomen Society of the United States. "To stand here and read you Hugh's biographical sketch would not tell you very much about Hugh McColl," said Storrs, a man who chose his words as a London tailor selects his cloth. "The measure of the man is not in what he has accomplished but in how he has accomplished so much."

Even then, six years before McColl would plant his flag on the

Pacific shore, Tom Storrs recognized that his protégé had slipped the surly bonds of expectation. Storrs had been McColl's teacher, and good teachers know their pupils will achieve greatness only as greatness is expected of them. Hugh McColl was born into a so-called New South, in which the only expectations were limitations. His grandmother's fondest hope was that he would stay at home and become the rekindling of his great-grandfather's flame. She wanted only for "the Hugh" to reign as Merchant Prince of Bennettsville, South Carolina. McColl's mother, and eventually his father as well, would not have their son tethered to that dream. They cut him free and sent him off. Later, when McColl realized he was being held in bondage to the expectations of other bankers—that he must confine his goals to servicing smaller banks, that he must genuflect toward New York for favors—he cut himself, and his company, free from those limitations as well.

In 1940, when McColl was a boy of five, W. J. Cash concluded his classic book, *The Mind of the South*, by admitting it was far easier to criticize the South's failure to face up to its problems than it was to actually solve those problems. Like McColl, Cash grew up in Scotch-Irish, small-town South Carolina, then moved to Charlotte, where he did most of his writing. The South was corrupted, he insisted by "intolerance, aversion and suspicion to new ideas, an incapacity for analysis, an inclination to act from feeling rather than from thought, an exaggerated individualism and a too narrow concept of social responsibility."

The list of sins continued, but Cash's most stinging point was the observation that white Southerners preferred to blame the region's problems on the North, big business, Washington and blacks, than to examine their own reflection in a mirror. In the South, the greatest sin was to tell an ugly truth when a beautiful lie would serve. And what was to blame for the region's fatalistic complacency? Cash's answer was "the absence of leadership."

If Cash was right, then Hugh McColl's story goes against the grain not only of his profession, but of his birthright. McColl has embraced new ideas, has taught himself to be analytical, has rejected stereotyping by race and gender, and has broadened an entire nation's definition of social responsibility. Rather than blaming government or the money center for his shortcomings, McColl has first used them to gain equal footing, then maneuvered around legal and capital barriers to overwhelm his rivals. One may take issue with some of his methods; one may question his motives, but one cannot doubt his leadership skills.

Even McColl, who some days can be his harshest critic, is impressed at the degree to which he has exceeded Southern expectations. "I think what is really interesting to realize," he said, "is that we built a company that dwarfs the huge banks, the ones we used to think of as *giants*. And we have surpassed them, Chase and Morgan. Morgan can't even get up on a radar screen with us."

In the fall of 1998, McColl relaxed in his study, trying to put his career in the context of history. The assets of his family's bank in Bennettsville hit an all-time high of just over six hundred thousand dollars in 1911 when Duncan Donald McColl died, he recalled. Twenty years later his sons could not find a buyer for that bank at thirty thousand dollars. McColl smiled, pulled off his boots. "And his great-grandson will end the century running a company of $570 billion or $600 billion by then. That's even more interesting to me than being bigger than Mr. Morgan's bank." In fact, before the end of 1998, the new Bank of America already would be worth more than $624 billion, exceeding even Hugh McColl's expectations.

Getting ready for his first annual shareholders' meeting of his new company—the name of which would become Bank *of* America Corporation, once the votes were tallied—McColl was clear of the clouds that had him in a funk the worse part of a year. He could even smile when he came across a wryly apropos line in the book he was reading, James H. Webb's *The Emperor's General*. Webb had written: "When one measures life by the enemies he has conquered rather than the friends he has made, it becomes important not to run out of battles."

Although McColl was fairly certain he'd fought his last major campaign, at least his fears of having taken his troops "a bridge too far" were behind him. "My trepidation has gone away," he confided. "By October 1999 we'll be rolling. Where we are today is a whole new world."

Ebullience overcame his customary annual-meeting jitters, because McColl was once again sure of his footing. He was marching like old times, in front of his own cadre of field marshals; former BankAmerica CFO Mike O'Neill was gone, his exit considerably more graceful than

Coulter's, leaving only Mike Murray from the former West Coast Group on the senior management team as president of Global Corporate and Investment Banking. Ken Lewis, back in Charlotte, was secure in the position of president of the corporation, the title Coulter had enjoyed, and that fueled external speculation that now Ken Lewis must certainly be McColl's heir apparent. Since the board had asked the CEO to stay on until 2002—the first guaranteed stretch of employment he'd ever known—McColl had another two years before he left his company in the hands of people he'd brought up through the ranks. There was no sign of a letup in his commitment to America's cities; in fact, the philanthropic community was left speechless when Bank of America Foundation announced its intention to contribute $100 million in cash to United Way and other charitable causes during 1999. The amount dwarfed any other gift of corporate cash. No question about it: the hands-down number-one bank in the United States was Hugh McColl's company.

April 28, 1999, McColl took the stage at Belk Theater of the North Carolina Blumenthal Performing Arts Center, the glittering symphony hall at the base of his tower. Forty years ago, almost to the day, he'd been sitting at that old kitchen table in Bennettsville, listening to his daddy on the phone with a banker in Charlotte who didn't want to hire another short, slow-talking country boy. He'd showed up for work in a poor-fitting suit with his hair still growing out from the bush-cut into the Elvis-look. He'd talked his way around the company till he caught the fever of maybe working for the biggest bank in all North Carolina one day.

Now, there he was, almost alone on that wide empty stage. The only other person up there was the corporation secretary, Jim Kiser, one of the few males in the company shorter than McColl. The chairman's suit looked good, as did his gray, short-cropped hair. There was still the South Carolina country boy in his voice, natural though, not laid on thick for effect. There was no cutting edge about his style, nothing suggesting haughtiness, though his voice and his posture were secure. He seemed, for a change, not playing a role, but simply being himself.

"Our relationship with Shaw has been restructured," he told the crowd. "And the first-quarter earnings we reported last week beat Wall Street estimates by a healthy margin." In fact, the stock of the combined banks was just now climbing toward the numbers NationsBank stock had sold for prior to the merger. "I believe we have turned the corner. And I believe that we are now well-positioned to build the company we all envision."

Dick Rosenberg, the man who'd envisioned buying McColl's bank and replacing him with David Coulter, sat smiling in the second row, one of nineteen directors on a board weighted solidly in McColl's favor. The directors were there to hear McColl say that at last he had corralled all the old NationsBank banks, even those in Texas, under one charter. The western half of the franchise would soon be operating under that charter as well, meaning one corporation, headquartered in Charlotte.

Already, McColl told the crowd, Global Corporate and Investment Banking was doing business under the new flag, as were consumer banks in Texas and New Mexico and Military Banking. By summer's end, all but the Northwest, Florida and California would be wearing the new Bank of America brand, the Hugh McColl brand. But the work would not stop there, he said, "It will continue for as long as your company exists. This work is being carried out every day by the associates of your company who are serving customers by living out the core values of your company."

To some in the audience, McColl's remarks seemed uncharacteristically reserved. It may have been simply that he intended to let CFO Jim Hance's numbers do the boasting. Taking the stage before his computer-generated charts and graphs, Hance was like a virtuoso soloist, giving the performance of his life. Net revenues, he proclaimed, were up about 1 percent, to $30.7 billion, placing Bank of America second in operating earnings among the world's financial institutions.

Sitting at a little table to the side of the stage with Jim Kiser, McColl looked down at his notes and smiled. It seemed such a short time ago they'd been number two in their state. Then they took aim at number one in the Southeast. Last year, number-one bank in America. Now Jim Hance implicitly was laying down the next set of challenges.

At the close of the first quarter of '99, shareholders' equity stood at $46.8 billion, the largest of any financial institution in the world. Give Hance the right set of numbers and he could roll them off like Benny Goodman laying down a clarinet riff. In net income among all Fortune 500 companies—not just banks—McColl's was ranked fifth.

In shareholders' equity, he was second highest. In assets, second highest. And after every line of numbers McColl heard Hance's voice ring out clear in the big hall: ". . . in the world."

Maybe he heard his grandmother's voice, too:

"Second? That's all right, honey, I know you'll do better next time."

AFTERWORD
AUTHOR'S ACKNOWLEDGMENTS

I first met Hugh McColl in 1992, when my wife and I were putting together the computer-driven program on banking that would become part of the Museum of the New South's first exhibit. With our videographer, we arrived in the NationsBank Tower (the sixty-story Corporate Center still under construction across the street) and we were shown into a nondescript conference room by a cordial executive assistant, Pat Hinson. No sooner had we set up the lights than McColl arrived, lugging a large, frayed-flap carton. He introduced himself on the move—"Hugh McColl. How're y'all? Sorry I'm late."—and began unfolding yellowed newspapers onto the conference table.

He had dug up articles about the Charlotte Federal Reserve Bank, about Word Wood and Torrence Hemby, about the mergers between American Trust and Commercial National. He showed us old photos and articles from the *Marlboro Gazette*, about the banking achievements of earlier McColls, dating back to Reconstruction. For a man of his reputation and responsibility, he was remarkable in his informality, candor, lack of pretension. He could disarm you with aw-shucks humility; his family's bank had been small potatoes. He could run you through with confidence; one day "whoever's sitting in my seat will be running the largest bank in the United States." He seemed a man of many parts with no part he felt required to play.

It was not until nearly five years later that I encountered McColl again and learned, to my astonishment, that he recognized my name. This may have been as a result of his acquaintance with conductor Zubin Mehta, who had autographed to McColl a copy of his biography. The book happened to reside on a high shelf of the Scotland Avenue study, with the author's name, mine, staring at him from its spine. Perhaps that coincidence convinced him to let me write his story. Eighteen months later, McColl seemed to wish he'd never shaken hands on the agreement. Contemplating the publication of this book was a bit like contemplating his own death, he said.

Nevertheless, we did get it finished. Much of the credit for that is due to my wife, who helped me with many of the interviews. JoAnn transcribed hundreds of hours of recorded interviews, and, along with our daughter Beth, endured the agony of reading and rereading the manuscript, demanding clarification. If the complexities of banking and finance have been rendered comprehensible to the uninitiated reader, it is due entirely to the persistence of these two women and I thank them with all my heart. I am grateful also to my agent, Sally Hill McMillan, without whose Southern sagacity and mastery of the negotiator's art we might never have found the perfect publisher for this book, nor the perfect editor, John Yow.

There are several in the McColl-NationsBank-Bank of America family who should be singled out for their contributions. Most notably, Jane Spratt McColl, who agreed to be interviewed and, ultimately, put on public view—something she has avoided successfully most of her life. At the bank, Tom Storrs, Chuck Cooley, Vick Phillips and Pat Hinson, Lynn Drury and Dick Stilley helped out enormously. And it must be said that this book never would have come to be without the dedicated, unwavering commitment of Joe Martin, despite the communication challenges imposed on him by ALS. Thank you, Joe, for your inspiration, advice, encouragement and so much more.

In the research phase, we had access to archival materials from many sources, including interviews and documents at the University of North Carolina. Among the dozens of books consulted, by far the most helpful was *The Story of NationsBank* by Howard Covington and Marion Ellis. Yet, more than any publication, this book owes its vitality to the memories of those who lived the stories it attempts to record.

The ancient Greeks established Mnemosyne, Goddess of Memory, as mother of all the nine muses. Aeschylus credits her with spawning all human wisdom. Yet memory is not mathematics and her theorems stand mostly unprovable. Artifacts of fiction too often evolve into articles of faith. Yet we light our votive candles at Memory's altar and pray for Wisdom's enlightenment.

INDEX